JN086581

ハッカーズ・スーパーボキャブラリー

HACKERS
SUPER
VOCABULARY

ハッカーズ語学研究所
David Cho

IBCパブリッシング

Copyright © 2002 Hackers Language Research Institute Co., Ltd.
published in Japan, 2023

This edition is published in Japan under License Agreement
between Hackers Language Research Institute Co., Ltd.
and IBC PUBLISHING, INC.

All rights reserved. NO part of this Publication or related
audio files may be reproduced, stored in a retrieval system, or
transmitted, in any form or by any means, electronic or
mechanical, including photocopying, recording, or otherwise,
without the prior written permission of the copyright owner,
Hackers Language Research Institute Co., Ltd.

カバーデザイン　　岩目地英樹（コムデザイン）
編 集 協 力　　株式会社オフィス LEPS
　　　　　　　武市　圭子

はじめに

　本書は、ハイレベルな語彙の習得を目指す英語学習者のために企画・制作されたものです。大学院進学や研究課程での語学的な必要性や、英語で書かれた文献・論文などを読みこなして幅広い知識を獲得する目的を視野に入れ、さらには TOEFL、IELTS、GMAT、SAT、GRE といった各種進学・資格試験、加えて海外・英語圏での就職活動での有効性をも考慮した、非常に高度な英単語集です。

　高いレベルの語彙力を効率的に身につけるには、一定の基準で厳選された単語を、正確な意味・定義とともに素早く覚え込んでいくことが重要です。そうした観点に基づいて、本書には以下のような特徴があります。

　まず、各種試験に最も頻出する語彙を統計処理によって厳選し、その上で各単語の正確な意味を明示するために見出し語に英語の定義文を付しました。また、関連語を提示した上で見出し語と比較しながら、単語間の微妙な意味の違いを把握できるように構成されています。また、見出し語に別の単語を関連づけて提示することで、単語を簡単に、長期間にわたって記憶できるよう工夫しました。また、本書に収録されている 3,200 以上の単語を、語根に分解して立体的に学習できるように、Super Vocabulary Words Roots を追加しました。

　本書が、高度な英語の語彙力拡充を目指す皆さんが学習を進める上で、有効な一助となることを、編者一同、祈っています。

CONTENTS

本書の基本構成

01 見出し語

02 英語による定義

03 日本語による定義

04 例文

05 例文の日本語訳

06 関連語と類義語・反意語

07 Daily Check-up

08 Crossword Puzzle

09 Super Vocabulary
Words Pack

10 Super Vocabulary
Words Roots & Prefixes

11 Index

各ページの左側に大きく示されているのが、覚えるべき単語です。合計1,800語に及ぶ見出し語がリストアップされています。これらを30日間で覚えていきます。

各見出し語の語義が英文で定義されています。英語のまま、できるだけ正確に単語の意味を把握できるようになっています。

英語による定義の直後に示されています。より短時間で効率的に学習するために活用するといいでしょう。

定義の下に、見出し語を含んだ例文が示されています。単語のニュアンスと正確な用法を把握するうえで、例文が大いに役立つはずです。

各ページの下段に例文の日本語訳が示されています。各例文の意味を確認してください。

見出し語ごとに「関連語」と「類義語」「反意語」を紹介しています。他の語との比較や連想を行う中で、見出し語の意味やニュアンス、使い方をより明確に把握することを目的としています。

1日分の学習を終えたところで、60の単語を復習し、どこまで記憶・理解できているかを自己診断してください。

10日分の学習を終えたところで、そこまでの復習を兼ねて気軽にパズルを楽しんでください。

1,800の見出し語には含まれていないものの、重要度においては決して見出し語に引けを取らない500語を、追加で紹介してあります。学習に余裕があれば、ぜひ目を通してみてください。

本書に収載された3,200あまりの単語を200以上の語根を軸に再分類し、立体的に復習できるようにしました。一度学習した単語を、意味を持った語根に基づいて再度確認・学習することで、より確実に記憶に定着させることが可能です。

本書で取り上げたハイレベルな英単語を、辞書的に検索して日頃の学習効率を高められるように、巻末にまとめてあります。

本書の特徴

01 TOEFL、IELTS、GMAT、SAT、GRE などに頻出する単語を収載

02 学習者の現状に合った立体的な学習法の提示

03 効率的な確認学習のための Daily Check-up

04 見出し語の定義を英語と日本語の両方で提示

05 日常生活で活用できる例文と的確な和訳

06 見出し語と関連語を有機的に結びつけて覚える連想記憶法の提示

07 上級英語のための上級語彙を収載

08 意味を持つ語根で単語を再分類し、学習の繰り返しを提唱

09 MP3 形式の音声をダウンロードで提供

本書は、現在実施されている各種英語資格試験に共通して頻出する単語を中心に、ハイレベルな語彙力の拡充に必須の語彙を体系的に習得できるように構成されています。特に、他の試験に比べて高難易度の語彙力が求められるGMAT、SAT、GREの受験者にとって、大きな助けとなるでしょう。

試験を間近に控えた学習者と、長期的な目標の下で取り組む学習者では、最適な学習法が同じではありません。本書では、学習者一人ひとりが置かれた状況に最適な学習法を具体的に提示しています。

1日の学習を終えた後に、学習の進捗状況を効率よく自己診断できるように確認問題を設け、見出し語や関連単語がきちんと身についているか短時間で確認できるようになっています。

英単語の正確な意味を把握するための最良のツールは英語そのものだ、という考えの下、単語の語義や関連する別の単語の間にあるニュアンスの違いを正確につかめるように、シンプルで的確な英語による定義が提示されています。併記された日本語による定義と併せて読むことで、各単語の語義をスピーディーかつ容易に把握できるようになっています。

単語を説明するための複雑な例文をたくさん載せた既刊書とは一線を画し、簡単でありながら実生活ですぐに使える例文を提示しています。さらに、各ページの下部に各例文の日本語訳を示してあるので、文意が不確かな例文についてだけ確認するといった効率的な学習が可能になります。

本書では、すべての見出し語について、「関連語」と「類義語」「反意語」の情報が提示されています。見出し語を習得する際に、関連語や類義語・反意語との意味的な関係を把握することで、棒暗記に依存せず、比較・連想によって連鎖的に記憶に定着させられるよう配慮したものです。なお、関連語・類義語・反意語を用いて学習効率を高めるために、あえて見出し語と品詞が異なる語が提示されている場合もあります。

本書に収載された1,800の単語は、資格試験などに出題されるだけの、いわゆる試験対策用単語ではなく、現実のさまざまな場面で実際に役立つハイレベルな必須語彙です。試験対策になるのはもちろんのこと、本書の語彙を習得することによって、アカデミックな英文原書や英字新聞、各種英語論文などを読みこなせるだけの語彙力の総合的なレベルを向上させることができます。

見出し語と関連語、類義語・反意語を合わせた3,200以上の単語を、意味を持った語根に基づいて再分類し、一度学習した単語を意味別に再度学習できるようにしました。学習を多角的に進めることで、単語を退屈することなく確実に記憶に定着させることができます。

ネイティブスピーカーによる正確な発音で収録した本書の単語と英語による定義の音声を、各DAY冒頭のQRコードから聞いたり、次ページから音声ファイルを一括ダウンロードすることができます。音声が記憶の定着を助けるとともに、リスニング力の向上にも役立ちます。

● 音声一括ダウンロード ●

本書の朗読音声（MP3形式）を下記 URL と QR コードから無料で PC などに一括ダウンロードすることができます。

https://ibcpub.co.jp/audio_dl/0748/

※ダウンロードしたファイルは ZIP 形式で圧縮されていますので、解凍ソフトが必要です。

※ MP3 ファイルを再生するには、iTunes や Windows Media Player などのアプリケーションが必要です。

※ PC や端末、アプリケーションの操作方法については、編集部ではお答えできません。付属のマニュアルやインターネットの検索を利用するか、開発元にお問い合わせください。

SUPER VOCABULARY

1st DAY–30th DAY

さあ！　深呼吸をして、
30日間の単語の旅に出ましょう。

1st DAY

---

abscond
[æbskánd]

v. **to leave secretly and hide oneself**　　　　[動] 逃亡する、姿をくらます

Though the CEO *absconded* to another country, he was extradited and forced to stand trial for the company's disastrous bankruptcy.

関連語 abscond : depart [dipáːˈt]
人目を忍んで depart（去る）のが abscond。

---

adulate
[ǽdʒulèit]

v. **to flatter in a servile way**　　　　[動] 〜を過剰に持ち上げる

In order to get a raise, the employee *adulated* the boss.

関連語 adulate : flatter [flǽtər]
adulate は flatter（お世辞を言う）よりもはるかに程度が強い。

---

adulterate
[ədʌ́ltərèit]

v. **to make impure by adding or mixing with foreign or inferior substances**　　　　[動] 〜を（異物を加えたり、混ぜたりして）不純にする、劣化させる

Though the jeweler claimed it was pure, the gold had been *adulterated*.

関連語 adulterate : purity [pjúˤrəti]
adulterate は purity（純度）を落とすこと。

---

altruist
[ǽltruːist]

n. **one who is unselfishly devoted to improving the welfare of others**　　　　[名] 他人の福利を向上させるために献身する人、利他主義者

Perry was a great *altruist* that touched the lives of people from all over the world.

反意語 altruist : vulture [vʌ́ltʃəʳ]
altruist の反意語が vulture（ハゲタカの意。弱者を食い物にする人、冷血人間）

TRANSLATION | 例 文 の 訳

abscond	その最高経営責任者は他国へ逃亡したが、本国に引き渡され、当該企業の破滅的な破綻に対する裁判を受けるように要請された。
adulate	給料を上げてもらおうと、その職員は上司をひどく持ち上げた。
adulterate	その金は純金だと宝石商は主張したが、不純物が混ざっていた。
altruist	ペリーは偉大な利他主義者で、世界中の人の生活に影響を与えた。

anachronism
[ənǽkrənìzm]

n. a chronological error　　　　　　　　　　[名] 時代錯誤

It is an *anachronism* to attempt a life without technology in the modern world.

関連語 anachronism : chronology [krənálədʒi]
chronology（年代記、年代学）を理解しないと anachronism に結び付く。

awry
[ərái]

adj. turned or twisted out of place; not in proper position
[形]（本来の位置から外れて）曲がった、ねじれた；間違った

Anne rushed into the meeting late with her hair unbrushed and her clothes *awry*.

反意語 awry : orderly [ɔ́ːʳdəʳli]
awry の反意語が orderly（整った、整然とした）

blunt
[blʌnt]

v. to make dull　　　　　　　　　　　　　　[動] ～を鈍くする

adj. not sharp; direct or frank in speech or manner
[形] 鈍い；（発言や態度が）遠慮がない、率直な

Amy *blunted* the corners of the coffee table in order to ensure her toddler's safety.

I would rather have people be *blunt* with me than waste time beating around the bush.

反意語 blunt : whet [ʰwet]
blunt の反意語が whet（研ぐ）

browbeat
[bráubìːt]

v. to intimidate or discourage by being overbearing or domineering　　　　　　[動] ～を（威圧的な表情や行動で）威嚇する

Lawyers are not allowed to *browbeat* witnesses that are on the stand.

関連語 browbeat : bully [búli]
bully（弱い者いじめをする人、いじめっ子）は自分よりも弱い者を browbeat する。

TRANSLATION | 例 文 の 訳

anachronism　現代世界において、技術を使わずに生活しようとするのは時代錯誤だ。

awry　アンは髪の毛はぼさぼさ、服は乱れたままに、その会議に遅れて駆け込んできた。

blunt　エイミーは赤ん坊の安全を守るために、コーヒーテーブルの角を丸く削った。
遠回しな言い方で時間を無駄にされるより、遠慮なく話してもらったほうがいい。

browbeat　弁護士が証言台にいる証人を脅すことは許されていない。

canopy
[kǽnəpi]

n. **a covering usually made of cloth held on poles**

[名] 柱にかけられたカバー布、天蓋、ひさし

A *canopy* was added to the restaurant so that patrons could dine outdoors.

関連語 canopy : cover [kʌ́vəʳ]
canopy には cover (覆い) の機能がある。

clumsy
[klʌ́mzi]

adj. **awkward or lacking grace**

[形] 不器用な、無作法な

My sister is said to have *clumsy* feet because she is always tripping.

関連語 clumsy : knack [næk]
clumsy な人には knack (こつ、要領) が欠けている。

crucial
[krúːʃəl]

adj. **critical or extremely important**

[形] きわめて重要な、不可欠な

It is *crucial* that you get the package to the post office on time.

反意語 crucial : inconsequential [ìnkɑnsikwénʃəl]
crucial の反意語が inconsenquential (取るに足らない、重要でない)

crumble
[krʌ́mbl]

v. **to fall to pieces or collapse**

[動] 粉々になる、崩れる

The tall building *crumbled* from the earthquake.

関連語 crumble : friable [fráiəbl]
friable (砕けやすい) なものは crumble しやすい。

curt
[kəːʳt]

adj. **rudely short in speech or manner**

[形] (発言や態度が) ぶっきらぼうな、そっけない

The man at the counter was very *curt* when replying to my request.

反意語 curt : wordy [wə́ːʳdi]
curt の反意語が wordy (口数の多い)

TRANSLATION | 例 文 の 訳

canopy	客が屋外で食事ができるように、そのレストランに日よけがついた。
clumsy	妹はいつもつまづくので、歩くのが不器用だと言われる。
crucial	時間通りに郵便局に小包を持っていくことがきわめて重要だ。
crumble	その高い建物は地震で崩れた。
curt	カウンターの男は私の要求にぶっきらぼうに応じた。

curtail
[kəˈtéil]

v. to shorten or make less by cutting off some part

[動]〜を（一部を削除することで）短縮する、削減する

The executives *curtailed* negotiations after making no headway with the labor union.

反意語 curtail : protract [proutrǽkt]

curtailの反意語がprotract（〜を引き延ばす）

daunt
[dɔːnt]

v. to intimidate or lessen the courage of

[動]〜を怖気づかせる、気力をくじく

Being attacked in Russia was a *daunting* experience.

関連語 dauntless : trepidation [trə̀pidéiʃˀn]

dauntless（怖い）した人はtrepidation（恐怖、不安）をあまり感じない。

diocesan
[daiásəsən]

adj. related to the area or churches under a bishop's jurisdiction

[形]司教の管轄地域や教会の、教区の

The *diocesan* council overlooked the matter while the bishop was absent.

反意語 diocesan : ecumenical [èkjuménikəl]

diocesanの反意語はecumenical（キリスト教諸派を代表する、世界のキリスト教会の）

disaffected
[dìsəféktid]

adj. discontented and resentful, especially against authority

（政府等に）苦情を抱いた、憤慨した

Many of the Vietnam War Veterans have become *disaffected* to their country.

関連語 disaffected : contentment [kənténtmənt]

disaffected（不満な）人はcontentment（満足）を感じない。

disavow
[dìsəváu]

v. to disclaim knowledge of, responsibility for, or association with

[動]（知識・責任・関係などを）否定する、否認する

Jeff *disavowed* any knowledge of the robbery.

類義語 disavow : deny [dinái]

disavowの類義語がdeny（〜を否定する）

TRANSLATION | 例 文 の 訳

curtail　　　労働組合との話し合いに進展が見られず、幹部らは交渉期間を短縮した。

daunt　　　ロシアで攻撃されたのは恐ろしい経験だった。

diocesan　　司教の不在中、教区の評議会はその問題を見逃した。

disaffected　ベトナム戦争の従軍兵の多くは自国に不満を抱くようになっている。

disavow　　ジェフはその強盗事件について何も知らないと言った。

discern [disə́ːᵣn]	v. to see or understand as different; to recognize as distinct or separate [動]（違いを）見分ける；～を（別のものだと）識別する It is hard, at times, to *discern* between right and wrong. 反意語 discerning : myopic [maiápik] discerning（洞察力のある）の反意語は myopic（視野の狭い）

discomfit
[diskʌ́mfit]
	v. to disconcert; to upset or make uneasy
	    [動] 当惑させる；落ち着きを失わせる
	
	The president was *discomfited* by the terrorist threats.
	
	反意語 discomfit : pacify [pǽsəfài]
	    discomfit の反意語が pacify（～を落ち着かせる、なだめる）

discommode [dìskəmóud]	v. to trouble or cause inconvenience [動] ～を困らせる、不便にする The driver was *discommoded* by the flat tire. 反意語 discommode : assist [əsíst] discommode の反意語が assist（～を助ける）
discompose [dìskəmpóuz]	v. to disturb the self-composure of [動] ～の平静を失わせる、不安にする The laughs of the other schoolchildren on the playground *discomposed* the young girl. 関連語 discompose : pacific [pəsífik] pacific（穏やかな、心が落ち着いている）な人は discompose されにくい。
discontent [dìskəntént]	adj. unhappy or dissatisfied [形] 不満な n. dissatisfaction [名] 不満 It was a point in my life when I was *discontent* and needed a change. The people had *discontent* against the newly launched policy. 類義語 discontent : gripe [graip] discontent の類義語が gripe（不平）

TRANSLATION | 例 文 の 訳

discern	正しいものと間違っているものを見分けるのは時に困難だ。
discomfit	大統領はテロリストの脅しに当惑した。
discommode	その運転手はタイヤがパンクして困った。
discompose	校庭にいる他の生徒たちの笑い声が、その小さな女の子を不安にさせた。
discontent	それは私の人生で、不満を感じ、変化を必要とした瞬間だった。 国民は新たに施行された政策に不満を抱いていた。

6

drudgery
[drʌ́dʒəri]

n. uninspiring and fatiguing work　　　　　　　　　[名] 退屈な仕事、骨折り仕事

Unskilled labor workers spend their entire lives in *drudgery*.

反意語 drudgery : rewarding work [riwɔ́ːʳdiŋ wəːʳk]
drudgeryの反意語がrewarding work（やりがいのある仕事）

earsplitting
[íəʳsplìtiŋ]

adj. excessively loud　　　　　　　　　　　　　　[形] 耳をつんざくような

Clubs are only good for people who enjoy dancing and *earsplitting* music.

関連語 earsplitting : loud [laud]
earsplittingはloud（大きい、うるさい）よりもはるかに騒がしい。

ecumenical
[èkjuménikəl]

adj. universal; promoting worldwide Christian cooperation
　　　　　　　　[形] 普遍的な；キリスト教諸派を代表する、世界のキリスト教会の

Saving the environment is of *ecumenical* importance.

類義語 ecumenical : general [dʒénªrəl]
ecumenicalの類義語がgeneral（一般的な、全体的な）

elucidate
[ilúːsədèit]

v. to make clear by explanation; to render more intelligible
　　　　　　　　　　　　　[動] 〜を明確に説明する；はっきりさせる

Mary *elucidated* her actions by explaining her perspective and intentions.

反意語 elucidate : garble [gáːʳbl]
elucidateの反意語がgarble（〜を誤って伝える、歪曲する）

emulate
[émjulèit]

v. to imitate or strive to equal　　　　　　　　　[動] 〜をまねる、〜と競う

Carrie *emulated* her older sister in appearance and personality.

関連語 emulate : exemplary [igzémpləʳi]
exemplary（模範的な）なものを求めてemulateする。

TRANSLATION | 例文の訳

drudgery　　技術のない労働者たちは退屈な仕事をして一生を送る。
earsplitting　クラブは、ダンスと耳をつんざくような音楽が好きな人々のみ楽しめるものだ。
ecumenical　環境を守ることには普遍的な意義がある。
elucidate　　メアリーは自分の見通しと意図を説明して、自分の行動を明確にした。
emulate　　キャリーは姉の外見と性格をまねた。

equipoise
[ékwəpɔ̀iz]

n. a state of equilibrium　　　　　　　　[名] 平衡（状態）、均衡、つり合い

Will the world ever reach an *equipoise*?

関連語 equipoise : vacillate [vǽsəlèit]
　　equipoise にあるものは vacillate（揺れる）ことがない。

fervid
[fə́ːʳvid]

adj. impassioned or having intense feelings　　　　[形] 熱烈な、熱情的な

The missionary is absolutely *fervid* about her faith.

反意語 fervid : impassive [impǽsiv]
　　fervid の反意語が impassive（無感動の、感情を表さない）

forthright
[fɔ́ːʳθràit]

adj. frank or direct　　　　　　　　[形] 率直な、素直な、隠し立てのない

The father was *forthright* with his son about the dangers of drinking.

関連語 forthright : circumlocution [sə̀ːʳkəmloukjúːʃən]
　　forthright ではなく、遠回しに話すのが circumlocution（遠回し、回りくどい表現）で
　　ある。

fortify
[fɔ́ːʳtəfài]

v. to strengthen physically, emotionally, or mentally
　　　　　　　　　　　　　[動] 〜を（物理的・感情的・精神的に）強くする、強化する

The Venetians *fortified* their Cretan castle with huge defensive walls.

反意語 fortify : enervate [énəʳvèit]
　　fortify の反意語が enervate（〜を弱くする）

furtive
[fə́ːʳtiv]

adj. deceptively secret or sly　　　　　　[形] こっそりとした、うさんくさい

The politician's *furtive* behavior was attacked by journalists in the
newspaper.

反意語 furtive : overt [ouvə́ːʳt]
　　furtive の反意語が overt（明白な、隠し立てのない）

TRANSLATION | 例 文 の 訳

equipoise	世界が平衡状態に達することはあるだろうか。
fervid	その宣教師は自分の信仰に情熱を持っている。
forthright	その父親は飲酒の危険性について息子に率直に話した。
fortify	ベネチア人はクレタ城を巨大な防御壁で強化した。
furtive	その政治家のうさんくさい行動が新聞でジャーナリストたちに非難された。

husband
[hʌ́zbənd]

v. **to use sparingly or economically** [動] (金・資源などを) 節約する、大切に使う

Billy *husbanded* his monthly allowance in order to save for a new bicycle.

反意語 husbandry : prodigality [prɑ̀dəgǽləti]
   hasbandry (節約) の反意語が prodigality (浪費、道楽)

martinet
[mɑ̀ːˈtⁱnét]

n. **a person who is strictly disciplined and adherent to forms**
   [名] (規則や命令に絶対に従う) 厳格な人

It takes a *martinet* to run a military operation.

関連語 martinet : leniency [líːniənsi]
   martinet は leniency (寛大さ、慈悲) を持ちにくい。

mirth
[məːˈθ]

n. **happiness or gaiety expressed with laughter**　[名] 歓喜；浮かれ騒ぎ

Elizabeth responded with *mirth* when her boyfriend proposed to her.

関連語 mirth : laughter [lǽftər]
   mirth は laughter (笑い) で表現される。

misanthrope
[mísənθròup]

n. **one who dislikes or distrusts mankind**　[名] 人間嫌いの人

Polly Whitney once pointed out the irony of a *misanthrope* needing people to hate.

関連語 misanthrope : humane [ʰjuːméin]
   misanthrope は humane (思いやりのある、心の優しい) な人ではない。

misbehave
[mìsbihéiv]

v. **to behave improperly**　[動] 無作法にふるまう、行儀悪くする

It is typical for children to *misbehave*.

関連語 misbehave : reprobate [réprəbèit]
   reprobate (道楽者、放蕩者) は misbehave しがちである。

TRANSLATION | 例 文 の 訳

husband	ビリーは新しい自転車を買うために、月々の小遣いを節約した。
martinet	軍事作戦の遂行には、厳格な人間が必要だ。
mirth	恋人が結婚を申し込んだとき、エリザベスは喜んで応じた。
misanthrope	ポリー・ウィットニーはかつて、人間嫌いの人は嫌うための人間を必要とするという皮肉を指摘した。
misbehave	子供が無作法にふるまうのはよくあることだ。

mischievous
[místʃivəs]

adj. tending to cause trouble; harmful　　　　　[形] いたずら好きな、有害な

The mother could not control her *mischievous* teen.

関連語 mischievous : brat [bræt]
brat (行儀の悪い子供) には mischievous という特性がある。

partial
[pá:ʳʃəl]

adj. having prejudice; being favorably disposed
　　　　　　　　　　　　　　　　　　　　　　　[形] 不公平な；えこひいきをする

The manager was *partial* to his hirees and tended to promote them above others.

反意語 partial : dispassionate [dispǽʃənət]
partial の反意語は dispassionate (冷静な、公平な)

類義語 bias [báiəs]
名詞の類義語は bias (偏見、先入観)

partisan
[pá:ʳtizᵊn]

n. one who strongly adheres to a cause, party or faction
　　　　　　　　　　　　　　　　[名] (主義・党派・派閥などの) 熱心な支持者

Lee is a *partisan* for anti-globalization.

関連語 partisan : allegiance [əlí:dʒəns]
partisan は強い allegiance (忠誠、忠節) を持っている。

persuade
[pəʳswéid]

v. to convince or urge someone by argument or entreaty
　　　　　　　　　　　　　　　　[動] (議論や懇願を通して人を) 説得する、求める

You can try to *persuade* him, but I guarantee he won't be moved.

関連語 persuade : obstinate [ábstənət]
obstinate (頑固な) 人を persuade するのは非常に難しい。

pertinacity
[pə̀:ʳtənǽsəti]

n. an obstinate adherence to a cause, position, or purpose
　　　　　　　　　　　　　　[名] (主義・地位・目的などに対する) 頑固な執着

Darcy could not believe Elizabeth's *pertinacity* to feminism.

関連語 pertinacity : refractory [rifrǽktᵊri]
形容詞の類義語が refractory (手に負えない、強情な)

TRANSLATION | 例 文 の 訳

mischievous　その母親はいたずら好きな10代の子供をコントロールできなかった。

partial　その支配人は自分が雇った従業員たちをひいきし、他の者より重用しがちだった。

partisan　リーは反グローバル化の熱心な支持者である。

persuade　あなたが彼を説得しようと試みることはできるが、私は彼が動かされないことを保証する。

pertinacity　エリザベスのフェミニズムへの頑固な執着がダーシーには信じられなかった。

pertinent
[pə́ːʳtᵊnənt]

adj. relevant　　　　　　　　　　　　　　　　　[形] 関連のある、適切な

The judge ruled the evidence *pertinent* to the case.

反意語 pertinent : immaterial [ìmətíᵊriəl]
pertinentの反意語がimmaterial (〜にとって重要でない、関連のない)

perturb
[pəʳtə́ːrb]

v. to disturb or cause confusion to someone's peace of mind
[動] (人を) 悩ませる、不安にさせる

The new employee *perturbed* the manager with his lazy work habits.

関連語 perturb : stoic [stóuik]
stoic (禁欲的な、冷静な) 人はperturbされにくい。

pervade
[pəʳvéid]

v. to permeate through every part　　　　　[動] 全体に広がる、充満する

The scent of flowers from the garden *pervaded* the cottage.

関連語 pervasive : avoid [əvɔ́id]
pervasive (浸透性の、普及力のある) ことをavoid (避ける) のは難しい。

portentous
[pɔːʳténtəs]

adj. arousing amazement; being an important or serious matter; ominous
[形] 尊大な；ゆゆしい；不吉な

His *portentous* words left the crowd in amazement and fear.

反意語 portentous : auspicious [ɔːspíʃəs]
portentousの反意語がauspicious (幸先のよい)

portrait
[pɔ́ːʳtrit]

n. a picture or portrayal in words of a person　　[名] 肖像画、人物描写

There is a *portrait* of Mona Lisa hanging in the Louvre in Paris.

関連語 portrait : person [pə́ːʳsn]
person (人物) を描写した絵がportrait。

TRANSLATION | 例 文 の 訳

pertinent 判事はその証拠が事件に関連していると裁定した。
perturb 新しい従業員はその怠惰な勤務態度で課長を悩ませた。
pervade 庭の花の香りがそのコテージ全体に広がっていた。
portentous 彼の不吉な言葉が群衆を驚きと恐怖に陥れた。
portrait パリのルーブル美術館にモナリザの肖像画が展示されている。

purvey
[pəˈvéi]
	v. **to supply provisions or materials** [動]（食糧や材料を）供給する
	
	The committee *purveyed* food and other supplies for the conference.
	
	関連語 purvey : vendor [véndəʳ]
	    vender（売り手、販売業者）は物を purvey する役割を果たす。
	    cf) vendee（買い手、買い主）

ribald [ríbəld]	adj. **offensive; containing indecent humor** [形] みだらな；下品な Politicians must be careful not to make *ribald* comments during speeches. 反意語 ribald : seemly [síːmli] ribald の反意語が seemly（場にふさわしい、上品な）
rescind [risínd]	v. **to remove, take back, or revoke** [動]〜を廃止する、撤回する、無効にする The judgement was *rescinded* by the committee due to new evidence. 関連語 rescind : law [lɔː] rescind する対象は law（法律）など。
sanguine [sǽŋgwin]	adj. **being of the color of blood; of a cheerful and confident disposition** [形] 赤ら顔の；楽天的な、自信がある Derek had a *sanguine* temperament and always had a smile on his face. 反意語 sanguine : despondent [dispándənt] sanguine の反意語が despondent（元気のない、落胆した）
servile [sə́ːʳvil]	adj. **subservient or submissive** [形] 言いなりになる、追従的な、従順な Debbie is a quiet and *servile* young woman who never raises her voice. 反意語 servile : imperious [impíʳriəs] servile の反意語が imperious（傲慢な、横柄な）

TRANSLATION | 例 文 の 訳

purvey	委員会はその会議のために食料やその他の必需品を供給した。
ribald	政治家は演説中に下品な発言をしないように注意しなければならない。
rescind	新しい証拠が理由で、その判断は委員会によって撤回された。
sanguine	デレクは楽天的な気質で、いつも笑顔を浮かべていた。
servile	デビーは決して声を上げない静かで従順な若い女性だ。

squander
[skwάndəʳ]

v. **to spend foolishly; to scatter**   [動] 浪費する、散財する；散布する

Michael *squandered* his entire first paycheck at the casino.

反意語 squander : conserve [kənsə́ːʳv]
squanderの反意語がconserve（大切に使う、節約する）

steadfast
[stédfæst]

adj. **immovable; loyal and unchanging**   [形] 不動の；忠実で不変の

There is nothing more valuable than a *steadfast* friendship.

反意語 steadfast : capricious [kəpríʃəs]
steadfastの反意語がcapricious（気まぐれな、不安定な）

strut
[strʌt]

v. **to walk in a proud or arrogant way**   [動] 気取って歩く、横柄な態度で歩く

Kathy *strutted* down the hallways of her corporation, flaunting her attractiveness.

関連語 strut : walk [wɔːk]
傲慢な態度でwalkするのがstrut。

verve
[vəːʳv]

n. **energy or vitality; the spirit of enthusiasm**   [名] 活気、元気；熱意

The surfer goes at life just as he does a wave, with *verve* and confidence.

反意語 verve : listlessness [lístlisnis]
verveの反意語がlistlessness（無気力、やる気がないこと）

virtuous
[və́ːʳtʃuəs]

adj. **exhibiting excellent moral virtue**   [形] 徳の高い、高潔な

The princess was not only kind but *virtuous*.

反意語 virtuous : base [beis]
virtuousの反意語がbase（卑劣な、卑しい）

TRANSLATION | 例 文 の 訳

squander	マイケルはカジノで初任給を全部浪費した。
steadfast	変わらない友情より価値あるものはない。
strut	キャシーは魅力をふりまきながら、会社の廊下を気取って歩いた。
verve	そのサーファーは波に乗るときと同じように、活気と自信を持って人生を生きている。
virtuous	その王女は優しいのみならず、徳が高かった。

virulent
[vír(j)ulənt]

adj. being able to cause disease by breaking down bodily defense mechanisms; malignant

［形］（免疫系を壊すことで病気を引き起こす）伝染力の強い、悪性の；有毒な

Without proper treatment, the *virulent* HIV will spread throughout his body quickly and debilitate him.

反意語 virulent : salubrious [səlú:briəs]

virulentの反意語がsalubrious（健康によい、快適な）

wary
[wέəri]

adj. cautious or watchful of danger ［形］用心深い、慎重な

When walking alone at night, one should be *wary* of strangers.

関連語 wary : gulled [gʌld]

注意深くwaryする人はgulled（だまされる）ことはない。

TRANSLATION | 例 文 の 訳

virulent　適切な治療をしなければ、悪性のHIVが彼の体全体に急速に広がり、彼を衰弱させるだろう。

wary　夜、1人で歩くときには知らない人に用心しなければならない。

■ Fill in the blanks with the correct letter that matches the word with its definition.

1. virulent _____
2. curt _____
3. drudgery _____
4. furtive _____
5. purvey _____
6. emulate _____
7. misanthrope _____
8. disaffected _____
9. portentous _____
10. husband _____

a. to imitate or strive to equal

b. one who dislikes or distrusts mankind

c. being able to cause disease by breaking down bodily defense mechanisms; malignant

d. rudely short in speech or manner

e. to supply provisions or materials

f. deceptively secret or sly

g. arousing amazement or being an important or serious matter; ominous

h. to use sparingly or economically

i. discontented and resentful especially against authority

j. uninspiring and fatiguing work

■ Put the correct word in each blank from the list of words below.

11. adulate は_____よりお世辞の程度がはるかに強い。

12. 傲慢な態度で walk することを_____すると表現する。

13. _____は misbehave する傾向がある。

14. _____の類義語は discontent（苦情）である。

15. loud よりはるかに騒々しいとき_____と言う。

16. _____せずに遠回しに話すのが circumlocution である。

17. _____の反意語は impassive（情熱のない）である。

18. _____な人は容易に discompose されない。

19. 注意深く wary する人は_____することはない。

20. _____は leniency を持ちにくい。

| a. reprobate | b. gripe | c. earsplitting | d. forthright | e. pacific | f. gulled |
| g. flatter | h. martinet | i. fervid | j. bale | k. prodigality | l. strut |

Answer key

11. g 12. l 13. a 14. b 15. c 16. d 17. i 18. e 19. f 20. h
1. c 2. d 3. j 4. f 5. e 6. a 7. b 8. i 9. g 10. h

15

1日を3.333…パーセントと考えて単語を
覚えていけば、30日後には100パーセントになる。

2nd DAY

---

assent
[əsént]

v. **to agree to or approve of** 　　　　　[動] 同意する、賛成する

Max *assented* to the conditions and terms of the job.

反意語 assent : object [əbdʒékt]
　　assentの反意語はobject（反対する）

---

assert
[əsə́ːʳt]

v. **to forcefully state or declare an opinion or position; to defend one's rights** 　　[動]（意見・立場・権利などを）主張する、断言する；擁護する

Tom *asserts* relentlessly that the judge is corrupt.

関連語 assertive : bumptious [bʌ́mpʃəs]
　　assertive（はっきり自分の意見を述べる）な態度が行き過ぎるとbumptious（傲慢な）になる。

---

assiduity
[æ̀sid(j)úːəti]

n. **the quality of being extremely hard working and diligent** 　　[名] 勤勉、精励

It is *assiduity*, not necessarily intelligence, that will take you far in the world.

関連語 assiduity : slothful [slɔ́ːθfəl]
　　slothful（怠惰な、不精な）人はassiduityがない。

---

badger
[bǽdʒəʳ]

v. **to tease or annoy persistently** 　　[動] ～をしつこくからかう、困らせる

The boy *badgered* his sister until she started to cry.

関連語 badger : bother [bɑ́ðəʳ]
　　badgerはひどくbother（～を困らせる）すること。

TRANSLATION | 例文の訳

assent	マックスはその仕事の条件に同意した。
assert	トムはその裁判官が不正だとしつこく主張した。
assiduity	この世界であなたを進歩させてくれるのは、必ずしも知力というわけではなく、勤勉さだ。
badger	その少年は妹が泣き出すまでしつこくからかった。

banish
[bǽniʃ]

v. **to expel or exile from a country**　[動]（国などから）追放する、強制退去させる

Nick was *banished* from his country for treason.

関連語 banish : country [kʌ́ntri]
banishはcountry（国など）から追放すること。

carouse
[kəráuz]

v. **to drink excessively and be boisterous**　[動] 大酒を飲んで楽しむ

Japanese businessmen work diligently all day and let out their stress by *carousing* until the wee hours of the morning.

関連語 carouse : roisterer [rɔ́istəʳəʳ]
carouseはroisterer（どんちゃん騒ぎをする人）がすること。

desecrate
[désikrèit]

v. **to damage or defile the sanctity or sacredness of**　[動]〜の神聖を汚す、冒涜する

The church was *desecrated* by the graffiti spray-painted on its front doors.

反意語 desecrate : sanctify [sǽŋktəfài]
desecrateの反意語はsanctify（〜を神聖にする）

desiccate
[désikèit]

v. **to dehydrate or absorb moisture**　[動]〜を乾燥させる、水分を吸収する

Due to the drought, the land was barren and *desiccated*.

関連語 desiccate : moisture [mɔ́istʃəʳ]
desiccateはmoisture（水分）を取り除くこと。

discredit
[diskrédit]

v. **to question the accuracy or authority of; to damage a reputation**　[動]（学説や権威などを）信用できないものとする、疑う；評判を悪くする

The attorney *discredited* the witness's character by revealing his criminal history.

関連語 discredit : invective [invéktiv]
discreditするためにinvective（悪口、非難）を流布する。

TRANSLATION | 例 文 の 訳

banish　ニックは反逆罪で国外追放された。
carouse　日本のサラリーマンは一日懸命に働き、真夜中過ぎまで酒を飲んで騒いでストレスを発散する。
desecrate　正面ドアにスプレーで落書きされて、その教会は冒涜された。
desiccate　干ばつのせいで、その土地は荒れ、乾燥していた。
discredit　弁護士はその証人の犯罪歴を明かして、彼の人格を疑った。

discrete
[diskríːt]

adj. having a separate or distinct identity

[形] ばらばらの、別々の、個別的な

Only in recent years have homosexual couples been recognized as *discrete* under the law in some countries.

関連語 discrete : overlap [òuvəʳlǽp]

discreteなものはoverlap（重複する）されることがない。

discriminate
[diskrímənèit]

v. to perceive differences or distinctions between; to treat unfairly due to race, religion, age, or other features

[動] ～を識別する、区別する；（人種、宗教、年齢などの理由で）～を差別する

Avid watchers can *discriminate* between the various species of birds.

関連語 discriminate : difference [dífʳrəns]

discriminateはdifference（差異）を見つけること。

discursive
[diskə́ːʳsiv]

adj. changing topics without order; covering a wide range of subjects

[形] 脈絡のない；（話題などが）広範囲にわたる

The *discursive* lecture left the students informed, but a little confused.

類義語 discursive : digressive [daigrésiv]

discursiveの類義語はdigressive（主題から離れがちな、脱線する）

disdain
[disdéin]

v. to treat with haughty contempt

[動] ～を軽蔑する

n. a feeling of contempt

[名] 軽蔑

The Hispanic population charges that the U.S. *disdains* their people and heritage.

Young prince David III, looked at the common people in *disdain*.

類義語 disdain : snub [snʌb]

disdainの類義語はsnub（冷たくあしらう、無視する）

TRANSLATION | 例 文 の 訳

discrete　ここ数年でようやく、いくつかの国で法的に同性のカップルの独立性が認定されるようになった。

discriminate　観察好きな人はさまざまな種類の鳥を識別できる。

discursive　その広範囲にわたる内容を扱った講義は学生に知識を与えたが、少し混乱させた。

disdain　ヒスパニック系の人々は米国が自分たちの民族と伝統を軽蔑していると非難する。
　若き王子デイビッド３世は平民を軽蔑の目で見た。

disembody
[dìsembádi]

v. to free from corporeal existence　　　　[動] 肉体から離れる

It is said that through meditation people have *disembodied* themselves and elevated to a purely spiritual existence.

反意語 disembodied : corporeal [kɔːrpɔ́ːriəl]
　　disembodied の反意語は corporeal（肉体の、有形の）

disgruntle
[disgrʌ́ntl]

v. to make discontented or dissatisfied　　[動] 不満にさせる、不機嫌にさせる

The *disgruntled* postal workers eventually went on strike.

反意語 disgruntled : contented [kənténtid]
　　disgruntled の反意語は contented（満足な）

disguise
[disgáiz]

v. to change the appearance of; to conceal　　[動] 〜を変装させる；隠す

n. a costume or change of appearance used to hide one's identity or imitate another's identity　　[名] 変装、仮装用具

The thief could not be identified because he *disguised* himself with a used military uniform.

What *disguise* will you wear for Halloween?

関連語 disguise : camouflage [kǽməflùːʒ]
　　disguise は camouflage（カムフラージュ、偽装）に使用される。

disgust
[disgʌ́st]

v. to offend with distastefulness　　　　[動] 嫌がらせをする、うんざりさせる

n. a strong aversion or dislike　　　　[名] 嫌悪、反感

Melanie was *disgusted* by the rude behavior of the people sitting at the next table.

Ellie sat in *disgust* while her date ate three plates of food.

関連語 disgust : odious [óudiəs]
　　odious（非常に不愉快な）なことは disgust の要因になる。cf) odious は人・ものの状態を表し、disgust はその人・ものを見ている人の感覚を表す。

TRANSLATION | 例 文 の 訳

disembody　瞑想を通して、人々は肉体から離れ、純粋な霊的存在に高まると言われている。

disgruntle　不満な郵便局員たちはついにストライキを起こした。

disguise　その泥棒は中古の軍服で変装したため、正体を見破られずにすんだ。
　　　　　あなたはハロウィーンでどんな仮装をしますか。

disgust　メラニーは隣のテーブルに座る人々の無礼なふるまいにうんざりした。
　　　　　エリーはデートの相手が3皿食べる間、うんざりして座っていた。

disingenuous
[dìsindʒénjuəs]

adj. insincere or lacking in candor 　　　　　　[形] 不誠実な、不正直な

The poem criticized *disingenuous* expressions of love.

関連語 disingenuous : sincerity [sinsérəti]
disingenuous なものには sincerity (誠実、誠意) がない。

equivocate
[ikwívəkèit]

v. to use uncertain or ambiguous language to avoid committing to a perspective or statement
　　　　　　　　　　[動] (明言を避けるために) ごまかす、あいまいなことを言う

John intentionally *equivocated* his position on abortion to avoid controversy in the office.

関連語 equivocation : clarity [klǽrəti]
equivocation には clarity (明快さ、明晰さ) がない。

erudite
[ér(j)udàit]

adj. learned or scholarly 　　　　　　　　　　[形] 学識のある、博学な

The *erudite* graduate student finished his Ph.D. in 4 years.

関連語 erudite : fathom [fǽðəm]
erudite な人は fathom (〜を推測する、測る) することができる。

eschew
[istʃúː]

v. to avoid deliberately; to shun 　　　　　　[動] 〜を (意図的に) 避ける；控える

Phil found it difficult to *eschew* Paul because they had the same circle of friends.

反意語 eschew : welcome [wélkəm]
eschew の反意語は welcome (〜を歓迎する)

exultant
[igzʌ́ltˀnt]

adj. filled with great joy or triumph 　　　　　[形] 大喜びで、勝ち誇った

The newly engaged man is *exultant* because his girlfriend said yes to his proposal.

反意語 exultant : crestfallen [kréstfɔːlən]
exultant の反意語は crestfallen (意気消沈した、がっかりした)

TRANSLATION ｜ 例 文 の 訳

disingenuous　その詩は誠実さを欠く愛の表現を批判したものだ。

equivocate　ジョンは会社で議論が起こらないように、中絶についての自分の立場を意図的にごまかした。

erudite　その博学な大学院生は4年で博士課程を修了した。

eschew　友人関係が共通しているので、フィルはポールを避けることは難しいことに気づいた。

exultant　その婚約したての男性は、恋人がプロポーズを承諾してくれたことに大喜びしている。

1st
2nd
3rd
4th
5th
6th
7th
8th
9th
10th

fluent
[flúːənt]

adj. facile in language; capable of flowing with ease

[形] 流暢な；すらすらと操れる

To make it in the career world today, one must be *fluent* in at least two languages.

関連語 fluent : glib [glib]

fluentと glib（口の達者な）の違いは、後者が言語とは関係のない、口の上手さを言う点にある。

frugal
[frúːgəl]

adj. sparing or thrifty

[形] 倹約する、質素な

The *frugal* man lived in a relatively modest home despite his substantial wealth.

関連語 frugal : parsimonious [pàːˈsəmóuniəs]

frugalの度が過ぎると parsimonious（けちな）と言われる。

反意語 frugal : profligate [práfligət]

frugalの反意語は profligate（乱費する）

gouge
[gaudʒ]

v. to cut or scoop out

[動] ～を彫る、掘り出す

The archeologist began to delicately *gouge* the sedimentary rock surrounding the fossil.

関連語 gouge : engrave [ingréiv]

gougeは engrave（彫刻する）よりも狭い範囲を深く掘る。

gush
[gʌʃ]

v. to emit in a large flow or rush

[動] 流れ出す

Water *gushed* out of the broken hose.

関連語 gush : trickle [tríkl]

gushは trickle（少しずつ流れる）よりも勢いよく流れる様子を表す。

hash
[hæʃ]

v. to mince or chop finely

[動] 細かく刻む、みじん切りにする

After seeing the dentist, all of his food had to be *hashed* before he could eat it.

関連語 hash : pestle [péstl]

hashするために pestle（すりこぎ）を使用する。

TRANSLATION | 例 文 の 訳

fluent	現代のキャリア社会で成功するには、少なくとも２つの言語が流暢でなければならない。
frugal	その倹約家の男性はかなりの資産があるにもかかわらず比較的地味な家に住んでいた。
gouge	その考古学者は化石の周りの堆積石を慎重に掘り出し始めた。
gush	破れたホースから水が流れ出した。
hash	歯科医の診察後、彼の食べる物はすべて食べやすいように細かく刻まれなければならなかった。

haunt
[hɔːnt]

v. to frequent or continually visit; to troublingly reappear continually
[動] 頻繁に訪れる；出没する、付きまとう

n. a well-frequented place
[名] よく行く場所

Larry and his friends *haunted* the local bar and were well acquainted with the owner.

The library is the *haunt* of diligent students.

関連語 haunt : familiar [fəmíljəʳ]
人にとって、haunt は familiar（よく知っている）な場所である。

insensible
[insénsəbl]

adj. apathetic; incapable of feeling sensation
[形] 無関心な；無反応な、意識のない

Ryan's *insensible* demeanor was often mistaken for arrogance and afforded him few friends.

関連語 insensible : affect [əfékt]
insensible な人を affect（感動させる、影響する）するのは難しい。

insight
[ínsàit]

n. the ability or act of understanding the true nature of things
[名] 洞察力、理解

The wise person has *insight* into every situation.

関連語 insight : discerning [disə́ːʳniŋ]
insight と似た意味で形容詞 discerning（洞察力のある）がある。

laud
[lɔːd]

v. to praise
[動] ～を賞賛する

The young woman was *lauded* for her efforts in the match, despite the fact that she lost.

反意語 laud : berate [biréit]
laud の反意語は berate（～を叱責する）

TRANSLATION | 例 文 の 訳

haunt　ラリーと友人たちはその地元のバーによく行くので、店主をよく知っていた。
図書館は勉強熱心な学生がよく行く場所だ。

insensible　ライアンの無関心な態度がよく傲慢だと誤解されるので、彼には友達がほとんどいなかった。

insight　賢明な人にはあらゆる状況についての洞察力がある。

laud　その若い女性は負けたにもかかわらず、試合中の努力を賞賛された。

22

lint
[lint]

n. scraped linen used for dressing wounds

[名]（傷の手当てに使われる）ガーゼ、包帯用の布

Rick looked through the first aid kit, but could not find the *lint* to cover Anne's wound.

関連語 lint : bleeding [blí:diŋ]

lintは bleeding（出血）を止めるために使われる。

lush
[lʌʃ]

adj. growing thick and healthily; fertile or plentiful

[形] 緑豊かな；多産の、豊かな

The *lush* garden would soon provide an abundance of vegetables.

反意語 lush : sere [siəʳ]

lushの反意語は sere（干からびた）

maudlin
[mɔ́:dlin]

adj. extremely sentimental or emotionally weak　　[形] ひどく感傷的な

Kelly always cries at *maudlin* movies.

関連語 maudlin : sentimental [sèntəméntl]

maudlinは sentimental（感傷的な）の度が強い様子。

miscreant
[mískriənt]

n. a villain; a heretic　　　　　　　　　　　[名] 悪者；異教徒

The *miscreant* was exiled out of Greece.

反意語 miscreant : saint [séint]

miscreantの反意語は saint（聖者、聖人のような人）

misdemeanor
[mìsdimí:nəʳ]

n. a minor legal offense less serious than a felony

[名] 非行、不品行、軽犯罪

The *misdemeanor* cost Frank a $100 fine.

関連語 misdemeanor : crime [kraim]

misdemeanorは crime（犯罪）よりも程度の軽い違法行為を指す。

TRANSLATION | 例 文 の 訳

lint　　　　リックは救急箱の中を見渡したが、アンの傷を覆う布を見つけられなかった。

lush　　　　その緑豊かな庭からはまもなく豊富な野菜が収穫できるだろう。

maudlin　　ケリーはとても感傷的な映画を見るといつも泣く。

miscreant　その異教徒はギリシャから追放された。

misdemeanor フランクはその軽犯罪のために100ドルの罰金を納めなければならなかった。

miser
[máizəʳ]

n. a person who is cruel and stingy with money [名] 守銭奴、けち

The *miser* refused to tip his waiter more than 5% of the bill.

関連語 miser : hoard [hɔːʳd]
miser には hoard (財宝や食料などをこっそり蓄える) するという特徴がある。

mishap
[míshæp]

n. an unfortunate accident or occurrence [名] 不運な出来事

The airport lost her luggage in a *mishap*.

関連語 mishap : catastrophe [kətǽstrəfi]
catastrophe (大災害、大惨事) は mishap よりも程度の大きい不運を表す。

obscure
[əbskjúəʳ]

adj. unclear or hidden; not easily understood
[形] 不明瞭な、隠れた：わかりにくい

The professor's explanation was full of *obscure* jargon and beyond my scope of comprehension.

関連語 obscure : comprehend [kàmprihénd]
obscure なことは簡単に comprehend (～を理解する) ができない。

obsequious
[əbsíːkwiəs]

adj. over attentive and obedient [形] 過度に気を使った、卑屈な

The student's *obsequious* behavior toward his teacher was a source of ridicule for the other kids.

関連語 obsequious : deferential [dèfərénʃəl]
deferential (丁重な) の度が過ぎた状態が obsequious である。

obsess
[əbsés]

v. to have something haunt and control one's mind and actions
[動] (妄想などが) 人に取りつく、考えと行動を規制する

Jack was so *obsessed* with Jill that he moved to another country just to be near her.

関連語 obsessed : attracted [ətrǽktid]
obsessed は attracted (引かれている) というレベルを超え、すっかり心が奪われている状態を表す。

TRANSLATION | 例 文 の 訳

miser	その守銭奴はウェイターに請求額の5パーセントを超えるチップを渡すことを拒否した。
mishap	不運なことに、空港が彼女の手荷物を紛失した。
obscure	その教授の説明にはわかりにくい専門用語が満載で、私の理解できる範囲を超えていた。
obsequious	その生徒の教師に対する卑屈な態度は、他の子供の嘲笑の種になった。
obsess	ジャックはジルに心を奪われ、彼女のそばにいるだけのために他国へ引っ越した。

opulent
[ápjulənt]

adj. **wealthy**   [形]富裕な、豊かな

The *opulent* businessman tipped the waiter almost 50% of the bill.

反意語 opulent : indigent [índidʒənt]
opulentの反意語はindigent（極貧の）

ossify
[ásəfài]

v. **to change into bone; to become inflexible or rigid**
    [動]骨化する；硬化する、固定化する

After the September 11th attacks, many Americans who were democratic and liberal *ossified*.

関連語 ossification : flexible [fléksəbl]
ossification（固定化、硬化）しているものはflexible（柔軟な）ではない。

paunchy
[pɔ́:ntʃi]

adj. **having a potbelly**   [形]太鼓腹の

Soren's *paunchy* father had obviously drunk too many beers in his day.

反意語 paunchy : svelte [svelt]
paunchyの反意語はsvelte（ほっそりした）

pluck
[plʌk]

n. **nerve**   [名]度胸、勇気

v. **to pick or pull quickly; to remove or separate forcibly; to play by sounding the strings with the fingers**
    [動]引き抜く；むしり取る；（楽器の弦を）指でかき鳴らす

The new reporter was known for his *pluck* when investigating a story.
Patrick *plucked* a few stray hairs around his eyebrows.

反意語 pluck : cowardice [káuəʳdis]
pluckの反意語はcowardice（臆病、小心）

関連語 pluck : harp [hɑː'p]
harp（ハープ）はpluckする楽器。

TRANSLATION | 例 文 の 訳

opulent その富裕な企業家はウェイターに請求額の50パーセント近いチップを渡した。
ossify 9月11日のテロ攻撃後、民主的でリベラルだった多くのアメリカ人の態度が硬化した。
paunchy ソーレンの父親が太鼓腹なのは、明らかに若い頃にビールを飲みすぎたからだ。
pluck その新しい記者は事件を調べるときの度胸で知られていた。
パトリックは眉毛の周りのむだ毛を数本引き抜いた。

plumb
[plʌm]

n. a lead weight strung at the bottom of a line to determine a true vertical　　　[名]（深度を測るために糸にくくりつけた）鉛錘

v. to measure depth　　　[動] 深さを測る

The carpenter measured the angle of the wall with a *plumb*.

The oceanographers had to *plumb* the site to see where they could release the new scientific equipment.

関連語 plumb : depth [depθ]
　　　plumbはdepth（深さ）を測ること。

plummet
[plʌ́mit]

v. to fall or drop rapidly　　　[動] 急落する

Diving to catch its prey, the inexperienced hawk accidently *plummeted* into the ground.

関連語 plummet : descend [disénd]
　　　plummetはまっすぐ急速にdescend（下降する）こと。

poseur
[pouzə́ːʳ]

n. one who habitually pretends to be what he/she is; an insincere person　　　[名] 気取り屋、偽善者

The *poseur* dressed as a rock star, even though he was a janitor.

関連語 poseur : sincerity [sinsérəti]
　　　poseurにはsincerity（誠実、誠意）がない。

prudence
[prúːdns]

n. the ability and good judgment to govern oneself with the use of reason　　　[名] 用心深さ、慎重さ、分別

The King used *prudence* in making decisions about his kingdom.

関連語 prudence : daredevil [déəʳdèvəl]
　　　daredevil（向こう見ずな人）はprudenceを持ちにくい。

TRANSLATION | 例 文 の 訳

plumb　　　その大工は鉛錘で壁の角度を測った。
　　　　　　　その海洋学者たちは、どこにその新しい科学装置を置けるかを判断するために、その地点の深度を測らなければならなかった。

plummet　　その未熟なタカは餌を捕まえようと急降下し、誤って地面に激突してしまった。

poseur　　その気取り屋は管理人なのに、ロックスターのように着飾っていた。

prudence　　その王は自国に関する決定を慎重に下した。

26

pusillanimous
[pjùːsəlǽnəməs]

adj. afraid, timid, or lacking courage　　　　　[形] 気の弱い、臆病な

The onlooker was too *pusillanimous* to help the man being robbed.

反意語 pusillanimous : stouthearted [stáuthάːʳtid]
　　　pusillanimous の反意語は stouthearted（勇敢な）

rash
[ræʃ]

adj. reckless or hasty and done without thinking
　　　　　　　　　　　　　　　　　　　　[形] 向こう見ずな、性急な、軽率な

n. a red spot which appears on skin as a biological reaction　[名] 発疹

Her decision to quit school was *rash* and she later regretted it.
The *rashes* around my neck are very sore.

関連語 rash : adventurous [ædvéntʃərəs]
　　　rash と adventurous（大胆な）の違いは、後者には軽率なという意味がないこと。

reserved
[rizə́ːʳvd]

adj. characterized by reticence and self-restraint; set aside
　　　　　　　　　　　　　　　[形] 控えめな、無口な、内気な；残された

Darcy is a rather *reserved* man, keeping to himself most of the time.

反意語 reserved : expansive [ikspǽnsiv]
　　　reserved の反意語は expansive（朗らかな、気さくな）

resilience
[rizíljəns]

n. the capability to recover one's original form or health
　　　　　　　　　　　　　　　　　　　　　　　[名] 弾力性、回復力

The gymnast's *resilience* allowed him to recover quickly from a sprained ankle.

反意語 resilience : inability to recover [ìnəbíləti tə rikʌ́vər]
　　　resilience の反意語は inability to recover（回復力がない）

TRANSLATION | 例 文 の 訳

pusillanimous その見物人は気が弱すぎて、男性が強盗に襲われるところを助けられなかった。

rash 退学するという彼女の決心は軽率で、彼女はやがて後悔した。
　　　　首の周りの発疹がとても痛い。

reserved ダーシーはほとんどの時間を1人で過ごす、どちらかというと控えめな男性だ。

resilience その体操選手は自身の回復力のおかげで、足首の捻挫からすぐに復帰できた。

27

sculpt
[skʌlpt]

v. to carve or make a sculpture　　　　　[動]〜を彫ること、彫刻すること

The artist *sculpted* an image of the beautiful woman he fell in love with in his youth.

関連語 sculpture : cameo [kǽmiòu]
cameo（カメオ）は宝石や貝殻に顔を彫ったsculuptureの一種。

scrupulous
[skrúːpjuləs]

adj. having moral integrity; attentive to detail and exactness
[形] 良心的な、誠実な；綿密な

The congregation couldn't have asked for a more *scrupulous* pastor.

反意語 unscrupulousness : probity [próubəti]
反意語はunscrupulousness（破廉恥、不実）。似た意味の名詞にprobity（正直、誠実）がある。

sluggard
[slʌ́gəʳd]

n. a person who is continually lazy　　　　　[名] 怠け者、不精者

The *sluggard* showed up to work late every day and slept most of the time.

関連語 sluggard : lazy [léizi]
sluggardはlazy（怠惰な）だという特徴がある。

smug
[smʌg]

adj. self-satisfied; offensively arrogant　　　　　[形] 自己満足した；偉そうな

Chloe didn't like the *smug* attitude of the professional wrestlers when she asked for their autographs.

関連語 smugness : smirk [sməːʳk]
smirk（にやにや笑い、薄笑い）をする背後にはsmugness（ひとりよがり、うぬぼれ）がある。

TRANSLATION | 例 文 の 訳

sculpt	その芸術家は彼が若いときに恋した美しい女性の姿を彫刻した。
scrupulous	信徒たちにはこれ以上良心的な牧師は望めなかっただろう。
sluggard	その怠け者は毎日遅刻して職場に現れ、ほとんどの時間、眠っていた。
smug	クロウはサインを頼んだときのプロレスラーたちの偉そうな態度が気に入らなかった。

1st
2nd
3rd
4th
5th
6th
7th
8th
9th
10th

smuggle
[smʌ́gl]

v. **to illegally import or export things** [動] ～を密輸する

Five people were arrested yesterday for *smuggling* drugs into England.

関連語 smuggle : convey [kənvéi]
smuggle は違法に外国との間で物品を convey (運ぶ、運搬する) こと。

snub
[snʌb]

v. **to treat with neglect or impoliteness** [動] ～を無視する、冷たくあしらう

The arrogant actress *snubbed* the man offering her his coat.

関連語 snub : politeness [pəláitnis]
snub する人は politeness (礼儀正しさ、丁寧さ) のある態度を取らない。

stultify
[stʌ́ltəfài]

v. **to render useless or ineffectual; to cause to appear stupid**
[動] ～を台無しにする、無効にする；～を愚かに見せる

Johnson's previous prison record *stultified* any chances of him getting into medical school.

反意語 stultifying : stirring [stə́ːriŋ]
stultifying (無効にする) の反意語は stirring (呼び起こす)。

TRANSLATION | 例 文 の 訳

smuggle 昨日、麻薬をイギリスに密輸したかどで5人が逮捕された。
snub その傲慢な女優は自分にコートを差し出した男性を無視した。
stultify ジョンソンは逮捕歴があったため、医科大学に入れる可能性がまったくなくなった。

29

■ Fill in the blanks with the correct letter that matches the word with its definition.

1. assiduity _____
2. desiccate _____
3. gush _____
4. maudlin _____
5. obsequious _____
6. disgruntle _____
7. ossify _____
8. lush _____
9. discursive _____
10. plummet _____

a. to change into bone; to become conventional
b. the quality of being extremely hard working and diligent
c. to dehydrate or absorb moisture
d. growing thick and healthily; fertile or plentiful
e. to emit in a large flow or rush
f. extremely sentimental or emotionally weak
g. changing topics without order; covering a wide range of subjects
h. to fall or drop rapidly
i. to make discontented or dissatisfied
j. over attentive and obedient

■ Put the correct word in each blank from the list of words below.

11. _____ な態度が行き過ぎると bumptious に見える。
12. 無分別に adventurous した場合は _____ という。
13. snub（無視、冷たい）の類義語は _____ である。
14. _____ の度が過ぎると parsimonious だと言われる。
15. _____ は engrave より狭い範囲を深く掘るものである。
16. crestfallen（落胆した）の反意語は _____ である。
17. welcome（歓迎する）の反意語は _____ である。
18. _____ は camouflage（偽装）に使用される。
19. _____ は difference（差異）を見つけることである。
20. _____ なものには sincerity（誠実、誠意）がない。

| a. assertive | b. eschew | c. poseur | d. rash | e. disguise | f. disdain |
| g. exultant | h. disingenuous | i. frugal | j. gouge | k. discriminate | l. resilience |

Answer key

11. a   12. d   13. f   14. i   15. j   16. g   17. b   18. e   19. k   20. h
1. b   2. c   3. e   4. f   5. j   6. i   7. a   8. d   9. g   10. h

この単語集を制覇して、
あなたの実力を見せましょう！

3rd DAY

---

aboveboard
[əbʌ́vbɔ̀ːʳd]

adj. **honest and open; being without deception**　［形］公明正大な；正直な

In the antique business, it is absolutely imperative that one have an *aboveboard* reputation.

反意語 aboveboard action : chicanery [ʃikéinəri]
aboveboard action の反意語は chicanery（ごまかし、策略）

---

absorb
[æbsɔ́ːʳb]

v. **to take up or acquire**　［動］〜を吸収する、取り入れる

Most flowers take in nutrients by *absorbing* water and minerals from the soil.

反意語 absorb : secrete [sikríːt]
absorb の反意語は secrete（〜を分泌する）

---

advertent
[ædvə́ːʳtnt]

adj. **heedful**　［形］注意深い

David makes a good husband because he is *advertent* to the needs of others.

反意語 advertent : inattentive [ìnəténtiv]
advertent の反意語は inattentive（不注意な）

---

assist
[əsíst]

v. **to aid or help**　［動］〜を手伝う、助ける

Jess *assisted* her friends with their move to their new home.

反意語 assist : discommode [dìskəmóud]
assist の反意語は discommode（〜を不便にする、困らせる）

TRANSLATION | 例 文 の 訳

aboveboard　骨董品業界では、公明正大な評判を取ることが絶対に必要だ。

absorb　ほとんどの花は土壌から水分とミネラルを吸収することで栄養分を得る。

advertent　デイビッドは人の要求によく注意するという点で、良い夫だ。

assist　ジェスは友人たちが新居に引っ越すのを手伝った。

associate
[əsóuʃièit]

v. **to work or socialize with; to become partners with**

[動] 関係する；連携する

Kids are taught not to *associate* with people who use drugs.

関連語 associate : aloof [əlúːf]
aloof（よそよそしい、無関心な）な人たちは互いに associate することがない。

auspicious
[ɔːspíʃəs]

adj. **favorable or prosperous; having signs or omens of a positive nature**

[形] 好ましい、前途有望な；幸先のいい

New Year's is an *auspicious* time to set goals for one's personal wellbeing.

反意語 auspicious : unfavorable [ʌnféivˀrəbl]
auspicious の反意語は unfavorable（好ましくない、不都合な）

besmirch
[bismə́ːʳtʃ]

v. **to make dirty or soil; to sully**

[動] 〜を汚す；〜をけがす

President Clinton *besmirched* his reputation by having an affair.

反意語 besmirch : honor [ánəʳ]
bersmirch の反意語は honor（栄誉を授ける）

blurb
[bləːʳb]

n. **a brief, written publicity notice**

[名] 短い宣伝文

There was a *blurb* in the paper about the upcoming convention.

関連語 blurb : notice [nóutis]
bulb な notice（掲示、広告）の一種。

blurt
[bləːʳt]

v. **to speak abruptly and impulsively**

[動] うっかり口に出す

Daniel *blurted* out his love for her in a moment of overwhelming emotion.

関連語 blurt : speak [spiːk]
blurt は前置きなく speak（話す、口にする）する状態を表す。

TRANSLATION | 例文の訳

associate	子供は、麻薬を使用している人間とは関わらないようにと教えられる。
auspicious	新年は個人の幸せに向けて目標を定めるには好ましい時だ。
besmirch	クリントン大統領は不倫して名声をけがした。
blurb	来たる大会について新聞に短い宣伝文があった。
blurt	ダニエルは感情があふれ出した瞬間、彼女への愛を思わず口に出した。

bluster [blʌ́stəʳ]	v. to utter or act with noisy threats　　　　　[動] 怒鳴る Samuel came home drunk and *blustered* at the cat. 関連語 bluster : speak [spiːk] 　　blusterは大声で相手を威嚇するようにspeak（話す、口にする）する状態を表す。
caustic [kɔ́ːstik]	adj. corrosive or capable of destroying through chemical reaction; 　　sarcastic　　　　　　　　　　　　　　　　　[形] 腐食性の；辛辣な Henry was not enjoying the *caustic* jokes that Daniel was saying about his old car. 関連語 caustic : barb [bɑːʳb] 　　barb（とげのある発言、いやみ）にはcausticという特徴がある。
cavern [kǽvəʳn]	n. a large cave　　　　　　　　　　　　　　　　　[名] 大洞窟 The *caverns* of the west coast are a humbling sight. 関連語 cavern : spelunker [spilʌ́ŋkəʳ] 　　cavernはspelunker（洞窟探検家）が探検するものだ。
cessation [seséiʃən]	n. a stopping of an action; discontinuance　　　[名] 中断；停止 The treaty put a *cessation* to the war. 反意語 cessation : commencement [kəménsmənt] 　　cessationの反意語はcommencement（開始）
cosmopolitan [kàzməpálətn]	adj. pertinent to the whole world; found in all parts of the world; 　　having worldwide scope 　　　　　　　　　[形] 国際的な；世界じゅうに分布した；国際的な視野を持った Most professors today are *cosmopolitan* and reside in multiple countries. 反意語 cosmopolitan : insular [ínsələʳ] 　　cosmopolitanの反意語はinsular（島国根性の、狭量な）

TRANSLATION | 例 文 の 訳

bluster	サミュエルは酔っぱらって帰宅し、ネコに向かって怒鳴った。
caustic	ヘンリーは、彼の古い車についてのダニエルの辛辣な冗談が不愉快だった。
cavern	西海岸の大洞窟はつまらない景観だ。
cessation	その条約でその戦争は休戦になった。
cosmopolitan	今日の大学教授のほとんどが国際的で、さまざまな国に住んでいる。

33

cosset [kásit]	v. **to pamper** 　　　　　　　　　　　　　　　[動] ～を甘やかす n. **a pet** 　　　　　　　　　　　　　　　　　　[名] ペット If you *cosset* your child, he or she will never learn self-responsibility. Nobody wants to be treated like a *cosset*. 反意語 cosset : slight [slait] 　　cosset の反意語は slight（～を侮辱する、無視する）
court [kɔːʳt]	v. **to seek the affections or good will of** 　　　　　　　　　　　　　[動] ～と交際する、機嫌を取ろうとする It is customary in certain cultures for a young couple to *court* each other before getting married. 反意語 court : snub [snʌb] 　　court の反意語は snub（冷たくあしらう、無視する）
coven [kʌ́vən]	n. **a collection of people with similarities; a group of about 13 witches** 　　　　　　　[名]（類似点を持つ人々の）集会；13人の魔女の集会 The *coven* of Dutch students met every week to socialize and practice speaking. 関連語 coven : witch [witʃ] 　　witch（魔女）は coven のメンバーである。
despicable [déspikəbl]	adj. **contemptible or arousing moral indignation** 　　[形] 卑しい、卑劣な The capture and torture of civilians in Argentina was a *despicable* act. 反意語 despise : venerate [vénərèit] 　　despise（～を軽蔑する）の反意語は venerate（～を敬う）
despondent [dispándənt]	adj. **depressed or discouraged** 　　　　　　　　[形] 元気のない、落胆した Soren has been *despondent* for almost two weeks now. 反意語 despondent : sanguine [sǽŋgwin] 　　despondent の反意語は sanguine（楽天的な、自信がある）

TRANSLATION | 例 文 の 訳

cosset	子供は、甘やかすと絶対に自己責任感を身につけないだろう。 ペットのように扱われたい人はいない。
court	若いカップルが結婚前に交際するのは、ある文化圏では当たり前のことだ。
coven	交流と弁論の練習のために、オランダの学生たちが毎週集会を開いた。
despicable	アルゼンチンでの市民の逮捕と拷問は卑劣な行為だった。
despondent	ソレンは2週間近く落ち込んでいる。

disintegrate
[disíntəgrèit]

v. **to break into parts or components**　　[動] 分解する、崩壊する

The dominant political party *disintegrated* into belligerent factions under the pressure of corruption investigations.

反意語 disintegrate : amalgamate [əmǽlgəmèit]
disintegrate の反意語は amalgamate（合併する、融合する）

disinterest
[disínt°rist]

n. **an impartiality; a lack of interest**　　[名] 公平さ；無関心

Her *disinterest* in the outcome of the trial makes her a reliable witness.

反意語 disinterested : prejudiced [prédʒədist]
disinterested（公平な）の反意語は prejudiced（不公平な、偏見を持った）

dismantle
[dismǽntl]

v. **to take apart; to destroy the integrity of**　　[動] 〜を分解する；解体する

The technician *dismantled* the computer in order to identify the hardware problem.

関連語 dismantle : unity [júːnəti]
dismantle する対象は 1 つの unity（統一体、まとまり）である。

disparage
[dispǽridʒ]

v. **to degrade or belittle through speech**　　[動] 〜をけなす、非難する

The tennis player *disparaged* her opponents' abilities publicly prior to the match.

関連語 disparage : ignore [ignɔ́ːʳ]
disparage は ignore（〜を無視する）よりも深刻だ。

disparate
[díspərət]

adj. **distinctly marked in quality or character; totally different**
　　[形]（質や特徴が）まったく異なる

Globalization allows people of *disparate* backgrounds to interact and conduct business.

反意語 disparate : similar [símələʳ]
disparate の反意語は similar（類似した）

TRANSLATION | 例 文 の 訳

disintegrate	政権与党は汚職捜査の圧力を受けて、対立派閥に分裂した。
disinterest	彼女は裁判の結果に無関心なので、信頼に足る証人になれる。
dismantle	その技術者はハードウェアの問題を特定するためにコンピューターを分解した。
disparage	そのテニス選手は試合前に相手選手の力を公にけなした。
disparate	グローバル化によって、全く異なる背景の人々が交流し、事業を行えるようになっている。

dispassionate
[dispǽʃənət]

adj. **unaffected by passion, emotion, or prejudice; calm; impartial**

[形] 感情に動かされない；冷静な；公平な

It is very difficult to take a *dispassionate* position on major issues such as abortion and capital punishment.

反意語 dispassionate : partial [páːˈʃəl]

dipassionateの反意語は partial（不公平な、偏った）

disprove
[disprúːv]

v. **to prove untrue or wrong**

[動] 誤りを立証する、反証する

In order to *disprove* his guilt, the accused prisoner took a lie detector test.

関連語 disprove : syllogism [sílədʒìzm]

相手の意見に disprove するための手法として syllogism（演繹法）がよく使われる。

dispute
[dispjúːt]

v. **to oppose or debate with**

[動] 議論する、反論する

n. **an argument or verbal controversy**

[名] 議論、反論

The two companies *disputed* over the rights to produce a new flavor of coffee.

The *dispute* over child support took five hours of court time to settle.

関連語 dispute : incontrovertible [ìnkàntrəvɔ́ːˈtəbl]

incontrovertible（議論の余地がない）というのは dispute する必要がないことを表す。

disregard
[dìsrigáːˈd]

v. **to ignore or pay no attention to**

[動] 〜を無視する、軽視する

Please *disregard* that last statement.

関連語 disregard : flout [flaut]

flout（〜を破る、無視する）は disregard よりも態度が強い。

TRANSLATION | 例 文 の 訳

dispassionate 中絶や死刑などの重要な問題について冷静な立場を取ることはとても難しい。

disprove 彼の有罪を立証するため、被告人は嘘発見器にかけられた。

dispute 2社がコーヒーの新風味を生産する権利をめぐって議論した。

親権をめぐる争いが解決するのに5時間の裁判を要した。

disregard その最後の発言は無視してください。

disrespect
[dìsrispékt]

v. to show a lack of respect for　　　　　[動] 〜に失礼をする、〜を軽視する

n. a lack of respect　　　　　　　　　　　　　[名] 失礼、軽視

The defendant was careful not to *disrespect* the judge during her trial.

The explorer's *disrespect* for local customs was less due to his ignorance than his arrogance.

反意語 disrespect : homage [ʰámidʒ]
　　　disrespectの反意語はhomage（敬意、尊敬）

disrupt
[disrʌ́pt]

v. to throw into confusion; to interrupt or cause a break in the normal flow of; to rupture or break
　　　　　　　　　　　　　[動] 混乱させる；中断させる；崩壊させる

The appearance of the bride's ex-boyfriend *disrupted* the wedding.

関連語 disrupt : saboteur [sæ̀bətɔ́ːʳ]
　　　saboteur（サボタージュを行う人、破壊工作員）とはdisruptする人のこと。

dissemble
[disémbl]

v. to pretend; to put on the appearance of　　　[動] ふりをする；隠す、偽る

On her job application Jackie *dissembled* the fact that she was a college graduate even though she hadn't even finished high school.

関連語 dissemble : honesty [ánisti]
　　　dissembleする人はhonesty（正直、誠実）を持ち合わせていない。

disseminate
[disémənèit]

v. to make known or disperse throughout; to throw about
　　　　　　　　　　　　　[動] 〜を広める、普及させる；〜をまき散らす

The news of the attack was *disseminated* rapidly throughout the world.

関連語 disseminate : information [ìnfəʳméiʃən]
　　　disseminateするものはinformation（情報）である。

TRANSLATION | 例 文 の 訳

disrespect　その被告人は彼女の裁判中、裁判官に無礼にならないように気をつけた。
　　　　　　　その探検家が現地の習慣を軽視したのは、彼の無知というより傲慢さによるものだった。

disrupt　　その花嫁の元恋人が現れて、結婚式は混乱した。

dissemble　仕事の応募書類で、ジャッキーは高校も卒業していなかったにもかかわらず、自分が大卒者だと偽った。

disseminate　その攻撃のニュースはすぐ世界中に知れわたった。

dissent
[disént]

n. a disagreement   [名] 異議、反対

v. to differ in opinion   [動] 意見が違う、異議を唱える

The protesters illustrated their *dissent* against the government's position.

The group of students *dissented* with the principal's new dress code.

反意語 dissent : concur [kənkə́ːʳ]
    dissent の反意語は concur（意見が一致する、同意する）

dyspeptic
[dispéptik]

adj. having indigestion; being of ill humor   [形] 消化不良の；機嫌が悪い

John couldn't help but notice Niki's *dyspeptic* appearance when he mentioned he had set her up on a blind date.

反意語 dyspeptic : genial [dʒíːnjəl]
    dyspeptic の反意語は genial（愛想のよい、朗らかな）

eavesdrop
[íːvzdràp]

v. to listen to other people's conversation without them knowing   [動]（他人の会話を）盗み聞きする

Helen discovered a horrible secret while *eavesdropping* on her sister's phone conversation.

関連語 eavesdrop : listen [lísn]
    eavesdrop は listen（聞く）するやり方の一つ。

edifice
[édəfis]

n. a large building of imposing appearance   [名] 大建造物

Many of the *edifices* found on the university campus have been standing there for over a hundred years.

関連語 edifice : buttress [bʌ́tris]
    buttress（控え壁）は edifice を支えるのに用いられる。

TRANSLATION | 例 文 の 訳

dissent　抗議者たちは政府の立場への反対意見を説明した。
生徒たちは校長による新しい服装規定に異議を唱えた。

dyspeptic　ジョンはニキにブラインドデートを取りはからったことを伝えたとき、彼女の不機嫌な表情に気づかずにはいられなかった。

eavesdrop　ヘレンは妹の電話での会話を盗み聞きするうち、恐ろしい秘密を知った。

edifice　その大学のキャンパスに見られる大規模建造物の多くは100年を超えてそこに建っている。

elated
[iléitid]

adj. **full of high spirited pride and joy** ［形］大得意の、有頂天の

The young man was *elated* after his girlfriend's father consented to their marriage.

反意語 elated : hangdog [hǽŋdɔ̀(ː)g]
elated の反意語は hangdog（しょんぼりした）

enslave
[insléiv]

v. **to subjugate or put into slavery** ［動］〜を従わせる、奴隷にする

The African people have been kidnapped and *enslaved* by many different countries and peoples.

反意語 enslave : manumit [mæ̀njəmít]
enslave の反意語は manuimit（〜を解放する）

filly
[fíli]

n. **a young female horse; a lively young woman** ［名］若い牝馬；おてんば娘

The farmers had a hard time bringing the excited *filly* in from the field.

関連語 filly : horse [hɔːrs]
filly は若い雌の horse（馬）を指す。

finesse
[finés]

n. **skillful and tactful handling of a situation** ［名］手際のよさ、巧妙さ

John's *finesse* with cars made him the most sought after car mechanic in town.

関連語 finesse : gauche [gouʃ]
gauche（未熟な、ぎこちない）人には finess がない。

fuss
[fʌs]

v. **to take care with excessive concern; to complain**
［動］騒ぎ立てる、やきもきする；文句を言う

The mother *fussed* incessantly over the newborn's slight fever.

関連語 fuss : tend [tend]
fuss は過度に心配して tend（注意する、面倒を見る）状態を言う。

TRANSLATION | 例 文 の 訳

elated	その若い男性は恋人の父親が結婚に同意してくれたので有頂天だった。
enslave	アフリカ人はさまざまな国や人々に誘拐され、奴隷にされてきた。
filly	その農夫たちは興奮した若い牝馬を牧草地から連れ戻すのに苦労した。
finesse	ジョンは手際よく車を扱えるので、町で一番引っぱりだこの自動車整備士になった。
fuss	その母親は生まれたばかりの赤ん坊の微熱に絶えずやきもきした。

gossamer [gásəməʳ]	n. thin and soft threads produced by spiders [名] クモの巣 adj. very light or thin [形] 非常に軽い、繊細な The old abandoned house was covered in dust and *gossamers*. Daniel had to work carefully with the *gossamer* material to keep from tearing it accidentally. 反意語 gossamer : ponderous [pánd³rəs] 　　gossamerの反意語は ponderous(大きくて重い)
hesitance [hézət³ns]	n. reluctance or delay [名] 躊躇、ためらい I have some *hesitance* about buying such an expensive house right now. 関連語 hesitance : impetuous [impétʃuəs] 　　impetuous(軽率な)な人は hesitanceなく行動する。
insipid [insípid]	adj. tasteless or lacking interesting qualities [形] 味のない、面白みのない Plain popcorn has a rather *insipid* flavor. 反意語 insipid : piquant [píːkənt] 　　insipidの反意語は piquiant(食欲をそそる、興味をそそる)
insolent [ínsələnt]	adj. rude, arrogant, or disrespectful in speech or conduct [形] 無礼な、横柄な、生意気な Most teenagers are *insolent* when it comes to authority figures. 関連語 insolent : veneration [vénərèiʃ³n] 　　insolentな人は veneration(尊敬の念)に欠けている。
insouciant [insúːsiənt]	adj. being lightheartedly unconcerned [形] 無頓着な、のん気な An *insouciant* attitude about life will guarantee peace, but may lead to unproductiveness. 関連語 insouciant : worry [wə́ːri] 　　insouciantな人は worry(心配する)することがない。

TRANSLATION | 例 文 の 訳

gossamer	その古い廃屋はほこりとクモの巣で覆われていた。 ダニエルは繊細な生地を誤って破らないように注意して作業しなければならなかった。
hesitance	私はいますぐそんなに高価な家を買うことには躊躇する。
insipid	未加工のポップコーンは味気ない。
insolent	10代の若者のほとんどは権威のある人物に対して生意気な態度をとる。
insouciant	生きることに無頓着だと平穏無事な日々は保証されるだろうが、非生産的な結果につながるかもしれない。

1st

2nd

3rd

4th

5th

6th

7th

8th

9th

10th

inspire
[inspáiə^r]

v. **to motivate or stimulate to work hard or be creative; to affect by divine influence**　　[動] 鼓舞する、奮起させる；神から影響を受ける

Encouragement and praise always *inspire* my dreams and goals.

関連語 inspire : infuse [infjúːz]
inspire は infuse（吹き込む、影響する）よりも強い。

mislead
[mislíːd]

v. **to lead astray or down the wrong path**
[動] 欺く、誤解させる、誤った方向へ導く

His e-mail *misled* me to believe that he was coming to visit.

関連語 misleading : equivocation [ikwìvəkéiʃən]
equivocation（あいまいな言葉）は misleading しがちである。

resist
[rizíst]

v. **to withstand or fend off; to oppose; to keep from enjoying**
[動] 抵抗する；反抗する；我慢する

The German forces *resisted* the American assault for two months.

反意語 resist : capitulate [kəpítʃulèit]
resist の反意語は capitulate（抵抗をやめる、降伏する）

resolute
[rézəlùːt]

adj. **steady or firm in purpose or dedication**　　[形] 決心の堅い、断固たる

Bill made a *resolute* decision to quit smoking.

関連語 resolute : dissuade [diswéid]
resolute した人を dissuade（思いとどまらせる）のは難しい。

respite
[réspit]

n. **a short interval of rest; a pause or period of temporary delay**
[名] 小休止、一時的な中断；猶予

The Memorial Union is a place for students to go for a *respite* from their studying.

関連語 respite : labor [léibə^r]
respite は labor（労働）から離れて休む状態を言う。

TRANSLATION | 例 文 の 訳

inspire	励ましや賞賛は常に私を夢と目標に駆り立ててくれる。
mislead	彼のEメールを読んで、私は彼が訪ねて来るものと思い込んでしまった。
resist	ドイツ軍はアメリカの攻撃に2カ月間抵抗した。
resolute	ビルはたばこをやめることを固く決意した。
respite	その記念会館は学生たちが学業を離れて小休止しに行く場所だ。

41

resplendent
[rispléndənt]

adj. **brilliant or shiny; splendid**   [形] キラキラ輝く、まばゆい；華麗な

Our kids love to walk through the department stores and see the many Christmas trees with all their *resplendent* decorations on display.

関連語 resplendent : appearance [əpíʳrəns]
resplendentは appearance（外観）を表す言葉の1つ。

---

taunt
[tɔ:nt]

v. **to ridicule or challenge by mocking**   [動] からかう、あざける

The football player *taunted* the scholarly boy until he ran home crying.

関連語 taunt : provoke [prəvóuk]
provoke（挑発する）は tauntよりも攻撃性が高い。

---

truculent
[trʌ́kjulənt]

adj. **savage or destructive, sometimes belligerent**
[形] 野蛮な、破壊的な、敵意のある

Brett's moment of *truculent* behavior won him a night in prison.

関連語 truculent : gentleness [dʒéntlnis]
truculentな人には gentleness（親切、優しさ）がない。

---

trudge
[trʌdʒ]

v. **to walk or march with difficulty**   [動] 重い足取りで歩く

The soldiers *trudged* through the jungle, weary and afraid.

関連語 trudge : walk [wɔ:k]
trudgeは重い足取りでwalk（歩く）すること。

---

truncate
[trʌ́ŋkeit]

v. **to shorten or cut in length**   [動] 短縮する

The presentation was *truncated* by about 15 minutes to make it fit the schedule.

反意語 truncate : prolong [prəlɔ́:ŋ]
truncateの反意語は prolong（延長する）

> TRANSLATION | 例 文 の 訳
>
> **resplendent** うちの子供たちは、デパートの中を歩き、まばゆい飾りつけをされたたくさんのクリスマスツリーを見るのが大好きだ。
>
> **taunt** そのサッカー選手はガリ勉の少年をからかい、少年はとうとう泣きながら家に走って帰ってしまった。
>
> **truculent** ブレットは一瞬の野蛮な行為のせいで、留置場で一晩過ごす羽目に陥った。
>
> **trudge** 兵士たちは疲れ、おびえながらジャングルを重い足取りで歩いた。
>
> **truncate** その発表は予定に合うように約15分間短縮された。

vault
[vɔːlt]

n. a storage compartment or room used for the safekeeping of valuables　　　[名] 金庫室、貴重品保管室

The items in our *vault* included a diamond necklace, our wills, and $3000.

関連語 vault : valuables [vǽljuːəblz]
vault は valuables（貴重品）を保管する場所である。

vaunt
[vɔːnt]

v. to brag of one's own worth　　　[動] 自慢する、威張る

Vaunting and gloating, the winner of the contest left the ceremony to celebrate.

類義語 vaunt : boast [boust]
vaunt の類義語は boast（自慢する）

unsound
[ʌnsáund]

adj. not true or logically valid; not healthy or whole　　　[形] 根拠のない；不健全な

In a rage of anger, Kevin made an *unsound* and fatal decision to drink and drive.

反意語 unsound : tenable [ténəbl]
unsound の反意語は tenable（弁護できる）

visionary
[víʒənèri]

adj. illusory; imaginary; incapable of being realized　　　[形] 架空の；想像力豊かな

n. a daydreamer; a seer　　　[名] 夢想家；占い師

Dave was entirely haunted by the *visionary* scene.
It takes a *visionary* to spark a revolution.

関連語 visionary : delusion [dilúːʒən]
visionary に似た意味に名詞の delusion（錯覚、妄想）がある。

TRANSLATION | 例 文 の 訳

vault 私たちの金庫室にある物にはダイヤのネックレス、遺言状、現金3,000ドルなどが含まれていた。
vaunt そのコンテストの優勝者はうぬぼれ、満悦して、表彰式から立ち去った。
unsound ケビンは激怒して、酒を飲んで運転するという不健全かつ致命的な決断を下した。
visionary デイブはその架空の光景に完全に取りつかれていた。
革命を起こすには夢想家が必要だ。

43

■ Fill in the blanks with the correct letter that matches the word with its definition.

1. besmirch	_____	a. honest and open; being without deception
2. insipid	_____	b. tasteless or lacking interesting qualities
3. truculent	_____	c. to pamper; a pet
4. unsound	_____	d. to make dirty or to soil; to sully
5. truncate	_____	e. brilliant or shiny; splendid
6. aboveboard	_____	f. savage or destructive, sometimes belligerent
7. despondent	_____	g. not healthy or whole; not true or logically valid
8. resplendent	_____	h. to shorten or cut in length
9. dyspeptic	_____	i. depression or discouragement
10. cosset	_____	j. having indigestion; being of ill humor

■ Put the correct word in each blank from the list of words below.

11. aloof な人たちは互いに _____ することがない。

12. _____ は短い推薦文で notice の一種である。

13. _____ な人は worry することがない。

14. equivocation は _____ しがちである。

15. delusion の意味を持つ形容詞は _____ である。

16. _____ に valuables を保管する。

17. syllogism は、相手の意見を論理的に _____ する手段として使用される。

18. secrete（分泌する）の反意語は _____ である。

19. _____ は ignore よりも深刻である。

20. _____ は spelunker の探検の対象である。

a. misleading	b. disparage	c. cavern	d. resist	e. insouciant	f. associate
g. blurb	h. disprove	i. vault	j. prolong	k. visionary	l. absorb

Answer key

11. f 12. g 13. e 14. a 15. k 16. i 17. h 18. l 19. b 20. c
1. d 2. b 3. f 4. g 5. h 6. a 7. i 8. e 9. j 10. c

44

重要なのは、
出発点ではなく到達点。

4th DAY

abstemious
[æbstíːmiəs]

adj. characterized by restraint in indulgences such as food and drink　　　　[形] 禁欲的な、（食事・酒などを）節制して

The overweight woman was *abstemious* because of her desire to lose weight.

関連語 abstemious : indulge [indʎldʒ]
abstemiousな人は indulge（ふける、～を飽食する）することがない。

abstract
adj.[ǽbstrækt]
n.[ǽbstrækt]

adj. relating to that which is not concrete; expressing a quality apart from an object　　　　[形] 抽象的な；空想的な

n. a statement summarizing the important points of a text　　[名] 要約

Philosophy studies the world of *abstract* objects while biology that of the real.

The editor demanded that the author write an *abstract* for the new textbook.

関連語 abstract : condensed [kəndénst]
abstract には condensed（凝縮された）であるという特徴がある。

aesthete
[ésθiːt]

n. one having sensitivity to beauty, mostly in art　　　　[名] 美的感覚の鋭い人、芸術愛好家

The *aesthete's* entire home was devoted to the collection and display of scenic paintings.

関連語 aesthete : art [ɑːʳt]
aesthete は art（芸術）に優れた感覚を持っている。

assuage
[əswéidʒ]

v. to calm; to ease pain, grief, or burden　　　　[動] ～をなだめる；（苦痛や悲しみ、不安などを）静める

My fears were *assuaged* by the presence of my best friend.

関連語 assuage : sorrow [sárou]
assuage とは sorrow（悲しみ）をなだめること。

TRANSLATION | 例 文 の 訳

abstemious	その太った女性は減量したいという欲望から節制していた。
abstract	生物学は現実世界を、哲学は抽象的な世界を探究する。
	その編集者は著者に新しい教科書の要約を書くように要求した。
aesthete	その芸術家の家全体が風景画の収集と展示に使われていた。
assuage	親友の存在が私の不安を和らげてくれた。

austere
[ɔːstíəʳ]

adj. **cold and grave in appearance or manner; morally selfdisciplined; having no adornment**

[形] 飾り気のない；厳しい、厳格な；質素な

The dean appeared at the banquet with an *austere* demeanor.

The poor woman's apartment was *austere* and empty, reflecting her cold and uninviting personality.

類義語 austere : Spartan [spɑ́ːrtn]
austereの類義語は Spartan（スパルタ式の、厳格な）

関連語 austere : decorate [dékərèit]
austereとは decorate（飾る）していない状態を表す。

barefaced
[béərfèist]

adj. **open and shameless**　　　　[形] あからさまな、しらじらしい

Hogan couldn't believe that his brother told a *barefaced* lie to his parents.

反意語 barefaced : surreptitious [sə̀ːrəptíʃˀs]
barefacedの反意語は surreptitous（内密の、こそこそした）

bathetic
[bəθétik]

adj. **marked by banality and triviality; insincerely emotional**

[形] 陳腐な、平凡な；わざとらしい、感傷的な

The *bathetic* course of his life frustrated Tom because he had dreamed of great things in his youth.

反意語 bathetic : offbeat [ɔːfbíːt]
batheticの反意語は offbeat（風変わりな）

castigate
[kǽstəgèit]

v. **to rebuke or subject to severe criticism**　　　[動] 〜を懲戒する、酷評する

The traveler was *castigated* harshly by the immigration officer for overstaying his visa.

関連語 castigation : admonishment [ædmɑ́niʃmənt]
castigationは admonishment（訓戒）よりも程度が強い。

TRANSLATION | 例 文 の 訳

austere　その学長は厳しい表情で宴席に現れた。
その貧しい女性のアパートは、彼女の冷たく不愉快な人格を反映して、質素で空疎だった。

barefaced　ホーガンは自分の兄が両親にあからさまな嘘をついたとは信じられなかった。

bathetic　若い頃に大きな夢を抱いていたので、人生の平凡な成り行きがトムをいら立たせた。

castigate　その旅行者はビザの期限を超えて不法滞在していたことで入国管理局職員から厳しく懲戒された。

cistern
[sístə^rn]

n. a reservoir used to store water　　　　　[名] 貯水タンク

A *cistern* was added to the village during war time as a precaution.

関連語 cistern : liquids [líkwidz]
　　　cistern は liquids（液体）を保存しておくタンクを言う。

crutch
[krʌtʃ]

n. a support put under the arm and used to assist people to walk

[名] 松葉杖

The football player was given *crutches* to use while his sprained foot was healing.

関連語 crutch : walk [wɔːk]
　　　crutch は walk（歩く）するために使われる。

crux
[krʌks]

n. the essential point or main feature　　　[名] 核心、重要な点

The *crux* of the negotiations dealt with the equitable distribution of the corporation's stock.

類義語 crux : gist [dʒist]
　　　crux の類義語は gist（要点）

dissolute
[dísəlùːt]

adj. lacking restraint in the indulgence of vices

[形] ふしだらな、放蕩な

The hedonistic and *dissolute* man's vices included drinking and gambling.

関連語 dissolute : libertine [líbə^rtìːn]
　　　dissolute な人のことを libertine（放蕩者）という。

dissolve
[dizálv]

v. to disappear or disperse; to liquefy　　[動] 消える、なくなる；溶解する

The cold tablets *dissolve* in hot water or cold water.

関連語 dissolve : solvent [sálvənt]
　　　材料を dissolve するために使われるのが solvent（溶剤、溶媒）である。

関連語 dissolve : insoluble [insáljubl]
　　　insoluble（溶けない、不溶解の）物質は dissolve されない。

TRANSLATION | 例文の訳

cistern	戦時中、その村に予防措置として貯水タンクが設置された。
crutch	そのサッカー選手は足の捻挫が治るまでの間使うように松葉杖を与えられた。
crux	その交渉の核心は、その企業の株を公平に分配することだった。
dissolute	その快楽主義でふしだらな男は飲酒や賭博などの悪行に手を染めていた。
dissolve	その風邪薬は湯や水に溶ける。

dissuade
[diswéid]

v. to persuade someone against something　[動] 説得して思いとどまらせる

I tried hard to *dissuade* my friend from quitting his job.

関連語 dissuade : remonstrator [rimánstreitəʳ]
remonstrator（抗議する人）は他人を dissuade しようとする。

distort
[distɔ́ːʳt]

v. to twist out of true meaning or shape
[動]（事実などを）曲げる、（形を）ゆがめる

Some people will *distort* the truth to get what they want.

関連語 distortion : caricature [kǽrikətʃəʳ]
distortion（事実の歪曲）は caricature（風刺画・文）の特徴と言える。

distract
[distrǽkt]

v. to divert or turn one's attention away
[動]（気持ち・注意などを）そらす、散らす

The loud music was *distracting* me from my studies.

関連語 distract : rapt [ræpt]
rapt（夢中になっている、没頭している）人を distract するのは難しい。

dour
[duəʳ]

adj. gloomy or unhappy; stern or obstinate
[形] 落ち込んで、不幸で；厳格な、気難しい

It would be very nice if that *dour* man would smile for once.

関連語 dour : geniality [dʒìːniǽləti]
dour な人には geniality（愛想、朗らかさ）がない。

excursive
[ikskə́ːʳsiv]

adj. tending to digress　[形] 散漫な

The professor's *excursive* lecture lacked focus and confused the students.

関連語 excursive : digress [daigrés]
excursive なものには digress（わき道にそれる、脱線する）するという特徴がある。

TRANSLATION | 例 文 の 訳

dissuade	私は友人が仕事を辞めないように説得しようと懸命に努力した。
distort	自分の欲しいものを手に入れるために真実を曲げる人もいる。
distract	騒々しい音楽のせいで勉強に集中できなかった。
dour	もしあの気難しい男が一度でも笑ったら素晴らしいだろうに。
excursive	その教授の散漫な講義には焦点がなく、学生を混乱させた。

exempt
[igzémpt]

v. **to free or release from obligation or duty**　[動]（義務などから）免除する

Due to diplomatic immunity, Luke was *exempted* from all the criminal charges filed against him.

関連語 exempt : liability [làiəbíləti]
　人を liability（責任、義務）から exempt する。

fast
[fæst]

v. **to abstain from eating**　[動] 断食する

adj. **stuck or firmly fixed; rapidly moving**　[形] しっかり固定された；素早い

The whole family *fasts* one day a month to cleanse their bodies.
The door is bolted *fast*.

反意語 fast : eat [iːt]
　fast の反意語は eat（食べる）
反意語 fast : loosely attached [lúːsli ətǽtʃt]
　fast の反意語は loosely attached（ゆるく付いている）

fastidious
[fæstídiəs]

adj. **extremely careful or concerned with details**　[形] 最新の注意を払う、潔癖な

Paul is so *fastidious* about cleanliness that he will do any dishes left in the sink for 10 minutes.

関連語 fastidious : careful [kɛəʳfəl]
　過度に careful（注意深い）な人を fastidious だと言う。

fervor
[fə́ːʳvəʳ]

n. **the passion or intensity of feeling or expression**　[名] 熱情、熱烈

The painter worked on his art piece with incredible *fervor*.

関連語 fervor : zealot [zélət]
　fervor の大きな人を zealot（熱狂する人）と言う。

TRANSLATION | 例 文 の 訳

exempt　外交特権のおかげで、ルークは自分に対するあらゆる犯罪告発から免除された。
fast　体を清めるために、その一家では全員が月1日断食する。
　そのドアはボルトでしっかりと固定されている。
fastidious　ポールは清潔さにとてもうるさいので、どんな皿でも流しに10分間つけておく。
fervor　その画家は驚くほどの情熱で自分の芸術作品に取り組んだ。

foster
[fɔ́ːstəʳ]

v. to encourage and support in development or growth

[動] (発達や成長を) 促進する、育成する

By reading to your children at an early age, you *foster* their educational development.

反意語 foster : stifle [stáifl]
foster の反意語は stifle (〜を抑制する)

glut
[glʌt]

n. an excess

[名] 超過、供給過剰

v. to overfill or overeat, especially regarding food

[動] 過剰供給する、食べ過ぎる

There was a *glut* of spare parts that had to be stockpiled in the storage room.

Look at the girl! She is *glutting* with every sweet in sight!

関連語 glutton : overindulge [òuvərindʌ́ldʒ]
glutton (大食家) とは overindulge (食べ過ぎる) 人のこと。

gourmet
[guəʳméi]

n. a connoisseur of food and drink

[名] 美食家

The *gourmet* ordered a succulent five course meal and an expensive bottle of wine for his dinner guests.

関連語 gourmet : cuisine [kwizíːn]
gourmet とは cuisine (高級料理) に精通している人のこと。

hasten
[héisn]

v. to act or move quickly; to accelerate

[動] 急ぐ；加速する

Already ten minutes late, Becky *hastened* to class.

反意語 hasten : retard [ritáːʳd]
hasten の反意語は retard (遅らせる)

TRANSLATION | 例 文 の 訳

foster	子供が小さいときに読み聞かせをすることで、彼らの教育的な発達を促進することができる。
glut	交換部品が過剰にあり、倉庫に備蓄しなければならなかった。
	あの女の子を見て！　目の前の甘いものを全部食べている！
gourmet	その美食家は夕食に招いた客人のために、おいしい5品のコースと高価なワインボトルを注文した。
hasten	すでに10分遅れていたベッキーは急いで授業に行った。

histrionic
[hìstriánik]

adj. **dramatic or excessively emotional**　　　[形] 芝居じみた、過度に感情的な

Stan's *histrionic* reaction to the announcement made everyone laugh.

関連語 histrionic : actor [ǽktə^r]
histrionic に行動するのが actor（俳優）の特徴である。

instigate
[ínstəgèit]

v. **to incite or provoke**　　　[動] 〜を刺激する、扇動する

The school board *instigated* a protest advocating equal rights for students of color.

反意語 instigate : quell [kwel]
instigate の反意語は quell（〜を鎮圧する）

instill
[instíl]

v. **to infuse slowly; to give gradually by example or teaching**
　　　[動] しみこませる；徐々に教え込む

Traveling *instills* an appreciation and tolerance for other cultures.

類義語 instill : implant [implǽnt]
instill の類義語が implant（教え込む、移植する）

instruct
[instrʌ́kt]

v. **to teach or direct**　　　[動] 教える、指示する

The chef *instructed* his class on how to make a cheese cake.

関連語 instruction : apothegm [ǽpəθèm]
apothegm（格言）は人に instruction するためのもの。

inure
[in(j)úə^r]

v. **to make used to tolerating something undesirable**
　　　[動]（困難などに）慣れさせる

The captain forced the new recruits to run three miles daily *inuring* them to the strict physical regime of military life.

関連語 inured : tolerance [tάlərəns]
inured（慣れさせた、鍛えられた）した人は tolerance（忍耐、我慢）を持つようになる。

TRANSLATION | 例 文 の 訳

histrionic　その発表に対するスタンの芝居じみた反応は皆を笑わせた。

instigate　教育委員会は非白人学生への平等な権利を主張する抗議行動を扇動した。

instill　旅行によって異文化への理解と寛容さが徐々に身についてくる。

instruct　シェフはチーズケーキの作り方についての教室を指導した。

inure　その将校は新兵たちに毎日３マイル走るように強制して、軍隊生活の過酷な体力的水準に慣れさせた。

invective
[invéktiv]

n. insulting or abusive language or speech   [名] 悪口、ののしり

adj. marked by abusive language   [形] 悪口の、ののしる

The angry woman yelled *invectives* at her son, but immediately regretted it.

In court, the separated couple shouted *invective* remarks to each other from across the room.

反意語 invective : accolade [ǽkəlèid]
invective の反意語は accolade（賞賛）

investigate
[invéstəgèit]

v. to observe or examine closely and systematically   [動] ～を調査する、捜査する

It is the detective's job to *investigate* crimes.

類義語 investigate : probe [proub]
investigate の類義語は probe（～を調査する、探る）

inveterate
[invetˀrət]

adj. habitual or firmly established   [形] 習慣的な、根深い

The German tendency to close doors at all times is an *inveterate* character of the culture.

反意語 inveterate : casual [kǽʒuəl]
inveterate の反意語は casual（臨時の、一時的な）

jest
[dʒest]

n. a joke or humorous remark; a gay and playful mood or manner   [名] 冗談；いたずら、戯れ

Larry's *jests* often offended those around him though it was never intended.

反意語 jest : solemn utterance [sáləm ʌ́tərəns]
jest の反意語は solemn utterance（まじめな言葉）

jovial
[dʒóuviəl]

adj. good humored and cheerful   [形] 陽気な、快い

John was attracted to her *jovial* nature.

反意語 jovial : morose [məróus]
jovial の反意語は morose（不機嫌な）

TRANSLATION | 例 文 の 訳

invective 怒った女性は息子をののしったが、すぐにそれを後悔した。
法廷で、その別れた夫婦は部屋の両端から互いに悪口を叫んだ。

investigate 犯罪を捜査するのが刑事の仕事だ。

inveterate ドイツでは常にドアを閉めておく傾向があるが、それは、ドイツ文化にしみ付いた特徴だ。

jest ラリーの冗談は決して意図的なものではなかったが、周りの人々を不快にすることが多かった。

jovial ジョンは彼女の陽気な性格に引かれた。

1st

2nd

3rd

4th

5th

6th

7th

8th

9th

10th

listless [lístlis]	adj. lacking interest or energy　　　　　　　　[形] つまらなそうな、無気力そうな
	Anne usually comes home from work tired and *listless*.
	反意語 listlessness : verve [vəːʳv] 　listlessness（無気力）の反意語は verve（活力、活気）
massive [mǽsiv]	adj. bulky or heavy; serious　　　　　　　　　[形] 巨大な、重大な；深刻な
	Grandfather died after a *massive* heart attack.
	反意語 massive : trivial [tríviəl] 　massive の反意語は trivial（ささいな）
maven [méivən]	n. an expert　　　　　　　　　　　　　　　　　　　　[名] 専門家
	The government called him in because he is a negotiation *maven*.
	関連語 maven : experience [ikspíˀriəns] 　maven は特定の分野についての experience（経験）を多く持っている人。
maverick [mǽvˀrik]	n. an independent person who resists adherence to a group; a 　　dissenter　　　　　　　　　　　　　　　　[名] 異端者、一匹狼；反対者
	William had earned the reputation of *maverick* because he never did what was expected and always did things on his own.
	反意語 maverick : follower [fálouəʳ] 　maverick の反意語は follower（支持者、追従者）
obstinate [ábstənət]	adj. stubbornly adhering to an opinion or purpose　　[形] 頑固な
	Grandma is *obstinate* about not getting on planes because of her great fear of flying.
	関連語 obstinate : firm [fəːʳm] 　firm（堅い、断固とした）な態度が過度になると obstinate になる。

TRANSLATION | 例 文 の 訳

listless	アンはたいてい疲れて、無気力になって職場から家に帰ってくる。
massive	祖父は深刻な心臓発作のあとに亡くなった。
maven	政府が彼を呼び寄せたのは、彼が交渉の専門家だったからだ。
maverick	ウイリアムは期待されていることを決して行わず、いつも自分勝手に行動したので、一匹狼の評判を取っていた。
obstinate	祖母が頑なに飛行機に乗ろうとしないのは、空を飛ぶことへの恐怖が大きいからだ。

obstruct [əbstrʌ́kt]	v. **to block with obstacles; to impede or hinder** [動] ～をふさぐ；妨害する、妨げる The enforcement of the ruling was *obstructed* by a large group of protesters. 関連語 obstruct : progress [prágrəs] 物事が progress（進行）するのを obstruct する。
obviate [ábvièit]	v. **to do away with; to anticipate; to make unnecessary** [動] ～を取り除く；未然に防ぐ Fail-safe precautions built into the design of nuclear reactors do not *obviate* the need for vigilance against accidents and catastrophe. 関連語 obviate : unnecessary [ʌ̀nnésəsèri] ある行為を unnecessary（無用の、無駄な）ものにするために obviate する。
pastiche [pæstíːʃ]	n. **a work of art that imitates the style of some previous work** [名] 模倣作品 Modern Greek architecture is a *pastiche* of Turkish, Venetian, and Western architecture. 反意語 pastiche : original work [ərídʒənl wəːrk] pastiche の反意語は original work（独創的な作品）
pantechnicon [pæntéknikàn]	n. **a van used for moving furniture** [名]（家具を運搬する）大型トラック The Watsons had to order two *pantechnicons* to move all the furniture to their new house. 関連語 pantechnicon : furniture [fə́ːrnitʃər] pantechnicon は furniture（家具）を運ぶ仕様になっている車。
paroxysm [pǽrəksìzm]	n. **a sudden outburst or attack of emotion; convulsion** [名]（感情の）爆発；発作 The patient took a turn for the better after his *paroxysm* of laughing at the antics of Dr. Adams. 関連語 paroxysm : sudden [sʌ́dn] paroxysm には sudden（突然な）という特徴がある。

TRANSLATION | 例 文 の 訳

obstruct	大勢の抗議者が、その裁定の実施を妨げた。
obviate	核原子炉の設計に安全装置を組み込んでも、事故や大災害への警戒の必要性が取り除かれるわけではない。
pastiche	現代のギリシャ建築はトルコ、ベネチア、西洋の建築の模倣だ。
pantechnicon	ワトソン家は新居にすべての家具を移動するのに、2台の大型トラックを手配しなければならなかった。
paroxysm	その患者はアダムス医師の滑稽なしぐさに大笑いしたあと、症状が好転した。

parrot
[pǽrət]

v. **to mindlessly repeat or imitate words or actions of another**
[動] (言葉や行動を) を意味もなくおうむ返しする、まねる

n. **a tropical bird with a curved beak and vividly colored feathers**
[名] オウム、曲がったくちばしと鮮やかな色の羽を持つ熱帯の鳥

Children often *parrot* the adults around them as the most efficient way to learn language or other new skills.

A *parrot's* plumage and verbal potential make it a target of tropical poachers.

関連語 parrot : originality [ərídʒənǽləti]
originality (独創性) を持たずに他人をまねるのが parrot である。

restive
[réstiv]

adj. **fidgety or agitated; unable to rest**
[形] 興奮した、じっとしていない；落ち着きのない

The children were *restive* and grouchy from riding in the back of the car for 5 hours.

関連語 restive : calmness [kɑ́:mnis]
restive なものには calmness (静けさ、落ち着き) がない。

restrain
[ristréin]

v. **to hold back or control; to prevent from doing something**
[動] 〜を抑える；やめさせる

John had to *restrain* himself from killing the man who had kidnapped his son.

関連語 restrain : irrepressible [ìriprésəbl]
irrepressible (抑えられない) というのは restrain できない状態を言う。

revere
[rivíər]

v. **to admire fondly and show devoted honor to**
[動] 〜をあがめる、崇敬する

The teacher is *revered* highly by all her students.

関連語 revere : respect [rispékt]
revere は respect (〜を尊敬する) よりも程度が強い。

TRANSLATION | 例 文 の 訳

parrot 子供たちは言葉などの技能を身につけるための最も効果的な方法として、周りにいる大人を意味もなくまねることが多い。
オウムはその羽毛と潜在的な言語能力によって熱帯の密猟者の標的になる。

restive 子供たちは車の後部に5時間乗っていたことでじっとしていられず、不機嫌になった。

restrain ジョンは息子を誘拐した男を殺したい気持ちを抑えなければならなかった。

revere その教師は全学生から大変尊敬されている。

55

roster
[rástər]

n. **a list of names** [名] 名簿

The coach posted the *roster* of the starting players for the new season.

関連語 roster : personnel [pə̀ːrsˤnél]
roster とは personnel（職員、社員、隊員など）の名簿を言う。

rustic
[rʌ́stik]

adj. **relating to the countryside or old buildings; rough or coarse**
[形] 田舎の、丸太づくりの；粗野な、下品な

In Wyoming there are *rustic* cabins for rent everywhere.

反意語 rustic : polished [pɑ́liʃt]
rustic の反意語は polished（洗練された）

scurrilous
[skə́ːrələs]

adj. **using or containing vulgar or abusive language**
[形] 中傷的な、口汚い

The student was suspended for using *scurrilous* language in class.

関連語 scurrilous : propriety [prəpráiəti]
scurrilous なものには propriety（礼儀正しさ）がない。

sentinel
[sént³nl]

v. **to guard or watch over** [動] 〜を見張る、番をする
n. **one who keeps guard** [名] 見張り、番人

John was to *sentinel* the grounds and report anything out of the ordinary.

The *sentinels* decided to go to sleep when they realized they had been sent to guard a dog house.

関連語 sentinel : watchful [wátʃfəl]
sentinel には watchful（用心深い）という特徴がある。

spurious
[spjúˤriəs]

adj. **marked by absence of authenticity or validity**
[形] 偽の、偽造の

The antique the traveler purchased turned out to be *spurious*.

反意語 spurious : genuine [dʒénjuin]
spurious の反意語は genuine（本物の）

TRANSLATION | 例 文 の 訳

roster	その監督は新シーズンの先発選手の名簿を掲示した。
rustic	ワイオミングにはどこにでも丸太造りのキャンプ小屋がある。
scurrilous	その学生は授業中に中傷的な言葉を使って停学になった。
sentinel	ジョンは構内を見張り、異常があればすべて報告することになっていた。
	見張りたちは自分たちが犬小屋の番をするために送られたことに気づくと、眠りに行くことに決めた。
spurious	その旅行者が買った骨董品は偽物であることがわかった。

spurn
[spəːʳn]

v. to reject or treat in a contemptible or scornful way

[動] 〜をはねつける、拒絶する

The company *spurned* the proposal to merge with the weak competitor.

反意語 spurn : embrace [imbréis]
spurn の反意語は embrace（喜んで応じる）

systematic
[sìstəmǽtik]

adj. based on a system; methodical or orderly in procedure or plan

[形] 組織的な；体系的な

The school was run *systematically*.

反意語 systematic : haphazard [hæphǽzəʳd]
systematic の反意語は haphazard（でたらめの、計画性のない）

testimony
[téstəmòuni]

n. a solemn declaration made under oath; evidence

[名] 宣誓、証言；証拠

The witness gave his *testimony* in tears.

反意語 testimony : perjury [pə́ːʳdʒəʳri]
testimony の反意語は perjury（偽証）

testy
[tésti]

adj. irritable or easily angered

[形] 短気な、怒りっぽい

In the mornings, Kelly is *testy* and sluggish.

類義語 testy : irascible [irǽsəbl]
testy の類義語は irascible（怒りっぽい、短気な）

unsteady
[ʌnstédi]

adj. changeable or unstable

[形] 変わりやすい、不安定な

The vase fell off the *unsteady* book shelf.

関連語 unsteady : dodder [dádəʳ]
dodder（よろよろ歩く）とは unsteady な歩き方だということ。

TRANSLATION | 例 文 の 訳

spurn	その企業は弱小の競合会社と合併するという提案をはねつけた。
systematic	その学校は組織的に運営されていた。
testimony	その目撃者は泣きながら証言した。
testy	午前中、ケリーは怒りっぽく、だらだらしている。
unsteady	その花びんは不安定な本棚から落ちた。

■ Fill in the blanks with the correct letter that matches the word with its definition.

1. cistern _____
2. fastidious _____
3. aesthete _____
4. histrionic _____
5. listless _____
6. invective _____
7. pastiche _____
8. obviate _____
9. instigate _____
10. foster _____

a. a reservoir used to store water
b. extremely careful or concerned with details
c. one having sensitivity to beauty, mostly in art
d. dramatic or excessively emotional
e. a work of art that imitates the style of some previous works
f. to do away with; to anticipate; to make unnecessary
g. to incite or provoke
h. lacking interest or energy
i. insulting or abusive language or speech
j. to encourage and support in development or growth

■ Put the correct word in each blank from the list of words below.

11. _____ な人は indulge（飽食する）しない。
12. _____ は admonishment に比べてその程度が強い。
13. casual（一時的な）の反意語は _____ である。
14. _____ は respect より尊敬の度合いが大きい。
15. _____ なものには calmness がない。
16. gist（要点）の類義語は _____ である。
17. _____ とは overindulge する人である。
18. _____ が非常に大きな人を zealot と言う。
19. _____ な人は geniality を持っていない。
20. insoluble な物質は _____ されない。

a. dour　　b. dissolve　　c. crutch　　d. revere　　e. roster　　f. abstemious
g. castigation　h. restive　　i. crux　　j. inveterate　　k. glutton　　l. fervor

Answer key

1. a　2. b　3. c　4. d　5. h　6. i　7. e　8. f　9. g　10. j
11. f　12. g　13. j　14. d　15. h　16. i　17. k　18. l　19. a　20. b

58

Track 05

この本に載っている単語だけ覚えれば
大丈夫だ！

5th DAY

advocate v.[ǽdvəkèit] n.[ǽdvəkət]	v. **to speak, plead, or argue in favor of**	[動]〜を主張する、擁護する
	n. **a worker or supporter of a cause**	[名]主張者、支持者

Cesar Chavez was the founder of the United Farm Workers and strongly *advocated* the reform of labor laws in America.

The president had to be an *advocate* of disarmament for his political stability.

関連語 advocate : exponent [ikspóunənt]
　　　exponent（主張者、支持者）とは自分の信念をadvocateする人を言う。

---

antagonize
[æntǽgənàiz]

v. **to counteract or provoke the anger of; to offend**
[動]〜に反感を持たせる；〜を敵にする

Presidents usually try to avoid *antagonizing* senators with long recess appointments.

反意語 antagonize : propitiate [prəpíʃièit]
　　　antagonizeの反意語はpropitiate（人の機嫌をとる）

---

attenuate
[əténjuèit]

v. **to make thin; to lessen the force, magnitude, or value of**
[動]〜を補足する；（力などを）弱める、減ずる

A long-distance relationship will *attenuate* any love.

関連語 attenuate : thickness [θíknis]
　　　attenuateはあるもののthickness（厚さ、太さ、濃さ）を減らすという意味。

TRANSLATION | 例 文 の 訳

advocate	セサール・チャベスは米国農場労働者連合の創立者で、アメリカの労働法改正を強く主張した。 大統領は自身の政治的安定のために軍備縮小の主張者になる必要があった。
antagonize	大統領はたいてい、長期の休会中に任命することで上院議員たちを敵に回すのを回避しようとする。
attenuate	長距離恋愛はどのような愛情をも弱めてしまうだろう。

59

busybody
[bízibàdi]

n. an inquisitive person, often too interested in the lives of others

[名] 詮索好き、出しゃばり

Every society has its *busybodies* who spend half their life gossiping.

関連語 busybody : intrusive [intrúːsiv]

busybodyとは他人の問題にintrusive（でしゃばりの、押し入る）な人を表す。

caprice
[kəpríːs]

n. a sudden change in feeling, action, or opinion

[名] 気まぐれ、むら気

Most people did not trust Tom because he was known for his many *caprices*.

関連語 caprice : whimsical [ʰwímzikəl]

capriceと似た意味の形容詞whimsical（気まぐれな、むら気な）がある。

catalyst
[kǽtᵊlist]

n. a substance that speeds up a chemical reaction; an agent that provokes change

[名] 触媒；触発物

The bombing of Pearl Harbor was America's *catalyst* into World War II.

関連語 catalyst : enzyme [énzaim]

enzyme（酵素）はcatalystの一種だ。

categorical
[kæ̀təgɔ́ːrikəl]

adj. having no exceptions or conditions; absolute or unequivocal

[形] 全面的な、無条件の；絶対的な、断言的な

Robert made a *categorical* denial of any wrongdoing in his statement to the press.

反意語 categorical : qualified [kwáləfàid]

categoricalの反意語はqualified（条件付きの、制限された）

TRANSLATION | 例 文 の 訳

busybody　　人生の半分を噂話をして過ごす詮索好きが、どの社会にもいるものだ。

caprice　　　トムはよく気が変わることで有名だったので、ほとんどの人は彼を信頼していなかった。

catalyst　　　真珠湾攻撃はアメリカを第二次世界大戦へと導いた。

categorical　ロバートはメディアに対してすべての悪行を全面的に否定した。

cavil
[kǽvəl]

v. **to raise trivial objections or criticisms** [動] 難癖、揚げ足取り

Bobby loves to *cavil* at his mother just to annoy her.

関連語 cavil : quibbler [kwíblər]
いつも cavil しようとする人が quibbler（言いがかりをつける人）

cavort
[kəvɔ́ːʳt]

v. **to bound about in a sprightly manner; to have lively fun**
[動]（楽しそうに）飛び回る；浮かれ騒ぐ

The leprechauns *cavorted* around their pot of gold.

関連語 cavort : sprightly [spráitli]
cavort には sprightly（活発な、陽気な）な特徴がある。

civilize
[sívəlàiz]

v. **to bring out of a primitive state; to refine or socialize**
[動] 〜を文明化する；洗練させる

Missionaries *civilized* the tribes of New Guinea, teaching many members how to read and write.

反意語 civilize : barbarize [báːʳbəràiz]
civilize の反意語は barbarize（〜を野蛮にする、粗野にする）

cowardice
[káuəʳdis]

n. **lack of courage** [名] 臆病、卑怯

Failing to stand up for his girlfriend exhibited *cowardice* on Ron's part.

反意語 cowardice : pluck [plʌk]
cowardice の反意語は pluck（勇気）

cryptic
[kríptik]

adj. **secret or with hidden meaning** [形] 暗号の、隠れた意味を持つ

The *cryptic* message puzzled the CIA.

関連語 cryptic : cipher [sáifəʳ]
cipher（暗号）は cryptic だという特徴がある。

TRANSLATION | 例 文 の 訳

cavil	ボビーは母親を困らせるだけのために難癖をつけるのが大好きだ。
cavort	レプラコーンたちは金のつぼの周りで浮かれ騒いだ。
civilize	宣教師たちはニューギニアの部族の大勢に読み書きを教えて、彼らを文明化した。
cowardice	恋人を守れなかったことは、ロンの臆病さを示していた。
cryptic	その暗号メッセージは CIA を悩ませた。

desultory
[désəltɔ̀ːri]

adj. **lacking in plan or purpose; lacking rational sequence or connection** [形] 散漫な、気まぐれな；とりとめのない

Chuck's parents began to worry when he turned 35 and showed no signs of changing his *desultory* ways.

関連語 desultory : plan [plæn]
> desultory なことの中に plan（計画）を見いだすのは難しい。

detach
[ditǽtʃ]

v. **to separate or disengage** [動] 切り離す、分離する

Once he became a teenager, Jim gradually *detached* himself emotionally from his family.

反意語 detach : tether [téðəˈ]
> detach の反意語は tether（つなぐ、しばる）

devout
[diváut]

adj. **religiously devoted; serious about a belief or cause** [形] 信心深い、敬虔な；熱烈な

The *devout* Christian went to church every Sunday.

関連語 devout : sanctimonious [sæ̀ŋktəmóuniəs]
> sanctimonious（信心深げな）とは外面だけ devout に見せることを表す。

dexterous
[dékstˈrəs]

adj. **skillful or clever; artful** [形] 器用な；巧みな

The *dexterous* pitch at the end of the game brought victory to the East Coast team.

関連語 dexterous : manipulate [mənípjulèit]
> manipulate（巧みに扱う）することには dexterous な特徴がある。

ditch
[ditʃ]

n. **a long narrow hole dug in the earth, usually used for water drainage or containment** [名] 溝

The car went into the *ditch* because it spun out of control.

関連語 ditch : canyon [kǽnjən]
> ditch は canyon（深い峡谷）よりも狭くて浅い溝を言う。

TRANSLATION | 例 文 の 訳

desultory	チャックには35歳になってもはっきりしない生活態度を変える気配が見えず、両親が心配し始めた。
detach	10代になると、ジムはしだいに家族から感情面で離れていった。
devout	その敬虔なキリスト教徒は毎週日曜日に教会に行った。
dexterous	試合最後の巧みな投球が東海岸チームに勝利をもたらした。
ditch	その車は制御不能になってスピンし、溝に落ちた。

downpour
[dáunpɔ̀:ʳ]

n. **a heavy rain**　　　　　　　　　　　　　　[名] どしゃ降り

Just as we were walking out of the park, a *downpour* came and ruined our evening.

関連語 downpour : flooding [flʌ́diŋ]
downpour が flooding（洪水）を引き起こす。

doyen
[dɔ́ien]

n. **an experienced and senior member of a body or group**
　　　　　　　　　　　　　　[名] 最古参者、長老、第一人者

The *doyen* of the company suggested that it make the deal with Intel.

関連語 doyen : uninitiated [ʌ̀nɪníʃièitid]
doyen は uninitiated（経験が乏しい）なことがない。

drawl
[drɔ:l]

v. **to talk using lengthened vowel sounds**
　　　　　　　　　　　　[動]（母音を長く伸ばして）ゆっくり話す

n. **a manner of speaking slowly**　　　　[名] ゆっくりした話し方

Erica *drawled* her speech when she first began to study English.

It is difficult to understand people who speak with a Southern *drawl*.

関連語 drawl : slow [slou]
drawl には slow（ゆっくりした）という特徴がある。

envious
[énviəs]

adj. **feeling or showing jealousy or envy**
　　　　　　　　　　　　[形] うらやましく思っている、ねたんでいる

Jinny became increasingly *envious* of Trisha after hearing that her boyfriend had bought her a new coat.

関連語 envious : greedy [grí:di]
greedy（貪欲な、欲深い）は envious よりも望む程度が強い。

TRANSLATION | 例 文 の 訳

downpour	ちょうど歩いて公園から出ようとしたとき、どしゃ降りに見舞われてしまい、せっかくの晩が台無しになった。
doyen	その企業の長老がインテル社と取引するように提案した。
drawl	エリカは英語を学びたてのころ、母音を伸ばしてゆっくりと話していた。
	南部なまりで話す人の言うことを理解するのは難しい。
envious	トリシャの恋人が彼女に新しいコートを買ったと聞いて、ジニーはますます彼女がうらやましくなった。

esteem
[istíːm]

v. **to regard with respect or reverence; to consider**

[動] 尊敬する；～と見なす

n. **the high regard in which a person is held**　[名] 尊敬

The president had met many great men during his career, but he *esteemed* his father above them all.

Colin Powell is a man who has earned the *esteem* of the American people.

関連語 esteem : idolize [áidᵊlàiz]

度を越えて esteem すると idolize（偶像化する）ことにつながる。

extant
[ékstənt]

adj. **currently or still existing**　[形] 現存している

The largest *extant* reptile found in Asia is the Komodo dragon.

反意語 extant : extinct [ikstíŋkt]

extant の反意語は extinct（絶滅した）

favorable
[féivᵊrəbl]

adj. **expressing or facilitating approval or favor; advantageous**

[形] 好意的な；好都合な

The weather on our trip was *favorabl*e to our outdoor plans.

反意語 unfavorable : propitious [prəpíʃəs]

反意語は unfavorable（好ましくない、不都合な）。類義語に propitious（幸運な）がある。

fawn
[fɔːn]

v. **to seek favor by groveling or flattery**　[動] へつらう、こびる

The nobles *fawned* over the King as they asked for more titles and land grants.

関連語 fawning : hauteur [houtə́ːʳ]

fawning（へつらっている、こびている）人たちは hauteur（高慢、横柄）な態度はとらない。

TRANSLATION | 例 文 の 訳

esteem　大統領は在任中に多くの偉大な人物に会ったが、だれよりも自分の父親を尊敬していた。
コリン・パウエルはアメリカ人に尊敬されている人物だ。

extant　アジアで発見された現存する最大の爬虫類はコモドオオトカゲである。

favorable　旅行中の天気は私たちの屋外で過ごす予定に好都合なものだった。

fawn　その貴族たちはより多くの称号と土地を手に入れようと国王にこびた。

faze
[feiz]

v. **to disturb or disconcert**　　　　　[動] ～を驚かせる、困らせる

The accident didn't *faze* him a bit for some reason.

反意語 fazed : undisturbed [ʌndistə́ːʳbd]

fazed (驚いた、困った) の反意語は undisturbed (平静な)

indict
[indáit]

v. **to formally accuse of a crime**　　　　[動] ～を (罪で) 起訴する

People continued to treat Mr. Johnson with suspicion though he was never *indicted* for the murder.

関連語 indict : accused [əkjúːzd]

accused (被疑者) を indict する。

insubordinate
[ìnsəbɔ́ːʳdᵊnit]

adj. **disobedient; refusing to adhere to authority**

[形] 服従しない；反抗的な

The officer announced that he would not tolerate *insubordinate* behavior.

反意語 insubordinate : submissive [səbmísiv]

insubordinate の反意語は submissive (従順な)

intangible
[intǽndʒəbl]

adj. **not tangible; incapable of being defined or realized**

[形] 触れることができない；実体のない、不可解な

The *intangible* aura of the old man made me weak in his presence.

関連語 intangible : perceive [pəʳsíːv]

intangible なものは perceive (知覚する) ことができない。

integral
[íntigrəl]

adj. **consisting of essential parts; entire**　　　[名] 不可欠な；全体の

Happiness is an *integral* ingredient for a long life.

反意語 integral : peripheral [pərífᵊrəl]

integral の反意語は peripheral (周辺にある、あまり重要でない)

TRANSLATION | 例 文 の 訳

faze	ある理由で、彼はその事故に全然驚かなかった。
indict	ジョンソン氏は殺人罪で起訴されることはなかったが、人々は彼に疑いの目を向け続けた。
insubordinate	その将校は反抗的な行動は許さないと告げた。
intangible	その年配の男性がいると、つかみどころのない雰囲気のために私は強く出られなかった。
integral	幸福は長い人生にとって不可欠な要素である。

intensify
[inténsəfài]

v. **to strengthen or increase in density or intenseness**

[動] 〜を強める、強化する；強くなる

The noise of the crowd *intensified* as the final minutes of the game wore down.

反意語 intensify : wane [wein]

intensify の反意語は wane（弱くなる、衰える）

intent
[intént]

n. **the purpose or plan**

[名] 意図、趣旨

It was my *intent* to exercise every night, but I didn't do it.

反意語 intentional : accidental [æ̀ksidéntl]

intentional（意図的な）の反意語は accidental（偶然の）

invigorate
[invígərèit]

v. **to stimulate or give energy to**

[動] 〜を元気づける、活気づける、励ます

A cold shower in the morning *invigorates* me during the hot summer months.

関連語 invigorate : tonic [tánik]

tonic（強壮剤）には invigorate する働きがある。

inviolable
[inváiələbl]

adj. **secure from profanation, assault, or violation**

[形] 犯してはならない、神聖な

Christians regard the Bible as an *inviolable* source for inspiration and wisdom.

関連語 inviolable : profane [prouféin]

inviolable は profane（冒涜する）することができないということ。

TRANSLATION | 例 文 の 訳

intensify	試合の残り時間が減っていくに従って、群衆はますます騒がしくなった。
intent	毎晩運動するつもりだったが、しなかった。
invigorate	暑い夏の朝の冷たいシャワーは、私を元気にしてくれる。
inviolable	キリスト教徒たちは聖書を霊感と英知の神聖な源だと考えている。

invulnerable
[inv∧ln°rəbl]

adj. incapable of being wounded or conquered

[形] 傷つくことがない、不死身の；難攻不落の

The *invulnerable* Superman flew through the burning fire to save the family.

関連語 invulnerable : injure [índʒəʳ]

invulnerabule なものを injure（傷つける）ことは難しい。

latent
[léitnt]

adj. present but not currently active; dormant

[形] 潜在的な、隠れた；休止状態にある

Lyme Disease can stay *latent* in a body for years before it affects one's health.

反意語 latent : manifest [mǽnəfèst]

latent の反意語は manifest（明らかな、はっきりした）

lavish
[lǽviʃ]

adj. generous in using or spending; extravagant

[形] 気前のよい；豪華な、ぜいたくな

The *lavish* wedding was held at a posh mansion and adorned with ice sculptures.

反意語 lavish : penurious [pən(j)úʳriəs]

lavish の反意語は penurious（極貧の）

lax
[læks]

adj. careless or slacking; negligent to details　[形] 手ぬるい、甘い；ゆるい

Toward the end of a semester, students tend to become *lax* with their studies.

類義語 lax : loose [luːs]

lax の類義語は loose（ゆるんだ、ゆるい）

TRANSLATION | 例 文 の 訳

invulnerable	不死身のスーパーマンはその家族を救うために燃える炎の中を飛んだ。
latent	ライム病は何年も体内に潜んだのちに健康に害を及ぼすことがある。
lavish	その贅沢な婚礼は豪華な大邸宅で行われ、会場は氷の彫刻で飾られた。
lax	学期末が近づくと、学生たちは勉強の手をゆるめがちだ。

lethal [líːθəl]	adj. **devastatingly harmful to the point of causing death** <div align="right">[形] 致命的な、致死の</div>Juliet woke up a moment after Romeo had drunk the *lethal* poison. 関連語 lethal : harmful [háːˈmfəl] lethalは死をもたらすほどharmful（有害な）であることを表す。
loyalty [lɔ́iəlti]	n. **faithfulness or allegiance**<div align="right">[名] 忠誠、忠実</div>His *loyalty* makes him a good solider. 関連語 loyalty : perfidious [pəˈfídiəs] 他者にprefidious（不誠実な、不実な）な人にはloyaltyがない。
luxuriant [lʌgʒúˈriənt]	adj. **abundant or rich; marked by luxury**<div align="right">[形] 豊かな；華麗な</div>My family took a *luxuriant* vacation to the tropics. 反意語 luxuriant : Spartan [spáːrtn] luxuriantの反意語はSpartan（スパルタ式の、質素な）
meteoric [mìːtiɔ́ːrik]	adj. **of or relating to meteors; relating to the speed of meteors** <div align="right">[形] 流星の；急速な</div>For her role in the movie Basic Instinct, Sharon Stone experienced a *meteoric* rise to fame. 関連語 meteoric : constancy [kánstənsi] meteoricなものにはconstancy（不変、安定）がない。

TRANSLATION | 例 文 の 訳

lethal	ジュリエットはロミオが毒薬を飲んだ直後に目覚めた。
loyalty	彼は忠実なのでいい兵士になる。
luxuriant	私の家族は熱帯地方で贅沢な休暇を過ごした。
meteoric	映画『氷の微笑』でシャロン・ストーンは名声を手に入れた。

1st
2nd
3rd
4th
5th
6th
7th
8th
9th
10th

patent
[pǽtnt]

n. the written rights given to an inventor by the government to exclusively make, use, or sell an invention for a set number of years　[名] 特許、特許権

adj. obvious　[形] 明白な

A *patent* was given to Alexander Graham Bell for the invention of the telephone.

Rick spends five hours each day in front of the computer and is a *patent* addict to computer games.

反意語 patent : occult [əkʌ́lt]
patent の反意語は occult（魔術的な、秘密の）

potable
[póutəbl]

adj. drinkable　[形] 飲用に適した

Contrary to popular belief, the tap water in New York City is *potable* and of good quality.

関連語 potable : beverage [bévˀridʒ]
beverage（飲料）は potable である。

potentate
[póutntèit]

n. ruler or one who holds great power　[名] 支配者、権力者

In a democracy, there is no true *potentate*, only popular icons called politicians.

関連語 potentate : power [páuəʳ]
potentate は power（力、権力）をもつ人のこと。

resurgence
[risə́ːʳdʒəns]

n. the coming again into activity and prominence　[名] 復活、再起

After the wild tech stock speculations of the 1990's, there was a *resurgence* of investment in traditionally stable companies.

反意語 resurgent : moribund [mɔ́(ː)rəbʌnd]
形容詞 moribund（活気を失った、ひん死の）は、品詞は違うが resurgent の反対の意味になる。

TRANSLATION | 例 文 の 訳

patent　アレクサンダー・グラハム・ベルに電話の発明の特許が与えられた。
リックは毎日パソコンの前で5時間を費やすのだから、明らかなパソコンゲーム中毒者だ。

potable　一般に信じられていることとは反対に、ニューヨークの水道水は飲用に適しており、水質もよい。

potentate　民主主義には真の権力者はおらず、政治家と呼ばれる大衆の象徴がいるだけだ。

resurgence　1990年代にハイテク株への著しい投機があったのち、伝統的な安定企業への投資が復活した。

69

retain [ritéin]	v. **to keep in possession; to maintain in a certain place, condition, or position** [動] 保つ；(状態、地位などを) 維持する
	Bob *retains* most of his income and stores it in savings accounts.
	反意語 retain : proffer [práfər]
	retainの反意語はproffer（差し出す、提供する）
retaliate [ritǽlièit]	v. **to repay an injury in kind; to return like for like** [動] 報復する、復讐する；仕返しする
	The French *retaliated* against the Spanish for invading Cotignac.
	反意語 retaliate : forgive [fəˈgív]
	retaliateの反意語はforgive（許す）
retard [ritáːˈd]	v. **to slow up or delay** [動] ～を遅らせる、妨げる
	Caffeine is thought to *retard* growth in children.
	反意語 retard : hasten [héisn]
	retardの反意語はhasten（～を急がせる、早める）
shackle [ʃǽkl]	v. **to restrain or confine to prevent from action** [動] 拘束する、束縛する
	David felt *shackled* by his wife, children, job, and financial obligations.
	反意語 shackle : emancipate [imǽnsəpèit]
	shackleの反意語はemancipate（～を解放する、自由にする）
suture [súːtʃəˈ]	n. **the act of surgically closing a wound** [名] (傷口などの) 縫合
	If the *sutures* left an unsightly scar, Kara's hopes to be a model would be lost.
	反意語 suture : incision [insíʒən]
	sutureの反意語はincision（切開）

TRANSLATION | 例 文 の 訳

retain	ボブは収入のほとんどを使わずに、預金口座にためている。
retaliate	フランスはスペインがコティニャックを侵略したことに報復した。
retard	カフェインは子供たちの成長を遅らせると考えられている。
shackle	デイビッドは妻、子供たち、仕事、経済的な義務に束縛されていると感じた。
suture	もし、縫合によって醜い傷が残ったら、カラのモデルになるという希望は失われてしまうだろう。

testimonial
[tèstəmóuniəl]

n. **something given as an expression of thanks or admiration**

[名] 推薦文、功労賞、感謝状

The enormous statue of the mayor served as a *testimonial* to his great service to the city.

関連語 testimonial : appreciation [əprì:ʃiéiʃᵊn]
appreciation（感謝）を示すために testimonial を与える。

tinker
[tíŋkəʳ]

v. **to fix experimentally or unskillfully**   [動] 下手な修理をする、いじくる

Janet finally called the plumber after *tinkering* with the sink by herself for an hour.

関連語 tinker : adjust [ədʒʌ́st]
tinker は adjust（調整する）に比べて不器用な技術でものをさわるという意味がある。

tonic
[tánik]

n. **a medicine or agent that invigorates and refreshes**   [名] 強壮剤

adj. **causing mental, physical, or emotional vigor**

[形] 元気づける、強壮にする

Balding men hope for a hair *tonic* that will re-grow lost hair.

Helen believed the secret to her youthful appearance was the daily *tonic* juice she drank.

関連語 tonic : invigorate [invígərèit]
tonic には invigorate（元気づける、活気づける）という機能がある。

unsuitable
[ʌ̀nsú:təbl]

adj. **not suitable or appropriate; not acceptable or wanted**

[形] 不適切な、ふさわしくない ; 受け入れられない

The retinue found the hotel room to be entirely *unsuitable* for the movie star.

反意語 unsuitable : meet [mi:t]
動詞 meet（〜を満たす、かなえる）は品詞は違うが unsuitable と反対の意味をもつ。

TRANSLATION | 例 文 の 訳

testimonial	市長の巨大な銅像は、彼の市に対する多大な貢献への感謝を示している。
tinker	ジャネットは自分で流しを1時間いじってみたあと、最終的には配管工を呼んだ。
tonic	頭がはげている男性たちは、ヘアトニックが抜けた髪を再び生やしてくれることを願っている。
	ヘレンは自分の若々しい外見の秘訣が毎日飲んでいる栄養ジュースだと信じていた。
unsuitable	付き人たちは、そのホテルの部屋が映画スターにとってまったくふさわしくないことに気づいた。

untenable
[ʌnténəbl]

adj. unable to be defended　　　　　　　　　　　[形] 支えきれない、防御できない

The captain determined that their position on the field was *untenable*, so the soldiers moved back several miles.

関連語 untenable : defend [difénd]
　　　untenableというのは defend（防御、防衛）できない状態。

usurp
[juːsə́ːʳp]

v. to seize in possession of rights, power, or role of another

[動]（権力・地位などを）暴力で入手する、強奪する

The commander in chief was *usurped* by the opposing general.

関連語 usurp : power [páuəʳ]
　　　usurpとは power（権力）などを奪うことをいう。

vital
[váitl]

adj. essential to life; lively, full of energy or spirit

[形] 不可欠な；活気のある、生き生きとした

Nutrients and clean water are *vital* to maintaining good health.

関連語 vitality : languish [lǽŋgwiʃ]
　　　languish（弱まる、低迷する）とは vitalの名詞 vitality（活気、元気）がなくなること。

vivacious
[vivéiʃəs]

adj. lively or sprightly　　　　　　　　　　　　　[形] 快活な、陽気な

The boy had a *vivacious* and pleasant character.

反意語 vivacious : lifeless [láiflis]
　　　vivaciousの反意語は lifeless（元気のない、生気のない）

votary
[vóutəri]

n. a committed follower of a religion or cult; an enthusiast or devoted admirer　　　　　　　　　　　　　　[名] 信者、崇拝者；支持者

Bush's *votaries* waited three days outside the White House to see him in person.

反意語 votary : skeptic [sképtik]
　　　votaryの反意語は skeptic（懐疑論者、疑い深い人）

TRANSLATION | 例文の訳

untenable	将校は戦場で自分たちの陣地を守り切れないと判断し、兵士たちは数マイル退却した。
usurp	その最高司令官の地位は敵対する司令官に奪われた。
vital	栄養ときれいな水は健康を維持するのに不可欠だ。
vivacious	その少年は快活で気持ちのいい性格の持ち主だった。
votary	ブッシュの支持者たちは、彼に直接会うためにホワイトハウスの外で3日間待った。

■ Fill in the blanks with the correct letter that matches the word with its definition.

1. categorical	_____	a. absolute or unequivocal
2. desultory	_____	b. necessary or essential; consisting of essential parts
3. retain	_____	c. currently or still existing
4. vivacious	_____	d. lacking in plan or purpose; lacking rational sequence or connection
5. usurp	_____	e. an experienced and senior member of a body or group
6. potentate	_____	f. to keep in possession; to maintain in a certain place, condition, or position
7. integral	_____	g. lively or sprightly
8. extant	_____	h. to seize in possession of rights, property, or role of another
9. doyen	_____	i. a ruler or one who holds great power
10. cavort	_____	j. to bound about in a sprightly manner; to have lively fun

■ Put the correct word in each blank from the list of words below.

11. exponent は自分の信念を _____ する。

12. pluck（容器、胆力）の反意語は _____ である。

13. _____ の反意語は tether（つかむ）である。

14. tinker は _____ に比べて不器用な技術でものを扱うという意味だ。

15. drawl には _____ という特徴がある。

16. greedy は _____ よりもその渇望の程度が強い。

17. _____ は死に至るほど非常に harmful という意味である。

18. sanctimonious は表面的に _____ な様子を言う。

19. quibbler はいつも _____ しようとする。

20. _____ は他人の仕事に intrusive する人である。

a. slow	b. adjust	c. detach	d. cowardice	e. advocate	f. envious
g. lethal	h. devout	i. cavil	j. drinkable	k. unsuitable	l. busybody

Answer key

11. e   12. d   13. c   14. b   15. a   16. f   17. g   18. h   19. i   20. l

1. a   2. d   3. f   4. g   5. h   6. i   7. b   8. c   9. e   10. j

73

覚えるべき単語が多すぎる？
心配するよりも行動しよう。

6th DAY

anthology
[ænθálədʒi]

n. a collection of selected literary or artistic pieces compiled into one work　　　　　　　　　　　　　　[名] アンソロジー；詩選集、作品集

This *anthology* is regarded as the first Korean literary work to be translated into Mongolian for publication.

関連語 anthology : poem [póuəm]
anthology は厳選された poem（詩）を収録している。

antipathy
[æntípəθi]

n. aversion or strong dislike　　　　　　　　　　　　　[名] 反感、嫌悪

The president made clear his *antipathy* to the opposition by vetoing their legislation 3 times.

反意語 antipathy : affinity [əfínəti]
antipathy の反意語は affinity（親近感、愛着）

artless
[á:ʳtlis]

adj. uncultured; made without skill; having or displaying no guile
[形] 洗練されていない；素朴な；不器用な

Blake enrolled in a poetry class to improve his reputation as a crass and *artless* football player.

Americans are thought to have an *artless* attitude about other peoples and cultures.

反意語 artlessness : urbanity [ə:ʳbǽnəti]
artlessness（素朴、不器用）の反意語は urbanity（都会風、洗練）

関連語 artless : guile [gail]
artless な人は guile（狡猾さ）を持たない。

TRANSLATION | 例 文 の 訳

anthology　この選集はモンゴル語に翻訳されて出版された最初の韓国文学作品とされている。

antipathy　大統領は立法案に3回拒否権を行使して、野党への嫌悪感をあらわにした。

artless　ブレイクは、無神経で洗練されていないアメフト選手という評判を払しょくするために、詩の授業に参加した。

アメリカ人は、他の民族や文化に対する姿勢に問題があると考えられている。

authentic
[ɔːθéntik]

adj. **genuine or real**   [形] 真の、本物の

The painting was deemed to be *authentic* after much inspection and scrutiny.

関連語 authenticity : fabricate [fǽbrikèit]

fabricate(作り上げる、捏造する)したものにはauthenticity(本物であること、確実性)がない。

authorize
[ɔ́ːθəràiz]

v. **to grant permission; to invest with legal authority**   [動] 承認する；権限を与える

John *authorized* his wife to have access to his bank accounts.

反意語 authorize : interdict [ìntəʳdíkt]

authorizeの反意語はinterdict(〜を禁ずる)

bequest
[bikwést]

n. **a gift left in a will**   [名] 遺産

Edward's educational trust fund was a *bequest* left to him by his rich uncle.

関連語 bequest : testator [tésteitəʳ]

testator(遺言人)が残すものがbequest。

catholic
[kǽθəʳlik]

adj. **broad in scope; universal**   [形] 広範な；普遍的な

Amy was a woman of *catholic* interests, ranging from bungee jumping to stamp collecting.

反意語 catholic : narrow [nǽrou]

catholicの反意語はnarrow(狭量な、偏狭な)

cement
[simént]

v. **to bind or bring together; to unite**   [動] 結ぶ；固める

The marriage of their children *cemented* the two families' friendship.

反意語 cement : fracture [frǽktʃəʳ]

cementの反意語はfracture(分裂させる)

TRANSLATION | 例 文 の 訳

authentic	多くの調査と審査を経て、その絵画は本物であると判定された。
authorize	ジョンは妻が自分の銀行口座を利用するのを認めた。
bequest	エドワードの教育信託資金は裕福なおじから残された遺産だった。
catholic	エイミーはバンジージャンプから切手収集まで幅広い趣味を持つ女性だった。
cement	子供同士の結婚が両家の友情を強固にした。

charade
[ʃəréid]

n. a pretense or mockery
[名] ごまかし、見せかけ

Though they loathed each other, the couple managed the *charade* of a marriage for the sake of their children.

関連語 charade : dissimulate [disímjulèit]
charadeと品詞は違うが、似た意味の単語が動詞dissimulate（相違させる、異化させる）

connive
[kənáiv]

v. to work together in a secret or illegal manner; to collude
[動] 共謀する、陰謀を企てる；結託する

The bank robbers *connived* for 3 months to plan the perfect robbery.

関連語 conniver : conspiratorial [kənspìrətɔ́:riəl]
conniver（共謀者）には conspiratorial（共謀の、陰謀の）という特徴がある。

deter
[ditə́:ʳ]

v. to inhibit or prevent from acting by means of fear or doubt
[動]（不安や恐怖から）〜するのを思いとどまらせる、防止する

D.A.R.E. is a drug prevention program aimed to *deter* children from taking drugs.

関連語 deter : intrepid [intrépid]
intrepid（恐れを知らない）な人をdeterするのは難しい。

determination
[ditə́:ʳmənéiʃən]

n. the conclusion or the act of deciding definitely; strong will or resoluteness
[名] 決断；決意、決心

Her *determination* is what got Sally to the top of the corporate ladder.

反意語 determination : irresolution [irèzəlú:ʃən]
determinationの反意語はirresolution（優柔不断）

TRANSLATION | 例 文 の 訳

charade　　お互いに憎み合っていたが、その夫婦は子供たちのためにどうにか見せかけだけの結婚生活を送った。

connive　　その銀行強盗たちは、完璧な強盗を計画するのに３カ月間共謀した。

deter　　D.A.R.E.とは、子供に麻薬を使用させないようにするための薬物抑止プログラムだ。

determination　　意志の強さがあったから、サリーはその会社のトップに上り詰めた。

detour
[díːtuəʳ]

n. **a deviation from the normal route or direct course; a path or road replacing a temporarily disabled one**　　[名] 迂回路；回り道

v. **to go or cause to go by a roundabout way**
　　　　　　　　　　　　　　　　[動] 回り道をする、回り道をさせる

The cab driver took a *detour* down the alley in order to avoid traffic.

We had to *detour* through Minnesota because the highway was under construction.

関連語 detour : route [ruːt]
　　detour するのは route (道、ルート) である。

encumber
[inkʌ́mbəʳ]

v. **to obstruct or impede**　　[動] 妨げる、邪魔する

Drinking in moderation is fine, but it becomes a problem when it *encumbers* one's ability to make decisions.

反意語 encumber : remove impediment [rimúːv impédəmənt]
　　encumber の反意語は remove impediment (障害を取り除く)

enthusiasm
[inθúːziǽzm]

n. **intense interest or involvement**　　[名] 熱中、熱意

The teacher's *enthusiasm* kept the children attentive in class.

関連語 enthusiasm : mania [méiniə]
　　enthusiasm の度が強いものが mania (異常な熱意、熱狂)

entice
[intáis]

v. **to tempt or lure by arousing hope or desire**　　[動] そそのかす、誘惑する

The brightly lit store window with its display of all the latest toys *enticed* the little boy.

類義語 entice : allure [əlúəʳ]
　　entice の類義語は allure (〜を魅惑する)

TRANSLATION | 例 文 の 訳

detour　　そのタクシー運転手は交通渋滞を避けるために路地を迂回した。
　　　　　　幹線道路が工事中だったので、私たちはミネソタを通って迂回しなければならなかった。

encumber　　節度ある飲酒はいいが、それが人の判断力を妨げるほどになると問題だ。

enthusiasm　　その教師の熱意のおかげで、子供たちは授業に集中していた。

entice　　あらゆる最新のおもちゃが並ぶ明るく照らされたショーウインドーに、その小さな男の子は誘惑された。

77

estimable
[éstəməbl]

adj. **capable of being valuable; worthy of esteem**

[形] 尊敬すべき；尊重できる

The king was impressed by the *estimable* young knight's heroic deeds in battle.

反意語 estimable : contemptible [kəntémptəbl]

estimable の反意語は contemptible (軽蔑すべき)

extinguish
[ikstíŋgwiʃ]

v. **to stop from burning**

[動] 消火する

Luckily, the firemen *extinguished* the flames before they burned down the entire house.

反意語 extinguish : kindle [kíndl]

extinguish の反意語は kindle (火をつける、点火する)

extol
[ikstóul]

v. **to praise or glorify**

[動] 激賞する、絶賛する

The evangelist *extolled* the virtues of his religion to every person he encountered.

反意語 extol : excoriate [ikskɔ́:rièit]

extol の反意語は excoriate (〜を激しく非難する)

extort
[ikstɔ́:ʳt]

v. **to obtain by force or illegal power**

[動] ゆすり取る、奪う

The bully *extorted* money from the boy everyday by threatening to beat him up.

関連語 extortionist : intimidation [intìmədéiʃən]

extortionist (強奪者) の武器は intimidation (脅し) である。

fathom
[fǽðəm]

n. **a measurement of water equal to six feet**

[名] 6フィートの水深

v. **to come to understanding through probing or thinking**

[動] (深く考えて) 理解する

The nuclear submarine was cruising undetected in the *fathoms* below.

Tim couldn't *fathom* why she would do that.

関連語 fathom : erudite [ér(j)udàit]

erudite (博学な) な人は fathom するものだ。

TRANSLATION | 例 文 の 訳

estimable	その尊敬すべき若い騎士が戦闘中に見せた英雄的行為に、国王は感銘を受けた。
extinguish	幸いにも、消防士たちは家が全焼してしまう前に消火した。
extol	その福音主義者は、出会うすべての人の前で自分の宗教の美点を絶賛した。
extort	そのいじめっ子は殴ると脅して、その少年から毎日金を奪い取った。
fathom	その原子力潜水艦は、水深数十フィートを検知されることなく進んでいた。
	ティムは、彼女がなぜそのようなことをしようとしているのか理解できなかった。

fatigue
[fətíːg]

n. exhaustion from labor or stress　　　　　　[名] 疲労、疲れ

v. to exhaust with labor or intensive stress　　[動] 疲れさせる

After the hard fought soccer game, a few of the players collapsed on the field in *fatigue*.

After hiking in the mountains for two hours, the hunter was *fatigued* and ready to give up the chase.

関連語 fatigue : repose [ripóuz]
　　　repose（休息）をとって、fatigueから回復する。

futile
[fjúːtl]

adj. useless or completely ineffective　　　　[形] 無駄な、効果のない

It is *futile* to argue with her when she has made up her mind like that.

反意語 futile : efficacious [èfəkéiʃəs]
　　　futileの反意語はefficacious（有効な）

intercessor
[ìntəʳsésəʳ]

n. one who mediates between two parties to reconcile differences
　　　　　　　　　　　　　　　　　　　　　　[名] 調停人、仲裁者

To make money, the marriage counselor has even served as an *intercessor* for couples she thought should be apart.

関連語 intercessor : mediate [míːdièit]
　　　intercessorの主要な任務はmediate（仲裁する）することだ。

interdict
[ìntəʳdíkt]

v. to prohibit or forbid in a formal or authoritative manner
　　　　　　　　　　　　　　　　　　　　　　[動] ～を禁ずる、禁止する

The role of the guards is to *interdict* anyone from entering the compound.

反意語 interdict : authorize [ɔ́ːθəràiz]
　　　interdictの反意語はauthorize（権限を与える）

interrogate
[intérəgèit]

v. to question formally and aggressively　　　[動] ～を尋問する

The inspector *interrogated* the suspect for three hours, but wasn't able to extract new information.

類義語 interrogate : examine [igzǽmin]
　　　interrogateの類義語はexamine（～を尋問する、調査する）

TRANSLATION | 例文の訳

fatigue　サッカーの激戦が終わると、数名の選手が疲労のためにピッチで倒れた。
　　　　　2時間山を歩いたあと、その狩猟者は疲れ切って追跡をあきらめようと思った。
futile　彼女がそのように決心してしまっているときには、議論しても無駄だ。
intercessor　金を稼ぐために、その結婚カウンセラーは別れるべきだと思う夫婦さえ仲裁した。
interdict　警備員たちの役割は、構内に入ろうとするあらゆる人を止めることだった。
interrogate　その捜査員は容疑者を3時間尋問したが、新たな情報を聞きだすことはできなかった。

intimate
[íntəmət]

adj. marked by close association in a very private and personal matter　　　[形] 親密な、親しい

n. a very close friend　　　[名] 親友

The relationship between the co-workers grew very *intimate* after a couple of months.

Most people meet their *intimate* either in childhood, or while attending college.

関連語 intimate : clique [kliːk]
　clique (派閥、党派) の構成員は互いに intimate な関係を持っている。

intimidate
[intímədèit]

v. to make timid; to frighten　　　[動] 怖がらせる；脅迫する、脅す

You can't *intimidate* me with your childish threats!

関連語 intimidate : bully [búli]
　bully (弱い者いじめをする人、いじめっ子) は他人を intimade する。

latitude
[lǽtət(j)ùːd]

n. angular distance north or south of the Earth's equator measured up to 90 degrees; freedom to act　　　[名] 緯度；自由

White, middle-class Americans take for granted the *latitude* bestowed to them by their social position in today's world.

反意語 latitude : strict limitation [strikt lìmətéiʃⁿn]
　latitude の反意語は strict limitation (厳しい制限)

literal
[lítⁿrəl]

adj. being in accordance with the primary or exact meaning of words; true to fact　　　[形] 文字通りの；正確な

New branches of Christianity diverge from a *literal* interpretation of the bible.

反意語 literal : figurative [fígjurətiv]
　literal の反意語は figuative (比喩的な)

TRANSLATION | 例 文 の 訳

intimate　　数カ月すると、職場の人々の人間関係は非常に親密なものになった。
　　　　　　　ほとんどの人たちは子供時代あるいは大学生時代に親友と出会う。

intimidate　子供じみた脅迫で私を怖がらせることなどできない！

latitude　　白人で中流のアメリカ人は、今の世の中における自分たちの社会的地位によって与えられた自由を当たり前のものと思っている。

literal　　　キリスト教の新しい分派は、聖書の文字通りの解釈から離れている。

lithe
[laið]

adj. **flexible; easily bent or flexed**　　　　　　[形] 柔軟な；しなやかな

Fortunately the gymnast was *lithe* enough to handle the difficult move.

類義語 lithe : lissome [lísəm]
　　lithe の類義語は lissome（柔軟な、しなやかな）

mawkish
[mɔ́:kiʃ]

adj. **excessively sentimental; having a bad taste**

[形] 非常に感傷的な、趣味の悪い

The critic's review of the movie seems *mawkish* and overwrought.

類義語 mawkish : maudlin [mɔ́:dlin]
　　mawkish の類義語は maudlin（感傷的な）

meticulous
[mətíkjuləs]

adj. **excessively thorough and careful with details**

[形] 慎重な、非常に注意深い

It takes a *meticulous* person to be a good editor.

関連語 meticulous : careful [kɛ́əˈfəl]
　　careful（注意深い）の度が強くなると meticulous になる。

mitigate
[mítəgèit]

v. **to reduce the severity or pain of; to mollify or alleviate**

[動] ～を和らげる、軽減する；なだめる

The camper *mitigated* the itch of his mosquito bites by applying a cream.

関連語 mitigate : severity [səvérəti]
　　mitigate は severity（厳しさ、深刻さ）を軽減することをいう。

motivate
[móutəvèit]

v. **to impel or provide a reason to do something**

[動] やる気を与える、動機づける

The possibility of making money *motivates* people to work hard.

関連語 motivate : exhortation [ègzɔːˈtéiʃən]
　　exhortation（奨励）の目的は motivate すること。

TRANSLATION | 例 文 の 訳

lithe	幸運なことに、その体操選手はこの難しい動きをこなせるだけの柔軟性をもっていた。
mawkish	その批評家の映画評は、過度に感傷的で大げさすぎるようだ。
meticulous	非常に慎重な人がいい編集者になる。
mitigate	そのキャンパーは、クリームを塗って蚊に刺されたところのかゆみを和らげた。
motivate	お金を稼げる可能性があると、人は熱心に働く気になる。

noxious
[nákʃəs]

adj. poisonous or harmful to living creatures; obnoxious

[形] 有毒な、有害な；不快な

The city was evacuated to save them from the *noxious* fumes coming out of the fast food restaurants.

関連語 noxious : venom [vénəm]

venom（毒液）は noxious だという特徴がある。

orthodox
[ɔ́ːʳθədɑ̀ks]

adj. conforming to generally accepted doctrine　[形] 正統的な、正統派の

Orthodox Jews must follow strict dietary laws.

反意語 orthodoxy : heresy [hérəsi]

orthodoxy（背移設、正教）の反意語は heresy（異端、異論）

oxymoron
[ɑ̀ksimɔ́ːrɑn]

n. a combination of contradictory words　[名] 矛盾語法

The phrase just war is an *oxymoron* that is often used by politicians to alleviate fears that innocent civilians will be killed accidently.

関連語 oxymoron : contradictory [kɑ̀ntrədíktəri]

oxymoron には contradictory（矛盾した）という特徴がある。

pith
[piθ]

n. the core or essential part　[名] 要点、核心

The *pith* of humanity is love.

反意語 pith : unimportant point [ʌ̀nimpɔ́ːʳtᵊnt pɔint]

pith の反意語は unimportant point（重要ではない点）

ratification
[ræ̀təfikéiʃən]

n. formal approval and confirmation　[名] 批准、承認

The *ratification* of the handgun law shocked the public.

反意語 ratify : repeal [ripíːl]

ratify（〜を批准する、承認する）の反意語は repeal（〜を廃止する、撤回する）

TRANSLATION | 例 文 の 訳

noxious　そのファストフードレストランが吐き出す有害な煙からのがれるために、全市民が避難した。

orthodox　正統派ユダヤ教徒は厳格な食事の規則を守らなければならない。

oxymoron　正義の戦いという言葉は、罪のない民間人が誤って命を落とすかもしれないことへの恐怖を和らげるために政治家がよく使う矛盾語法だ。

pith　人間性の核心にあるものは愛だ。

ratification　その銃器法の承認は一般大衆に衝撃を与えた。

rational
[rǽʃənl]

adj. **reasonable** [形] 合理的な

I habitually went for advice to my grandmother because she was a *rational* and compassionate person.

関連語 rationalization : plausible [plɔ́:zəbl]
rationalization（合理化）されたものは plausible（妥当な、もっともな）だという特徴がある。

reticence
[rétəs³ns]

n. **the quality of being reserved or restrained**
[名] 無口、沈黙；控えめ

Jim has some *reticence* about expressing emotion.

関連語 reticent : talk [tɔ:k]
reticent（無口な）な人はあまり talk（話す）することがない。

retinue
[rét³n(j)ù:]

n. **a group of retainers or followers** [名] 従者、随行団

Queen Elizabeth had a *retinue* of 30 servants that accompanied her on any of her travels.

関連語 retinue : attendant [əténdənt]
attendant（参加者）は retinue の一員である。

retort
[ritɔ́:ʳt]

v. **to reply rapidly and sharply, sometimes in jest; to present a count argument; to return in kind**
[動] 素早く言い返す；反論する；仕返しをする

n. **a sharp reply or counterargument** [名] 応酬、口答え

The receptionist *retorted* with a sarcastic comment.
His father's stinging *retort* wounded Aaron.

類義語 retort : repartee [rèpəʳtí:]
retort の類義語は repartee（会話、やりとり）

TRANSLATION | 例文の訳

rational 祖母は合理的で思いやりのある人だったので、私はしょっちゅう彼女に助言を求めに行った。

reticence ジムはあまり感情を表に出さない。

retinue エリザベス女王は30人の召使いを従えて、どのような旅にも同行した。

retort その受付係は皮肉な言葉で応酬した。
父親のとげのある返事にアーロンは傷ついた。

revive
[riváiv]

v. to reawaken to consciousness or life; to renew something; to revitalize　　　　　[動] 意識を回復させる；よみがえらせる；復活させる

I tried to *revive* her spirits, but she was hopelessly gloomy.

反意語 revive : wither [wíðəʳ]
　　revive の反意語は wither（衰えさせる）

satiate
[séiʃièit]

v. to fully satisfy; to sate　　　　　[動] 十分に満足させる；（欲望などを）満たす

After the feast, my stomach was *satiated*.

関連語 satiated : food [fuːd]
　　food（食べ物）を食べることで、satiated（満腹な）になる。

satisfaction
[sæ̀tisfǽkʃən]

n. fulfillment of needs or desire; contentment; reparation for a sin or payment of a debt　　　　　[名] 充足；満足；贖罪、賠償

My morning coffee brings me great *satisfaction*.

関連語 satisfy : exacting [igzǽktiŋ]
　　exacting（厳格な、多くを求める）人は、簡単に satisfy（満足させる）させることはできない。

savor
[séivəʳ]

n. the taste or smell of something　　　　　[名] 味、におい

v. to taste or enjoy an experience　　　　　[動] 〜を味わう、楽しむ

Roxanne enjoyed the *savor* of the meal and left no food to waste.

While in Thailand, I *savored* every bite of their fantastic cuisine.

類義語 savory : palatable [pǽlətəbl]
　　savory（おいしい）の類義語は palatable（味のよい）

TRANSLATION | 例 文 の 訳

revive	私は彼女を元気づけようとしたが、彼女は望みのないほど落ち込んでいた。
satiate	ごちそうを食べて、私は満腹だった。
satisfaction	朝のコーヒーは私にすばらしい満足感を与える。
savor	ロクサーヌは料理の味を楽しみ、何も残さずに食べた。
	タイにいる間、私はすばらしい料理を一口ごとに味わった。

savvy
[sǽvi]

n. **knowledge of affairs; shrewdness**   [名] 物知り；実務能力

adj. **knowledgeable and perceptive**   [形] 物知りな；有能な

The senator's political *savvy* has won him more than 5 re-elections.

Savvy presidential advisors knew of the scandal well before the media broke the story.

反意語 savvy : tactless [tǽktlis]
    savvyの反意語は tactless（融通の利かない）

sly
[slai]

adj. **clever, usually implying deceptiveness**   [形] 狡猾な

The *sly* fox outsmarted the owl, or so the fable goes.

反意語 sly : artless [áːᵊtlis]
    slyの反意語は artless（不器用な、飾らない）

tawdry
[tɔ́ːdri]

adj. **gaudy in brightness of appearance**   [形] 派手な；下品な

Cynthia failed to achieve an air of elegance with that *tawdry* dress she wore.

関連語 tawdry : garment [gáːᵊmənt]
    tawdryは主に garment（衣服）の様子を表すのに使われる。

tether
[téðəᵊ]

v. **to fasten with a rope**   [動] 綱でしばる心

n. **a chain**   [名] 鎖

While sailing on the boat, Micky had to *tether* the sail tighter so it wouldn't flap around.

The neighbor's dog could not reach our yard because his *tether* was only five feet long.

反意語 tether : loose [luːs]
    tetherの反意語は loose（～をほどく）

TRANSLATION | 例 文 の 訳

savvy　その上院議員は政治的な手腕のおかげで、5回を超えて再選されている。
　　　　有能な大統領補佐官たちは、メディアが暴露する前に、そのスキャンダルについてすっかり知っていた。

sly　狡猾なキツネがフクロウを出し抜いた、とその寓話は語る。

tawdry　シンシアは、着ていた派手なドレスのせいで上品な雰囲気を出せなかった。

tether　船で航行する間、ミッキーは帆を強くしばってはためかないようにしなければならなかった。
　　　　隣家のイヌがうちの敷地に入れなかったのは、つないである鎖の長さが5フィートしかなかったからだ。

thwart
[θwɔːʳt]

v. **to prevent occurrence, realization, or attainment of; to baffle**
[動] ～を妨げる、くじく；当惑させる

The nation *thwarted* the war by giving back the hostages.

反意語 thwart : aid [eid]
thwartの反意語は aid (～を助ける、促進する)

toxic
[táksik]

adj. **poisonous or harmful**
[形] 有毒な、有害な

The Mr. Yuk stickers are put on bottles to warn children that the contents are *toxic* and dangerous.

関連語 toxic : venom [vénəm]
venom (毒液) には toxic な成分が含まれている。

untoward
[ʌntóuəʳd]

adj. **unlucky or unfavorable; improper**
[形] 困った、不利な；不適切な

Julian found himself in a very *untoward* situation, having no money and no place to stay for the night.

反意語 untoward : fortunate [fɔ́ːrtʃənət]
untowardの反意語は fortunate (運のいい、幸運な)

utter
[ʌ́təʳ]

v. **to speak or give utterance**
[動] 話す、発言する

adj. **complete or total**
[形] 完全な、まったくの

The groom *uttered* a few words of thanks to each of his guests at the wedding.

The flashlight's batteries gave out, leaving the campers in *utter* darkness.

関連語 utter : blurt [bləːʳt]
blurt (うっかり口にする) は utter の一種である。

TRANSLATION | 例 文 の 訳

thwart	人質を解放することで、その国は戦争を回避した。
toxic	ユック氏のシールが瓶に貼りつけられているのは、内容物が有毒で危険なことを子供たちに警告するためだ。
untoward	お金がなく、泊まるところもなく、ジュリアンは自分が非常に困った立場にいることに気づいた。
utter	新郎は婚礼の招待客一人ひとりに感謝の言葉を述べた。
	懐中電灯の電池がなくなり、キャンプをしている人たちは完全な暗闇の中に残された。

venial
[víːniəl]

adj. **easily excused or forgiven**　　　　　　　　[形] 軽微な、ささいな

In Singapore, littering is not considered a *venial* offense.

関連語 venial : excuse [ikskjúːz]
venialな行為には excuse（許す）することができるという特徴がある。

veto
[víːtou]

n. **an authoritative prohibition**　　　　　　　　　[名] 拒否権

v. **to prohibit, especially the passage of a law**　　[動]（特に法案を）拒否する

The plan was circumvented by the president's *veto*.

In the end, the president *vetoed* the law legalizing marijuana.

関連語 veto : prohibitive [prouhíbitiv]
vetoは prohibitive（禁止するための）なものである。

watershed
[wɔ́ːtərʃèd]

n. **a divided region that drains into another (usually larger) body of water; a critical point that marks a change of course**

[名] 分岐点；転機

The Vietnam war was an important *watershed* in modern American history marking the end of easily justified military interventions abroad.

反意語 watershed : routine [ruːtíːn]
watershedの反意語は routine（日課）

wither
[wíðər]

v. **to dry up or shrivel; to lose vitality or freshness**

[動] しおれる、枯れる；衰える、弱る

The rose *withered* in the sun and the petals fell off.

関連語 wither : vitality [vaitǽləti]
witherは vitality（活気、元気）を失うこと。

TRANSLATION | 例 文 の 訳

venial　シンガポールでは、ごみを捨てることが軽微な違反行為では済まされない。

veto　その計画は大統領の拒否権で回避された。
　　　　結局、大統領はマリファナを合法化する法律を拒否した。

watershed　安易に正当化された海外での軍事介入に終わりを告げたベトナム戦争は、現代アメリカ史の重要な転機であった。

wither　バラが日光を浴びてしおれ、花びらが落ちた。

■ Fill in the blanks with the correct letter that matches the word with its definition.

1. interdict _____
2. estimable _____
3. fathom _____
4. lithe _____
5. tawdry _____
6. untoward _____
7. savvy _____
8. reticence _____
9. noxious _____
10. mawkish _____

a. knowledgeable; practical knowledge
b. to prohibit or forbid in a formal or an authoritative manner
c. valuable; worthy of esteem
d. the quality of being reserved or restrained; to be hesitant
e. to come to understanding through probing or thinking
f. flexible; easily bent or flexed
g. poisonous or harmful to living creatures; obnoxious
h. sentimental or having a bad taste
i. difficult to work with; unlucky or unfavorable
j. gaudy in brightness of appearance

■ Put the correct word in each blank from the list of words below.

11. _____ には厳選された poem が収録されている。
12. kindle（火をつける）の反意語は _____ である。
13. _____ の主な使命は mediate することである。
14. intrepid な人を _____ するのは難しい。
15. venom には _____ な成分が含まれている。
16. bully は主に他の人を _____ する。
17. _____ を感じたら repose を取る。
18. _____ は contradictory である。
19. blurt は突然 _____ することである。
20. attendant は _____ の一員である。

a. anthology b. fatigue c. tawdry d. extinguish e. oxymoron f. intercessor
g. intimidate h. retinue i. deter j. toxic k. utter l. sly

Answer key

11. a 12. d 13. f 14. i 15. j 16. g 17. b 18. e 19. k 20. h
1. b 2. c 3. e 4. f 5. j 6. i 7. a 8. d 9. g 10. h

88

私って健忘症？
いいえ、普通に怠けているだけです。

7th DAY

abstruse
[æbstrú:s]

adj. **difficult to understand** [形] 難解な、難しい

The *abstruse* terminology used in the economist's presentation confused most of his audience.

反意語 abstruse : accessible [æksésəbl]
abstruseの反意語は accessible（わかりやすい、アクセスしやすい）

astronomy
[əstrúnəmi]

n. **the science of matter outside the Earth's atmosphere** [名] 天文学

For Jeff's *astronomy* course, the teacher took them outside to look at the stars.

関連語 astronomer : planet [plǽnit]
astronomer（天文学者）は planet（惑星）を研究する。

attractive
[ətrǽktiv]

adj. **charming; causing interest or pleasure** [形] 魅力的な；興味をそそる

The *attractive* woman caught the eyes of many men as she walked down the street.

反意語 attractive : unprepossessing [ʌnpri:pəzésiŋ]
attractiveの反意語は unprepossessing（印象のよくない）

buttress
[bʌ́tris]

n. **a structure giving stability to a wall or building** [名] 支え

v. **to sustain or support** [動] 〜を支える、支持する

The city mandated the addition of *buttresses* to all multi-story buildings in preparation of future earthquakes.

The well-built skyscraper was *buttressed* with reinforced steel and a stable foundation.

関連語 buttress : edifice [édəfis]
buttressは edifice（大建造物）を支えるのに使われる。

TRANSLATION | 例 文 の 訳

abstruse その経済学者の発表では難解な専門用語が使われていたので、聴衆のほとんどが混乱した。
astronomy ジェフが受けている天文学の授業で、星を見るために教員が学生たちを外に連れ出した。
attractive その魅力的な女性が通りを歩く姿は、多くの男性の目を引いた。
buttress 将来の地震に備えるため、その都市ではすべての高層建築に支柱を追加することが義務付けられた。
強固に建築されたその高層ビルは、補強用の鋼鉄と安定した基盤に支えられていた。

carp
[kɑːʳp]

v. **to find fault or complain querulously**   [動] 文句を言う、あら捜しをする

The old man was always *carping* at anyone who sat near him.

関連語 carp : complain [kəmpléin]
    carp は complain (不平を言う) よりも強く苦情を言い、批判するという意味がある。

caulk
[kɔːk]

v. **to make something airtight or watertight**   [動] すき間などを詰める

n. **a stopper**   [名] 詰めもの

To prevent the wind from coming in, Andrew tried to *caulk* the cracks with sealant.

The plumber used *caulk* around the elbow joint to stop the leaking water.

類義語 caulk : seal [siːl]
    caulk の類義語は seal (〜を密閉する)

convivial
[kənvíviəl]

adj. **festive; fond of good company**   [形] 陽気な；社交的な

The *convivial* young boy was the most popular student in his class.

類義語 convivial : sociable [sóuʃəbl]
    convivial の類義語は sociable (社交的な)

destruction
[distrʌ́kʃən]

n. **the act of destroying**   [名] 破壊

The *destruction* of the ozone layer is a significant challenge for scientists to solve.

類義語 destruction : demolition [dèməlíʃən]
    destruction の類義語は demolition (取り壊し、破壊)

disturb
[distə́ːʳb]

v. **to interrupt or put into disorder**   [動] 〜を邪魔する、妨げる

The constant nightmares *disturbed* his sleep.

関連語 disturb : serenity [sərénəti]
    serenity (静穏) なものが disturb される。

TRANSLATION | 例 文 の 訳

carp	その老人は自分の近くに座るあらゆる人のあら捜しをいつもしていた。
caulk	風が入ってこないように、アンドリューは密封材ですき間をふさごうとした。
	その配管工は水漏れを止めるために、L字型の部品の周りを詰め物で覆った。
convivial	その陽気な少年はクラスで一番人気のある生徒だった。
destruction	オゾン層の破壊は科学者たちが解決しなければならない重大な課題だ。
disturb	絶え間ない悪夢が彼の睡眠を妨げた。

entrap
[intrǽp]

v. **to catch in a trap; to lure into danger** [動] ～をわなにかける；だます

Many well-intentioned public servants are unwittingly *entrapped* by the political machinery.

関連語 entrap : vigilant [vídʒələnt]
vigilant（常に警戒している）と簡単にentrapされることがない。

equable
[ékwəbl]

adj. **uniform or steady; even-tempered** [形] 変化のない、安定した；落ち着いた

The new principal's *equable* demeanor was appreciated and respected by the community.

反意語 equable : intemperate [ɪntémpʰrit]
equableの反意語はintemperate（節度のない、激しい）

extract
[ikstrǽkt]

v. **to pull out with force; to excerpt** [動] ～を引き出す；引用する

The FBI *extracted* a confession from the accused spy.

関連語 extract : milk [milk]
milk（搾り取る）はextractよりも程度が強い。

extraneous
[ikstrǽiniəs]

adj. **irrelevant or unrelated to the topic at hand; extrinsic or coming from the outside** [形] ～と無関係な；外部からの

Harry quickly became annoyed at the *extraneous* chatter that filled the discussion group.

関連語 extraneous : essence [ésns]
extraneousなものにはessence（本質、重要な部分）が欠けている。

extraordinary
[ikstrɔ́ːˈdənèri]

adj. **not usual; remarkable** [形] 異常な；驚くべき

The trip to Southern Europe was an *extraordinary* experience.

反意語 extraordinary : mundane [mʌ́ndein]
extraordinaryの反意語はmundane（日常の、ありふれた）

TRANSLATION | 例 文 の 訳

entrap	多くの善意の公務員が、気づかないうちに政治組織の罠にかかっている。
equable	新しい校長の落ち着いた態度は、その地域住民の評価と尊敬を集めた。
extract	FBIはスパイの容疑者から自白を引き出した。
extraneous	ハリーは、その討議グループの中で関係のない雑談ばかり交わされていることにすぐにうんざりした。
extraordinary	南欧旅行は驚くべき経験だった。

extravagant [ikstrǽvəgənt]	adj. **recklessly wasteful; excessively expensive; exceeding the limits of reason** [形] 無駄遣いする；ぜいたくな；法外な
	Sally considered her boyfriend's tastes to be too *extravagant* for her simple lifestyle.
	反意語 extravagant : parsimonious [pɑ̀ːˈsəmóuniəs] extravagantの反意語は parsimonious（極度にけちな、けちけちした）
extrinsic [ikstrínsik]	adj. **external or outside of; unessential** [形] 外部の、外側の；本質から外れた
	The *extrinsic* stain on the man's teeth was caused by years of habitual coffee drinking.
	反意語 extrinsic : immanent [ímənənt] extrinsicの反意語は immanent（内在する）
fatuous [fǽtʃuəs]	adj. **foolish; unreal** [形] 愚かな；非現実的な
	Kenny's dream of becoming a race car driver was considered *fatuous* by his peers.
	反意語 fatuous : scintillating [síntᵊlèitiŋ] fatuousの反意語は scintillating（興味深い、おもしろい）
fetter [fétəˈ]	v. **to put fetters on; to confine** [動] 〜に足かせをする；束縛する
	n. **a chain or shackle for the ankles** [名] 足かせ
	After graduation, Jennifer longed to move away where she wouldn't be *fettered* by family obligations.
	The *fetters* of the prisoners clinked as they marched to the fields to work.
	反意語 fetter : release [rilíːs] fetterの反意語は release（〜を解放する）

TRANSLATION | 例 文 の 訳

extravagant	サリーは彼の好みが自分の質素な生活に比べて贅沢すぎると思った。
extrinsic	その男性の歯の表面の着色は、習慣的にコーヒーを飲むことが原因だった。
fatuous	カーレーサーになるというケニーの夢は、仲間たちから愚かだと見なされた。
fetter	卒業後、ジェニファーは家族に束縛されない場所に転居することを切望した。
	作業をするために畑に向かって行進するうち、囚人たちの足かせがからまった。

institute
[ínstət(j)ùːt]

v. **to initiate or establish** [動] 〜を導入する、設立する

n. **an organization usually for education and research**
[名] 研究所、研究機関

In the early 1900s, Ataturk *instituted* what is now known as Istanbul University.

The CDC is an *institute* that researches diseases and viruses.

反意語 institute : abrogate [ǽbrəgèit]
institute の反意語は abrogate（〜を廃止する）

intractable
[intrǽktəbl]

adj. **not easily directed or manipulated; unruly**
[形] 手に負えない、扱いにくい；強情な

Erica soon discovered that children at day care are *intractable* and frustrating.

関連語 intractable : manage [mǽnidʒ]
intractable な人々を簡単に manage（うまく扱う、操る）することはできない。

intrepid
[intrépid]

adj. **fearless or courageous** [形] 恐れを知らない、大胆な

The *intrepid* climber reached the top of Mount Everest alone.

反意語 intrepid : timorous [tímərəs]
intrepid の反意語は timorous（ひどく臆病な）

intricacy
[íntrikəsi]

n. **the quality or state of being complex and elaborately detailed**
[名] 複雑さ、込み入っている状態

For English speakers, the *intricacies* of the Chinese language are far too difficult.

関連語 intricacy : tapestry [tǽpəstri]
tapestry（タペストリー）は intricacy を特徴として持っている。

TRANSLATION | 例 文 の 訳

institute 1900年代初頭、アタテュルクは現在のイスタンブール大学を設立した。
CDCは疾病やウイルスについて研究する機関だ。

intractable エリカはすぐに、保育園の子供たちが扱いにくく、いらいらさせられるものだと気づいた。

intrepid その大胆な登山家はエベレストに単独で登頂した。

intricacy 英語話者にとって、中国語の複雑さはあまりにも難しい。

intrude [intrúːd]	v. **to enter without permission or invitation; to interrupt** <div align="right">[動] 侵入する；妨げる</div>Jack *intruded* on the party in order to talk to his ex-girlfriend. 類義語 intrude : trespass [tréspəs] 　intrude の類義語は trespass（不法侵入する）
jittery [dʒítəri]	adj. **suffering from irregular random movements, often caused by stress, chemical stimulants, or excitement** <div align="right">[形] 神経質な、不安な</div>The three cups of coffee made her *jittery* and unable to sit still. 反意語 jittery : resolute [rézəlùːt] 　jittery の反意語は resolute（決心の堅い、断固とした）
lassitude [lǽsət(j)ùːd]	n. **fatigue or listlessness** <div align="right">[名] 疲労、脱力感</div>After a night of drinking, Brian's *lassitude* was clearly apparent to his co-workers. 反意語 lassitude : vim [vim] 　lassitude の反意語は vim（活力、元気）
miff [mif]	v. **to insult or offend slightly** <div align="right">[動] 怒らせる</div>Mr. Kronkite was *miffed* by reporter's tardiness for the interview. 反意語 miff : appease [əpíːz] 　miff の反意語は appease（〜をなだめる）
mottle [mátl]	n. **a spot or blotch** <div align="right">[名] まだら、斑点</div>v. **to mark with spots** <div align="right">[動] 〜をまだらにする</div>The painting was a random arrangement of *mottles*. The tree had *mottled* leaves indicating it was dying of disease. 関連語 mottled : spot [spɑt] 　mottled（まだらの）の似た意味の名詞が spot（まだら、斑点）

TRANSLATION | 例 文 の 訳

intrude	ジャックは昔の恋人と話すために、そのパーティーに無断で入り込んだ。
jittery	彼女はコーヒーを3杯飲んだために神経質になり、静かに座っていられなくなった。
lassitude	一晩飲み明かしたあとのブライアンが疲れていることは、同僚には明らかだった。
miff	クロンカイト氏は記者が取材に遅れてきたことに腹を立てた。
mottle	その絵画はランダムに斑点を並べたものだった。
	その木にはまだら模様の葉が付いており、病気で死にかけていることがわかった。

natty
[nǽti]

adj. stylish and tidy, usually in reference to a man
[形] しゃれた、粋な（通常、男性に使う）

The actor looked *natty* at the Oscars in his long black tuxedo.

反意語 natty : slovenly [slʌ́vənli]
nattyの反意語はslovenly（だらしない、ずさんな）

nettle
[nétl]

n. a stinging plant with needles
[名] イラクサ

v. to arouse irritation or annoyance
[形] 〜をいらだたせる

The campers avoided walking through an open field after seeing bunches of *nettles* in it.

The waiter's arrogant attitude *nettled* me.

反意語 nettle : conciliate [kənsílièit]
nettleの反意語はconciliate（〜をなだめる）

nitpick
[nítpìk]

v. to criticize small and unimportant details
[動] あら探しをする

Mothers are always *nitpicking* about their children's appearance.

関連語 nitpicker : criticize [krítəsàiz]
nitpicker（あら探しをする人）はいつもcriticize（批判する）という特徴がある。

obstreperous
[əbstrép°rəs]

adj. characterized by unruly noise or clamor; stubbornly resistant to control
[形] 騒がしい；手に負えない

The birthday party became *obstreperous* as soon as the parents left.

関連語 obstreperous : control [kəntróul]
obsteperousなものをcontrol（制御する）することは難しい。

obtuse
[əbt(j)ú:s]

adj. slow to understand or lacking sharpness of intellect
[形] 鈍い、鈍感な

The man was too *obtuse* to catch the humor and wit of the play.

関連語 obtuseness : keen [ki:n]
keen（頭の切れる）な人にobtuseness（鈍感さ）は見いだせない。

TRANSLATION | 例 文 の 訳

natty	アカデミー賞の授賞式で、その俳優は黒の長いタキシードに身を包み、粋だった。
nettle	キャンパーたちは大量のイラクサが生えているのを見て、広い草原を歩き抜けることをやめた。
	そのウェイターの偉そうな態度は私をいら立たせた。
nitpick	母親はいつも自分の子供たちの外見にあら探しをするものだ。
obstreperous	親たちがいなくなるとすぐに、その誕生日パーティは手に負えなくなった。
obtuse	その男は鈍感すぎて、その演劇のユーモアと機知がわからなかった。

ostracize
[ástrəsàiz]

v. to exclude or exile from a group or society by popular consent
[動] 〜を追放する、のけ者にする

Themistokles, the Ancient Greek politician, was *ostracized* from Athens for three years in the 5th century BC.

類義語 ostracize : exile [égzail]
ostracize の類義語は exile (〜を追放する)

parsimonious
[pà:ˈsəmóuniəs]

adj. excessively stingy; unwilling to spend
[形] ひどくけちな；出し惜しむ

Frugality was a quality she admired, but Frank's *parsimonious* habits were too much for her.

関連語 parsimonious : frugal [frú:gəl]
frugal (質素な) が度を過ぎると parsimonious と言われる。

patronize
[péitrənàiz]

v. to act condescendingly towards someone; to provide support for or be a customer of
[動] 〜をひいきにする；〜を後援する、取引する

As a rule, I try to *patronize* the local community businesses rather than large national chain stores.

関連語 patron : support [səpɔ́:ˈt]
patron (後援者) は support (〜を支持する) してくれる人のこと。

pedagogue
[pédəgàg]

n. one who teaches or instructs
[名] 教育者、教師、先生

The greatest *pedagogues* in the world are the ones who impart both wisdom and knowledge.

関連語 pedagogue : indoctrinate [indáktrənèit]
pedagogue には indoctrinate (教える) という特徴がある。

petrography
[pitrágrəfi]

n. the scientific description and classification of rocks [名] 岩石分類学

For lack of better options, Jack took a class in *petrography* to fulfill his science requirements.

関連語 petrography : rock [rɑk]
petrography は rock (岩石) を分類する学問だ。

TRANSLATION | 例 文 の 訳

ostracize 紀元前5世紀、古代ギリシャの政治家テミストクレスはアテネから3年間追放された。

parsimonious 質素であることは彼女が重んじる資質だったが、フランクのひどくけちな習慣は彼女には限度を超えていた。

patronize 原則として、私は全国規模の大きなチェーン店よりも地元と店を利用することにしている。

pedagogue 世界で最も偉大な教育者は、知恵と知識をともに与えてくれる人だ。

petrography 他にいい選択肢がなかったので、ジャックは理系科目の履修要件を満たすために岩石分類学のクラスを取った。

petty
[péti]

adj. having little or no significance　　　[形] ささいな、つまらない

The two friends fought over something *petty* that managed to destroy their friendship.

関連語 petty : noticeable [nóutisəbl]
pettyなものは noticeable（目立つ、注目に値する）なことがない。

pittance
[pítns]

n. a small portion or allowance　　　[名] 少量、少額の手当

Jackie's mother gives her a *pittance* every month for taking out the garbage.

関連語 pittance : allowance [əláuəns]
pittanceとは少額の allowance（手当、小遣い）を表す。

pity
[píti]

n. the feeling of sympathetic sorrow for another; something to be regretted　　　[名] 哀れみ、同情；残念なこと

It was a *pity* we didn't get to see Jill before she left for Hawaii.

関連語 pity : lamentable [læməntəbl]
pityに意味が似ている形容詞が lamentable（悲しむべき、嘆かわしい）

playbill
[pléibìl]

n. printed program of a play with a listing of cast members
[名] キャストの名簿が印刷されている演劇プログラム

Harry was very upset when he found out his name was misprinted in the *playbill*.

関連語 playbill : cast [kæst]
playbillは cast（配役）を紹介するもの。

polarize
[póuləràiz]

v. to cause to concentrate about two conflicting or contrasting positions　　　[動] ～を分裂させる、対立させる

The police brutality case *polarized* the community.

反意語 polarize : make compatible [meik kəmpætəbl]
polarizeの反意語は make compatible（共存させる）

TRANSLATION | 例文 の 訳

petty	その2人の友人同士はささいなことでけんかし、友情が壊れることになった。
pittance	ジャッキーのごみ捨てに対して母親は毎月わずかな小遣いを与えている。
pity	残念ながら、われわれはハワイに向かう前のジルに会わなかった。
playbill	ハリーはプログラムに自分の名前が間違って印刷されていることに気づき、ひどく怒った。
polarize	警察による残虐な事件が地域を分断した。

posture
[pástʃəˈr]

n. the position of the body　　　　　　　　　　　　[名] 姿勢

v. to assume a pose or behave in an artificial manner to impress others　　　　　　　　　　　　　　[動] ～を気取る

Her *posture* was so bad that the chiropractor recommended a back brace.

When Dave was threatening me, he was just *posturing*.

関連語 posturer : unaffected [ʌ̀nəféktid]
posturer（気取り屋）は unaffected（気取らない、ありのままの）なことがない。

potter
[pátəˈr]

n. a person who makes pottery　　　　　　　　　　[名] 陶工

The *potter* sold some of his brightly painted vases at the craft show.

関連語 potter : artisan [ɑ́ːˈtəzən]
potter は artisan（職人）の一種。

retrench
[ritréntʃ]

v. to cut down or reduce　　　　　　　　[動] ～を節約する、減らす

The family *retrenched* their monthly expenses to save for a big trip.

関連語 retrench : expense [ikspéns]
expense（費用）を retrench する。

routine
[ruːtíːn]

n. a regular or habitual procedure　　　　　[名] いつもの手順、日課

Without my morning *routine* of exercise and breakfast, I can't get through the day awake and alert.

反意語 routine : watershed [wɔ́ːtəˈʃed]
routine の反意語は watershed（転機）

saturate
[sǽtʃərèit]

v. to treat with a liquid until no more can be absorbed; to fully satisfy or complete　　[動] ～を水浸しにする；～でいっぱいにする；飽和させる

The rainstorm *saturated* the football field with muddy puddles of water.

関連語 saturated : moisture [mɔ́istʃəˈr]
moisture（水分）を多く含んだ結果、saturated（水浸しの）な状態になる。

TRANSLATION | 例 文 の 訳

posture　　彼女は姿勢が悪すぎるので、カイロプラクターが背骨の矯正器を勧めた。
デイブが私を威嚇したが、それはただのポーズだった。

potter　　その陶工は工芸品見本市で明るく色を塗った花びんをいくつか売った。

retrench　その一家は大がかりな旅行に備えてお金をためるために、月々の出費を切り詰めた。

routine　　毎朝の運動と朝食を抜くと、私はすっきり目覚めた状態で一日を過ごすことができない。

saturate　どしゃ降りでサッカー場が水びたしになり、泥水でいっぱいになった。

squabble
[skwábl]

n. a small argument over trivial matters [名] 口げんか

v. to quarrel or argue about unimportant things
[動] つまらないことで言い争う

All of our *squabbles* are about Jack's smoking habit.
Married couples are always *squabbling* about money.

関連語 squabble : dispute [dispjúːt]
squabble は dispute（論争、口論）に比べると些細なものを表す。

squalid
[skwálid]

adj. very dirty or filthy [形] 不潔な、むさくるしい

The *squalid* streets of the impoverished neighborhood can be very depressing.

反意語 squalid : immaculate [imǽkjulət]
squalid の反意語は immaculate（しみひとつない）

squall
[skwɔːl]

n. a sudden windstorm followed by rain or snow; a short-lived commotion [名]（雨や雪を伴う）突風；騒動

The *squall* came upon the countryside without warning.

関連語 squall : commotion [kəmóuʃən]
squall は commotion（騒ぎ、騒動）に比べて規模が小さい。

squalor
[skwálər]

n. a quality or condition of filth or degradation caused by poverty or neglect [名] 不潔さ、堕落

Due to current political and economic problems, *squalor* is the norm in the inner cities of America.

反意語 squalor : splendor [spléndər]
squalor の反意語は splendor（豪華さ、壮麗）

TRANSLATION | 例 文 の 訳

squabble　私たちの口げんかはすべてジャックの喫煙習慣についてのものだった。
　　　　　　　夫婦はいつもお金のことで言い争う。

squalid　その貧困地区の不潔な通りにはとても気がめいる。

squall　その騒動は前触れもなく農村で起きた。

squalor　現在の政治・経済問題のせいで、生活の悪化はアメリカの内陸都市で一般的なものになった。

tatty	adj. **worn or shabby**	[形] ぼろぼろの、みすぼらしい
[tǽti]	The homeless man near my work dresses in *tatty* clothes and carries a garbage bag.	
	反意語 tatty : smart [smɑːˈt]	
	tattyの反意語はsmart（身なりのきちんとした、洗練された）	

taut	adj. **tight or tense**	[形] ぴんと張った、緊張した
[tɔːt]	His nerves were *taut* during the interview.	
	関連語 tautness : slacken [slǽkən]	
	tautness（ぴんと張っていること、緊張）をslacken（～をゆるめる）する。	

truant	adj. **absent without permission, especially from school; shirking duty**	[形] 無断欠席の；怠惰な
[trúːənt]	The *truant* father abandoned his wife and children in order to pursue his dream of being a singer.	
	反意語 truant : dutiful [d(j)úːtifəl]	
	truantの反意語はdutiful（義務を果たす、忠実な）	

unwonted	adj. **out of the ordinary or unusual**	[形] ふつうでない、まれな
[ʌnwɔ́ːntid]	We experienced *unwonted* freezing this past autumn.	
	反意語 unwonted : usual [júːʒuəl]	
	unwontedの反意語はusual（ふつうの）	

vex	v. **to irritate or distress**	[動] ～をいらだたせる、悩ませる
[veks]	Mike could not help but be *vexed* by the troubling news.	
	反意語 vex : conciliate [kənsílièit]	
	vexの反意語はconciliate（～をなだめる）	

TRANSLATION | 例 文 の 訳	
tatty	私の職場のそばにいる浮浪者は、ぼろぼろの服を着てごみ袋を持ち歩いている。
taut	彼はその取材の間、神経を張り詰めていた。
truant	その怠惰な父親は、歌手になるという夢を追いかけるために妻と子供たちを捨てた。
unwonted	私たちはこの秋、まれにない寒さを経験した。
vex	マイクはその面倒な知らせにいら立たずにはいられなかった。

vituperate
[vait(j)ú:pərèit]

v. to scold or censure severely or abusively

[動] 〜を叱責する、非難する

Jessie Ventura, the Minnesota governor, was harshly *vituperated* by politicians nationwide when he was first elected.

反意語 vituperate : admire [ædmáiər]
vituperateの反意語は admire（〜を賞賛する）

waylay
[wéilèi]

v. to be lying in wait to ambush; to attack from a hiding place

[動] 〜を待ち伏せする；〜を物陰から襲う

Bret was *waylaid* by a mugger from the dark alley way off the main boulevard.

関連語 waylaid : vigilant [vídʒələnt]
vigilant（常に警戒している）な人は waylaid されることがない。

wizen
[wí(:)zn]

v. to become wrinkled and begin exhibiting signs of aging; to cause to wither, shrivel, or dry up　[動] 縮んでしわが寄る；しなびる；しぼむ

It is hard to see your own parents become *wizened* by time.

反意語 wizen : rejuvenate [ridʒú:vənèit]
wizenの反意語は rejuvenate（〜を若返らせる、元気を回復させる）

wry
[rai]

adj. bent out of shape or twisted; dryly humorous

[形] しかめた、ゆがめた；皮肉たっぷりの

The student showed an almost *wry* attitude towards his teacher.

関連語 wry : humorous [ʰjú:mᵊrəs]
humorous（ユーモアのある、こっけいな）が度を越えた状態を wry と表す。

TRANSLATION | 例 文 の 訳

vituperate ミネソタ州知事のジェシー・ベンチュラは初当選時に全国の政治家からひどく非難された。

waylay ブレットは大通りから離れた暗い路地で強盗に襲われた。

wizen 自分の両親が時とともに老いていくのを見るのはつらい。

wry その生徒は教師にほとんど皮肉ともとれる態度を見せた。

■ Fill in the blanks with the correct letter that matches the word with its definition.

1. extrinsic _____
2. jittery _____
3. lassitude _____
4. mottle _____
5. squalor _____
6. squabble _____
7. ostracize _____
8. retrench _____
9. obstreperous _____
10. nettle _____

a. external or outside of
b. suffering from irregular random movements, often caused by stress, chemical stimulants, or excitement
c. fatigue or listlessness
d. to mark with spots; a spot or blotch
e. to exclude or exile from a group or society by popular consent
f. to cut down or reduce
g. characterized by unruly noise or clamor
h. a place or situation of filth or degradation caused by poverty or neglect
i. to quarrel or argue about unimportant things
j. to arouse irritation or annoyance

■ Put the correct word in each blank from the list of words below.

11. demolition（破壊）の類義語は _____ である。
12. _____ なものは noticeable ではない。
13. commotion に比べて小さな騒動を _____ という。
14. intemperate（乱暴な）の反意語は _____ である。
15. _____ は rock を分類するための学問である。
16. _____ は、edifice を支持するために使用される。
17. _____ は playbill の内容を構成する一部である。
18. scintillating の反意語は _____ である。
19. keen な人からは _____ を見いだすことができない。
20. parsimonious（ひどくけちな）の反意語は _____ である。

a. obtuseness   b. extravagant   c. inherent   d. equable   e. vituperate   f. destruction
g. petty   h. petrography   i. buttress   j. squall   k. cast   l. fatuous

今日私が覚える単語は、
昨日試験を受けた人が
とても気にしていた単語です。

8th DAY

abdicate [ǽbdəkèit]	**v.** **to give up power or resign from high position** ［動］〜を退く、放棄する The Allies forced Napoleon to *abdicate* his emperorship and exiled him to the island of Elba. **関連語** abdicate : throne [θroun] abdicateとは throne (王位) を退くことを言う。
addict v.[ədíkt] n.[ǽdikt]	**v.** **to cause to be habitually dependent on a substance** ［動］(麻薬などの) 中毒にさせる **n.** **one who is addicted** ［名］常習者 The teenager became *addicted* to cigarettes and soon started smoking two packs a day. We became online *addicts* with the release of the new computer game. **関連語** addicted : dependency [dipéndənsi] 酒や薬物に addicted (〜に依存している、中毒な) になると、それに対する dependency (依存) が生じる。
ameliorate [əmíːljərèit]	**v.** **to make better or more tolerable; to ease; to get better** ［動］〜を改善する；和らげる；よくする We may be able to *ameliorate* the suffering of patients with the new drug. **類義語** ameliorate : improve [imprúːv] ameliorate の類義語は improve (〜を改善する)

TRANSLATION | 例 文 の 訳

abdicate	連合軍はナポレオンを皇帝から退位させ、エルバ島に追放した。
addict	その10代の若者は喫煙中毒になり、すぐに1日2箱たばこを吸い始めた。 その新しいコンピューターゲームが発売されると、私たちはオンライン中毒になった。
ameliorate	私たちはその新薬で患者の痛みを和らげることができるかもしれない。

amend
[əménd]

v. **to make right, usually through change; to correct**

[動] ～を修正する；訂正する

Congress *amended* the bill to include a more comprehensive tax plan.

関連語 amend : incorrigible [inkɔ́ːridʒəbl]

incorrigible（矯正できない、手に負えない）なものは amend できない。

blemish
[blémiʃ]

n. **a noticeable imperfection; a tainted reputation**

[名] 目に見える欠点；汚点

v. **to stain or spoil by a flaw**

[動]（名声などを）傷つける、汚す

The Watergate scandal was a huge *blemish* for the Nixon administration.

Jason's perfect report card was *blemished* with a B in science.

関連語 blemish : impeccable [impékəbl]

impeccable（欠点のない、完璧な）な人の blemish を見つけるのは難しい。

bode
[bóud]

v. **to be an omen of; to foreshow**

[動] ～の前兆となる

The policy *bodes* ill for the future of international cooperation on environment.

反意語 boding ill : auspicious [ɔːspíʃəs]

boding ill（悪い前兆である）の反意語は auspicious（幸先のいい）

cleft
[kleft]

n. **an opening or fissure indicating division or splitting**

[名] 裂け目、割れ目

adj. **divided**

[形] 分裂している

The tremors of the earthquake created a massive *cleft* in the street.

A *cleft* lip is one of the most common facial congenital anomalies.

関連語 cleft : chasm [kǽzᵊm]

chasm（亀裂）は cleft よりも深く割れているもの。

TRANSLATION | 例 文 の 訳

amend	国会はより包括的な税制を含むように法案を修正した。
blemish	ウォーターゲイト事件はニクソン政権にとって大きな汚点だった。
	理科でBを取ったことでジェイソンの完璧な成績表に傷がついた。
bode	その政策は環境に対する国際協力の未来にとって悪い前兆である。
cleft	地震の揺れによってその通りに巨大な地割れができた。
	口唇裂は最もよくある顔面の先天性奇形の一つだ。

clement
[klémənt]

adj. lenient or merciful　　　　　　　　　　　[形] 温和な、寛大な

The *clement* woman took in the deserted stray and nourished it back to health.

反意語 clement : pitiless [pítilis]
　　clementの反意語は pitiless（無慈悲な）

credence
[krí:dⁿns]

n. a mental belief in something as true　　　　[名] 信頼、信用

Galileo disputed the *credence* that the world was flat.

反意語 credence : doubt [daut]
　　credenceの反意語は doubt（疑い）

creep
[kri:p]

v. to move slowly and quietly close to or on the ground
　　　　　　　　　　　　　　　　　[動] ゆっくり近づく、這う

The boy and his mother saw the cat *creep* into the door of the bakery.

反意語 creep : move swiftly [mu:v swíftli]
　　creepの反意語は move swiftly（素早く動く）

dedicate
[dédikèit]

v. to set apart for sacred purposes; to commit oneself to a goal of life; to open to the public use
　　　　　　　　　　[動] ～に捧げる；～に打ち込む；（建物などを）ささげる

The men and women who immigrated to the United States from Korea *dedicated* their lives to providing their children with the best possible education.

関連語 dedication : zeal [zi:l]
　　zeal（熱意、熱狂）は dedication（献身）よりも特定の仕事や理想に対する強い熱意を示す。

diehard
[dáihà:ʳd]

n. one who is strongly devoted and resists any change
　　　　　　　　　　　　　　　　[名] 頑固な保守主義者、意固地な人

Many in the firm viewed Aaron as a *diehard* who would never approve the new budget plan.

関連語 diehard : budge [bʌdʒ]
　　diehardは簡単に budge（意見などを変える）することがない。

TRANSLATION | 例 文 の 訳

clement　その寛大な女性は捨てられた動物を引き取って栄養を与え、健康な状態に回復させた。

credence　ガリレオは、当時浸透していた世界は平面だという考えに異を唱えた。

creep　その少年と母親はネコがパン屋のドアにゆっくり近づくのを見た。

dedicate　韓国からアメリカに移民してきた人々は、子供たちに可能な限り良い教育を受けさせることに自分たちの人生を捧げた。

diehard　その会社にいる多くの人たちがアーロンのことを、新しい予算計画を決して承認しない意固地な人間だと見ていた。

endorse
[indɔ́:ʳs]

v. to sign one's name on the back of; to give approval of

[動] (小切手など) に裏書きする；支持する

Mr. Derrick offers this only as a suggestion, and will *endorse* any decision you arrive at.

関連語 endorse : approval [əprú:vəl]

endorseとは approval (承認、認可) を下すことをいう。

endure
[ind(j)úəʳ]

v. to sustain; to bear or tolerate a lasting and usually suffering state; to exist through time

[動] 我慢する；～に耐える；持ちこたえる

What cannot be cured must be *endured*.

関連語 endure : affliction [əflíkʃən]

affliction (苦痛、苦悩) を endure する。

erect
[irékt]

adj. upright in position

[形] 直立した、まっすぐな

v. to be or place in an upright or raised position; to build

[動] 直立させる、～を立てる；～を建てる

Buckingham Palace guards are renowned for their *erect* posture.

Verena Tarrant was *erected* on her little platform, dressed in white, with flowers in her bosom.

反意語 erect : prostrate [prástreit]

erectの反意語は prostrate (横たわった)

execrate
[éksikrèit]

v. to denounce; to feel loathing for

[動] ～をののしる；強く嫌悪する

Conservative Christians often *execrate* cinema and television, claiming that it corrupts the youth.

反意語 execrate : exalt [igzɔ́:lt]

execrateの反意語は exalt (～を賛美する)

TRANSLATION | 例 文 の 訳	
endorse	デリク氏は単に提案としてこれを申し出ているだけで、あなたが下すどんな決定をも支持するだろう。
endure	治療できないものは耐えるしかない。
erect	バッキンガム宮殿の近衛兵は直立不動の姿勢で有名だ。
	ヴェレーナ・タラントは白い服を着て、胸に花を差し、小さな踏み台の上に立っていた。
execrate	保守的なキリスト教徒は映画やテレビが若者を堕落させると主張して、ひどく嫌うことが多い。

exemplify
[igzémpləfài]

v. to show by example; to serve as an example of
[動] ～を例示する；～を体現する

The mother asked her eldest son to *exemplify* good behavior to the younger children.

関連語 exemplify : archetype [ɑ́ːˈkitàip]
archetype（典型、代表例）は exemplify している。

fleet
[fliːt]

v. to fade away quickly
[動] 飛び去っていく、消えていく

adj. moving swiftly; evanescent
[形] 速い、素早い；はかない

Being in the spot light for just a *fleeting* moment was enough to make the old singer smile.

The warrior had to be *fleet* of foot to escape from the pursuing enemies.

類義語 fleeting : meteoric [mìːtióːrik]
fleeting の類義語は meteoric（急速な、流星の）

greet
[griːt]

v. to welcome or address someone
[動] ～を迎える、挨拶する

When George Willard came to the door, he *greeted* Belle effusively.

反意語 greeting : valediction [væ̀lədíkʃən]
greeting の反意語は valediction（告別、いとまごい）

gregarious
[grigéəriəs]

adj. sociable; preferring the company of others
[形] 社交的な；群居する

The once shy and reticent girl had become a *gregarious* young lady.

関連語 gregariousness : recluse [rékluːs]
recluse（隠遁者）には gregariousness（社交性）が欠けている。

TRANSLATION | 例文の訳

exemplify その母親は長男に年下のきょうだいたちのいい手本になるように頼んだ。
fleet 一瞬でもスポットライトが当たったことは、その年老いた歌手を笑顔にするのに十分だった。
その戦士は追っ手から逃れるために素早く走らなければならなかった。
greet ジョージ・ウィラードはドアのところに来て、ベルを熱烈に迎えた。
gregarious かつては内気で無口だった少女が、社交的な若い女性になっていた。

107

hedge
[hedʒ]

n. a bush or shrub used to line an edge [名] 生垣、垣根

v. to evade or to protect oneself from danger

[動] 〜を取り囲む、〜を予防する

The *hedges* served as a boundary between the two estates.

On her way home, Jackie *hedged* hitting the deer by swerving off of the road.

関連語 hedge : fence [fens]
hedge は fence（フェンス、塀）の一種。

hodgepodge
[hádʒpàdʒ]

n. a mixture of many different things [名] ごたまぜ、寄せ集め

America is a *hodgepodge* of cultures from all over the world.

関連語 hodgepodge : homogeneous [hòumədʒíːniəs]
hodgepodge は homogeneous（同質の、均質な）なものからはかけ離れている。

hovel
[hʌ́vəl]

n. a small poor dwelling place; a hut [名] あばらや；小屋

Compared to the mansion we used to live in, this place is a *hovel*.

関連語 hovel : palatial [pəléiʃəl]
hovel が palatial（宮殿のような、豪華な）なことはない。

hue
[hju:]

n. gradation of color; color [名] 色合い；色

All of the rooms in the resort are painted in various *hues* of red and blue.

関連語 hue : achromatic [ækrəmǽtik]
achromatic（無色な）なものには hue が欠けている。

indifferent
[indífʳrənt]

adj. impartial; lacking interest or concern [形] 公平な；無関心な

Mary's *indifferent* attitude towards school frustrated her parents.

反意語 indifferent : avid [ǽvid]
indifferent の反意語は avid（熱心な、渇望している）

TRANSLATION | 例 文 の 訳

hedge　その生け垣は2つの私有地の境界になっていた。
家に帰る途中、ジャッキーはシカと衝突するのを避けるために急ハンドルを切って道路から外れた。

hodgepodge　アメリカは世界中の文化の寄せ集めだ。

hovel　私たちが前に住んでいた邸宅に比べると、この家はあばらやだ。

hue　そのリゾートホテルの全客室が赤と青のさまざまな色合いで塗られている。

indifferent　メアリーの学校に対する無関心な態度は、彼女の両親をいら立たせた。

indigenous [indídʒənəs]	adj. **native to a particular region**	[形] 先住の
	The Aborigines are the *indigenous* people of Australia.	
	反意語 indigenous : exotic [igzátik] indigenousの反意語は exotic（外来の、異国風の）	
indolent [índələnt]	adj. **lazy; causing no pain**	[形] 怠惰な；無痛性の
	Clare's *indolent* partner caused them to receive a poor grade on the project.	
	反意語 indolent : sedulous [sédjuləs] indolentの反意語は sedulous（勤勉な、よく働く）	
indomitable [indámətəbl]	adj. **incapable of being stopped or subdued; unconquerable**	[形] 不屈の；断固とした
	The Greeks besieged the *indomitable* city of Troy with the gift of a wooden horse.	
	関連語 indomitable : subdued [səbd(j)úːd] indomitableとは決して subdued（征服された、支配された）な状態にできないことを表す。	
indubitable [ind(j)úːbətəbl]	adj. **unable to be doubted**	[形] 疑う余地のない、明白な
	The *indubitable* truth of Pierre's testimony could not be argued.	
	反意語 indubitable : doubtful [dáutfəl] indubitableの反意語は doubtful（疑わしい）	
indulge [indʌ́ldʒ]	v. **to give in to desire; to free from inhibitions or restrictions**	[動]（快楽などに）ふける；〜をほしいままにする
	People in Las Vegas *indulge* themselves in the wildest of vices.	
	関連語 indulge : abstemious [æbstíːmiəs] abstemious（禁欲的な）な人々は快楽に indulge することがない。	

TRANSLATION | 例 文 の 訳

indigenous	アボリジニはオーストラリアの先住民だ。
indolent	クレアの怠惰なパートナーのせいで、彼らはそのプロジェクトで低い評価を受けることになった。
indomitable	ギリシャ人は木馬をうまく利用して、不落の都市トロイを包囲した。
indubitable	ピエールの証言が疑いのない真実であることに議論の余地はない。
indulge	人々はラスベガスで不道徳の限りを尽くす。

ineluctable [ìnilʌ́ktəbl]	adj. **unchangeable or inevitable**　　　　　[形] 変えられない、避けられない Fate is the belief that all of life is *ineluctable*. 類義語 ineluctable : inescapable [ìnəskéipəbl] 　　ineluctableの類義語は inescapable（避けられない）
judicious [dʒu:díʃəs]	adj. **having sound judgment**　　　　　　[形] 判断力の確かな、賢明な A good mediator and friend, Karen is respectable and *judicious* at all times. 反意語 judicious : daft [dæft] 　　judiciousの反意語は daft（愚かな、まぬけな）
lethargic [liθá:ʳdʒik]	adj. **lacking vitality or energy; apathetic**　　　[形] 無気力な；昏睡状態の Alex was so *lethargic* from oversleeping that he didn't care that his favorite show was on. 関連語 lethargic : energy [énərdʒi] 　　lethargicな人には energy（活力、エネルギー）が欠けている。
ludicrous [lú:dəkrəs]	adj. **humorous in its absurdity**　　　　　[形] こっけいな、ばかげた It's *ludicrous* to think that a teen-ager has the freedom to make a choice, Blaine said. 関連語 ludicrous : farce [fɑ:ʳs] 　　farce（笑劇、茶番）には ludicrousだという特徴がある。
mediate [mí:dièit]	v. **to act as the middle-man for two opposing parties who are trying to reach a resolution**　　　　　　　[動] 仲裁する Razali *mediated* between Myanmar's military junta and the opposition in a bid to restore democracy. 関連語 mediate : intercessor [ìntəʳsésəʳ] 　　intercessor（仲裁者）は紛争を mediateするという特徴がある。

TRANSLATION | 例 文 の 訳

ineluctable	運命とは、人生のすべてが避けられないものだと信じることだ。
judicious	よき仲裁者であり友人であるカレンは、常に立派で判断力がある。
lethargic	アレックスは眠りすぎて無気力になり、好きな番組が放送されていることも気にしなかった。
ludicrous	10代に選択の自由があると考えるなんてばかげている、とブレインは言った。
mediate	ラザリは民主主義を復活させようとして、ミャンマーの軍事政権と反対派を仲裁した。

mediocre
[mìːdióukəʳ]

adj. **of moderate or middle-ground quality** [形] 並みの、二流の

The poet's work was considered *mediocre* at best.

反意語 mediocrity : virtuosity [vəːʳtʃuásəti]
mediocrity (並み、二流) の反意語は virtuosity (名人芸)

moderate
[mádʳrət]

v. **to lessen the intensity of; to lead a discussion** [動] ～を和らげる；～の議長をする

adj. **not excessive or extreme; mediocre; temperate** [形] 適度の；ふつうの；穏やかな

Annie *moderated* her anger after realizing it would lead to further conflict with her employer.

Many tourists are attracted to Florida due to its *moderate* climate and beautiful beaches.

反意語 moderate : intensify [inténsəfài]
moderate の反意語は intensify (～を強める)

modest
[mádist]

adj. **showing a moderate estimation of one's own talents, abilities, and value; decent in speech and demeanor; not too large or too small** [形] 控えめな、謙虚な；(特に女性が) 内気な；適度な

The athlete was *modest* in victory, giving full credit to his coaches and teammates.

反意語 modest : brazen [bréizn]
modest の反意語は brazen (ずうずうしい)

関連語 modest : prudish [prúːdiʃ]
modest な態度が過度になると prudish (堅い、潔癖な) だと言われる。

modicum
[mádikəm]

n. **a small amount or quantity** [名] 少量

Even a *modicum* of moisture would be greatly appreciated by farmers in the dry season.

反意語 modicum : large amount [láːrdʒ əmáunt]
modicum の反意語は large amount (大量)

TRANSLATION | 例 文 の 訳

mediocre その詩人の作品はよく言って二流だと見なされた。

moderate アニーは自分の怒りが雇用主とのさらなる争いにつながると気づいたので、怒りを抑えた。
フロリダの穏やかな気候と美しい浜辺に、多くの観光客が引き付けられている。

modest その選手は勝利を謙遜し、すべて自分のコーチとチームメイトのおかげだとした。

modicum 乾期には少量の雨でも農民にとても感謝される。

meek [miːk]	adj. **mild, soft, or submissive** [形] おとなしい、従順な
	Daniel's *meek* personality was often taken as a sign of weakness by others.
	関連語 meek : arrogance [ǽrəgəns] meekな人にはarrogance（傲慢さ）が欠けている。
mnemonic [nimánik]	n. **a phrase or device that helps one remember** [名] 記憶を助ける語呂合わせや装置
	Children use *mnemonics* to help them remember difficult problems.
	関連語 mnemonic : remember [rimémbəʳ] mnemonicはremember（〜を覚える）するのを助けるもの。
nudge [nʌdʒ]	v. **to bump or push in a very gentle manner** [動] そっと押す
	Steve *nudged* me with his elbow when I began dozing off in the meeting.
	関連語 nudge : prod [prɑd] nudgeは軽くprod（〜を突く、押す）することを表す。
obdurate [ábd(j)urət]	adj. **stubborn in perspective** [形] 頑固な、強情な
	The captain was *obdurate* to their appeals.
	関連語 obdurate : firm [fəːʳm] obdurateはfirm（断固とした、堅い）の度が過ぎた状態を表す。
obedient [oubíːdiənt]	adj. **submissive to commands** [形] 従順な
	Obedient students rarely defy their teachers.
	反意語 obedient : contumacious [kànt(j)uméiʃəs] obedientの反意語はcontumacious（反抗的な）

TRANSLATION | 例 文 の 訳

meek	ダニエルのおとなしい性格は、他の人々に弱さの印だと見なされることが多かった。
mnemonic	子供たちは難しい問題を覚える助けに語呂合わせを使う。
nudge	私が会議で居眠りを始めると、スティーブが私を肘でそっと突いた。
obdurate	大尉は彼らの訴えをはねのけた。
obedient	従順な学生たちは教師にめったにそむかない。

precis
[preisíː]

n. a brief and accurate summary　　　　　　　　　[名] 要約

Karen's *precis* highlighted all the points of the arguments.

関連語 precis : concise [kənsáis]
precis には concise（簡潔な）であるという特徴がある。

predict
[pridíkt]

v. to foretell based on scientific or personal observation

[動] 予測する

Economists *predict* that the global economy will experience a recession early next year.

関連語 prediction : augur [ɔ́ːgəʳ]
未来について prediction（予言）を述べるのが augur（占い師）。

preen
[priːn]

v. to excessively groom oneself; to pride oneself on

[動] 入念に身支度する、得意になる

Mary *preened* herself for two hours on the night of the school dance.

関連語 preen : dandy [dǽndi]
dandy（しゃれた男性、粋な男）は preen するという特徴がある。

quell
[kwel]

v. to calm or quiet down; to suppress　　　　[動] 〜を抑える；鎮圧する

Liz *quelled* the crying baby with a pacifier.

反意語 quell : stir [stəːʳ]
quell の反意語は stir（駆り立てる、奮起させる）

quench
[kwentʃ]

v. to put out; to satisfy a thirst or desire

[動]（火などを）消す；（渇きや欲望を）いやす

The fire fighters were unable to *quench* the forest fire and it raged out of control.

反意語 quench : ignite [ignáit]
quench の反意語は ignite（点火する）

TRANSLATION | 例 文 の 訳

precis	カレンの要約はすべての論点に言及していた。
predict	経済学者たちは来年の初めに世界経済が低迷するだろうと予測している。
preen	メアリーは学校のダンスパーティーの日、2時間かけて身支度をした。
quell	リズは泣く赤ん坊をおしゃぶりでなだめた。
quench	消防士たちはその山火事を消火できず、火は制御できぬまま広がった。

seemly
[síːmli]

adj. **proper and agreeable**　　　　　[形] ふさわしい、上品な

A *seemly* gentleman entered the room and caught her attention.

反意語 seemly : ribald [ríbəld]
　　seemlyの反意語は ribald（下品な、みだらな）

sneer
[sniəʳ]

v. **to speak in a scornful, contemptuous, or derisive manner**
　　　　　　　　　　　　　　　　　　　　[動] あざ笑う、冷笑する

n. **a facial expression that exhibits scorn**　　[名] 冷笑、あざけり

The crowd *sneered* at the poor attempts of the magician.

A *sneer* crossed the suspect's face as the lawyer began questioning him.

類義語 sneer : derision [diríʒən]
　　sneerの類義語は derision（あざけり、嘲笑）

speculate
[spékjulèit]

v. **to take a guess about something; to ponder**　　[動] 推測する；思案する

Some researchers *speculate* that the dinosaurs died off because of an increase in global volcanic activity.

類義語 speculate : conjecture [kəndʒéktʃəʳ]
　　speculateの類義語は conjecture（推測する）

spendthrift
[spéndθrìft]

n. **a person who wastefully spends his money**　[名] 金遣いの荒い人、浪費家

Kimberly was known as a *spendthrift* because of her penchant for impulse buys.

関連語 spendthrift : improvidence [imprávədᵊns]
　　spendthrift には improvidence（将来の見通しがない）という特徴がある。

TRANSLATION ｜ **例 文 の 訳**

seemly　　上品な紳士が部屋に入ってきて、彼女の目を引いた。

sneer　　群衆はその手品師の貧弱な技をあざ笑った。
　　　　　　弁護士が質問を始めると、容疑者の顔に冷笑が広がった。

speculate　恐竜は世界の火山活動の増加によって絶滅した、と推測する研究者もいる。

spendthrift　キンバリーは衝動買いが好きなので、浪費家として知られていた。

steep
[sti:p]

adj. **at an excessively high angle**   [形]（角度が）急な、険しい

v. **to soak in a liquid**   [動]〜を（液体に）つける、浸す

The *steep* angle of the mountain made it impossible to climb without aid of a rope.

The hint to making better raisin muffins is to *steep* the raisins in sherry.

関連語 steepness : precipice [présəpis]
precipice（絶壁）には steepness（急なこと）という特徴がある。

stench
[stentʃ]

n. **a foul smell**   [名]悪臭

The *stench* of rotting corpses filled the air around the river.

関連語 stench : nose [nouz]
nose（鼻）が感知するものが stench。

svelte
[svelt]

adj. **slender or graceful in outline**   [形]ほっそりした、洗練された

James Levine was investigating why some people can gorge themselves with food and stay *svelte*.

反意語 svelte : paunchy [pɔ́:ntʃi]
svelte の反意語は paunchy（太鼓腹の）

sweltering
[swéltəriŋ]

adj. **very hot and humid; suffering from intense heat**
    [形]ひどく蒸し暑い；蒸し暑さで苦しんでいる

The *sweltering* heat in Cambodia was unbearable for the tourists.

関連語 sweltering : heat [hi:t]
sweltering と似た意味の名詞が heat（熱）

TRANSLATION | 例 文 の 訳

steep   その山は急峻で、ロープの助けがないと登るのが不可能だった。
おいしいレーズンマフィンを作るコツは、レーズンをシェリー酒にひたすことだ。

stench   腐乱死体の悪臭が川の周囲に立ち込めた。

svelte   ジェームズ・レヴァインはなぜ人によってお腹いっぱい食べ物を食べてもほっそりとしていられるのかを調べていた。

sweltering   旅行者たちはカンボジアの蒸し暑さに耐えられなかった。

trenchant [tréntʃənt]	adj. **incisive; vigorous and effective; clear-cut** [形] 鋭い；強力な；明確なる The *trenchant* facts of the case left little for the jury to deliberate on. 反意語 trenchant : vague [veig] 　trenchantの反意語はvague (あいまいな)
troupe [tru:p]	n. **a group of traveling performers of an opera or a play** [名] オペラや演劇の一座 The strain of 2 months of traveling and performing was beginning to wear the *troupe* down. 関連語 troupe : actor [ǽktəʳ] 　actor (俳優) は troupe を構成する。
wheedle [ʰwíːdl]	v. **to gain or entice by flattery or guile** [動] 口車に乗せる、甘い言葉で誘惑する、取り入る Developers of some projects are *wheedling* potential clients with free food and entertainment. 関連語 wheedle : cajolery [kədʒóuləri] 　wheedleと似た意味の名詞にcajolery (甘言、おべっか) がある。

TRANSLATION | 例 文 の 訳

trenchant	事件の事実関係は明らかで、陪審員が審議する余地はほとんどなかった。
troupe	２カ月に及ぶ旅と公演の重圧で、一座は消耗し始めていた。
wheedle	いくつかのプロジェクトの開発者たちが、無料の食べ物や接待で潜在顧客を誘い込んでいる。

8th Day *Daily Check-up*

■ Fill in the blanks with the correct letter that matches the word with its definition.

1. abdicate   _____
2. boding   _____
3. hodgepodge   _____
4. mediocre   _____
5. stench   _____
6. preen   _____
7. mnemonic   _____
8. obdurate   _____
9. modicum   _____
10. diehard   _____

a. to give up power or resign from high position
b. a phrase or device that helps one remember
c. stubborn in perspective
d. to be an omen of; to foreshow
e. a small amount or quantity
f. a mixture of many different things
g. of moderate or middle-ground quality
h. a foul smell
i. to excessively groom oneself; to pride oneself on
j. one who is strongly devoted and resists any change

■ Put the correct word in each blank from the list of words below.

11. 酒や薬物に _____ されると、それに対する dependency が生じる。
12. _____ な人は arrogance を持っていない。
13. hovel は _____ なことがない。
14. impeccable な人は _____ を見つけにくい。
15. farce には _____ という特徴がある。
16. recluse には _____ が不足している。
17. execrate（非常に非難する）の反意語は _____ である。
18. chasm は _____ より深く割れた隙間を指す。
19. valediction（別れ）の反意語は _____ である。
20. _____ は concise である。

a. ludicrous	b. blemish	c. palatial	d. meek	e. addicted
f. gregariousness		g. exalt	h. cleft	i. greeting	j. paunchy
k. frigid	l. precis			

Answer key

11. e 12. d 13. c 14. b 15. a 16. f 17. g 18. h 19. i 20. l
1. a 2. d 3. f 4. g 5. h 6. i 7. b 8. c 9. e 10. j

117

Track 09

昨日の愛はあなたの元を去って行く
かもしれないが、今日学ぶ単語が
あなたを置き去りにすることはない。

9th DAY

aberrant [əbérənt]	adj. deviating from the norm	[形] 異常な、常軌を逸した

The mother began to worry when all of her son's teachers complained of his *aberrant* behavior.

関連語 aberrant : standard [stǽndəʳd]
aberrant は standard（基準、標準）から外れているという意味。

---

abet
[əbét]

v. to actively encourage or support　　[動] ～を積極的に励ます、支持する

The protesters gathered to *abet* the legalization of same-sex marriages.

関連語 abet : encouragement [inkə́:ridʒmənt]
abet と似た意味の名詞に encouragement（激励、励まし）がある。

---

acerbic
[əsə́:ʳbik]

adj. sour or bitter in taste; harsh or acidic in mood
[形]（味が）酸っぱい、苦い；（態度などが）厳しい、鋭いる

The medicine's *acerbic* flavor caused the child to flinch.

反意語 acerbic : saccharine [sǽkərin]
acerbic の反意語は saccharine（ひどく甘い）

---

alert
[ələ́:ʳt]

adj. watchful and aware　　　　　　　[形] 警戒した、油断のない

v. to notify of approaching danger or action　　[動] ～に警戒させる

An *alert* security guard triggered the silent alarm during the bank robbery.

Health officials *alerted* the public about the possible outbreak of mad cow disease.

関連語 alert : somnolence [sámnələns]
alert な人は somnolence（眠気）に陥ることはない。

TRANSLATION | 例 文 の 訳

aberrant　母親は、息子の教師の全員が彼の異常な行動に不満を述べるのを聞いて、不安になった。

abet　その抗議者たちは同性婚の合法化を支持するために集まった。

acerbic　薬の苦さにその子はしり込みした。

alert　銀行が強盗に遭っている間、抜け目のない警備員が無音の警報装置を作動させた。

公衆衛生担当の役人が人々に狂牛病発生の危険性を知らせた。

118

amenity
[əménəti]

n. the quality of being pleasant or agreeable; something that is conducive to convenience and pleasure

[名] 心地よさ、快適さ；生活を便利に楽しくするもの

Proponents say specialty hospitals offer hotel-like *amenities* to patients.

関連語 amenity : comfortable [kʌ́mfɚ'təbl]
amenity には comfortable（快適な）だという特徴がある。

anesthetic
[æ̀nəsθétik]

n. a drug used by doctors to prevent a patient from feeling pain

[名] 麻酔薬

adj. causing anesthesia; insensitive　　[形] 麻酔の；無感覚の

Operations on the battlefield are often performed without *anesthetics*.

Ms. Park was under the influence of *anesthetic* medications.

関連語 anesthetic : pain [pein]
anesthetic には pain（痛み）を取り除く機能がある。

aversion
[əvɔ́ːrʒən]

n. a feeling of strong dislike　　[名] 嫌悪

A young man naturally conceives an *aversion* to labor when he receives no benefit from it.

関連語 aversion : disinclination [disìnklənéiʃ°n]
aversion は disinclination（気が進まないこと）よりも嫌な気持ちが大きい。

brevity
[brévəti]

n. shortness of speech or writing　　[名] 簡潔さ、短さ

For the sake of *brevity*, you can call me Bill.

関連語 brevity : aphorism [ǽfərìzm]
aphorism（金言、格言）は brevity を特徴として持っている。cf) epigram（警句）

caveat
[kǽviɑ̀ːt]

n. a warning, caution, or protest　　[名] 警告、注意、抗議

Samantha did not heed the *caveat* given by her father.

関連語 caveat : cautionary [kɔ́ːʃənèri]
caveat と似た意味の形容詞に cautionary（警告的な）がある。

TRANSLATION | 例文の訳

amenity	提唱者たちによると、専門病院は患者にホテルのような快適さを提供するのだという。
anesthetic	戦場での手術は往々にして麻酔なしで行われる。
	パークさんには麻酔の影響が残っていた。
aversion	若い男性は、労働から何の利益も得られなければ当然、嫌悪感を抱く。
brevity	そのほうが簡単なので、私のことをビルと呼んでください。
caveat	サマンサは父親の警告を気にとめなかった。

charlatan
[ʃáːˈlətn]

n. **one who deceivingly claims to know much**

[名] 知ったかぶりをする人、ペテン師

Charlatans use their deceptive abilities to con wealthy people of their money.

関連語 charlatan : deceive [disíːv]

charlatan には deceive（人をあざむく）傾向がある。

crest
[krest]

n. **a showy tuft on the head of a bird; the top of a hill or wave; the peak**

[名] とさか；山頂；絶頂

During the hurricane, the *crest* of the waves would reach incredible heights.

関連語 crest : wave [weiv]

crest は wave（波）の最も高いところをいう。

crestfallen
[kréstfɔːlən]

adj. **having a drooping crest; depressed or dejected**

[形] しおれた；意気消沈した、がっかりした

The employee to whom the manager had been talking went away quite *crestfallen*.

反意語 crestfallen : exultant [igzʌ́ltᵊnt]

crestfallen の反意語は exultant（歓喜した、有頂天の）

deterrent
[ditə́ːrənt]

n. **something that discourages or prevents**

[名] 妨害物、引き止めるもの

The claim that corporal punishment is an effective *deterrent* against future crimes is false.

反意語 deterrent : inducement [ind(j)úːsmənt]

deterrent の反意語は inducement（報酬、誘因）

devastate
[dévəstèit]

v. **to bring to destruction by violent action; to overwhelm or confound**

[動] ～を破壊する、荒廃させる；打ちのめす

Rob was *devastated* when he didn't get the toy truck he wanted from Santa.

反意語 devastated : spry [sprai]

devastated（破壊された、打ちのめされた）の反意語は spry（活気のある、元気な）

TRANSLATION | 例 文 の 訳

charlatan	ペテン師には人をだます才能があり、それを発揮して金持ちから金を詐取する。
crest	ハリケーンが来ると、波頭が信じられない高さまで上がる。
crestfallen	その従業員は課長と話していたが、かなり気を落として去って行った。
deterrent	体罰が将来に対する効果的な抑止力になる、という主張は間違っている。
devastate	ロブは欲しがっていたおもちゃのトラックをサンタクロースからもらえず、完全に気落ちした。

dilapidate
[dilǽpədèit]

v. **to bring into a state of decay or partial ruin; to squader**

[動] 荒廃させる、破損する；散財する

The riots left the streets *dilapidated*.

反意語 dilapidated : restored [ristɔ́ːʳd]
dilapidated（破損した、荒廃した）の反意語は restored（回復した、復活した）

earshot
[íəʳʃàt]

n. **the distance over which a sound can be heard**   [名] 声の届く範囲

Tom made sure we were out of *earshot* before he began telling me the latest rumors.

関連語 earshot : hear [hiəʳ]
earshot は hear（～を耳にする、聞く）することができる範囲のこと。

enervate
[énəʳvèit]

v. **to drain of physical or mental energy**   [動]（力を）弱める、気力を奪う

The long work day and lack of sleep *enervated* Marie.

関連語 enervate : vigor [vígəʳ]
enervate する対象は vigor（活力、活気）である。

frenetic
[frənétik]

adj. **frantic and nervously excited**   [形] 熱狂した

The children were *frenetic* on the last day of school.

関連語 frenetic : energetic [ènəʳdʒétik]
frenetic は energetic（熱心な）よりも程度が強い。

frenzy
[frénzi]

n. **a temporary state of chaos and panic**   [名] 熱狂、逆上

The scuba divers witnessed feeding *frenzy* as the sharks devoured the bait.

関連語 frenzy : emotion [imóuʃən]
frenzy は emotion（感情）がひどく高ぶっている状態をいう。

TRANSLATION | 例 文 の 訳

dilapidate	暴動によって通りは荒廃した。
earshot	トムは周囲に声が届かないことを確かめてから、私に最近の噂話を聞かせた。
enervate	長時間の勤務と睡眠不足でマリーの気力が奪われた。
frenetic	子供たちは学校の最終日に熱狂していた。
frenzy	スキューバダイバーたちはサメが狂ったように餌をむさぼるところを目撃した。

121

gorge
[gɔːˈdʒ]

v. **to eat excessively and greedily** [動] 腹いっぱいに食べる

After 3 days of fasting, Amy *gorged* herself on anything she could get her hands on.

関連語 gorge : abstemious [æbstíːmiəs]
abstemious（禁欲的な、節制して）な人は gorge することがない。

grimace
[gríməs]

v. **to twist one's face in an ugly way to show pain, strong dislike, etc.** [動] 顔をゆがめる[しかめる]

Francis *grimaced* whenever she was reminded of her painful past.

関連語 grimace : pain [pein]
pain（痛み、苦しみ）が grimace を引き起こす。

inept
[inépt]

adj. **not apt; not skilled in; lacking in reason or sense** [形] 不適当な；不器用な；ばかげた

The boy's *inept* sense of direction led us to the wrong side of the state.

関連語 inept : adroitness [ədrɔ́itnis]
inept な人には adroitness（巧みさ、器用さ）が欠けている。

inert
[inə́ːˈt]

adj. **unable to move or resist motion** [形] 動けない、動かない

The ropes bound the *inert* hostage to the chair.

関連語 inert : react [riːǽkt]
inert なものは簡単に react（反応する）することができない。

inevitable
[inévətəbl]

adj. **unavoidable** [形] 不可避の、避けられない

Historians regarded the war as an *inevitable* conclusion to the enmity between the two countries.

関連語 inevitable : avoid [əvɔ́id]
inevitable とは avoid（〜を避ける）することができないことを表す。

TRANSLATION | 例 文 の 訳

gorge	3日間の絶食を終えると、エイミーは手に入るものは何でもおなかに詰め込んだ。
grimace	フランシスはつらい過去を思い出すたびに顔をゆがめた。
inept	その少年が方向音痴だったせいで、私たちは州の間違った側に出てしまった。
inert	ぐったりした人質がロープで椅子に縛られていた。
inevitable	歴史家たちは、その戦争が2国間の対立から生じた避けられない結末だったと考えた。

ode
[oud]

n. a lyrical poem written in praise of a particular person, thing, or event [名] オード、頌歌（特定の人やものに呼びかける叙情詩）

The young poet sang an *ode* to Odysseus, the clever and courageous hero.

関連語 ode : poem [póuəm]
ode は poem（詩）の一種。

overbearing
[òuvəˈbéˈriŋ]

adj. marked by the ability to force into submission; arrogant [形] 威圧的な、横柄な

The *overbearing* commander shouted at and threatened his troops.

反意語 overbearing : meek [mi:k]
overbearing の反意語は meek（従順な、おだやかな）

overexpose
[òuvərikspóuz]

v. to expose too much or too long; to expose film to excessive light [動] 〜を過度にさらす；〜を露出過度にする

It is well known that today's youth are *overexposed* to sex and violence because of television and the internet.

関連語 overexposure : jaded [dʒéidid]
overexposure された結果、jaded（飽き飽きした）な状態になる。

overindulge
[òuvərindʌ́ldʒ]

v. to indulge excessively in some action [動] 〜を食べすぎる、飲みすぎる

It is hard to not *overindulge* during the holidays and vacations.

関連語 overindulge : glutton [glʌ́tn]
glutton（大食家）は食べ物を overindulge するのが特徴だ。

TRANSLATION | 例 文 の 訳

ode その若い詩人は賢く勇敢な英雄、オデッセウスのための頌歌を歌った。

overbearing その威圧的な司令官は、部下の兵士たちをどなっておびえさせた。

overexpose 現代の若者がテレビとインターネットのせいでセックスや暴力にさらされすぎていることは、よく知られている。

overindulge 休みや休暇中に食べすぎずにいるのは難しい。

123

overture
[óuvəˈtʃùəˈ]

n. an introductory musical piece; a proposal　　　　　[名] 序曲；提案

The composer's *overture* to the opera was enthusiastically received by the crowd.

反意語 overture : coda [kóudə]
　　　overtureの反意語は coda（コーダ、終結部）

pedestrian
[pədéstriən]

adj. ordinary; lacking wit or imagination　　　[形] 平凡な；想像力に欠ける

n. a person who is walking　　　　　　　　　　　　　　[名] 歩行者

The company's *pedestrian* advertisements failed to generate sales.

There were so many *pedestrians* on the street on Sunday.

反意語 pedestrian : imaginative [imǽdʒənətiv]
　　　pedestrianの反意語は imaginative（想像力豊かな）

peeve
[pi:v]

v. to cause to be annoyed or resentful　　　[動] ～をいら立たせる、怒らせる

The housekeeper was *peeved* at his boss for leaving such a mess.

反意語 peeve : placate [pléikeit]
　　　peeveの反意語は placate（～をなだめる）

pierce
[piəˈs]

v. to cut or pass through; to make a hole in　[動] ～を突き通す；穴を開ける

Lily's father would not allow her to *pierce* her ears until she turned 16.

関連語 pierce : awl [ɔ:l]
　　　awl（千枚通し）は pierceするための道具だ。

precarious
[prikɛ́ˀriəs]

adj. unstable or insecure　　　　　　　　　　　[形] 不安定な、危険な

You don't seem to realize that we are in a *precarious* condition.

関連語 precarious : stability [stəbíləti]
　　　precariousなものには stability（安定）が欠けている。

TRANSLATION ｜ 例 文 の 訳

overture	その作曲家が書いたオペラの序曲は聴衆に熱狂的に受け入れられた。
pedestrian	その企業の広告は平凡で、売り上げを生むことなどできなかった。
	日曜日、その通りにはとても多くの歩行者がいた。
peeve	その家政婦はそのような散らかった状態を放置した雇い主に腹を立てた。
pierce	リリーの父親は彼女が16歳になるまで耳にピアスを着けるのを許そうとしなかった。
precarious	あなたは私たちが危険な状況にいることを理解していないようだ。

precede
[prisí:d]

v. to occur before in time; to come before in order or rank

[動]〜より先に起こる；〜の前に来る

Mr. Roberts made it very clear that his opinion *precedes* any of his employees'.

関連語 precedent : unique [ju:ní:k]

precedent（前例、先例）がないものは unique（独創的な）だ。

precipitate
[prisípətèit]

v. to cause to occur suddenly or abruptly　[動]〜を突然引き起こす

The accident was *precipitated* by the younger driver not paying attention to the road.

関連語 precipitate : symptom [símptəm]

precipitate するとは、なんの symptom（兆候）もなく突然発生することをいう。

preponderance
[pripánd³rəns]

n. superiority in weight, power, or importance

[名]（重さ・力などで）まさること、優勢

A *preponderance* of evidence against the defendant made the prosecution's job easy.

関連語 preponderance : weight [weit]

preponderance は weight（重さ）などでまさっていることをいう。

preposterous
[pripást³rəs]

adj. inverted in order; contrary to reason, nature, or commom sense　[形]逆の；不合理な、ばかげた

No one paid any attention to Bill because everything he said was *preposterous*.

反意語 preposterous : commonsensical [kàmənsénsikəl]

preposterous の反意語は commonsensical（常識的な）

TRANSLATION | 例 文 の 訳

precede	ロバーツ氏は自分の意見がどの部下のものよりも重要なことを非常に明確にした。
precipitate	その事故は道路状況に注意していなかった若い運転者によって突然引き起こされた。
preponderance	被告人に不利な証拠が大半で、検事は仕事が楽になった。
preposterous	ビルの言ったことはすべてばかげていたので、だれも彼に注意を払わなかった。

preserve
[prizə́ːˈv]

v. **to guard from destruction or injury and to maintain good condition** 　　　[動]（破壊、損傷されないように）保護する、保存する

National parks *preserve* endangered animals and the habitats they live in.

関連語 preservative : spoilage [spɔ́ilidʒ]
preservative（防腐剤）は spoilage（腐敗）を防ぐ。

prestige
[prestíːdʒ]

n. **qualities that are regarded highly in the general opinion**
[名]名声、威信

Despite the *prestige* that accompanied his occupation, Larry was discontented with the long hours.

関連語 prestige : eclipse [iklíps]
eclipse（〜を失墜させる）とは prestige などを落とすという意味だ。

prevail
[privéil]

v. **to triumph over in strength or influence; to be common or frequent** 　　　[動]〜に打ち勝つ；普及する、まん延する

In the Civil War, the North *prevailed* over the South.

類義語 prevalent : predominant [pridámənənt]
prevalent（普及している）の類義語は predominant（卓越した、支配的な）

prevaricate
[privǽrəkèit]

v. **to cover up the truth; to misrepresent** 　　　[動]真実を隠す；嘘を言う

The guilty child *prevaricated* to his mother when she asked who broke the vase.

関連語 prevarication : truth [truːθ]
prevarication（真実を隠すこと）には truth（真実）が欠けている。

querulous
[kwér(j)uləs]

adj. **continually whining or complaining** 　　　[形]不満の多い、不平を言う

The traveler could not stand taking trips with *querulous* people.

関連語 querulous : grouch [grautʃ]
grouch（不平をいう人、気難し屋）は常に querulous だという特徴がある。

TRANSLATION | 例 文 の 訳

preserve	国立公園は絶滅が危惧される動物とその生息地を保存している。
prestige	職務に伴う名声があるにもかかわらず、ラリーは長い勤務時間に不満だった。
prevail	南北戦争で北軍が南軍に勝った。
prevaricate	母親にだれが花瓶を割ったのかと聞かれ、罪悪感を抱いた子供はうそをついた。
querulous	その旅行者は不平の多い人々と旅行することに耐えられなかった。

126

redolent
[réd°lənt]

adj. **giving off an odor or fragrance**　　　　　　[形] 香りがする

Sara's hair was *redolent* of sweet perfume.

類義語 redolent : fragrant [fréigrənt]
　　redolentの類義語はfragrant（香りのよい、いいにおいのする）

redoubtable
[ri:dáutəbl]

adj. **deserving of respect; causing a scare**　　　[形] 尊敬すべき；恐るべき

The counselor was a *redoubtable* member of the faculty who many students turned to for advice.

関連語 redoubtable : regard [rigáːʳd]
　　redoubtableの似た意味の名詞にregard（尊敬、敬意）がある。

rudiment
[rúːdəmənt]

n. **a basic and essential element or principle**　　[名] 基本（原理）、初歩

Primary school educates youth in the *rudiments* of human knowledge.

類義語 rudiment : fundament [fʌ́ndəmənt]
　　rudimentの類義語はfundament（基本、原理）

rue
[ruː]

n. **a regret about something**　　　　　　　　　[名] 後悔

v. **to regret; to grieve for**　　　　　　　　[動] 後悔する、悲しむ

The old man has *rue* regarding his failed first marriage.
Mike *rued* that he asked his wife to divorce.

類義語 rue : remorse [rimɔ́ːʳs]
　　rueの類義語はremorse（激しい後悔）

scent
[sent]

n. **a smell or perfumed fragrance**　　　　　　　[名] におい、香り

The faint sharp *scent* of the geraniums mingled with the odor of Ethan's smoke.

関連語 scent : malodor [mælóudəʳ]
　　malodor（悪臭）はscentの中でもひどいもののことを言う。

TRANSLATION | 例 文 の 訳

redolent	サラの髪から甘い香水の匂いがただよった。
redoubtable	そのカウンセラーは、たくさんの学生がアドバイスを求めにいく尊敬すべき職員だった。
rudiment	小学校では子供たちに人の知識の基本を教える。
rue	その年老いた男性は、失敗に終わった自分の最初の結婚を後悔している。
	マイクは妻に別れてくれと頼んだことを後悔した。
scent	ゼラニウムのかすかで鮮明な香りが、イーサンのたばこの臭いと混ざった。

sedulous [sédʒuləs]	adj. **steadily industrious; assiduous** [形] 勤勉な；よく働く The *sedulous* student was on the honor roll every semester. 反意語 sedulous : indolent [índələnt] 　sedulousの反意語は indolent（怠惰な）
sidereal [saidíˀriəl]	adj. **of or related to constellations or stars** [形] 星座の、恒星の Although a normal year is based on the time it takes Earth to go around the sun, a *sidereal* year is based on the movement of the stars. 関連語 sidereal : star [stɑːʳ] 　siderealと似た意味の名詞が star（星）。
skeptic [sképtik]	n. **one who doesn't easily believe or is prone to disbelieving; one inclined to skepticism regarding religion** [名] 懐疑論者、疑い深い人；無神論者 The Wright Brothers proved their *skeptics* wrong by building the first working airplane. 関連語 skeptic : credulous [krédʒələs] 　skepticは credulous（信じやすい、だまされやすい）なことがない。
specious [spéːʃəs]	adj. **appearing true although it is false** [形] 見せかけだけの The man's *specious* reasoning nearly convinced the couple to sign the contract. 反意語 specious : valid [vǽlid] 　speciousの反意語は valid（妥当な、正当な）
stentorian [stentɔ́ːriən]	adj. **very loud** [形]（音が）大きい The *stentorian* speeches of the artillery continued in some distant encounter, but the crashes of the musketry had almost ceased. 関連語 stentorian : audible [ɔ́ːdəbl] 　stentorianは audible（聞こえる）よりもずっと騒々しい状態を表す。

TRANSLATION | 例 文 の 訳

sedulous	その勤勉な学生は、毎学期、優等生名簿に名前が載った。
sidereal	通常の1年は地球が太陽の周りを回る時間に基づくが、恒星年は星の動きに基づいている。
skeptic	ライト兄弟は最初の実用的な飛行機を作ったことで、彼らを疑った人々が間違っていたことを証明した。
specious	その夫婦は男のもっともらしい理屈にだまされて、もう少しで契約書にサインするところだった。
stentorian	砲兵隊による騒がしい演説は遠くから聞こえ続けていたが、小銃射撃のすさまじい音はほとんど途絶えていた。

sterile
[stéril]

adj. **absolutely clean; unable to reproduce**　[形] 殺菌した；不妊の、不毛な

It is very important that a doctor's instruments are *sterile* before use to ensure that germs are not spread.

関連語 sterile : germ [dʒəːˈm]
germ（細菌）のない状態を sterile と言う。

tedious
[tíːdiəs]

adj. **boring or tiresomely elongated**　[形] 退屈な、冗長な

Editing papers is a long and *tedious* process.

反意語 tedious : absorbing [əbsɔːˈbiŋ]
tedious の反意語は absorbing（夢中にさせる）

teeter
[tíːtəʳ]

v. **to waver or move unsteadily**　[動] ぐらつく、ふらつく

A Chinaman went by, *teetering* under the weight of the market baskets slung on a pole across his shoulders.

類義語 teeter : totter [tátəʳ]
teeter の類義語は totter（よろめく、揺れる）

theatrical
[θiǽtrikəl]

adj. **relating to the theater; unnaturally extravagant in behavior and expression**　[形] 劇場の、演劇の；芝居じみた

The *theatrical* performance by the thespian enhanced the play greatly.

反意語 theatrical : sober [sóubəʳ]
theatrical の反意語は sober（ありのままの、誇張のない）

torrid
[tɔ́ːrid]

adj. **intensely hot or scorching**　[形] 焼けつくように暑い、灼熱の

In South America, siestas are taken in the middle of the day to hide from the *torrid* sun.

反意語 torrid : arctic [áːʳktik]
torrid の反意語は arctic（厳寒の）

TRANSLATION ｜ 例 文 の 訳

sterile	確実に細菌が広がらないようにするために、医師が用いる器具は使用前に殺菌されていることが非常に大切だ。
tedious	論文の編集は長くて退屈な作業だ。
teeter	中国人の男が、肩にかけた棒からぶら下げた商品かごの重さでふらつきながら、通り過ぎた。
theatrical	その俳優の大げさな演技が芝居の質を高めた。
torrid	南米では、焼けつくような日光を避けるために真っ昼間に昼寝をする。

trepidation
[trèpədéiʃən]

n. anxiety or fear

[名] 不安、恐怖

The dog's enormous size caused the little boy to approach it with *trepidation*.

関連語 trepidation : dauntless [dɔ́ːntlis]
dauntless (勇敢な) な人は trepidation を感じることはない。

trespass
[tréspəs]

v. to enter unlawfully onto another's property or land; to commit an offense or sin

[動] 不法侵入する；罪を犯す

The hunter was arrested for *trespassing* on private property.

関連語 trespass : enter [éntəʳ]
違法に enter (入る) するのが trespass だ。

upset
[ʌpsét]

v. to cause emotional or physical distress to

[動] 〜をろうばいさせる、苦しませる

Axel was *upset* that his parents wouldn't let him go to the concert.

関連語 upset : unflappable [ʌ́nflǽpəbl]
unflappable (動揺しない、冷静な) な人は簡単に upset されることがない。

TRANSLATION | 例 文 の 訳

trepidation	その犬が巨大だったので、小さな少年は近づきながら恐怖を感じた。
trespass	その狩猟者は私有地に不法侵入して逮捕された。
upset	アクセルは両親が彼をコンサートに行かせようとしないことに怒った。

■ Fill in the blanks with the correct letter that matches the word with its definition.

1. abet _____
2. dilapidate _____
3. teeter _____
4. gorge _____
5. peeve _____
6. redolent _____
7. prevaricate _____
8. amenity _____
9. frenetic _____
10. crest _____

a. giving off an odor or fragrance
b. to cover up the truth; to misrepresent
c. to actively encourage or support
d. to squander or bring into ruin
e. to cause to be annoyed or resentful
f. to eat excessively and greedily
g. frantic and nervously excited
h. the top of a hill or wave; the peak
i. the quality of being pleasant or agreeable; something that is conducive to convenience and pleasure
j. to waver or move unsteadily

■ Put the correct word in each blank from the list of words below.

11. saccharine（非常に甘い）の反意語は _____ である。
12. dauntless な人は _____ を感じない。
13. valid（妥当な、正当な）の反意語は _____ である。
14. grouch はいつも _____ である。
15. malodor は _____ の中でもひどいものを意味する。
16. imaginative（想像力豊かな）の反意語は _____ である。
17. _____ することは、いかなる symptom もなく突然発生することである。
18. _____ した状態は、audible なものよりはるかに騒々しいことを言う。
19. earshot は _____ できる範囲を指す。
20. _____ には pain を取り除く機能がある。

a. specious b. querulous c. scent d. pedestrian e. stentorian
f. hear g. acerbic h. anesthetic i. precipitate j. tidy k. theatrical
l. trepidation

Answer key

11. g 12. l 13. a 14. b 15. c 16. d 17. i 18. e 19. f 20. h
1. c 2. d 3. j 4. f 5. e 6. a 7. b 8. i 9. g 10. h

131

Out of sight, out of mind!
単語は見ていないと
忘れてしまいます。毎日続けましょう！

10th DAY

---

affability
[ǽfəbíləti]

n. the quality of being pleasant and easy to talk to

[名] 愛想のよさ、人好きがすること

His *affability*, even to those whom he disliked, was unfailing.

反意語 affability : surliness [sə́ːrlinis]
affabilityの反意語はsurliness（不愛想、不機嫌）

affiliate
[əfílièit]

v. to accept as a member or branch; to become closely connected or associated

[動] 〜を提携させる；加入する、加わる

Lawrence only *affiliated* with such seedy characters under the most dire of circumstances.

反意語 affiliate : dissociate [disóuʃièit]
affiliateの反意語はdissociate（〜を分離する；関係を絶つ）

affinity
[əfínəti]

n. an interest or attraction to, often based on similarity

[名] 親近感

The two young lovers felt an *affinity* for each other at first sight.

反意語 affinity : antipathy [æntípəθi]
affinityの反意語はantipathy（反感、嫌悪感）

TRANSLATION | 例 文 の 訳

affability	彼の愛想のよさは、彼が嫌っている人々に対しても変わらなかった。
affiliate	ローレンスはこれ以上ない悲惨な状況でしか、そのようないかがわしい人々に加わることはなかった。
affinity	その若い恋人たち2人は一目でお互いに親近感を抱いた。

affirm
[əfə́ːʳm]

v. to maintain to be true; to confirm or ratify　　[動] 証言する；断言する、承認する

Today, we *affirm* a new commitment to live out our nation's promise through civility, courage, compassion, and character.

反意語 affirm : gainsay [gèinséi]
　　affirm の反意語は gainsay（〜を否定する、反対する）

affluent
[ǽfluənt]

adj. abundant or wealthy　　[形] 豊富な、裕福な

Hank had grown up in an *affluent* family and always had his material needs met.

反意語 affluent : impecunious [ìmpikjúːniəs]
　　affluent の反意語は impecunious（金がない）

buffoon
[bəfúːn]

n. a clown; a foolish and uneducated person　　[名] ピエロ、馬鹿者

The man acted like a *buffoon* in front of the kids to amuse them.

関連語 buffoon : ludicrous [lúːdəkrəs]
　　buffoon には ludicrous（こっけいな）であるという特徴がある。

coward
[káuəʳd]

n. a person disgracefully exhibiting lack of courage　　[名] 臆病者、卑怯者

The *coward* was ostracized by his community for his lack of bravery.

類義語 coward : dastard [dǽstəʳd]
　　coward の類義語は dastard（卑劣な人）

daft
[dæft]

adj. foolish or insane　　[形] 愚かな、まぬけな

Brian's parents labeled his plans to forgo college as a *daft* decision.

反意語 daft : judicious [dʒuːdíʃəs]
　　daft の反意語は judicious（判断力の確かな、賢明な）

TRANSLATION | 例 文 の 訳

affirm　今日、私たちは礼儀、勇気、思いやり、品性を通じて我が国の使命の実現に新たに取り組むことを宣言します。

affluent　ハンクは裕福な家庭で育ち、物質的要求は常に満たされていた。

buffoon　その男性は子供たちを楽しませようと、彼らの前でピエロのように振舞った。

coward　その臆病者は勇気がないために仲間うちからのけ者にされた。

daft　ブライアンの両親は、大学に行かないという彼の計画は愚かな判断だと決めつけた。

133

defend
[difénd]

v. to protect from danger; to keep safe; to argue sympathetically for
[動] ～を守る；防衛する；擁護する

Children depend upon adults to *defend* and protest their rights.

関連語 defend : apologist [əpálədʒist]
apologist（擁護者）には政策や制度などをdefendするという特徴がある。

defer
[difə́ːʳ]

v. to postpone or move to a later time; to submit to another's wishes or opinions through respect
[動] ～を延期する；（敬意から）人の希望や意見に従う

It was impossible to *defer* the journey to Moscow any longer.

Lieberman has said he would *defer* to Gore if the former vice president decides to seek the presidency.

反意語 deferrable : exigent [éksədʒənt]
deferrable（引き延ばせる）の反意語は exigent（差し迫った）

関連語 defer : leader [líːdəʳ]
leader（指導者）の意見などを defer する。

defile
[difáil]

n. a narrow valley or passage
[名] 谷間の狭い道

v. to make impure or despicably unclean; to desecrate
[動] ～を汚す；～を冒涜する

Many wild dogs lurk in the shadows of the *defile*, looking for prey.

The church had been broken into and *defiled* by vandals.

関連語 defile : narrowness [nǽrounis]
defileには narrowness（狭さ）という特徴がある。

類義語 defile : taint [teint]
defileの類義語は taint（～を汚す）

TRANSLATION | 例 文 の 訳

defend　子供たちは自分たちの権利を守り、主張することを大人に依存している。

defer　モスクワへの旅行をこれ以上延期することは不可能だった。

リーバーマンはもしもゴア元副大統領が大統領選への出馬を決めた場合には、彼に従うと述べていた。

defile　たくさんの野生のイヌが狭い谷間の物陰で獲物を待ち伏せしている。

その教会は破壊者たちに壊され、汚された。

definitive
[difínətiv]

adj. **supplying a final decision; precisely explicit** [形] 最終的な；決定的な

The judgement of the case was *definitive* with no hope of appeal.

反意語 definitive : provisional [prəvíʒənl]
definitive の反意語は provisional（一時の、暫定的な）

deft
[deft]

adj. **quick and skillful; adroit** [形] 手際のよい；器用な

The magician baffled the young child with his *deft* sleight of hand.

反意語 deft : maladroit [mælədrɔ́it]
deft の反意語は maladroit（不手際な、不器用な）

defuse
[difjúːz]

v. **to remove the fuse from a bomb; to make less dangerous, tense, or hostile**
[動]（爆弾から）信管を取り除く；（危険・緊張・敵意など）を和らげる

The police *defused* the situation and coaxed the kidnappers into releasing the hostages.

反意語 defuse : foment [foumént]
defuse の反意語は foment（〜を誘発する、扇動する）

diffidence
[dífədəns]

n. **the state of lacking self-confidence; shyness** [名] 自信のなさ；内気

His *diffidence* became evident in his speech and mannerisms.

反意語 diffidence : brazenness [breiznnis]
diffidence の反意語は brazenness（厚顔無恥、ずうずうしさ）

dissonance
[dísənəns]

n. **a combination of discordant sounds; an inconsistency or lack of agreement** [名] 不協和音；（言行の）不一致、不和

The *dissonance* in their relationship grew until they finally broke up.

反意語 dissonance : concord [kɑ́ŋkəʳd]
dissonance の反意語は concord（一致）

TRANSLATION | 例 文 の 訳

definitive	その事件の判決は上訴の望みがない決定的なものだった。
deft	その手品師は器用な手先の早わざでその小さな子供を煙に巻いた。
defuse	警察は状況を落ち着かせ、人質を解放するように誘拐犯たちを説得した。
diffidence	彼の自信のなさが、話し方や身ぶりの癖にはっきり表れた。
dissonance	彼らの人間関係の不和はどんどん大きくなり、とうとう別れてしまった。

135

dissipate
[dísəpèit]

v. **to disperse; to disappear by dispersion; to spend or use up carelessly** [動] 〜を散らす；〜を晴らす；浪費する

The heavy clouds *dissipated* and the sun shone through.

In one week, Michael had *dissipated* his entire paycheck.

関連語 dissipate : diminish [dimíniʃ]
　dissipateはdiminish (〜を減らす) した結果、なくなってしまうことをいう。

関連語 dissipate : husbandry [hʌ́zbəndri]
　dissipateする人にはhusbandry (節約、倹約) が欠けている。

distillate
[dístələt]

n. **the condensed liquid product resulting from distillation; an essence** [名] 蒸留液；エキス、エッセンス

Whiskey is a *distillate* of grain.

関連語 distillate : purity [pjúʲrəti]
　distillateにはpurity (純度) が高いという特徴がある。

divergent
[divə́ːʳdʒənt]

adj. **moving apart from a common point; differing from a standard** [形] 分岐する；逸脱した

The salesman eventually convinced his boss of the financial benefits of following his unorthodox and *divergent* strategies.

関連語 divergent : aside [əsáid]
　aside (余談) にはdivergentだという特徴がある。

efface
[iféis]

v. **to obliterate or make indistinct; to make inconspicuous** [動] 〜を消し去る、目だたなくする；〜を消す

Michelle often *effaced* herself in an attempt to avoid being the object of attention.

反意語 efface : bring to prominence [briŋ tə prámənəns]
　effaceの反意語はbring to prominence (目立たせる)

TRANSLATION | 例 文 の 訳

dissipate　厚い雲が消え、太陽が輝いた。
　　　　　　　　１週間でマイケルは給料を全部使ってしまった。

distillate　ウイスキーは穀類の蒸留液だ。

divergent　その販売員は、自分の型破りで特異な戦略に基づく財政的恩恵を、とうとう上司に納得させた。

efface　ミッシェルは注目されないように、人目を避けることが多かった。

effervesce
[èfə'vés]

v. to emit small bubbles of gas; to be high spirited or excited

[動] 泡出つ；熱狂する、はしゃぐ

Jane *effervesced* with joy upon hearing the news of her husband's successful surgery.

反意語 effervesce : droop [dru:p]
effervesce の反意語は droop（垂れ下がる、衰える、気が沈む）

effete
[ifí:t]

adj. depleted of vitality; weak; infertile　　[形] 活力のない；弱い；不毛な

The *effete* senior citizen walked feebly and only with aid of a cane.

反意語 effete : hale [heil]
effete の反意語は hale（剛健な）

efficacious
[èfəkéiʃəs]

adj. effective or able to produce an intended effect

[形] 効き目のある、有効な

The old woman wore the pained expression that she had long since found to be much more *efficacious* than anger.

反意語 efficacious : futile [fjú:tl]
efficacious の反意語は futile（無益な、効果のない）

effulgent
[ifʌ́ldʒənt]

adj. shining brilliantly; splendid　　[形] 燦然と輝いている、まばゆい；素晴らしい

The stars in the sky produced an *effulgent* sight.

関連語 effulgent : resplendence [rispléndəns]
effulgent と似た意味の名詞に resplendence（光輝、華麗）がある。

enfeeble
[infí:bl]

v. to deprive of strength; to make weak or feeble

[動] ～を衰弱させる；弱める

The reliance on funding has gradually *enfeebled* every state which has adopted it.

関連語 enfeeble : strength [streŋkθ]
strength（力）を enfeeble する。

TRANSLATION | 例 文 の 訳

effervesce	ジェーンは夫の手術が成功したという知らせを聞き、喜び、はしゃいだ。
effete	その衰弱した老人は杖の助けだけを借りて、よろよろと歩いた。
efficacious	その老女は、長年しみついている苦悶の表情を浮かべた。そのほうが怒りを見せるよりも効果があるとわかっていたからだ。
effulgent	空に光る星が素晴らしい光景を作り出した。
enfeeble	財政支援に依存することで、それを取り入れてきた各国が徐々に弱体化している。

enfranchise
[infrǽntʃaiz]

v. **to confer a franchise on; to admit a right; to set free**

[動] ～に選挙権を与える；権利を与える；～を自由にする

The Emancipation Proclamation *enfranchised* American slaves.

反意語 enfranchise : enfetter [infétəʳ]

enfranchiseの反意語はenfetter（足かせをする、束縛する）

fanatic
[fənǽtik]

n. **a person who is marked by excessive enthusiasm**

[名] 狂信者、熱狂的愛好者

My father is a cheese cake *fanatic*.

関連語 fanatic : devoted [divóutid]

fanaticは devoted（熱心な、熱烈な）だという特徴がある。

gloat
[glout]

v. **to think about something with victorious and malicious gratification**

[動] 満足して眺める、いい気味だと思う

The victor of the election *gloated* at his opponent.

関連語 gloat : smug [smʌg]

gloatするという行為にはsmug（うぬぼれの強い、自己満足した）であるという特徴がある。

impartial
[impáːʳʃəl]

adj. **treating all sides equally; not partial**

[形] 公平な；偏りのない

The coach couldn't find an *impartial* referee to work the game.

関連語 impartiality : arbitrator [áːʳbitrèitəʳ]

arbitrator（仲裁者）にはimpartiality（公平、中立）がなければならない。

impassion
[impǽʃən]

v. **to arouse the passions or feelings of**

[動] ～を熱狂させる、～の心に訴える

The president's rousing speech *impassioned* the nation to fight illiteracy.

関連語 impassion : callous [kǽləs]

callous（冷淡な）な人をimpassionするのは難しい。

TRANSLATION | 例 文 の 訳

enfranchise	奴隷解放宣言によって、アメリカの奴隷が解放された。
fanatic	私の父はチーズケーキのマニアだ。
gloat	その選挙の当選者は満足気に対立候補を眺めた。
impartial	その監督は、試合を公平に進めてくれる審判が一人もいないと思った。
impassion	その大統領の心を揺さぶる演説は国民を熱狂させ、無学文盲を克服しようという意識を高めた。

imperative
[impérətiv]

adj. **should not be avoided; mandatory or orderly**

[形] 必須の；強制的な、命令的な

It is *imperative* that the doctor's instructions be carried out precisely.

関連語 imperative : order [ɔ́ːᵊrdəʳ]
imperativeと似た意味の名詞にorder（命令）がある。

infinite
[ínfənət]

adj. **extending indefinitely**

[形] 無限な

There is an almost *infinite* variety of people in American society.

関連語 infinite : exhaust [igzɔ́ːst]
infiniteなものをexhaust（〜を使い果たす）することはできない。

inflame
[infléim]

v. **to set on fire; to arouse to excessive action or feeling; to make more violent**

[動] 火をつける；（行動や感情を）かき立てる；〜を悪化させる

The students further *inflamed* the heated situation by insulting the intelligence of the teacher.

反意語 inflame : assuage [əswéidʒ]
inflameの反意語はassuage（〜を和らげる）

jaundice
[dʒɔ́ːndis]

v. **to affect adversely**

[動] 悪影響を与える

Diane's previous marriage had *jaundiced* her opinion of men until she met Josh.

反意語 jaundice : dispose favorably [dispóuz féivᵊrəbli]
jaundiceの反意語はdispose favorably（よい影響を与える）

lofty
[lɔ́ːfti]

adj. **having great height; exalted or noble**

[形] 非常に高い；地位の高い、高貴な

The prosecutor pleaded with the *lofty* judge to make a just decision.

反意語 lofty : ignoble [ignóubl]
loftyの反意語はignoble（卑劣な）

TRANSLATION | 例 文 の 訳

imperative	医師の指示には正確に従わなければならない。
infinite	アメリカ社会には、ほとんど無限と言えるほどさまざまな人々がいる。
inflame	生徒たちはその教師の知性を侮辱したことで、加熱した状況をさらに悪化させた。
jaundice	ジョッシュに会うまで、ダイアンの前の結婚生活が男性に対する彼女の見方に悪影響を与えていた。
lofty	検事はその高潔な裁判官に公正な判決を下すように懇願した。

139

metaphor
[métəfɔːʳ]

n. a figure of speech where something is used in place of another to suggest a likeness or analogy between them　　　[名] 隠喩

Homeric epic is famous for its extended *metaphors*.

関連語 metaphor : literal [lítᵊrəl]
　　metaphorは literal（文字通りの）ではないという特徴がある。

morbid
[mɔ́ːʳbid]

adj. characterized by excessively gloomy or unwholesome thoughts and feelings; relating to disease
　　　[形] 恐ろしい、ぞっとするような；病的な、不健全な

His *morbid* thoughts nearly led him to commit suicide.

反意語 morbid : wholesome [hóulsəm]
　　morbidの反意語は wholesome（健康によい、健全な）

muffle
[mʌ́fl]

v. to wrap up or cover, in order to deaden sound
　　　[動]（音が出ないように）包む；（音を）消す

He put a pillow over his head in an attempt to *muffle* the sound of his roommate's snoring.

反意語 muffled : plangent [plǽndʒənt]
　　muffled（音が殺されてはっきり聞こえない）の反意語は plangent（鳴り響く）

nefarious
[niféᵊriəs]

adj. wicked or evil　　　[形] 邪悪な

Al Capone was the *nefarious* mastermind behind the St. Valentine's day massacre.

関連語 nefarious : wickedness [wíkidnis]
　　nefariousと似た意味の名詞に wickedness（邪悪）がある。

obey
[oubéi]

v. to follow orders or comply with commands　　　[動]（命令に）従う

The troops *obeyed* every command the officer made.

関連語 obey : recalcitrant [rikǽlsitrənt]
　　recalcitrant（反抗的な、手に負えない）な人は他人に obeyすることがない。

TRANSLATION | 例 文 の 訳

metaphor	ホメロスの叙事詩は、多くの隠喩が使われていることで有名だ。
morbid	彼は病的な考えを抱いたことで自殺しかけた。
muffle	彼は、同居人のいびきの音を消そうと、頭に枕をかぶった。
nefarious	アル・カポネは聖バレンタインデーの虐殺の裏にいた邪悪な黒幕だった。
obey	その軍隊は将校が下すすべての命令に従った。

obfuscate
[ábfʌskeit]

v. **to make obscure or unclear; to confuse or baffle**

[動] ～をぼんやりさせる；わかりにくくする

The president's staff *obfuscated* the story concerning the president's alleged affair.

反意語 obfuscate : clarify [klǽrəfài]
obfuscateの反意語は clarify（～を明らかにする）

---

offbeat
[ɔ:fbìt]

adj. **unexpected or unusual**

[形] 想像と違う、ふつうでない

The new student was too *offbeat* to fit in with the other students.

反意語 offbeat : bathetic [bəθétik]
offbeatの反意語は bathetic（陳腐な）

---

offend
[əfénd]

v. **to cause hurt feelings or resentment**

[動] 感情を害する、立腹する

Offended by the students' harsh criticism, the teacher left the room.

関連語 offense : euphemism [júːfəmìzm]
euphemism（婉曲語法）には offence（気持ちを害すること、無礼）が欠けている。

---

officious
[əfíʃəs]

adj. **meddlesome; unofficial**

[形] おせっかいな；非公式な

The *officious* neighbor was known for giving unwanted advice and being noisy.

関連語 officious : attentive [əténtiv]
attentive（気配りのある）な行為が度が過ぎると officious になる。

---

offish
[ɔ́(ː)fiʃ]

adj. **prone to be reserved and aloof**

[形] 人と関わらない、よそよそしい

I asked my sister why she was being so *offish*, but she gave no reply.

反意語 offish : sociable [sóuʃəbl]
offishの反意語は sociable（愛想のいい、社交的な）

TRANSLATION | 例 文 の 訳

obfuscate	側近たちは、大統領の不倫が疑われていることについて話をぼかした。
offbeat	その新入生はとても変わっていて、他の生徒たちになじめなかった。
offend	生徒たちからの厳しい批判に腹を立てて、その教員は部屋を出て行った。
officious	そのおせっかいな隣人は、望まれない助言をすることと口うるさいことで有名だった。
offish	私は妹に、なぜそんなによそよそしいのかと尋ねたが、彼女は返事をしなかった。

parry [pǽri]	v. **to deflect or evade** [動] ～をかわす、受け流す Smith had been a politician for 10 years and could *parry* any reporter's question. **関連語** parry : question [kwéstʃən] question（質問）を parry する。
parse [pɑːᵊs]	v. **to take a sentence and analyze each component grammatically** [動] 文の構成要素を文法的に分析する Angela *parsed* over the letter and found no mistakes. **関連語** parse : sentence [séntəns] sentence（文）を parse する。
penitent [pénətⁿnt]	adj. **feeling sorrow and shame over acts of sin committed** [形]（罪を）悔い改めた、後悔している A truly *penitent* person makes amends to the people he has hurt. **類義語** penitence : remorse [rimɔ́ːᵊs] penitence（悔い改め、ざんげ）の類義語は remorse（激しい後悔、自責）
perforate [pɔ́ːᵊfərèit]	v. **to punch a row of holes in order to allow for easy separation** [動] ミシン目を入れる Enid preferred the notebook with the *perforated* pages so she could tear them out. **関連語** perforate : hole [houl] perforate は hole（穴）を開けること。
raffish [rǽfiʃ]	adj. **cheaply or showily vulgar; characterized by a carefree unconventionality** [形] 低俗な；型破りな Amy's father worried about her becoming friendly with the *raffish* bunch of hoodlums. **関連語** raffish : decorum [dikɔ́ːrəm] raffish なものには decorum（礼儀正しい行動、上品さ）が欠けている。

TRANSLATION | 例 文 の 訳

parry	スミスは10年間も政治家をしているので、記者のどのような問題もかわすことができた。
parse	アンジェラはその手紙を文法的に分析したが間違いはなかった。
penitent	本当に罪を後悔している人は、自分が傷つけた人々に償いをする。
perforate	エニドは、破りやすいようにページにミシン目の入っているノートのほうが好きだった。
raffish	エイミーの父親は、彼女が低俗なちんぴらたちと親しくなっていることを心配した。

refined
[ri:fáind]

adj. **free from vulgarity; purified** [形] 洗練された；純粋な

Tom has always lived among *refined* and cultivated people.

反意語 refined : uncouth [ʌnkúːθ]
refined (洗練された) の反意語は uncouth (粗野な)

refractory
[rifrǽktᵊri]

adj. **resistant to authority, control, pressure, or heat** [形] 手に負えない、扱いにくい、耐熱性の

The frustrated teacher quickly sent her *refractory* student to the principal's office.

関連語 refractory : authority [əθɔ́:rəti]
refractory とは authority (権威) などに抵抗することを表す。

safeguard
[séifgàːʳd]

v. **to ensure the safety of; to protect** [動] ～を守る；保護する

My aim is simply to *safeguard* my reputation.

関連語 safeguard : accident [ǽksədᵊnt]
safeguard とは accident (事件、事故) から守ることを表す。

snobbish
[snábiʃ]

adj. **being a snob, one who thinks himself/herself too good for others; vulgarly pretentious** [形] お高くとまった；俗物の

A *snobbish* attitude will bring you nothing but loneliness.

関連語 snobbish : refined [rifáind]
refined (洗練された) な行動が過度になると snobbish になってしまう。

suffuse
[səfjúːz]

v. **to fill or spread over with fluid, color, or light** [動] ～を (液体、色、光で) いっぱいにする、覆う

The room was *suffused* with sunlight when she opened the window shades.

関連語 suffuse : tint [tint]
tint (～に色合いをつける) に対して、suffuse には全体を完全に覆うという意味合いがある。

TRANSLATION | 例 文 の 訳

refined	トムはいつも、洗練された教養のある人々の中で暮らしてきた。
refractory	いら立ちがたまったその教師は、自分の手に負えない生徒をすぐに校長室に送り込んだ。
safeguard	私の目的は単純に自分の評判を守ることだ。
snobbish	お高くとまった態度をとっていると、孤独になるだけだろう。
suffuse	彼女が窓の日よけを開けると、部屋に日光があふれた。

surrender
[səréndəʳ]

v. to resign or give up　　　　　　　　　　[動] 譲る、あきらめる

James *surrendered* his job in New York to return home and care for his ailing mother.

反意語 surrender : appropriate [əpróuprièit]
　　surrenderの反意語はappropriate (〜を横領する、盗む)

unfit
[ʌnfít]

adj. unsuitable; unqualified　　　　　　　[形] 適さない；資格のない

It was obvious that the man was *unfit* to be a soldier.

反意語 unfit : meet [miːt]
　　unfitの反意語はmeet (適した)

unflappable
[ʌnflǽpəbl]

adj. not easily perturbed; persistently calm　　[形] 動揺しない；落ち着いた

One sign of a true leader is an *unflappable* reaction to crisis.

関連語 unflappable : upset [ʌpsét]
　　unflappableな人は簡単にupset (ろうばいさせる、心を乱す) されることがない。

vagrant
[véigrənt]

adj. moving around without direction; wandering and unsettled
　　　　　　　　　　　　　　　　　　　　　[形] まよう；放浪する

During the depression, the streets were filled with *vagrant* children who had nowhere to go.

反意語 vagrant : fixed [fikst]
　　vagrantの反意語はfixed (固定した、確固たる)

veer
[viər]

v. to shift direction sharply　　　　　　　[動] 向きを変える

The driver *veered* off the road to avoid oncoming traffic.

関連語 veer : course [kɔːʳs]
　　course (方向) をveerする。

TRANSLATION | 例 文 の 訳

surrender　ジェームズは故郷に帰って病気の母親の世話をするために、ニューヨークでの仕事をあきらめた。

unfit　その男が兵士に向かないのは明らかだった。

unflappable　真の指導者を示す1つの指標は、危機に際して動揺しないことだ。

vagrant　不景気の間、通りは行くあてなくさまよう子供たちであふれた。

veer　その運転手は予測された交通渋滞を避けるため、道路からそれた。

10th Day *Daily Check-up*

■ Fill in the blanks with the correct letter that matches the word with its definition.

1. affability _____
2. daft _____
3. effete _____
4. defer _____
5. morbid _____
6. refined _____
7. obfuscate _____
8. defuse _____
9. snobbish _____
10. effulgent _____

a. free from vulgarity; purified
b. foolish or insane
c. shining brilliantly; splendid
d. the quality of being pleasant and easy to talk to
e. characterized by excessively gloomy or unwholesome thoughts and feelings; relating to disease
f. weak; infertile; depleted of vitality
g. to submit to another's wishes or opinions through respect
h. to lessen the danger; to remove the fuse from a bomb
i. to make obscure or unclear
j. being a snob, one who thinks himself/herself too good for others

■ Put the correct word in each blank from the list of words below.

11. _____ な人は簡単に upset されない。
12. _____ の類義語は dastard である。
13. _____ する行為には smug という属性が含まれている。
14. _____ は ludicrous な点を持っている。
15. narrowness は _____ の特徴である。
16. _____ は authority などに抵抗することを言う。
17. impecunious（金がない）の反意語は _____ である。
18. _____ する人には husbandry（節約）が欠けている。
19. _____ は何かに devoted（熱心な、熱烈な）な人である。
20. _____ には purity が高いという特徴がある。

| a. buffoon | b. fanatic | c. distillate | d. suffuse | e. gloat | f. unflappable |
| g. coward | h. affluent | i. refractory | j. meet | k. defile | l. dissipate |

Answer key

11. f 12. g 13. e 14. a 15. k 16. i 17. h 18. l 19. b 20. c
1. d 2. b 3. f 4. g 5. e 6. a 7. i 8. h 9. j 10. c

145

Answer Page 436

Questions

across

2. the ability and good judgment to govern oneself with the use of reason
4. to speak abruptly and impulsively
5. lacking interest or energy
8. a chronological error
10. cold and grave in appearance or manner; morally self-disciplined; having no adornment
16. growing thick and healthily; fertile or plentiful
17. skillful or clever; artful
18. to ridicule or challenge by mocking
19. to interrupt or put into disorder
20. to oppose or obstruct; to baffle

down

1. to shorten or make less by cutting off some part
3. to subjugate or put into slavery
6. to obtain by force or illegal power
7. a substance that speeds up a chemical reaction; an agent that provokes change
9. awkward or lacking grace
11. to show by example; to serve as an example of
12. to offend with distastefulness; a strong aversion or dislike
13. learned or scholarly
14. to disturb or cause confusion to someone's peace of mind
15. drinkable

147

英単語は70万語以上ありますが、
頻繁に使われる単語は意外と多くありません。

11thDAY

alacrity
[əlǽkrəti]

n. eagerness; speed or quickness　　　　[名] やる気；素早さ、速さ

Bryan carried on his mission with great *alacrity*.

関連語 alacrity : apathetic [æ̀pəθétik]
apathetic（無関心な、やる気のない）な人には alacrity が欠けている。

albino
[ælbáinou]

n. abnormal pigmentation causing such characteristics as milky skin or white hair; a person or animal lacking normal pigmentation　　　[名] アルビノ（色素が少ない先天性の病気）

A U.S.-based Korean researcher has succeeded in changing white *albino* mice hairs to black by correcting their genetic mutation.

関連語 albinism : pigment [pígmənt]
albinism（アルビノであること）とは pigment（色素）が少ない症状をいう。

ambivalent
[æmbívələnt]

adj. characterized by a mixture of opposite attitudes or feelings; fluctuating in opinion　　　[形] 両面価値的な、相反する；どちらとも決めかねる

Even though Malcolm played a role in the company's technological revolution, he is *ambivalent* about the changes.

関連語 ambivalent : commitment [kəmítmənt]
ambivalent な態度の人は確実に commitment（約束、公約）することがない。

TRANSLATION ｜ 例 文 の 訳

alacrity　ブライアンは即座に任務を遂行した。

albino　アメリカを拠点に活動する韓国人研究者が、遺伝子変異を修正することで白いアルビノのネズミの毛を黒くすることに成功した。

ambivalent　マルコムはその会社の技術革新に一定の役割を果たしたにもかかわらず、その変化についてはどっちつかずの態度をしている。

ancillary
[ǽnsəlèri]

adj. **not of primary importance**   [形] 補助の、副次的な

After the pressing matters are discussed, the *ancillary* topics will be covered if there is leftover time.

反意語 ancillary : paramount [pǽrəmàunt]
ancillaryの反意語はparamount（最高の、最も重要な）

artifact
[áːrtəfækt]

n. **a manmade object of historical or archaeological interest**
                                        [名]（歴史的価値のある）人工遺物

The *artifacts* that were discovered in Italy have provided valuable information about how people lived thousands of years ago.

関連語 artifacts : museum [mjuːzíːəm]
museum（博物館）はartifactsを展示する場だ。

aseptic
[əséptik]

adj. **clear of pathogenic microorganisms**   [形] 無菌の

Doctors have to use *aseptic* instruments when treating patients to prevent infections.

関連語 aseptic : disinfection [dìsinfékʃən]
disinfection（消毒、滅菌）はものをasepticにすること。

atrocious
[ətróuʃəs]

adj. **appallingly inhumane; wicked**   [形] 残虐な、ひどい

Surviving *atrocious* living conditions, the family was finally able to move out of the slums.

関連語 atrocious : bad [bæd]
atrociousはbad（悪い）よりも程度が強い。

babble
[bǽbl]

v. **to utter meaningless sounds**   [動] 意味のないことを言う、ベラベラしゃべる

The stranger *babbled* endlessly about the reasons why I should buy his product.

反意語 babble : express succinctly [iksprés sʌksíŋktli]
babbleの反意語はexpress succinctly（簡潔に話す）

TRANSLATION | 例 文 の 訳

ancillary　緊急の問題を話し合ったあとで、もし時間が余れば補助的な話題が取り上げられる。

artifact　イタリアで発見された人工遺物は、数千年前に人々がどのように暮らしていたかについての貴重な情報を提供してきた。

aseptic　医師たちは患者を処置する際に、感染症を防ぐために無菌の器具を使わなければならない。

atrocious　ひどい生活状況を生き延びて、その家族はとうとうスラムから出ることができた。

babble　その見知らぬ人物は、なぜ私が彼の商品を買うべきなのかをまくしたてた。

beacon
[bíːkən]

n. a signaling device, such as a lighthouse; a signal fire

[名] (灯台などの) 灯火；信号灯

The *beacon* gave the lost sailors hope.

関連語 beacon : light [lait]
beacon には light (光) を出すという機能がある。

blazon
[bléizn]

n. a coat of arms

[名] 紋章

v. to adorn or embellish with

[動] 〜を飾る

A dove was added to the country's *blazon* following the ratification of the peace treaty.

The knight, *blazoned* with armor, charged the gates of the castle.

関連語 blazon : adorn [ədɔ́ːˈn]
blazon (紋章) は adorn (〜を飾る) することに使われる。

brattish
[brǽtiʃ]

adj. often used in reference to a spoiled child

[形] しつけのなっていない

The *brattish* child was scolded by his mother for his rude behavior in front of the guests.

類義語 brattish : mischievous [místʃivəs]
brattish の類義語は mischievous (有害な、いたずら好きな)

chagrin
[ʃəgrín]

n. a feeling of frustration or embarrassment caused by failure or disappointment

[名] (失敗による) くやしさ、無念

Much to his *chagrin*, Phillip didn't receive the promotion his boss promised.

反意語 chagrin : elation [iléiʃən]
chagrin の反意語は elation (大喜び、意気揚々)

coagulate
[kouǽgjulèit]

v. to transform from a liquid into a mass

[動] 液体を凝固させる

There was *coagulated* blood at the corners of Hector's mouth.

関連語 coagulant : clot [klɑt]
coagulant (凝固剤) には clot (〜を凝固させる) するという機能がある。

TRANSLATION | 例 文 の 訳

beacon	その灯台の光は漂流する船員たちに希望を与えた。
blazon	平和条約を批准してから、その国の紋章にハトが加わった。
	鎧で身を固めた騎士が、その城の門に突撃した。
brattish	しつけのなっていないその子供は、客たちの前での無礼な態度を母親に叱られた。
chagrin	実に残念なことに、フィリップは上司が彼に約束していた昇進がかなわなかった。
coagulate	ヘクターの口の脇には固まった血がついていた。

craven
[kréivən]

adj. **lacking courage; cowardly** [形] 勇気のない；臆病な

The *craven* soldiers were the first to die on the battlefield.

関連語 craven : dastard [dǽstərd]
dastard（臆病者）には craven だという特徴がある。

dabble
[dǽbl]

v. **to engage in or do something superficially; to splash and play in water** [動] ～をかじる；水しぶきを上げて遊ぶ

Although Tyrone *dabbled* in learning many languages, he was fluent in none.

反意語 dabbler : specialist [spéʃəlist]
dabbler（道楽半分でする人）の反意語は specialist（専門家）

deadpan
[dédpæ̀n]

adj. **marked by a void of expression** [形] 無表情な

His face remained *deadpan* throughout the poker game.

関連語 deadpan : impassive [impǽsiv]
deadpan と似た意味の形容詞に impassive（無表情な、無感動な）がある。

debase
[dibéis]

v. **to lower in value or quality** [動] ～の価値や質を落とす

The euro has dramatically *debased* the value of the Turkish lira.

関連語 debase : value [vǽlju:]
value（価値）を dabase する。

debate
[dibéit]

v. **to engage in a formal discussion** [動] ～を討論する
n. **a formal argument or a discussion with opposing points** [名] 討論、議論

The two presidential candidates *debated* on public television.
Both the participants brought up points during the *debate*.

類義語 debate : issue [íʃu:]
debate の類義語は issue（問題、争点）

TRANSLATION | 例 文 の 訳

craven 臆病な兵士たちが真っ先に戦場で死んだ。
dabble ティローンはたくさんの言語をかじったが、一つも流ちょうに話せない。
deadpan ポーカーをしている間、彼の顔はずっと無表情だった。
debase ユーロに対するトルコリラの価値が暴落した。
debate 2人の大統領候補が公営テレビで討論した。
参加者双方が討論中に重要な論点を持ち出した。

debilitate [dibílətèit]	v. **to weaken the strength of**	[動] 〜を衰弱させる、弱体化させる

Throwing for nine innings *debilitated* the pitcher's arm.

関連語 debilitate : strength [streŋkθ]
　　　strength（力、強さ）を debilitate する。

draconian [dreikóuniən]	adj. **very severe or harsh**	[形] （法などが）厳しい、過酷な

Many people believe that modern immigration laws are *draconian*.

関連語 draconian : severity [səvérəti]
　　　draconian と似た意味の名詞に severity（厳格さ、厳しさ）がある。

drain [drein]	v. **to cause liquid to go out from**	[動] 〜を排水させる、〜の水を抜く

When the lake was *drained*, the lost boat was found.

関連語 drain : colander [kʌləndəʳ]
　　　colander（料理用の水切りボール）には drain する機能がある。

dubious [d(j)ú:biəs]	adj. **having or showing doubt; creating uncertainty**	[形] 疑わしいと思う；疑わしい

Coach Nelson was *dubious* about his team's chances of winning after they failed to score.

関連語 dubious : conviction [kənvíkʃən]
　　　dubious な人には conviction（信念、確信）が欠けている。

embarrass [imbǽrəs]	v. **to place in doubt, perplexity, or difficulties**	[動] 困らせる、恥をかかせる、〜を追い詰める

The young lady was *embarrassed* by the man's attention.

関連語 embarrassment : humiliation [ʰju:mìliéiʃºn]
　　　humiliation（恥、屈辱）は embarrassment（当惑、恥ずかしさ）よりももっと恥ずかしく、不安な感情を表す。

TRANSLATION | 例 文 の 訳

debilitate	9回にわたる投球がそのピッチャーの腕を疲弊させた。
draconian	多くの人々が現在の移民法を厳しいと思っている。
drain	湖の水が抜かれると、行方不明の船が見つかった。
dubious	チームが得点できなかったので、ネルソン監督は勝利の可能性を疑った。
embarrass	その若い女性は、男性に注目されて恥ずかしくなった。

11th
12th
13th
14th
15th
16th
17th
18th
19th
20th

exacerbate
[igzǽsəᶃbèit]

v. **to increase the severity of** 　　　　　[動] ～をさらに悪化させる

Pollution *exacerbates* the depletion of the ozone layer.

類義語 exacerbate : deprave [dipréiv]
　exacerbate の類義語は deprave（～を堕落させる、腐敗させる）

exaggerate
[igzǽdʒərèit]

v. **to overstate the truth** 　　　　　[動] ～を大げさに言う、誇張するな

We couldn't trust what she said because she always *exaggerates*.

関連語 exaggerated : hyperbole [haipə́ᶃbəli]
　hyperbole（誇張法、誇張）は exaggerated（誇張された、大げさな）だという特徴がある。

fidget
[fídʒit]

v. **to move uneasily due to anxiety or restlessness** 　　　　　[動] そわそわする、もじもじする

During a job interview, one must remember to appear calm and confident by not *fidgeting*.

関連語 fidget : nervousness [nə́ᶃvəsnis]
　fidget は nervousness（神経質、いらいら）を持った結果、現れる。

flaccid
[flǽksid]

adj. **lacking normal firmness** 　　　　　[形] しまりのない、軟弱な

Many months of not exercising made Andrew's body *flaccid*.

関連語 flaccid : firmness [fə́ᶃmnis]
　flaccid なものには firmness（堅さ、堅いなこと）がない。

flatter
[flǽtəᶃ]

v. **to excessively compliment with self-directed intentions** 　　　　　[動] おだてる、～にお世辞を言う

A person who knows how to *flatter* also knows how to slander.

関連語 flatter : adulate [ǽdʒəlèit]
　adulate（～を過度に絶賛する）は flatter よりも程度が強い。

TRANSLATION | 例 文 の 訳

exacerbate 汚染がオゾン層の破壊を促進させる。

exaggerate 彼女はいつも物事を誇張するので、私たちは彼女の言ったことを信じられなかった。

fidget 就職の面接の間は、そわそわせずに落ち着いて、自信のある様子を見せることを忘れてはならない。

flaccid 何カ月も運動していなかったせいで、アンドリューの体にはしまりがなかった。

flatter お世辞の上手な人間は人を中傷するのも上手い。

153

flaw
[flɔː]

n. a fault or imperfection that devalues the whole

[名] 傷、不備、欠陥、欠点

Anne's lack of experience was the only *flaw* on her resume.

関連語 flaw : glitch [glitʃ]
glitch（問題、不調）は重大ではないflawを表す。

fragile
[frǽdʒəl]

adj. weak and easily broken

[形] もろい、壊れやすい

All the *fragile* china broke when the mover dropped the box.

類義語 fragile : frail [freil]
fragileの類義語がfrail（壊れやすい）

frailty
[fréilti]

n. physical weakness; a fault, especially a moral weakness

[名] 体の弱さ；欠点、性格の弱さ

You should be very careful when you are handling babies because of their *frailty*.

関連語 frailty : spindly [spíndli]
frailtyと似た意味の形容詞にspindly（弱々しい）がある。

fraud
[frɔːd]

n. an intentional deception of the truth committed for personal gain at the expense of another

[名] 詐欺

Force and *fraud* are the two cardinal virtues in war.

関連語 fraudulent : hoax [houks]
hoax（いたずら、悪ふざけ）にはfraudulent（詐欺の、不正な）という特徴がある。

gibberish
[dʒíbəriʃ]

n. unintelligible or nonsensical talk or writing

[名] ちんぷんかんぷん、理解できない言葉

Mrs. Earnshaw repeated over and over again some *gibberish* that nobody could understand.

関連語 gibberish : intelligible [intélədʒəbl]
gibberishは intelligible（理解できる、わかりやすい）なものではない。

TRANSLATION | 例 文 の 訳

flaw	経験不足がアンの経歴における唯一の欠点だった。
fragile	引っ越し業者が箱を落としたときに、壊れやすい陶器がすべて割れてしまった。
frailty	赤ん坊は体が弱いので、扱いには十分に注意すべきだ。
fraud	力を行使することと裏をかくことが、戦争における2つの枢要である。
gibberish	アーンショー夫人は、だれにもわからないちんぷんかんぷんな言葉を何度も繰り返した。

gibe
[dʒaib]

n. a mocking or derisive comment　　　　　[名] 嘲笑、からかい

v. to tease with taunting remarks　　　　　[動] あざける、からかう

The crowd gave a *gibe* to the old king as he marched in the town.

The young maid *gibed* the young shepherd.

類義語 gibe : derision [diríʒən]
　gibeの類義語は derision（あざけり、嘲笑）

glaze
[gleiz]

v. to apply a smooth, glossy surface to　　　　　[形] 〜に釉薬を塗る

The chef *glazed* the pastries with a thin layer of strawberry syrup.

関連語 glaze : porcelain [pɔ́ːˤsˤlin]
　porcelain（磁器）を glaze する。

gratify
[grǽtəfài]

v. to give pleasure or satisfaction to　　　　　[動] 〜を喜ばせる、満足させる

It would *gratify* grandmother if you would stop cursing.

関連語 gratify : desire [dizaiəˤ]
　gratifyは desire（願望、欲望）を満足させるという意味。

gratuitous
[grət(j)úːətəs]

adj. unwarranted; free　　　　　[形] 根拠のない；無料の

The doctor claimed that the charges of malpractice were *gratuitous* but the prosecutor insisted he had evidence to back up the charge.

反意語 gratuitous : warranted [wɔ́(ː)rəntid]
　gratuitousの反意語は warranted（保証された、正当化された）

gravity
[grǽvəti]

n. the severe importance and seriousness of a person or situation　　　　　[名]（人や事態の）重大さ、深刻さ、真剣さ

The *gravity* of the situation hit the group like a ton of bricks.

関連語 gravity : frivolous [frívələs]
　frivolous（軽薄な）な人は gravity が欠けている。

TRANSLATION | 例文の訳

gibe 　群衆は年老いた王が町を行進すると嘲笑した。
その少女は若い羊飼いをあざ笑った。

glaze 　そのシェフはペストリーにイチゴシロップを薄く塗ってつやを出した。

gratify 　あなたが悪態をつくのをやめたら、祖母は喜ぶだろう。

gratuitous 　医師はその医療ミスの告発に根拠がないと主張したが、検察官は告発を裏づける証拠があると主張した。

gravity 　事態の深刻さが、その集団に大打撃を与えた。

green [griːn]	adj. **marked by lack of experience or sophistication** [形] 未熟な、経験不足の The veteran could see that though the young man was *green* he had a great deal of potential. 関連語 green : experience [ikspíˀriəns] greenな人には experience（経験）が欠けている。
headlong [hédlɔ̀ːŋ]	adj. **marked by impulse and little or no forethought** [形] 向こう見ずに、軽率に Tom always fell *headlong* in love with beautiful women before he really got to know them. 反意語 headlong : deliberate [dilíbərət] headlongの反意語は deliberate（慎重な、よく考えた）
inaugurate [inɔ́ːg(j)urèit]	v. **to bring into office with a ceremony; to begin with a ceremony** [動] 〜の就任式を行う；（式をして施設などを）開く The president was *inaugurated* with the biggest celebration ever seen in Washington D.C. 関連語 inauguration : official [əfíʃəl] inauguration（就任式、落成式）は officialな始まりを示すもの。
leaden [lédn]	adj. **heavy and inert; downcast and depressed** [形] 重い、だるい；がっかりした、落ち込んだ The woman's heart was *leaden* upon hearing the news of her friend's passing. 反意語 leaden : vivacious [vivéiʃəs] leadenの反意語は vivacious（活発な、元気な）

TRANSLATION | 例 文 の 訳

green	そのベテランは、未熟とはいえ、その若者には大きな可能性があることがわかった。
headlong	トムはいつも、よく知りもしない美女と軽々しく恋に落ちた。
inaugurate	大統領はワシントンDCで、これまでで最大規模の就任式を開いた。
leaden	友人の死去の知らせを聞いて、その女性の心は重くなった。

lien
[liːn]

n. a legal claim to take over another's property if an obligation is not met or debt repaid　［名］先取特権、留置権

The *lien* gave the bank possession of the house unless a deposit was made within the next 24 hours.

関連語 lien : claim [kleim]
lien は claim（要求、請求）という属性を持っている。

matriculation
[mətrìkjuléiʃən]

n. admission of students into a college or group　［名］大学入学許可

Matriculation at Harvard is considered to be a great accomplishment.

関連語 matriculation : student [st(j)úːdnt]
matriculation は student（学生）に与えるものだ。

meager
[míːgəʳ]

adj. lacking in quality or quantity　［形］貧弱な、不十分な

Dan's monthly salary was too *meager* for him to afford a new car.

反意語 meagerness : amplitude [ǽmplət(j)ùːd]
meagerness（貧弱、不十分）の反意語は amplitude（大きさ、強さ、豊かさ）

nucleate
[n(j)úːklièit]

v. to gather together into a nucleus　［動］中心に集まる

The students had already *nucleated* around the campfire.

反意語 nucleate : scatter [skǽtər]
nucleate の反意語は scatter（散らばる）

opacity
[oupǽsəti]

n. the quality of not being transparent; the state of mental dullness　［名］不透明；愚鈍

The curtain's *opacity* was just perfect for my room.

関連語 opacity : translucent [trænsljúːsnt]
translucent（半透明の）なものには opacity が欠けている。

TRANSLATION | 例 文 の 訳

lien 24時間以内に保証金が払われなければ、抵当権に基づいて銀行がその家を所有することになっていた。

matriculation ハーバード大に合格することは偉業だと考えられている。

meager 月給が少なすぎて、ダンに新しい車を買う余裕がなかった。

nucleate 学生たちはすでにキャンプファイヤーの周りに集まっていた。

opacity そのカーテンは不透明で、私の部屋にぴったりだった。

placate
[pléikeit]

v. **to appease by making concessions**
[動] 〜をなだめる、慰める、（怒りなどを）和らげる

William *placated* his girlfriend's anger by sending her flowers.

関連語 placate : irascible [irǽsəbl]
irascible（怒りっぽい）な人を placate するのは難しい。

placebo
[pləsí:bou]

n. **a medication prescribed more for the mental relief of the patient than for its actual effect on a disorder** [名] プラシーボ、偽薬

The doctor gave the paranoid patient a *placebo*.

関連語 placebo : noxious [nákʃəs]
placebo は noxious（有害な、健康に悪い）ではない。

prairie
[préºri]

n. **a large area of treeless grassland** [名] 大草原

Prairies are good grazing lands for cattle.

関連語 prairie : tree [tri:]
prairie は tree（木）のない草原を表す。

praise
[preiz]

n. **expression of approval or admiration; the exaltation of a deity or ruler** [名] 賞賛；崇拝

The ancient Egyptians' *praise* for the sun god Ra was an integral part of their religion.

関連語 praise : hymn [him]
hymn（讃美歌、聖歌）は praise する歌である。

slacken
[slǽkən]

v. **to slow down; to make less tense** [動] 〜を遅くする；緩める

The prisoner's handcuffs were *slackened* after complaining they were too tight.

関連語 slacken : tension [ténʃən]
tension（緊張）を slacken する。

TRANSLATION | 例 文 の 訳

placate ウィリアムは花を送って恋人の怒りを和らげた。
placebo その医師は偏執狂の患者に偽薬を与えた。
prairie 大草原は、優れた家畜の放牧地だ。
praise 古代エジプト人の太陽神ラーへの崇拝は、彼らの宗教における肝要な部分だった。
slacken その囚人は、手錠がきつすぎると苦情を言って緩めてもらった。

slake
[sleik]

v. **to satisfy a craving**　　　[動]（飢え・渇きなどを）いやす、（欲望などを）満たす

Tarzan went to the brook first and *slaked* his thirst.

関連語 slake : thirst [θəːˈst]
slakeはthirst（渇き）をいやすという意味。

soak
[souk]

v. **to make saturated by placing in liquid**
　　　　　　　　　　　　　　[動] 〜を液体に浸す、つける；びしょぬれにする

The following Monday morning a heavy rain *soaked* the yard around Barbara's house.

関連語 soak : damp [dæmp]
soakはdamp（〜を湿らす）よりも全体を濡らす。

stability
[stəbíləti]

n. **resistance to change of position or condition**　　　[名] 安定（性）

The *stability* of a nation depends on its people.

関連語 stability : ballast [bǽləst]
ballast（船を安定させるために船底に積む砂利など）によってstabilityを維持する。

staff
[stæf]

n. **a long stick used for support of the body during walking; the persons assigned to assist a commander or director**　　　[名] 杖；職員

The man carried his *staff* and bundle in hand.

The director announced that there would be a *staff* meeting at 8 a.m. the next morning.

関連語 staff : walk [wɔːk]
walk（歩くこと）を支える補助器具がstaff。

関連語 staff : roster [rɑ́stəˈ]
staffの名前が書かれているのがroster（職員名簿）。

TRANSLATION | 例 文 の 訳

slake	ターザンは最初に小川に行き、渇きをいやした。
soak	翌月曜日の朝に大雨が降り、バーバラの家の周りの庭は水浸しになった。
stability	国の安定はその国民に依存している。
staff	その男は手に杖と包みを持って運んでいた。
	その役員は翌朝8時に職員会議があると発表した。

staid
[steid]

adj. having a state of permanence or sedateness

[形] まじめな、古風な、堅苦しい

Darcy is typically a *staid* and unanimated person.

反意語 staid : jaunty [dʒɔ́:nti]
staid の反意語は jaunty（軽快な、陽気な）

swagger
[swǽgəʳ]

v. to walk with an air of arrogance

[動] いばって歩く

The prince has a tendency to *swagger* as he walks through the palace.

類義語 swagger : strut [strʌt]
swagger の類義語は strut（気取って歩く）

tractable
[trǽktəbl]

adj. easily handled or controlled

[形] 扱いやすい

Parents are happy with their children so long as they are *tractable* and obedient.

反意語 tractable : balky [bɔ́:ki]
tractable の反意語は balky（言うことを聞かない、強情な）

zeal
[zi:l]

n. passionate devotion and eager pursuit of something

[名] 熱意、熱心さ

Bryan contributed much *zeal* and enthusiasm to the project.

関連語 zeal : dedication [dèdikéiʃən]
zeal は dedication（献身）よりも特定の物事に対する強い熱意を表す。

TRANSLATION | 例 文 の 訳

staid	ダーシーはいつも、まじめで陰気な人物だ。
swagger	その王子は宮殿の中をいばって歩くたちだ。
tractable	親は、扱いやすくて従順でいる限り、子供たちに満足するものだ。
zeal	ブライアンはそのプロジェクトに大変な熱意と情熱を注いだ。

160

■ Fill in the blanks with the correct letter that matches the word with its definition.

1. tractable _____
2. brattish _____
3. exacerbate _____
4. gratuitous _____
5. chagrin _____
6. deadpan _____
7. ambivalent _____
8. meager _____
9. staid _____
10. debilitate _____

a. a feeling of frustration or embarrassment caused by failure or disappointment
b. easily handled or controlled
c. characterized by a mixture of opposite attitudes or feelings; fluctuating in opinion
d. often used in reference to a spoiled child
e. to increase the severity of
f. unwarranted; free
g. to weaken the strength of
h. having a state of permanence or sedateness
i. lacking in quality or quantity
j. marked by a void of expression

■ Put the correct word in each blank from the list of words below.

11. humiliation は_____よりもより恥ずかしく、不安な感情を示す。

12. irascible な人を_____することは容易ではない。

13. hoax は_____という特徴を持つ。

14. _____は bad (悪い) よりも強い表現である。

15. damp よりもしっかり濡らすのが_____である。

16. _____は adorn することに使用される。

17. roster には_____の名前が書かれている。

18. _____は jaunty (軽快な、陽気な) の反意語である。

19. _____の反意語は balky (言うことを聞かない、強情な) である。

20. _____は液体を clot させる。

| a. soak | b. atrocious | c. staid | d. placate | e. staff | f. blazon |
| g. fraudulent | h. embarrassment | i. slake | j. coagulant | k. craven | l. tractable |

Answer key

11. h 12. d 13. g 14. b 15. a 16. f 17. e 18. c 19. l 20. j
1. b 2. d 3. e 4. f 5. a 6. j 7. c 8. i 9. h 10. g

161

ある日突然、その単語が
必要になるかもしれません。
そのときに備えて、覚えておきましょう。

12th DAY

---

abandon
[əbǽndən]

v. to give up a person, objects, or responsibility with the
intention of never returning to it　　[動] 〜を見捨てる；〜を捨てる、手放す

As time passed, some rituals were *abandoned*.

反意語 abandon : retain [ritéin]
abandonの反意語は retain（〜を保つ、保持する）

---

adamant
[ǽdəmənt]

adj. stubbornly unyielding; inflexible　　[形] 断固として譲らない；屈しない

n. a very hard substance　　[名] 非常に堅いもの

The boy's *adamant* refusal to do his chores angered his mother.

The knights made their hearts hard as *adamant*.

関連語 adamant : flexibility [flèksəbíləti]
adamantな人やものには flexibility（柔軟性）が欠けている。

---

alienable
[éiljənəbl]

adj. transferable to another person's ownership　　[形] 譲渡できる

Grandfather Jefferson arranged the inheritance to be legally *alienable*, in
case his son made poor decisions with the money.

反意語 inalienable : surrendered [səréndəʳd]
alienableの反意語は inalienable（譲渡できない）。似た意味の形容詞に surrendered
（譲渡された、引き渡された）がある。

---

amalgamate
[əmǽlgəmèit]

v. to combine into a single unit or whole　　[動] 〜を合併する；〜と融合する

The two companies, both fearing bankruptcy, *amalgamated* into one
corporation to minimize expenses.

反意語 amalgamate : disintegrate [disíntigrèit]
amalgamateの反意語は disintegrate（〜を分解する、崩壊させる）

TRANSLATION | 例 文 の 訳

abandon　　時間がたつにつれて、儀式のいくつかは行われなくなった。

adamant　　その少年は、家の手伝いを断固拒否して母親を怒らせた。
　　　　　　　騎士たちはこの上なく強く心を決めた。

alienable　　祖父のジェファーソンは、息子がお金の判断を誤った場合に備えて、遺産を法的に譲渡できるよ
　　　　　　　うにした。

amalgamate　その2社はともに倒産を懸念しており、損失を最小限に抑えるために合併して1つの企業になった。

analgesia
[ǽnəldʒíːziə]

n. the inability to feel pain but without a loss of consciousness
[名] 無痛、痛覚の消失

The patient asked the doctor to put her into a state of *analgesia* before the operation.

関連語 analgesic : ache [eik]
analgesic（鎮痛剤）は ache（痛み）をなくすためのもの。

antidote
[ǽntidòut]

n. an agent used to counteract a poisonous or noxious substance
[名] 解毒剤

This is a deadly poison because there is no known *antidote* in existence.

関連語 antidote : poisoning [pɔ́izᵊniŋ]
antidote は poisoning（中毒）を解毒するもの。

aqueduct
[ǽkwədʌkt]

n. a pipe or channel that usually supplies large cities with its water supply
[名] 水道、送水路

A malfunction in the city's main *aqueduct* would inconvenience thousands of households.

関連語 aqueduct : water [wɔ́ːtəʳ]
aqueduct には water（水）を供給する機能がある。

barb
[baːʳb]

n. a cutting comment
[名] とげのある言葉

Jim was hurt by the sarcastic *barb* made by his boss at his expense.

関連語 barb : caustic [kɔ́ːstik]
barb は caustic（辛辣な、手厳しい）だという特徴がある。

blanch
[blæntʃ]

v. to take the color out of; to cause to become pale
[動] 〜を漂白する；青ざめさせる

The dry cleaner *blanched* Steve's favorite white shirt for his upcoming job interview.

反意語 blanch : mottle [mάtl]
blanch の反意語は mottle（〜をまだらにする）

TRANSLATION | 例 文 の 訳

analgesia	その患者は、手術前に自分を無痛状態にしてくれるように医者に頼んだ。
antidote	まだ解毒剤が見つかっていない以上、これは致命的な毒物だ。
aqueduct	都市の主要な水道管が機能を失うと、何千世帯もに不便が生じる。
barb	ジムは、彼の出費に対する上司の皮肉っぽくとげのある言葉に傷ついた。
blanch	クリーニング店が、スティーブのお気に入りの白いシャツを就職の面接に備えて漂白してくれた。

bland
[blænd]

adj. gentle in manner; lacking distinctive flavor; not stimulating

[形] 感情を示さない；味のない；退屈な

Although fresh, the food was rather *bland*.

反意語 bland : tangy [tǽŋi]
bland の反意語は tangy（味の強い）

blandish
[blǽndiʃ]

v. to persuade in a flattering manner

[動] 〜をおだてて丸め込む、こびへつらう

The employee *blandished* her boss into giving her a promotion.

関連語 blandishment : coax [kouks]
blandishment（追従、甘言）は他人を coax（なだめすかす、〜へと誘う）するために使用する言葉。

chameleon
[kəmíːliən]

n. a lizard with the ability to change color of the skin; a changeable or inconstant person

[名] カメレオン；気まぐれな人

My boyfriend changes hairstyles like a *chameleon*.

関連語 chameleon : herpetologist [hə̀ːˈpətálədʒist]
herpetologist（爬虫類・両生類学者）は chameleon などの爬虫類を研究する。

coalesce
[kòuəlés]

v. to come together

[動] 合体する、結合する

Two stars *coalesced* and shone brightly as one.

反意語 coalesce : disaggregate [disǽgrigèit]
coalesce の反意語は disaggregate（要素に分ける）

TRANSLATION | 例 文 の 訳

bland	新鮮ではあったが、その食べ物には味があまりなかった。
blandish	その従業員は上司をおだてて昇進させてもらった。
chameleon	私のボーイフレンドはカメレオンのように髪形を変える。
coalesce	2つの星が合体し、1つの星のように明るく輝いた。

cramp
[kræmp]

n. a sharp pain caused by a sudden contraction of a muscle; something that restrains freedom of function

[名] けいれん；束縛するもの

Mrs. Hooven found herself assailed by sharp pains and *cramps* in her stomach.

反意語 cramped : commodious [kəmóudiəs]
cramped（手狭な、狭苦しい）の反意語は commodious（広々している）

deploy
[diplɔ́i]

v. to spread out men in battle systematically or strategically

[動]（部隊などを）配置する

U.S. troops were *deployed* in order to cover the border area.

反意語 deploy : concentrate [kánsəntrèit]
deploy の反意語が concentrate（～を集める）

depose
[dipóuz]

v. to make a statement under oath

[動] 証言する

Irene was brought to the stand and she *deposed* that she had seen the murder.

反意語 depose : perjure [pə́ːrdʒər]
depose の反意語は perjure（偽証する）

desiccant
[désikənt]

n. a substance that absorbs moisture or water; a drying agent

[名] 乾燥剤

Desiccants are used in packages to keep the products from getting wet.

関連語 desiccant : dry [drai]
desiccant は dry（～を乾燥させる）という機能がある。

TRANSLATION | 例 文 の 訳

cramp   フーヴェン夫人は鋭い腹痛と胃けいれんに襲われた。
deploy   国境地帯を守るために米軍が配置された。
depose   アイリーンは証言台に上がり、殺人を目撃したと証言した。
desiccant 乾燥剤は、製品が湿らないように包装の中に入れられる。

11th
12th
13th
14th
15th
16th
17th
18th
19th
20th

165

disentangle
[dìsentǽŋgl]

v. to free from entanglement or difficulty　　　[動] ～を解放する、解き放つ

In order to *disentangle* himself from the whole mess, he would have to go to the police and turn himself in.

反意語 disentangle : snarl [snɑːʳl]
　　　disentangleの反意語は snarl（～をもつれさせる）

emancipate
[imǽnsəpèit]

v. to free from oppression or bondage　　　[動]（圧迫、束縛などから）解放する

Abraham Lincoln helped to *emancipate* the slaves of North America.

反意語 emancipate : shackle [ʃǽkl]
　　　emancipateの反意語は shackle（～を拘束する、束縛する）

evanescent
[èvənésnt]

adj. vanishing like vapor　　　[形] 一瞬の、すぐに消えていく

The change was subtle, *evanescent*, and hard to define, but unmistakable.

関連語 evanescent : permanency [pə́ːʳmᵊnᵊnsi]
　　　evanescentなものには permanency（永続性）が欠けている。

exalt
[igzɔ́ːlt]

v. to intensify; to elevate in rank, power, or character; to extol
　　　　　　　　　　　　　　　　　　[動] ～を強める；昇進させる；絶賛する

The people *exalted* the newly elected prime minister for his charisma and insight.

反意語 exalt : execrate [éksəkrèit]
　　　exaltの反意語は execrate（～をののしる）

ford
[fɔːʳd]

n. a shallow area in a body of water where it is possible to cross
　　　　　　　　　　　　　　　　　　　　　　　　　　　[名] 浅瀬

The boys could not cross the river because it was still a mile away to the next *ford*.

関連語 ford : river [rívəʳ]
　　　fordは river（川）の浅い個所をさす。

TRANSLATION | 例 文 の 訳

disentangle	そのひどい混乱から逃れるためには、彼は警察に行って自供しなければならないだろう。
emancipate	エイブラハム・リンカーンは北米の奴隷解放を助けた。
evanescent	その変化は些細で、一瞬で、わかりにくいが、紛れもないものだった。
exalt	人々は新しく選出された首相のカリスマ性と洞察力を絶賛した。
ford	次の浅瀬がまだ1マイルも先だったので、少年たちは川を渡ることができなかった。

11th
12th
13th
14th
15th
16th
17th
18th
19th
20th

fungi
[fʌ́ndʒai]

n. a subdivision of plants which include molds, mushrooms, and mildews　　　　　　　　　　　　　　　　　　[名] 菌類、キノコ類

Diane was a botanist who specialized in the study of *fungi*.

関連語 fungi : ecologist [iːkálədʒist]
fungiは ecologist（生態学者）の研究対象になる。

fury
[fjúˀri]

n. intense anger or rage　　　　　　　　　　　　　　　　　　　[名] 激怒

The father hid his *fury* in front of the guests.

関連語 fury : anger [ǽŋgəˀ]
furyは anger（怒り）がさらに強くなった状態を表す。

grandeur
[grǽndʒəˀ]

n. the quality of being grand or magnificent　　　　　　　[名] 壮大さ、雄大さ

Everyone who sees the mountains is impressed by their *grandeur*.

反意語 grandeur : frivolousness [frívələsnis]
grandeurの反意語は frivolousness（軽薄、浅薄）

grandiloquent
[grændíləkwənt]

adj. extravagant in language or manner　　　　　[形]（言葉や態度が）おおげさな

The winner's *grandiloquent* speech was too much for the audience.

関連語 grandiloquent : language [lǽŋgwidʒ]
grandiloquentはおおげさな language（言葉遣い）を表す。

inane
[inéin]

adj. lacking substance or meaning; void of sense or intelligence
　　　　　　　　　　　　　　　　　　　　　　　　　　[形] ばかげた；意味のない

Jack suddenly came to the realization that his life thus far had been *inane* and purposeless.

反意語 inane : meaningful [míːniŋfəl]
inaneの反意語は meaningful（重要な、意味のある）

TRANSLATION | 例 文 の 訳

fungi　　　　ダイアンは菌類の研究が専門の植物学者だった。
fury　　　　父親は客たちの前では怒りを隠した。
grandeur　　山を見る人は皆、その雄大さに感動する。
grandiloquentその勝者のおおげさな演説に聴衆はうんざりした。
inane　　　　ジャックは、それまでの自分の人生がばかげて意味のないものだったことに突然気づいた。

167

liberal
[líbərˀl]

adj. **marked by generosity; not limited to established attitudes or views** [形] 寛大な；自由主義の

Monet's *liberal* use of color in his paintings became a trademark for his later works.

関連語 liberality : generous [dʒénˀrəs]
liberality（理解、寛容さ）に似た意味の形容詞がgenerous（気前のよい、寛容な）

libertine
[líbəʳtìːn]

n. **a person free of moral restrictions usually in reference to men** [名] 放蕩者（主に男性をいう）

The *libertine* was known as a Casanova who sought the company of women.

関連語 libertine : dissolute [dísəlùːt]
libertineにはdissolute（ふしだらな、放蕩な）だという特徴がある。

nibble
[níbl]

v. **to eat in small bites** [動] 少しずつかじる

Tom divided the cake, and Becky *nibbled* at her piece.

関連語 nibble : gobble [gábl]
gobble（がつがつ食べる）はnibbleよりも一度にたくさん食べる様子を表す。

nuance
[n(j)úːɑːns]

n. **a subtle distinction or variation** [名] 微妙な違い、ニュアンス

There were *nuances* in the artist's paintings that only the trained eye could catch.

関連語 nuance : distinction [distíŋkʃən]
nuanceはdistinction（区別、違い）よりも非常に微妙である。

plangent
[plǽndʒənt]

adj. **having a loud and resounding sound** [形] 大きく鳴り響く

From across the street I could hear the demonstrators' *plangent* cries.

反意語 plangent : muffled [mʌfld]
plangentの反意語はmuffled（はっきり聞こえない）

TRANSLATION | 例 文 の 訳

liberal	モネの絵画における自由な色使いは、彼の後期の作品の特徴になった。
libertine	その放蕩者は、常に女性と一緒にいたがる女たらしとして知られていた。
nibble	トムがケーキを分けると、ベッキーは自分の分を少しずつかじった。
nuance	その画家の絵画には、目利きだけが気づくことができる微妙なニュアンスがあった。
plangent	道路の反対側から、抗議者たちの大きな叫び声が聞こえた。

plausible
[plɔ́:zəbl]

adj. logically possible or seemingly true　　　[形] もっともな、ありうる

It is *plausible* that two people could fall in love at first sight, but it doesn't happen often.

関連語 plausible : rationalization [ræ̀ʃⁿəlizèiʃən]
　　rationalization（合理化）しているものは plausible な特徴がある。

primp
[primp]

v. to take excessive care in dressing; to groom oneself
　　　　　　　　　　　　　　　　　　　　　　　[動] 着飾る；めかしこむ

All the girls met at Becky's house to *primp* themselves before the prom.

類義語 primp : preen [pri:n]
　　primp の類義語は preen（入念に身づくろいをする、着飾る）

qualify
[kwáləfài]

v. to make eligible for a job; to modify or restrict by giving exceptions　　　[動] 〜の資格を与える；（前言などを）修正する、制限する

Edgar was asked to *qualify* his remark about the president's inadequacy.

反意語 qualified : categorical [kæ̀təgɔ́:rikəl]
　　qualified（資格を有する、条件付きの）の反意語は categorical（無条件の）

rabble
[rǽbl]

n. a confused or complicated crowd that lacks control; a tumultuous crowd of vulgar, noisy people　　　[名] 野次馬；暴徒

The police soon lost all control as the *rabble* swarmed the barricades.

類義語 rabble : mob [mɑb]
　　rabble の類義語は mob（暴徒）

rabid
[rǽbid]

adj. crazy or extreme in actions and thought　　　[形] 過激な、猛烈な

The *rabid* protestors took the streets of Milan with a fury.

関連語 rabid : composure [kəmpóuʒəʳ]
　　rapid な人には composure（落ち着き、平静）が欠けている。

TRANSLATION | 例 文 の 訳

plausible	2人が互いに一目ぼれすることはありうるだろうが、しょっちゅう起きることではない。
primp	プロムに備えて着飾るために、女の子たちは全員ベッキーの家に集まった。
qualify	エドガーは、社長が不適格だという彼の発言を撤回するよう求められた。
rabble	暴徒がバリケードに群がると、警察はすぐに制御できなくなった。
rabid	その過激な抗議者たちは激怒してミラノの通りを埋め尽くした。

rebel

v.[ribél]
n.[rébəl]

v. to fight against an established government　[動] 反乱を起こす

n. a person who rebels　[名] 反乱者、反逆者

The people *rebelled* against the socialist regime due to famine and poor living conditions.

The northern *rebels* were in hiding after defying the laws of the new regime.

関連語 rebel : anarchist [ǽnərˈkist]
政府に rebel する人が anarchist（無政府主義者）だ。

rubicund

[rú:bikʌnd]

adj. having a healthy reddish color　[形] 赤ら顔の、血色のよい

The typical images of Santa Clause depict a *rubicund* old man.

反意語 rubicund : wan [wɑn]
rubicund の反意語は wan（青ざめた、血の気のない）

scan

[skæn]

v. to examine quickly and systematically; to analyze into metrical patterns　[動] ～をざっと見る；（詩の）韻律を調べる

The literature major *scanned* the poem in search of iambic pentameter.

関連語 scan : metrical [métrikəl]
scan は metrical（韻律の）な面を分析するという意味がある。

scant

[skænt]

adj. having an inadequate or insufficient supply　[形] 十分でない；乏しい

Society has made *scant* progress in its efforts to curb environmental pollution.

反意語 scant : profuse [prəfjú:s]
scant の反意語は profuse（豊富な）

TRANSLATION | 例 文 の 訳

rebel	飢餓と貧しい生活環境のせいで、人々は社会主義体制に対して反乱を起こした。
	北部の反乱軍は新体制の法に公然と逆らった後、姿を隠していた。
rubicund	典型的なサンタクロースの姿は、血色のよい年老いた男性として描かれている。
scan	その文学専攻の学生は、弱強五歩格の研究でその詩の韻律を調べた。
scant	社会は環境汚染を抑制する取り組みにおいて、ほとんど進展を見せていない。

sham
[ʃæm]

adj. not genuine; fake　　　　　　　　　　[形] 見せかけの；偽の

n. a deceptive act of imitation; a counterfeit

[名] 見せかけ、いんちき；偽物

v. to pretend to be something; to feign　[動] ～のふりをする；～と見せかける

The *sham* diamonds were sold at an exorbitant price to unsuspecting customers.

She tried to be calm and indifferent, but it was a *sham*.

He *shamed* being ill to get out of the date.

反意語 sham : genuine [dʒénjuin]
　　sham の反意語は genuine（本物の）

sinew
[sínju:]

n. a cord or band that connects muscle and bone　　　[名] 腱

Having strong *sinews* means having muscular power.

類義語 sinewy : tendinous [téndənəs]
　　sinewy（腱のような）の類義語は tendinous（腱の）

spelunker
[spilʌ́ŋkəʳ]

n. one whose hobby is to explore caves　　　[名] 洞窟探検家

Spelunkers are daring people who like to discover new things and explore the unknown.

関連語 spelunker : cavern [kǽvəʳn]
　　spelunker は cavern（洞窟）を探検する。

stalemate
[stéilmèit]

n. the state of being deadlocked　　　[名] 行き詰まり

The industrial dispute at Waikato University remains at a *stalemate*.

関連語 stalemate : negotiations [nigòuʃiéiʃənz]
　　stalemate は negotiations（交渉）に進展がない状態を表す。

TRANSLATION | 例文の訳

sham　偽のダイヤモンドが、何の疑いも抱かない顧客たちに法外な値段で売られた。
　　彼女は落ち着いて無関心でいようと努めたが、それは見せかけだけに終わった。
　　彼はデートから逃げ出すために病気のふりをした。
sinew　強い腱を持っているということは、筋力があることを意味する。
spelunker　洞窟探検家は、新しいものを発見し、未知のものを探究することを好む勇気ある人々だ。
stalemate　ワイカト大学の労働争議は依然、膠着状態だ。

171

stalwart
[stɔ́:lwəʳt]

adj. characterized by outstanding strength of the body, mind, or spirit　　　　　　　[形] 断固とした、不屈の

n. one who is strong and sturdy in body; an unwavering supporter of an organization or cause　[名] 丈夫な人、がっしりとした人；忠誠心の強い人

The Secret Service is the *stalwart* security of the White House.

Without its usual band of *stalwarts*, the fundraising committee fell short of the target goal.

> 関連語 stalwart : constancy [kánstənsi]
> stalwart には constancy（安定、忠実）という特徴がある。

stammer
[stǽməʳ]

v. to speak with involuntary repetitions or stops　[動] どもる、口ごもる

Alexei was speaking so quickly that he began to *stammer*, unable to articulate the word suffering.

> 関連語 stammer : speak [spi:k]
> stammer は speak（話す）の一種。

stifle
[stáifl]

v. to smother or suffocate by confinement　　　　　　　　　　　　　　[動] 〜を抑制する、（声などを）抑える

Joanne's dreams of becoming an artist were *stifled* by her oppressive parents who wanted her to be a doctor.

> 反意語 stifle : foster [fɔ́(:)stəʳ]
> stifle の反意語は foster（〜を育成する、助長する）

subdue
[səbd(j)ú:]

v. to defeat; to reduce or tone down the intensity of　　　　　　　　　　[動] 〜を征服する；〜を抑える

Virtuous people have the ability to *subdue* the desire for power.

> 関連語 subdued : indomitable [indámətəbl]
> indomitable（不屈の、断固とした）な人は subdued（弱められた、ふさぎこんだ）になることがない。

TRANSLATION | 例 文 の 訳

stalwart	シークレットサービスはホワイトハウスの強固な安全保障を担う。
	常時、強力な支持者たちを集めておけなかったら、その資金調達委員会は目標金額を達成できなかっただろう。
stammer	アレクセイはあまりにも早口で話したためにどもってしまい、「苦しみ」という単語を明瞭に発音できなくなった。
stifle	ジョアンの芸術家になりたいという夢は、医者になってほしいと圧力をかける両親によって抑え込まれた。
subdue	高潔な人には権力欲を抑える力がある。

subjugate
[sʌ́bdʒugèit]

v. **to bring under authority or control** ［動］〜を征服する、支配する

The fascist dictator *subjugated* the people of the country with his strong military force.

反意語 subjugate : manumit [mæ̀njumít]
subjugateの反意語はmanumit（〜を解放する）

sway
[swei]

v. **to move back and forth; to cause to change a decision or opinion** ［動］前後に揺れる；揺れ動く

The lobbyist *swayed* many politicians to repeal the latest income tax on small business.

関連語 sway : resolute [rézəlùːt]
resolute（決心の堅い、断固たる）な人をswayすることは難しい。

sybarite
[síbəràit]

n. **one who is luxurious or extremely sensual** ［名］快楽主義者

Sybarites are practitioners of hedonism.

反意語 sybarite : ascetic [əsétik]
sybariteの反意語はascetic（禁欲主義者）

tranquil
[trǽŋkwil]

adj. **free from anxiety or disturbance** ［形］平静な；穏やかな

The youth developed a *tranquil* philosophy for these moments of irritation.

反意語 tranquil : topsy-turvy [tápsitə́ːʳvi]
tranquilの反意語はtopsy-turvy（混乱した、逆さまの）

transgress
[trænsgrés]

v. **to exceed or go beyond set limits; to break a law** ［動］（限界などを）超える；（法律など）に違反する

The felon *transgressed* a recent city ordinance, which was in direct violation of his parole.

関連語 transgress : rectitude [réktət(j)ùːd]
transgressすることにはrectitude（正直、実直）が欠けている。

TRANSLATION | 例文の訳

subjugate	その独裁者は強力な軍隊を使って国民を支配した。
sway	そのロビイストは、小企業への新たな所得税を廃止するよう多くの政治家に働きかけた。
sybarite	快楽主義者とは、快楽主義を実践する人々だ。
tranquil	その若者はこのような腹立たしい瞬間に備えて穏やかな心持ちを身につけていた。
transgress	その重罪犯は最近の市条例を破ったが、それは彼の刑の執行猶予に直接違反する行為だった。

173

transient [trǽnʃənt]	adj. **passing through with only a brief stay** 　　　[形] 一時的な、つかの間の Outer beauty is *transient*, but inner beauty lasts forever. 反意語 transient : lasting [lǽstiŋ] 　　transientの反意語は lasting（永続的な）
translate [trænsléit]	v. **to convert written or spoken words into another language** 　　　　　　　　　　　　　　　　　　　　[動] 翻訳する、通訳する The interpreter *translated* the coach's words, trying hard not to lose the meaning and humor of the original language. 関連語 translate : interpreter [intə́ːr pritər] 　　translate する人が interpreter（通訳者）
translucent [trænslúːsnt]	adj. **transmitting but diffusing light so that objects beyond cannot be seen clearly; lucid** 　　　[形] 半透明の；明解な The brand new car has four *translucent* windows. 反意語 translucent : impervious to light [impəːrviəs tə lait] 　　translucentの反意語は impervious to light（光を通さない）
transparent [trænspéⁱrənt]	adj. **permitting the passage of light and a clear view of object on the other side; free from guile; clear** 　　　　　　　　　　　　　　　　　[形] 透明な；率直な；わかりやすい The *transparent* look on his face convinced the store owner of the boy's veracity. 反意語 transparent : deceitful [disíːtfəl] 　　transparentの反意語は deceitful（不正直な、だます）

TRANSLATION | 例 文 の 訳

transient	外面の美しさは一時的なものだが、内面の美しさは永遠に続く。
translate	その通訳者は元の言葉の意味とユーモアを失わないように懸命に努力しながら、監督の言葉を訳した。
translucent	その新車には半透明の窓が４つある。
transparent	彼の率直な表情を見て、店主はその少年が正直だと確信した。

urbane
[əːˈbéin]

adj. **notably well-mannered and worldly**　　　[形] 洗練された、あか抜けした

Although *urbane* in appearance, Jerry displayed his lack of etiquette when refusing to greet his guests.

反意語 urbane : rustic [rʌ́stik]
urbaneの反意語は rustic（粗野な、下品な）

vanish
[vǽniʃ]

v. **to disappear from sight**　　　[動] 消える、消滅する

David Copperfield was a great magician who could make elephants *vanish* in the blink of an eye.

関連語 vanish : evanescent [èvənésnt]
evanescnent（すぐに消えていく、はかない）ものは vanish するという特徴がある。

TRANSLATION | 例 文 の 訳

| urbane | 見かけは洗練されていたが、ジェリーは客への挨拶を拒否して、礼儀に欠けているところを見せてしまった。 |
| vanish | デイビッド・カッパーフィールドは、一瞬でゾウを消すことができる偉大な奇術師だった。 |

11th / 12th / 13th / 14th / 15th / 16th / 17th / 18th / 19th / 20th

■ Fill in the blanks with the correct letter that matches the word with its definition.

1. rubicund _____
2. alienable _____
3. stalemate _____
4. plangent _____
5. evanescent _____
6. blanch _____
7. tranquil _____
8. cramp _____
9. transient _____
10. inane _____

a. having a loud and resounding sound
b. a sharp pain caused by a sudden contraction of a muscle; something that restrains freedom of function
c. lacking substance or meaning; void of sense or intelligence
d. to take the color out of; to cause to become pale
e. vanishing like vapor
f. free from anxiety or disturbance
g. transferable to another person's ownership
h. passing through with only a brief stay
i. having a healthy reddish color
j. the state of being deadlocked

■ Put the correct word in each blank from the list of words below.

11. mob（暴徒）の類義語は_____である。

12. _____は他人を coax するために使用する言葉である。

13. _____は dissolute な人を指す。

14. execrate（非難する）の反意語は_____である。

15. _____な人やものには flexibility がない。

16. deceitful（欺く）の反意語は_____である。

17. _____には constancy という特徴がある。

18. _____は disintegrate（～を分解する、崩壊させる）の反意語である。

19. resolute な人を_____させることは難しい。

20. shackle（拘束する）の反意語は_____である。

a. exalt b. emancipate c. amalgamate d. sway e. transparent
f. libertine g. blandishment h. rabble i. adamant j. transgress
k. stalwart l. sham

Answer key

11. h 12. g 13. f 14. a 15. i 16. e 17. k 18. c 19. d 20. b
1. i 2. g 3. j 4. a 5. e 6. d 7. f 8. b 9. h 10. c

あなたは強い。今日も昨日と
同じくらいできることを願っています。

13th DAY

---

abase
[əbéis]

v. **to lower in office or esteem**　　　　［動］（地位・品位などを）落とす、下げる

The *abased* executive was embarrassed by his recent demotion.

関連語 abase : prestige [prestíːdʒ]
abase は prestige（名声、威信）を失うことをいう。

---

abash
[əbǽʃ]

v. **to embarrass or make ashamed**　　　［動］恥ずかしい思いをさせる、恥をかかせる

Abashed glances of wonder were exchanged by the sailors.

反意語 abash : embolden [imbóuldⁿn]
abash の反意語は embolden（〜を大胆にする、励ます）

---

abate
[əbéit]

v. **to lessen in amount, degree, or intensity**　　　［動］〜を減ずる、やわらげる

The installation of insect light traps did little to *abate* the problem.

関連語 abate : degree [digríː]
abate は degree（程度）を弱めるということ。

---

amuse
[əmjúːz]

v. **to please or appeal to one's sense of humor**

［動］楽しませる、笑わせる

The comic performer was able to *amuse* the crowd for hours.

関連語 amusement : anecdote [ǽnikdòut]
anecdote（逸話）は人に amusement（楽しさ、おもしろさ）を与える短い話だ。

TRANSLATION | 例 文 の 訳

abase　　　権威を失墜したその重役は、最近降格したことを恥ずかしく思った。

abash　　　船員たちは当惑して、きまり悪そうに目くばせした。

abate　　　殺虫ランプを設置したが、問題の軽減にはほとんど役に立たなかった。

amuse　　　そのお笑い芸人は何時間も観衆を笑わせることができた。

apathetic [æ̀pəθétik]	adj. **having or exhibiting a lack of feeling or concern** [形] 無関心な、やる気のない Alfred stood motionless, in what seemed to be an *apathetic* attitude. 関連語 apathetic : fervor [fə́ːʳvəʳ] apathetic な人は fervor (熱情) が欠けている。
avarice [ǽvəris]	n. **an excessive desire for wealth**　　　[名] (金銭に対する) 貪欲、強欲 The *avarice* of the man caused his neighbors and friends to spite him. 反意語 avarice : generosity [dʒènərásəti] avarice の反意語は generosity (寛大さ、気前のよさ)
blast [blæst]	n. **a violent outburst of air or sound; an explosion**　[名] 爆風；爆発 When the bomb exploded, the sound of the *blast* could be heard from far away. 関連語 blast : whiff [ʰwif] blast は whiff (そよ風) よりも風の強さが強い。
blatant [bléitᵊnt]	adj. **completely obvious or vulgarly conspicuous; unpleasantly loud especially in a vulgar or offensive manner** [形] 見え透いた；露骨な The oil tycoon's *blatant* show of wealth was epitomized by his gold encrusted belt buckle. 関連語 blatant : ignore [ignɔ́ːʳ] blatant なものを ignore (無視する) するのは難しい。
blush [blʌʃ]	v. **to become red in the face from shame or nervousness** [動] 顔を赤らめる Surprised and a little embarrassed by his flattery, Tonya *blushed*. 関連語 blush : embarrassment [imbǽrəsmənt] embarrassment (当惑、恥ずかしさ) を感じると blush する。

TRANSLATION | 例文の訳

apathetic	アルフレッドはじっと立っていた。それは無関心な態度に見えた。
avarice	その男は強欲だったので、隣人や友人たちの恨みを買った。
blast	爆弾が爆発したとき、その爆風音は遠くからでも聞こえた。
blatant	その石油王は富を露骨に見せびらかしていた。金ピカのベルトのバックルに、それが表れていた。
blush	彼のお世辞に驚き、少し恥ずかしくなって、トーニャは顔を赤らめた。

brash [bræʃ]	adj. hasty and lacking in regard for consequences　[形] 性急な、無謀な
	Tony's *brash* manner has gotten him in a lot of trouble.
	反意語 brash: deliberate [dilíbərət] brashの反意語はdeliberate（意図的な、よく考えた）
charitable [tʃǽrətəbl]	adj. liberal in benediction to the needy　[形] 慈善の、人助けの、寛大な
	Tom has a *charitable* heart because he makes donations to various needy organizations on an annual basis.
	反意語 charitableness : rancor [rǽŋkəʳ] charitableness（寛大さ、慈悲）の反意語はrancor（怨恨、憎しみ）
chary [tʃéəri]	adj. very cautious; slow to give　[形] 用心深い；細心な
	Clara knew that Mr. Gryce was *chary*, not prone to rash or impulsive decisions.
	反意語 chary : bold [bould] charyの反意語はbold（大胆な）
chasm [kǽzm]	n. a deep opening in the surface of the Earth; a marked difference　[名] 地面の亀裂；意見の食い違い
	The rock climbers looked down into the *chasm*.
	関連語 chasm : cleft [kleft] chasmはcleft（地面の裂け目）よりもさらに深く割れているものをいう。
clarify [klǽrəfài]	v. to make clear or understandable　[動] ～を明らかにする、明確にする
	Could you please *clarify* that statement for me?
	関連語 clarify : misunderstood [mìsʌndərstúd] misunderstood（誤解された）されたものをclarifyする。

TRANSLATION | 例文の訳

brash	トニーは性急な行動のせいで多くのトラブルに陥ってきた。
charitable	トムは寛大な心の持ち主で、援助が必要ないろいろな組織に毎年寄付している。
chary	クララは、グライス氏が用心深く、軽率で衝動的な判断を下したりしないことを知っていた。
chasm	そのロッククライマーは地面の亀裂を見下ろした。
clarify	その意見について私にわかりやすく説明していただけますか。

179

concede [kənsíːd]	v. **to accept that something is true; to yield** [動] 〜を (正しいと) 認める；譲歩する
	It is generally *conceded* that humans are social beings.
	反意語 concede : disavow [dìsəváu] concede の反意語は disavow（〜を否定する）
consent [kənsént]	v. **to give approval of; to agree to**　[動] 〜を承認する；同意する n. **an agreement**　[名] 同意、承諾
	Dirk *consented* to the drug test because he had no other options. I asked my mother's *consent* to marry Shannon.
	反意語 consent : dissent [disént] consent の反意語は dissent（意見が違う、意見の相違）
cursory [kə́ːʳsəri]	adj. **superficial; hasty; careless**　[形] 表面的な；早まった；せっかちな
	The editor's *cursory* review of the document failed to reveal its structural flaws.
	反意語 cursory : fastidious [fæstídiəs] cursory の反意語は fastidious（最新の注意を払う、厳格な）
dearth [dəːʳθ]	n. **a lack or shortage of supply, especially of food**　[名] 不足、欠乏
	The drought in Bengal a few years ago caused a great *dearth* of food supplies.
	反意語 dearth : plethora [pléθərə] dearth の反意語は plethora（過多、過度）
diaphanous [daiǽfənəs]	adj. **characterized by such fineness of texture as to permit seeing through**　[形] (布繊維などが) 薄くて透けている
	In the gloom, the girls' wraps glowed pallid and *diaphanous*.
	反意語 diaphanous : opaque [oupéik] diaphanous の反意語は opaque（不透明な、光を通さない）

TRANSLATION |　例 文 の 訳

concede	人間は社会的な存在であると一般的に認められている。
consent	ダークが薬物検査に同意したのは、そうするしかなかったからだ。
	私はシャノンとの結婚について母の承諾を求めた。
cursory	その編集者は原稿を表面的に見ただけだったので、その構成上の問題点を見落とした。
dearth	数年前のベンガル地方の干ばつは、深刻な食糧危機をもたらした。
diaphanous	暗闇の中で、少女たちのショールは青白く透き通ったように輝いた。

discharge
[distʃáːʳdʒ]

v. **to release from an obligation or from employment; to dismiss; to send out or shoot** [動] ～を解放する、解雇する；放電する；～を発射する、撃つ

The captain was *discharged* from the army after 30 years of loyal service.

反意語 discharge : induct [indʌkt]
dischargeの反意語はinduct（～を任命する、就任させる）

disclosure
[disklóuʒəʳ]

n. **the exposure or revelation of something that was hidden or secret** [名] 暴露、公開

The *disclosure* of FBI reports has raised many doubts as to the actions of President Bush prior to Sept. 11th.

反意語 disclosure : stealth [stelθ]
disclosureの反意語はstealth（密かな行為）

discord
[dískɔːʳd]

n. **conflict or a lack of agreement** [名] 不和、不一致

Wars arise from *discord* between political bodies.

反意語 discord : rapport [ræpóːʳ]
discordの反意語はrapport（信頼関係、一致、調和）

drab
[dræb]

adj. **dull in appearance; cheerless** [形] 単調な、退屈な

The man's entire wardrobe is rather *drab*.

関連語 drab : resplendence [rispléndəns]
drabなものにはresplendence（華やかさ、華麗、まぶしさ）が欠けている。

elate
[iléit]

v. **to make full of pride or joy** [動] ～の意気を高める、喜びにあふれさせる

Patrick was *elated* when he was accepted into the Naval Academy.

反意語 elation : sullenness [sʌlənnis]
elation（意気揚々、大喜び）の反意語はsullenness（落ち込み、不機嫌）

TRANSLATION | 例 文 の 訳

discharge その大尉は30年間忠実に軍務に携わったあと、除隊した。
disclosure FBIの報告書が公開され、9月11日以前のブッシュ大統領の行動について多くの疑問が挙がった。
discord 戦争は政府間の不和から起きる。
drab その男性が持っている衣類は、あまりパッとしない。
elate パトリックは海軍士官学校に合格したとき大喜びだった。

181

enact
[inǽkt]

v. **to make or pass a law; to act out**

[動]（法律を）制定する；（劇などを）上演する

Congress *enacted* a new law that prohibits college students from drinking during the school year.

反意語 enact : rescind [risínd]

enactの反意語は rescind（法律などを無効にする、廃止する）

ensconce
[inskáns]

v. **to settle in a comfortable and secure place; to conceal in a secure place**

[動]〜に落ち着く；安置する

Norma deals with stress by *ensconcing* herself in her apartment and reading.

反意語 ensconce : unsettle [ʌnsétl]

ensconceの反意語は unsettle（〜を乱す、不安定にする）

extrovert
[ékstrəvə̀ːʳt]

n. **an gregarious and social person**

[名]外交的な人、社交的な人

Typically the *extroverts* are the popular people in high school.

関連語 extrovert : outgoing [áutgòuiŋ]

extrovertは outgoing（社交的な）だという特徴がある。

flirt
[fləːʳt]

v. **to show light amorous interest in someone; to treat something not seriously**

[動]浮気をする；もてあそぶ

Sunny *flirted* with the bartender in hopes of receiving a free beverage.

関連語 flirtatious : coquette [koukét]

coquette（コケティッシュな女性）は flirtatious（媚を売る）という特徴がある。

forbear
[fɔːʳbɛ́əʳ]

v. **to refrain from; to hold back from; to be patient**

[動]自制する；控える；我慢する

Although Kelly could hardly wait to give her Mom the present, she *forbore* the urge until Christmas Day.

類義語 forbear : forgo [fɔːʳgóu]

forbearの類義語は forgo（〜を差し控える）

TRANSLATION | 例 文 の 訳

enact	議会は、大学生が在学中に飲酒することを禁じる新しい法律を制定した。
ensconce	ノーマは自分のアパートで落ち着いて読書することでストレスを解消する。
extrovert	一般に、外交的な人は高校で人気がある。
flirt	サニーは、飲み物がただになればいいと思いながら、バーテンダーにお世辞を言った。
forbear	ケリーは母親に贈り物を渡したくて仕方がなかったが、クリスマス当日までその衝動を抑えた。

fulsome
[fúlsəm]

adj. excessively complimentary or flattering; offensive

[形]（お世辞などが）大げさな、度を越した

The bartender's *fulsome* compliments did not impress the lady server.

関連語 fulsome : complimentary [kàmpləméntəri]

fulsomeは過度にcomplimentary（挨拶の、賞賛を表す）なことをいう。

gobble
[gábl]

v. to eat greedily and quickly

[動] がつがつと急いで食べる

As children, my siblings and I would make fun of our dad for always *gobbling* his dinner.

関連語 gobble : nibble [níbl]

gobbleはnibble（少しずつかじる）に比べ、がつがつ食べることをいう。

graceful
[gréisfəl]

adj. beautiful or attractive in motion or style

[形]（物腰などが）優雅な、上品な

The ballerina's dancing was *graceful*, a true pleasure to watch.

反意語 graceful and light : ponderous [pándªrəs]

graceful and light（優雅で軽やか）の反意語はponderous（重苦しい、大きくて重い）

harsh
[hɑːrʃ]

adj. causing pain or irritation; severe or crude

[形] 辛辣な；厳しい、下品な

The father's *harsh* words deeply wounded his son.

関連語 harsh : pan [pæn]

pan（酷評、厳しい批評）はharshだという特徴がある。

hearten
[háːrtn]

v. to give courage or spirit to

[動] ～を勇気づける、励ます

Malcolm *heartened* the brave volunteers before flying to their posts in Africa.

関連語 hearten : dejection [didʒékʃən]

heartenはdejection（意気消沈、落胆）を取り除き、励ますこと。

TRANSLATION | 例 文 の 訳

fulsome	バーテンダーは大げさなお世辞を言ったが、その女性の給仕係は感心を示さなかった。
gobble	子供の頃、きょうだいたちと私は夕食をがつがつと食べる父をいつもからかったものだ。
graceful	そのバレリーナの踊りは優雅で、見ていて本当に楽しかった。
harsh	父親の辛辣な言葉が息子を深く傷つけた。
hearten	マルコムは、勇敢なボランティアたちを、アフリカの任地に飛び立つ前に勇気づけた。

irascible
[irǽsəbl]

adj. characterized by a tendency toward anger and a hot temper

[形] 怒りっぽい、かんしゃく持ちの

All the tenants tried to avoid the *irascible* landowner whenever possible.

関連語 irascible : placate [pléikeit]
irascible な人を placate（〜をなだめる、静める）することは難しい。

liability
[làiəbíləti]

n. a legal or pecuniary obligation; a drawback or disadvantage

[名]（法的）責任、義務；欠点、不利な点

The company went out of business because their *liabilities* far outweighed their assets.

関連語 liability : exempt [igzémpt]
liability は exempt（〜を免除する）する対象である。

反意語 liability : asset [ǽset]
liability の反意語は asset（資産、有用なもの）

loathe
[louð]

v. to feel extreme aversion for

[動] 〜をひどく嫌う

Commuters often *loathe* the drive to work because of perpetual traffic and hazardous road conditions.

関連語 loathe : dislike [disláik]
loathe はひどく dislike（〜を嫌う）ことを表す。

measly
[míːzli]

adj. despicably small; meager

[形] 取るに足りない；わずかな

The *measly* salary of the factory workers gave them reason to strike.

反意語 measly : grand [grænd]
measly の反意語は grand（壮大な、雄大な）

TRANSLATION | 例 文 の 訳

irascible	借地人たちはその怒りっぽい地主をできるだけ避けようとした。
liability	その企業は、法的負債が資産をはるかに超えたために倒産した。
loathe	絶え間ない交通渋滞と危険な道路状況のせいで、通勤者はあまり車で出勤したがらない。
measly	賃金が少ないことが、工場労働者がストライキをする理由だった。

mince
[mins]

v. to chop or cut into little pieces; to walk with very short steps or with exaggerated primness　　[動] 細かく刻む；気取って小またで歩く

The princess had *minced* her way across the ballroom to attract attention to her new gown.

関連語 mince : walk [wɔːk]
　　minceはwalk（歩く）することの一種。

opaque
[oupéik]

adj. impenetrable by light　　[形] 光を通さない、不透明な

The *opaque* curtains covered the room in darkness.

反意語 opaque : diaphanous [daiǽfənəs]
　　opaqueの反意語はdiaphanous（薄くて透けている）

orate
[ɔːréit]

v. to speak in an elevated and arrogant manner　　[動] 演説する、演説口調で話す

Pericles *orated* to the Athenians, persuading them to go to war.

関連語 oratory : modesty [mάdəsti]
　　oratory（雄弁）にはmodesty（謙遜、節度）が欠けている。

oust
[aust]

v. to kick out or force out of a position　　[動]（職や地位から）追い出す

The mayor was *ousted* from office after a huge scandal broke loose.

関連語 oust : incumbent [inkΛmbənt]
　　incumbent（現職者）をoustする。

outgoing
[áutgòuiŋ]

adj. friendly and sociable　　[形] 親しみやすい、社交的な

Although they were twins, Edward was shy and Edwin was *outgoing*.

関連語 outgoing : extrovert [ékstrəvə̀ːʳt]
　　extrovert（外交的な人、社交的な人）にはoutgoingだという特徴がある。

TRANSLATION | 例文の訳

mince 王女は新しいドレスに注目が集まるように、気取って小股でダンスホールを横切った。
opaque その不透明なカーテンによって、部屋は暗闇に覆われた。
orate ペリクレスはアテネの人々に戦争に参加するように演説した。
oust 巨大な不祥事が明るみに出て、その市長は職から追放された。
outgoing 彼らは双子だったが、エドワードは内気でエドウィンは社交的だった。

185

palmy
[pá:mi]

adj. **prosperous and profitable**   [形] 繁栄している、利益を生む

The 1990's was a *palmy* time for technology companies.

関連語 palmy : prosperity [prɑspérəti]
palmyと似た意味の名詞に prosperity（繁栄）がある。

penchant
[péntʃənt]

n. **a special fondness or continued inclination**   [名] 強い好み、偏愛

Lee has a *penchant* for percussion instruments.

反意語 penchant : aversion [əvə́:ˈʒən]
penchantの反意語は aversion（嫌悪）

placid
[plǽsid]

adj. **calm or serene**   [形] おとなしい、穏やかな

Jeremy was a *placid* man who rarely got angry.

反意語 placid : truculent [trʌ́kjulənt]
placidの反意語は truculent（気難しい、反抗的な）

prescience
[préʃ(i)əns]

n. **knowledge of the future or foresight**   [名] 予知、先見の明

The ancient wise men claimed to have a *prescience* which all the citizens listened to and followed.

反意語 prescience : myopia [maióupiə]
prescienceの反意語は myopia（近視的なこと）

quarrel
[kwɔ́:rəl]

n. **a dispute or verbal conflict**   [名] 口論、口げんか

The shouting from their *quarrel* attracted a crowd.

関連語 quarrel : spat [spæt]
spat（ちょっとしたけんか）はささいな quarrelのことである。

TRANSLATION | 例 文 の 訳

palmy	1990年代はテクノロジー企業の繁栄の時代だった。
penchant	リーは打楽器が大好きだ。
placid	ジェレミーはめったに怒ることのない穏やかな男だった。
prescience	古代の賢人たちは、自分たちには先見の明があり、市民は全員言うことを聞いて従うべきだと主張した。
quarrel	彼らが大声で口論したので、人々が集まってきた。

quarry
[kwɔ́ːri]

v. to extract by long, careful searching　　［動］〜を採掘する、捜し出す

n. an open pit from which building stone, limestone, or slate are acquired; a productive source　　［名］採石場；源泉

The police *quarried* the location of the fugitive through an exhaustive manhunt.

We paved our driveway with stone purchased from the local *quarry*.

関連語 quarry : marble [máːʳbl]
　　quarry で marble（大理石）を採掘する。

quash
[kwɑʃ]

v. to extinguish forcibly and completely　　［動］（反乱など）を鎮圧する、〜を鎮める

Modred was slain in his attempt to *quash* the revolt.

反意語 quash : engender [indʒéndər]
　　quash の反意語は engender（〜を発生させる）

reassure
[rìːəʃúəʳ]

v. to relieve; to restore confidence　　［動］安心させる；自信を回復させる

Bryan *reassured* Amelia with his friendly chuckle.

関連語 reassure : uneasiness [ʌníːzinis]
　　reassure するとは uneasiness（不安、心配）を取り除くこと。

reluctant
[rilʌ́ktənt]

adj. hesitant or unwilling　　［形］〜したくない、気が進まない

Elizabeth was *reluctant* to give up her weekends for work.

反意語 reluctance : alacrity [əlǽkrəti]
　　reluctance（気が進まないこと）の反意語は alacrity（乗り気）

scarce
[skɛəʳs]

adj. insufficient in quantity or inadequate to meet a demand　　［形］乏しい、不十分な

Truly gifted mechanics are *scarce*.

反意語 scarce : superfluous [suːpə́ːrfluəs]
　　scarce の反意語は superfluous（過分の、十二分な）

TRANSLATION | 例 文 の 訳

quarry　警察は徹底的な捜索を通じて、逃亡犯の居場所を突き止めた。
　　　　　私たちは地元の採石場で購入した石で私道を舗装した。

quash　モードレッドは反乱を鎮圧しようとして殺された。

reassure　ブライアンは人なつこい笑い声でアメリアを元気づけた。

reluctant　エリザベスは週末を仕事に充てることに気が進まなかった。

scarce　本当に才能のある機械工が不足している。

187

shard
[ʃɑːʳd]

n. **a piece of broken pottery, glass, or metal**　　　［名］（陶器などの）破片

There were *shards* everywhere on the floor from the broken mirror.

関連語 shard : pottery [pátəri]
　　　shard は pottery（陶磁器類）などの破片。cf) ケーキのくずは crumb。

snarl
[snɑːʳl]

v. **to make tangle and intertwined**　　　［動］〜をもつれさせる、混乱させる

The fly was *snarled* in the black widow's spider web with no prospects of escaping.

反意語 snarl : disentangle [dìsentǽŋgl]
　　　snarl の反意語は disentangle（〜を解き放す、もつれをほどく）

Spartan
[spáːrtn]

n. **a person with self-discipline and courage**　　　［名］質実剛健な人

adj. **austere or simple**　　　［形］厳格な、簡素な

Mike is such a *Spartan* who rarely strays from his beliefs.

Janet's dedication to giving up worldly goods could be observed in her *Spartan* apartment.

反意語 Spartan : luxurious [lʌgʒúˀriəs]
　　　Spartan の反意語は luxurious（贅沢な、豪華な）

spate
[speit]

n. **a sudden outburst or flood; a large amount or number**　　　［名］多発、洪水；多数

Alice was a popular columnist and received a *spate* of letters everyday.

反意語 spate : dearth [dəːʳθ]
　　　spate の反意語は dearth（不足、欠乏）

TRANSLATION ｜ 例 文 の 訳

shard　　床一杯に割れた鏡の破片が散らばっていた。

snarl　　そのハエはクロゴケグモの巣にからまってしまい、逃げられる見込みがなかった。

Spartan　マイクはとても質実剛健な人で、自分の信念から外れることがほとんどない。
　　　　　　財産を放棄しようというジャネットの強い意志が、彼女の質素なアパートに見て取れた。

spate　　アリスは人気コラムニストで、毎日たくさんの手紙を受け取った。

11th

12th

13th

14th

15th

16th

17th

18th

19th

20th

startle
[stάː^{r}tl]

v. to cause to move involuntarily; to surprise suddenly

[動] 驚かせて～させる；～をびっくりさせる

n. a sudden start　　　　　　　　　　　　　　　[名] 驚き

Dad *startled* me yesterday while I was brushing my teeth.

The *startle* of his wife falling out of bed woke Bradley up.

反意語 startle : lull [lʌl]
　　startleの反意語は (落ち着かせる、静める)

stasis
[stéisis]

n. a state of balance or motionlessness　　　[名] 平衡状態、停滞状態

The Russia-U.S. relationship appears to have reached a *stasis*.

関連語 stasis : motility [moutíləti]
　　stasisは motility (運動性) のない平衡状態を表す。

weary
[wíˀri]

adj. fatigued or exhausted in strength; having little patience or tolerance　　　　　　　　　　[形] 疲れた；うんざりした、我慢できない

Grandma is *weary* from the trip and must take a nap.

反意語 weary : vivid [vívid]
　　wearyの反意語は vivid (生き生きとした)

TRANSLATION | 例 文 の 訳

startle　　昨日、歯を磨いているとき、父に驚かされた。
　　　　　　妻がベッドから落ちたことに驚いて、ブラッドリーは目が覚めた。

stasis　　ロシアとアメリカの関係は平衡状態に達しているように見える。

weary　　祖母は旅行で疲れているので、昼寝をしたほうがいい。

■ Fill in the blanks with the correct letter that matches the word with its definition.

1. liability _____
2. cursory _____
3. abase _____
4. shard _____
5. ensconce _____
6. blatant _____
7. chary _____
8. penchant _____
9. apathetic _____
10. drab _____

a. very cautious; slow to give
b. to settle in a comfortable and secure place
c. having or exhibiting a lack of feeling or concern
d. a special fondness or continued inclination
e. dull in appearance; cheerless
f. unpleasantly loud in a vulgar or offensive manner
g. a piece of broken pottery, glass, or metal
h. to lower in office or esteem
i. a legal or pecuniary obligation; a drawback or disadvantage
j. superficial; hasty; careless

■ Put the correct word in each blank from the list of words below.

11. _____は whiff よりも強い風である。

12. complimentary も_____になると不快感を与える。

13. _____は engender（発生させる）の反意語である。

14. plethora（過多、過度）の反意語は_____である。

15. _____は motility のない平衡状態である。

16. _____は sullenness（落ち込み）の反意語である。

17. spat はささいな_____である。

18. _____は generosity（寛大さ）の反意語である。

19. disentangle（もつれをほどく）の反意語は_____である。

20. _____には modesty がない。

| a. fulsome | b. quarrel | c. blast | d. quarry | e. oratory | f. dearth |
| g. gobble | h. elation | i. snarl | j. stasis | k. quash | l. avarice |

Answer key

11.c 12.a 13.k 14.f 15.j 16.h 17.b 18.l 19.i 20.e
1.i 2.j 3.h 4.g 5.b 6.f 7.a 8.d 9.c 10.e

友人や家族に覚えた単語を
テストしてもらうのもいい勉強になります。

14th DAY

---

abbreviate
[əbríːvièit]

v. to shorten by contraction, especially of words

[動] (語句など) を短縮する、省略する

The word 'Mister' has come to be *abbreviated* as 'Mr.'

関連語 abbreviate : word [wəːrd]
長い word (単語) を abbreviate する。

---

abhor
[æbhɔ́ːr]

v. to regard with intense loathing or horror　[動] 〜を忌み嫌う、憎悪する

Carrie *abhorred* the condescending manner in which her classmate spoke.

関連語 abhor : dislike [disláik]
abhor は dislike (〜を嫌う) よりも嫌う程度が強い。

---

abide
[əbáid]

v. to endure; to remain fixed in a state or condition

[動] 〜を持続する；〜に住む、とどまる

The composer's passion for writing music *abided* until his untimely death.

反意語 abiding : evanescent [èvənésnt]
abiding (永続的な) の反意語は evanescent (すぐに消えていく、はかない)

---

accessible
[æksésəbl]

adj. able to be influenced; approachable; easily understandable

[形] 影響されやすい；行きやすい、入手可能な；理解しやすい

The university lecture was not *accessible* to the high school students.

関連語 accessible : abstruse [æbstrúːs]
abstruse (難解な) な思想は accessible ではない。

TRANSLATION | 例 文 の 訳

abbreviate	Mister という単語は Mr. と略されるようになった。
abhor	キャリーは同級生の見下すような話し方が大嫌いだった。
abide	その作曲家の作曲への情熱は、彼が早すぎる死を迎えるまで絶えなかった。
accessible	その大学の講義は、高校生の受講が許されていなかった。

achromatic [æ̀krəmǽtik]	adj. **having no hue; consisting of black, gray, or white** [形] 色のない；黒、グレー、白の The *achromatic* door caused many visitors to miss the entrance completely. 関連語 achromatic : hue [hju:] achromaticなものには hue（色、色合い）がない。
adhere [ædhíəʳ]	v. **to hold on to or stick to something** [動] ～にしがみつく、くっつく、付着する The glue will *adhere* with remarkable tenacity. 関連語 adhere : slippery [slípəʳi] slippery（滑りやすい）な表面に他のものは adhere できない。
alibi [ǽləbài]	n. **the verifiable claim to have been in a place other than where and when a crime occurred** [名] アリバイ、現場不在証明 He fabricated an incongruous *alibi*. 関連語 alibi : exculpate [ékskʌlpèit] exculpate（～を無罪にする）するために alibi を利用する。
amble [ǽmbl]	v. **to walk slowly** [動] ぶらぶら歩く、ゆっくり歩く The couple *ambled* lazily through their garden after dinner. 関連語 amble : walk [wɔːk] amble はゆっくりと walk（歩く）すること。
ambrosial [æmbróuʒ(i)əl]	adj. **pleasing to the taste or smell** [形] 美味な、香り高い The *ambrosial* drink was heralded by many as the nectar of the gods. 関連語 ambrosial : food [fuːd] ambrosial は food（食べ物）を修飾する単語だ。

TRANSLATION | 例 文 の 訳

achromatic	ドアが無色だったので、まったく入り口を見つけられない訪問者が多かった。
adhere	その接着剤は強力な粘着力で物をくっつける。
alibi	彼はつじつまの合わないアリバイを捏造した。
amble	その夫婦は夕食後、のんびりと庭を歩いた。
ambrosial	その香り高い飲み物は、多くの人々に神の飲み物だと賞賛された。

amicable
[ǽmikəbl]

adj. **friendly and peaceful**   [形] 友好的な、平和的な

The *amicable* men came to a settlement quickly.

反意語 amicable : inimical [inímikəl]
amicable の反意語は inimical（敵意のある）

ancestor
[ǽnsestəʳ]

n. **a family member from whom one is descended**   [名] 先祖

Our family tree traces our *ancestors* back to the 14th century.

関連語 ancestor : heirloom [ɛ́əʳlùːm]
ancestor が残したものは heirloom（先祖伝来の家財、家宝）。cf) testator（遺言人）が残したものは bequest（遺産、形見）

aphorism
[ǽfərìzəm]

n. **a short saying containing a principle**   [名] 金言、格言

People who practice Confucianism use *aphorisms* to guide their lives.

関連語 aphorism : brevity [brévəti]
aphorism は brevity（簡潔さ）が特徴である。

archaic
[ɑːˈkéiik]

adj. **referring to the time up to the Classical period in Ancient Greece; old fashioned or antiquated**
    [形] 古代ギリシャの；古風な、旧式の、古代の

The factory's *archaic* methods of production slowed the growth of the company.

反意語 archaism : neologism [niːálədʒìzm]
archaism（古語、古語表現）の反意語は neologism（新語、新表現）

arid
[ǽrid]

adj. **extremely dry; lacking rain or water supply**
    [形] ひどく乾燥した；雨が少ない

The *arid* acres of his farm scarcely yielded enough to keep his household fed through the winter.

関連語 arid : desert [dézəʳt]
desert（砂漠）の特徴は arid なこと。

TRANSLATION | 例 文 の 訳

amicable その友好的な男たちはすぐに合意に達した。
ancestor 私たちの家系図は14世紀までさかのぼる。
aphorism 儒教に従う人々は格言を人生の指針にする。
archaic 工場の古い生産方式が、その企業の成長を遅らせた。
arid 彼の農場は土地が乾燥しているので、冬の間家族を食べさせるだけの作物を産出することがほとんどできなかった。

193

ascetic
[əsétik]

adj. strict self-discipline for religious reasons [形] 修行の、禁欲主義の

n. one who lives a severe and disciplined life for the purpose of religious devotion [名] 修行者、禁欲主義者

John had lived an *ascetic* life until he came to the very liberal and adventurous lifestyle of the Korean peninsula.

After his accident, Peter gave up his material possessions and moved to India where he lived as an *ascetic*.

関連語 ascetic : self-denial [sélfdináiəl]
ascetic な人は強い self-denial（自制）が特徴である。

aside
[əsáid]

n. deviation; a message that strays from the main theme [名] 逸脱；余談

adv. away from other people [副] わきへ、外れて

The lecturer's *asides* were becoming increasingly divergent from the subject matter.

Matt stood *aside* while he waited for the speaker to introduce him.

関連語 aside : divergent [divə́:ʳdʒənt]
aside には divergent（逸脱した）だという特徴がある。

augur
[ɔ́:gəʳ]

n. one who foretells using omens [名] 占い師、預言者

Louis went to the *augur* to discover his fate.

関連語 augur : prediction [pridíkʃən]
augur には prediction（予言）をする力がある。

avid
[ǽvid]

adj. enthusiastically dedicated; desirous to the point of greed [形] 熱心な；貪欲な

So *avid* was Jamie in his pursuit of affluence that he soon forgot the friends who aided him in his quest.

反意語 avid : indifferent [indífərənt]
avid の反意語は indifferent（無関心な、冷淡な）

TRANSLATION | 例 文 の 訳

ascetic　ジョンは、朝鮮半島の非常に進歩的で大胆な生活様式に触れるまで、禁欲的な生活を送ってきた。
事故のあと、ピーターは持ち物をすべて処分し、インドに移って禁欲主義者として生活した。

aside　その講師の余談は主題からどんどん離れていっていた。
マットは、講演者が彼を紹介するのを待つ間、わきに立っていた。

augur　ルイは自分の運命を知るために占い師のところに行った。

avid　ジェイミーは富の追求に貪欲すぎて、自分の望みをかなえることに手を貸してくれた友人たちのことなどすぐに忘れてしまった。

bribe
[braib]

n. money or favors given to a person in a position of judgment or authority for personal gain or relief from legal trouble　[名] わいろ

v. to offer a bribe　　　　　　　　　　[動] 〜をわいろを贈る；買収する

The mobster offered the judge a *bribe* to rule in his favor.

The vice-president was arrested for trying to *bribe* a politician to award a contract to his company.

関連語 bribe : incorruptible [ìnkərʌ́ptəbl]
incorruptible（買収されない、高潔な）な人を bribe することはできない。

chiaroscuro
[kià:rəskjúˀrou]

n. an artistic method or design that employs light and dark shades without concern for color　　　　[名] 明暗の配合；明暗法

Chiaroscuro was employed by the artist to create a perception of shadows in the sketch.

関連語 chiaroscuro : contrast [kántræst]
chiaroscuro は contrast（明暗の対比）を特徴とする技法だ。

chicanery
[ʃikéinəri]

n. illegal deception or trickery　　　　　　　[名] ごまかし、策略

Many Americans think that President Bush used *chicanery* to win the last election.

反意語 chicanery : aboveboard action [əbʌ́vbɔ̀ːʳd ǽkʃən]
chicanery の反意語は aboveboard action（公明正大な、正直な行動）

cliche
[kli(:)ʃéi]

n. an overly familiar phrase　　　　　　　[名] 陳腐な決まり文句

A typical American *cliche* is "Cat got your tongue?"

関連語 cliche : hackneyed [hǽknid]
cliche には hackneyed（陳腐な、紋切り型の）だという特徴がある。

TRANSLATION | 例 文 の 訳

bribe　　　その暴力団員は、自分に有利な判決を求めて裁判官にわいろをもちかけた。
　　　　　　副社長は、政治家に賄賂を渡して自分の会社に契約をさせようとしたため逮捕された。

chiaroscuro　その芸術家はスケッチに陰影を出すために明暗法を使った。

chicanery　多くのアメリカ人は、ブッシュ大統領が最後の選挙に勝つために謀略を図ったと考えている。

cliche　　アメリカ人の典型的な決まり文句の一つに「どうして黙っているの」がある。

deception
[disépʃən]

n. something that tricks or makes something untrue seem true

[名] だますこと、欺瞞

The master criminal was skilled at the art of *deception*.

関連語 deceptive : ruse [ruːz]
　　　ruse（計略、策略）の特徴は deceptive（人をだますような、惑わせる）であることだ。

dehydrate
[diːháidreit]

v. to remove water from

[動] 〜から水分を抜く、乾燥させる

Mummification involves *dehydrating* the corpse for longer preservation.

関連語 dehydrate : water [wɔ́ːtəʳ]
　　　water（水）を抜いて dehydrate する。

eccentric
[ikséntrik]

adj. deviating far from the norm; odd

[形] ふつうでない、奇妙な

Carrington was the most *eccentric* person Gore had ever met.

類義語 eccentric : offbeat [ɔːfbíːt]
　　　eccentric の類義語は offbeat（風変わりな、ふつうでない）

embolden
[imbóuldən]

v. to make bold; to encourage

[動] 〜を大胆にする；励ます

Sybil was *emboldened* by her sister's words and confronted her boss about the problem.

反意語 embolden : appall [əpɔ́ːl]
　　　embolden の反意語は appall（〜をぞっとさせる、ぎょっとする）

embrace
[imbréis]

v. to hold close with the arms; to take up willingly or eagerly

[動] 〜を抱擁する；〜を喜んで受け入れる

Roger quickly *embraced* the idea of expanding his business.

反意語 embrace : spurn [spəːʳn]
　　　embrace の反意語は spurn（〜をはねつける）

TRANSLATION | 例 文 の 訳

deception	その熟練犯罪者は、人をだます手口に長けていた。
dehydrate	ミイラ化の工程には遺体を長期保存するための乾燥が含まれる。
eccentric	カリングトンは、ゴアがそれまでに会った中で最も変わった人だった。
embolden	シビルは妹の言葉に励まされ、その問題について上司に抗議した。
embrace	ロジャーは、事業拡大のアイデアをすぐに喜んで受け入れた。

excerpt [éksəːʰpt]	n. a part or quote taken from a larger work; an abstract [名] 引用；抜粋
	Heather keeps a book with all her favorite *excerpts* that she reads for inspiration.
	関連語 excerpt : summary [sʌ́məri] excerptの関連語は summary（要約）
fabric [fǽbrik]	n. the underlying structure or matrix; cloth material [名] 基本構造、基盤；布地
	The *fabric* of the dress is not exactly what she wants.
	関連語 fabric : linen [línin] linen（リネン）は fabricの一種だ。
fabricate [fǽbrikèit]	v. to create or make, often with the purpose of lying [動]（嘘・言い訳など）を作り上げる、捏造する
	The student *fabricated* a story to tell his teacher that explained why his homework was late.
	関連語 fabricate : authenticity [ɔ̀ːθentísəti] fabricate したものには authenticity（本物であること、確実性）が欠けている。
facetious [fəsíːʃəs]	adj. merry or jocular [形]（言葉などが）こっけいな、ふざけた
	Victor's *facetious* comment was met with great amusement by his coworkers.
	関連語 facetious : speech [spiːtʃ] facetiousは speech（話、言葉）を描写する単語。
gash [gæʃ]	n. a deeply cut flesh wound [名] 長く深い切り傷
	The paramedics found a large *gash* in the stabbing victim's right side.
	関連語 gash : cut [kʌt] gashは cut（切り傷）よりも深い。

TRANSLATION | 例文の訳

excerpt	ヘザーはお気に入りの引用を全部ノートにまとめて、インスピレーションを得るために読んでいる。
fabric	そのドレスの生地は、彼女が本当に望んでいるものではない。
fabricate	その学生は話をでっち上げて、なぜ宿題を出すのが遅れたのかを教師に説明した。
facetious	ビクターのこっけいな発言は、同僚たちを大いに楽しませた。
gash	その救命救急士は、刺された犠牲者の右腹部に大きな切り傷を見つけた。

197

genteel [dʒentíːl]	adj. **elegant and refined in manner; polite** ［形］上品な、優雅な；礼儀正しい Brad's *genteel* demeanor belied his true maliciousness. 反意語 genteel : churlish [tʃə́ːʻliʃ] genteelの反意語はchurlish（無作法な、失礼な）
incendiary [inséndièri]	n. **a person who intentionally sets fires; an agitator** ［名］放火犯；扇動者 As a result of the man's *incendiary* speech, the protest became violent. 関連語 incendiary : agitate [ǽdʒitèit] incendiaryはagitate（扇動する）する人である。
incense [ínsens]	v. **to make very angry** ［動］〜を激怒させる The recollection of Alexei's last act *incensed* his wife. 反意語 incense : propitiate [prəpíʃièit] incenseの反意語はpropitiate（〜の機嫌をとる、なだめる）
labor [léibəʻ]	n. **physical or mental exertion; work** ［名］（肉体的・精神的）骨折り；労働 One reason that prices are going up is that *labor* costs have been rising. 関連語 labor : respite [réspit] laborしない時間がrespite（小休止）だ。
labyrinth [lǽbərìnθ]	n. **a complicated maze where someone is easily lost** ［名］迷宮、迷路 McDougal's cave was a vast *labyrinth* of crooked walkways. 関連語 labyrinth : tortuous [tɔ́ːʻtʃuəs] labyrinthにはtortuous（煩雑な、ねじれた、曲がりくねった）だという特徴がある。

TRANSLATION | 例 文 の 訳

genteel	ブラッドは上品にふるまうことで、彼が本来持っている悪意を隠した。
incendiary	その男の煽動的な演説の結果、抗議デモは暴力的になった。
incense	アレクセイの最近の行動を思い出して、彼の妻は激怒した。
labor	物価が上がっている理由の1つは、人件費が上がっていることだ。
labyrinth	マクドゥーガルの洞窟は、曲がりくねった通路のある巨大な迷宮だった。

lacerate
[lǽsərèit]

v. to cut or tear open; to cause deep mental or emotional pain to

[動] ～を深く切り裂く；（心や感情などを）傷つける

His colleague's tragic death *lacerated* the fireman, and his guilty conscience drove him to see a therapist.

類義語 lacerate : distress [distrés]
lacerateの類義語は distress（～を悩ませる、～の心を痛める）

licentious
[laisénʃəs]

adj. not having moral restraints, especially sexual restraints

[形] みだらな、放蕩にふける

The man went to the cathedral and confessed of his *licentious* behavior.

反意語 licentiousness : moral restraint [mɔ́:rəl ristréint]
licentiousness（みだら、放蕩、不道徳）の反意語は moral restraint（道徳的自制心）

nebulous
[nébjuləs]

adj. lacking distinct form; unclear

[形] 漠然とした、不明瞭な

Banks and investors prefer the structure of a corporation to the often more *nebulous* organization of a sole proprietorship.

反意語 nebulous : unambiguous [ʌnæmbígjuəs]
nebulousの反意語は unambiguous（不明瞭なところのない、明らかな）

nicety
[náisəti]

n. delicacy or exactness of perception; a subtle distinction

[名] 精密さ、正確さ；微妙な相違

The consultant's *nicety* of the situation allowed her to immediately think of an alternative remedy.

類義語 nicety : precision [prisíʒən]
nicetyの類義語は precision（正確さ、精密さ）

11th
12th
13th
14th
15th
16th
17th
18th
19th
20th

TRANSLATION | 例文の訳

lacerate	同僚の悲劇的な死が、その消防士を深く傷つけ、彼は罪悪感に苦しんでセラピストに会いに行った。
licentious	その男性は大聖堂に行って、自分のみだらな行動を告白した。
nebulous	銀行や投資家は、あいまいな自営業の形態よりも法人組織を好む。
nicety	そのコンサルタントは状況把握が正確で、すぐに代替の解決策を思いついた。

noble
[nóubl]

adj. **having or showing high qualities; being of high birth**

[形] 高潔な、気高い；高貴な

The actions of virtue are *noble* and require no other reward.

類義語 noble : lofty [lɔ́:fti]
nobleの類義語はlofty（高尚な）

peccadillo
[pèkədílou]

n. **a slight sin or fault**

[名] 軽い罪、ちょっとした過ち

The conquistador committed a *peccadillo* to the priest but quickly made amends for it.

関連語 peccadillo : sin [sin]
peccadilloは小さなsin（罪）をいう。

recalcitrant
[rikǽlsitrənt]

adj. **opposing or defiant of authority**

[形]（権威などに）反抗的な、手に負えない

In general, the people of France have been historically *recalcitrant*.

関連語 recalcitrant : obey [oubéi]
recalcitrantな人は簡単にobey（〜に従う）することがない。

recant
[rikǽnt]

v. **to renounce a previous belief or statement**

[動] 〜を取り消す、撤回する；改宗する

Helen's refusal to *recant* her Christian faith led to her imprisonment for more than a year.

関連語 recant : belief [bilí:f]
recantはbelief（信仰）を撤回することをいう。

TRANSLATION | 例 文 の 訳

noble	善行は高潔なもので、他にほうびを求めない。
peccadillo	その征服者は司祭に対して軽い罪を犯したが、すぐにわびた。
recalcitrant	概して、フランス人は歴史的に権威に反抗してきた。
recant	ヘレンはキリスト教から改宗することを拒否したことで、1年以上服役しなければならなかった。

saboteur
[sæ̀bətə́ːʳ]

n. one who sabotages　　　　　　　　[名] サボタージュをする人、破壊工作員

The *saboteurs'* underhanded tactics led to the demise of the agency.

関連語 saboteur : disrupt [disrʌ́pt]

saboteurは社会をdisrupt（〜を混乱させる、崩壊させる）する目的で破壊工作をする人をいう。

sobriety
[səbráiəti]

n. seriousness in manner; self-restraint　　　　[名] 真面目、謹厳；自制

Sobriety is one of the most important tenets of Buddism.

関連語 sobriety : sumptuous [sʌ́mptʃuəs]

sumptuous（豪華な、贅沢な）な暮らしにはsobrietyがない。

sublime
[səbláim]

adj. majestic; lofty and eminent; impressive and noble

[形] 雄大な；崇高な；すばらしい

There is but one step from the *sublime* to the ridiculous.

反意語 sublime : base [beis]

sublimeの反意語はbase（卑劣な、いやしい）

submerge
[səbmə́ːʳdʒ]

v. to put completely under water　　　　　　[動] 〜を水に沈める、潜水する

When the submarine was completely *submerged*, the sailors on shore let out a great cheer.

関連語 submerge : buoyant [bɔ́iənt]

buoyant（浮力のある）ものはsubmergeすることができない。

subside
[səbsáid]

v. to fall downward; to become less active

[動] 陥没する；おさまる、静まる

The storm eventually *subsided*.

反意語 subside : intensify [inténsəfài]

subsideの反意語はintensify（〜を強める、強くなる）

TRANSLATION | 例 文 の 訳

saboteur	その破壊工作員のひきょうな策謀によって、その機関は消滅した。
sobriety	謹厳は仏教の最も重要な教義の一つだ。
sublime	崇高さとこっけいさは紙一重だ。
submerge	その潜水艦が完全に水に潜ると、陸にいた水兵たちは大きな歓声を上げた。
subside	嵐はとうとう収まった。

subsidiary
[səbsídièri]

adj. of the second importance; furnishing support

[形] 二次的な；補助的な

Truancy was a *subsidiary* reason for why Dan was let go.

関連語 subsidy : supportive [səpɔ́ːrtiv]

subsidy（補助金）には何かに対して supportive（〜を支持する、補助する）だという特徴がある。

substantial
[səbstǽnʃəl]

adj. material; considerable in importance or amount

[形] 実体のある；重要な、相当な

The bank would not finance Kelly's loan without *substantial* personal property.

類義語 substantial : corporeal [kɔːrpɔ́ːriəl]

substantial の類義語は corporeal（有形の）

subterfuge
[sʌ́btərfjùːdʒ]

n. a deceptive artifice that conceals the truth

[名] ごまかし、策略

Roberta's apparent happiness with her domestic life was nothing more than *subterfuge* that masked a lonely and empty existence.

関連語 subterfuge : candor [kǽndər]

subterfuge には candor（率直さ、正直さ）が欠けている。

subvert
[səbvə́ːrt]

v. to overturn from the foundation

[動] 〜を破壊する、転覆させる

The rebels *subverted* the existing regime and replaced it with a democratic system of government.

類義語 subvert : sabotage [sǽbətùːʒ]

subvert の類義語は sabotage（〜を破壊する）

TRANSLATION | 例 文 の 訳

subsidiary 無断欠勤はダンが解雇された二次的な理由だった。

substantial 銀行は十分な個人財産がなければケリーに融資しないだろう。

subterfuge ロバータの家庭生活での見かけの幸福は、孤独で空虚な暮らしぶりを隠すごまかしにすぎなかった。

subvert 反乱者たちはそれまでの政権を転覆させ、民主的な政治体制に置き換えた。

succinct
[sʌksíŋkt]

adj. precise and clear expression in writing and speaking

[形] 簡潔な、明解な

Mrs. Fisher summed it up to her friend in a *succinct* remark: You must marry as soon as you can.

反意語 express succinctly : babble [bǽbl]
express succinctly（簡潔に表現する）の反意語は babble（意味のないことを言う）

succor
[sʌ́kəʳ]

n. help when in trouble or need

[名] 援助、支援

The homeless woman found *succor* at the local shelter.

類義語 succor : relief [rilíːf]
succorの類義語は relief（救済、救援）

taciturn
[tǽsətəːʳn]

adj. not talkative; uncommunicative

[形] 無口な；不愛想な

Alex enjoyed Beth's company even though she was *taciturn* by nature.

反意語 taciturn : loquacious [loukwéiʃəs]
taciturnの反意語は loquacious（おしゃべりの）

vaccinate
[vǽksənèit]

v. to prevent disease by giving an injection of dead virus

[動] ～に予防接種する

Children must be *vaccinated* for the flu in the winter months.

関連語 vaccination : immunity [imjúːnəti]
vaccination（予防接種）の目的は immunity（免疫）をつけることだ。

vibrant
[váibrənt]

adj. full of life

[形] 生き生きとした、活気に満ちた

A *vibrant* complexion can signal younger, healthier individuals.

反意語 vibrant : flagging [flǽgiŋ]
vibrantの反意語は flagging（衰えつつある）

TRANSLATION | 例 文 の 訳

succinct フィッシャー夫人は話をまとめ、友人に簡潔に言った。「あなたはできるだけ早く結婚しないとね」

succor そのホームレスの女性は地元の保護施設で支援を受けた。

taciturn ベスは生まれつき無口だったが、アレックスは彼女といっしょにいると楽しかった。

vaccinate 冬の間のインフルエンザに備えて、子供たちは予防接種を受けなければならない。

vibrant 生き生きとした顔色は、若くて健康な人の印だ。

waver
[wéivəʳ]

v. **to be indecisive or vacillate**　　　　　　　　　　[動] 迷う、ためらう

Alex finally made a decision after two weeks of *wavering* back and forth.

関連語 waver : irresoluteness [irézəlùːtnis]
　　　waverと似た意味の名詞に irresoluteness（決断力のなさ、優柔不断）がある。

TRANSLATION | 例 文 の 訳

waver　　　　アレックスは2週間あれこれと迷った末、ようやく決心した。

■ Fill in the blanks with the correct letter that matches the word with its definition.

1. recalcitrant	_____	a. to make very angry
2. facetious	_____	b. to renounce a previous belief or statement
3. aphorism	_____	c. illegal deception or trickery
4. recant	_____	d. help when in trouble or need
5. excerpt	_____	e. a part or quote taken from a larger work; an abstract
6. succor	_____	f. a deceptive artifice that conceals the truth
7. chicanery	_____	g. lacking distinct form; unclear
8. nebulous	_____	h. a short saying containing a principle
9. incense	_____	i. opposing or defiant of authority
10. subterfuge	_____	j. merry or jocular

■ Put the correct word in each blank from the list of words below.

11. spurn（〜をはねつける）の反意語は_____である。

12. desert は_____である。

13. _____は小さな sin である。

14. exculpate するために_____が手段として使用される。

15. _____は supportive な働きを持つお金である。

16. _____したものには authenticity がない。

17. evanescent（すぐに消えていく）の反意語は_____である。

18. _____は社会を disrupt させる目的で破壊行為に手を染める人である。

19. _____には tortuous という特徴がある。

20. _____には prediction する能力がある。

a. fabricate	b. sublime	c. arid	d. alibi	e. abiding	f. licentious
g. subsidy	h. embrace	i. augur	j. saboteur	k. peccadillo	l. labyrinth

Answer key

11. h   12. c   13. k   14. d   15. g   16. a   17. e   18. j   19. l   20. i
1. i   2. j   3. h   4. b   5. e   6. d   7. c   8. g   9. a   10. f

15th DAY

今日で単語集の半分が
終わります。頑張りましょう！

accolade [ǽkəlèid]	n. praise or honor　　　　　　　　　　　　　　　[名] 賞賛、賛辞 In 1967 Michael won *accolades* for his role as a mass murderer in In Cold Blood. 反意語 accolade : invective [invéktiv] 　accoladeの反意語は invective（悪口、非難、ののしり）
anchor [ǽŋkəʳ]	v. to fasten by an anchor　　　　　　　　　[動]（船など）を錨で止める n. a heavy object that holds a ship in place　　　　　[名] 錨 Bryan *anchored* the ship as far off shore as possible. Nautilus used the air brake instead of an *anchor* to stop moving. 関連語 anchor : shift [ʃift] 　anchorには shift（～を移す、移動させる）しないようにする機能がある。
archetype [áːʳkitàip]	n. a prototype; an ideal example of a type　　　[名] 典型、代表例 The *archetype* of an Ancient Greek woman was Aphrodite. 関連語 archetype : exemplify [igzémpləfài] 　archetypeは exemplify（例示する）する要素を持っている。

TRANSLATION | 例 文 の 訳

accolade	1967年、マイケルは映画『冷血』の殺人鬼の役で賞賛を博した。
anchor	ブライアンは、できるだけ海岸から離れたところで船から錨を下ろした。
	ノーチラス号は静止するために、錨の代わりに空気ブレーキを使った。
archetype	古代ギリシャの女性の代表例がアフロディーテだった。

archive
[áːʳkaiv]

n. the place where historical documents and records are kept

[名]（古文書、公文書、記録文書などの）保管所

According to the suit, the National *Archives* and Records Administration first learned that Zimet was trying to sell the documents in late February and early March.

関連語 archive : manuscript [mǽnjuskrìpt]
archiveには manuscript（原稿）を保管する機能がある。

bucolic
[bjuːkálik]

adj. referring to the rural life of the herdsman　[形]田園的な、田舎的な

I don't love the hectic urban lifestyle, but I prefer it to a *bucolic* life here.

反意語 bucolic : urban [əːʳbən]
bucolicの反意語は urban（都市の、都会の）

constellation
[kànstəléiʃən]

n. the formation of stars that make a shape or design　[名]星座

Mary and John stared at the sky identifying as many *constellations* as they could.

関連語 constellation : star [stɑːʳ]
star（星）が constellationを構成する。

constitute
[kánstət(j)ùːt]

v. to lay the foundation for or set up; to appoint one to a high office or place of dignity　[動]の基礎を築く、設立する；任命する

Henderson was *constituted* as the new ambassador in July.

反意語 constitute : abdicate [ǽbdikèit]
constituteの反意語は abdicate（〜を放棄する、退く）

cower
[káuəʳ]

v. to shrink in fear　[動]恐怖に縮み上がる

Every time the owner raised his voice, the dog *cowered* in the corner.

関連語 cower : fear [fiəʳ]
fear（恐れ、恐怖）のために cowerする。

TRANSLATION | 例 文 の 訳

archive	その訴状によると、アメリカ国立公文書記録管理局はジメットがその文書を売ろうとしたことを、2月下旬から3月上旬に初めて知った。
bucolic	私はせわしない都市生活が大好きなわけではないが、ここでの田舎生活よりは好きだ。
constellation	メアリーとジョンはなるべく多くの星座を見つけようと空を見つめた。
constitute	ヘンダーソンは7月に新しい大使に任命された。
cower	飼い主が声を上げるたびに、そのイヌは隅で縮み上がった。

delirium
[dilíªriəm]

n. a state of mental confusion and disorientation

[名] 一時的な精神錯乱

The force of the blow put Liz into a temporary *delirium*.

関連語 delirium : confusion [kənfjúːʒən]
deliriumは一時的に confusion（混乱）している状態。

exhaust
[igzɔ́ːst]

v. to use up completely

[動] 〜を使い果たす

The small clinic's resources were *exhausted* while treating patients from the bus accident.

関連語 exhaust : infinite [ínfənət]
infinite（無限な）ものを exhaust することはできない。

exhort
[igzɔ́ːʳt]

v. to urge strongly with argument

[動] 〜を奨励する、熱心に勧める

Mr. Smith *exhorted* the company's administrative committee to cut down on expenditures.

関連語 exhortative : urge [əːrdʒ]
exhortative（熱心に勧める、推奨する）なものには urge（勧める）する性質が備わっている。

facile
[fǽsil]

adj. easily accomplished; superficial

[形] 簡単に手に入る；皮相的な

The bachelor's *facile* reasons for marriage turned off any woman he dated.

関連語 facile : profundity [prəfʌ́ndəti]
facile なものには profundity（深さ、強さ）がない。

facilitate
[fəsílətèit]

v. to help make easier; to help in progress

[動] 〜を容易にする；〜を促進する

Technology has unarguably *facilitated* communication.

反意語 facilitate : impede [impíːd]
facilitate の反意語は impede（〜を妨げる）

TRANSLATION | 例 文 の 訳

delirium	衝撃を受けて、リズは一時的に錯乱した。
exhaust	バスの事故の負傷者を治療しているうちに、その小さな診療所の備品は使い果たされた。
exhort	スミス氏は、その企業の経営委員会に支出を減らすように強く勧めた。
facile	その独身男性にとっての結婚の理由は底が浅く、交際する女性が皆、嫌悪感を抱いた。
facilitate	技術がコミュニケーションを容易なものにしてきたことに、議論の余地はない。

feckless
[féklis]

adj. **irresponsible or feeble** [形] 無責任な、意志の弱い

The father was upset at his daughter's *feckless* behavior at school.

反意語 feckless : responsible [rispánsəbl]
　feckless の反意語は responsible（責任のある）

foible
[fɔ́:ibl]

n. **a minor fault in someone's character** [名]（性格上のささいな）欠点、弱点

The father's *foibles* did not prevent his son from admiring him.

関連語 foible : failing [féiliŋ]
　foible はささいな failing（欠点、弱点）をいう。

friable
[fráiəbl]

adj. **easily breakable; easily reduced to powder** [形] 砕けやすい；もろい

The water filtered into underlying, particularly *friable* soil.

関連語 friable : crumble [krʌ́mbl]
　friable なものは簡単に crumble（割れる）する。

glib
[glib]

adj. **able to speak smoothly and easily without hesitation stemming from superficiality** [形] 口の達者な、よくしゃべる

The *glib* speaker told his life story to an enraptured audience.

関連語 glib : fluent [flú:ənt]
　glib は fluent（流ちょうな）に比べて、特に言葉だけが上手いという意味を含んでいる。

grieve
[gri:v]

v. **to feel sorrow and grief over something** [動] ～を深く悲しむ、嘆く

We were shocked and *grieved* at the wanton murder he had committed.

関連語 grieve : sorrow [sárou]
　grieve と似た意味の名詞に sorrow（悲しみ、悲哀）がある。

11th　12th　13th　14th　15th　16th　17th　18th　19th　20th

TRANSLATION | 例 文 の 訳

feckless	父親は、娘の学校での無責任な行動に怒っていた。
foible	父親にはささいな欠点があったが、息子の父への賞賛を妨げるものではなかった。
friable	水が地下の特にもろい土壌にしみ込んだ。
glib	その能弁な講演者は、魅了された聴衆に向かって自分の人生の話をした。
grieve	私たちは彼が犯した理不尽な殺人にショックを受け、悲しんだ。

guidance
[gáidns]

n. direction as to a decision; counselling　　　　[名] 指導；支援

His uncle's *guidance* helped Patrick through adolescence.

関連語 guidance : mentor [méntəʳ]
mentor (助言者) とは guidance をしてくれる人をいう。

hackneyed
[hǽknid]

adj. common or dull　　　　[形] 陳腐な、紋切り型の

The *hackneyed* sentiments of the play caused people to audibly groan at its triteness.

関連語 hackneyed : cliche [kli(:)ʃéi]
cliche (陳腐な決まり文句) には hackneyed だという特徴がある。

ichthyologist
[ìkθiálədʒist]

n. one who studies fish　　　　[名] 魚類学者

The number of fish in Long Lake was determined by the *ichthyologist*.

関連語 ichthyologist : salmon [sǽmən]
ichthyologist は salmon (サケ) などの魚を研究する学者だ。

incipient
[insípiənt]

adj. beginning to exist　　　　[形] (存在の) 始まりの、初期の

The work is still in the *incipient* stage.

関連語 incipient : realized [ríːəlàizd]
incipient なものはまだ realized (達成された、実現された) されていない。

incite
[insáit]

v. to move to action; to provoke or stir up
[動] (人を) 駆り立てる；扇動して～させる

William *incited* a physical altercation with the police officer by resisting arrest.

関連語 extant : incite : persiflage [pə́ːʳsəflàːʒ]
persiflage (軽□、からかい) を叩いて、incite する。

TRANSLATION | 例 文 の 訳

guidance	叔父の指導は、パトリックが思春期を過ごすうえで役立った。
hackneyed	その芝居で描かれた陳腐な心情に、人々はありふれた不満の声を上げて応えた。
ichthyologist	ロング湖の魚の生息数が、その魚類学者によって明らかにされた。
incipient	その仕事はまだ初期の段階にある。
incite	ウィリアムは、逮捕に抵抗して警察官ともみ合いになった。

inclement
[inklémənt]

adj. severe or merciless　　　　　　　　　　　[形] 厳しい、無慈悲な

The *inclement* man's heart was not touched by the starving children.

反意語 inclement : balmy [bá:mi]
　　inclementの反意語はbalmy（温和な、おだやかな）

incogitant
[inkádʒətənt]

adj. inconsiderate or thoughtless　　　　　　[形] 思慮のない、軽率な

I found my brother's teasing of my boyfriend to be extremely *incogitant*.

関連語 incogitant : thought [θɔːt]
　　incogitantなものにはthought（考え、考慮）が欠けている。

inherent
[inhíʳrənt]

adj. existing as an essential constituent or characteristic; intrinsic　　　　　　　　[形] 本来備わっている；生まれつきの

Religious freedom was the *inherent* reason why the Pilgrims settled in America.

反意語 inherent : extrinsic [ikstrínsik]
　　inherentの反意語はextrinsic（外部からの、外部の）

inhibit
[inhíbit]

v. to discourage or restrain from doing something
　　　　　　　　　　　　　　　　[動]～を抑制する、抑える、妨げる

Most parents *inhibit* their children from staying up late at night.

反意語 inhibit : foment [foumént]
　　inhibitの反意語はfoment（～を助長する）

laconic
[ləkánik]

adj. using few words; brief to the point　　　　[形] 口数の少ない；簡潔な

Chris didn't enjoy trying to make conversation with the *laconic* guest.

関連語 laconic : volubility [vàljʲbíləti]
　　laconicな人はvolubility（能弁、口達者）を持たない。

TRANSLATION | 例 文 の 訳

inclement	その無慈悲な男の心は、飢えた子供たちを見ても動かされなかった。
incogitant	私の恋人をからかう兄の態度は、ひどく軽率なものだと思った。
inherent	宗教の自由は、清教徒がアメリカに定住した本来の理由だった。
inhibit	ほとんどの親は子供たちに夜ふかしさせないようにする。
laconic	クリスは、その口数の少ない客と喜んで会話しようとは思わなかった。

211

lucid
[lú:sid]

adj. **easily understood; clear**　　　　　　[形] わかりやすい；明解な

The student wrote a *lucid* explanation of his behavior, expressing regret.

関連語 lucid : obfuscate [ábfʌskeit]
lucid なものは obfuscate（〜をぼんやりさせる、わかりにくくする）することがない。

---

mockery
[mákəri]

n. **derision; a subject of ridicule**　　[名] あざけり、からかい；笑いもの

Lily's *mockery* of his obesity drove him to lose weight.

関連語 mockery : burlesque [bəᵣlésk]
burlesque（パロディー、風刺画）は mockery を特徴として持っている。

---

outmaneuver
[àutmənjú:vəᵣ]

v. **to defeat or overcome by skillful maneuvering**

[動] 〜に策略で勝つ、裏をかく

In martial arts, speed and precision are important in *outmaneuvering* your opponent.

反意語 outmaneuver : yield [ji:ld]
outmaneuver の反意語は yield（屈する、降伏する）

---

pacific
[pəsífik]

adj. **peaceful; appeasing**　　　　　　[形] 平和な；なだめるような

The *pacific* demeanor of the kindergarten teacher was unappreciated by her students.

関連語 pacific : discompose [dìskəmpóuz]
pacific な人を discompose（〜の平静を失わせる）することは難しい。

---

palatable
[pǽlətəbl]

adj. **satisfactory or acceptable to the taste**　　[形] 味のよい、口に合う

Hunger makes any fare *palatable*.

類義語 palatable : savory [séivəri]
palatable の類義語は savory（味のよい、食欲をそそる）

TRANSLATION | 例 文 の 訳

lucid	その学生は、後悔を表明しながらも、自分の行動についてはっきりと綴った。
mockery	リリーに肥満をからかわれたことで、彼は減量に駆り立てられた。
outmaneuver	格闘技では、敵の裏をかくうえで速さと正確さが大事だ。
pacific	その幼稚園教諭の穏やかな話し方は、園児たちには喜ばれなかった。
palatable	空腹なら、どんな食べものでもおいしく感じる。

paucity [pɔ́:səti]	n. smallness in number or quantity [名] 少数、少量
	The *paucity* of the group allowed them to travel together.
	反意語 paucity : slew [slu:]
	paucity の反意語は slew (たくさん、多数)

pliant [pláiənt]	adj. easily flexed; compliant [形] 柔らかい、曲がりやすい；従順な
	The wire coat hanger was *pliant* enough to bend into different shapes.
	類義語 pliant : lithe [laið]
	pliant の類義語は lithe (しなやかな、柔軟な)

preclude [priklú:d]	v. to make impossible or prevent for the future; to exclude [動] 〜を不可能にする、妨げる；排除する
	His choice not to go to college has *precluded* any possibility for a good career.
	反意語 preclude : enclose [inklóuz]
	preclude の反意語は enclose (〜を入れる)

pristine [prísti:n]	adj. belonging to the earliest period; pure or unspoiled [形] 初期の、本来の；汚れのない
	The *pristine* beauty of the lake caused everyone to stare in awe.
	関連語 pristine : taint [teint]
	pristine なものは taint (〜を汚す、汚染する) されていない。

pliable [pláiəbl]	adj. flexible and easily bent; yielding readily to others [形] 柔軟な、曲げやすい；影響されやすい
	The *pliable* gymnast was able to do the splits with the greatest of ease.
	類義語 pliable : supple [sʌ́pl]
	pliable の類義語は supple (柔軟な、しなやかな)

TRANSLATION | 例 文 の 訳

paucity	少人数の集団だったので、旅行中いっしょに行動できた。
pliant	その針金で出来たコートハンガーは柔軟で、いろいろな形に曲げられた。
preclude	大学に進学しないことを選んだので、彼が良い職に就ける可能性はいっさいなくなった。
pristine	その湖のけがれのない美しさを、みな息をのんで見つめた。
pliable	その柔軟な体操選手は、いとも簡単に開脚ができた。

pucker [pʌ́kər]	v. **to contract into wrinkles** [動] ～にしわを寄せる、(唇など) をすぼめる Her lips were *puckered* in anticipation of a kiss. 関連語 pucker : mouth [mauθ] mouth (口) を pucker する。
puckish [pʌ́kiʃ]	adj. **mischievous or impish** [形] いたずら好きな、腕白な With a *puckish* gleam in her eye, Sarah ate the cake that was meant for the dinner guests. 反意語 puckish : sober [sóubər] puckish の反意語は sober (しらふの、真面目な)
quibble [kwíbl]	v. **to find fault for trivial reasons** [動] 言いがかりをつける、揚げ足をとる The heirs *quibbled* over the equitable distribution of the inheritance. 関連語 quibbler : cavil [kǽvəl] quibbler (言いがかりをつける人、揚げ足をとる人) は常に cavil (～に難癖をつける) しようとする。
quiescence [kwaiésns]	n. **inactivity or silence** [名] 無活動；静止 The night's *quiescence* lulled Sarah to sleep. 反意語 quiescence : tumult [t(j)úːmʌlt] quiescence の反意語は tumult (騒動、大騒ぎ)

recidivism
[risídəvìzm]
	n. **continual return to bad habits, especially criminal relapse**
	     [名] 常習性；常習的な犯行
	
	The drug user's *recidivism* made any attempts at rehabilitaion useless.
	
	関連語 recidivism : relapse [rilǽps]
	    recidivism は relapse (再発する、ぶり返す) する犯罪などの特徴である。

TRANSLATION | 例 文 の 訳

pucker	彼女はキスを期待して唇をすぼめた。
puckish	瞳をいたずらっぽく輝かせて、サラは夕食の招待客に用意されたケーキを食べた。
quibble	相続人たちは遺産の公平な配分について難癖をつけた。
quiescence	夜の静寂の中、サラは眠りに就いた。
recidivism	その薬物使用者は、常習癖のせいで回復への試みをすべて無駄にした。

reciprocate
[risíprəkèit]

v. **to move backward and forward; to give things or feelings in return** ［動］往復運動する；返礼する、報いる

The pendulum of the clock *reciprocated* slowly once every hour.

反意語 reciprocate : move unidirectionally [muːv jùːnidirékʃənəli]
reciprocateの反意語は move unidirectionally（一方向に動く）

reckless
[réklis]

adj. **disregardful of consequences; heedless** ［形］無謀な；向こう見ずな

Many wars have been avoided by patience but have also been precipitated by *reckless* haste.

反意語 reckless : circumspect [sə́ːʳkəmspèkt]
recklessの反意語は circumspect（慎重な、用心深い）

recluse
[rékluːs]

n. **one who lives in solitude** ［名］世捨て人、隠遁者

For two years John wandered through Arizona, living as a *recluse* in the desert.

関連語 recluse : gregariousness [grigéəriəsnis]
recluse は gregariousness（社交性）を持たない。

recondite
[rékəndàit]

adj. **abstruse or obscure** ［形］難解な、知られていない

Quantum physics is a *recondite* subject for the average layman.

反意語 recondite : widely understood [wáidli ʌndəʳstúd]
reconditeの反意語は widely understood（広く理解されている）

reconnoiter
[rìːkənɔ́itəʳ]

v. **to conduct a preliminary survey, especially in order to gather military information** ［動］〜を予備調査する、偵察する

A scout was sent ahead to *reconnoiter* the position of the enemy.

関連語 reconnoiter : information [ìnfəʳméiʃən]
information（情報）を得るために reconnoiter する。

TRANSLATION | 例 文 の 訳

reciprocate その時計の振り子は1時間に1度だけゆっくりと往復する。
reckless 多くの戦争が忍耐によって回避されてきたが、一方で無謀な性急さによって引き起こされたものもある。
recluse 2年の間、ジョンは砂漠で世捨て人のように暮らしながら、アリゾナを歩き回った。
recondite 量子物理学は一般の人にとっては難しい科目だ。
reconnoiter 敵の位置を偵察するために斥候が前線に送られた。

rehabilitate
[rìːʰəbílətèit]

v. to fix or restore to proper condition; to restore to a healthy condition
[動] ～を修復する；～の機能回復訓練をする

After the accident, James had to *rehabilitate* his broken leg.

関連語 rehabilitation : convalesce [kànvəlés]
rehabilitationと似た意味の動詞にconvalesce（次第に回復する、快方に向かう）がある。

rickety
[ríkiti]

adj. being in an unstable condition; weak or inclined to break
[形] 不安定な；弱い、がたつく

The *rickety* floor of the old house creaked as Michelle walked across it.

関連語 rickety : furniture [fɔ́ːrnitʃər]
furniture（家具）などが古くなるとricketyになる。

schism
[sízm]

n. a division or disharmonic situation
[名] 分裂、分離

A *schism* arose between Turkey and Greece after a group of illegal immigrants were found living in Athens.

反意語 schism : unanimity [jùːnəníməti]
schismの反意語はunanimity（全員の合意、満場一致）

secondary
[sékəndèri]

adj. of second importance
[形] 二次的な

My primary responsibility is to my family; my *secondary* responsibility to my job.

反意語 secondary : preponderant [pripándərənt]
secondaryの反意語はpreponderant（優勢な、圧倒的な、主要な）

sociable
[sóuʃəbl]

adj. naturally enjoying the companionship of others
[形] 社交的な

Kelly is a gay and *sociable* girl who loves parties.

類義語 sociable : convivial [kənvíviəl]
sociableの類義語はconvivial（陽気な、親しみのある）

TRANSLATION | 例 文 の 訳

rehabilitate	事故のあと、ジェームズは骨折した脚のリハビリをしなければならなかった。
rickety	ミッシェルが歩いて渡ると、その古い家のがたついた床にひびが入った。
schism	不法移民の集団がアテネに住んでいることが明らかになると、トルコとギリシャの間が分裂した。
secondary	私の第1の責任は家族に対するもの、第2の責任は仕事に対するものだ。
sociable	ケリーは、パーティーが大好きな陽気で社交的な女の子だ。

11th
12th
13th
14th
15th
16th
17th
18th
19th
20th

stickler
[stíklər]

n. one who insists on exactness or completeness in the observance of something　　　　　[名] ～にうるさい人、こだわる人

My grammar teacher is a *stickler* for correcting grammar errors.

関連語 stickler : exacting [igzǽktiŋ]
stickler には exacting（厳格な、多くを要求する）であるという特徴がある。

synopsis
[sinápsis]

n. a summary capturing the main points　　[名]（小説、詩などの）概要、大意

The busy professor asked his assistant to give him a *synopsis* of the article.

関連語 synopsis : conciseness [kənsáisnis]
synopsis は conciseness（簡潔）を特徴として持つ。

tacit
[tǽsit]

adj. implied without being spoken　　　　　　　　　　　　[形] 暗黙の

The face she made at that moment was a *tacit* cue for me to leave.

関連語 tacit : infer [infə́ːr]
tacit なことを infer（推測する）する。

ticklish
[tíkliʃ]

adj. sensitive to tickling; easily offended or upset
　　　　　　　　　　　　　[形] くすぐったがりの；感情を害しやすい、やっかいな

Jane's *ticklish* disposition made her sensitive to criticism.

反意語 ticklish : imperturbable [ìmpərtə́ːrbəbl]
ticklish の反意語は imperturbable（動揺しない、冷静な）

vacillate
[vǽsəlèit]

v. to sway from one side to the other; to fluctuate in mind or opinion　　　　　　　　　　　　　　　　　　[動] 揺れ動く；心を決めかねる

The dancer's body rhythmically *vacillated* to the beat of the music.

関連語 vacillate : equipoise [ékwəpɔ̀iz]
vacillate するものには equipoise（つり合い、平衡）が欠けている。

TRANSLATION | 例 文 の 訳

stickler	私の文法の先生は、文法の間違いを正すことにこだわる。
synopsis	その多忙な教授は、助手にその記事の概要をまとめるように頼んだ。
tacit	そのときの彼女の顔の表情は、もう帰るという私への無言の合図だった。
ticklish	ジェーンは感情を害しやすい性分で、批判に敏感だった。
vacillate	そのダンサーの体は、音楽のビートに合わせてリズミカルに揺れ動いた。

vociferous
[vousífᵊrəs]

adj. offensively loud; given to vehement outcry

[形] やかましい、騒がしい；絶叫する

The fans' *vociferous* voices attempted to distract opposing teams.

反意語 vociferous : serene [sərí:n]
vociferousの反意語は serene (平静な、穏やかな)

wicked
[wíkid]

adj. vicious or evil

[形] 邪悪な、悪の

The truly *wicked* people of the world live alone.

関連語 wickedness : nefarious [nifέᵊriəs]
wickedness (邪悪、悪意) と似た意味の形容詞に nefarious (極悪な) がある。

TRANSLATION | 例 文 の 訳

| vociferous | ファンたちは、相手チームの注意力を乱すために絶叫した。 |
| wicked | 世の中の本当に邪悪な人々は、孤立して生きている。 |

218

■ Fill in the blanks with the correct letter that matches the word with its definition.

1. inclement _____
2. pliant _____
3. quiescence _____
4. laconic _____
5. bucolic _____
6. hackneyed _____
7. feckless _____
8. tacit _____
9. exhort _____
10. palatable _____

a. common or dull
b. satisfactory or acceptable to the taste
c. to urge strongly with argument
d. implied without being spoken
e. inactivity or silence
f. severe or merciless
g. using few words; brief to the point
h. referring to the rural life of the herdsman
i. easily flexed; compliant
j. irresponsible or feeble

■ Put the correct word in each blank from the list of words below.

11. extrinsic（外部からの、外部の）の反意語は_____である。
12. _____はささいな failing である。
13. _____は taint（汚染する）されていない。
14. _____は fluent と比較して言葉だけが上手いという意味を内包する。
15. _____は manuscript を保管する機能がある。
16. supple（柔軟な、しなやかな）は_____の類義語である。
17. _____は relapse する犯罪を意味する。
18. infinite なものは_____できない。
19. _____は exemplify する要素がある。
20. _____は impede（〜を妨げる）の反意語である。

a. vacillate b. archetype c. pristine d. exhaust e. archive f. glib g. foible
h. inherent i. pliable j. facilitate k. incogitant l. recidivism

Answer key

11. h 12. g 13. c 14. f 15. e 16. i 17. l 18. d 19. b 20. j
1. f 2. i 3. e 4. g 5. h 6. a 7. j 8. d 9. c 10. b

この単語集もすでに半分が
過ぎました。この調子で頑張りましょう。

16th DAY

accrete [əkríːt]	v. to increase gradually by addition　　　　　　　　[動] 次第に増大する The money that Fred had invested 14 years ago had *accreted* to a large amount. 関連語 accrete : grow [grou] 　accrete は grow（増す、育つ）の一種で、徐々に増える様子をいう。
align [əláin]	v. to put or fall into line　　　　　　　[動] ～を一直線に並べる、一列に並べる The interior decorators *aligned* the coffee table with the couches. 反意語 aligned : askew [əskjúː] 　aligned（一直線に並んだ）の反意語は askew（斜めに、ゆがんで）
animate [ǽnəmèit]	v. to enliven or fill with life　　　　　[動] ～に命を吹き込む、～を生き生きとさせる Seth was a smart and *animated* boy with enthusiasm and expression. 反意語 animation : lassitude [lǽsət(j)ùːd] 　animation（活発、熱心）の反意語は lassitude（だるさ、脱力感）
ardent [áːʳdʰnt]	adj. passionate and torrent; displaying strong enthusiasm 　　　　　　　　　　　　　　　　　　　　　　　　　[形] 熱心な；熱狂的な The *ardent* opponents to the death penalty lined up to protest outside the prison walls. 反意語 ardent : tepid [tépid] 　ardent の反意語は tepid（なまぬるい、熱意のない）

TRANSLATION | 例 文 の 訳

accrete	フレッドが14年前に投資した資金が次第に増えて、大きな金額になった。
align	その室内装飾家は、ソファとコーヒーテーブルを一列に並べた。
animate	セスは情熱的で表情豊かな、賢く生き生きとした少年だった。
ardent	熱心な死刑廃止論者たちが刑務所の塀の外に並んで抗議した。

audacious
[ɔːdéiʃəs]

adj. recklessly adventurous or brave　　　　[形] 大胆な、無謀な、勇敢な

The *audacious* tricks of the stuntman awed the audience.

関連語 audacious : trepidation [trèpədéiʃən]
audaciousな人はtrepidation（恐怖、不安）を抱くことがない。

blight
[blait]

n. a disease which destroys or ruins plants　[名] 胴枯れ病（植物を枯らす病気）

v. to wither up; to frustrate or destroy
　　　　　　　　　　　[動] ～を枯らす；～をだめにする、～をくじく

The pine tree was dying of *blight*.

The disease *blighted* the entire crop, leaving the farmer with nothing to harvest.

類義語 blight : ruin [rúːin]
blightの類義語はruin（～を台無しにする、だめにする）

cacophony
[kəkáfəni]

n. dissonant sounds　　　　　　　　　　[名] 不協和音

The Sirens tortured their victims with a *cacophony* of singing and wailing.

反意語 cacophony : melody [mélədi]
cacophonyの反意語はmelody（メロディー、旋律）

coda
[kóudə]

n. an independent concluding part of an artistic work
　　　　　　　　　　[名]（音楽や物語の）コーダ、終結部

Finally in the *coda*, the book moves forward to 1999 for its embracing, reflective conclusion.

反意語 coda : prelude [prél(j)uːd]
codaの反意語はprelude（前置き、前奏曲）

decorous
[dékərəs]

adj. being decent or proper　　　　　　[形] 礼儀正しい、上品な

The *decorous* young man never lost his temper or said anything out of line.

反意語 decorous : mangy [méindʒi]
decorousの反意語はmangy（見苦しい）

TRANSLATION | 例 文 の 訳

audacious そのスタントマンの大胆な技に、観客はあっけにとられた。
blight その松の木は胴枯れ病で枯れかけていた。
この病気は作物全体を枯らし、農家は収穫するものを失ってしまった。
cacophony セイレーンたちは歌と嘆きの不協和音で犠牲者たちをひどく苦しめた。
coda 終結部になってようやく、その本は1999年の話に進み、包括的で思慮深い結論が提示される。
decorous その礼儀正しい若者は、決して機嫌を損ねたり、不適切な発言をしたりしなかった。

221

decrepit
[dikrépit]

adj. weakened, worn out, or impaired by old age or much use

[形] 衰弱した、よぼよぼの、老朽化した

The *decrepit* old man spent the last ten years of his life in bed.

反意語 decrepit : vigorous [vígərəs]
decrepit の反意語は vigorous（力強い、元気のある）

didactic
[daidǽktik]

adj. tending to teach or moralize

[形] 教訓的な、説教的な

Although he was an extremely intelligent man, his *didactic* attitude was not liked by anyone.

関連語 didactic : teach [tiːtʃ]
didactic な人は teach（〜を教える）しようとする特徴がある。

dodder
[dádəʳ]

v. to shake from age or overall weakness of the body; to totter

[動]（老齢・病気などで）よろよろ歩く；震える

Grandmother Betty *doddered* on her way from the house to the car.

関連語 dodder : unsteady [ʌnstédi]
dodder には unsteady（不安定な）だという特徴がある。

emigrate
[émigrèit]

v. to leave one's country to live in another

[動]（自国から他国へ）移住する

Andy's parents *emigrated* to Canada in search of a better future for their family.

反意語 emigrate: repatriate [riːpéitrièit]
emigrate の反意語は repatriate（〜を本国へ送還する）

eminent
[émənənt]

adj. highly ranked or prominent

[形] 高名な、際立った、卓越した

Dressed in full attire, the *eminent* General led the parade through the town's main street.

関連語 eminence : luminary [lúːmənèri]
luminary（ある分野の権威、指導的人物）は eminence（名声、著名）を有している。

TRANSLATION | 例 文 の 訳

decrepit	その衰弱した老人は人生最後の10年間をベッドの上で過ごした。
didactic	彼はとても知的な男だったが、説教がましい態度はだれにも好かれなかった。
dodder	祖母のベティは、家から車までよろよろと歩いた。
emigrate	アンディの両親は家族のよりよい未来を求めてカナダに移住した。
eminent	その高名な将軍は正装し、町の目抜き通りでパレードを先導した。

encourage
[enkə́:ridʒ]

v. **to inspire or give hope to someone**　　　[動]〜を励ます、勇気づける

Criticism of the government should not only be tolerated, but *encouraged*.

関連語 encourage : hortatory [hɔ́ːˈtətɔ̀ːri]
hortatory（奨励の、激励の、勧告的な）なものは encourage するのが特徴だ。

enigma
[ənígmə]

n. **something puzzling or hard to explain and understand**
[名] 不可解なもの、謎

Kay's recent behavior was an *enigma* to those who knew her.

関連語 enigma : impenetrable [impénətrəbl]
enigma には impenetrable（不可解な、理解できない）だという特徴がある。

epigram
[épəgræm]

n. **a wise saying, often in poetic form**　　[名] 警句、エピグラム、短い風刺

Sometimes the doctor made philosophic *epigrams* which he used as encouragement through the hardships in his life.

関連語 epigram : wise [waiz]
epigram は wise（賢い、賢明な）なものだ。

epilogue
[épəlɔ̀ːg]

n. **the conclusion to a literary work or play; afterword**
[名]（文学作品や演劇の）結末、結びの言葉；終局

The *epilogue* of Don Quixote's first book foretells the coming of a second adventure for the valiant knight.

反意語 epilogue : preface [préfis]
epilogue の反意語は preface（序文、はしがき）

excoriate
[ikskɔ́:rièit]

v. **to censure harshly**　　　　　　　[動]〜を激しく非難する

Mr. Arafat has been *excoriated* harshly by President Bush because of the many Palestinian suicide bombings.

反意語 excoriate : extol [ikstóul]
excoriate の反意語は extol（〜を激賞する、絶賛する）

TRANSLATION | 例文の訳

encourage 政府への批判は単に許容されればいいのではなく、むしろ奨励されるべきだ。

enigma ケイの最近の行動は、彼女を知る人々にとっては謎だった。

epigram その医者はときどき哲学的な警句を作り、人生の困難をくぐり抜けるうえでの励ましとした。

epilogue ドン・キホーテの第1作の結末に、この勇敢な騎士の第2の冒険が予見される。

excoriate パレスチナ人による多数の自爆テロが理由で、アラファト議長はブッシュ大統領に激しく非難されてきた。

exculpate
[ékskʌlpèit]

v. **to forgive or excuse of a criminal charge**　　　　[動]〜を無罪にする

The defendant argues that the new evidence should *exculpate* him.

関連語 exculpate : alibi [ǽləbài]
exculpate するために alibi（アリバイ、現場取材証明）を利用する。

faction
[fǽkʃən]

n. **a select group within a larger group**　　　　[名]党派、派閥、少数派

Only the most outstanding *faction* of students was selected to represent the school at the ceremony.

類義語 faction : clique [kliːk]
faction の類義語は clique（徒党、派閥）

fade
[feid]

v. **to slowly disappear; to lose freshness**　　　[動]〜から消えていく；色あせる

Old soldiers never die; they just *fade* away.

関連語 fade : loudness [láudnis], brightness [bráitnis]
loudness（音の大きさ）や brightness（光の明るさ）が fade していく。

faint
[feint]

adj. **weak or dizzy; lacking courage or strength; lacking clarity or loudness**　　　[形]ふらふらして；かすかな、ほのかな；おぼろげな

The *faint* voices began to grow louder as Mary got closer to the door.

反意語 faint : stentorian [stentɔ́ːriən]
faint の反意語は stentorian（声が大きい）

fecundity
[fikʌ́ndəti]

n. **the productiveness of a person, thing, or animal**　　　[名]多産、肥沃

Research shows that high *fecundity* is often balanced by high mortality.

反意語 fecundity : barrenness [bǽrənnis]
fecundity の反意語は barrenness（不毛、不妊）

TRANSLATION | 例 文 の 訳

exculpate	被告人はその新しい証拠が自分の無罪を立証すると主張している。
faction	学生の中で唯一、最もずば抜けた少数派が、その式典で学校代表に選ばれた。
fade	老兵は決して死なない。ただいなくなるだけだ。
faint	メアリーがドアに近づくにつれて、かすかだった声が大きくなってきた。
fecundity	研究によると、高い出産率と高い死亡率が均衡することが多いという。

frigid
[frídʒid]

adj. extremely cold [形] 寒冷な、極寒の

Mars has *frigid* weather conditions.

関連語 frigid : cool [kuːl]
frigid は cool (涼しい、冷たい) よりもはるかに寒い状態を表す。

gainsay
[gèinséi]

v. to oppose or state as untrue [動]〜を否定する；反論する

I *gainsaid* my sister's claim that I had stolen Mom's money.

反意語 gainsay : affirm [əfə́ːrm]
gainsay の反意語は affirm (〜と断言する、確認する)

grind
[graind]

v. to reduce to powder by friction; to wear down or polish by friction [動]〜を挽く；〜を研ぐ

Flour is made by *grinding* wheat.

関連語 grind : pestle [péstl]
pestle (すりこぎ) は grind するために使う棒。cf) mortar (すり鉢) は pestle といっしょに grind するために使う。

guile
[gail]

n. deceit or trickery [名] 欺くこと、詐欺

Looking into her large clear eyes, Bruce could see nothing that would indicate *guile*.

関連語 guile : naive [nɑːíːv]
naive (世間知らずの、だまされやすい、無邪気な) な人には guile がない。

hamstring
[hǽmstrìŋ]

v. to cripple or incapacitate [動]〜を損なわせる、だめにする、挫折させる

The relief efforts were *hamstrung* by the unexpected storm.

関連語 hamstring : effectiveness [iféktivnis]
effectiveness (効果、効力) を hamstring する。

TRANSLATION | 例 文 の 訳

frigid 火星の気象条件は極寒だ。

gainsay 私は、私が母のお金を盗んだという姉の主張に反論した。

grind 小麦粉は小麦を挽いて作られる。

guile ブルースは彼女の大きく澄んだ目を覗き込んだが、裏切りの色は見えなかった。

hamstring 予期せぬ嵐で救護活動は頓挫した。

heinous
[héinəs]

adj. hatefully wicked   [形] 極悪な、凶悪な、非道な

Many consider Hitler's extermination of the Jews to be the most *heinous* act in history.

反意語 heinous : venial [ví:niəl]
    heinousの反意語は venial（[罪などが] ささいな、許される）

hidebound
[háidbàund]

adj. stubbornly conservative; having dry skin adhering closely to underlying flesh   [形] 狭量な、因習的な；(家畜が) 骨と皮だけの

Some critics say that present-day Korean society is much less hierarchical and *hidebound* than it was during the country's long pre-modern period.

関連語 hidebound : conservative [kənsə́:ˈvətiv]
    hideboundは conservative（保守的な）よりもさらに保守的な様子を表す。

hideous
[hídiəs]

adj. ugly to the point of being offensive   [形] ひどく醜い、ぞっとする

The Medusa was a mythological *hideous* creature whose face would turn any men to stone.

関連語 hideous : pulchritude [pʌ́lkrət(j)ùːd]
    hideousなものには pulchritude（身体の美しさ）が欠けている。

incontrovertible
[inkàntrəvə́:ˈtəbl]

adj. not open to argument; unquestionable   [形] 議論の余地がない；明白な

Despite *incontrovertible* evidence, the jury found the defendant innocent.

関連語 incontrovertible : dispute [dispjú:t]
    incontrovertibleなものは dispute（〜を議論する、討論する）する余地がない。

incorrigible
[inkɔ́:ridʒəbl]

adj. unruly; unable to reform   [形] 手に負えない；矯正できない

The *incorrigible* young man could not be controlled by anyone, not even his parents.

関連語 incorrigible : amend [əménd]
    incorrigibleなものは amend（〜を修正する、改正する）ことができない。

TRANSLATION | 例 文 の 訳

heinous	多くの人が、ヒトラーのユダヤ人虐殺を歴史上最も非道な行為だと考えている。
hidebound	何人かの批評家たちは、現在の韓国社会は長期にわたった前近代よりもずっと階級にしばられず、因習的でもないと言っている。
hideous	メデューサは神話に出てくるひどく醜い怪物で、その顔であらゆる人間を石に変えてしまう。
incontrovertible	明白な証拠があるにもかかわらず、陪審員団は被告人を無罪とした。
incorrigible	その救い難い若者はだれの手にも負えず、両親さえもが抑えられなかった。

226

inculpate
[inkʌ́lpeit]

v. to blame or convict of a wrongful act with the use of evidence or proof 　[動]（証拠を使って）人に罪を負わせる；〜をとがめる

Pierre was *inculpated* by the new evidence brought forth by the prosecution.

反意語 inculpate : exonerate [igzánərèit]
inculpateの反意語はexonerate（〜の無実を証明する）

indefensible
[ìndifénsəbl]

adj. incapable of being defended or excused
[形] 弁護の余地のない、言い訳できない

The company's decision not to recall the defective laptop is *indefensible*.

反意語 indefensible : tenable [ténəbl]
indefensibleの反意語はtenable（批判に耐えられる、弁護できる）

inimical
[inímikəl]

adj. being hostile or opposed to someone or something
[形] 敵意のある、敵対的な

Peter's cold, *inimical* voice towards Michael indicated the bad blood between the two.

反意語 inimical : amicable [ǽmikəbl]
inimicalの反意語はamicable（友好的な、社交的な）

inimitable
[inímətəbl]

adj. not able to be mimicked　[形] 真似できない、無比の

The actor's stellar performance was *inimitable*.

関連語 inimitable : copy [kápi]
inimitableなものをcopy（模倣する、真似る）することはできない。

jaded
[dʒéidid]

adj. being worn out and tired　[形] 疲れ切った、あきあきした

Jack seemed *jaded*, but he interrupted his comrade with a voice of calm confidence.

関連語 jaded : overexposure [òuvərikspóuʒəʳ]
overexposure（表舞台に立ちすぎる）した結果、jadedな状態になる。

TRANSLATION | 例文の訳

inculpate ピエールは検察が提出した新しい証拠によって有罪となった。
indefensible その企業が、欠陥品のノートパソコンを回収しないと決定したことは、言語道断だ。
inimical ピーターがマイケルに向けた冷たく敵意のある声は、2人の不和を浮き彫りにした。
inimitable その俳優のきわだった演技は、まねできないものだった。
jaded ジャックは疲れ切っているようだったが、穏やかな自信のある声で仲間の話をさえぎった。

jocund
[dʒákənd]

adj. **being in high spirits**　　　　　　　　　　　[形] 陽気な、快活な

After the football victory, the fans were *jocund* and celebrated all night.

反意語 jocund : morose [məróus]
　　jocundの反意語は morose（不機嫌な、気難しい）

occult
[əkʌlt]

adj. **hidden from general view or knowledge**　　　[形] 秘密の、不思議な

The *occult* entrance to the club was only accessible with a special key.

反意語 occult : patent [pǽtnt]
　　occultの反意語は patent（明白な）

orderly
[ɔ́ːʳdəʳli]

adj. **neatly organized**　　　　　　　　　　　　[形] 整然とした、整頓された

The secretary's desk had been arranged in a neat and *orderly* fashion.

反意語 orderly : awry [ərái]
　　orderlyの反意語は awry（曲がった、ゆがんだ）

pedantic
[pədǽntik]

adj. **being a pedant; ostentatious of learning**
　　　　　　　　　　　　　　　　　　[形] 細部にこだわる；学者ぶる

She had a reputation for being *pedantic* in her work, always double-checking every calculation.

関連語 pedantic : scholarly [skálərli]
　　pedanticは scholarly（学識のある、学問好きの）なふりをすることをいう。

persiflage
[pə́ːʳsəflɑ̀ːʒ]

n. **light teasing or banter**　　　　　　　　　[名] 軽口、冗談、からかい

The *persiflage* between the old friends belied the actual tension that strained their relationship.

関連語 persiflage : incite [insáit]
　　persiflageの目的は incite（怒りなどを起こさせる）することだ。

TRANSLATION ｜ 例 文 の 訳

jocund	勝利を収めたサッカーチームのファンたちは、一晩中陽気に浮かれ騒いだ。
occult	そのクラブの秘密の入口は、特別な鍵がないと入れなかった。
orderly	その秘書の机は、きちんと整理されていた。
pedantic	彼女は仕事に対して几帳面で、計算をするたびに必ずダブルチェックをするという評判であった。
persiflage	長年の友人同士の間での軽口が、実際の彼らの緊張関係を覆い隠した。

philistine
[fíləstìːn]

n. one who is uncultured and ignorant [名] 凡俗な人、俗物、教養のない人

The world is full of *philistines* who care only for money and nothing for culture and the arts.

関連語 philistine : cultivated [kʌ́ltəvèitid]
philistine は cultivated（教養のある、洗練された）な人ではない。

plagiarism
[pléidʒərìzm]

n. the use of another's words and ideas as one's own [名] 剽窃、盗用

Plagiarism is practiced by students now more than ever as the internet has made it easier to copy others' works.

関連語 plagiarism : ideas [aidíːəz]
ideas（考え、思想）は plagiarism の対象になる。

rectify
[réktəfài]

v. to make right; to correct [動] 〜を訂正する；直す

The businessman tried to *rectify* his mistakes of being an absentee father by spending more time with his children.

関連語 rectify : treaty [tríːti]
treaty（条約、協定）を rectify する。

rectitude
[réktət(j)ùːd]

n. the state of right and good morals; the quality of being correct in judgment [名] 正直、実直

The moral *rectitude* of humanity is of the utmost concern, especially for world religious leaders.

関連語 rectitude : corruptionist [kərʌ́pʃᵊnist]
corruptionist（背徳漢）には rectitude が欠けている。

TRANSLATION | 例 文 の 訳

philistine	この世界はお金のことだけを考え、文化や芸術のことなどかまわない無教養な人々でいっぱいだ。
plagiarism	インターネットによって他人の作品を簡単にコピーできるようになり、かつてないほど多くの学生が剽窃を行っている。
rectify	その実業家は子供たちといっしょに過ごす時間を増やすことで、留守がちだった父親としての過ちを正そうとした。
rectitude	人類の道徳的な誠実さは、特に世界の宗教指導者にとっての最大の関心事だ。

secure
[sikjúəʳ]

v. to protect from risk of loss and danger; to guarantee

[動] 確保する、守る；保証する

adj. free from danger

[形] 安全な、安定した

Laws alone cannot *secure* freedom of expression; in order that every man present his views without penalty there must be a spirit of tolerance in the entire population.

The commander had his entire unit make a *secure* temporary defensive site.

反意語 secure : precarious [prikέəriəs]
　　　secureの反意語はprecarious（不安定な、危険な）

sedate
[sidéit]

v. to make calm

[動] 人を落ち着かせる

adj. keeping a serious and quiet manner

[形] 真面目な、落ち着いた

The lawyer had to *sedate* his client from yelling against the judge to avoid the maximum sentence.

Jane looked a little more pale than usual, but more *sedate* than Elizabeth had expected.

反意語 sedate : roil [rɔil]
　　　sedateの反意語はroil（～を怒らせる、いらだたせる）

stiff
[stif]

adj. firm and difficult to bend

[形] 堅い、曲がりにくい

Thomas woke up with a *stiff* neck after sleeping in an awkward position.

関連語 stiff : suppleness [sʌ́plnis]
　　　stiffなものにはsuppleness（柔軟性、しなやかさ）が欠けている。

sycophant
[síkəfənt]

n. one who flatters those in power to get what he/she wants

[名] おべっか使い、ごまをする人

Hollywood stars often complain that true friends are hard to find among the plethora of *sycophants*.

関連語 sycophant : fawn [fɔːn]
　　　sycophantはfawn（へつらう、おもねる）する。

TRANSLATION | 例文の訳

secure　法律だけで表現の自由を守ることはできない。あらゆる人が罰せられることなく自分の意見を述べるためには、すべての人が寛容さを身につけなければならない。
その司令官は指揮下にある全部隊に、安全な臨時の防衛基地を作らせた。

sedate　その弁護士は極刑を避けるために、裁判官をどなりつけたりしないよう依頼人を落ち着かせなければならなかった。
ジェーンはいつもよりも少し青ざめて見えたが、エリザベスが予想していたよりは落ち着いていた。

stiff　トーマスは変な姿勢で眠っていたので、起きたら首が動かなくなっていた。

sycophant　ハリウッドスターたちは、ごますりが多すぎる中で本当の友人を見つけるのが難しい、とよく不満を言う。

tact
[tækt]

n. the capability to act so as not to offend people

[名] 機転、如才なさ、こつ

Tom was completely lacking *tact* and was of no romantic interest to Sue.

関連語 tactless : offend [əfénd]

tactless(融通が利かない、鈍感な)な人は offend(人の感情を害する、傷つける)する特徴がある。

thicken
[θíkən]

v. to make more thick; to increase the density of

[動] 厚くする；濃くする

Coagulants *thicken* blood which aid in the clotting of injured vessels.

関連語 thicken : coagulant [kouǽgjulənt]

coagulant(凝固剤)には液体を thicken する機能がある。

trickle
[tríkl]

v. to drip or fall as drops

[動] したたらせる、ぽたぽたと落ちる

Pierre felt the tears *trickle* under his spectacles and hoped they would not be noticed.

関連語 trickle : gush [ɡʌʃ]

gush(流れ出る、ほとばしる)は trickle よりも流れる勢いが激しい。

uncouth
[ʌnkúːθ]

adj. lacking in tact and grace

[形] 礼儀に反する、粗野な

Mattie remembered the shyness he had felt at approaching her in his *uncouth* clothes.

関連語 uncouth : churl [tʃɚl]

churl(無作法な男、育ちのいやしい男)は uncouth だという特徴がある。

TRANSLATION | 例 文 の 訳

tact	トムはまるで気が利かない人物なので、スーにまったく恋愛対象として見てもらえなかった。
thicken	凝血剤は血液を濃くすることで、傷ついた血管を固めるのを助ける。
trickle	ピエールは眼鏡の下で涙が流れ落ちるのを感じ、気づかれないことを願った。
uncouth	マティは、見苦しい服を着て彼女に会ったときの恥ずかしさを思い出した。

231

unctuous
[ʌ́ŋktʃuəs]

adj. **characterized by insincere kindness; having the quality of oil**

[形] 調子のいい；脂っこい

Many products, such as candles and oil, are made from the body parts of *unctuous* animals, such as whales.

関連語 unctuous : salve [sæv]
salve (軟膏) はたいてい unctuous だ。

uphold
[ʌphóuld]

v. **to support or sustain something to ensure its proper use**

[動] 〜を支持する、擁護する

It is the job of every citizen to *uphold* the law.

反意語 uphold : abrogate [ǽbrəgèit]
uphold の反意語は abrogate (〜を廃止する)

vague
[veig]

adj. **unclear or inexplicit**

[形] 不明瞭な、あいまいな

Nicholas formed a *vague* mental picture from the short description he had been given.

反意語 vague : trenchant [tréntʃənt]
vague の反意語は trenchant (はっきりした、痛烈な)

vehement
[víːəmənt]

adj. **intensely emotional; marked by forceful energy**

[形] 激しい、強烈な、熱烈な

In a rage of anger she shouted *vehement* words at the group of onlookers.

反意語 vehement : apathetic [ǽpəθétik]
vehement の反意語は apathetic (無関心な、やる気のない)

TRANSLATION | 例 文 の 訳

unctuous	ろうそくや油など、たくさんの製品が、クジラのような脂肪の多い動物の体の一部から作られている。
uphold	法を支持することは、すべての市民の義務だ。
vague	ニコラスは、与えられた短い説明の中から漠然としたイメージを膨らませた。
vehement	彼女は激怒して、見物人に向かって激しい言葉をぶつけた。

■ Fill in the blanks with the correct letter that matches the word with its definition.

1. enigma   _____

2. audacious   _____

3. rectitude   _____

4. dodder   _____

5. fecundity   _____

6. inculpate   _____

7. decorous   _____

8. uncouth   _____

9. excoriate   _____

10. jocund   _____

a. to censure harshly

b. to shake from age or overall weakness of the body

c. lacking in tact and grace

d. to blame or convict of a wrongful act with the use of evidence or proof

e. the state of right and good morals; the quality of being correct in judgement

f. being of decent or good taste

g. something puzzling or hard to explain and understand

h. the productiveness of a person, thing, or animal

i. being in high spirits

j. recklessly adventurous or brave

■ Put the correct word in each blank from the list of words below.

11. _____なものは amend できない。

12. _____は wise な内容を含んでいる。

13. patent（明白な）は_____の反意語である。

14. amicable（友好的な）の反意語は_____である。

15. luminary は_____を有している。

16. _____は fawn する。

17. _____は impenetrable という性質を持っている。

18. salve は通常_____である。

19. _____は ruin（〜を台無しにする）の類義語である。

20. _____は、cool の程度を超えてはるかに寒い状態を意味する。

| a. enigma | b. decrepit | c. occult | d. eminence | e. sedate | f. epigram |
| g. frigid | h. blight | i. unctuous | j. incorrigible | k. inimical | l. sycophant |

Answer key

11. j   12. f   13. c   14. k   15. d   16. l   17. e   18. i   19. h   20. g

1. g   2. j   3. e   4. b   5. h   6. d   7. f   8. c   9. a   10. i

17th DAY

今さら元には戻れない道を歩いているなら、最後まで進みましょう。

abstain
[æbstéin]

v. to prevent oneself from; to avoid doing something deliberately

[動] ～を避ける；控える

It is a common traditional practice to *abstain* from sex until marriage.

関連語 abstain : forbidden [fəˈbídn]
forbidden（禁止されている）ことを abstain する。

acute
[əkjúːt]

adj. sharp or severe; characterized by penetrating intellectual perception

[形] 深刻な、激しい；鋭い、鋭敏な

The professor is brilliant because she is an *acute* thinker.

関連語 acute : discerner [disə́ːˈnər]
discerner（目利き、識別する人）は acute な識別力を持つ。

aggrandize
[əgrǽndaiz]

v. to increase in strength or importance

[動]（権力など）を拡大する、増大する

Over the past decade China has *aggrandized* its influence in world affairs.

関連語 aggrandize : strength [streŋkθ]
aggrandize は strength（強さ、力）を増大することをいう。

aggravate
[ǽgrəvèit]

v. to irritate or make worse

[動] 人を怒らせる、（悩み、病気など）を悪化させる

The loud construction *aggravated* many nearby residents.

類義語 aggravate : exacerbate [igzǽsəˈbèit]
aggravate の類義語は exacerbate（～をさらに悪化させる）

TRANSLATION | 例文の訳

abstain	結婚するまで性行為を控えるのはよくある伝統的慣習だ。
acute	その大学教授は鋭い思考力をもっているので、きわめて優秀である。
aggrandize	この10年間で中国は国際問題への影響力を拡大してきている。
aggravate	工事の騒音が多くの近隣住民を怒らせた。

aggrieve
[əgríːv]

v. **to distress or bring trouble to**   [動]～を苦しませる、悩ませる

Eva looked downcast and *aggrieved* after her father's surgery.

反意語 aggrieve : gratify [grǽtəfài]
aggrieveの反意語はgratify（～を喜ばせる、満足させる）

argot
[áːʳgou]

n. **a secret language or idiom specific to the context**

[名] 隠語、業界用語

The two uttered an *argot* so as not to be understood by the others.

類義語 argot : jargon [dʒáːʳgən]
argotの類義語はjargon（専門用語、業界用語）

augment
[ɔːgmént]

v. **to make larger, greater, or more intense**   [動]～を増大させる、増やす

Chad *augmented* his income by working an extra part time job.

反意語 augment : abate [əbéit]
augmentの反意語はabate（～を減ずる、やわらげる）

bedlam
[bédləm]

n. **a state of extreme confusion or noisy uproar**   [名] 大騒ぎ、大混乱

Weddings are such a *bedlam* of activities that the bridal party is always exhausted afterwards.

反意語 bedlam : serenity [sərénəti]
bedlamの反意語はserenity（静けさ、穏やかさ）

bigot
[bígət]

n. **one who holds strong to their own prejudices and opinions about other's race or religion**

[名]（人種・宗教などについて）頑迷な人、偏狭な人

In the rural areas of the country there are more *bigots* because they have less exposure to different kinds of people.

関連語 bigot : tolerance [tálərəns]
bigotにはtolerance（寛容、寛大さ）がない。

TRANSLATION | 例 文 の 訳

aggrieve	エヴァは父親の手術のあと、落ち込んで悩んでいるように見えた。
argot	その2人は他の人たちにわからないように隠語を使って話した。
augment	チャドはパートタイムの仕事をすることで収入を増やした。
bedlam	結婚式はやることが多すぎて混乱気味になるので、続く披露宴には常に疲労感がある。
bigot	その国の農村部に頑迷な人が多いのは、多様な人々と出会う機会が少ないからだ。

235

cantankerous
[kæntǽŋkərəs]

adj. **difficult to deal with; ill-tempered**　　　[形] 扱いにくい；怒りっぽい

If Ron doesn't have his espresso in the morning, he becomes *cantankerous* for the whole day.

反意語 cantankerous : genial [dʒíːnjəl]
　　cantankerousの反意語は genial（愛想のよい、温和な）

circumference
[səʳkʌ́mfərəns]

n. **the distance around a closed circle**　　　[名] 円周

The *circumference* of the watermelon is triple that of the pear.

関連語 circumference : circle [sə́rkl]
　　circumferenceは circle（円）の一部だ。

cogent
[kóudʒənt]

adj. **very compelling; appealing to the mind or reason**
　　　　　　　　　　　　　　　　　　[形] 説得力のある；適切な

A missionary's job is to be *cogent* in delivering the message of God.

関連語 cogent : convince [kənvíns]
　　cogentな人は他人を convince（～を納得させる、説得する）しようとする。

cognizant
[kágnəzᵊnt]

adj. **having an awareness or knowledge**　　　[形] ～を認識して、知って

It is said that the oracles of Ancient Greece were *cognizant* of the ways of the gods.

反意語 cognizant : unaware [ʌnəwɛ́əʳ]
　　cognizantの反意語は unaware（～に気がつかない、知らない）

TRANSLATION | 例 文 の 訳

cantankerous	朝、エスプレッソを飲まないと、ロンは一日中怒りっぽくなる。
circumference	そのスイカの周囲の長さは、ナシの3倍だ。
cogent	宣教師の仕事は神のメッセージを説得力を持って伝えることだ。
cognizant	古代ギリシャの神官たちは神の行いを知っていたと言われる。

consummate
v.[kánsəmèit]
adj.[kánsəmit]

v. **to complete or finish** 　　　　　　[動] 〜を完成する、頂点に高める

adj. **skilled or perfect** 　　　　　　　　[形] 熟練した、完璧な

The two corporate leaders *consummated* their merger with a glass of wine.

Hiller was the *consummate* politician with his brilliant smile and excellent speaking skills.

反意語 consummate : amateurish [æ̀mətʃúəriʃ]
consummateの反意語はamateurish（素人っぽい、下手な）

digress
[daigrés]

v. **to move away from the main subject** 　[動] 話がわき道にそれる、脱線する

Our conversation *digressed* from academia to our plans for Friday night.

関連語 digress : subject [sʌ́bdʒikt]
subject（主題、話題）をdigressする。

dogged
[dɔ́(:)gid]

adj. **stubbornly unyielding** 　　　　　　[形] 頑固な、容易に屈しない

Sherlock Holmes was *dogged* in his pursuit to solve a mystery.

反意語 dogged : yielded [jíːldid]
doggedの反意語はyielded（降伏した、認めた）

doggerel
[dɔ́:gərəl]

n. **irregular and awkward poetry, usually used in a comic sense**
　　　　　　　　　　　　　　　　　　　　　　[名] へぼ詩、こっけい詩

As the soldier marched he sang a bit of a *doggerel* in a high and quavering voice.

関連語 doggerel : verse [vəːʳs]
doggerelはverse（詩、韻文）の一種。

effusive
[ifjúːsiv]

adj. **excessively demonstrative; gushy** 　[形] 気持ちをあらわにした；大げさな

Mrs. Lee's *effusive* personality began to grate on her dinner guests.

反意語 effusive : reticent [rétəsᵊnt]
effusiveの反意語はreticent（無口な、話したがらない）

TRANSLATION | 例 文 の 訳

consummate	その2社のトップは、合併交渉の締めくくりにワインで乾杯した。
	ヒラーはまぶしい笑顔と卓越した演説能力を持つ、完璧な政治家だった。
digress	私たちの会話は、学術的な話題から金曜の夜の過ごし方へと脱線した。
dogged	シャーロック・ホームズは謎解きを追求することにかけては頑固だった。
doggerel	その兵士は行進しながら、高く震える声で下手な詩の一節を詠んだ。
effusive	リー夫人の感情的な性格は、夕食に招かれた客たちの気分を害し始めた。

engender
[indʒéndəʳ]

v. **to produce or bring into being** [動]〜を生じる、発生させる

There had been so much enthusiasm *engendered* that Carrie believed herself deeply in love.

反意語 engender : quash [kwɑʃ]
engenderの反意語はquash（〜を鎮圧する、抑える）

engross
[engróus]

v. **to take all the attention of; to occupy completely** [動]〜を夢中にさせる、没頭させる

The book *engrossed* readers with an intense and imaginative plot.

類義語 engrossed : absorbed [əbsɔ́ːʳbd]
engrossed（夢中で、没頭して）の類義語はabsorbed（夢中になって）

fiasco
[fiǽskou]

n. **a complete and utter failure** [名]大失敗

Terry's friends had procrastinated too long in planning his birthday party and as a result it was a *fiasco*.

反意語 fiasco : notable success [nóutəbl səksés]
fiascoの反意語はnotable success（注目すべき成功）

frustrate
[frʌ́streit]

v. **to make discouraged; to block or prevent someone from doing something** [動]いらだたせる；〜するのを妨げる

I was *frustrated* that he didn't show up on time.

反意語 frustrate : abet [əbét]
frustrateの反意語はabet（〜をそそのかす）

infuse
[infjúːz]

v. **to introduce or put into by pouring; to fill with something** [動]〜を吹き込む；注入する

The newly wed wife *infused* her husband's bachelor pad with a homely atmosphere.

関連語 infuse : inspire [inspáiəʳ]
inspire（鼓舞する、強い感情を抱かせる）はinfuseよりも程度が強い。

TRANSLATION | 例 文 の 訳

engender	あまりにもたくさんの思いがこみ上げてきたので、キャリーは自分がどっぷりと恋に落ちているのだと思った。
engross	その本は感動的で想像力豊かな筋書きで読者を夢中にさせた。
fiasco	テリーの友人たちは、彼の誕生日パーティーの計画を遅らせすぎてしまい、結果的に大失敗だった。
frustrate	彼が定刻に現れなかったので、私はいらいらした。
infuse	その新婚の妻は、夫が独身時代に住んでいた部屋に家庭的な雰囲気を吹き込んだ。

ingenious
[indʒíːnjəs]

adj. **having or showing cleverness or creativity, especially in designing or in solving problems** [形] 巧みな、独創的な

Cornell's *ingenious* orchestral score was lauded as a masterpiece.

反意語 ingenious : prosaic [prouzéiik]
ingenious の反意語は prosaic (想像力に欠ける、つまらない)

ingenue
[ǽndʒən(j)úː]

n. **a naive young lady** [名] 無邪気な少女

The actress played the role of the *ingenue* who the lead male fell in love with.

関連語 ingenue : sophistication [səfistəkéiʃən]
ingenue には sophistication (洗練されていること、教養のあること) は見られない。

negligent
[néglidʒənt]

adj. **tending to neglect; careless or casual** [形] 怠慢な；不注意な

The doctor's *negligent* actions resulted in a permanent impairment for the patient.

反意語 negligent : vigilant [vídʒələnt]
negligent の反意語は vigilant (警戒している、油断のない)

odious
[óudiəs]

adj. **very unpleasant; causing disgust** [形] 非常に不愉快な；嫌悪を抱かせる

The *odious* smell in the kitchen emanated from the spoiled food.

関連語 odious : disgust [disgʌ́st]
odious なものを見ると、disgust (嫌悪) を感じる。

ominous
[ámənəs]

adj. **of a bad omen; threatening** [形] 不吉な；縁起の悪い

The *ominous* occurrence of events this week foretells of a greater disaster.

反意語 ominous : auspicious [ɔːspíʃəs]
ominous の反意語は auspicious (前途有望な、幸先のよい)

TRANSLATION | 例 文 の 訳

ingenious	コーネルの独創的な交響曲は傑作だと賞賛された。
ingenue	その女優は、主人公の男が恋に落ちる無邪気な少女の役を演じた。
negligent	医師の不注意な行為のせいで、その患者に一生の障害が残った。
odious	台所の不愉快な臭いは、腐った食べ物から出ていた。
ominous	今週起きた不吉な出来事は、より大きな災難を予告している。

opine
[oupáin]

v. **to state as one's own opinion; to express an opinion**

[動] ～という意見を述べる；意見を言う

The doctor *opined* that the indisposition arose from fatigue and he prescribed rest.

関連語 opine : pundit [pʌ́ndit]

pundit（専門家）はいつも opine する傾向がある。

ostentation
[àstentéiʃən]

n. **a showy display to impress others**

[名] 見せびらかし、誇示

The wealthy are not disliked for their riches, but rather for their *ostentatious* behavior.

反意語 ostentation : artlessness [ɑ́ːˈtlisnis]

ostentation の反意語は artlessness（飾らないこと）

persevere
[pə̀ːˈsəvíəˈ]

v. **to persist in an undertaking despite difficulties or obstacles**

[動]（困難や障害に耐えて）～をやり抜く

Those who keep their goals in mind shall *persevere*.

反意語 persevere : give up [giv ʌp]

persevere の反意語は give up（あきらめる）

philanthropist
[filǽnθrəpist]

n. **one who acts in goodwill towards others**

[名] 博愛主義者、慈善家

The noted *philanthropist* was known for his generous donations and benevolent spirit.

関連語 philanthropist : eleemosynary [èlimásənèri]

philanthropist は eleemosynary（慈善的な）だ。

pigment
[pígmənt]

n. **a color created for decoration (i.e., makeup); a coloring matter in a cell of animals and plants**

[名] 顔料；色素

The *pigment* in her lips and cheeks were red from the cold.

関連語 pigment : albinism [ǽlbənìzm]

albinism（色素欠乏症）の人は pigment が不足している。

TRANSLATION | 例 文 の 訳

opine その医者は、気分がすぐれないのは疲労が原因だろうという見解を述べ、休息をとるよう促した。

ostentation 金持ちが嫌われるのは豊かだからではなく、これ見よがしの態度をとるからだ。

persevere 心に目標を抱いている人々はやり抜くだろう。

philanthropist その高名な慈善家は、気前のよい寄付と慈悲深い心で知られていた。

pigment 寒さで彼女の唇と頬が赤かった。

rage
[reidʒ]

n. **uncontrolled anger** [名] 激怒

Aaron's bouts of *rage* when drinking scared his family members.

関連語 rage : anger [ǽŋɡəʳ]
rageは抑えられない強いanger（怒り）を表す。

rant
[rænt]

v. **to speak or write in a violent or angry manner**
[動] 大声を張り上げる、わめく

The townspeople had grown accustomed to the crazy man *ranting* about his life.

関連語 rant : anger [ǽŋɡəʳ]
anger（怒り）のためにrantする。

rapprochement
[ræ̀prouʃmáːŋ]

n. **the establishment or renewal of good relations, especially between two nations; the state of reconciliation**
[名]（国家間の）和解、親交関係、親善

The *rapprochement* of the two nations is necessary for trade negotiations to take place.

反意語 rapprochement : estrangement [istréindʒmənt]
rapprochementの反意語はestrangement（不和、離反）

refuse
n.[réfjuːs]
v.[rifjúːz]

n. **waste or garbage** [名] ごみ

v. **to turn down or express a desire to not comply** [動] 〜を拒否する

The city's *refuse* was dumped at a nearby landfill.

I wouldn't *refuse* any invitation to a free meal.

関連語 refuse : landfill [lǽndfil]
refuseを埋め立てる場所がlandfill（埋め立て地）。

TRANSLATION | 例 文 の 訳

rage	酒を飲むと激怒するアーロンの癖は、家族を怖がらせた。
rant	町の人々は、大声で自分の人生の不満を語る狂人に、だんだん慣れてきた。
rapprochement	その二国間の和解は貿易交渉を実現させるために不可欠だ。
refuse	市のごみは近くの埋め立て地に捨てられた。
	無料で食事をとれるなら、どのような招待でも拒否するつもりはない。

241

regimen [rédʒəmən]	n. a plan or system for daily life usually intended to improve health　　　　　　[名] (食事や運動などの) 養生規則、養生計画
	Soldiers in any army follow a strict *regimen* of diet, exercise, and discipline.
	関連語 regimen : health [helθ] 　regimen は health (健康) を促進するための規則、計画をいう。
reign [rein]	n. rule by a monarch; the period during which a royalty has power; pervasive dominance　　　　　　[名] 治世、統治
	The *reign* of King Louis XIII brought much prosperity to France.
	関連語 reign : coronation [kɔ̀:rənèiʃən] 　coronation (戴冠式) は reign を授ける儀式だ。
righteous [ráitʃəs]	adj. upright according to moral law　　[形] (道徳的に) 正しい、公正な、正義の
	Hector prides himself on his *righteous* and proper character.
	反意語 righteous : reprobate [réprəbèit] 　righteous の反意語は reprobate (節操のない、品行の悪い)
roil [rɔil]	v. to stir up or cause to move quickly　　[動] ～をかき混ぜる、混乱させる
	Throwing rocks into a pond always *roils* the fish.
	反意語 roil : sedate [sidéit] 　roil の反意語は sedate (～を落ち着かせる)
sagacious [səgéiʃəs]	adj. keen; having the ability to discern judgment　　[形] 機敏な；しっかりした判断力を持った
	It is said the most *sagacious* are the slowest to speak.
	関連語 sagacity : simpleton [símplt°n] 　simpleton (馬鹿者、間抜け) には sagacity (聡明さ、判断力) が欠けている。

TRANSLATION | 例 文 の 訳

regimen	どんな軍の兵士も食事、運動、訓練から成る厳格な養生規則に従う。
reign	ルイ13世の治世にフランスは大きく繁栄した。
righteous	ヘクターは自分の公正できちんとした性格に誇りを持っている。
roil	池に石を投げると魚はいつも驚く。
sagacious	最も賢いのは最も無口な人だと言われる。

242

11th
12th
13th
14th
15th
16th
17th
18th
19th
20th

sage
[seidʒ]

n. **a wise man** [名] 賢人

The *sage* was often sought by the people of the village for advice.

関連語 sage : judicious [dʒuːdíʃəs]

sageとは judicious (思慮深い、賢明な) な人だ。

scintillate
[síntˀlèit]

v. **to give off sparks; to be brilliant** [動] 火花を発する；きらめく

The *scintillating* story kept Anne up all night.

反意語 scintillating : fatuous [fǽtʃuəs]

scintillating (面白い；きらめく) の反意語は fatuous (愚かな、無能な)

shift
[ʃift]

v. **to move slightly; to change ideas or position**

[動] 位置を変える；意見や立場を変える

Eugene *shifted* on the couch to make room for his friend.

関連語 shift : anchor [ǽŋkərʳ]

anchor (錨) には船を shift しないようにする機能がある。

significant
[signífikənt]

adj. **having consequence or meaning; fairly large in amount or quantity** [形] 重要な、意義のある；かなりの

William Shakespeare is ranked as a *significant* literary figure.

反意語 significant : paltry [pɔ́ːltri]

significant の反意語は paltry (つまらない、ごくわずかな)

skimp
[skimp]

v. **to put forth minimal attention, money, or effort**

[動] けちけちする、節約する；〜を出し惜しむ

The employer was in the habit of *skimping* his workers.

関連語 skimp : parsimony [páːrsəmòuni]

skimp と似た意味の形容詞に parsimony (極度の倹約、けち) がある。

TRANSLATION | 例 文 の 訳

sage	その賢人はよく村人たちからアドバイスを求められた。
scintillate	アンはその面白い物語を夜通し読んだ。
shift	ユージーンは友達が座れるようにソファの上で横にずれた。
significant	ウィリアム・シェイクスピアは重要な文人と位置づけられている。
skimp	その雇用主は従業員に対して出し惜しむ癖があった。

243

slight
[slait]

v. to treat as small or unimportant　　　　　　[動] ～を侮辱する、軽蔑する

The *slighted* worker continued to keep his discontent hidden under a cheerful smile.

反意語 slight : cosset [kásit]
slight の反意語は cosset（～を甘やかす、過保護に育てる）

stimulant
[stímjulənt]

n. that which creates a temporary increase of energy or activity　　　　　　[名] 興奮剤、刺激剤

As coffee contains a *stimulant*, drinking it can result in increased alertness.

反意語 stimulant : soporific [sàpərífik]
stimulant の反意語は soporific（催眠剤、睡眠薬）

swift
[swift]

adj. able to move rapidly　　　　　　[形] 速やかな、すばやい

The danger of capsizing increases when rafting in *swift* currents.

反意語 move swiftly : creep [kri:p]
move swiftly（素早く動く）の反意語は creep（ゆっくり動く、徐行する）

swill
[swil]

v. to drink rapidly or greedily　　　　　　[動] ～をがぶがぶ飲む

He *swilled* the last of his coffee before getting up from the table.

関連語 swill : sip [sip]
sip（少しずつ飲む）に比べて、swill は速くどんどん飲むことをいう。

taint
[teint]

v. to corrupt or spoil　　　　　　[動] 堕落させる、汚す、傷つける

Tracy's fall off the bike *tainted* her image of motorcycling.

関連語 taint : pristine [prísti:n]
pristine（新鮮な、汚れのない）なものは taint されていない。

TRANSLATION | 例 文 の 訳

slight	その冷遇された従業員は、陽気な笑顔の下に不満を隠し続けた。
stimulant	コーヒーは刺激物質を含んでいるので、飲むと覚醒することがある。
swift	急流の中でラフティングをすると、転覆の危険が増す。
swill	彼はコーヒーを飲み干すと、テーブルから立ち上がった。
taint	トレーシーはバイクから落ちたので、オートバイに乗ることに悪いイメージを持つようになった。

tease
[tiːz]

v. **to annoy by provoking or pestering; to mock playfully**

[動] いじめる；からかう、冷やかす

The other kids *teased* Bill everyday because he wore glasses.

関連語 tease : ruffian [rʌ́fiən]
ruffian（悪漢、ならず者）は他人をteaseする。

ungainly
[ʌngéinli]

adj. **lacking grace or ease of movement or form; clumsy**

[形] 見苦しい、ぎこちない

Alex's *ungainly* gait concealed his natural athletic prowess.

反意語 ungainly : lissome [lísəm]
ungainlyの反意語はlissome（柔軟な、しなやかな）

urge
[əːrdʒ]

v. **to advise someone strongly; to impel; to present a forceful argument**

[動] 強く勧める；催促する；力説する

City officials *urged* the public to use water sparingly until the drought passed.

関連語 urge : exhortative [igzɔ́ːˈtətiv]
exhortative（強要する、激励する）なものはurgeする。

vagary
[véigəri]

n. **an unpredictable happening; an erratic action**

[名] 予測できないこと、予期せぬ行動

The *vagary* of the horse races is the very excitement of them.

関連語 vagary : predict [pridíkt]
vagaryはpredict（予測する）することができない。

vigilant
[vídʒələnt]

adj. **keenly alert; watchful for danger**   [形] 絶えず警戒している；油断のない

The *vigilant* guards kept watch over the town as everyone slept.

関連語 vigilant : entrap [intrǽp]
vigilantな人は簡単にentrap（罠にかける、だます）されることがない。

TRANSLATION | 例 文 の 訳

tease	眼鏡をかけているという理由で、他の子供たちが毎日ビルをいじめた。
ungainly	アレックスのぎこちない足取りは、彼が生来持っている運動能力を隠した。
urge	市の職員たちは、干ばつが終わるまで水を控えめに使うように市民に強く勧めた。
vagary	競馬は予想できないからこそ、面白いのだ。
vigilant	用心深い警備員たちは、皆が眠っている間、村を監視し続けた。

vignette
[vinjét]

n. **a brief scene in a play or movie**　　　　　[名]（演劇や映画の）短いシーン

Thankfully the movie's pedestrian love *vignette* was brief.

関連語 vignette : scene [si:n]
vignetteはscene（シーン）の一種。

vigor
[vígəʳ]

n. **active force of the body or mind**　　　　　[名] 活力、活気

They rowed with *vigor* using quick strokes.

関連語 vigor : enervate [énəʳvèit]
vigorをenervate（〜の力を弱める、気力を奪う）する。

whim
[ʰwim]

n. **a sudden and unreasonable change of mind**　　　[名] 気まぐれ、心変わり

Tracy skipped work and went to Atlantic City on a *whim*.

関連語 whimsical : caprice [kəprí:s]
whimsical（気まぐれな、移り気な）と似た意味の名詞にcaprice（気まぐれ、むら気）がある。

TRANSLATION | 例 文 の 訳

vignette	ありがたいことに、その映画の退屈なラブシーンは短かった。
vigor	彼らは素早いストロークで元気よくボートを漕いだ。
whim	トレーシーは気まぐれで仕事を休み、アトランティック・シティに行った。

246

■ Fill in the blanks with the correct letter that matches the word with its definition.

1. philanthropist _____
2. skimp _____
3. aggrieve _____
4. swill _____
5. regimen _____
6. dogged _____
7. vagary _____
8. cognizant _____
9. roil _____
10. engross _____

a. to take all the attention of; to occupy completely
b. an unpredictable happening; an erratic action
c. a plan or system for daily life usually intended to improve health
d. to put forth minimal attention, money, or effort
e. to stir up or cause to move quickly
f. having an awareness or knowledge
g. to drink a large amount of something
h. stubbornly unyielding
i. one who acts in goodwill towards others
j. to distress or bring trouble to

■ Put the correct word in each blank from the list of words below.

11. subject を_____する。
12. _____していると簡単に entrap されない。
13. _____には tolerance がない。
14. abet（〜をそそのかす）の反意語は_____である。
15. _____は cosset（〜を甘やかす）の反意語である。
16. forbidden されたことを_____する。
17. _____は strength を増やすことを言う。
18. _____なものを見た結果、disgust を感じる。
19. _____は amateurish（素人っぽい）の反意語である。
20. _____は scene の一種である。

a. slight　b. consummate　c. opine　d. aggrandize　e. vigilant　f. bigot
g. abstain　h. vignette　i. ungainly　j. frustrate　k. digress　l. odious

Answer key

11. k　12. e　13. f　14. j　15. a　16. g　17. d　18. l　19. b　20. h
1. i　2. d　3. j　4. g　5. c　6. h　7. b　8. f　9. e　10. a

247

「この単語を覚えるのは無理」
という言葉が意味するのは、
「もう一度この単語を覚える
ように努力しなければ」ということだ。

18th DAY

abject
[ǽbdʒekt]

adj. in a miserable or low condition; lacking in pride or spirit

[形] ひどい、みじめな、みすぼらしい；卑屈な

The *abject* neighborhood was often the scene of violent crimes.

反意語 abject : spirited [spíritid]
abjectの反意語はspirited（元気のいい、活発な）

abjure
[æbdʒúəʳ]

v. to reject or renounce something under oath

[動]（信条や主義などを宣誓して）捨てる、放棄する

Mr. Linton *abjured* his involvement with the cult.

反意語 abjure : espouse [ispáuz]
abjureの反意語はespouse（~を支持する、採用する）

adjust
[ədʒʌ́st]

v. to bring to a more satisfactory state; to adapt or conform

[動] 調整する；慣れる、順応する

Laura settled herself comfortably far back in her corner, *adjusting* her skirt and murmuring.

関連語 adjust : tinker [tíŋkəʳ]
tinker（下手な修理をする、いじくり回す）はadjustに比べて不器用にものを扱うことをいう。

agitate
[ǽdʒətèit]

v. to disturb or irritate the mind or emotions

[動] 扇動する、（心や感情を）かき乱す

The revolution leader *agitated* the frenzied crowd into storming the city hall.

関連語 agitate : incendiary [inséndièri]
incendiary（扇動する人）はagitateする。

TRANSLATION | 例文の訳

abject	その貧しい地域では、よく暴力犯罪が目撃された。
abjure	リントン氏は、その新興宗教団体とのかかわりを放棄した。
adjust	ローラは自室の奥にくつろいで座ると、スカートを整え何かをつぶやいていた。
agitate	その革命指導者は熱狂的な群衆を扇動して、市役所に押し入らせた。

askew
[əskjúː]

adj. **not straight; awry** [形] 斜めに；ゆがんで

The artist complained that one of his paintings in the gallery was *askew*.

反意語 askew : aligned [əláind]
askew の反意語は aligned（一直線に並べた）

awkward
[ɔ́ːkwəʳd]

adj. **lack of ease or skill** [形] ぎこちない、不器用な

Lewis' *awkward* social skills were a hinderance of his job.

反意語 awkward : dexterous [dékstˤrəs]
awkward の反意語は dexterous（器用な、巧妙な）

bait
[beit]

v. **to lure; to tease** [動] いじめる；怒らせる

The terrorists *baited* their hostages with the tips of their rifles.

反意語 bait : mollify [mάləfài]
bait の反意語は mollify（〜をなだめる、静める）

banal
[bənǽl]

adj. **uninteresting or trite** [形] 陳腐な、ありふれた

Brian did poorly on his creative writing assignment because the professor thought it was a *banal* piece of writing.

関連語 banal : platitude [plǽtət(j)ùːd]
platitude（平凡な言葉・発言）は banal だという特徴がある。

belabor
[biléibəʳ]

v. **to attack verbally; to explain or insist on excessively; to hit vigorously** [動] 言葉で攻撃する；くどくどと論じる；強く打つ

The speaker *belabored* the point, repeating it several times to make sure it was understood.

関連語 belabor : assert [əsə́ːʳt]
belabor は assert（主張する）に比べて、執拗に論じるという意味がある。

11th 12th 13th 14th 15th 16th 17th 18th 19th 20th

TRANSLATION | 例 文 の 訳

askew	その芸術家は画廊で、自分の絵の1枚が曲がっていると文句を言った。
awkward	ルイスは社交が苦手で、それが彼の仕事の障害になった。
bait	テロリストたちはライフルの先端で人質をいびった。
banal	ブライアンの作文の課題の評価が低かったのは、教授がありふれた文章だと思ったからだ。
belabor	話し手はその点を理解できるようにと、何度も繰り返しくどくどと説明した。

249

bristle
[brísl]

v. **to stand stiffly on end like bristles in anger; to show anger**

[動] いらだつ、毛を逆立てる；けんか腰になる

The hair on Peter's head *bristled* even after many brushings with a comb.

関連語 bristle : anger [ǽngər]
anger（怒り）によって髪の毛が bristle する。

cajole
[kədʒóul]

v. **to coax or persuade with charm**   [動] ～を甘言でだます、おだてて～させる

The salesman *cajoled* the woman into buying a new car.

類義語 cajole : wheedle [ʰwíːdl]
cajole の類義語は wheedle（甘言で誘う）

candid
[kǽndid]

adj. **honest and straightforward**   [形] 率直な、遠慮のない

Charles' *candid* story did not leave out his own role in the crime.

反意語 candid : furtive [fə́ːʳtiv]
candid の反意語は furtive（こっそりなされた）

candor
[kǽndəʳ]

n. **the quality of honesty and straightforwardness in expression; impartiality**   [名] 率直さ、誠実さ；公平

The political candidate's *candor* won over many voters who were impressed by his frankness.

関連語 candor : palter [pɔ́ːltəʳ]
palter（ごまかす、いい加減なことを言う）する人には candor がない。

clique
[kliːk]

n. **an exclusive group of people**   [名] 徒党、派閥

The jock's *clique* was comprised of fellow football players and their cheerleader girlfriends.

類義語 clique : faction [fǽkʃən]
clique の類義語は faction（派閥、党派）

TRANSLATION | 例 文 の 訳

bristle	ピーターの髪の毛は、くしで何度もといたのに逆立っていた。
cajole	その販売員は女性をおだてて新車を買わせた。
candid	チャールズは、犯行での自分自身の役割を割愛することなく正直に供述した。
candor	その候補者は誠実だったので、率直さに感銘を受けた多くの有権者を味方につけた。
clique	そのスポーツ好きの集団は、フットボール選手仲間と彼らのチアリーダーの恋人たちで構成されていた。

conceal
[kənsíːl]

v. **to hide or keep secret** [動] 隠す、秘密にする

The widow could not *conceal* her tears at her late husband's funeral.

反意語 conceal : divulge [diváldʒ]
conceal の反意語は divulge (～を漏らす、暴露する)

concentrate
[kánsəntrèit]

v. **to bring or direct toward a common center; to make less dilute**
[動] ～に集中する、～を集める；～を濃縮する

The endangered species were found in a highly *concentrated* area, allowing the conservationists to locate them easily.

反意語 concentrate : deploy [diplɔ́i]
concentrate の反意語は deploy (展開する)

conciliate
[kənsílièit]

v. **to gain or win back the good feelings of**
[動] ～をなだめる、手なずける；なだめる、和解する

The new president tried to *conciliate* the press after the sordid scandal.

関連語 conciliatory : sop [sɑp]
sop (甘言、わいろ) は conciliatory (なだめる、懐柔的な) という特性を含む。

concise
[kənsáis]

adj. **brief and exact** [形] 簡潔な、簡明な

The style of the letter was decidedly terse and *concise*.

反意語 concise : verbose [vəːˈbóus]
concise の反意語は verbose (言葉数が多い、くどい)

concord
[kánkɔːˈd]

n. **an agreement** [名] 一致、調和

The sisters finally reached a *concord* about the layout of their bedroom.

関連語 concord : inconsonant [inkánsˈnənt]
inconsonant (一致しない) なものには concord が欠けている。

TRANSLATION | 例 文 の 訳

conceal	その未亡人は、亡くなった夫の葬式で涙を隠すことができなかった。
concentrate	その絶滅危惧種は1カ所で集中的に見つかったので、自然保護者たちはすぐにそれとわかった。
conciliate	新大統領は、その下劣なスキャンダルが発覚すると、記者たちを手なずけようとした。
concise	その手紙の様式はとても単純で簡潔だった。
concord	その姉妹は寝室内の物の配置についてようやく意見が一致した。

concur
[kənkə́ːʳ]

v. **to approve or agree**

[動] 意見が一致する、同意する

Representatives of the two countries *concur* that the trade agreement will be highly beneficial.

反意語 concur : dissent [disént]
concur の反意語は dissent（意見が違う、異議を唱える）

condemn
[kəndém]

v. **to find guilty by law; to express extreme disapproval of**

[動] 有罪判決を下す；責める、非難する

Paul *condemned* nothing hastily, or without taking account of circumstances.

反意語 condemn : countenance [káuntᵊnəns]
condemn の反意語は countenance（～を支持する、是認する）

condense
[kəndéns]

v. **to thicken or make more dense; to abridge or make more concise**

[動] 濃縮する；要約する、短縮する

Cliff's notes are *condensed* versions of books that can be read instead of the actual novel.

関連語 condensed : abstract [ǽbstrækt]
abstract（要約、要旨）は condensed（要約された、短縮された）されているのが特徴だ。

condescend
[kàndəsénd]

v. **to talk at someone in an arrogant manner; to descend to a less formal or dignified level**

[動] えらそうに話す；（階級が下の者に合わせて）へりくだる

The magazine article was *condescending* in its sympathy for the plight of the impoverished nation.

関連語 condescending : patronize [péitrənàiz]
patronize（いばった態度をとる、～をひいきにする）する行為は condescending（えらそうな、いばった）な特徴がある。

TRANSLATION | 例 文 の 訳

concur	その2国の代表者は、貿易協定が非常に有益なものになるだろうという点で意見が一致している。
condemn	ポールは、あわてて状況を考えずに何かを非難するようなことをしなかった。
condense	クリフのメモは本を要約したものなので、実際の小説の代わりに読むことができる。
condescend	その雑誌記事は、貧困にあえぐその国に同情しながらも見下すような論調だった。

252

condone
[kəndóun]

v. **to pardon, disregard, or overlook voluntarily; to accept but not completely agree with** ［動］〜を許す、大目に見る

The mother didn't *condone* the outlandish behavior of her daughter.

反意語 condone : denounce [dináuns]
condoneの反意語はdenounce（公然と非難する）

dappled
[dǽpld]

adj. **marked with spots; spotted** ［形］まだらの；ぶちの

Virginia preferred her *dappled* horse to all the other plain horses.

関連語 dappled : spot [spɑt]
dappledと意味の似た名詞にspot（まだら、ぶち）がある。

deject
[didʒékt]

v. **to make sad or tired** ［動］悲しくさせる、意気消沈させる

Though Jane generally had a positive attitude, there were periods when she was *dejected*.

関連語 dejection : hearten [hɑ́ːrtn]
hearten（励ます、元気づける）はdejection（落胆、失意）をなくして励ましているという意味。

drivel
[drívəl]

v. **to speak carelessly and senselessly** ［動］たわごとを言う

The actor *driveled* all over the media looking for any kind of publicity.

関連語 drivel : nonsensical [nɑnsénsikəl]
drivelする人にはnonsensical（無意味な、ばかげた）だという特徴がある。

eleemosynary
[èlimásənèri]

adj. **relating to charity; benevolent** ［形］慈善の；善意からの

The unexpected outpouring of *eleemosynary* gifts touched the missionaries deeply.

関連語 eleemosynary : philanthropist [filǽnθrəpist]
philanthropist（博愛主義者、慈善家）はeleemosynaryだという特徴がある。

TRANSLATION | 例 文 の 訳

condone	母が娘の奇行に目をつぶることはなかった。
dappled	バージニアは自分のまだらのウマのほうが模様のない他のウマよりも好きだった。
deject	ジェーンはたいてい前向きだったが、意気消沈している時期もあった。
drivel	その俳優は、どうであれ注目されたかったので、あらゆるメディアでたわごとを言った。
eleemosynary	予期せぬ善意の贈り物を大量に受け取り、宣教師たちは深く感銘を受けた。

253

enlarge
[inlάːʳdʒ]

v. **to expand or make larger**   [動] 拡大する、広げる

In 1697 the bank was allowed to *enlarge* its capital stock.

反意語 enlarge : retrench [ritréntʃ]
　　enlargeの反意語はretrench（〜を切り詰める、削除する）

fetid
[fétid]

adj. **stinky; horribly malodorous**   [形] 悪臭のする、臭い

The *fetid* odor made the girls nauseous.

関連語 fetid : smell [smel]
　　fetidはsmell（におい）を修飾する形容詞だ。

flit
[flit]

v. **to dart across or move quickly**   [動] 通り過ぎる、素早く引っ越す

Tracy's role as the angel in the school play was to *flit* across the stage gracefully.

関連語 flit : move [muːv]
　　flitとは素早くmove（動く）すること。

frivolity
[frivάləti]

n. **the act of being light-hearted**   [名] 軽率さ

He did not like to combine *frivolity* with the serious business of hunting.

関連語 frivolous : gravity [grǽvəti]
　　frivolous（軽率な）な人にはgravity（真剣さ、まじめさ）が欠けている。

gait
[geit]

n. **the way a person walks or moves**   [名] 足取り

Diana walked into the meeting with a confident *gait*.

関連語 gait : walk [wɔːk]
　　gaitは人のwalk（歩く）する姿を表す。

TRANSLATION | 例 文 の 訳

enlarge	1697年にその銀行は増資を許可された。
fetid	悪臭でその女の子たちは吐き気をもよおした。
flit	トレイシーは学校演劇に天使役で出演し、舞台を優雅に横切る演技を見せた。
frivolity	彼は、軽率さと狩猟という重大な問題を結びつけたくなかった。
gait	ダイアナは自信に満ちた足取りで会議の場に足を踏み入れた。

grouch
[grautʃ]

n. a habitually complaining person; a sulky or peevish mood

[名] 気難し屋；怒りっぽい人

The children were all afraid of the *grouch* who sat in front of the corner store.

関連語 grouch : querulous [kwér(j)uləs]

grouchとは querulous（不満の多い、不平を言う）な人のこと。

hike
[haik]

n. a long walk for leisure; an abrupt increase

[名] ハイキング；（大幅な）値上げ、高騰

v. to increase; to rise upward

[動] 急に引き上げる；上がる

The government's tax *hike* caused a sudden increase in product price.

The Federal Reserve Chairman *hiked* the interest rate in hopes of slowing inflation.

反意語 hike : backset [bǽksèt]

hikeの反意語は backset（逆行、逆転）

idolater
[aidάlətəʳ]

n. one who worships idols; one who blindly adores another

[名]（偶像）崇拝者、心酔者

In today's society, most people are *idolaters* of money.

関連語 idolater : reverent [révʳrənt]

idolaterには reverent（敬虔な、うやうやしい）という特徴がある。

iniquitous
[iníkwətəs]

adj. unjust; wicked or sinful

[形] 不正な；非道な、邪悪な

The *iniquitous* freight rates were due to a lack of competition in the shipping industry.

反意語 iniquity : rectitude [réktət(j)ù:d]

iniquity（不正、不法）の反意語は rectitude（正直、実直）

TRANSLATION | 例 文 の 訳

grouch	子供たちはみな、角の店の前に座っている気難し屋を怖がっていた。
hike	政府が大幅に税率を引き上げたことで、商品価格が突然上がった。
	連邦準備制度理事会の会長が、インフレを遅らせようと金利を上げた。
idolater	今日の社会では、ほとんどの人がお金を崇拝している。
iniquitous	運賃が高いのは、海運業に競争がないためだ。

255

irk [ə:ʳk]	v. **to make irritated or annoyed** It *irked* Helen that Matt forgot her birthday. 関連語 irk : enrage [inréidʒ] 　　enrage (～を激怒させる) は irk よりも怒らせる程度が強い。	[動] ～をいらいらさせる、困らせる
jejune [dʒidʒú:n]	adj. **lacking in interest; dull and boring** The *jejune* novel put me to sleep after the first page. 関連語 jejune : interest [íntʰrəst] 　　jejune なことには interest (興味、おもしろみ) が欠けている。	[形] 面白くない；退屈な
lugubrious [lug(j)ú:briəs]	adj. **sad or mournful** A dog let out a long, *lugubrious* howl outside. 反意語 lugubrious : jovial [dʒóuviəl] 　　lugubrious の反意語は jovial (陽気な、気持ちのいい)	[形] 悲しげな、落ち込んだ
maladroit [mælədrɔ́it]	adj. **inept; lacking in skill or grace** The *maladroit* young lady is not fit to be a dancer. 反意語 maladroit : deft [deft] 　　maladroit の反意語は deft (手際のよい、器用な)	[形] 不器用な；不手際な
morose [məróus]	adj. **sullen and glum** Janet guessed from Jason's *morose* mood that the test did not go very well. 反意語 morose : jocund [dʒákənd] 　　morose の反意語は jocund (陽気な、快活な)	[形] 不機嫌な、気難しい

TRANSLATION | 例 文 の 訳

irk	ヘレンはマットが誕生日を忘れたので怒った。
jejune	その小説は退屈で、最初のページを読み終えたところで眠くなってしまった。
lugubrious	イヌが外で長く悲し気な遠吠えをした。
maladroit	その若い女性は不器用で、ダンサーには向いていない。
morose	ジャネットは、ジェイソンの不機嫌な様子から、テストが上手くいかなかったのだろうと推測した。

naive
[nɑːíːv]

adj. **marked by unaffected simplicity; childlike** ［形］世間知らずの；無邪気な

The *naive* young lawyers were still full of ideal hopes as they entered the work force.

反意語 naive : worldly [wə́ːˈldli]
naive の反意語は worldly（現世の、世俗的な）

nonentity
[nɑ̀néntəti]

n. **a person of no significance, importance, or influence**
［名］取るに足りない人

Having been considered a *nonentity* his whole life, Albert aspired to be a world renowned author one day.

関連語 nonentity : consequence [kɑ́nsəkwèns]
nonentity には consequence（重要さ、重大さ）が欠けている。

pontificate
[pɑntífəkèit]

v. **to speak in an arrogant and dogmatic manner**
［動］傲慢で独断的な話し方をする

The brilliant professor was disliked because he had a tendency to *pontificate* during his lectures.

関連語 pontificate : speak [spiːk]
pontificate は speak（話す）の一種。

procrastinate
[proukrǽstənèit]

v. **to delay or put off doing something** ［動］〜を引き延ばす

The jury *procrastinated* their decision, asking the judge for more time to deliberate.

関連語 procrastinate : alacrity [əlǽkrəti]
alacrity（乗り気、敏捷さ）がない人は procrastinate する。

reject
[ridʒékt]

v. **to refuse or decline** ［動］拒否する、断る

Union leaders *rejected* the latest counteroffer by the steel industry due to an insufficient health plan.

関連語 reject : scorn [skɔːˈn]
scorn（軽蔑して拒絶する）は軽蔑しながら reject することをいう。

TRANSLATION | 例 文 の 訳

naive その世間知らずの若い弁護士たちは、働き始めたときにはまだ希望でいっぱいだった。

nonentity それまで取るに足りない人物だと見なされてきたアルバートは、ある日、世界的に有名な作家になることを熱望した。

pontificate その有能な大学教授は、講義中に傲慢で独断的に話す傾向があるせいで、嫌われていた。

procrastinate 陪審員団は裁判官にさらに検討する時間を求めて、決断を先延ばしにした。

reject 健康保険制度が不十分なために、組合の幹部らは鉄鋼業界側からの最新の対案を拒否した。

257

shirk [ʃəːʳk]	v. **to avoid responsibility or duty; to neglect** [動]（仕事や義務から）逃避する；怠る John has tried to *shirk* the responsibility. 関連語 shirk : malingerer [məlíŋgəʳəʳ] 　malingerer（仮病を使う人）は自分の仕事や義務を shirk しようとしている。	
skirt [skəːʳt]	v. **to avoid**　[動] 避ける Tom *skirted* the issue of his family by changing the subject. 類義語 skirt : evade [ivéid] 　skirt の類義語は evade（～を避ける）	
skit [skit]	n. **a short and comic or dramatic performance**　[名] 寸劇、スキット Our *skit* at summer camp had the children in stitches. 関連語 skit : drama [drɑ́ːmə] 　skit は drama（演劇）の中でも短くておもしろいもの。	
slipshod [slípʃɑ̀d]	adj. **carelessly wearing loose shoes; carelessly done; looking shabby**　[形] ほどけた靴を履いた；いい加減な；みすぼらしい A *slipshod* man passed me on the street, wearing a ragged coat and torn pants. 類義語 slipshod : slovenly [slʌ́vənli] 　slipshod の類義語は slovenly（だらしない、ぞんざいな）	
smirk [sməːʳk]	n. **an arrogant and self-satisfied smile**　[名] にやにや笑い Emily's *smirk* upon hearing the news of her rival company's demise indicated she knew of it beforehand. 関連語 smirk : smugness [smʌ́gnis] 　smirk には smugness（うぬぼれ、自己満足）という特徴がある。	

TRANSLATION | 例 文 の 訳

shirk	ジョンはその責任から逃れようとしている。
skirt	トムは話題を変えて、家族の問題に触れるのを避けた。
skit	夏のキャンプで私たちが披露した寸劇に、子供たちは笑い転げた。
slipshod	ぼろぼろのコートと破れたズボンを身に着けたみすぼらしい男が、路上で私とすれ違った。
smirk	ライバル企業の倒産のニュースを聞いたときのエミリーのにやにや笑いで、彼女がそれを事前に知っていたことがわかった。

spiritual
[spírit∫uəl]

adj. **regarding the spirit; incorporeal**　　　[形] 精神的な；霊的な

Religion addresses purely *spiritual* concerns.

反意語 spiritual : carnal [ká:ʳnl]
spiritualの反意語はcarnal（世俗的な）

stir
[stə:ʳ]

v. **to mix together; to cause movement; to provoke deliberately**
[動] 混ぜる；動かす；刺激する

The news writer *stirred* controversy when she wrote an editorial on the legislation of gun control.

反意語 stir : quell [kwel]
stirの反意語はquell（〜を鎮圧する、抑える）

thirsty
[θə́:ʳsti]

adj. **desiring to drink; strongly craving something**
[形] のどの渇いた；切望する

The *thirsty* man greedily drank from the water fountain.

関連語 thirsty : imbibe [imbáib]
thirstyになるとimbibe（〜を飲む）する。

trite
[trait]

adj. **commonplace or stale**　　　[形] 使い古された、陳腐な

The maxim is so old that it is *trite* — it is laughable.

類義語 trite : hackneyed [hǽknid]
triteの類義語はhackneyed（陳腐な、紋切り型の）

turncoat
[tə́:ʳnkòut]

n. **a traitor; one who switches allegiances**　　　[名] 反逆者；裏切り者

One of the greatest crimes is to be a *turncoat* against your country.

関連語 turncoat : constancy [kánstənsi]
turncoatにはconstancy（忠実）が欠けている。

TRANSLATION | 例 文 の 訳

spiritual	宗教は純粋に霊的な関心事に取り組むものだ。
stir	その新聞記者が銃規制の法制化についての社説を書くと、論争が起こった。
thirsty	その男はのどが渇いていたので、水飲み場でごくごくと水を飲んだ。
trite	その金言はとても古く、陳腐だ。つまり、くだらない。
turncoat	最大の犯罪の1つは、母国の反逆者になることだ。

unique
[juːníːk]

adj. being the one of its kind; very unusual   [形] 唯一の；独特の

This *unique* individual was an ex-soldier turned religionist.

関連語 unique : precedent [présədnt]
uniqueなものにはprecedent（前例）がない。

unjustifiable
[ʌndʒʌ́stəfàiəbl]

adj. impossible to justify or excuse   [形] 正当化できない、弁解できない

Harry could not explain his *unjustifiable* absence to his teacher.

反意語 unjustifiable : tenable [ténəbl]
unjustifiableの反意語はtenable（批判に耐えられる、弁護できる）

unkempt
[ʌnkémpt]

adj. messy or not clean   [形] 乱れた、だらしない

Mr. Gracie was short and *unkempt*, almost rustic.

反意語 unkempt : dapper [dǽpəʳ]
unkemptの反意語はdapper（こざっぱりした、粋な）

TRANSLATION | 例 文 の 訳

unique	このユニークな人物が、宗教家に転じた退役軍人だった。
unjustifiable	ハリーは、正統な理由なく欠席したことについて教師に説明できなかった。
unkempt	グレイシー氏は背が低くて、だらしのない、ほとんど下品なほどの人物だった。

■ Fill in the blanks with the correct letter that matches the word with its definition.

1. deject   _____
2. flit   _____
3. slipshod   _____
4. bristle   _____
5. iniquitous   _____
6. condone   _____
7. abject   _____
8. procrastinate   _____
9. clique   _____
10. shirk   _____

a. an exclusive group of people
b. unjust; wicked or sinful
c. to dart across or move quickly
d. to avoid responsibility or duty; to neglect
e. to stand stiffly on end like bristles; to show anger
f. to accept but not completely agree with
g. to delay or put off doing something
h. in a miserable or low condition; lacking in pride or spirit
i. carelessly wearing loose shoes; looking shabby
j. to make sad or tired

■ Put the correct word in each blank from the list of words below.

11. _____は assert よりも執拗に論じるという意味だ。
12. tenable（批判に耐えられる、弁護できる）の反意語は_____である。
13. _____は hackneyed（陳腐な）の類義語である。
14. dexterous（器用な、巧妙な）は_____の類義語である。
15. _____には smugness（うぬぼれ、自己満足）という特徴がある。
16. scorn は軽蔑と嘲りの感情を持って_____することである。
17. _____の反意語は rectitude（正直、実直）である。
18. _____することには nonsensical（無意味な、ばかげた）という属性が含まれている。
19. tinker は_____に比べて不器用な技量で物を扱うという意味だ。
20. _____は countenance（～を支持する、是認する）の反意語である。

| a. reject | b. iniquity | c. unjustifiable | d. belabor | e. awkward | f. condemn |
| g. cajole | h. adjust | i. maladroit | j. drivel | k. trite | l. smirk |

Answer key

11.d 12.c 13.k 14.e 15.l 16.a 17.b 18.j 19.h 20.f
1.j 2.c 3.i 4.e 5.b 6.f 7.h 8.g 9.a 10.d

261

単語征服！この単語集の
おかげで進んでいます。

19th DAY

allay [əléi]	v. **to relieve; to calm**	[動]〜を鎮める；やわらげる

The travel agent *allayed* the man's concerns about airsafety.

反意語 allay : aggravate [ǽgrəvèit]
allayの反意語はaggravate（〜を悪化させる）

alleviate [əlí:vièit]	v. **to lessen; to make pain more bearable**	[動]〜を軽減する、緩和する

By putting forth a new reform bill, the president took measures to *alleviate* poverty.

関連語 alleviate : stress [stres]
stress（緊張、ストレス）をalleviateする。

anterior [æntíˤriər]	adj. **occurring before or earlier**	[形]以前の、前方の

Anterior events have led investors to believe that the technology sector is extremely volatile.

反意語 anterior : ensuing [insú:iŋ]
anteriorの反意語はensuing（あとの、次の）

antic [ǽntik]	n. **ludicrous or funny actions**	[名]こっけいな態度、おかしな行動
	adj. **odd or fanciful**	[形]奇妙な、おかしな

The comedy show was full of *antics* that had us bursting with laughter.
A clown's *antic* foolery entertains young and old audience members.

関連語 antic : behavior [bihéivjəʳ]
anticはbehavior（行動）を描写する単語。cf) facetious（こっけいな、ふざけた）は
speech（言葉、話）を描写する単語。

TRANSLATION | 例文の訳

allay	その旅行代理店の担当者は飛行機の安全性に関する男性の不安を鎮めた。
alleviate	新しい改革法案を提示することで、大統領は貧困の緩和策をとった。
anterior	以前の出来事によって、投資家たちはテクノロジー業界がきわめて不安定だと考えるようになった。
antic	そのコメディー番組はこっけいな振る舞いでいっぱいで、私たちは爆笑した。
	ピエロのこっけいでばかばかしい振る舞いが、年齢を問わず観衆を楽しませる。

bale
[beil]

n. great evil; anguish; large and closely pressed bundles of goods
[名] 災い；苦痛、悲惨；（圧縮梱包された）大荷物

The news of great *bale* in the neighboring town caused immense chaos.

反意語 bale : mirth [məːʳθ]
baleの反意語はmirth（陽気、歓喜）

beleaguer
[bilíːgəʳ]

v. to annoy persistently; to besiege　　[動] しつこく困らせる；〜を包囲する

The children *beleaguered* their parents for a vacation to Disney World.

反意語 beleaguer : mollify [máləfài]
beleaguerの反意語はmollify（〜をなだめる、静める）

belie
[bilái]

v. to give a wrong impression; to contradict; to show to be wrong
[動] 〜を誤って伝える；矛盾する；〜が誤りだと示す

The generally cold first impression I often give people *belies* my soft and caring heart.

反意語 belie : confirm [kənfɔ́ːʳm]
belieの反意語はconfirm（〜を確認する）

braggart
[brǽgəʳt]

n. one who boasts about oneself loudly　　[名] うぬぼれ屋

Brandon's accomplishments were numerous, but he could never be accused of being a *braggart*.

類義語 braggart : braggadocio [brægədóuʃiòu]
braggartの類義語はbraggadocio（自慢する人）

calibrate
[kǽləbrèit]

v. to determine by comparison with a standard
[動] 〜を調整する、（計量器などの）目盛りを決める

Thermometers should be *calibrated* daily to ensure accurate readings.

反意語 calibrated : unstandardized [ʌnstǽndəʳdàizd]
calibrated（調整された）の反意語はunstandardized（規格化されていない）

TRANSLATION | 例文の訳

bale	隣町の災害に関するニュースが大混乱を招いた。
beleaguer	子供たちはディズニーワールドで休暇を過ごしたいとしつこく迫り、両親を困らせた。
belie	私の第一印象は概して冷たいので、本当は柔和で思いやりがあることが、なかなかうまく伝わらない。
braggart	ブランドンの業績は数知れないが、彼がうぬぼれていると責めることなどありえない。
calibrate	間違いなく正確に読み取れるように、温度計は毎日調整すべきだ。

cipher
[sáifəʳ]

n. a message created using a cryptographic system　　[名] 暗号、暗号文

The intelligence agency is reading through thousands of e-mails and trying to figure out which are *ciphers*.

関連語 cipher : cryptic [kríptik]
　　cipher には cryptic（隠れた、秘密の）な特徴がある。

dandy
[dǽndi]

n. a man with extravagant outer appearance　　[名] しゃれた男性

What a *dandy* you are today, dressed in your Sunday best!

関連語 dandy : preen [priːn]
　　dandy は preen（入念に身づくろいをする）する。

debrief
[diːbríːf]

v. to interrogate for the purpose of finding out information that was discovered during a military operation　　[動] 軍務で得た情報を聞く

The pilot was *debriefed* by the airline after the emergency landing.

関連語 debrief : information [ìnfəʳméiʃən]
　　information（情報）を debrief する。

deleterious
[dèlitíʳriəs]

adj. harmful or noxious　　[形] 有害な、有毒な

George's indigestion was caused by the *deleterious* ingredients in his soup.

反意語 deleterious : salutary [sǽljutèri]
　　deleterious の反意語は salutary（有益な、健康によい）

TRANSLATION | 例 文 の 訳

cipher　　情報機関では何千通ものEメールに目を通し、どれが暗号文かを見きわめようとしている。

dandy　　一張羅を着て、今日のあなたはなんとおしゃれなのだろう！

debrief　　パイロットは緊急着陸の後、航空会社から報告を受けた。

deleterious　　ジョージの消化不良は、彼が飲んだスープの中の有害な食材が原因だった。

deliberate
v. [dilíbərèit]
adj. [dilíbərət]

v. to consider carefully　　　　　　　　　　　　　[動] 〜を熟慮する

adj. intended; resulting from careful and thorough consideration
　　　　　　　　　　　　　　　[形] 故意の；よく考えた、慎重な

The jury *deliberated* the case for five long hours before reaching a verdict.

The *deliberate* nature of the interview process allowed the company to selectively screen all the candidates.

反意語 deliberate : impetuous [impétʃuəs]
　　deliberateの反意語はimpetuous（性急な、軽率な）

---

delicate
[délikət]

adj. very fine or subtle; easy to break　　　　[形] 繊細な；壊れやすい

Despite her *delicate* physical appearance, Nancy enjoyed outdoor activities and camping.

反意語 delicate : husky [hʌski]
　　delicateの反意語はhusky（がっちりした、頑丈な）

---

dilate
[dailéit]

v. to discourse at length; to swell or widen
　　　　　　　　　　　　　　　[動] 広げる；膨張させる、拡張させる

The heavy torrents of rain *dilated* the river causing it to flood.

反意語 dilate : contract [kántrækt]
　　dilateの反意語はcontract（〜を縮小する、収縮させる）

---

dilettante
[dílità:nt]

n. an admirer of the arts; a person having a superficial interest in an art　　　　　　　　　　　[名] 美術愛好家；芸術を道楽でする人

Matt had never studied art formally, but he was a *dilettante* who appreciated artistic works on his own.

関連語 dilettante : superficial [sù:pərfíʃəl]
　　dilettanteにはsuperficial（表面的な）だという特徴がある。

TRANSLATION | 例 文 の 訳

deliberate 陪審員団は5時間にわたってその事件について熟慮したのちに、評決に達した。
よく練られた面接プロセスのおかげで、その企業は応募者全員を入念に選考することができた。

delicate ナンシーは体つきが弱々しいのに、アウトドア活動やキャンプを楽しんだ。

dilate 猛烈な雨で川幅が広がり、氾濫した。

dilettante マットは美術を正式に学んだことはなかったが、個人的に芸術作品を鑑賞する愛好家だった。

eclipse
[iklíps]

v. **to make obscure or darker; to cause to decline in importance, fame, or reputation** ［動］〜の影を薄くする；（競争相手などを）失墜させる

n. **the complete or partial blocking out of one celestial body over another** ［名］（太陽・月の）食

Modern technology has *eclipsed* the innovations of early American inventors such as Benjamin Franklin.

To witness a total *eclipse* of the sun is a once in a lifetime opportunity.

関連語 eclipse : prestige [prestí:dʒ]
eclipse は prestige（名声、威信）を失墜させるという意味。

elliptical
[ilíptikəl]

adj. **shaped like an ellipse; marked by economy of expression; relating to deliberate obscurity** ［形］楕円のような；省略の；わかりにくい

No one knew exactly what inspired Anna's *elliptical* comments.

反意語 elliptical : palpable [pǽlpəbl]
elliptical の反意語は palpable（明白な、簡単にわかる）

enlighten
[enláitn]

v. **to give knowledge to; to provide with previously lacking insight or information** ［動］人に教える；説明する、啓蒙する

Jerry *enlightened* the young woman on the dangers of smoking.

関連語 enlighten : explanation [èksplənéiʃən]
enlighten するために explanation（説明）を与える。

filibuster
[fíləbʌstəʳ]

n. **the use or an instance of delaying or preventing legislative action by making long speeches** ［名］（長い演説などによる）議事の妨害

The senator attempted to use a *filibuster* in hopes of staving off a vote on the floor.

関連語 filibuster : delay [diléi]
fillbuster は議事進行を delay（〜を遅らせる）するものだ。

TRANSLATION | 例 文 の 訳

eclipse	現代のテクノロジーの発展は、ベンジャミン・フランクリンのような初期のアメリカの発明家たちによる技術革新の影を薄くしてきた。
	皆既日食を見られる機会はめったにない。
elliptical	だれも、なぜアナがあいまいな発言をしたのか、よくわからなかった。
enlighten	ジェリーはその若い女性に喫煙の危険性を説明した。
filibuster	その上院議員は、議場での採決を阻止できればと思い、議事妨害を試みた。

filigree
[fíləgrìː]

n. **detailed ornamentation of fine gold or silver wire** ［名］金［銀］線細工

Alice took from one of the drawers a black leather card-case lined with silver *filigree*.

関連語 filigree : delicacy [délikəsi]
filigree は delicacy（繊細さ）を特徴に持つ金や銀の線細工だ。

flannel
[flǽnl]

n. **a blend of wool and cotton used for clothing**

［名］フランネル、ウールと綿の混紡

Flannel pajamas are the warmest thing to wear to sleep in the winter.

関連語 flannel : cloth [klɔ(ː)θ]
flannel は cloth（布地）の一種。

fondness
[fándnis]

n. **a warm affection; a strong liking or inclination** ［名］愛情、愛着

Maggie had a particular *fondness* for plants.

関連語 fondness : adoration [æ̀dəréiʃən]
神への崇拝や情熱的な愛を意味する adoration（愛慕、熱愛、崇拝）は fondness よりも程度が強い。

hale
[heil]

adj. **healthy or sound; retaining exceptional health and vigor**

［形］剛健な

At the age of eighty my grandfather was strong and *hale*.

反意語 hale : effete [ifíːt]
hale の反意語は effete（活力のない、衰えた）

ken
[ken]

n. **range of sight; abstract range of perception** ［名］視野；理解の範囲

The poor ship sank in *ken* of the shore.

関連語 ken : see [siː]
ken は see（目に入る、見える）できる範囲のこと。

TRANSLATION | 例 文 の 訳

filigree アリスは、銀線細工で縁取られた黒革のカードケースを引き出しから取り出した。
flannel フランネルのパジャマは冬の寝間着で最も温かいものだ。
fondness マギーは植物に特別な愛着をもっている。
hale 私の祖父は80歳の時点で、丈夫で剛健だった。
ken その船は、残念なことに、海岸が見えるところで沈没した。

267

landfill
[lǽndfil]

n. an area of land used to dump refuse in and continuously cover with land　　　　　　　　　　　　　　　　　　[名] 埋め立て地

The city of New York puts its trash in a *landfill* on Staten Island.

関連語 landfill : refuse [réfju:s]
landfill は refuse (ごみ) を埋め立てる場所のこと。

malicious
[məlíʃəs]

adj. arising from the desire to cause pain or stress to someone　　　　　　　　　　　　　　　　　　[形] 悪意のある、意地の悪い

Barry's vindictiveness towards his rival was often viewed in a *malicious* light.

反意語 malicious : benevolent [bənévələnt]
malicious の反意語は benevolent (慈悲深い)

malign
[məláin]

v. to speak or write evil about someone　　　[動] 〜をけなす、中傷する

adj. evil　　　　　　　　　　　　　　　　　　[形] 有害な、悪意のある

The food critic *maligned* the restaurant in his weekly column for poor service and barely edible food.

The press made a *malign* comment about the governor for accepting campaign funds from a major crime syndicate.

反意語 malign : eulogize [jú:lədʒàiz]
malign の反意語は eulogize (〜を賞賛する)

malinger
[məlíŋgəʳ]

v. to pretend to be sick or incapable in order to avoid work or duty　　　　　　　　　　　　　　　　　　[動] 仮病を使う

After a long night at the disco, I *malingered* to stay home and sleep.

関連語 malingerer : shirk [ʃəːʳk]
malingerer (仮病を使う人) は自分の仕事や義務から shirk (逃避する) する人だ。

TRANSLATION | 例 文 の 訳

landfill　ニューヨーク市はスタテン島の埋め立て地にごみを捨てている。

malicious　バリーはライバルを執念深く攻めるので、悪意があると見なされることが多かった。

malign　その料理評論家は、週刊のコラム記事でそのレストランをけなし、サービスが悪いうえに料理はほとんど食べられないと書いた。
そのメディアは知事を中傷する論評を出し、大規模な犯罪組織から選挙資金を受け取ったと報じた。

malinger　ディスコで長い夜を過ごしたあと、私は仮病を使って家で眠った。

mend
[mend]

v. **to repair or reform; to improve in health**

［動］繕う、直す、修理する；（病人が）回復する

It was not easy for Frank's mother to *mend* the tattered shirt he ruined while playing football.

反意語 mend : rend [rend]

mendの反意語はrend（〜を引き裂く）

mendacious
[mendéiʃəs]

adj. **dishonest; marked by deception**

［形］不正直な；偽りの

The press secretary's *mendacious* statement was later discovered by the media.

関連語 mendacious : truth [truːθ]

mendaciousなものには truth（真実）が欠けている。

mulish
[mjúːliʃ]

adj. **excessively obstinate**

［形］強情な

The two senators appeared equally *mulish* in their debate, neither would yield even the smallest concession.

関連語 mulish : flexibility [flèksəbíləti]

mulishな人には flexibility（柔軟性）が欠けている。

mundane
[mándein]

adj. **relating to the everyday activities of life; secular**

［形］日常の、ありふれた；世俗的な

Even the most *mundane* jobs are appreciated by the unemployed.

反意語 mundane : extraordinary [ikstrɔ́ːrdənèri]

mundaneの反意語は extraordinary（驚くべき、並外れた）

nondescript
[nàndiskrípt]

adj. **lacking any outstanding features or qualities; common or normal**

［形］特徴のない；ありきたりの

To Betty's dismay, her blind-date was a rather *nondescript* man.

反意語 nondescript : conspicuous [kənspíkjuəs]

nondescriptの反意語は conspicuous（人目を引く、目立つ）

TRANSLATION | 例 文 の 訳

mend	フランクがフットボールでぼろぼろにしたシャツを繕うのは、母親には容易ではなかった。
mendacious	その報道官の声明の内容が虚偽だったことが、のちにマスコミによって明らかにされた。
mulish	その2人の上院議員は、討論会の場で同じように強情で、2人とも一歩も譲ろうとしなかった。
mundane	この上なくありふれた仕事であっても、失業者にとってはありがたいものだ。
nondescript	ベティががっかりしたのは、ブラインドデートの相手がこれといって特徴のない男だったことだ。

obligate
[ábləgèit]

v. **to legally or morally commit** [動] ～する義務がある、～せざるを得ない

The conditions of settlement to which the railroad *obligated* itself are very explicit.

反意語 obligatory : discretionary [diskréʃənèri]
obligatory（義務的な、強制的な）の反意語は discretionary（任意の、自由裁量の）

panache
[pənǽʃ]

n. **a feathered plume on a helmet; flamboyance in style and action** [名]（かぶとの）羽飾り；華々しさ、堂々とした態度

The singer performed the routine with plenty of *panache.*

反意語 panache : humility [hju:míləti]
panache の反意語は humility（謙虚、謙遜）

phlegmatic
[flegmǽtik]

adj. **showing a slow and stolid temperament** [形] 冷静な、沈着な、鈍感な

Brian's *phlegmatic* nature prevented him from succeeding in the world of day trading.

関連語 phlegmatic : arouse [əráuz]
phlegmatic な人を arouse（刺激する）することは難しい。

polish
[páliʃ]

v. **to make glossy and smooth; to refine in manners**
[動] 磨く；洗練させる

Robert's language became more *polished* year after year.

反意語 polished : rustic [rʌ́stik]
polished（洗練された）の反意語は rustic（粗野な、下品な）

prate
[preit]

v. **to talk or chatter foolishly with little purpose**
[動] ぺちゃくちゃしゃべる、無駄話をする

n. **foolish or idle talk** [名] 無駄話

Lucy *prated* about the latest gossip with Ethel.

関連語 prate : aimless [éimlis]
prate には aimless（目的がない）という特徴がある。

TRANSLATION | 例 文 の 訳

obligate	その鉄道会社が責任を負った和解条件は非常に明解なものだ。
panache	その歌手は堂々といつもどおりの演目をこなした。
phlegmatic	ブライアンはおとなしい性格なので、デイトレーディングの世界では成功しなかった。
polish	ロバートの言葉は年々洗練されていった。
prate	ルーシーはエセルと最近のうわさ話をした。

prospect
v.[prəspékt]
n.[práspekt]

v. **to examine and explore an area for mineral deposits**
[動] 探し求める、試掘する

n. **something expected**
[名] 可能性、見込み

The panhandlers *prospected* the area for gold and other minerals.

Having many job *prospects*, the employee was free to leave her job at will.

関連語 prospect : mineral [mínᵊrəl]
mineral (鉱物) を prospect する。

prowl
[praul]

v. **to search with predatory intent**
[動] 獲物を求めてうろつく

Large cats will *prowl* stealthily in search of prey to eat.

関連語 prowl : prey [prei]
prey (獲物) を探して prowl する。

pulchritude
[pʌ́lkrət(j)ùːd]

n. **physical beauty or attractiveness**
[名] (女性の体の) 美しさ、魅力

The prince was taken aback by the maiden's exquisite *pulchritude*.

反意語 pulchritude : homeliness [hóumlinis]
pulchritude の反意語は homeliness (不器量)

relapse
[rilǽps]

v. **to worsen after getting better; to go back to bad habits**
[動] 病気を再発する、ぶり返す；悪習に再び陥る

n. **the recurrence of symptoms of a disease after a period of improvement**
[名] (病気の) 再発

Mr. Miles *relapsed* into drug use after many years of staying clean.

Don't forget to keep taking these medications to prevent a possible *relapse*.

関連語 relapse : recidivism [risídəvìzm]
recidivism (常習性、常習的な犯行) は relapse するものである。

release
[rilíːs]

v. **to set free; to open to the public**
[動] 解放する：公開する

The prisoner was *released* early from jail for good behavior.

反意語 release : constrain [kənstréin]
release の反意語は constrain (〜を制限する)

TRANSLATION | 例 文 の 訳

prospect その物乞いたちは、金やそのほかの鉱物を求めてその一帯を掘り返した。
いろいろな就職口が見込めたので、その従業員は自由に仕事を辞められた。

prowl 大型のネコ科の動物は、食べる獲物を求めてひっそりとうろつく。

pulchritude 王子はその少女のあまりの美しさにあっけにとられた。

relapse マイルズ氏は何年間も手を出していなかった薬物に再びおぼれてしまった。
再発の可能性を防ぐために、これらの薬を飲み続けるのを忘れないでください。

release その囚人は行いがよかったので、早く刑務所から釈放された。

| **relevant**
[réləvənt] | adj. **having a connection; applicable**   [形] 関連する；適切な
The judge deemed the evidence *relevant* to the case and admitted it. |
| | **類義語** relevant : pertinent [pə́ːᵗtᵊnənt]
relevant の類義語は pertinent（関連のある、適切な） |

| **relieve**
[rilíːv] | v. **to ease pain or suffering; to liberate from worries or fears; to take the place of someone**
    [動] 痛みを楽にする；（苦痛・心配など）をやわらげる；〜と交替する
Relieved that her husband was safe, Elizabeth began to scold him for not calling. |
| | **関連語** relieve : anodyne [ǽnoudàin]
anodyne（鎮痛剤）には relieve する働きがある。 |

| **relinquish**
[rilíŋkwiʃ] | v. **to give up or withdraw from; to release**   [動] 〜を断念する；〜を放棄する
Rhea *relinquished* custody rights to her children in exchange for weekly visits and alimony. |
| | **反意語** relinquish : procure [proukjúəʳ]
relinquish の反意語は procure（〜を手に入れる、獲得する） |

| **reward**
[riwɔ́ːrd] | v. **to recompense for a worthy or evil act**
    [動] 〜に報酬を与える、〜に報いる
Everything we do to others will one day come back to us and we will be *rewarded* for our actions. |
| | **反意語** rewarding work : drudgery [drʌ́dʒəri]
rewarding work（やりがいのある仕事）の反意語は drudgery（骨折り仕事、つまらない仕事） |

| **rile**
[rail] | v. **to agitate or enrage**   [動] 〜を怒らせる、いらだたせる
The animals were *riled* by the intruding zoo-keeper. |
| | **関連語** rile : choleric [kálərik]
choleric（怒りっぽい）な人は簡単に rile される。 |

> TRANSLATION | 例 文 の 訳
>
> **relevant** 　判事はその証拠が事件に関連していると見なし、採用した。
> **relieve** 　エリザベスは夫が無事に安堵して、電話をよこさなかったことを叱り始めた。
> **relinquish** 　リアは、毎週子供たちを訪問し、養育費を受け取ることと引き換えに、親権を手放した。
> **reward** 　私たちが他人に対して行うことのすべてはいつか自分に戻ってきて、その報いを受ける。
> **rile** 　動物たちは侵入してきた飼育員にいら立った。

salient
[séiliənt]

adj. noticeable or conspicuous; jutting out

[形] 顕著な、目立つ；突き出した

Bright neon lights were the most *salient* features of the building.

反意語 salient : inconspicuous [ìnkənspíkjuəs]

salient の反意語は inconspicuous（目立たない、注目されない）

sensation
[senséiʃən]

n. a perception by means of one of the sense organs; excitement or heightened feeling

[名] 感覚；大騒ぎ、センセーション

The heat from the sun sent a wave of *sensation* through my body.

関連語 sensation : numb [nʌm]

numb（感覚のなくなった、麻痺した人）には sensation が欠けている。

solemn
[sáləm]

adj. serious or sacred

[形] まじめな、荘重な、神聖な

The cadet's *solemn* face conveyed the importance of the responsibilities bestowed upon him.

反意語 solemn utterance : jest [dʒest]

solemn utterance（真剣な言葉）の反意語は jest（冗談）

solicitous
[səlísətəs]

adj. expressing concern; eagerly desirous; extremely careful

[形] 心配した；切望した、強く望んだ；よく気の付く

Steven's *solicitous* attention to his wife endeared him to the in-laws.

関連語 solicitous : insouciance [insú:siəns]

solicitous な人は insouciance（無頓着、のんき）を持たない。

tolerance
[tálərəns]

n. the ability of accepting beliefs or practices differing from one's own; the ability to endure pain or hardship; the capacity to become less responsive to a substance with repeated use or exposure

[名] 寛容；忍耐；耐性

Al gradually built up his *tolerance* to alcohol while attending college.

関連語 tolerance : inured [in(j)úəʳd]

ものに inured（慣れた、鍛えられた）な状態とは、そのものに対して tolerance が生じているということ。

TRANSLATION | 例 文 の 訳

salient	明るいネオンがその建物の最も目立つ特徴だった。
sensation	太陽の熱が次々と体を通り抜けるような感覚を抱いた。
solemn	その士官候補生の真剣な表情から、彼に課された責任の重さがうかがえた。
solicitous	スティーブンはこまごまと妻に気を使うので、彼女の親きょうだいに気に入られた。
tolerance	アルは大学在学中に酒に強くなった。

unlimited [ʌnlímitid]	adj. **having no restrictions; infinite** [形] 無制限の；無限の
	Olive's health club membership was for *unlimited* use during the weekdays.
	反意語 unlimited : circumscribed [sə̀ːˈkəmskráibd] unlimited の反意語は circumscribed（制限された）
valiant [vǽljənt]	adj. **brave or exhibiting courage** [形] 勇敢な、勇ましい
	The *valiant* knight was welcomed home with a celebratory feast at the palace.
	関連語 valiance : pusillanimous [pjùːsəlǽnəməs] pusillanimous（気の弱い、臆病な）な人には valiance（勇敢、勇壮）が欠けている。
vilify [víləfài]	v. **to slander or harshly criticize** [動] ～を中傷する、けなす
	Propaganda *vilified* the British government during the Revolutionary War.
	反意語 vilify : adulate [ǽdʒulèit] vilify の反意語は adulate（～を絶賛する）
volatile [válətil]	adj. **evaporating rapidly without much change in temperature or pressure; tending to become violent; ever-changing** [形] 揮発性の；激しやすい；変わりやすい、不安定な
	Jane had grown up with a *volatile* father who would get violent when angered.
	関連語 volatile : stabilize [stéibəlàiz] volatile な人を stabilize（～を安定させる）するのは難しい。
vulgarity [vʌlgǽrəti]	n. **that which offends good tastes or manners** [名] 低俗、下品、悪趣味、俗悪
	The fan's *vulgarity* offended the spectators sitting in close proximity and he was soon escorted out of the stadium.
	関連語 vulgarity : gentle [dʒéntl] gentle（優しい、穏やかな）な人に vulgarity を見いだすことはできない。

TRANSLATION | 例 文 の 訳

unlimited	オリーブのフィットネスクラブの会員権は、平日には無制限に使えるものだった。
valiant	その勇敢な騎士は宮殿での祝賀会で歓待された。
vilify	独立戦争中、プロパガンダによってイギリス政府が中傷を受けた。
volatile	ジェーンは、怒ると暴力的になる激しやすい父の下で育った。
vulgarity	そのファンは低俗な振る舞いで近くに座っていた観客たちを不快にさせ、すぐにスタジアムの外に連れ出された。

■ Fill in the blanks with the correct letter that matches the word with its definition.

1. fondness	_____	a. harmful or noxious
2. belie	_____	b. to slander or harshly criticize
3. pulchritude	_____	c. to pretend to be sick or incapable in order to avoid work
4. ken	_____	d. physical beauty or attractiveness
5. filigree	_____	e. detailed ornamentation of fine gold or silver wire
6. vilify	_____	f. to agitate or enrage
7. malinger	_____	g. to morally or legally commit
8. deleterious	_____	h. to give a wrong impression; to contradict; to show to be wrong
9. rile	_____	i. range of sight; abstract range of perception
10. obligate	_____	j. a warm affection

■ Put the correct word in each blank from the list of words below.

11. numb した人は_____がない。

12. _____は、議事進行を delay することである。

13. _____な人を arouse するのは難しい。

14. _____は専門的な知識なしでただ趣味として superficial に芸術を扱う人である。

15. eulogize（〜を賞賛する）の反意語は_____である。

16. _____したものには truth がない。

17. _____は pertinent（関連する、適切な）の類義語である。

18. mollify（〜をなだめる）は_____の反意語である。

19. _____な人を stabilize することは難しい。

20. _____な人には flexibility が欠けている。

a. relevant	b. filibuster	c. mulish	d. dilettante	e. elliptic	f. malign
g. sensation	h. mendacious	i. volatile	j. beleaguer	k. phlegmatic	l. alleviate

11. g 12. b 13. k 14. d 15. f 16. h 17. a 18. j 19. i 20. c

1. j 2. h 3. d 4. i 5. e 6. b 7. c 8. a 9. f 10. g

275

20th DAY

Track 20

もう見なくてもいいですかって？
冗談もお上手ですね〜

aloft
[əlɔ́(:)ft]

adj. high above in the air　[形] 高く、空中に

The sight of the eagles soaring *aloft* inspired Amos to paint a picture.

反意語 stay aloft : founder [fáundəʳ]
stay aloft（空中に浮いている）の反意語は founder（沈む）

amphibian
[æmfíbiən]

n. an animal that can live in water and on land　[名] 両生類

Amphibians have physical attributes which allow them to survive on land and in water.

関連語 amphibian : frog [frɔːg]
frog（カエル）は amphibian の一種。

arctic
[áːʳktik]

adj. extremely cold and frigid　[形] 厳寒の、極寒の

The *arctic* tundra is home to only the fittest of wildlife.

反意語 arctic : torrid [tɔ́ːrid]
arctic の反意語は torrid（灼熱の）

balk
[bɔːk]

v. to stop short and refuse to go on; to thwart　[動] 急に止まる、止まって動かない；妨げる、妨害する

The horse *balked* and would not proceed into the dark forest.

反意語 balk : move ahead willingly [muːv əhéd wíliŋli]
balk の反意語は move ahead willingly（喜んで前に進む）

TRANSLATION | 例文の訳

aloft　ワシが空高く飛んでいく光景を見て、エイモスは絵を描く気になった。
amphibian　両生類には陸上と水中の両方で生きていける身体的特性がある。
arctic　極寒のツンドラ地帯には、そこに適応した野生動物だけが住める。
balk　その馬は急に止まり、暗闇の森の中に進もうとはしなかった。

276

ballast
[bǽləst]

n. a heavy substance used to improve the stability of a ship

[名] バラスト（船を安定させるために船底に積む重い荷）

Without the *ballast*, the ship will roll too much.

関連語 ballast : stability [stəbíləti]
ballastを使ってstability（安定）を維持する。

balm
[bɑːm]

n. a balsamic resin; a soothing, healing, or comforting agent

[名] 芳香性樹脂；鎮痛剤

Lip *balm* is an essential for people who live in cold winter climates.

関連語 balm : irritation [ìrətéiʃən]
balmにはirritation（炎症、過敏症）を抑える働きがある。

belligerent
[bəlídʒərənt]

adj. inclined to fight; pertaining to war　　　[形] けんか腰の；好戦的な

The *belligerent* drunks were arrested by the police after harassing a group of young men.

反意語 belligerent : conciliatory [kənsíliətɔ̀:ri]
belligerentの反意語はconciliatory（なだめる、懐柔的な）

beloved
[bilʌ́vid]

adj. dearly or highly loved　　　[形] 愛されて、人気のある、最愛の

Princess Diana, *beloved* by all, was greatly mourned after the tragic car accident.

反意語 beloved : spurned [spəː'nd]
belovedの反意語はspurned（拒絶された、振られた）

TRANSLATION | 例 文 の 訳

ballast	バラストがなければ、その船はひどく揺れるだろう。
balm	リップクリームは寒い冬を過ごす人々には不可欠だ。
belligerent	けんかっ早い酔っ払いたちが、若い男性のグループに嫌がらせをして、警察に逮捕された。
beloved	ダイアナ妃はだれからも愛されながら、悲惨な自動車事故に遭い、大いに追悼された。

bolster
[bóulstəʳ]

n. a long pillow or cushion　　　　　　　　　　　　[名] 長枕

v. to support with a bolster; to give a boost to
　　　　　　　　　　　　　　　　[動] 長枕で支える ; ～を元気づける

Most people with back problems use a *bolster* for support when sitting in a chair.

An extended rest and a good meal *bolstered* the morale of the troops.

関連語 bolster : support [səpɔ́:rt]
　　bolster には support（支える）する機能がある。

bully
[búli]

n. one who repeatedly harasses and intimidates those weaker than himself　　　　　　[名] いじめっ子、弱い者いじめをする人

Poor little John has his lunch money taken away daily by the school *bully*.

関連語 bully : browbeat [bráubì:t]
　　bully は自分より弱い人を browbeat（脅す、威嚇する）するのが特徴だ。

callous
[kǽləs]

adj. hardened and thickened; having calluses ; unfeeling
　　　　　　　　　　　[形] 堅くなった ; たこのある ; 無感覚な、冷淡な

Greg's finger tips have become *callous* from playing guitar.

関連語 callous : friction [fríkʃən]
　　friction（摩擦）することが続くと、皮膚が callous になる。

callow
[kǽlou]

adj. immature and inexperienced　　　　　　[形] 未熟な、経験の乏しい

The man's *callow* ways often caused him to be shortsighted in his goals.

反意語 callow : mature [mət(j)úəʳ]
　　callow の反意語は mature（成熟した）

cart
[kɑ:ʳt]

n. a wheeled vehicle used to transport goods, often pulled by animals　　　　　　　　　　[名] 荷車、カート

My grandfather started making money by selling watermelons from a *cart* he would pull into the city.

関連語 cart : caisson [kéisn]
　　caisson（弾薬車）は cart の一種。

TRANSLATION | 例 文 の 訳

bolster　腰を痛めている人の大半が、椅子に座るときに長枕を支えに使う。
　　　　　長期間の休息と質の高い食事が、軍隊の士気を高めた。

bully　かわいそうなことに、小さなジョンは毎日学校のいじめっ子に昼食代を巻き上げられてきた。

callous　グレッグの指先には、ギターの演奏によるたこができてきている。

callow　その男は未熟さが災いして、自分の目標に対して短絡的になることが多かった。

cart　祖父は荷車を引いて町へ行き、そこに積んだスイカを売ってお金を稼ぎ始めた。

278

collapse
[kəlǽps]

v. **to lose strength; to fall or break down**　　　　[動] 崩壊する

The poorly built building *collapsed* once the storm hit.

関連語 collapse : implode [implóud]
　　implode（内破する）は建物の内部が破壊されること、collapseは全体が崩壊すること。

collude
[kəlúːd]

v. **to conspire**　　　　[動] 結託する、共謀する

Anarchists *collude* against the government.

関連語 collude : cooperate [kouápərèit]
　　colludeは陰謀のために複数の人々とcooperate（協働する）すること。

culpable
[kʌ́lpəbl]

adj. **guilty; deserving blame**　　　　[形] 有罪の；非難に値する

Are video games *culpable* for the recent violence in school?

関連語 culpable : blame [bleim]
　　culpableはblame（非難する）されるのに値するということ。

disgorge
[disgɔ́ːˈdʒ]

v. **to discharge or eject from the throat and mouth**　　　[動] ～を吐き出す

People in Ancient Rome often ate for 6 hours because they would excuse themselves to *disgorge* throughout the meal.

類義語 disgorge : vomit [vάmit]
　　disgorgeの類義語はvomit（～を吐く）

errant
[érənt]

adj. **deviating or straying from the established course**
　　　　　　　　　　　　　　　　　　　[形] 逸脱した、道から外れた

Tom's *errant* behavior worried his father greatly.

関連語 errant : course [kɔ́ːˈs]
　　errantは一定のcourse（道、方向）から外れている。

TRANSLATION | 例 文 の 訳

collapse　　その脆弱な建造物は、ひとたび嵐が直撃すると崩壊した。

collude　　無政府主義者は結託して政府に対抗する。

culpable　　ビデオゲームが最近の校内暴力の原因なのだろうか。

disgorge　　古代ローマの人々は食事中に食べ物を吐き出すことを良しとしていたので、ときには6時間にわたって食べ続けることもあった。

errant　　トムの道を踏み外した行動は、父を非常に心配させた。

eulogize
[júːlədʒàiz]

v. **to extol or speak highly of**　　　　　　　　[動] 賞賛する、賛辞を送る

President Bush *eulogized* the citizens of New York City for their reaction to the September 11th attacks.

関連語 eulogize : encomiast [enkóumiæst]
encomiast（賛辞を述べる人）は eulogize するのが特徴だ。

fallacious
[fəléiʃəs]

adj. **based on false information or ideas; tending to deceive**
　　　　　　　　　　　　　　　　[形] 誤った推論に基づく；人を惑わす、虚偽の

The product's *fallacious* advertising swindled many consumers of their hard earned money.

反意語 fallacious : veracious [vəréiʃəs]
fallacious の反意語は veracious（誠実な、本当の）

falter
[fɔːltəʳ]

v. **to move unsteadily; to speak or act hesitantly**　　[動] ゆらぐ；口ごもる

Michael *faltered* for a few moments before finally speaking.

類義語 falter : hesitate [hézətèit]
falter の類義語は hesitate（躊躇する、ためらう）

gall
[gɔːl]

v. **to vex or become irritated**　　　　　　　　[動] いらだたせる、怒らせる

n. **bile in liver; rudeness**　　　　　　　　　　[名] 胆汁、厚かましさ、無礼

The teacher was *galled* by Daniel's actions.

Richard Nixon had the *gall* to deny on national television any connection to Watergate.

反意語 gall : assuage [əswéidʒ]
gall の反意語は assuage（～を静める、やわらげる）

TRANSLATION | 例 文 の 訳

eulogize　　ブッシュ大統領は、9.11の攻撃へのニューヨーク市民の対応に賛辞を送った。

fallacious　その製品に関する虚偽広告によって、多くの消費者が苦労して稼いだお金をだまし取られた。

falter　　　マイケルはしばらく口ごもってから、ようやく話し出した。

gall　　　　その教師はダニエルの行動に怒った。
　　　　　　　リチャード・ニクソンは厚かましくも、国内のテレビでウォーターゲートとの関わりをいっさい否定した。

gull
[gʌl]

v. **to cheat or trick** [動] だます

n. **a large sea bird that has a loud call** [名] カモメ

People are willing to *gull* for what they desire.

The incoming ship was followed by a flock of curious *gulls*.

関連語 gull : chicanery [ʃikéinəri]
gull するために chicanery (ごまかし、策略) を練る。

illiterate
[ilítərət]

adj. **unable to read or write** [形] 読み書きのできない

The *illiterate* man attempted to conceal his secret by pretending to be an erudite.

反意語 illiterate : erudite [ér(j)udàit]
illiterate の反意語は erudite (博学な、学問的な)

jolt
[dʒoult]

v. **to strike suddenly and forcefully so as to cause movement; to move or disturb with a sudden, hard blow**
[動] ～を急にゆする；衝撃を与える

Rachael was *jolted* backwards by the collision of the cars.

関連語 jolt : move [muːv]
jolt には move (動く、動かす) と比べて、強さと勢いがある。

lull
[lʌl]

v. **to calm or soothe** [動] なだめる、落ち着かせる、うとうとさせる

Every night the mother *lulls* her baby to sleep with a song.

反意語 lull : gall [gɔːl]
lull の反意語は gall (いらだたせる、怒らせる)

TRANSLATION | 例 文 の 訳

gull 人は、自分の欲しいもののためなら他人をだますこともいとわない。
入港する船に好奇心をもったカモメの群れがついてきた。

illiterate その男は読み書きができなかったが、博学なふりをして自分の秘密を隠そうとした。

jolt レイチェルは、車の衝突によって激しく後方へ飛ばされた。

lull 母は毎晩、歌を歌って赤ん坊を寝かしつけた。

malleable
[mǽliəbl]

adj. capable of being shaped, as by hammering or rolling; tractable　　　　　　　　　[形] 形になりやすい、可鍛性の；影響されやすい

Copper was the first *malleable* metal to be uncovered and its flexibility led to rapid innovations.

関連語 malleable : shape [ʃeip]
　　melleableなものは簡単にshape（形）を変えられる。

malodor
[mælóudəʳ]

n. a horrid, offensive smell　　　　　　　　　　　　[名] 悪臭

Oral *malodor* is often the result of irregular brushing and improper hygiene.

関連語 malodor : scent [sent]
　　malodorはscent（におい）の中でも悪臭を指す。

mellifluous
[məlífluəs]

adj. having a rich, sweet, and smooth flow
　　　　　　　　　　　　　[形]（音楽などが）甘美な、流ちょうな

A beautiful *mellifluous* melody floated into the room.

関連語 mellifluous : music [mjúːzik]
　　mellifluousは耳障りのいいmusic（音楽）に対して使う。

mollify
[máləfài]

v. to ease or appease　　　　　　　　　　[動] 〜をなだめる、静める

The wife *mollified* her enraged husband.

反意語 mollify : beleaguer [bilíːgəʳ]
　　mollifyの反意語はbeleaguer（困らせる）

oblige
[əbláidʒ]

v. to constrain by physical, moral, or legal force; to render a service to　　　　　　[動] 〜することを義務付けられている；〜に親切にする

Kent *obliged* Mary by helping her move to a new apartment.

反意語 oblige : discommode [dìskəmóud]
　　obligeの反意語はdiscommode（〜を困らせる、悩ます）

TRANSLATION | 例 文 の 訳

malleable	銅は最初に発見された可鍛性の金属で、その柔軟性によって急速な技術革新が起こった。
malodor	口臭は不定期な歯磨きと不適切な衛生状態から生じることが多い。
mellifluous	美しく甘美なメロディーが部屋に流れ込んだ。
mollify	妻は怒っている夫をなだめた。
oblige	ケントはメアリーが新しいアパートに引っ越すのを手伝った。

obliterate
[əblítəréit]

v. **to destroy or remove all traces of**   [動] 〜を破壊する、取り除く

The city was *obliterated* from the war.

関連語 obliterate : remove [rimúːv]
    obliterate は痕跡もなく完全に remove（取り除く）することだ。

oblivion
[əblívian]

n. **the state of being forgotten; the act of forgetting**
    [名] 無意識状態；忘却

The young delinquent's misdeeds were buried as an act of *oblivion* the moment he turned eighteen.

関連語 oblivion : forget [fəɾgét]
    oblivion と似た意味の動詞に forget（〜を忘れる）がある。

palliate
[pǽlièit]

v. **to lessen the effect of; to make less severe**
    [動] 〜をやわらげる；一時的にいやす

Doctors hoped the new drug would *palliate* the side effects of chemotherapy on cancer patients.

関連語 palliate : severity [səvérəti]
    severity（厳しさ、激しさ）を palliate する。

pallid
[pǽlid]

adj. **looking pale; lacking liveliness**   [形] 青白い；退屈な

Watching television became a *pallid* substitute for exercise after James broke his leg.

類義語 pallid : wan [wɑn]
    pallid の類義語は wan（青ざめた、血の気のない）

palpable
[pǽlpəbl]

adj. **obvious or capable of being felt**
    [形] 明白な、簡単にわかる、触れることができる

The scar on his knee is *palpable* to the touch.

反意語 palpable : elliptical [ilíptikəl]
    palpable の反意語は elliptical（省略された、わかりにくい）

TRANSLATION | 例 文 の 訳

obliterate	その都市は戦争で跡形もなく消えた。
oblivion	その非行少年の悪事は、彼が18歳になるとともに記憶の彼方へ葬られた。
palliate	医師たちは、その新薬ががん患者の化学療法による副作用をやわらげるだろうと期待した。
pallid	脚を折ったジェームズにとって、テレビを見ることが、退屈ながら運動の代わりとなった。
palpable	彼の膝の傷は、触るとよくわかる。

palter
[pɔ́:ltəʳ]

v. to act or speak in a deceitful way; to equivocate

[動] ごまかす；いい加減なことを言う

Phillip *paltered* in front of the principal, hoping to get his classmate in trouble.

関連語 palter : candor [kǽndəʳ]
palter する人には candor（正直、率直）がない。

pellucid
[pəlú:sid]

adj. allowing for light to pass without diffusing or distorting; easily comprehensible

[形] 透明な、澄んだ；明瞭な

The professor's *pellucid* method of teaching was popular among his students.

反意語 pellucid : evasive [ivéisiv]
pellucid の反意語は evasive（回避的な、責任逃れの）

pillory
[píl°ri]

n. a wooden device with holes for a head and hands that is used to publicly display a criminal as punishment; laughingstock

[名] さらし台（犯罪者の頭と手を固定する木の道具）；笑い者

The villagers threw tomatoes at the man in the *pillory*.

関連語 pillory : punish [pʌ́niʃ]
pillory は punish（～を罰する）するために使う道具。

pine
[pain]

n. a type of coniferous evergreen tree

[名] 松の木

v. to fail in health because of sorrow; to desire intensely

[動]（悲しみなどで）やつれる；～を思いこがれる

Throughout the world *pines* are cultivated for their use as Christmas trees.

Justin *pined* for the opportunity to paint in Italy.

関連語 pine : longing [lɔ́(:)ŋiŋ]
pine と似た意味の名詞に longing（あこがれ、思慕）がある。

TRANSLATION | 例文の訳

palter	フィリップは同級生を困らせようとして、校長の前でいい加減なことを言った。
pellucid	その教授のわかりやすい指導法は、学生の間で人気があった。
pillory	村人たちが、さらし台にいる男にトマトを投げつけた。
pine	世界中で松の木が栽培されているのは、クリスマスツリーとして使われるからだ。
	ジャスティンはイタリアで絵を描く機会を切望した。

pollster
[póulstər]

n. a person who conducts a poll [名] 世論調査員

The *pollsters* are busy during election time.

関連語 pollster : canvass [kǽnvəs]
pollster は canvass (聞き込みをする、意見調査をする) する。

ponder
[pándəʳ]

v. to carefully think on and reflect about [動] ～を熟考する

Eric *pondered* all day over the social questions that his professor raised in class.

関連語 ponder : imprudence [imprú:dns]
ponder する人には imprudence (軽率さ、無分別) がない。

punctilious
[pʌŋktíliəs]

adj. concerned with every detail; strictly adhering to etiquette or formalities [形] 几帳面な；厳格な

Soren is an honest and very *punctilious* German, very much representing the general German culture.

反意語 punctilious : remiss [rimís]
punctilious の反意語は remiss (怠慢な、いい加減な)

pundit
[pándit]

n. a learned person [名] 専門家、情報通

The *pundit* gave lectures on globalization at universities across the world.

関連語 pundit : opine [oupáin]
pundit にはいつも opine (～という意見を述べる) する傾向がある。

rafter
[rǽftəʳ]

n. a sloping beam that is used to support the roof [名] 垂木 (屋根を支えるために斜めにわたされる木)

Once the *rafters* were put in, the house started to take shape.

関連語 rafter : roof [ru:f]
rafter には roof (屋根) を支える機能がある。

TRANSLATION | 例 文 の 訳

pollster	世論調査員は選挙期間中、忙しい。
ponder	エリックは、教授が授業で提起した社会問題について一日中熟考した。
punctilious	ソレンは正直でとても几帳面なドイツ人で、一般的なドイツ人気質を体現している。
pundit	その専門家は世界中の大学でグローバル化の講義をした。
rafter	いったん垂木が据えられると、その家は形になり始めた。

285

rancor
[ráŋkə^r]

n. long-lived and bitter hatred　　　　　　　[名] 怨恨、憎しみ

The doctor's *rancor* towards the tobacco industry emanated from treating lung cancer patients.

反意語 rancor : charitableness [tʃǽrətəblnis]
　　rancorの反意語は charitableness（慈善、寛大）

random
[rǽndəm]

adj. lacking a fixed goal, plan, or procedure; happening accidentally or haphazardly　　　[形] 手当たり次第の、無計画な；無作為の

Martin's *random* business proposal failed to attract any investors.

関連語 random : pattern [pǽtərn]
　　randomなものには pattern（傾向、型、パターン）が欠けている。

rend
[rend]

v. to tear apart violently　　　　　　[動] 〜を引き裂く、引きちぎる

Kathy's unfaithful husband *rent* her heart.

関連語 rend : tear [tɛə^r]
　　rendは乱暴に tear（破る）することを意味する。

sanctimonious
[sæ̀ŋktəmóuniəs]

adj. claiming to be more holy than one really is
　　　　　　　　　　　　　　[形] 信心深そうな、神聖らしく見せかけた

The preacher's *sanctimonious* spiel about tithing had many of the congregation shaking their heads.

関連語 sanctimonious: devout [diváut]
　　sanctimoniousは表面的に devout（信心深い、敬虔な）な様子をいう。

sincere
[sinsíə^r]

adj. honest and true in one's thoughts, actions, and expressions
　　　　　　　　　　　　　　　　　　[形] 心からの、偽りのない

Everyone trusts Lily because of *sincere* concern for others.

関連語 sincerity : poseur [pouzə́:^r]
　　poseur（気取り屋）には sincerity（誠実、誠意）が欠けている。

TRANSLATION | 例 文 の 訳

rancor	その医者のたばこ業界に対する怨恨は、肺がん患者の治療から生じた。
random	マーティンの無計画な事業案は、どの投資家の関心も引かなかった。
rend	キャシーの夫は不誠実で、彼女の心を引き裂いた。
sanctimonious	その牧師による10分の1税に関する聖人ぶった説教に、信徒たちは首を横に振った。
sincere	皆がリリーを信頼するのは、彼女が他人のことを心から気にかけているからだ。

solidify [səlídəfài]	v. **to make hard or solid; to make strong or united** [動] ～を凝固させる；固くする Dropping temperatures *solidified* the freezing pond into ice. 反意語 solidify : pulverize [pʌ́lvəràiz] solidify の反意語は pulverize（～をひいて粉にする、粉々にする）
sparse [spɑːrs]	adj. **existing in small amounts; scanty; thinly scattered** [形] 少ない；乏しい；まばらな Water is often *sparse* in the desert. 反意語 sparse : copious [kóupiəs] sparse の反意語は copious（多い、豊富な）
spleen [spliːn]	n. **an organ of the body involved in the filter and restoration of blood; ill temper**　[名] 脾臓；不機嫌、短気 Nicholas vented his *spleen* on his wife. 類義語 spleen : malice [mǽlis] spleen の類義語は malice（悪意、敵意）
sullen [sʌ́lən]	adj. **resentfully irritated and silent**　[形] むっつりした、不機嫌な、すねた The *sullen* little boy's mood was lifted with a trip to the amusement park. 反意語 sullenness : elation [iléiʃən] sullenness（むっつりすること、不機嫌）の反意語は elation（意気揚々、大喜び）
sunder [sʌ́ndər]	v. **to break apart; to separate by violence**　[動] ～を切断する；分断する The tree was *sundered* after the lightening strike. 関連語 sunder : divide [diváid] sunder は divide（分配する）よりも語感が強い。

TRANSLATION | 例 文 の 訳

solidify	気温が下がり、冷たい池の水が固まって氷になった。
sparse	砂漠では常に水が不足している。
spleen	ニコラスは妻に怒りをぶちまけた。
sullen	その少年はすねていたが、遊園地に出かけると機嫌が直った。
sunder	その木は落雷で裂けてしまった。

syllogism
[sílədʒìzm]

n. a deductive structure of an argument that includes a major premise, a minor premise, and a conclusion; deduction

[名] 三段論法、演繹法

Aristotle's doctrine of *syllogism* was the basis of formal logic.

関連語 syllogism : disprove [disprúːv]

syllogism は相手の意見を disprove（〜を反証する）するために使われる。

tangy
[tǽŋi]

adj. having a sharp, distinctive flavor or odor

[形] 風味が強い、香りが強い

Japanese cooking often uses the kabosu to produce a *tangy* flavor.

反意語 tangy : bland [blænd]

tangy の反意語は bland（味がほとんどない、薄味の）

tarnish
[táːʳniʃ]

v. to dull the luster of; to discolor; to bring disgrace upon

[動] 光沢を失う；〜を変色させる；（名誉など）を汚す、傷つける

The once shiny trophy had become *tarnished* over time.

関連語 tarnish : silver [sílvər]

silver（銀）の光沢を tarnish する。

veneer
[vəníəʳ]

n. a superficial or false appearance; a thin layer of wood or plastic that covers a cheap material

[名] 見せかけ、うわべの飾り；化粧板

The wooden *veneer* on the table was beautiful.

関連語 veneer : furniture [fáːʳnitʃəʳ]

veneer は furniture（家具）の表に貼り付ける薄い木やプラスチックの板のこと。

volition
[voulíʃən]

n. an act of free will; the power of determining

[名] 意志；決断力

Voting is an act of intelligent *volition*.

関連語 volition : vacillating [væsəléitiŋ]

vacillating（優柔不断な）な人には volition が欠けている。

TRANSLATION | 例 文 の 訳

syllogism	アリストテレスの三段論法は形式論理学の基礎だった。
tangy	日本料理では強い香りを出すためによくカボスを使う。
tarnish	かつて輝いていたトロフィーが、時間とともに光沢を失った。
veneer	そのテーブルの表面の化粧板は美しかった。
volition	投票は知的判断を伴う行動だ。

■ Fill in the blanks with the correct letter that matches the word with its definition.

1. pellucid _____
2. mellifluous _____
3. callow _____
4. spleen _____
5. balm _____
6. rend _____
7. lull _____
8. fallacious _____
9. bolster _____
10. punctilious _____

a. based on false information or ideas; tending to deceive
b. immature and inexperienced
c. to violently tear apart
d. an organ of the body involved in the filter and restoration of blood; ill temper
e. to enhance strength or give a boost to
f. allowing for light to pass without diffusing or distorting; easily comprehensible
g. concern about precise behavior according to conventions; scrupulous
h. to calm or soothe
i. having a rich, sweet and smooth flow
j. a balsamic resin; a cream that soothes when applied to the skin

■ Put the correct word in each blank from the list of words below.

11. _____は陰謀を図るために cooperate するという意味である。
12. _____は単に move するのではなく、より強さと勢いを持って動くという意味だ。
13. _____にはいつも opine（～という意見を述べる）する傾向がある。
14. _____するために chicanery を練る。
15. _____する人は candor がない。
16. _____は自分よりも弱い人を browbeat する。
17. silver の光沢が_____する。
18. friction の結果、肌が_____になる。
19. discommode（～を困らせる、悩ます）の反意語は_____である。
20. _____は船の stability のために使用されるものである。

| a. jolt | b. palter | c. malleable | d. collude | e. gull | f. bully |
| g. pundit | h. ballast | i. tarnish | j. culpable | k. callous | l. oblige |

Answer key

20. h | 19. l | 18. k | 17. i | 16. f | 15. b | 14. e | 13. g | 12. a | 11. d
10. g | 9. e | 8. a | 7. h | 6. c | 5. j | 4. d | 3. b | 2. i | 1. f

289

Answer Page 436

Questions

across

3. looking pale; dull
4. having or showing doubt; creating uncertainty
5. a stubbornly unyielding; inflexible
8. to extract by long, careful searching
9. the inability to feel pain but without a loss of consciousness
14. logically possible or seemingly true
15. to lessen; to make pain more bearable
18. to wear down into powder using friction
19. an overly familiar phrase
20. to thicken or make more dense

down

1. to lose strength and to fall or break down
2. tending to teach or moralize
6. a large area of treeless grassland
7. messy or not clean
10. to put completely under water
11. to give courage or spirit to
12. the state of being forgotten; the act of forgetting
13. to move backward and forward
16. to introduce or put into
17. to lower in value or quality

皆さん！ 昨日覚えたはずの
sanctimoniousを
まだ覚えていますか？

21st DAY

acme
[ǽkmi]

n. the highest point 　　　　　　　　　　　　　　[名] 絶頂、頂点

Having reached the *acme* of her political career, the woman planned to retire after the end of her second presidential term.

反意語 acme : nadir [néidəʳ]
　　acmeの反意語はnadir（どん底）

admirable
[ǽdmərəbl]

adj. deserving admiration 　　　　　　　　　　[形] 賞賛に値する、見事な

Ms. Johnson possessed many *admirable* qualities, but it was her patience and commitment to her students' academic welfare that earned her the prestigious Distinguished Teaching Award.

反意語 admirable : vituperative [vait(j)ú:pərèitiv]
　　admirableの反意語はvituperative（ののしりの、敵意に満ちた）

beneficial
[bènəfíʃəl]

adj. advantageous to personal or social well-being 　　　[形] 有益な

Volunteer work is *beneficial* to all parties involved.

反意語 beneficial : noisome [nɔ́isəm]
　　beneficialの反意語はnoisome（有害な、不快な）

bombast
[bάmbæst]

n. pretentious speech or writing; grandiloquence
　　　　　　　　　　　　　　　　　　　　　[名] 大げさな言葉、大言壮語

The professor's article, no more than a *bombast*, was denied publication.

関連語 bombast : pompous [pάmpəs]
　　bombastにはpompous（おおげさな、仰々しい）だという特徴がある。

TRANSLATION | 例 文 の 訳

acme 　　その女性は政治家としての経歴の頂点に達したので、2期目の大統領の任期を終えたら引退しようと考えた。

admirable 　　ジョンソンさんには多くの賞賛すべき資質があったが、彼女が栄誉ある「最優秀教員賞」を獲得できたのは彼女の忍耐と生徒の学業に対する献身の賜物だった。

beneficial 　　ボランティア活動はすべての関係者にとって有益だ。

bombast 　　その教授の論文は大言壮語でしかなく、出版は拒否された。

bromide
[bróumaid]

n. a commonplace or trite remark　　　　[名] 陳腐な慰めの言葉

The *bromides* offered to the crying girl did nothing to ease her pain and sorrow.

関連語 bromide : hackneyed [hǽknid]
　bromide は hackneyed（陳腐な、紋切り型の）な言葉だ。

calumniate
[kəlʌ́mnièit]

v. to injure someone's reputation by making cruel false statements about him/her　　　　[動] 誹謗中傷する

To divert attention from his own poor performance, Jason *calumniated* a co-worker, going so far as to accuse him of embezzlement.

関連語 calumniate : falsehood [fɔ́:lshùd]
　他人を calumniate するために falsehood（嘘、虚言）を使う。

comfort
[kʌ́mfərt]

v. to console or make another feel at peace [動] ～を慰める、快適にさせる

There was nothing I could say to *comfort* my grieving friend over the loss of his pet rabbit.

反意語 comfort : aggrieve [əgríːv]
　comfort の反意語は aggrieve（～を怒らせる）

confession
[kənféʃən]

n. the religious act of admitting guilt　　　　[名] 罪の告白、懺悔

Prisoners on death row are permitted a *confession* with a priest before their execution.

関連語 confession : guilt [gilt]
　confession とは guilt（罪）を認めて、打ち明けること。

confirm
[kənfə́ːrm]

v. to make certain or attest to the truth; to make valid by a legal act　　　　[動] ～を確認する；承認する

Before approving a new medical product, the country's food and drug administration must *confirm* the validity of the company's claims.

関連語 confirm : hypothesis [haipáθəsis]
　hypothesis（仮説）を confirm する。

TRANSLATION | 例 文 の 訳

bromide 泣いている少女に陳腐な慰めの言葉をかけたところで、彼女の苦痛や悲しみをいやす上で何の役にも立たなかった。

calumniate 自分のみじめな業務成績から注意をそらすために、ジェイソンは同僚を誹謗中傷し、彼を横領で訴えることまでした。

comfort 私は、ペットのウサギを亡くして悲しんでいる友達を慰めるための言葉など何も持ち合わせていなかった。

confession 死刑囚監房にいる囚人たちには、死刑執行前に牧師に懺悔をすることが許されている。

confirm 新薬を承認する前に、当該国の食品医薬品局は製薬会社の申請の妥当性を確認しなければならない。

conform
[kənfɔ́ːʳm]

v. to obey or comply with; to follow the actions and manners of others

[動] ～に従う；順応する

Young people have always refused to *conform* to the conventional standards of the day.

関連語 conformity : maverick [mǽvəʳrik]
　maverick（異端者、一匹狼）は慣習に conformity（服従、従順）しない。

confuse
[kənfjúːz]

v. to disturb or mix up; to make unclear or incomprehensible

[動] ～を混乱させる、困惑させる；～をあいまいにする

Too much alcohol *confuses* the senses and slows the brain.

関連語 confusion : delirium [dilíˀriəm]
　delirium（一時的精神錯乱）に陥った人は、confusion（混乱）を経験する。

congeal
[kəndʒíːl]

v. to solidify or harden

[動] 凝固する、固まる

The blood had *congealed* around the wound on his head.

反意語 congeal : liquefy [líkwifài]
　congeal の反意語は liquefy（～を液化する）

congenial
[kəndʒíːnjəl]

adj. warm and friendly; of the same nature or disposition

[形] 愛想のいい；同じ性質の、気心の合う

Stepan was *congenial* and kind to all his co-workers.

反意語 congenial : draconic [dreikánik]
　congenial の反意語は draconic（厳しい、過酷な）

congruent
[kəngrúːənt]

adj. being in agreement or harmony; in geometry, exactly the same in shape and size

[形] ～と一致する、調和する；合同の

The company's long-range goals are *congruent* with my own.

関連語 congruent : dimension [diménʃən]
　数学で congruent（合同の）な状態とは、2つの図形の dimension（寸法）が同じなことをいう。

TRANSLATION | 例 文 の 訳

conform	若者はいつもその時代の伝統的な基準に従うことを拒否してきた。
confuse	アルコールを飲みすぎると感覚が混乱し、脳の働きが鈍くなる。
congeal	彼の頭の傷の周囲で血が固まっていた。
congenial	ステパンはすべての同僚に対して愛想がよく親切だった。
congruent	その企業の長期目標は、私自身の目標と一致する。

convalesce
[kɑ̀nvəlés]

v. **to recover or recuperate from illness** [動] 次第に回復する、快方に向かう

When Samantha was *convalescing* after her surgery, the nurses insisted she get up and walk even though it was painful.

関連語 convalesce : rehabilitation [rìːʰəbìlətéiʃən]
convalesce するために rehabilitation（リハビリテーション）をする。

cultivate
[kʌ́ltəvèit]

v. **to prepare land for growing crops; to develop an understanding or interest through study** [動] 耕す；学問を修める

The Minister of Agriculture had a keen interest in *cultivating* barren land with new irrigation systems.

反意語 cultivate : stunt [stʌnt]
cultivate の反意語は stunt（～を妨げる、～の成長を妨げる）

decode
[diːkóud]

v. **to convert code into an understandable language** [動] 解読する

By *decoding* the cryptic emails, the FBI was able to uncover a huge drug trade.

関連語 decode : encoded [inkóudid]
encoded（暗号化された）されたものを decode する。

deluge
[déljuːdʒ]

n. **a great flow; a heavy downpour; an overwhelming amount or number** [名] 洪水；豪雨；多数、多量

A *deluge* hit Napier, flooding streets and property.

関連語 deluge : drizzle [drízl]
drizzle（霧雨）は deluge よりもはるかに雨量が少ない。

delusion
[dilúːʒən]

n. **an erroneous belief or opinion; an idea that is not true** [名] 錯覚；思い違い

Charles lived his life under the *delusion* that money brings happiness.

関連語 delusion : visionary [víʒənèri]
delusion と似た意味の形容詞に visionary（架空の、幻想的な）がある。

TRANSLATION | 例 文 の 訳

convalesce サマンサが手術後に快方に向かうと、看護師たちは、痛みがあっても起上がって歩くよう求めた。
cultivate 農業大臣は新しいかんがい設備を使って不毛な土地を耕すことに強い興味を持っていた。
decode 暗号化されたEメールを解読することで、FBIは巨大な薬物取引を明らかにすることができた。
deluge 豪雨がネーピアを襲い、道路や敷地が冠水した。
delusion チャールズは金が幸せをもたらすという誤った考えの下で生涯を送った。

dilute
[dilúːt]

v. **to weaken or thin by adding a liquid**　[動]〜を（液体で）薄める、希釈する

In Greece, wine is *diluted* with water to avoid heavy intoxication.

反意語 dilute : concentrate [kάnsəntrèit]
dilute の反意語は concentrate（濃くする、濃縮する）

diminish
[dimíniʃ]

v. **to decrease in number, quality, or force**　[動]〜を減らす、小さくする

Yesterday's thunderstorm *diminished* into a slight drizzle overnight.

反意語 diminution : augmentation [ɔ̀ːgmentéiʃən]
diminution（減少、縮小）の反意語は augmentation（増加、増大）

ditty
[díti]

n. **a short, simple song**　[名]短い簡単な歌

Mothers usually sing a *ditty* to put their baby to sleep.

関連語 ditty : song [sɔːŋ]
ditty は song（歌）の一種で短いもの。

flinch
[flintʃ]

v. **to recoil or shrink in fear or pain**　[動]（痛みや恐怖から）たじろぐ、ひるむ

After years of abuse, the dog *flinched* every time anyone raised their voice.

関連語 flinch : fear [fiəʳ]
fear（恐怖）が元になって flinch する。

foment
[foumént]

v. **to stir up trouble; to enhance the development of something; to incite**　[動]（不和・反乱など）を扇動する；〜を助長する；誘発する

Authorities accused opposition parties of using the media to *foment* widespread public discord.

反意語 foment : defuse [diːfjúːz]
foment の反意語は defuse（〜を静める、やわらげる）

TRANSLATION | 例 文 の 訳

dilute　　　ギリシャでは悪酔いしないようにワインを水で割る。
diminish　　昨日の雷雨が一晩で弱い霧雨になった。
ditty　　　母親は赤ん坊を寝かしつけるために、たいてい短い簡単な歌を歌う。
flinch　　　何年間も虐待を受けたので、そのイヌはだれかが声を上げるたびにたじろいだ。
foment　　　当局は野党を非難し、マスコミを利用して、広がる国民の不和を助長したと断じた。

296

galvanize
[gǽlvənàiz]

v. **to shock with an electric current; to arouse to action**

[動] 電流で刺激する；〜するようにショックを与える

Campaigns designed to *galvanize* the public into action by appealing to reason can be sustained over those that appeal to emotions.

関連語 galvanize : stimulate [stímjulèit]

galvanizeは stimulate（〜を刺激する）するよりも刺激の強度が大きい。

hem
[hem]

n. **the edge of a garment**

[名]（布や衣服の）へり

v. **to surround or confine; to fold back and stitch down the edge of**

[動] 包囲する；〜のへりを縫う、まつる

The mother helped her daughter to shorten the *hem* of her dress.

The valley was not discovered until recently because large mountains *hemmed* it in.

関連語 hem : garment [gάːˈmənt]

hemは garmentの端のこと。

homage
[ˈhάmidʒ]

n. **expression of high regard**

[名] 敬意、尊敬

Two hundred football players came to pay *homage* to the great coach who had been dear to them all.

反意語 homage : disrespect [dìsrispékt]

homageの反意語は disrespect（無礼、失礼）

humane
[ˈhjuːméin]

adj. **characterized by concern or compassion for human or animal life**

[形] 思いやりのある、心の優しい

Harvey had the *humane* habit of rescuing and caring for stray dogs.

関連語 humane : misanthrope [mísənθròup]

misanthrope（人間嫌いの人）は humaneではない。

TRANSLATION | 例 文 の 訳

galvanize 感情よりも理性に訴えかけて大衆を動かす運動のほうが、長続きする。

hem 母親は娘がドレスの裾を上げるのを手伝った。

その谷は、大きな山々に囲まれていたために、最近まで発見されなかった。

homage 200人のアメリカンフットボールの選手が、その偉大な監督に敬意を表しにやって来た。全員にとって大切な人物だったのだ。

humane ハービーには迷い犬を保護して、世話するような心優しいところがあった。

humble
[ʰʌmbl]

adj. **not arrogant or proud; modest**

[形] 謙虚な、つつましい

The Dali Lama remains a *humble* man, untouched by his fame and notoriety.

反意語 humble : imperious [impíˀriəs]
humble の反意語は imperious（傲慢な、尊大な）

humility
[hju:míləti]

n. **the quality of being humble**

[名] 謙虚、謙遜

Humility is considered a virtue, but one should really testify to one's own achievements.

関連語 humility : supplicant [sʌ́plikənt]
supplicant（嘆願者、懇願者）には humility がある。

illuminate
[ilú:mənèit]

v. **to fill with light; to make clear**

[動] 〜を照らす；明らかにする

Rather than interpreting, Terry prefers reading painting descriptions that can *illuminate* the painter's intention.

反意語 illuminate : obfuscate [ábfʌskeit]
illuminate の反意語は obfuscate（〜をぼんやりさせる、わかりにくくする）

immanent
[ímənənt]

adj. **existing or remaining within; inherent**

[形] 内在する

Atheists believe that a spiritual being is *immanent* in people.

反意語 immanent : extrinsic [ikstrínsik]
immanent の反意語は extrinsic（外部からの、外来性の）

immaterial
[ìmətíˀriəl]

adj. **unimportant or irrelevant; having no substance or body**

[形] 重要でない、不適切な；実体のない、無形の

The judge declared the evidence *immaterial* and would not allow it in court.

反意語 immaterial : pertinent [pə́ːˀtˀnənt]
immaterial の反意語は pertinent（関係のある；適切な）

TRANSLATION | 例 文 の 訳

humble	ダライ・ラマは自分の名声や悪名に惑わされることのない、謙虚な人間であり続けている。
humility	謙遜は美徳とされているが、自分の業績はきちんと示すべきだ。
illuminate	テリーは解釈することより、画家の意図を明らかにする絵画の説明文を読むほうが好きだ。
immanent	無神論者たちは、霊的な存在は人の中にあると信じている。
immaterial	裁判官は、その証拠が重要性に乏しく、法廷で認められるものではないと宣言した。

imminent
[ímənənt]

adj. **ready or about to happen** [形] 差し迫った

The soldier, fighting in the midst of a bloody battle, knew he was in *imminent* peril.

類義語 imminent : forthcoming [fɔːˈθkʌmiŋ]
imminentの類義語はforthcoming（近々来る、来たるべき）

lament
[ləmént]

v. **to express sadness or mourning for** [動] 〜を悲しむ、嘆く

The entire town *lamented* the death of its popular mayor.

類義語 lament : deplore [diplɔ́ːˈ]
lamentの類義語はdeplore（嘆かわしく思う、〜を強く非難する）

lexicographer
[lèksəkágrəfəˈ]

n. **one who edits and compiles a dictionary** [名] 辞書編集者

Lexicographers must be diligent and meticulous to produce an accurate dictionary.

関連語 lexicographer : dictionary [díkʃənèri]
lexicographerはdictionaryを作る人。

limerick
[límərik]

n. **a humorous poem of around five lines**
[名] リメリック（こっけいな五行詩）

The Irish are famous for their *limericks*.

関連語 limerick : poem [póuəm]
limerickはpoemの一種。

luminary
[lúːmənéri]

n. **a prominent or respected person, usually in a specific field of academia; something that gives off light**
[名] 権威、指導的人物；照明灯、発光体

The *luminary* professor Richard Feynman is best known for his revision of the theory of quantum electrodynamics.

関連語 luminary : eminence [émənəns]
luminaryはeminence（名声）を持っている。

TRANSLATION | 例 文 の 訳

imminent	残虐な戦場のただ中で戦っていたその兵士は、自分が差し迫った危険の中にいることを知っていた。
lament	町中が、人気の高かった市長の死を嘆いた。
lexicographer	辞書編集者は、正確な辞書を作るために勤勉で注意深いことが必要だ。
limerick	アイルランド人はリメリックで有名だ。
luminary	権威ある大学教授リチャード・ファインマンは、何よりも量子電気力学の理論を修正したことで知られている。

membrane
[mémbrein]

n. a thin layer covering living tissue; cell membrane　　[名] 膜；細胞膜

Both plant and animal cells have *membranes* to protect the nucleus and to filter incoming and outgoing substances.

関連語 membrane : cell [sel]
membrane は cell（細胞）の一部だ。

momentous
[mouméntəs]

adj. of very great importance or significance　　[形] 重要な、重大な

For many teenagers, the day that they graduate from high school is a *momentous* occasion.

関連語 momentous : important [impɔ́ːʳtʰnt]
momentous なものは important（重要な）なものよりも重要度が高い。

nomad
[nóumæd]

n. a person with no fixed home who moves with his/her tribe depending on season and resources　　[名] 遊牧民

As a prisoner of Ottoman Turks, the young girl was sold to an Arabic *nomad* and thus sentenced to serve the wandering man until death.

関連語 nomad : abode [əbóud]
nomad には決まった abode（住居、住まい）がない。

numb
[nʌm]

adj. without any sensation; apathetic or indifferent
[形] 無感覚の；無関心な

v. to make unresponsive or insensitive　　[動] 麻痺させる、感覚をなくさせる

The dentist used a drug to make the patient's mouth *numb* before extracting a tooth.

Alice didn't bother to *numb* her ear before she pierced it because everyone said it would not hurt.

関連語 numb : anesthetic [æ̀nəsθétik]
anesthetic（麻酔薬）には手術する箇所を numb にする機能がある。

TRANSLATION | 例 文 の 訳

membrane　植物細胞と動物細胞の両方に、細胞核を守り、細胞に出入りする物質をろ過する細胞膜が備わっている。

momentous　多くの10代の若者にとって、高校を卒業する日は大きな節目だ。

nomad　オスマン・トルコの囚人だったその若い少女は、あるアラブの遊牧民に売られ、死ぬまでその放浪者に仕えるように言い渡された。

numb　その歯科医は薬を使って、抜歯前に患者の口の感覚を麻痺させた。
皆が痛くないと言ったので、アリスはピアスの穴を開ける前にわざわざ耳に麻酔をかけたりしなかった。

paltry
[pɔ́ːltri]

adj. small or meager; despicable [形] ごくわずかな

The laborer received a *paltry* wage for his week's work, barely enough to feed his small family.

反意語 paltry : significant [signífikənt]
paltry の反意語は significant（かなりの）

premeditate
[priːmédətèit]

v. to plan or consider in advance [動] 前もって計画する、熟慮する

Sentencing is more severe for convicted individuals who *premeditate* their crimes because the planning implies cruelty.

反意語 premeditated : offhand [ɔːfhǽnd]
premeditated（前もって計画された）の反意語は offhand（即座の、用意のない）

remiss
[rimís]

adj. negligent or careless in the performance of one's duties or responsibilities [形]（任務や仕事に）怠慢な、不注意な

The employee was reprimanded for being *remiss* and forgetting to lock the office.

類義語 remiss : indolent [índələnt]
remiss の類義語は indolent（怠惰な、怠けた）

ruminate
[rúːmənèit]

v. to think over repeatedly [動]（繰り返し）思い巡らす

Tim grew restless as he *ruminated* over whether or not to accept the job offer.

反意語 ruminative : unreflective [ʌ̀nrifléktiv]
ruminative（考え込む）の反意語は unreflective（思慮の足りない、軽率な）

salubrious
[səlúːbriəs]

adj. promoting or favorable to health [形] 健康によい、快適な

A short workout every morning is a *salubrious* daily routine.

反意語 salubrious : baneful [béinfəl]
salubrious の反意語は baneful（致命的な、有害な）

TRANSLATION | 例 文 の 訳

paltry	その労働者が受け取った週給はごくわずかで、小さな家族をかろうじて養える程度の額だった。
premeditate	計画犯への判決内容がより厳しいものになるのは、計画性に残虐さが表れるからだ。
remiss	不注意にもオフィスに鍵をかけ忘れたことで、その従業員は叱責された。
ruminate	ティムは転職の誘いを受けるかどうか考えているうちに、落ち着かなくなった。
salubrious	毎朝の短い運動は健康によい習慣だ。

salve
[sæv]

n. a medical ointment   [名] 軟膏

v. to soothe or cure   [動] ～をやわらげる、癒やす

The veterinarian put a *salve* on the animal's wound to alleviate the pain.

After sitting in the sun for some time, Jimmy had to *salve* himself with aloe in order to lessen the discomfort from the sunburn.

> 関連語 salve : unctuous [ʌ́ŋktʃuəs]
> salve には unctuous (油っぽい、クリーム状の) だという特徴がある。

solvent
[sɑ́lvənt]

adj. able to pay all legal debts   [形] (負債などの) 支払い能力がある

n. a substance capable of dissolving another substance   [名] 溶剤

The gifted businessman managed to keep his company *solvent* throughout the long economic recession.

Many housewives use bleach as a *solvent* to get rid of stains around the house.

> 反意語 solvent : bankrupt [bǽŋkrʌpt]
> solvent の反意語は bankrupt (支払い能力のない、破産した)

somber
[sɑ́mbəʳ]

adj. dark colored; depressed or serious in mood or character   [形] 地味な；陰気な、落ち込んだ

Kitty's mood became *somber* when the policeman pulled her over for speeding.

> 反意語 somber : droll [droul]
> somber の反意語は droll (ひょうきんな、こっけいな)

symbiotic
[sìmbaiɑ́tik]

adj. characterized by the coexistence of two different organisms that may benefit both parties   [形] 共生の、共生している

A *symbiotic* relationship between two species develops over a long period of evolution.

> 関連語 symbiosis : interdependent [ìntəʳdipéndənt]
> symbiosis (共生) をする生物は interdependent (相互依存の、互いに頼り合う) な特徴がある。

TRANSLATION | 例 文 の 訳

salve 獣医師は、その動物の傷に軟膏を塗って痛みをやわらげてやった。
しばらく日なたに座ったあとで、ジミーは日焼けの痛みをやわらげなければならなかった。

solvent その有能な実業家は、長い不況の間、自分の会社の支払い能力をなんとか維持した。
多くの主婦が、家の周りの汚れを取るために漂白剤を溶剤として使っている。

somber 警察官がスピード違反で彼女の車を止めたとき、キティの気分は落ち込んだ。

symbiotic 2つの種の間の共生関係は、長期間の進化を経て発達する。

temerity
[təmérəti]

n. foolish boldness; recklessness   [名] 大胆さ、無謀さ

Alicia's *temerity* led her to scream at her boss.

関連語 temerity : timorous [tímərəs]
timorous（臆病な、腰抜けの）な人には temerity が欠けている。

vim
[vim]

n. a large amount of energy and vitality   [名] 元気、活力

The old grandmother was so full of *vim* and vigor that she tired out her grandchildren with her play.

反意語 vim : lassitude [lǽsət(j)ùːd]
vim の反意語は lassitude（だるさ、脱力感）

voluble
[váljubl]

adj. marked by knowledgeable and rapid speech
[形] 多弁な、よくしゃべる

Laura is *voluble* in her protestations, especially when discussing environmental issues.

反意語 voluble : reticent [rétəsˤnt]
voluble の反意語は reticent（無口な）

voluminous
[vəlúːmənəs]

adj. having great volume, size, or number   [形] 大きい、豊富な

Sharon's look of resignation indicated she had given up searching for her sister in the *voluminous* crowd.

反意語 voluminous : scanty [skǽnti]
voluminous の反意語は scanty（乏しい）

voluptuary
[vəlʌ́ptʃuèri]

n. a person addicted to luxury and sensual pleasures
[名] 快楽にふける人、享楽的な人

Bernice was a true *voluptuary* who enjoyed regular gourmet meals and weekend spa getaways.

反意語 voluptuous : ascetic [əsétik]
voluptuous の反意語は ascetic（禁欲主義の）

TRANSLATION | 例 文 の 訳

temerity　アリシアは大胆にも上司をどなりつけた。

vim　その年老いた祖母は元気と活力に満ちていて、いっしょに遊ぶ孫たちを疲れさせるほどだった。

voluble　ローラは自分が主張するとき、特に環境問題を議論するときに多弁になる。

voluminous　シャロンのあきらめの表情から、彼女が大勢の群衆の中で妹を探すことを断念したことがわかった。

voluptuary　バーニスは実に享楽的な人物で、定期的にグルメな食事を味わったり、週末に温泉で過ごしたりしていた。

wan [wɑn]	adj. **unnaturally pale; lacking strength or vigor** [形] 青ざめた；弱々しい
	The doctor's pale and *wan* face indicated that his 36 hour shift ran too long.
	反意語 wan : rubicund [rú:bikʌnd]
	wan の反意語は rubicund（赤ら顔の、血色のいい）

wander [wándəʳ]	v. **to roam aimlessly; to go astray** [動] ぶらつく；迷う、脱線する
	They had permitted him to freely *wander* about the prison.
	類義語 wander : drift [drift]
	wander の類義語は drift（漂う、ふらふらする）

wane [wein]	v. **to weaken or lessen in size; to diminish** [動] 衰える、弱くなる、小さくなる；減少する
	The heat of the sun had begun to *wane*, but the air was filled with a pink brightness.
	反意語 wane : intensify [inténsəfài]
	wane の反意語は intensify（～を強める、増大する）

windbag [wíndbæg]	n. **a talkative person who says nothing important** [名] むだ口ばかりたたく人、おしゃべり
	Nobody pays attention to that old *windbag* because he talks incessantly about the weather.
	関連語 windbag : verbosity [vəːʳbásəti]
	windbag は verbosity（冗舌、多弁なこと）を楽しむ。

TRANSLATION | 例 文 の 訳

wan	青白く弱々しい顔つきから、その医者の36時間の勤務が長すぎたことがわかった。
wander	彼らは彼が刑務所の中を自由に歩き回ることを許した。
wane	太陽の熱は弱まってきていたが、空気はピンク色の輝きに満ちていた。
windbag	その老人はおしゃべりだが、絶え間なく天気について話しているので、だれも気にしない。

■ Fill in the blanks with the correct letter that matches the word with its definition.

1. membrane _____
2. immanent _____
3. foment _____
4. solvent _____
5. congruent _____
6. paltry _____
7. deluge _____
8. remiss _____
9. confirm _____
10. temerity _____

a. to stir up trouble or enhance the development of something
b. small or meager; despicable
c. only existing in the mind
d. being negligent in one's duties or responsibilities
e. to make certain or attest to the truth; to make valid by a legal act
f. able to pay all legal debts
g. a great flow; a heavy downpour; an overwhelming amount or number
h. foolish boldness; recklessness
i. a thin layer covering living tissue; cell membrane
j. being in agreement or harmony; in geometry, exactly the same in shape and size

■ Put the correct word in each blank from the list of words below.

11. _____には一定の abode がない。

12. _____は verbosity を楽しむ人である。

13. _____する生物は interdependent している。

14. _____は draconic（厳しい、過酷な）の反意語である。

15. disrespect（無礼、失礼）の反意語は_____である。

16. _____は eminence を持っている。

17. reticent（無口な）の反意語は_____である。

18. noisome（有害な）の反意語は_____である。

19. _____は将来に影響を及ぼすので、important よりも重要なことを描写するために使用される。

20. falsehood は他人を_____するために使用する。

a. voluble	b. symbiosis	c. windbag	d. symbiotic
e. calumniate	f. beneficial	g. congenial	h. momentous
i. voluminous	j. luminary	k. nomad	l. homage

Answer key

20. e. | 19. h. | 18. f. | 17. a. | 16. j. | 15. l. | 14. g. | 13. b. | 12. c. | 11. k.
10. h | 9. e | 8. d | 7. g | 6. b | 5. j | 4. f | 3. a | 2. c | 1. i

305

食事をしながらでも、
単語を覚えなければならないかそれが問題だ。

22nd DAY

admonish [ædmɑ́niʃ]	v. **to reprove gently but seriously** 　　　　　[動] しかる、さとす、忠告する She softly *admonished* her husband for criticizing his brother's irresponsible lifestyle. 関連語 admonish : denounce [dináuns] admonishはdenounce（非難する）よりも穏やかに忠告することを表す。
arrhythmic [əríðmik]	adj. **lacking steady rhythm** 　　　　　　　　　[形] 不規則な、リズムのない Sandy brought the car to the mechanic because of an *arrhythmic* sound in the engine. 類義語 arrhythmic : erratic [irǽtik] arrhythmicの類義語はerratic（気まぐれな、不規則な）
brat [bræt]	n. **a spoiled, troublesome child** 　　　　　　　[名]（行儀の悪い）子供 Karen loved her nieces, but she had to admit that they were *brats*. 関連語 brat : mischievous [místʃivəs] bratにはmischievous（いたずら好きな、有害な）な特徴がある。
bumptious [bʌ́mpʃəs]	adj. **offensively self-assertive** 　　　　　　　[形] いばった、傲慢な The *bumptious* student didn't have many friends because of his aggressive attitude. 関連語 bumptious : assertive [əsə́ːᵣtiv] assertive（はっきり自分の意見を述べる、断定的な）な人はbumptiousに見える。

TRANSLATION | 例 文 の 訳

admonish	彼女は、夫が弟の無責任な生活態度を批判するのを、それとなくたしなめた。
arrhythmic	サンディが車を整備工場に持ち込んだのは、エンジンが異音を立てたからだ。
brat	カレンは姪たちが大好きだったが、彼女たちが行儀の悪いことは認めなければならなかった。
bumptious	その傲慢な学生にはあまり友達がいなかった。攻撃的な態度をとるからだ。

21st
22nd
23rd
24th
25th
26th
27th
28th
29th
30th

command
[kəmǽnd]

n. an order meant to be obeyed　　　　　　　[名] 命令、指令

The admiral sent a *command* for the fleet of ships to anchor in the bay.

関連語 command : entreaty [intríːti]
command は entreaty (懇願、嘆願) よりも強圧的な命令を指す。

commend
[kəménd]

v. to praise　　　　　　　　　　　　　　[動] ほめる、賞賛する

The brave citizen was *commended* for saving a child from drowning.

関連語 commend : esteem [istíːm]
esteem (〜を高く評価する、尊敬する) は commend よりも賞賛する程度が強い。

commodious
[kəmóudiəs]

adj. comfortably spacious　　　　　　　　[形] 広々している

The room was bright and *commodious*.

反意語 commodious : constricted [kənstríktid]
commodious の反意語は constricted (抑制された、収縮した)

commonplace
[kámənplèis]

adj. ordinary　　　　　　　　　　　[形] ありふれた、ごくふつうの

n. something that is common or frequent
　　　　　　　　　　　　　　[名] ありふれたもの、よくあること

The *commonplace* practice of shaking hands as a greeting can be found in many cultures.

All over Korea, it was *commonplace* to see fans wearing Red Devil shirts.

関連語 commonplace : originality [ərìdʒənǽləti:]
commonplace なものには originality (独創性) がない。

commonsensical
[kàmənsénsikəl]

adj. having a practical way of thinking　　　[形] 常識のある、常識的な

The philosopher is the antithesis to the *commonsensical* person.

反意語 commonsensical : preposterous [pripástᵊrəs]
commonsensical の反意語は preposterous (不合理な、ばかげた)

TRANSLATION | 例 文 の 訳

command	提督は艦隊に湾に停泊するように命令を出した。
commend	その勇敢な市民は、溺れそうな子供を救ったことで賞賛された。
commodious	その部屋は明るく広々としていた。
commonplace	挨拶のために握手をするという当たり前の習慣は、多くの文化に見られる。
	韓国全域で、Red Devil のシャツを着ているファンをよく見かけた。
commonsensical	その哲学者は常識人とは正反対の人だった。

commotion
[kəmóuʃən]

n. a condition of excitement and confusion　　[名] 突然の騒ぎ、興奮

Curious upon hearing the *commotion* in the boss's office, Mina decided to investigate.

関連語 commotion : squall [skwɔ:l]
squall (一時的な騒動) は commotion よりも小さな騒ぎをいう。

comparable
[kámpərəbl]

adj. equal in value to; similar　　[形] 比較できる、同種の；匹敵する、同等の

The atmosphere of Saturn is *comparable* to that of Jupiter.

反意語 comparable : disparate [díspərət]
comparable の反意語は disparate (まったく異なる、共通点のない)

compendious
[kəmpéndiəs]

adj. characterized by concise expression　　[形] 簡潔な、的を射た

The professor's *compendious* remarks impressed the faculty board.

関連語 compendious : encyclopedia [ensàikləpí:diə]
encyclopedia (百科事典) には説明が compendious だという特徴がある。

complacence
[kəmpléisᵊns]

n. contented satisfaction with oneself　　[名] 自己満足

Steve's *complacence* infuriated his ambitious girlfriend and eventually resulted in their break-up.

関連語 complacence : anxiety [æŋzáiəti]
complacence を持つ人には anxiety (悩み、不安) がない。

complain
[kəmpléin]

v. to express dissatisfaction or grief; to formally make a charge
[動] 不満を言う、文句を言う；訴える

It is common for students to *complain* about their teachers.

関連語 complain : carp [kɑːʳp]
carp (文句を言う、あら捜しをする) は complain よりも不満の程度が強い。

TRANSLATION | 例 文 の 訳

commotion　上司の部屋で騒ぎがあったと聞いて好奇心を持ったミナは、調べることを決めた。
comparable　土星の大気は木星のそれと同種のものだ。
compendious　その大学教授の的を射た発言は教授会を感心させた。
complacence　スティーブの自己満足は野心家の恋人を激怒させ、結局彼らは別れることになった。
complain　学生が担当教員の不満を口にするのはよくあることだ。

308

complexity
[kəmpléksəti]

n. the quality of being intricate; that which is complicated

[名] 複雑さ；複雑なもの

The *complexity* of life and the universe baffles the human mind.

関連語 complexity : convoluted [kánvəlù:tid]
complexity と同じ意味の形容詞に convoluted（複雑で難解な、入り組んだ）がある。

compliment
[kámpləmənt]

n. a positive expression of admiration or praise

[名] 賛辞、ほめ言葉

The gentleman's *compliment* was well received by the elegant lady.

反意語 compliment : invective [invéktiv]
compliment の反意語は invective（悪口、ののしり）

compose
[kəmpóuz]

v. to calm or tranquilize; to form

[動] ～を静める、やわらげる；～を組み立てる、構成する

It is imperative that emergency responders remain *composed* during a crisis situation.

反意語 composed : distraught [distrɔ́:t]
composed の反意語は distraught（取り乱した、ひどく困惑した）

comprehend
[kàmprihénd]

v. to understand the meaning or significance of

[動] ～を理解する

Cossette at first did not *comprehend* what the old woman was trying to tell her.

関連語 comprehend : ambiguous [æmbígjuəs]
ambiguous（あいまいな、不明瞭な）なことを comprehend するのは難しい。

TRANSLATION | 例文の訳

complexity 命と宇宙の複雑さに、人は途方に暮れるばかりだ。

compliment 紳士のほめ言葉を、その上品な女性は好意的に受け止めた。

compose 危機的な状況に際して、緊急時対応要員は落ち着いていなければならない。

comprehend コゼットは初め、その老女が自分に何を言おうとしているのかわからなかった。

compress
[kəmprés]

v. **to press together or compact**　　　　　　[動] 〜押しつける、〜を圧縮する

The best way to stop a nose bleed is to lean forward and *compress* the nose.

関連語 compression : clamp [klæmp]
clamp（留め具、クランプ）はしっかりと compression する機能を持つ道具。

compromise
[kámprəmàiz]

n. **an agreement or settlement reached in which all parties benefit and lose some**　　　　　　[名] 妥協

The two countries reached a *compromise* that would end the fighting.

関連語 compromise : mediation [mì:diéiʃən]
compromise に達するために mediation（調停）する。

compunction
[kəmpʌ́ŋkʃən]

n. **a sense of distress resulting from guilt**　　　　[名] ためらい、良心の痛み、やましさ

Cynthia had not the least *compunction* for what she had said.

関連語 compunction : unrepentant [ʌ̀nripéntənt]
unrepentant（自責の念のない）人は compunction を持たない。

conjecture
[kəndʒéktʃəʳ]

v. **to infer without evidence**　　　　　　　　　[動] 推測する

Elinor could only *conjecture* about their relationship because her husband didn't talk about it much.

類義語 conjecture : speculate [spékjulèit]
conjecture の類義語は speculate（憶測する、推測する）

damp
[dæmp]

adj. **wet; slightly moist**　　　　　　　　　　[形] 湿っぽい、じめじめした

v. **to moisten**　　　　　　　　　　　　　　　[動] 湿らせる

The morning dew left the ground *damp*.

Mike *damped* his handkerchief and wiped up the dust.

関連語 damp : soak [souk]
soak（〜を液体に浸す、つける）は damp よりもしっかりと水につける。

TRANSLATION | 例 文 の 訳

compress　　　鼻血を止める一番の方法は、前かがみになって鼻を強く押すことだ。
compromise　　その2国は妥協に至り、戦闘を終結させた。
compunction　シンシアは自分が言ったことに対して少しのやましさも感じなかった。
conjecture　　エリノアは、夫があまり語らなかったので、彼らの関係について推測するしかなかった。
damp　　　　　朝露が地面を濡らした。
　　　　　　　　マイクはハンカチを湿らせてほこりを拭き取った。

dank
[dæŋk]

adj. **unpleasantly wet and cool**　　　[形] じめじめした、湿っぽくて寒い

The air was *dank* and stale in the cargo hold of the huge freighter.

関連語 dank : moisture [mɔ́istʃəʳ]
dankと似た意味の名詞にmoisture（湿気）がある。

denigrate
[dénigrèit]

v. **to defame; to deny the value of**　　　[動] 人をけなす；（価値などを）軽視する

The coach *denigrated* the capabilities of the opposing team.

反意語 denigrate : honor [ánəʳ]
denigrateの反意語はhonor（〜を尊敬する、たたえる）

denounce
[dináuns]

v. **to openly declare as reprehensible**　　　[動] 非難する、告発する

Martin *denounced* the government for its tough new welfare policy.

関連語 denounce : admonish [ædmániʃ]
denounceはadmonish（しかる、さとす）よりも強く非難することを表す。

din
[din]

n. **a loud and persistent noise**　　　[名]（長く続く）やかましい音、不快な音

The *din* of the party inhibited the neighbor's sleep.

類義語 din : clamor [klǽməʳ]
dinの類義語はclamor（騒々しい音、大声）

enmity
[énməti]

n. **hatred or animosity**　　　[名] 敵意、悪意

Ratcliffe did not think Carrington's *enmity* a thing to be overlooked.

反意語 enmity : concord [kánkɔːʳd]
enmityの反意語はconcord（調和、友好）

TRANSLATION | 例 文 の 訳

dank 巨大な貨物船の荷室の空気は、じめじめとして、よどんでいた。
denigrate その監督は相手チームの能力を軽視した。
denounce マーティンは政府の達成困難な新しい福祉政策を非難した。
din パーティーの騒音のせいで、隣人は眠れなかった。
enmity ラトクリフはカリントンの敵意を、見逃せるものだとは思わなかった。

footloose
[fútlùːs]

adj. **having no attachments or ties; free to go as one pleases**

[形] 気の向くままの、気楽な

The man had been *footloose* most of his life, but now felt he wanted to settle down.

関連語 footloose : attachment [ətǽtʃmənt]

footlooseな人は attachment（何かにくっついていること）がない。

gargantuan
[gɑːˈɡǽntʃuən]

adj. **huge or massive in size**　　　　　　　　　　[形] 巨大な

The *gargantuan* redwood trees in California are the biggest in the world, growing over 100 meters tall.

関連語 gargantuan : large [lɑːˈdʒ]

gargantuanは非常に large（大きい）であることをいう。

genial
[dʒíːnjəl]

adj. **friendly and warm**　　　　　　　[形] 愛想のいい、朗らかな、温和な

Lyman seemed to be every man's friend, because his *genial* disposition even puts strangers at ease.

反意語 genial : mordant [mɔ́ːˈdᵊnt]

genialの反意語は mordant（皮肉な、辛辣な）

hamper
[hǽmpəˈ]

v. **to hinder or disrupt**　　　　　　　　　　[動] 妨げる、邪魔をする

Last-minute work at the office *hampered* Billy's plan to get an early start on the weekend.

反意語 hamper : facilitate [fəsílətèit]

hamperの反意語は faciliate（〜を促進する、容易にする）

hangdog
[hǽŋdɔ̀(ː)g]

adj. **dejected or depressed; feeling embarrassed over a guilty conscience**　　　　　　　　[形] しょんぼりした；恥じ入った、やましい

The boy left the classroom with a *hangdog* expression on his face when the teacher told him to go to the principal's office.

反意語 hangdog : elated [iléitid]

hangdogの反意語は elated（大喜びの、得意の）

TRANSLATION | 例 文 の 訳

footloose	その男性は人生のほとんどを気ままに過ごしたが、いまは落ち着きたいと思っている。
gargantuan	カリフォルニアの巨大なセコイアの木は世界で最も大きく、100メートルを超える高さにまで成長する。
genial	ライマンは朗らかな性格で、知らない人でも気楽に接することができるので、だれもが彼の友人のように見えた。
hamper	職場で土壇場になって仕事が入り、早めに週末を始めようというビリーの計画は妨げられた。
hangdog	教師に校長室へ行くように促され、その男の子はしょんぼりした表情で教室を出て行った。

21st
22nd
23rd
24th
25th
26th
27th
28th
29th
30th

hankering
[hǽŋkəriŋ]

n. **a strong desire or yearning** [名] 熱望、望み

Barney rummaged through the fridge to satisfy his *hankering* for a midnight snack.

反意語 hankering : dislike [disláik]
　　hankeringの反意語はdislike（嫌い）

hymn
[him]

n. **a song of praise to God; a song or poem of praise or joy** [名] 讃美歌；賛歌

The Church *hymns* filled the air on that Sunday morning.

関連語 hymn : praise [preiz]
　　hymnはpraise（賛美する）する歌。

ignite
[ignáit]

v. **to set on fire** [動] 火をつける

Richard *ignited* his match across the rough sandpaper.

反意語 ignite : quench [kwentʃ]
　　igniteの反意語はquench（消火する）

immune
[imjú:n]

adj. **free from or not susceptible to disease** [形] 免疫のある

Mike seems to be *immune* from illness because he never gets sick.

関連語 immunity : vaccination [væksənéiʃən]
　　vaccination（予防接種）の目的は、病気に対するimmunity（免疫）を持たせることだ。

immutable
[imjú:təbl]

adj. **unchangeable** [形] 不変の

Physicists like to believe that their discipline defines the *immutable* laws of nature.

関連語 immutable : vicissitude [visísət(j)ù:d]
　　immutableなものにはvicissitude（移り変わり）がない。

TRANSLATION | 例 文 の 訳

hankering	バーニーは夜食を食べたい欲求に駆られ、冷蔵庫をあさった。
hymn	その日曜日の朝、教会の讃美歌が響き渡った。
ignite	リチャードはきめの粗い紙やすりでマッチに火をつけた。
immune	マイクは決して体調を崩さないので、病気に免疫があるように見える。
immutable	物理学者たちは、自分たちの学問が自然界の不変の法則を定義づけるものだと考えたがる。

jingoism
[dʒíŋgouìzm]

n. strong nationalism and a hate for foreign countries

[名] 好戦的愛国主義

After the September 11th attacks, there was an excess of *jingoism* in America.

関連語 jingoism : nation [néiʃən]

jingoismは自分のnation（国家）に対する過度の愛国心を表す。cf) jingoismはchauvinism（熱狂的愛国主義）が他国への敵意で強まったもの。

languid
[læŋgwid]

adj. with minimal energy or excitement; listless

[形] けだるい、ものうい；無気力な

Barry's *languid* expression belied the excitement he felt inside.

関連語 languid : energy [énərdʒi]

languidな人にはenergy（元気、活力）が欠けている。

leniency
[líːniənsi]

n. a merciful or tolerant disposition or practice   [名] 寛大さ、慈悲、寛容

On occasion, the teacher exhibited *leniency* for her students' misbehavior, but usually she was very strict and quick to punish.

関連語 leniency : martinet [màːˈtˀnét]

martinet（厳格な人）の中にleniencyを見いだすのは難しい。

link
[liŋk]

n. a single connecting structure in a series; a relationship; connecting factor   [名] つながり；関連；連絡手段

Research has clearly established a *link* between cigarette smoking and lung cancer.

関連語 link : chain [tʃein]

linkが集まるとchain（鎖、チェーン、連鎖）になる。

longing
[lɔ́(ː)ŋiŋ]

n. a strong desire or emotional need; yearning   [名] 切望、憧れ

Miguel was full of *longing* for his girlfriend far away.

関連語 longing : pine [pain]

longingと似た意味の動詞にpine（恋い慕う）がある。

TRANSLATION | 例 文 の 訳

jingoism	9.11の攻撃以降、アメリカには過度の好戦的愛国主義が広がった。
languid	バリーのものうげな表情は、彼が内心感じている興奮を隠した。
leniency	その女性教師は、生徒たちの無作法に寛大なこともあったが、たいていはとても厳格ですぐに罰を与えた。
link	研究が喫煙と肺がんの関連性を明確に立証してきた。
longing	ミゲルは遠くにいる恋人が恋しくてたまらなかった。

314

mangy
[méindʒi]

adj. having blotches or bare spots on the skin; sordid

[形] できものののある、毛の抜けた；みすぼらしい、汚い

Homeless people are *mangy* looking because they lack life's necessities.

反意語 mangy : decorous [dékərəs]
mangyの反意語は decorous（礼儀正しい、上品な）

mania
[méiniə]

n. an excessively intense enthusiasm, interest, or desire

[名] 異常な熱意、熱狂

Christmas shopping *mania* turns ordinary people into frenzied, desperate customers.

関連語 mania : enthusiasm [inθúːziæzm]
enthusiasm（熱狂、熱中）が強くなると mania になる。

manifest
[mǽnəfèst]

n. a list of cargo or passengers on a ship or airplane

[名] 積荷リスト、乗客名簿

adj. obvious

[形] 明白な

Any freight that is not listed on the *manifest* cannot be cleared through customs.

His embarrassment was *manifest* in the way he avoided eye contact with us.

関連語 manifest : cargo [káːʳgou]
manifest は cargo（貨物）のリストである。

manipulate
[mənípjulèit]

v. to operate or control in a skillful manner; to control or change by deceitful means for a self-serving purpose

[動] 巧みに扱う；〜を操る

The tax broker *manipulated* his accounts in order to pocket some of the money.

関連語 manipulate : dexterous [dékstʳrəs]
manipulate には dexterous（器用な、巧妙な）な特徴がある。

反意語 manipulative : guileless [gáilis]
manipulative（巧みに扱う；ごまかしの）の反意語は guileless（たくらみのない、正直な）

TRANSLATION | 例 文 の 訳

mangy ホームレスの人たちは生活必需品がないためにみすぼらしい姿をしている。
mania クリスマスの買い物の熱狂によって、普通の人々が取り乱した死に物狂いの買い物客に変貌する。
manifest 積荷リストに記載されていない貨物は、どれも通関できない。
彼の照れくささが、私たちと目を合わせないようにしている姿に表れていた。
manipulate その税理士は、金の一部を着服するために自分の会計記録を操作した。

munificent [mju:nífəsnt]	adj. **very liberal or generous; lavish** [形] 気前のよい、寛大な The chief offered me a *munificent* benefits package to stay with the company longer. 反意語 munificent : parsimonious [pà:ˈsəmóuniəs] munificentの反意語は parsimonious（極度にけちな、けちけちした）

pompous
[pámpəs]
	adj. **exhibiting self-importance or arrogance; bombastic**
	                          [形] もったいぶった、尊大な；大げさな
	
	There is something very *pompous* in his style and mannerisms.
	
	関連語 pompous : bombast [bámbæst]
	    pompousは bombast（大げさな言葉）を特徴として持っている。

ramshackle
[rǽmʃæ̀kl]
	adj. **poorly constructed or likely to fall down; being in disrepair**
	                          [形] 今にも崩れそうな；破損した
	
	The *ramshackle* old vehicle sat rusting in the drive way.
	
	関連語 ramshackle : soundness [sáundnis]
	    ramshackleな車や建物には soundness（健全、堅実）が欠けている。

remonstrance [rimánstrəns]	n. **a formal statement that lists grievances; an expression of protest** [名] 強い抗議；反対表明 The workers submitted a *remonstrance* listing the reasons for their dissatisfaction with management. 関連語 remonstrator : dissuade [diswéid] remonstrator（抗議者）は他人を dissuade（説得して思いとどまらせる）する。
remorse [rimɔ́:ˈs]	n. **a sincere, often painful sense of regret** [名] 激しい後悔、良心のかしゃく I was full of *remorse* for having hurt my sister with my vicious criticism. 類義語 remorse：rue [ru:] remorseの類義語は rue（後悔）

TRANSLATION | 例 文 の 訳

munificent	課長は私が会社に留まるように、気前のよい諸手当の支給を提案してきた。
pompous	彼の態度や話しぶりには非常に尊大なところがある。
ramshackle	おんぼろの古い車が、私道に錆びたまま置かれていた。
remonstrance	労働者たちは、経営に対して不満な理由を並べた抗議文を提出した。
remorse	私は、悪意を込めた批判で姉を傷つけたことへの後悔でいっぱいだった。

remunerate
[rimjúːnərèit]

v. to compensate [動] 償う、賠償する

The company will *remunerate* their traveling salesmen for any reasonable expenses incurred.

反意語 remunerative : unrequited [ʌ̀nrikwáitid]
remunerative の反意語は unrequited（報われない）

somnolence
[sámnələns]

n. a state of sleepiness [名] 眠いこと、眠気

The students were nearing *somnolence* due to the teacher's monotone voice.

関連語 somnolence : alert [ələ́ːʳt]
alert（警戒している）な人は簡単に somnolence を持たない。

stalk
[stɔːk]

v. to observe and pursue someone out of derangement or obsession [動] しつこく付きまとう、ストーカー行為をする

Stella suspected the man was *stalking* her because he regularly waited outside her office and walked behind her a few blocks.

関連語 stalk : follow [fálou]
stalk は follow（あとに従う）の一種で否定的な意味がある。

summit
[sámit]

n. the highest point or highest attainable level [名] 頂点、頂上

Presley climbed to the *summit* of one of the hills.

類義語 summit : apex [éipeks]
summit の類義語は apex（頂点、絶頂）

sumptuous
[sámptʃuəs]

adj. luxurious or costly [形] 豪華な、高価な

The house had a very *sumptuous* appearance, so I knew I couldn't afford it.

関連語 sumptuous : sobriety [səbráiəti]
sumptuous なものには sobriety（謹厳）が欠けている。

TRANSLATION | 例 文 の 訳

remunerate	その会社は、外回りの販売員が負った合理性のある支出は、どのようなものであれ精算する。
somnolence	学生たちは教師の単調な声のせいで眠くなってきた。
stalk	ステラは、その男が定期的に会社の外で待ち伏せし、数ブロックにわたって跡をつけてきたので、ストーカーではないかと疑った。
summit	プレスリーは 1 つの丘の頂上に登った。
sumptuous	その家は外観がとても豪華だったので、自分には買えないものだとわかった。

sympathetic
[símpəθétik]

adj. exhibiting compassion; being able to associate with and understand another's situation or position

[形] 同情的な；思いやりのある

Harry's *sympathetic* words demonstrated his understanding of his friends suffering.

反意語 sympathetic : callous [kǽləs]
sympathetic の反意語は callous（人情味のない、無情な）

timorous
[tímərəs]

adj. fearful or timid

[形] 臆病な、ひどくこわがる

Worried about the cat, the *timorous* mouse never scampered about the house for very long.

関連語 timorous : temerity [təmérəti]
timorous な人には temerity（大胆さ）が欠けている。

tumult
[t(j)ú:mʌlt]

n. the disorderly noise of an excited crowd; mental or emotional agitation

[名] 騒動、大騒ぎ；精神の動揺、心の乱れ

The tiny earthquake left Paul in a *tumult* of fear and anxiety even though it hardly registered on the Richter Scale.

反意語 tumult : serenity [sərénəti]
tumult の反意語は serenity（平静、うららかさ）

TRANSLATION | 例 文 の 訳

sympathetic　思いやりのある言葉を聞いて、ハリーが友人の苦しみを理解していることがわかった。

timorous　ネコを恐れて、その臆病なネズミはずいぶん長い間、家の中を駆け回ることがなかった。

tumult　その地震は小規模で地震計に記録されない程度のものだったが、ポールは恐怖と不安で心が乱れた。

318

■ Fill in the blanks with the correct letter that matches the word with its definition.

1. jingoism _____

2. remonstrance _____

3. compendious _____

4. sympathetic _____

5. compliment _____

6. denigrate _____

7. munificent _____

8. commodious _____

9. hamper _____

10. dank _____

a. exhibiting compassion; being able to associate with and understand another's situation or position

b. strong nationalism

c. unpleasantly wet and cool

d. very liberal or generous; lavish

e. characterized by concise expression; comprehensive

f. a formal statement that lists grievances; an expression of protest

g. spacious and comfortable

h. to hinder or disrupt

i. a positive expression of admiration or praise

j. to defame; to deny the value of

■ Put the correct word in each blank from the list of words below.

11. unrepentant する人は_____を持っていない。

12. _____を成し遂げるために mediation する。

13. decorous（上品な）の反意語は_____である。

14. ambiguous なのものは_____するのが難しい。

15. rue（後悔）の類義語は_____である。

16. enthusiasm が過ぎると_____になる。

17. _____は clamor の類義語である。

18. 過度に assertive した人は_____に見える。

19. _____な人は temerity を持っていない。

20. vaccination の目的は、病気に対して_____を持たせることである。

a. remorse	b. comprehend	c. hangdog	d. mania	e. timorous
f. immunity	g. compunction	h. din	i. mangy	j. bumptious
k. compromise	l. sumptuous			

Answer key

11. g 12. k 13. j 14. b 15. a 16. d 17. h 18. j 19. e 20. f

1. b 2. f 3. e 4. a 5. i 6. j 7. d 8. g 9. h 10. c

どんな困難があっても、
私たちの単語を学ぶ旅は
ずっと続きます。頑張りましょう！

23rd DAY

acrimonious
[æ̀krəmóuniəs]

adj. bitter and caustic

[形] 辛辣な、とげとげしい

The memory of my parents' *acrimonious* divorce made me fear marriage for a long time.

関連語 acrimonious : goodwill [gúdwíl]
acrimoniousなものにはgoodwill（好意、善意）が欠けている。

apocalypse
[əpάkəlìps]

n. a prophetic revelation, usually concerning the end of the world

[名] 大惨事、大事件、ヨハネの黙示録

According to environmentalists, a sharp rise in global temperatures could portend an *apocalypse*.

類義語 apocalyptic : prophetic [prəfétik]
apocalyptic（終末論的な、世界が滅亡するような）の類義語はprophetic（予言の）

bare
[bɛəʳ]

adj. nude or exposed; unadorned and simple

[形] 裸の、むき出しの；衣服を着ていない、ありのままの

Telling the *bare* truth was easier than telling a complicated lie.

反意語 bare : occult [əkʌ́lt]
bareの反意語はoccult（秘密の）

berate
[biréit]

v. to scold or criticize severely

[動] ～をしかりつける、叱責する

The military unnecessarily *berates* its officers to instill blind obedience and devotion.

反意語 berate : laud [lɔːd]
berateの反意語はlaud（～を賞賛する）

TRANSLATION | 例文の訳

acrimonious	両親の険悪な離婚の記憶のせいで、私は長い間結婚を怖がっていた。
apocalypse	環境の専門家によると、世界の気温の急激な上昇は終末の予兆かもしれないという。
bare	ありのままの真実を話すほうが、複雑なうそをつくよりも簡単だった。
berate	軍は将校たちに盲目的な服従と献身を強いるために、不必要に叱責する。

canvass
[kǽnvəs]

v. **to discuss or examine carefully with other people; to take a poll** ［動］〜を徹底的に話し合う；（意見や情報を）聞いて回る

The group *canvassed* the neighborhood to determine if it was a conservative or liberal area.

関連語 canvass : pollster [póulstər]
> pollster（世論調査員）は canvass するという特徴がある。

circumlocution
[sə̀ːʳkəmloukjúːʃən]

n. **the use of an excessive quantity of words to express something** ［名］遠回し、回りくどい表現

Circumlocution is usually a sign of nervousness or anxiety.

関連語 circumlocution ： forthright [fɔ́ːʳθràit]
> circumlocution は forthright（率直な、素直な）ではない。

circumscribe
[sə́ːʳkəmskráib]

v. **to mark off or surround by a circle or boundary; to restrict** ［動］境界線を引く；制限する

The new law *circumscribed* the strength of unions by prohibiting strikes that lasted longer than a week.

反意語 circumscribed : unlimited [ʌnlímitid]
> circumscribed（制限された）の反意語は unlimited（際限のない、無制限の）

circumspect
[sə́ːʳkəmspèkt]

adj. **cautious in considering all the possible consequences; prudent** ［形］慎重な、用心深い

To be *circumspect* is necessary in life if one is to live wisely.

反意語 circumspect : rash [ræʃ]
> circumspect の反意語は rash（向こう見ずな、軽率な）

TRANSLATION | 例 文 の 訳

canvass	そのグループは近隣を調査して回り、そこが保守層・革新層のどちらが多い地区なのかを判断しようとした。
circumlocution	遠回しな表現は、たいていは緊張や不安の印だ。
circumscribe	その新しい法律は、1週間を超えるストライキを禁じることで、労働組合の力を制限するものだった。
circumspect	賢く生きようとするなら、用心深いことが必要だ。

circumvent
[sə̀ːˈkəmvént]

v. **to avoid; to go around**   [動] 〜をすり抜ける；迂回する

Rather than finish his assignment, the student *circumvented* it with excuses.

反意語 circumvent : confront [kənfrʌ́nt]
    circumvent の反意語は confront（直面する）

clog
[klɑg]

v. **to block or hinder; to become overfull**
    [動] 妨げる、ふさぐ；〜で詰まらせる

The stream was *clogged* by debris from the landslide.

関連語 clog : drainage [dréinidʒ]
    clog されてしまうと、drainage（排水）がなくなる。

coagulant
[kouǽgjulənt]

n. **an agent which causes a liquid to thicken into a semisolid state**   [名] 凝固剤

Corn starch is a *coagulant* used to make the sauce thicker.

関連語 coagulant : thicken [θíkən]
    coagulant には液体を thicken（濃くする）する働きがある。

contradictory
[kɑ̀ntrədíktəri]

adj. **unable to both be true at the same time; opposing**
    [形] 矛盾した、反対の

It is *contradictory* to pursue peace and plan for war at the same time.

関連語 contradictory : oxymoron [ɑ̀ksimɔ́ːrɑn]
    oxymoron（矛盾語法）は contradictory だという特徴がある。

contrite
[kəntráit]

adj. **feeling regret or sadness for having done wrong or caused harm**   [形] 悔恨の、深く後悔している

Catherine offered a *contrite* apology for having torn her sister's favorite sweater.

類義語 contrite : compunctious [kəmpʌ́ŋkʃəs]
    contrite の類義語は compunctious（悔恨の）

TRANSLATION | 例 文 の 訳

circumvent	その学生は、課題を終わらせるのではなく、むしろ言い訳して課題をすり抜けてしまった。
clog	その川は土砂崩れによる土砂で埋まった。
coagulant	コーンスターチは、ソースにとろみをつけるのに使われる凝固剤だ。
contradictory	平和を追求すると同時に戦争を計画するのは、矛盾している。
contrite	キャサリンは、姉のお気に入りのセーターを破ってしまったので、心から謝罪した。

contumacious
[kɑ̀nt(j)uméiʃəs]

adj. **disobedient or rebellious**　　　　　　[形] 反抗的な、命令に応じない

The *contumacious* anarchists refused to register for the draft.

反意語 contumacious : obedient [oubíːdiənt]
　　contumacious の反意語は obedient（従順な、忠実な）

convention
[kənvénʃən]

n. **a conference or meeting where people come to listen to lecturers; a social custom or rule of behavior**
　　　　　　　　　　　　　　　　　　　　[名] 大会、会議；しきたり、慣習

As Ray walked on with Verena, he asked her about the Women's *Convention*.

Cervantes' Don Quixote is a satire that pokes fun at the romantic chivalric *conventions* of 15th century Spain.

反意語 conventional : eccentric [ikséntrik]
　　conventional（伝統的な、慣習的な）の反意語は eccentric（奇妙な、変な）

convert
[kənvə́ːʳt]

v. **to change from one belief or view to another; to alter the nature of**　　　　　[動] ～に改宗させる、転向させる；～に変える

Due to the ardency and fervor of their belief, Muslims are almost impossible to *convert*.

関連語 convert : proselytizer [prásəlitàizər]
　　proselytizer（伝道師）には人を convert する特徴がある。

conviction
[kənvíkʃən]

n. **a strong belief or opinion; the process or act of finding someone guilty of a crime, especially in a court**
　　　　　　　　　　　　　　　　　　　　　　[名] 信念、確信；有罪判決

Hillary Clinton is a woman of strong political *convictions*.

関連語 conviction : dubious [djúːbiəs]
　　dubious（疑っている、迷っている）な人は conviction を持たない。

TRANSLATION | 例 文 の 訳

contumacious その反抗的な無政府主義者は徴兵に応じることを拒否した。

convention レイは歩きながら、ベレナに女性会議について尋ねた。
セルバンテスのドン・キホーテは、15世紀スペインのロマンチックな騎士道の伝統をからかった風刺だ。

convert イスラム教徒には信仰への情熱と信念があるので、改宗させることはほとんど不可能だ。

conviction ヒラリー・クリントンは強い政治的信念を持った女性だ。

convince
[kənvíns]

v. to make someone believe that something is true

[動] ～を確信させる、納得させる

Ma'am Bougon was *convinced* that Marius was an accomplice to the robbery the night before.

関連語 convince : cogent [kóudʒənt]

cogent（適切な、説得力のある）ものは convince する特徴がある。

convoluted
[kánvəlùːtid]

adj. twisted or coiled; complex or hard to understand

[形] 曲がりくねった、渦巻きの；複雑で難解な

The human maze was so *convoluted* that the students couldn't find their way out.

関連語 convoluted : complexity [kəmpléksəti]

convoluted と似た意味の名詞に complexity（複雑さ、複雑性）がある。

daredevil
[déərdèvəl]

n. one who is recklessly bold or performs dangerous and potentially harmful stunts

[名] 向こう見ずな人、恐れ知らずの人

The *daredevil* jumped off a 30 ft cliff with his bicycle into the river.

関連語 daredevil : prudence [prúːdns]

daredevil には prudence（用心深さ、慎重さ）がない。

derelict
[dérəlikt]

adj. abandoned, especially by the owner or occupant

[形] 見捨てられた、放棄された

n. a person without a home or means of support

[名] ホームレスの人、見捨てられた人

The *derelict* warehouse was used as a playground by the neighborhood children.

The *derelict* pleaded with passing pedestrians for some spare change or a bite to eat.

反意語 derelict : pillar of society [pílər əv səsáiəti]

derelict の反意語は pillar of society（社会の中心人物）

TRANSLATION | 例 文 の 訳

convince	ボーガン夫人は、マリウスが前夜の強盗の共犯者だと確信した。
convoluted	その迷路は複雑すぎて、学生たちは出口を見つけられなかった。
daredevil	その命知らずは、自転車に乗って高さ30フィートの崖の上から川に飛び込んだ。
derelict	その廃倉庫は近所の子供たちの遊び場になっていた。
	そのホームレスは、通行人に小銭か食べ物をくれるよう懇願した。

dire
[daɪəʳ]

adj. **terrible; desperately urgent**   [形] 恐ろしい、ひどい；差し迫った

With the economy in a *dire* situation, the unemployment rate was at its highest level since the Depression.

反意語 dire : pleasant [pléz³nt]
dire の反意語は pleasant（楽しい、心地よい）

dulcet
[dʌ́lsit]

adj. **extremely pleasant and melodious to the ear**
    [形]（耳に）快い；美しい音色の

The *dulcet* voices of the children's choir filled the church sanctuary every Sunday.

反意語 dulcet : cacophonous [kəkáfənəs]
dulcet の反意語は cacophonous（不協和音の、音調の悪い）

dune
[d(j)uːn]

n. **a hill or ridge created by the wind**
    [名]（風に吹かれて盛り上がった）砂の小山、砂丘

The sand *dunes* of the Egyptian desert appeared to go on forever.

関連語 dune : wind [wind]
dune は wind（風）によって作られる。

duration
[d(j)uréiʃən]

n. **the time that something continues or exists; the quality of lasting**   [名] 存続（持続）期間；耐久性

The *duration* of the flight from Frankfurt to Seoul is eleven hours.

関連語 duration : curtail [kəʳtéil]
duration を curtail（～を短くする、短縮する）する。

ennui
[ɑːnwíː]

n. **a feeling of boredom or dissatisfaction from lack of interest**
    [名] 倦怠、退屈、アンニュイ

It was only to her closest friends that she acknowledged she was tortured by *ennui*.

関連語 ennui : enthusiastic [inθúːziæ̀stik]
enthusiastic（情熱的な）な人は ennui を感じない。

TRANSLATION | 例 文 の 訳

dire	経済がひどい状況で、失業率は大恐慌以降の最高水準にあった。
dulcet	子供の聖歌隊の美しい声が、毎週日曜日、教会の礼拝堂に響き渡った。
dune	エジプトの砂漠の砂丘は、永遠に続くように見える。
duration	フランクフルトからソウルまでの飛行時間は 11 時間だ。
ennui	彼女は、最も親しい友人たちにだけ自分が退屈に苦しんでいることを認めた。

325

erode
[iróud]

v. to wear or wash away　　　　　　　　　　[動] 〜を侵食する

With time, a small creek can *erode* even solid granite.

類義語 erode : corrode [kəróud]
erodeの類義語はcorrode (〜を腐食させる、さびさせる)

erratic
[irǽtik]

adj. having no fixed course or regular pattern; eccentric
　　　　　　　　　　　　　　　　[形] 一定しない、不規則な；気まぐれな

Over the past few years, the Aegean winter has become more and more *erratic*.

反意語 erratic : permanent [pə́ːʳmᵊnənt]
erraticの反意語はpermanent (永続する、永久的な)

farce
[faːʳs]

n. a light comic play filled with ridiculous situations
　　　　　　　　　　　　[名] 笑劇、道化芝居、ファルス；茶番、ばかげたこと

The entire evening was such a disastrous *farce*!

関連語 farce : performance [pəʳfɔ́ːʳməns]
farceはperformance (公演、演技) の一種。

forbid
[fəʳbíd]

v. to hinder or prevent from　　　　　　[動] 〜を禁止する、妨げる

The law *forbids* the sale or use of marijuana.

関連語 forbidden : abstain [æbstéin]
forbidden (禁止された) されたものをabstain (〜を避ける、控える) する。

garble
[gáːʳbl]

v. to distort, confuse, or mix up
　　　　　　　　　　　[動] 〜を取り違える、誤って伝える、悪影響を与える

The static *garbled* Leslies' phone conversation with her friend.

反意語 garble : elucidate [ilúːsədèit]
garbleの反意語はelucidate (〜をはっきりさせる)

TRANSLATION ｜ 例 文 の 訳

erode	時間をかければ、小川が堅い花崗岩を侵食することもありうる。
erratic	ここ数年の間に、エーゲ海の冬の天候はますます不安定になった。
farce	その晩は、初めから終わりまでひどい茶番だった！
forbid	マリファナの売買と使用は法律で禁止されている。
garble	電波障害が、レスリーと友人の電話でのやり取りに影響を及ぼした。

genuine
[dʒénjuin]

adj. authentic or true; honest or sincere

[形] 本物の、真の；正直な、心からの

The appraiser deemed the Monet to be *genuine*.

反意語 genuine : spurious [spjúˠriəs]

genuine の反意語は spurious（にせの、不純な、偽造の）

harebrained
[hɛˠbrèind]

adj. foolish and reckless

[形] ばかげた、向こう見ずな、軽率な

The *harebrained* man decided to dance in the public fountain in his underwear.

類義語 harebrained : giddy [gídi]

harebrained の類義語は giddy（軽薄な、浮ついた）

larder
[láːˠdəˠ]

n. the place where the food supply is stored

[名] 食料貯蔵室

The *larder* for flour storage is the highest place in the house in order to keep out pests.

関連語 larder : food [fuːd]

larder には food（食べ物）を保管する機能がある。

manumit
[mænjumít]

v. to free from slavery

[動] 奴隷を解放する

As the Union Army invaded the South, it *manumitted* all the plantation slaves it encountered.

反意語 manumit : enslave [insléiv]

manumit の反意語は enslave（奴隷にする）

merchandise
[mɚ́ːˠtʃəndàiz]

n. the items or goods sold in business

[名] 商品

Good *merchandise* at good prices can only be found at the markets.

関連語 merchandise : warehouse [wɛˠhàus]

warehouse（倉庫）には merchandise を保存する機能がある。

TRANSLATION | 例 文 の 訳

genuine	鑑定家は、そのモネの作品を本物と見なした。
harebrained	その男は、軽率にも下着姿で噴水の中で踊ることに決めた。
larder	小麦粉を保管する貯蔵室は、害虫が近寄らないように家の一番高い場所にある。
manumit	連邦軍は南部に侵攻しながら、出くわした農場の奴隷たちを全員解放した。
merchandise	手ごろな価格の良い商品は、市場でしか見つからない。

minuscule
[mínəskjùːl]

adj. very small [形] 非常に小さい

His handwriting was so *minuscule* that I could only read it with a magnifying glass.

反意語 minuscule : enormous [inɔ́ːˈməs]
minuscule の反意語は enormous（巨大な）

minute
adj.[mainjúːt]
n.[mínit]

adj. very small [形] 微小な、微細な

n. 60 seconds [名] 分

Investigators are trained to pick up on the *minutest* clues that criminals leave behind.

Minute after *minute*, her hunger gnawed at her.

反意語 minute : gargantuan [gɑːˈgǽntʃuən]
minute の反意語は gargantuan（巨大な）

moratorium
[mɔ̀rətɔ́ːriəm]

n. a legally authorized delay of payment; a suspension of some activity considered to be bad [名] 支払い猶予；活動停止

Due to unstable political conditions, the U.S. put a *moratorium* on all flights to Pakistan.

関連語 moratorium : activity [æktívəti]
moratorium は activity（活動）が停止している状態だ。

mordant
[mɔ́ːˈdˀnt]

adj. biting or bitter in manner or style [形] 皮肉な、辛辣な

The movie received a *mordant* review.

反意語 mordant : genial [dʒíːnjəl]
mordant の反意語は genial（愛想のいい、朗らかな）

penurious
[pən(j)úˀriəs]

adj. very stingy; extremely poor [形] ひどくけちな；極貧の

The character Scrooge was the most *penurious* of men.

反意語 penurious : lavish [lǽviʃ]
penurious の反意語は lavish（豪華な、贅沢な）

TRANSLATION | 例文の訳

minuscule	彼の手書きの文字はとても小さくて、虫眼鏡を使わないと読めなかった。
minute	捜査員は犯罪者が残した最小限の手がかりでも見つけられるように訓練されている。
	1分ごとに、空腹が彼女を苦しめた。
moratorium	不安定な政治情勢のために、アメリカはパキスタンへのすべての便を欠航にした。
mordant	その映画は辛辣な批評を受けた。
penurious	スクルージという登場人物は、この上なくけちな男だった。

perceive
[pəˈsíːv]

v. **to become aware of through the senses; to understand**

[動] ～を知覚する；～を理解する

The way my friend and I *perceived* the movie was very different.

関連語 perceive : intangible [intǽndʒəbl]

intangible（触れることのできない、実体のない）ものは percieve することができない。

plod
[plɑd]

v. **to walk heavily and slowly**　　　[動] とぼとぼ歩く、ゆっくり進む

The young man *plodded* along the dark streets in silence to his house.

関連語 plod : walk [wɔːk]

plod はとぼとぼと walk（歩く）という意味。

probe
[proub]

v. **to investigate or examine**　　　　　[動] ～を調査する、調べる

n. **a penetrating inquiry or investigation**　　　[名] 徹底的な調査

The Senate *probed* the President about his involvement with Russian spies.

The *probe* uncovered fraud and bribery as an integral part of the company's dealings.

類義語 probe : investigate [invéstəgèit]

probe の類義語は investigate（調査する、研究する）

probity
[próubəti]

n. **integrity; honesty**　　　　　　　[名] 正直、誠実

The idea of *probity* in all financial dealings was deeply ingrained in him by his business class.

反意語 probity : shiftiness [ʃíftinis]

probity の反意語は shiftiness（ずるさ、うさんくささ）

21st
22nd
23rd
24th
25th
26th
27th
28th
29th
30th

TRANSLATION | 例 文 の 訳

perceive	友人と私では、その映画への理解の仕方がずいぶん違った。
plod	その若者は、暗い通り沿いに黙ってとぼとぼと家まで歩いた。
probe	上院は、大統領のロシアのスパイへの関与について調査した。
	その調査で、詐欺と賄賂がその企業の取引に不可欠であることが明らかになった。
probity	あらゆる金融取引における誠実さの概念が、商取引の授業によって彼の中に深く刻み込まれた。

proclivity
[prouklívəti]

n. an inclination or tendency [名] (悪い) 傾向、性向

Sam has a *proclivity* for drastic mood swings.

類義語 proclivity : propensity [prəpénsəti]
proclivityの類義語は propensity (傾向、性癖)

procure
[proukjúəʳ]

v. to obtain or take possession of [動] ～を手に入れる、獲得する

During the will reading, Georgia *procured* many worthless personal effects of her late great aunt.

反意語 procure : relinquish [rilíŋkwiʃ]
procureの反意語は relinquish (～を譲渡する、放棄する)

prod
[prɑd]

v. to incite into action with a pointed instrument; to urge or remind someone [動] ～を突く；～を駆り立てる、つっつく

The cowboy *prodded* the cattle to get them moving.

関連語 prod : nudge [nʌdʒ]
nudge (そっと押す、ひじで軽く押す) は軽く prod すること。

prodigal
[prɑ́digəl]

adj. recklessly wasteful with money [形] 浪費する、放蕩の

Larry was accused of being *prodigal* with company funds for expending a Learjet for his daily commute.

反意語 prodigality : husbandry [hʌ́zbəndri]
prodigality (浪費、放蕩) の反意語は husbandry (節約、倹約)

profane
[prəféin]

adj. debased; treating sacred things with contempt or disrespect [形] 卑しい；不敬な、神を汚す

The *profane* language used in the movie shocked many of the viewers.

反意語 profane : inviolate [inváiələt]
profaneの反意語は inviolate (聖なる)

TRANSLATION | 例 文 の 訳

proclivity	サムには気分がひどく揺れ動く傾向がある。
procure	遺言状が読み上げられる中で、ジョージアは亡くなった大おばから価値のない私物をたくさん受け取っていた。
prod	そのカウボーイは牛を突いて動かした。
prodigal	ラリーは毎日の通勤に小型ジェット機を使い、会社の資金を浪費したことで訴えられた。
profane	映画の中で使われた下品な言葉は、多くの視聴者にショックを与えた。

proffer
[práfəʳ]

v. to offer for acceptance [動] 物を差し出す、〜を申し出る

The defense rejected the plea bargain *proffered* by the prosecution.

反意語 proffer : retain [ritéin]
proffer の反意語は retain (〜を保つ、持ち続ける、保管する)

profligate
[práfligət]

adj. extravagant; dissolute [形] 乱費する、金遣いの荒い

n. one who is recklessly wasteful; a dissolute man [名] 放蕩者

The government officer was charged for *profligate* spending of the taxpayer's money.

The *profligate* could not control his credit spending and was mired in debt.

関連語 profligate : money [mʌ́ni]
profligate は money (お金) をむやみに使う様子を表す。

profuse
[prəfjúːs]

adj. plentiful; generous [形] 豊富な、物惜しみしない

No one enjoyed sitting next to Johnny in class because of his *profuse* perspiration all year round.

反意語 profuse : skimpy [skímpi]
profuse の反意語は skimpy (不十分な)

prohibit
[prouhíbit]

v. to forbid by law; to prevent someone from having or doing something [動] 法律で禁止する；〜を妨げる

Children easily maneuver around laws *prohibiting* minors from drinking by asking an adult to buy liquor for them.

関連語 prohibitive : veto [víːtou]
veto (拒否権) には prohibitive (禁止するための、抑制するための) だという特徴がある。

TRANSLATION | 例 文 の 訳

proffer 弁護団は検察が提示した司法取引を拒否した。

profligate その政府の役人は、納税者のお金を乱用したことで告発された。
その放蕩者はクレジットカードによる出費を抑えられず、借金の泥沼にはまった。

profuse ジョニーは年中、大量に汗をかくので、だれも喜んで教室で彼の隣に座りたがらなかった。

prohibit 子供たちは、大人に酒の購入を頼むことで、未成年者の飲酒を禁じる法律を簡単にすり抜けてしまう。

puny [pjú:ni]	adj. **weak and small** [形] 小さくて弱い、弱々しい
	The *puny* landowner looked silly next to his tall and strong field worker.
	類義語 puny : weakly [wí:kli] punyの類義語は weakly（弱い、病弱な、弱々しい）

riveting [rívitiŋ]	adj. **engrossing one's attention; fascinating** [形] 興味を引き付けられる；魅惑的な
	The lecture on The State of the Environment in East Asia was far from *riveting*, and everyone left in the middle of it.
	反意語 riveting : vapid [væpid] rivetingの反意語は vapid（退屈な、つまらない）

stodgy [stádʒi]	adj. **boring or tedious** [形] おもしろくない、退屈な
	Living in a small town becomes *stodgy* and predictable for most people.
	類義語 stodgy : dull [dʌl] stodgyの類義語は dull（退屈な、つまらない）

stoic [stóuik]	adj. **showing little or no feelings; dispassionated** [形] 禁欲的な、冷静な
	n. **one apparently unaffected by pleasure or pain** [名] 禁欲主義者
	The *stoic* look on Jeanie's face masked the disappointment she felt when passed over for the promotion.
	Alex's indifferent attitude towards everything caused people to refer to him as a *stoic*.
	関連語 stoic : perturb [pərtə́:rb] stoicな人は簡単に perturb（〜を不安にさせる、うろたえさせる）されることがない。

TRANSLATION | 例 文 の 訳

puny	その貧弱な地主は、長身で屈強な小作人の隣にいると間が抜けて見えた。
riveting	「東アジアの環境の現状」についての講演は、まるで魅力を欠いており、皆が途中で退席してしまった。
stodgy	小さな町での生活は、ほとんどの人にとって退屈でありきたりなものになってしまう。
stoic	ジェニーは平然とした表情を浮かべていたので、昇進が見送られたことで抱いた失望感が覆い隠された。
	アレックスは何事にも無関心な態度をとるので、人々は彼を禁欲主義者と呼んだ。

unobtrusive
[ʌ̀nəbtrúːsiv]

adj. **not obtrusive or blatant; inconspicuous**

［形］人目につかない、遠慮がちな；地味な

Catherine was soothed and calmed by his simple and *unobtrusive* demeanor.

反意語 unobtrusive : blatant [bléitᵊnt]

unobtrusive の反意語は blatant（見え透いた、露骨な）

variegate
[véᵊriᵊgèit]

v. **to make varied and diverse**

［動］多様化する、変化を加える

Variegating the menu brought in more new customers than the manager expected.

類義語 variegate : vary [véəri]

variegate の類義語は vary（～に変化を与える、変える）

TRANSLATION | 例 文 の 訳

unobtrusive キャサリンは、彼の飾り気のない地味なふるまいのおかげで落ち着き、冷静になった。

variegate メニューを多様化したことで、店長の予想を上回る大勢の新規顧客がやって来た。

■ Fill in the blanks with the correct letter that matches the word with its definition.

1. canvass _____
2. probity _____
3. penurious _____
4. convict _____
5. puny _____
6. mordant _____
7. circumvent _____
8. prodigal _____
9. derelict _____
10. manumit _____

a. a person without a home or means of support
b. to avoid; to go around
c. recklessly wasteful with money
d. weak and small
e. to free from slavery
f. integrity; honesty
g. to discuss or examine carefully with other people; to take a poll
h. extremely frugal; hating to spend money
i. to declare or prove someone guilty, especially in a court
j. biting or bitter in manner or style

■ Put the correct word in each blank from the list of words below.

11. _____は investigate（調査する）の類義語である。
12. _____は food を保管する機能を果たす。
13. _____は forthright ではない。
14. _____の反意語は elucidate（〜をはっきりさせる）である。
15. dull（退屈な）は_____の類義語である。
16. unlimited（無制限の）の反意語は_____である。
17. genial（愛想のいい）の反意語は_____である。
18. _____の類義語は propensity（傾向、性癖）である。
19. _____された状態になると drainage にならない。
20. _____には prudence がない。

a. proclivity   b. garble   c. stodgy   d. mordant   e. probe   f. circumscribed
g. daredevil   h. larder   i. clog   j. proffer   k. circumlocution
l. unobtrusive

Answer key

1.g   2.f   3.h   4.i   5.d   6.j   7.b   8.c   9.a   10.e
11.e   12.k   13.k   14.b   15.c   16.f   17.d   18.a   19.i   20.g

英語が上手になるという夢は
必ずかないます！
Dreams come true!

24th DAY

21st
22nd
23rd
24th
25th
26th
27th
28th
29th
30th

abridge
[əbrídʒ]

v. **to shorten or condense, especially written works**

[動] (本・物語など) を要約する、短縮する

The *abridged* version of Lonesome Dove is available for people who don't have the time to read it in its entirety.

関連語 abridge : length [leŋkθ]

abridgeとは length (長さ) を減らすこと。

acrid
[ǽkrid]

adj. **having an irritatingly pungent or harsh taste or odor**

[形] ぴりっとする、苦い、鼻をつく

The *acrid* smell of rotting garbage is revolting.

反意語 acrid : savory [séivəri]

acrid の反意語は savory (味のよい、香りのよい)

agonize
[ǽgənàiz]

v. **to suffer in agony or torture; to suffer great emotional, mental or physical pain**

[動] ひどく苦しむ

It is *agonizing* to see my clients remain in jail when they are innocent.

関連語 agonized : distressed [distrést]

agonized (苦痛の、苦しそうな) は distressed (悩んで、悲しんで、心を痛めて) よりも苦しみの程度が強い。

TRANSLATION | 例 文 の 訳

abridge　『ロンサム・ダブ』の簡約版は、同書を丸一冊読む時間がない人のためにある。

acrid　腐ったごみの鼻をつく臭いは不快だ。

agonize　私の依頼人が、無罪なのに刑務所にいるのを見るのはひどく苦しい。

aloof
[əlúːf]

adj. reserved and remote; indifferent　　　[形] よそよそしい；無関心な

The man remained *aloof* and refused to participate in the party games.

反意語 aloof : gregarious [grigéᵊriəs]
aloofの反意語は gregarious（社交的な）

amorphous
[əmɔ́ːᵣfəs]

adj. lacking shape or form; lacking organization

[形] 無定形の、特徴のない；一定の形をもたない

Gene could not appreciate the *amorphous* mass of clay as abstract art.

関連語 amorphous : conformation [kɑ̀nfɔːᵣméiʃən]
amorphous なものには conformation（形態、構造）が欠けている。

anecdote
[ǽnikdòut]

n. a short and humorous narrative about one's own experiences

[名] 逸話

Matthew, a journalist from Dublin, always has great *anecdotes* to share with his friends.

関連語 anecdote : amusement [əmjúːzmənt]
anecdote は amusement（楽しみ、おもしろさ）を与える短い体験談をいう。

anomalous
[ənámələs]

adj. irregular or differing from the norm　　　[形] 異例の、変な

The regulators recognized that events like the Enron bankruptcy are relatively *anomalous* in a well-functioning economy.

反意語 anomalous : typical [típikəl]
anomalous の反意語は typical（典型的な）

apologize
[əpálədʒàiz]

v. to express regret for a faulty action or behavior; to make a formal defense or justification　　　[動] 謝罪する；陳謝する

I am sorry it happened, and now I publicly *apologize* for what I did.

関連語 apologize : contrite [kəntráit]
contrite（悔恨の、深く後悔して）な人が apologize する。

TRANSLATION | 例 文 の 訳

aloof　　　その男性はずっとよそよそしいままで、パーティーゲームへの参加を断った。

amorphous　　　ジーンは、とらえどころのない粘土のかたまりを抽象芸術として鑑賞することなどできなかった。

anecdote　　　マシューはダブリン出身のジャーナリストで、いつもすばらしい逸話を友達に聞かせている。

anomalous　　　監視官たちは、エンロン社の倒産のような出来事を、正常な経済の下では比較的異例のことだと捉えた。

apologize　　　そのようなことが起きてしまい、申し訳なく思います。そして、私がしたことについて公に謝罪いたします。

apoplectic
[ǽpəpléktik]

adj. extremely and noticeably angry; furious　　　[形] 激怒した

Sheila was *apoplectic* with rage over the salesperson's comment about her waist size.

反意語 apoplectic : calm [kɑːm]
　　　apoplectic の反意語は calm（冷静な）

arrest
[ərést]

v. to take into custody by legal authority; to catch someone's attention; to make inactive

[動] 逮捕する；（人の注意など）を引く；（進行など）を止める、遅らせる

Three men were *arrested* for the bank robbery.

My attention was *arrested* by the mime performing on the street.

The plant's growth was *arrested* by lack of adequate sunlight and sufficient water.

反意語 arrest : vitalize [váitəlàiz]
　　　arrest の反意語は vitalize（～に生命を与える、～を活気づける）

bark
[bɑːrk]

v. to shout or snap at someone; to howl　　　[動] 叫ぶ；吠える

n. the hard outer layer of a tree　　　[名] 木の皮、樹皮

The dog's *barking* kept the neighbors up all night.

People collect sap from a rubber tree by stripping off a piece of *bark* and placing a container under the exposed area.

関連語 bark : tree [triː]
　　　bark は tree（木）の皮のこと。

burgeon
[bɔ́ːrdʒən]

v. to grow rapidly; to sprout　　　[動] 急成長する；芽を出す

Once the rain came, new wildflowers *burgeoned* all across the field.

反意語 burgeon : wither [wíðər]
　　　burgeon の反意語は wither（枯れる）

TRANSLATION | 例 文 の 訳

apoplectic	シーラは、彼女のウエストサイズについての販売員の言葉に激怒した。
arrest	3人の男が銀行強盗の容疑で逮捕された。
	路上でのパントマイムのパフォーマンスに注意を引き付けられた。
	適切な日当たりと十分な水が不足して、その植物の成長が遅れた。
bark	イヌの鳴き声で、近隣住民は一晩中眠れなかった。
	人々はゴムの木の皮をむき、むきだしになった部分の下に容器を置いて樹液を集める。
burgeon	ひとたび雨が降ると、新しい野生の花が草原中に芽吹いた。

burlesque
[bəˈlésk]

n. a comic literary or theatrical work that pokes fun at people or events with grotesque exaggeration　　　　[名] パロディー、戯画

Burlesques satirizing the president are a common feature on the Saturday Night Live show.

関連語 burlesque : mockery [mákəri]
　　burlesque は mockery（あざけり、からかい）を含む風刺の効いた喜劇。

choleric
[kálərik]

adj. easily irritated or upset　　　　[形] 怒りっぽい

The commander of the regiment was an elderly, *choleric* man who snapped angrily at every little thing.

関連語 choleric : rile [rail]
　　choleric な人は rile（～を怒らせる、いらだたせる）しやすい。

chord
[kɔːˈd]

n. three or more musical notes played together　　　　[名] 和音

Sonya struck the first *chord* of the prelude.

関連語 chord : note [nout]
　　複数の note（音）が集まって、1 つの chord になる。

choreograph
[kɔ́ːriəgræf]

v. to arrange the dances and movements for dancers to perform　　　　[動] 振り付ける

Madonna's concerts are always well *choreographed* and worth the money to see.

関連語 choreography : dance [dæns]
　　choreography は dance（踊り、ダンス）を作っていく行為だ。

combust
[kəmbást]

v. to burn　　　　[動] 燃焼する

The fireworks display was spectacular, with many of the rockets *combusting* in a shower of sparks and color.

反意語 combustible : nonflammable [nɑnflǽməbl]
　　combustible（可燃性の）の反意語は nonflammable（不燃性の）

TRANSLATION | 例文の訳

burlesque	大統領を風刺するパロディーは『サタデー・ナイト・ライブ』の番組の定番だ。
choleric	連隊の司令官は年老いた怒りっぽい男で、些細なことにもすぐにかみついた。
chord	ソニアは前奏曲の最初の和音を弾いた。
choreograph	マドンナのコンサートではいつも振り付けがよくできていて、お金を払って見る価値がある。
combust	花火大会は壮観で、多くのロケットが火花と色のシャワーを浴びて燃え上がった。

constrict
[kənstríkt]

v. **to cause something to become narrower and smaller**

[動] ～を締め付ける；～を収縮させる

The renovations opened up the kitchen, but *constricted* the living room space.

反意語 constricted : commodious [kəmóudiəs]

constricted（収縮した、抑制された）の反意語は commodious（広々としている）

contagion
[kəntéidʒən]

n. **a disease that can be transmitted through direct or indirect contact**

[名] 伝染病

The *contagion* spread quickly through the community because the doctors were unsure of the correct prevention methods.

関連語 contagion : cold [kould]

cold（風邪）は contagion の一種。

cooperate
[kouápərèit]

v. **to work together towards the same goal**

[動] 協力する

The governments of the two countries agreed to *cooperate* in the fight against terrorism.

関連語 cooperate : collude [kəlú:d]

collude（共謀する）とは陰謀を図るために複数の人々と cooperate すること。

cronyism
[króunìzəm]

n. **the partiality to one's friends in political appointments or business contracts**

[名] 縁故主義、ひいき

Cronyism was a big problem at the firm until the new owner took over the task of hiring.

関連語 cronyism : intimate [íntəmət]

cronyism は intimate（親友）の味方をすること。

TRANSLATION | 例 文 の 訳

constrict　リフォームしてキッチンは広くなったが、居間のスペースは狭くなった。

contagion　その地域に伝染病が一気に広がったのは、医師らが適切な予防措置をしっかり講じなかったからだ。

cooperate　両国政府は、テロとの戦いで協力することに合意した。

cronyism　新しいオーナーが採用業務を引き継ぐまで、縁故主義はその会社で大きな問題だった。

croon [kru:n]	v. **to sing or speak softly**	[動] ささやき声で歌う、感傷的に歌う
	Alice was softly *crooning* to herself during class.	
	関連語 croon : sing [siŋ] 静かに歌うことを意味する croon は sing の一種。	
curb [kəːʳb]	v. **to restrain or restrict**	[動] 抑制する、制限する
	Heather *curbed* her spending habit by cutting up all her credit cards.	
	反意語 curb : goad [goud] curb の反意語は goad（突き動かす、あおり立てる）	
distraught [distrɔ́:t]	adj. **greatly agitated by conflict of emotions; insane**	
		[形] 取り乱した、ひどく困惑した
	The couple was deeply *distraught* over the kidnapping of their child.	
	関連語 distraught : troubled [trʌ́bld] distraught は troubled（困った）の程度が強く、感情的な状態。	
droll [droul]	adj. **having a funny or odd character**	[形] ひょうきんな、おどけた
	Adults found his *droll* comments comical.	
	反意語 droll : somber [sámbəʳ] droll の反意語は somber（陰鬱な、深刻な）	
elongate [ilɔ́:ŋgeit]	v. **to make longer**	[動] 〜を長くする、引き伸ばす
	The speechwriter *elongated* the Presidential Address by adding a piece concerning world hunger.	
	反意語 elongate : shorten [ʃɔ́:rtn] elongate の反意語は shorten（〜を短くする）	

TRANSLATION | 例 文 の 訳

croon	アリスは授業中に静かな声で歌っていた。
curb	ヘザーはクレジットカードをすべて切り刻んで、自分の浪費癖を抑えた。
distraught	その夫婦は、自分たちの子どもが誘拐されてひどく取り乱した。
droll	大人たちは彼のおどけた発言を面白がった。
elongate	そのスピーチライターは、大統領の演説を引き延ばすために、世界飢饉に関する一節を追加した。

exonerate
[igzánərèit]

v. to clear of guilt; to relieve of responsibility

[動] 容疑を晴らす、無実を証明する；義務を免除する

I am relieved that I have been *exonerated* from the criminal charges.

反意語 exonerate : inculpate [inkʌ́lpeit]
exonerate の反意語は inculpate (〜に罪を負わせる)

gloom
[glu:m]

n. a feeling of despair or sadness　　　　　　[名] 憂鬱

A *gloom* set over the people as they heard that fighting in the Middle-East had broken out again.

反意語 gloom : glee [gli:]
gloom の反意語は glee (大喜び、歓喜)

glossy
[glási]

adj. having a smooth and shiny surface　　　[形] 光沢のある、つやつやした

The horses in his stable with their *glossy* manes were clearly well cared for.

関連語 glossy : varnish [vá:ʳniʃ]
varnish (ニス、マニキュア) には glossy にする機能がある。

groove
[gru:v]

n. a long narrow hole; a set routine　　　　[名] 溝；決まり切ったやり方

Grooves were placed onto handlebars for a better grip.

関連語 groove : striated [stráieitid]
groove と似た意味の形容詞に striated (筋・線・縞のある) がある。

harbinger
[há:ʳbindʒəʳ]

n. one that indicates or foreshadows what is to come

[名] 前触れ、前兆

In the Bible, the Book of Revelation contains several *harbingers* about the end of the world.

関連語 harbinger : presage [présidʒ]
harbinger は presage (〜の前兆となる、〜を予知する) する特徴がある。

TRANSLATION | 例文の訳

exonerate 私は犯罪の疑いが晴れてほっとしている。
gloom 中東で再び戦闘が起こったと聞いて、人々は憂鬱になった。
glossy 彼の馬小屋にいるウマたちはたてがみがつややかで、明らかに世話が行き届いていた。
groove 持ち手には握りやすいように溝が切ってあった。
harbinger 聖書の中の黙示録に、世界の終末に関するいくつかの前兆が書かれている。

341

myopia
[maióupiə]

n. a visual defect that causes short-sightedness; inability to think or plan into the future　　　[名] 近視；考え方が近視的なこと、視野の狭さ

Fun seekers who spurn life's responsibility are said to suffer from *myopia*.

反意語 myopia : prescience [préʃ(i)əns]
　　 myopia の反意語は prescience（予知、先見の明）

peremptory
[pərémptəri]

adj. not permitting refusal; offensively self-assured
　　　　　　　[形] 有無を言わさない；横柄な、独断的な、命令的な

The director became rather *peremptory* after the great success of his last film.

関連語 peremptory : fawn [fɔːn]
　　 peremptory な人は fawn（へつらう、こびる）することがない。

porcelain
[pɔ́ːrsᵊlin]

n. a hard, white ceramic ware often highly decorated　　　[名] 磁器

The girl's *porcelain* doll smashed to pieces when it fell on the floor.

関連語 porcelain : glaze [gleiz]
　　 procelain に glaze（陶器などにうわ薬をかける）する。

pore
[pɔːr]

n. a minute opening in tissue　　　[名] 毛穴、気孔

v. to read carefully or studiously　　　[動] 熟読する

Sun exposure, or any kind of heat, causes skin *pores* to open.

The night before the exam, the college student *pored* over her lecture notes.

関連語 pore : membrane [mémbrein]
　　 membrane（細胞膜）には pore がある。

TRANSLATION | 例 文 の 訳

myopia	人生の責任を拒否して楽しみを追求する人たちは、視野狭窄に陥っている。
peremptory	その監督は前作の映画が大成功して以来、かなり横柄になった。
porcelain	その少女の磁器人形は、床に落ちて粉々になってしまった。
pore	日光をはじめ、どんな熱にさらされても、皮膚の毛穴は開く。
	試験の前夜、その大学生は自分の講義ノートを熟読した。

proliferate
[prəlífərèit]

v. to increase in number or multiply at a rapid rate

[動] 激増する、繁殖する

Vaccines have stopped a number of diseases from *proliferating*.

反意語 proliferate : dwindle [dwíndl]
proliferate の反意語は dwindle（〜を少なくする、縮める、減らす）

prolix
[proulíks]

adj. drawn out too long; characterized by an excess of words

[形] 冗長な；くどい

The *prolix* style of his speech lost the audience's attention.

関連語 prolix : terseness [tə́:ʳsnis]
prolix な文には terseness（簡潔さ）が欠けている。

prominent
[prámənənt]

adj. standing out beyond a surface; well-known or eminent; obvious

[形] 突き出た；卓越した、有名な；目立った

The maiden had large and very *prominent* blue eyes.

反意語 prominent : inconspicuous [ìnkənspíkjuəs]
prominent の反意語は inconspicuous（目立たない、地味な）

promote
[prəmóut]

v. to advance in rank or position; to contribute to the progress of

[動] 昇進する；推進する

Having a famous athlete like Magic Johnson *promote* the fight against AIDS has helped raise awareness immeasurably.

反意語 promote : impede [impí:d]
promote の反意語は impede（邪魔する）

propitiate
[prəpíʃièit]

v. to pacify or appease; to obtain the good favor of

[動] 〜をなだめる；〜の機嫌をとる

I took an orange from my pocket in order to *propitiate* the belligerent monkey.

反意語 propitiate : incense [ínsens]
propitiate の反意語は incense（〜を激怒させる）

TRANSLATION | 例文の訳

proliferate ワクチンは、たくさんの病気が急速に拡大するのを防いできた。

prolix 彼の冗長なスピーチは、聴衆の関心を失わせた。

prominent その少女は、大きくてとても目立つ青い目を持っていた。

promote マジック・ジョンソンのような有名なスポーツ選手にエイズ撲滅運動を推進してもらうことで、意識の向上に計り知れない効果があった。

propitiate 私はポケットからオレンジを取り出し、その攻撃的なサルを手なずけた。

propitious [prəpíʃəs]	adj. favorable or lucky [形] 幸運な、好都合な
	The terrace at Bellomont on a September afternoon is *propitious* for sentimental musings.
	反意語 propitious : inauspicious [inɔːspíʃəs] propitious の反意語は inauspicious（不吉な、縁起の悪い、不運な）
propriety [prəpráiəti]	n. appropriateness; good manners [名] 妥当性；礼儀正しさ
	Susan's outdated ideas of *propriety* are better suited for someone living in Victorian England.
	反意語 propriety : presumption [prizʌ́mpʃən] propriety の反意語は presumption（図々しさ、厚かましさ）
prosaic [prouzéiik]	adj. ordinary or dull; lacking in imagination [形] 退屈な、つまらない；想像力に欠ける
	The book was derided by critics as a *prosaic* piece of fiction.
	関連語 prosaic : ingenuity [ìndʒən(j)úːəti] prosaic な文には ingenuity（創意工夫）がない。
proscribe [prouskráib]	v. to prohibit or banish publicly [動] ～を禁止する、～を追放する
	In the Johnson's household, phone calls after 9 p.m. were strictly *proscribed*.
	反意語 proscribe : sanction [sǽŋkʃən] proscribe の反意語は sanction（～を認可する、承認する）
proselytize [prásəlitàiz]	v. to try to persuade someone to change their belief or religion [動] 改宗させる
	The missionaries *proselytized* the people of Zimbabwe.
	関連語 proselytize : religion [rilídʒən] proselytize はだれかの religion（宗教）を変えること。

TRANSLATION | 例 文 の 訳

propitious	9月の午後のベルモントのテラスは、感傷に浸るには絶好の場所だ。
propriety	スーザンの礼儀正しさに関する時代遅れの考え方は、ビクトリア朝のイギリスに暮らす人にふさわしい。
prosaic	その本は、批評家たちにつまらない小説だとばかにされた。
proscribe	ジョンソンの家では、午後9時以降の電話は厳しく禁止されていた。
proselytize	その宣教師たちはジンバブエの人々を改宗させた。

prosper
[práspəʳ]

v. **to flourish or achieve; to grow in wealth**　　　[動] 繁栄する、栄える

Airline businesses *prosper* during the holiday seasons.

反意語 prosperous : impecunious [ìmpikjúːniəs]
　　prosperous（繁栄している）の反意語は impecunious（金がない、無一文の）

rarefy
[réᵊrəfài]

v. **to become thin or less dense; to become purer**　　[動] 薄くする；浄化する

Mixing in some water, the chemist *rarefied* the thick solution.

反意語 rarefy : condense [kəndéns]
　　rarefyの反意語は condense（凝縮する）

scorn
[skɔːʳn]

v. **to show disdain; to reject with extreme contempt**
　　　　　　　　　　　　　　　　[動] 軽蔑する；（軽蔑して）はねつける

n. **a feeling of disrespect or contempt**　　　　　　[名] 軽蔑

The bigoted townspeople *scorned* the disfigured man and cast him out of the community.

The single mother has unfairly become the target of *scorn* in modern society.

関連語 scorn : reject [ridʒékt]
　　scornは軽蔑して reject（拒絶）すること。

serendipity
[sèrəndípəti]

n. **something not earned but luckily found**
　　　　　　　　　[名] 掘り出しものを見つける才能、偶然いいことが起きる才能

Peggy discovered true love by *serendipity* and not by a well-planned endeavor.

関連語 serendipity : effort [éfəʳt]
　　serendipityは effort（努力）をすることなく、いいものを発見する才能を言う。

serene
[səríːn]

adj. **calm or free of unpleasant change**　　[形] 落ち着いた、平静な、穏やかな

The *serene* waters of Long Lake are a beautiful sight.

反意語 serene : tumultuous [t(j)uːmʌ́ltʃuəs]
　　sereneの反意語は tumultuous（騒々しい、動揺した）

TRANSLATION | 例 文 の 訳

prosper	航空会社は休暇シーズンに繁盛する。
rarefy	水に混ぜることで、その化学者は濃い溶液を薄めた。
scorn	頑固な市民たちはその醜い男を軽蔑し、地域から追放した。
	シングルマザーは現代社会で不当に軽蔑の対象となってきた。
serendipity	ペギーが真の愛を発見できたのは偶然によるもので、計画的にできることではない。
serene	ロングレイクの穏やかな湖水は美しい風景だ。

345

sordid
[sɔ́ːʳdid]

adj. **dirty or wretched; mean; vulgar** 　　[形] 汚い、悲惨な；卑しい；強欲な

Jack's reputation was forever tainted by his *sordid* extramarital affair.

反意語 sordid : noble [nóubl]
　　sordid の反意語は noble（高潔な、気高い）

spontaneous
[spɑntéiniəs]

adj. **happening without outward forces or causes; done without having been planned in advance** 　　[形] 自発的な；気の向くままの

Online ticketing has been a godsend for people who make *spontaneous* travel plans.

関連語 spontaneous : extemporization [ekstémpərizèiʃən]
　　extemporization（即興演奏）は spontaneous な特徴がある。

sporadic
[spərǽdik]

adj. **happening in irregular or scattered instances**
　　[形] 時折の、散発的な

Greg's *sporadic* coughing disturbed the other opera patrons.

反意語 sporadic : regular [régjulər]
　　sporadic の反意語は regular（定期的な、規則的な）

threadbare
[θrédbèəʳ]

adj. **worn and shabby, usually with thread showing; hackneyed**
　　[形] すり切れた、ぼろぼろの；陳腐な、使い古された

Barry's *threadbare* excuses for his financial problems ran thin with his parents.

関連語 threadbare : novelty [návəlti]
　　threadbare なものには novelty（目新しさ、斬新さ）が欠けている。

unremarkable
[ʌnrimáːʳkəbl]

adj. **unworthy of attention or praise** 　　[形] 目立たない、平凡な

Our trip to Cancun was rather *unremarkable*.

反意語 unremarkable : signal [sígnᵊl]
　　unremarkable の反意語は signal（重大な、目覚ましい）

TRANSLATION | 例 文 の 訳

sordid	ジャックの評判は、汚れた不倫関係によって永遠に傷つけられた。
spontaneous	オンライン発券は、気の向くままに旅行を計画する人にとって天の恵みとなってきた。
sporadic	グレッグは時折せき込むので、他のオペラの観客のじゃまになった。
threadbare	バリーは自分の金銭トラブルについて手垢のついた言い訳を並べるので、彼の両親は我慢できなくなっていた。
unremarkable	私たちのカンクン旅行は、ごく平凡なものだった。

unrepentant
[ʌnripéntənt]

adj. unwilling to ask forgiveness for a sin or wrong-doing

[形] 自責の念のない、後悔の気持ちを表さない

The killer was *unrepentant*, even at his execution.

反意語 unrepentant : penitential [pènəténʃəl]
unrepentantの反意語はpenitential（悔い改めの、ざんげの）

verbose
[vəːˈbóus]

adj. wordy or long-winded　　　　[形] 言葉数が多い、くどい

St. Augustine's writings are extremely *verbose*.

反意語 verbose : concise [kənsáis]
verboseの反意語はconcise（簡潔な）

verdant
[və́ːˈdnt]

adj. covered with green growth; green in the sense of naive or inexperienced　　[形] 新緑で覆われた、青々とした

The *verdant* prairies of South Dakota are ideal for grazing cattle.

反意語 verdant : sterile [stéril]
verdantの反意語はsterile（不毛な、やせた）

vicarious
[vaikéˈriəs]

adj. lived and understood through the experience of another; substitutionary　[形] 他人の経験を通して自分のことのように感じられる、代理の

People get a lot of *vicarious* excitement when their favorite team wins a championship.

反意語 vicarious : firsthand [fə́ːˈsthǽnd]
vicariousの反意語はfirsthand（じかの、実地の）

wholesome
[hóulsəm]

adj. promoting health of body, mind, or spirit; healthy

[形] 健康によい、健全な

Michael urged him to embrace the opportunity of taking *wholesome* exercise in the open air.

反意語 wholesome : morbid [mɔ́ːrbid]
wholesomeの反意語はmorbid（病的な、不健全な）

TRANSLATION | 例 文 の 訳

unrepentant	その殺人犯は、死刑執行時にも後悔の気持ちを表さなかった。
verbose	聖アウグスティヌスの文章は極端に冗長だ。
verdant	サウスダコタの青々とした大平原は牛を放牧するのに理想的だ。
vicarious	人々は、お気に入りのチームが優勝すると、自分のことのように興奮するものです。
wholesome	マイケルは彼に、戸外で健康的な運動をする機会を持つよう促した。

■ Fill in the blanks with the correct letter that matches the word with its definition.

1. anecdote _____
2. prolix _____
3. threadbare _____
4. burgeon _____
5. vicarious _____
6. propriety _____
7. groove _____
8. combust _____
9. sordid _____
10. anomalous _____

a. dirty or wretched; mean; vulgar
b. to burn
c. lived and understood through the experience of another; substitutionary
d. drawn out too long; characterized by an excess of words
e. to grow rapidly; to sprout
f. appropriateness or good manners
g. a short and humorous narrative about one's own experiences
h. irregular or differing from the norm
i. worn and shabby, usually with thread showing
j. a long narrow hole; a set routine

■ Put the correct word in each blank from the list of words below.

11. varnish には_____の状態にする機能がある。

12. _____は inauspicious（不運な）の反意語である。

13. _____は dance を組み立てる行為である。

14. _____は regular（定期的な、規則的な）の反意語である。

15. _____なものには conformation が欠けている。

16. extemporization（即興演奏）には_____な特徴がある。

17. _____は tree の外側部分のことである。

18. _____は、effort なしでいいものを発見する才能を意味する。

19. _____な文章には ingenuity がない。

20. gregarious（社交的な）の反意語は_____である。

a. apoplectic	b. choreograph	c. serendipity	d. spontaneous	e. amorphous
f. bark	g. verbose	h. prosaic	i. propitious	j. aloof
k. sporadic	l. glossy			

Answer key

11. l	12. i	13. b	14. k	15. e
16. d	17. f	18. c	19. h	20. j
1. g	2. d	3. i	4. e	5. c
6. f	7. j	8. b	9. a	10. h

Track 25

25th DAY

勉強をサボっても
単語は消えず。ただ忘れさるのみ。

---

apostate
[əpásteit]

n. one who renounces a faith or cause　　　［名］棄教者、離脱者、変節者

The *apostate* from the Republican Party was welcomed by the Democrats.

関連語 apostasy : faith [feiθ]
apostasy（棄教、変節）は faith（信仰、信念）を捨てること。

---

appall
[əpɔ́:l]

v. to cause one to be shocked or offended
［動］〜をぞっとさせる、ぎょっとさせる

The social worker was *appalled* by the working conditions of the sweatshop.

反意語 appall : embolden [imbóuldən]
appall の反意語は embolden（〜を大胆にする、〜を励ます）

---

appeal
[əpí:l]

v. to attract or please; to have a case reviewed by the court
［動］（人の）気に入る、興味を引く；上訴する、抗議する

Diamonds *appeal* to women more than any other precious stone.

関連語 appeal : applicant [ǽplikənt]
applicant（志願者）は自分の長所を appeal することで選ばれようとする。

---

appease
[əpí:z]

v. to calm or allay　　　　　　　　　　　　　　　［動］〜を懐柔する、なだめる

Nothing could *appease* her fears and worries.

反意語 appease : miff [mif]
appease の反意語は miff（〜を怒らせる）

TRANSLATION | 例 文 の 訳

apostate　その共和党からの離脱者は、民主党に歓迎された。
appall　ソーシャルワーカーは、その低待遇の工場の作業環境を見てぞっとした。
appeal　ダイヤモンドは、他のどの宝石よりも女性の興味を引く。
appease　彼女の恐怖心と不安を静められるものは何もなかった。

21st
22nd
23rd
24th
25th
26th
27th
28th
29th
30th

349

arouse [əráuz]	v. **to excite or stimulate; to awaken from sleep** 　　　　　　　　　　　　　　　　　[動] ～を刺激する；～を目覚めさせる The girl's interest was still further *aroused* by the spectacular show at the circus. 関連語 arouse : phlegmatic [flegmǽtik] 　phlegmatic（冷静な、沈着な）人を arouse することは難しい。
arrange [əréindʒ]	v. **to make preparations for; to put in proper order; to settle** 　　　　　　　　　　　[動] ～の準備を整える；～をきちんと並べる；～を取りきめる Julia *arranged* her new textbooks on her new desk. 反意語 orderly arrangement : welter [wéltər] 　orderly arrangement（きちんとした配置）の反意語は welter（混乱、騒動）
bootless [búːtlis]	adj. **unprofitable; ineffective**　　　　　　　[形] 無益な；役に立たない Your many *bootless* business ventures have also bankrupted you personally. 関連語 bootless : worth [wəːˈθ] 　bootless なものには worth（価値）がない。
breach [briːtʃ]	v. **to violate**　　　　　　　　　　　　　　　　[動] ～に違反する n. **a violation of a law or obligation**　　　[名] 法律や義務への違反 The man *breached* his contract with the school and left two months early. The guard was accused of a *breach* of protocol. 関連語 breach : covenant [kʌ́vənənt] 　breach する対象は covenant（約束、契約）。
buoyant [bɔ́iənt]	adj. **cheerful or happy; floatable**　　　　[形] 元気な、快活な；浮力のある A life vest is a very *buoyant* device. 関連語 buoyant : submerge [səbmə́ːˈdʒ] 　buoyant なものは submerge（水中に沈める）することができない。

TRANSLATION | 例 文 の 訳

arouse	その少女は、サーカスの華やかな出し物に、さらにいっそう興味をかき立てられた。
arrange	ジュリアは、新しい教科書を自分の新しい机の上に並べた。
bootless	あなたの多くの無益なベンチャー事業のせいで、あなたは個人的にも破産したのだ。
breach	その男は学校との契約に反して2カ月早く退職した。
	その警備員は服務規定に違反して訴えられた。
buoyant	救命胴衣はとても浮力の大きい器具だ。

350

chef
[ʃef]

n. a professional cook who heads a large kitchen staff　　　[名]シェフ

The aspiration of all students in culinary school is to be the head *chef* of their own restaurants one day.

関連語 chef : banquet [bǽŋkwit]
chefにとって、banquet（ごちそう、豪華な食事）は調理の対象だ。

clout
[klaut]

n. a heavy blow; power or influence　　　[名]コツンと叩くこと；勢力、影響力

The mayor had a lot of *clout* over the police department.

反意語 clout : impuissance [impjúːisns]
cloutの反意語はimpuissance（無気力）

colonnade
[kàlənéid]

n. a series of columns spaced out in regular intervals
[名]一定の間隔で並んでいる柱の列

Colonnades are used by architects to give a building a more stately and grand appearance.

関連語 colonnade : pillar [pílər]
pillar（柱）はcolonnadeの一部。

contraction
[kəntrǽkʃən]

n. the shortening and thickening of muscle; the process of becoming smaller　　　[名]筋肉の収縮；縮小

A *contraction* of muscle transforms into force.

関連語 contraction : convulsion [kənvʌ́lʃən]
convulsion（けいれん）は筋肉の極端なcontraction。

coquette
[koukét]

n. a woman who flirts to exploit men
[名]コケティッシュな女性、なまめかしい女

Jeannie had unknowingly gained the reputation of being a *coquette*.

関連語 coquette : flirtatious [fləːrtéiʃəs]
coquetteにはflirtatious（いちゃつく、セクシーな）な特徴がある。

TRANSLATION | 例 文 の 訳

chef	料理学校の全生徒の願いは、いつか自分の所有するレストランの料理長になることだ。
clout	その市長には警察に対する大きな影響力があった。
colonnade	建築家は柱を一定の間隔で並べることで、建物の外観をより堂々とした豪華なものにする。
contraction	筋肉が収縮すると力に変わる。
coquette	ジーニーはいつの間にかコケティッシュな女性だという評判を取っていた。

debacle
[deibá:kl]

n. a sudden destruction; a complete failure　　　[名] 瓦解；大失敗

The campaign was a *debacle* and a waste of money.

反意語 debacle : landslide [lǽndslàid]
　　debacle の反意語は landslide（地滑り的勝利、圧倒的勝利）

decadence
[dékədᵊns]

n. a period of decay; the condition of low morals; the state of being overindulgent　　　[名] 退廃、堕落

The *decadence* of April's spending habit was a constant source of contention between her and her husband.

反意語 decadence : wholesomeness [hóulsəmnis]
　　decadence の反意語は wholesomeness（健全さ）

dingy
[díndʒi]

adj. darkened or discolored with dirt　　　[形] 黒ずんだ；すすけた

The *dingy* motel room was badly in need of new wallpaper and other renovations.

関連語 dingy : glisten [glísn]
　　dingy なものは glisten（ぴかぴか光る）することがない。

disabuse
[dìsəbjú:z]

v. to free somebody from a falsehood or misconception
　　　[動] 〜を（迷い・誤解から）解放する、解く

Magellan *disabused* the belief that the world was flat.

関連語 disabuse : fallacy [fǽləsi]
　　fallacy（誤った考え、誤信）を disabuse する。

dread
[dred]

n. extreme fear or terror　　　[名]（極度の）恐怖

The people in the war-torn city live in *dread* of further shelling.

関連語 dread : cringe [krindʒ]
　　dread を感じると体が cringe（すくむ、縮こまる）する。

TRANSLATION | 例 文 の 訳

debacle	そのキャンペーンは大失敗で、金の無駄だった。
decadence	エイプリルの退廃的な浪費癖は、彼女と夫の間の絶え間ない争いの元だった。
dingy	そのすすけたモーテルの部屋は、壁紙の張り替えなどの修理が早急に必要だった。
disabuse	マゼランは地球が平らであるという思い込みから人々を解放した。
dread	戦火で荒れたその町の人々は、さらなる爆撃におびえながら暮らしている。

dupe
[d(j)u:p]

v. to trick or fool　　　　　　　　　　　[動]〜をだます

n. one who is easy to trick; a fool　　　[名]だまされやすい人

That he could have chosen to *dupe* her in so ready a manner seemed a cruel thing.

Mary's naive and innocent nature often made her seem like a *dupe*.

関連語 dupe : gullible [gΛləbl]
　　dupe は gullible（だまされやすい）だという特徴がある。

enhance
[inhǽns]

v. to advance or improve　　　　[動]〜を向上させる、高める

Tammy *enhanced* the softness of her hair by applying a heavy conditioner.

反意語 enhance : mar [mɑːʳ]
　　enhance の反意語は mar（〜を損なう、台無しにする）

exotic
[igzátik]

adj. excitingly different; foreign or not native
　　　　　　　　　　　　　　　　　[形]風変わりな；外来の、外国の

The *exotic* breed of panda was the most popular attraction at the zoo.

反意語 exotic : indigenous [indídʒənəs]
　　exotic の反意語は indigenous（土着の、原産の）

foot-dragging
[fútdræ̀giŋ]

n. deliberate slowness in action　　　　[名]遅延、引き延ばし

The employee's constant *foot-dragging* cost her job.

関連語 foot-dragging : expedite [ékspədàit]
　　expedite（〜を迅速に遂行する、手早く片付ける）する人は foot-dragging とは無縁だ。

grotesque
[groutésk]

adj. outlandish in character or appearance; differing greatly from the acceptable norm　　　[形]異様な、怪奇な；ひどい、とんでもない

It is always more fun to dress as something *grotesque* on Halloween.

関連語 grotesque : fantastic [fæntǽstik]
　　grotesque は fantastic（現実離れした、空想的な、風変わりな）の度を越えた様子を表す。

TRANSLATION | 例 文 の 訳

dupe　彼がそんなに簡単な方法で彼女をだませてしまったのは、残酷なことに思えた。
　　　メアリーは単純で無邪気なので、だまされやすく見えやすい。

enhance　タミーは強いコンディショナーを使って、自分の髪をさらに柔らかくした。

exotic　外来種のパンダは、その動物園で一番の人気者だった。

foot-dragging　その従業員は年中、業務を遅らせていたので、解雇されてしまった。

grotesque　ハロウィーンには怪奇な衣装を着たほうが、より楽しくなるものだ。

hive
[haiv]

n. **a place that is busy with activity** 　　　　　　　　[名] 忙しい人が集まる場所

The store became a *hive* during the Christmas season.

関連語 hive : active [ǽktiv]
　hive は active（活発な、元気な）な場所。

impact
n.[ímpækt]
v.[impǽkt]

n. **a forceful contact or consequence; a significant impression of one thing on another** 　　　[名] 衝撃；影響

v. **to forcefully strike or affect** 　　[動] 〜に衝突する、（大きな）影響を与える

An *impact* with the steering wheel during the accident bruised the driver's forehead.

The experiences in science high school *impacted* Daniel's personality a lot.

関連語 impact : buffer [bʌ́fəʳ]
　buffer（やわらげる人、緩衝器）は impact をやわらげるもの。

impassive
[impǽsiv]

adj. **unsusceptible to emotional or physical pain; showing no emotion** 　　　　　　　[形] 無感動の；感情を表さない

Fleming always sat with the same *impassive* and absent-minded air during the boss's rantings.

類義語 impassive : deadpan [dédpæ̀n]
　impassive の類義語は deadpan（無表情な）

impeccable
[impékəbl]

adj. **flawless; incapable of sinning or doing wrong**
　　　　　　　　　　　　　　　　　　　[形] 欠点のない；完璧な

Joe was an *impeccable* hero in his younger brother's eyes.

関連語 impeccable : blemish [blémiʃ]
　impeccable な人には blemish（汚点、欠点）がない。

TRANSLATION | 例 文 の 訳

hive　　　その店はクリスマスシーズンの間、活気にあふれた。

impact　　その事故でハンドルに頭をぶつけた衝撃で、運転手の額にあざができた。
　　　　　　科学高校での経験がダニエルの性格に大きく影響した。

impassive　フレミングは、上司が大声でわめいている間、いつも変わらず無感動でぼんやりと座っていた。

impeccable　ジョーは、弟の目から見ると完璧な英雄だった。

menace
[ménis]

n. something that poses a danger or threatens injury or harm

[名] 脅威、危険

v. to pose a threat or endanger against　　[動] 脅威を与える、脅かす

Drug dealers are a *menace* to society.

The Roman Empire was *menaced* by its barbaric neighbors.

関連語 menace : fear [fiə^r]
menace（脅す）することで相手は fear（恐れ、恐怖）を抱くようになる。

notable
[nóutəbl]

adj. impressive or worthy of notice　　[形] 著名な、顕著な、注目すべき

The professor was given an award for his *notable* research.

反意語 notable success : fiasco [fiǽskou]
notable success（大成功）の反意語は fiasco（大失敗）

parable
[pǽrəbl]

n. a brief fictitious story that illustrates a moral or religious value

[名] 寓話

Children's bedtime stories are often *parables*.

関連語 parable : story [stɔ́:ri]
parable は story（物語）の一種。

paranoia
[pæ̀rənɔ́iə]

n. a mental disorder characterized by persistent delusions of being grand, or of being persecuted by others; extreme suspicion and distrust of others　　[名] 妄想、被害妄想；偏執病

During a war there is always a general *paranoia* in society.

関連語 paranoia : suspicion [səspíʃən]
suspicion（疑い）が度を越えると paranoia になる。

TRANSLATION | 例 文 の 訳

menace　麻薬の売人は社会にとって脅威だ。
　　　　　　ローマ帝国は、その未開の隣国におびやかされていた。
notable　その大学教授は重要な研究業績に対して賞を与えられた。
parable　寝る前に子供が聞く話には寓話が多い。
paranoia　戦争中はいつも社会全体に被害妄想が広がる。

platitude
[plǽtət(j)ùːd]

n. a dull or banal remark; the state of being boring or insipid

[名] 決まり文句、平凡な言葉；平凡、陳腐

The preacher's sanctimonious *platitudes* wore on his congregation.

関連語 platitude : banal [bənǽl]
platitude には banal（陳腐な、平凡な）だという特徴がある。

plethora
[pléθərə]

n. an excessive or overabundant amount

[名] 過多、過度

The wedding couple received a *plethora* of gifts at their wedding reception.

反意語 plethora : dearth [dəːʳθ]
plethora の反意語は dearth（不足、欠乏）

plot
[plɑt]

n. the main story in a fictional work; a plan made in secret

[名]（創作作品の）筋、構想；陰謀、たくらみ

Although the book's writing style is intriguing, the *plot* is rather dull.

They laid out their little *plot* against Madeleine and elaborated it carefully.

関連語 plot : plan [plæn]
plot は密かに練られた plan（計画）。

preach
[priːtʃ]

v. to give a sermon; to advise earnestly

[動] 説教する、伝道する

One should only *preach* what they practice.

関連語 preacher : sermon [sə́ːʳmən]
preacher（牧師）は sermon（説教）をする人。

preamble
[príːæ̀mbl]

n. the introductory statement or fact

[名] 前置き、序言；前文

The *preamble* to the new law highlighted the government's commitment to protect forests.

関連語 preamble : introductory [ìntrədʌ́ktəri]
preamble は introductory（紹介の、前置きの）だという特徴がある。

TRANSLATION | 例 文 の 訳

platitude	信徒たちは、その牧師の聖人ぶった陳腐な話にうんざりしていた。
plethora	その新郎新婦は披露宴で贈り物を過剰に受け取った。
plot	その本は、文体に魅力があるが、筋はかなり退屈だ。
	彼らはマデリンに対抗する計画を企て、念入りに練り上げた。
preach	人は自分が実践できることだけを説くべきだ。
preamble	その新しい法律の前文では、政府の森林保護への取り組みが強調されていた。

prostrate
[prástreit]

adj. **lying flat and face down; completely exhausted**
[形] 横たわった、ひれ伏した；疲れ果てた

v. **to lie or throw flat with the face down**　[動] 身を伏せる、平伏する

After an incredibly long and strenuous day of work, Brian came home and lay down *prostrate* on his bed.

The beggar *prostrated* himself on the man's feet in hopes of some clemency.

反意語 prostrate : upright [ʌ́pràit]
prostrateの反意語はupright（直立した、まっすぐに立った）

protract
[proutrǽkt]

v. **to continue or prolong unnecessarily**
[動] ～を故意に長引かせる、引き延ばす

The teacher *protracted* the lesson by going into unnecessary detail, causing some of the students to lose interest.

反意語 protract : curtail [kəʳtéil]
protractの反意語はcurtail（～を短くする、短縮する）

protuberance
[prout(j)úːbərəns]

n. **the state or quality of bulging**　[名] こぶ、腫物

Nolan had a strange *protuberance* on his cheek that he asked the doctor to examine.

反意語 protuberance : concavity [kɑnkǽvəti]
protuberanceの反意語はconcavity（くぼみ、凹面）

provident
[právəd°nt]

adj. **providing money and other things you need for the future; prudent; economical**　[形] 将来に備えた、先見の明がある、つつましい

Lilly is a *provident* person who saves 15% of her paycheck each month.

関連語 improvidence : spendthrift [spéndθrìft]
spendthrift（金遣いの荒い人、浪費家）はimprovidence（先見の明のないこと、将来へのたくわえがないこと）だ。

TRANSLATION | 例 文 の 訳

prostrate 信じられないほど長くきつい1日の仕事を終えると、ブライアンは帰宅してベッドに横たわった。その物乞いは、慈悲を期待して男の足元にひれ伏した。

protract 教師が不必要に詳しく説明することで授業を長引かせ、生徒の何人かが興味を失ってしまった。

protuberance ノーランは、ほおに奇妙なこぶができたので、医者に検査してくれるように頼んだ。

provident リリーは将来に備えて毎月給料の15パーセントを貯蓄している。

provincial
[prəvínʃəl]

adj. **coming from a province; unsophisticated or narrowminded**

[形] 州の、地方の；田舎の、視野の狭い、偏狭な

The brilliant and sophisticated writer's *provincial* nature surprised his audience of readers.

反意語 provincial : cosmopolitan [kὰzməpálətn]

provincialの反意語はcosmopolitan（国際的な、国際感覚のある、国際的な視野を持った）

provisions
[prəvíʒənz]

n. **preparatory measures; a stock of needed food or supplies**

[名] 用意；食料、貯蔵品

The travelers stopped at the nearest town to get *provisions* for their hike.

関連語 provisions : larder [lάːʳdəʳ]

larder（食料貯蔵室）は provisions を保存する。

provoke
[prəvóuk]

v. **to cause anger; to evoke a feeling or emotional reaction**

[動] ～を怒らせる；（感情や反応など）を起こさせる

Elizabeth, looking to have a quarrel, *provoked* Darcy by shouting abuses at him.

関連語 provoke : taunt [tɔːnt]

provokeは taunt（～をなじる、あざける）よりも攻撃性が強い。

quotidian
[kwoutídiən]

adj. **occurring everyday**

[形] 毎日起こる、毎日の

Personal hygiene such as brushing one's teeth is a *quotidian* chore.

反意語 quotidian : striking [stráikiŋ]

quotidianの反意語はstriking（著しい、目立つ）

rapacious
[rəpéiʃəs]

adj. **grasping or taking by force; extremely greedy**

[形] 略奪する；どん欲な

Many hoped that the *rapacious* strangers would be induced to leave the town quickly.

関連語 rapacious : covetous [kʌ́vitəs]

rapaciousは covetous（欲しがる）より他人のものをもっと欲しがるという意味。

TRANSLATION | 例 文 の 訳

provincial	頭脳明晰で洗練されたその作家の偏屈な性格は、読者を驚かせた。
provisions	旅行客たちは一番近い町に立ち寄り、登山用の食料を手に入れた。
provoke	けんかの機会をうかがっていたエリザベスは、ダーシーに罵詈雑言を浴びせて彼を怒らせた。
quotidian	歯みがきのような個人衛生は日常の雑事の１つだ。
rapacious	強欲なよそ者たちがすぐに町から出て行ってくれることを、多くの人々が望んだ。

repartee
[rèpəˈtíː]

n. a quick, clever reply　　　　　　　　　　[名] 当意即妙のやりとり

Our neighbor was a witty man, famous for pleasant *repartees*.

類義語 repartee : retort [ritɔ́ːˈt]
repartee の類義語は retort（応酬、口答え）

repatriate
[riːpéitrièit]

v. to return to country of origin　　　　　[動] ～を本国に送還する

In the mid 1900s, Greece and Turkey *repatriated* each other's citizens to their home countries.

反意語 repatriate : emigrate [émigrèit]
repatriate の反意語は emigrate（他国へ移民させる）

riot
[ráiət]

v. to raise a riot; to practice unrestrained revelry
　　　　　　　　　　　　　　　　　　　[動] 暴動を起こす；放蕩する

n. public violence as a group, usually protesting power or authority　　　　　　　　　　　　　　　[名] 暴動

Rioting in Italy, especially Milan and Florence, is a common occurrence.

Most Korean stores in L.A. were known to have been robbed in the *riot*.

関連語 rioter : hodgepodge [hádʒpàdʒ]
rioter（暴徒）には hodgepodge（ごたまぜ、寄せ集め）という特徴がある。

route
[ruːt]

n. a traveled path; a designated course of action　[名] 道、道筋、ルート

The *route* to the top of that mountain is long and winding.

関連語 route : detour [díːtuəˈ]
route で detour（回り道をする）する。

TRANSLATION | 例 文 の 訳

repartee 私たちの隣人は軽妙な男で、愉快で気の利いた受け答えをすることで有名だった。
repatriate 1900年代半ば、ギリシャとトルコは互いに相手国の国民を送還し合った。
riot イタリア、特にミラノとフィレンツェでは暴動がよく起こる。
その暴動で、ロサンゼルスにある韓国系の店舗のほとんどが略奪に遭ったことが知られていた。
route その山の頂上へのルートは、長く曲がりくねっている。

359

separate [sépərèit]	v. **to set or move apart; to legally part before a divorce; to disunite** [動] 引き離す；別居する；分離する、離脱する
	The two students were *separated* after their fight in the playground.
	Kate and Tom didn't quite know how to break the news to their children that they were *separated*.
	反意語 separate : meld [meld] separateの反意語はmeld（～を併合する、混合する）
sip [sip]	v. **to take small drinks** [動] ちびちび飲む
	Sipping her coffee, Mary read the morning newspaper before heading to work.
	関連語 sip : swill [swil] swill（～をがぶがぶ飲む）はsipに比べて速いペースで飲むことを表す。
slouch [slautʃ]	v. **to let one's shoulders and neck fall forward** [動] 前かがみになる
	The young man *slouched* at his desk.
	反意語 slouch : stand erect [stænd irékt] slouchの反意語はstand erect（直立する）
slovenly [slʌ́vənli]	adj. **untidy or dirty** [形] だらしない、汚い
	Harran's groping hand met that of a *slovenly* little Dutchman.
	反意語 slovenly : natty [nǽti] slovenlyの反意語はnatty（しゃれた、粋な）
smother [smʌ́ðəʳ]	v. **to deprive of oxygen; to cover up and destroy** [動] 窒息させる；覆い包む、火を消す
	The fireman *smothered* the flames with a wet blanket.
	類義語 smother : choke [tʃouk] smotherの類義語はchoke（窒息させる）

TRANSLATION | 例 文 の 訳

separate	その２人の生徒は校庭でけんかしてから、疎遠になった。
	ケイトとトムは、自分たちが別居することを子供たちにどう知らせればいいか、よくわからなかった。
sip	メアリーは仕事に向かう前に、コーヒーをちびちび飲みながら朝刊を読んだ。
slouch	その若い男性は机に向かって前かがみになっていた。
slovenly	ハランが手探りすると、汚れた小柄なオランダ人の手に触れた。
smother	その消防士は濡れた毛布で火を消した。

soothe
[su:ð]

v. **to comfort or ease pain; to relax or calm**

[動] (痛みなどを) 和らげる；〜をなだめる、落ち着かせる

Alice tried unsuccessfully to *soothe* her sobbing friend.

反意語 soothe : rankle [ræŋkl]
soothe の反意語は rankle (心を苦しめる)

sop
[sɑp]

v. **to give a conciliatory gift or bribe; to take up liquid by absorbing it**
[動] 賄賂を与える；(液体を) 吸い取る

n. **a bribe**
[名] 賄賂

Grandpa would always *sop* up his soup with his bread.

The feuding tribes exchanged *sops* in order to maintain the accord of the two tribes.

関連語 sop : conciliatory [kənsíliətɔ̀:ri]
sop には conciliatory (なだめる、懐柔的な) な性質がある。

treacherous
[trétʃərəs]

adj. **characterized by betrayal of fidelity or trust; unreliable or dangerous**
[形] 裏切りの、不誠実な；危険な、油断できない

In the entertainment business, most people are *treacherous* and only befriend you while you're famous.

反意語 treacherous : faithful [féiθfəl]
treacherous の反意語は faithful (忠実な)

vertigo
[və́:ʳtigòu]

n. **dizziness or weakness; a disordered or confused state of mind**
[名] めまい

Beth went to the doctor because she was repeatedly experiencing *vertigo*.

類義語 vertigo : dizziness [dízinis]
vertigo の類義語は dizziness (めまい)

TRANSLATION | 例 文 の 訳

soothe アリスは泣いている友達をなだめようとしたが、無駄だった。
sop 祖父はいつもパンをスープに浸して食べた。
反目し合っていた両部族は、部族間の円満を維持するために賄賂を交換した。
treacherous 芸能界ではほとんどの人々が不誠実で、いま有名な人とだけ親しくなろうとする。
vertigo ベスは繰り返しめまいを感じるので、医者のもとへ行った。

voracious
[vɔːréiʃəs]

adj. **having an insatiable appetite**

[形] 大食の、食欲旺盛な

After playing football all day Timmy was *voracious* and ready for dinner.

関連語 voracious : satisfy [sǽtisfài]
　　　voraciousな人をsatisfy（満足させる）するのは難しい。

■ Fill in the blanks with the correct letter that matches the word with its definition.

1. debacle _____
2. repatriate _____
3. provident _____
4. plethora _____
5. quotidian _____
6. parable _____
7. preamble _____
8. voracious _____
9. breach _____
10. slouch _____

a. the introductory statement or fact
b. having an insatiable appetite
c. a sudden destruction; a complete failure
d. occurring everyday
e. an excessive or overabundant amount
f. a brief fictitious story that illustrates a moral or religious value
g. to return to country of origin
h. a violation of a law or obligation
i. to let one's shoulders and neck fall forward
j. providing money and other things you need for the future; prudent; economical

■ Put the correct word in each blank from the list of words below.

11. larder は_____を保存する機能を持っている。
12. dizziness（めまい）の類義語は_____である。
13. applicant は自分の長所を_____することで選んでもらおうとする。
14. fallacy を_____する。
15. suspicion が度を超すと_____になる。
16. _____なものには worth がない。
17. choke（窒息させる）の類義語は_____である。
18. _____は faith を捨てる行為である。
19. _____を感じた結果、体が cringe する。
20. convulsion は筋肉の極端な ___ のことである。

a.paranoia   b. enhance   c.provisions   d. platitude   e. appeal
f. smother   g. bootless   h. vertigo   i. disabuse   j. apostasy
k. contraction   l. dread

11.c 12.h 13.e 14.i 15.a 16.g 17.f 18.j 19.l 20.k
1.c 2.g 3.j 4.e 5.d 6.f 7.a 8.b 9.h 10.i

26th DAY

---

abundant
[əbʌ́ndənt]

adj. plentiful or amply supplied　　　　　　[形] 豊富な、ありあまる

The garden produced an *abundant* amount of vegetables this year.

反意語 abundant : scant [skænt]
　abundantの反意語は scant（十分でない、乏しい）

---

acquisition
[æ̀kwəzíʃən]

n. the attainment or purchase of something; the gaining of knowledge or information　　　　　　[名] 獲得、習得

David's most recent *acquisition* was a convertible car.

反意語 acquisition : divestiture [divéstətʃəʳ]
　acquisitionの反意語は divestiture（奪うこと、剥奪）

---

amenable
[əmíːnəbəl]

adj. responsible or answerable; readily brought to submission or obedience　　　　　　[形] 受け入れる；従いやすい、従順な

All citizens of the U.S. are *amenable* to the supreme law of the land—the U.S. Constitution.

反意語 amenable : querulous [kwér(j)uləs]
　amenableの反意語は querulous（不満の多い）

---

anonymous
[ənɑ́nəməs]

adj. not identified or of unknown authorship　　　　　　[形] 匿名の

Rosy received an *anonymous* bouquet of flowers at work.

関連語 anonymous : identify [aidéntəfài]
　anonymousなものはだれによるものか identify（特定する、確認する）ことができない。

TRANSLATION | 例 文 の 訳

abundant　　今年その菜園では、ありあまるほど野菜の収穫があった。
acquisition　デイビッドが一番最近買ったのはコンバーチブルの車だった。
amenable　　すべての米国民は国の最高法である合衆国憲法に従う。
anonymous　ロージーは職場で匿名の花束を受け取った。

ascend
[əsénd]

v. **to rise or move upward** [動] 登る、上がる

Tanner *ascended* to the penthouse by helicopter because the elevator was out of order.

反意語 ascend : descend [disénd]
ascend の反意語は descend（下る、降りる）

bleed
[bli:d]

v. **to lose blood; to ooze out** [動] 出血する；にじる

Mark lay on the street, *bleeding* profusely.

関連語 bleeding : tourniquet [túəˈnikit]
tourniquet（止血帯）は bleeding を防ぐもの。

burnish
[bə́ːˈniʃ]

v. **to polish or make shiny by rubbing; to shine forth**
[動] ～をこすって磨く；つやが出る

The maid spent the entire day *burnishing* the trophies and statues.

関連語 burnish : lustrous [lʌ́strəs]
burnish すると lustrous（光沢のある）になる。

candidate
[kǽndidèit]

n. **a person who aspires to be elected or appointed to a certain position** [名] 候補者、志願者

There are only three *candidates* for the job, and all are equally qualified.

関連語 candidate : slate [sleit]
slate（候補者名簿）は candidate の名前を書いておく名簿。

celebrity
[səlébrəti]

n. **a famous or widely known living person; fame** [名] 有名人、名士

Audrey Hepburn's role in Roman Holiday transformed her from an unknown actress into a *celebrity*.

反意語 celebrity : obscurity [əbskjúˈrəti]
celebrity の反意語は obscurity（無名）

TRANSLATION | 例 文 の 訳

ascend	エレベーターが故障していたので、タナーはヘリコプターでペントハウスに上がった。
bleed	マークはひどく血を流しながら通りに横たわっていた。
burnish	そのメイドはその日一日、トロフィーと銅像を磨いて過ごした。
candidate	その職には3人しか応募者がおらず、全員同じように資格を備えている。
celebrity	オードリー・ヘップバーンは『ローマの休日』での役で、無名女優から有名人になった。

contravene
[kὰntrəvíːn]

v. to violate; to oppose in argument   [動] 違反する；反対する

In Singapore, *contravening* even minor laws can bring severe punishments.

反意語 contravene : buttress [bʌ́tris]
> contraveneの反意語はbuttress（〜を支える、支持する）

convulsion
[kənvʌ́lʃən]

n. violent, involuntary muscular contractions   [名] けいれん、ひきつけ

During a seizure, people with epilepsy often experience *convulsions* that rack their whole bodies.

関連語 convulsion : contraction [kəntrǽkʃən]
> convulsionは筋肉のcontraction（収縮）が極端に進んだ状態。

coronation
[kɔ́ːrənèiʃən]

n. the act or occasion of crowning a sovereign   [名] 戴冠、戴冠式

The *coronation* ceremony of Queen Elizabeth II was extremely elaborate.

関連語 coronation : reign [rein]
> coronationはreign（治世、統治期間）を引き継ぐこと。

counterfeit
[káuntəʳfit]

adj. forged or falsified   [形] 偽造された、偽りの

v. to forge; to attempt to deceive by pretense   [動] 偽造する；〜を装う

n. a copy that is presented as the original; an act of forging   [名] 偽造品、にせ物

They had no way to differentiate the *counterfeit* product from the genuine one.
The business of *counterfeiting* luxuries seems to be expanding.
The new U.S. currency has reduced the amount of *counterfeits* circulating in the economy.

類義語 counterfeit : forgery [fɔ́ːʳdʒəri]
> counterfeitの類義語はforgery（偽造、偽造物、模造品）

TRANSLATION | 例 文 の 訳

contravene シンガポールでは、ささいな法律違反でも重い刑罰の対象になる。
convulsion てんかんの患者は、発作を起こすと、よく全身がけいれんする。
coronation 女王エリザベス2世の戴冠式は、とても凝っていた。
counterfeit 彼らには偽造品と純正品とを見分ける手段がなかった。
贅沢品を模造するビジネスが拡大しているようだ。
米国では、新しい貨幣のおかげで市場に流通している偽札の量が減ってきている。

countermand
[kàuntəˈmǽnd]

v. to take back or cancel an order   [動]（命令など）を変更する

The security advisor *countermanded* the operation in fear of causing too many civilian casualties.

関連語 countermand : order [ɔ́ːˈdəˈ]
> countermand は order（命令）を取り消すことを表す。

credulous
[krédʒuləs]

adj. overly eager to believe; naive   [形]信じやすい；だまされやすい

It was *credulous* of the tourist to believe the local salesman.

関連語 credulous : skeptic [sképtik]
> skeptic（懐疑論者）は credulous ではない。

delegate
n.[déligət]
v.[déligèit]

n. a representative with the power to speak or act on behalf of others   [名]代表、使節

v. to send as a representative; to entrust to another
     [動]〜を代表として派遣する；〜を委任する

Each state sent a number of *delegates* to the national convention.

Minister Kim was *delegated* to represent South Korea at APEC 2000.

関連語 delegation : represent [rèprizént]
> delegation（代表団、使節団）はある集団を represent（代表する）する。

detection
[ditékʃən]

n. the act of discovering the true character, fact, or existence of   [名]〜の発見、検知、探知

Early *detection* of most cancers ensures a high survival rate.

関連語 indetection : camouflage [kǽməflùːʒ]
> indetection（検知しないこと）のために camouflage（カムフラージュする、偽装する）する。

diatribe
[dáiətràib]

n. an abusive speech or writing, usually ironical or satirical   [名]痛烈な非難、批評

The protestant preacher went into a *diatribe* against the Catholic Church.

関連語 diatribe : abuse [əbjúːz]
> diatribe は abuse（ののしり、悪口）の程度が強いもの。

TRANSLATION | 例 文 の 訳

countermand	民間人の犠牲者が多く出すぎることを懸念して、国家安全保障担当補佐官は軍事作戦を変更した。
credulous	その旅行客はだまされやすかったので、地元の販売員を信じてしまった。
delegate	各州が全国大会に多数の代表者を派遣した。
	キム大臣は APEC2000 に韓国代表として派遣された。
detection	ほとんどのがんは早期発見によって高い生存率が保証される。
diatribe	そのプロテスタントの牧師は、カトリック教会に対する痛烈な非難を始めた。

21st | 22nd | 23rd | 24th | 25th | **26th** | 27th | 28th | 29th | 30th

dignify
[dígnəfài]

v. **to ennoble or give dignity to**　　　　[動] 〜に威厳をつける、〜を厳かにする

The senator's presence *dignified* the local charity's fund raising event.

反意語 dignify : demean [dimí:n]
dignifyの反意語はdemean（〜の品位を下げる）

distress
[distrés]

n. **physical or emotional pain or suffering; trouble or danger**
　　　　[名] 苦悩、心痛、苦痛；困窮、災難

v. **to upset or cause suffering**　　　　[動] 〜を悩ませる、悲しませる

Her husband's death caused her great *distress*.

The young boy was *distressed* by his parents' argument.

関連語 distress : alleviate [əlí:vièit]
distressをalleviate（〜を軽減する、緩和する）する。

drench
[drentʃ]

v. **to saturate or soak thoroughly**　　　　[動] 〜をびしょぬれにする

On the way home I was completely *drenched* by a rain shower.

関連語 drench : douse [daus]
drenchにはdouse（水に浸す、入れる）よりもびしょぬれなニュアンスがある。

dwindle
[dwíndl]

v. **to decrease or make steadily less**
　　　　[動] だんだん小さくなる、少なくなる、減少する

As the depression hit, sales at the Evans' family store *dwindled* to less than one third of normal volume.

反意語 dwindle : proliferate [proulífʳrèit]
dwindleの反意語はproliferate（激増させる）

embed
[imbéd]

v. **to put into another substance**　　　　[動] 埋め込む

The gardener carefully *embedded* the bulbs in the dirt.

反意語 embed : disinter [dìsintá:ʳ]
embedの反意語はdisinter（〜を掘り出す、明るみに出す）

TRANSLATION | 例 文 の 訳

dignify	その上院議員が出席したので、地域の慈善団体の資金集めに箔がついた。
distress	夫の死は彼女に大きな苦痛を与えた。
	その少年は両親の口論に苦しんだ。
drench	家に帰る途中、私は雨でびしょぬれになった。
dwindle	不況が襲い、エバンスの個人商店の売り上げは通常の3分の1以下に減った。
embed	その造園業者は球根を慎重に土に埋めた。

21st

22nd

23rd

24th

25th

26th

27th

28th

29th

30th

enunciate
[inʌ́nsièit]

v. to express or pronounce clearly and articulately

[動] 明確に発音する、明確に述べる

The teacher asked the presenting student to *enunciate* clearly for the class.

反意語 enunciate : waffle [wάfl]
enunciate の反意語は waffle（むだ口をたたく、言い逃れを言う）

extenuate
[iksténjuèit]

v. to lessen or diminish the seriousness or magnitude

[動]（罪・罰）を軽くする、情状酌量する

Mary's elaborate excuses did little to *extenuate* her mistake.

関連語 extenuate : seriousness [síᵊriəsnis]
extenuate は seriousness（重大性）を軽減するということ。

fidelity
[fidéləti]

n. faithfulness

[名] 忠誠、忠実

The *fidelity* of a henchman is always in question.

反意語 fidelity : apostasy [əpάstəsi]
fidelity の反意語は apostasy（離脱）

fortunate
[fɔ́ːʳtʃənət]

adj. lucky or receiving unexpected good fortune

[形] 幸運な

Beth is *fortunate* to have won the trip to New York.

反意語 fortunate : untoward [ʌntóuərd]
fortunate の反意語は untoward（困った、不利な）

grove
[grouv]

n. a group of trees cultivated for growing fruit

[名] 果樹園

The *grove* of orange trees in Oscar's backyard produced the most delicious oranges.

関連語 grove : tree [triː]
tree（木）は grove の一部。

TRANSLATION | 例 文 の 訳

enunciate	その教師は、発表する生徒に、クラスの皆のためにはっきりと発音するよう求めた。
extenuate	メアリーはあれこれ言い訳したが、それで自分のミスが軽くなることなどほとんどなかった。
fidelity	部下の忠誠心など、いつも疑問だ。
fortunate	ベスは運よくニューヨーク旅行に当選した。
grove	オスカーの家の裏にオレンジの果樹園があり、最高においしいオレンジが収穫された。

grudge
[grʌdʒ]

n. a feeling of resentment　　　　　　　　　[名]恨み、怨恨

v. to reluctantly give or admit　　　　　[動]〜を惜しむ、しぶる

I can't believe she still holds a *grudge* against me for a mistake I made three years ago!

We should not *grudge* helping any human being in need.

反意語 grudge : goodwill [gúdwil]
grudge の反意語は goodwill（善意）

infect
[infékt]

v. to contaminate with a disease or sickness; to corrupt
　　　　　　　　　　　　　　　　　[動] 感染させる；堕落させる

Many people became *infected* with the plague that spread throughout the country.

関連語 infection : antibiotic [æ̀ntaibaiɑ́tik]
antibiotic（抗生物質）は infection（感染症、伝染病）を治療するために使われる。

inveigle
[invíːgl]

v. to lure or entice　　　　　　　[動]〜を巧みに誘い込む、そそのかす

The charmer *inveigled* the young lady.

関連語 inveigle : interest [íntᵊrəst]
inveigle はだまして関心を引くという意味で、interest（関心を引く）の一種。

kindle
[kíndl]

v. to start a fire; to arouse or stir up
　　　　　　　　　　　　　[動] 火をつける；（感情・興味などを）かき立てる

Feelings of attraction and affection quickly *kindled* between them.

反意語 kindle : extinguish [ikstíŋgwiʃ]
kindle の反意語は extinguish（火を消す）

TRANSLATION | 例 文 の 訳

grudge 信じられないことだが、彼女はいまだに私の3年前の失敗を恨んでいるのだ！
　　　　　私たちは、困っている人を助けることをためらうべきではない。

infect 全国に広がった伝染病に、多くの人が感染した。

inveigle その女たらしは、若い女性をそそのかした。

kindle 彼らの間で、引かれ合う思いと愛情の火がすぐに燃え出した。

21st
22nd
23rd
24th
25th
26th
27th
28th
29th
30th

liken
[láikən]

v. **to regard or see as similar; to compare**

[動] ～をたとえる、～になぞらえる

A divorce is often *likened* to the death of a marriage.

関連語 liken : similarity [sìməlǽrəti]

likenは similarity（類似点）を比較してたとえる。cf) discriminate（～を識別する）は違いを比較する。

lustrous
[lʌ́strəs]

adj. **bright; radiant in character**

[形] 輝かしい；光沢のある

Brigette's *lustrous* hair shone under the afternoon sun.

関連語 lustrous : burnish [bə́ːʳniʃ]

burnish（～を磨く）すると lustrousになる。

mandatory
[mǽndətɔ̀ːri]

adj. **required or obligatory**

[形] 義務的な、強制的な

Every new employee must take a *mandatory* drug test.

関連語 mandatory : comply [kəmplái]

mandatoryなことには comply（～に従う）する。

mentor
[méntəʳ]

n. **a trusted tutor**

[名] 助言者、指導教官

The young boy's *mentor* was his older brother.

関連語 mentor : guidance [gáidns]

mentorは guidance（指導、支援）をくれる人。

murmur
[mə́ːʳməʳ]

v. **to speak or complain with an unclear tone**

[形] 低い声で言う、ささやく

David *murmured* foul words under his breath.

関連語 murmur : speak [spiːk]

murmurは speak（話す）の一種。

TRANSLATION | 例 文 の 訳

liken 離婚は、よく結婚の死に例えられる。

lustrous ブリジットのつやのある髪が、午後の日差しの下で輝いた。

mandatory 新入社員は全員、義務として薬物検査を受けなければならない。

mentor その少年の助言者は、彼の兄だった。

murmur デイビッドは小声で汚い言葉をつぶやいた。

371

painstaking
[pèinztéikiŋ]

adj. illustrating diligent care and work　　[形] 念入りな、丹精を込めた

Pat went to *painstaking* lengths to ensure the party was a success.

反意語 painstaking : slipshod [slípʃàd]
painstakingの反意語は slipshod（ずさんな）

permit
[pəˈmít]

v. to authorize or give consent　　[動] 許す、許可する

n. an official warrant or license　　[名] 認可書、免許証

Trespassers are not *permitted* on the Rosenbach's land.

反意語 permit : proscribe [prouskráib]
permitの反意語は proscribe（禁止する）

pernicious
[pəˈníʃəs]

adj. highly destructive or deadly　　[形] ひどく有害な、致命的な

Cocaine is illegal because of its *pernicious* effects on a user's mind and body.

関連語 pernicious : harmful [háːˈrmfəl]
perniciousは非常に harmful（有害な）であるという意味。

perspicacious
[pə̀ːˈrspəkéiʃəs]

adj. being of keen discernment　　[形] 鋭い判断力のある、洞察力のある

The *perspicacious* jury could clearly see all the flaws in the defense lawyer's argument.

反意語 perspicacious : stupid [st(j)úːpid]
perspicaciousの反意語は stupid（愚かな）

pledge
[pledʒ]

n. a binding promise or oath　　[名] 誓い、誓約

v. to make a pledge or swear　　[動] 誓う

Every morning the students said the *Pledge* of Allegiance to the flag.

Adam *pledged* his sword to the chieftain.

関連語 pledge : renounce [rináuns]
renounce（〜を放棄する）は前に立てた pledgeを破るということ。

TRANSLATION | 例 文 の 訳

painstaking　パットは、そのパーティーの成功を確実なものにするためなら何でもした。

permit　ローゼンバックの土地は立入禁止だ。

pernicious　コカインが違法なのは、使用者の体に致命的な影響を与えるからだ。

perspicacious　陪審団は高い判断力を備えており、被告側弁護人の主張のあらゆる不備をはっきりと見抜くことができた。

pledge　毎朝、学生たちは国旗に向かって忠誠を誓った。
　　　アダムは首長のために戦うことを誓った。

polemic
[pəlémik]

n. an aggressive attack on or disputation against

[名] 激しい論争、論戦、反論

The freedom fighter's *polemics* have already lasted over two hours!

反意語 polemic : agreement [əgrí:mənt]
polemic の反意語は agreement（同意、一致）

precursor
[pri:kə́:ˡsəˡ]

n. one that indicates the arrival of another; a predecessor

[名] 前兆；先駆者、前任者

The protests in the small town were seen as a *precursor* to the larger, nationwide movement for change.

反意語 precursory : derivative [dirívətiv]
precursory（先駆けの、前触れとなる）の反意語は derivative（独創性のない、模倣した）

prodigious
[prədídʒəs]

adj. huge in bulk or quantity; marvelous　　[形] 巨大な；すばらしい

The project will require a *prodigious* amount of money.

反意語 prodigious : pinpoint [pínpɔ̀int]
prodigious の反意語は pinpoint（極めて小さい）

prune
[pru:n]

n. a dried plum　　[名] プルーン

v. to reduce or cut off parts, usually of plants　　[動]（枝などを）切り取る

The children preferred to eat raisins over *prunes*.
The old woman *prunes* her hedges every Sunday.

関連語 prune : plum [plʌm]
prune は plum（プラム）を乾燥したもの。

rude
[ru:d]

adj. inelegant or impolite in manner or action; crude or simple

[形] 失礼な、無礼な；卑しい

It is *rude* to interrupt someone's conversation.

関連語 rude : churl [tʃə́(:)ˡl]
churl（無作法な男）には rude だという特徴がある。

TRANSLATION | 例文の訳

polemic その自由論者は、すでに2時間以上も反論を続けている！
precursor 小さな町での抗議行動は、より大きな、全国的な変革のための運動の前兆と見なされていた。
prodigious そのプロジェクトには莫大な資金が必要だろう。
prune 子供たちはプルーンよりもレーズンを食べたがった。
その老女は、毎週日曜日に生け垣を刈り込む。
rude 人の会話に割って入るのは失礼だ。

sanction
[sǽŋkʃən]

n. **official approval or permission**   [名] 許可、認可

v. **to formally approve**   [動] 許可する、認可する

The West imposed comprehensive *sanctions* on the autocratic country's banks, preventing its citizens from wiring money internationally.

Now, the President is ready to *sanction* the reinforcement of the local army.

反意語 sanction : interdict [ìntəˈdíkt]
    sanction の反意語は interdict (〜を禁ずる)

scheme
[ski:m]

n. **a plot or secret program of action**   [名] 筋書き、計画

v. **to plot**   [動] 〜をたくらむ

Soren and Heather came up with a *scheme* to make extra money.

Daniel has already noticed that the rival company is *scheming* against him.

関連語 scheme : plan [plæn]
    scheme は plan の一種。

sere
[siəˈ]

adj. **dried and withered**   [形] 干からびた、しおれた

The vase full of old flowers, wilted and *sere*, didn't look very cheerful on the kitchen table.

反意語 sere : lush [lʌʃ]
    sere の反意語は lush (青々と茂った)

sermon
[sə́:ˈmən]

n. **a speech on conduct or duty usually given by a religious leader**   [名] 説教

The *sermon* topic this Sunday was philanthropy.

関連語 sermon : preacher [prí:tʃəˈ]
    preacher (牧師、説教者) は sermon (説教) をする人。

TRANSLATION | 例 文 の 訳

sanction	欧米諸国は独裁国の銀行に包括的な制裁を課して、国民が国際的に送金することを不可能にした。今や大統領は地方の軍備強化を認可しようとしている。
scheme	ソレンとレザーは、副収入を得るための計画を思いついた。ダニエルは競合会社が自分を陥れようとしていることにすでに気づいている。
sere	花瓶にたくさんの古い花が差してあり、すっかりしおれているので、キッチンテーブルの上の眺めが生彩を欠いていた。
sermon	今週日曜日の説教の話題は博愛主義だった。

shun [ʃʌn]	v. **to avoid and stay away from**	[動]〜を避ける、遠ざける
	I was *shunned* by my co-workers.	
	反意語 shun : haunt [hɔːnt] shunの反意語はhaunt(〜へしばしば行く、つきまとう)	

stingy [stíndʒi]	adj. **lacking generosity; unwilling to spend money**	
		[形]〜を出し惜しみする、けちな
	Christmas is not the time to be *stingy*.	
	関連語 stingy : miser [máizəʳ] miser(守銭奴)とはstingyな人。	

submission [səbmíʃən]	n. **a surrender or compliance**	[名]降伏、服従
	The sieging army starved the city into *submission*.	
	関連語 submission : insubordinate [ìnsəbɔ́ːʳdⁿnit] insubordinate(服従しない、不従順な)な人はだれにもsubmissionしない。	

summon [sʌ́mən]	v. **to call or send for, usually officially**	[動]出廷を命じる、呼ぶ
	Tom has been *summoned* to court.	
	関連語 summon : citation [saitéiʃən] citation(法廷への召喚)は証人を法廷にsummonするための命令。	

tame [teim]	adj. **domesticated; submissive or harmless; spiritless or dull**	
		[形]飼いならされた;従順な;単調な、退屈な
	The party was considered *tame* by many of the guests who were in attendance.	
	反意語 tame : racy [réisi] tameの反意語はracy(生気のある)	

TRANSLATION | 例 文 の 訳

shun	私は同僚たちから疎まれた。
stingy	クリスマスは、出し惜しみすべき時期ではない。
submission	包囲軍はその都市への食糧の供給を断ち、市民を降伏させた。
summon	トムは出廷を命じられた。
tame	そのパーティーは多くの出席者から退屈だと思われた。

tender
[téndəʳ]

adj. **soft or delicate**   [形] 優しい、柔らかい、傷つきやすい

Nothing is more *tender* than the love of a doting grandmother.

反意語 tender : hardy [háːʳdi]
　　tender の反意語は hardy（頑丈な、丈夫な）

terminate
[táːʳmənèit]

v. **to close or end; to finish**   [動] ～を終わらせる、終結させる

The factory officially *terminated* her employment.

反意語 termination : inception [insépʃən]
　　termination（終了、満了）の反意語は inception（発足、始まり）

vindicate
[víndəkèit]

v. **to show the validity of; to defend; to free from an accusation, suspicion, or doubt with supporting proof**
    [動] 正当さを立証する；潔白を証明する、容疑などを晴らす

The jury's not-guilty verdict *vindicated* the defendent.

反意語 vindicate : impugn [impjúːn]
　　vindicate の反意語は impugn（～に疑いをはさむ）

void
[vɔ́id]

v. **to empty or clear; to nullify**   [動] 空にする；～を無効にする

n. **an empty space or absence**   [名] 空所、欠落

adj. **empty or containing nothing**   [形] 空の、～を描いている

The cashier *voided* the transaction.

After their child left for college, they tried to fill the *void* in their life with arts and crafts.

Void of contact with other monkeys, the captured monkey became listless and lethargic.

類義語 void : empty [émpti]
　　void の類義語は empty（空の）

TRANSLATION | 例 文 の 訳

tender	盲目的な祖母の愛ほど優しさに満ちたものはない。
terminate	その工場は彼女の雇用を正式に終わらせた。
vindicate	陪審員団による無罪評決で、被告人の容疑が晴れた。
void	レジ係は処理を取り消した。
	子供が大学に入学して家を出ると、彼らは生活に開いた穴を美術工芸の趣味で埋めようとした。
	捕えられたサルは、他の仲間との接触がないために、すっかり無気力になった。

■ Fill in the blanks with the correct letter that matches the word with its definition.

1. polemic _____
2. stingy _____
3. enunciate _____
4. amenable _____
5. grudge _____
6. lustrous _____
7. drench _____
8. sere _____
9. contravene _____
10. submission _____

a. to reluctantly give or admit
b. dried and withered
c. bright; radiant in character
d. to express or pronounce clearly and articulately
e. to violate; to oppose in argument
f. an aggressive attack on or disputation against
g. a surrender or compliance
h. responsible or answerable; readily brought to submission or obedience
i. lacking generosity; unwilling to spend money
j. to saturate or soak thoroughly

■ Put the correct word in each blank from the list of words below.

11. _____は非常に harmful という意味である。
12. _____は guidance をしてくれる人のことだ。
13. _____は proliferate（激増させる）の反意語である。
14. racy（生気のある）は_____の反意語である。
15. _____は interdict（〜を禁ずる）の反意語である。
16. derivative（独創性のない、模倣した）の反意語は_____である。
17. churl は_____である人を意味する。
18. _____は、程度の強い abuse のことである。
19. skeptic は_____ではない。
20. disinter（〜を掘り出す）の反意語は_____である。

a. dwindle　b. prune　c. precursory　d. pernicious　e. credulous　f. tame
g. mentor　h. rude　i. embed　j. diatribe　k. fidelity　l. sanction

Answer key

11. d　12. g　13. a　14. f　15. l　16. c　17. h　18. j　19. e　20. i
1. f　2. i　3. d　4. h　5. a　6. c　7. j　8. b　9. e　10. g

377

ここまででほとんどの単語を
覚えました。残るはあと4日です！

27thDAY

---

applause
[əplɔ́ːz]

n. the clapping of hands at a performance to express approval

[名] 拍手

The *applause* from the crowd filled the stadium.

関連語 applause : approval [əprúːvəl]
approval（賛成、承認）を表現するために applause を送る。

---

arduous
[áːˈdʒuəs]

adj. difficult or strenuous

[形] 困難な、努力を要する

The *arduous* climb up the mountain took three days.

反意語 arduous : facile [fǽsil]
arduous の反意語は facile（容易な、簡単に手に入る）

---

asperity
[əspérəti]

n. harshness or roughness

[名] とげとげしさ、荒々しさ

Todd spoke with an *asperity* during the meeting that intimidated
potential detractors.

反意語 asperity : mildness [máildnis]
asperity の反意語は mildness（温和、まろやかさ）

---

aspirant
[ǽspərənt]

n. one who seeks or desires to succeed or advance

[名]（成功や昇進を）熱望する人、大望を抱く人

Aspirants to the succession of leadership schemed for months before the
dictator's death.

関連語 aspirant : quarry [kwɔ́ːri]
aspirant は quarry（あさる）する。

TRANSLATION | 例 文 の 訳

applause	スタジアムが観客の拍手でいっぱいになった。
arduous	その登山は困難なもので、3日かかった。
asperity	トッドは会議中に辛らつな言葉で話し、批判を抑え込もうとした。
aspirant	後継の座を狙う者たちによる数カ月間の謀略の果てに、その独裁者は死んだ。

capitulate
[kəpítʃulèit]

v. **to surrender or acquiesce on agreed terms**

[動]〜に降伏する、黙って従う

I *capitulated* to the chief's request to work over-time.

反意語 capitulation : resistance [rizístᵊns]
capitulation（降伏）の反意語は resistance（抵抗）

comity
[kámǝti]

n. **a state of civility and respect between peoples or nations**

[名] 相互の礼節

The *comity* of races has been the goal of many great leaders such as Martin Luther King Jr. and Gandhi.

反意語 comity : enmity [énmǝti]
comity の反意語は enmity（敵意、悪意）

copious
[kóupiǝs]

adj. **abundant or plentiful in quantity or quality**

[形]（量が）多い、豊富な

The thunderstorm brought *copious* rain to the Serengeti Plains.

反意語 copious : sparse [spɑːʳs]
copious の反意語は sparse（まばらな、少ない）

curmudgeon
[kəʳmʌ́dʒən]

n. **an ill-tempered and hostile person**

[名] 気難しい人

No one knew how to act around the *curmudgeon* because everything seemed to set him off.

反意語 curmudgeon : agreeable person [əgríːəbl pəːʳsn]
curmudgeon の反意語は agreeable person（感じのよい人）

deafening
[défᵊniŋ]

adj. **excessively loud**

[形] 耳をつんざくような

Every time Korea scored a goal the crowd raised a *deafening* cheer.

関連語 deafening : loud [laud]
deafening は loud（騒がしい）よりもはるかに騒々しい様子を表す。

TRANSLATION | 例 文 の 訳

capitulate	私は係長の残業の要求に黙って従った。
comity	人種間で互いに礼節を保つことが、マーティン・ルーサー・キングやガンジーといった多くの偉大な指導者の目標であり続けてきた。
copious	その激しい嵐はセレンゲティ平原に豊富な雨をもたらした。
curmudgeon	その人は気難しく、何をしても怒りそうだったので、彼の周りでどう行動したらいいのかだれにもわからなかった。
deafening	韓国がゴールを決めるたびに、群衆は耳をつんざくような歓声を上げた。

379

demur
[dimə́ːʳ]

v. **to object** [動] 異議を唱える

n. **a protest or hesitation** [名] 異議、反対

It is my right to *demur* to vote.

David proposed to his girlfriend who agreed without *demur*.

類義語 demur : objection [əbdʒékʃən]
demurの類義語は objection（反対、異議）

deplete
[diplíːt]

v. **to use up; to lessen or reduce** [動] 〜を使い尽くす；激減させる

The army *depleted* its food supply quickly.

反意語 deplete : enrich [inrítʃ]
depleteの反意語は enrich（〜を向上させる、豊かにする）

deplore
[diplɔ́ːʳ]

v. **to express or feel sadness or regret; to condemn or strongly disapprove of** [動] 嘆く；強く非難する

The President stated that he *deplored* the deaths of the children in Somalia.

反意語 deplore : rejoice [ridʒɔ́is]
deploreの反意語は rejoice（〜を喜ぶ、うれしく思う）

divulge
[divʌ́ldʒ]

v. **to proclaim or disclose; to reveal and make known** [動] 〜を公表する；〜を漏らす

Fred *divulges* all his secrets to his best friend.

反意語 divulge : conceal [kənsíːl]
divulgeの反意語は conceal（隠す、秘密にする）

dolt
[doult]

n. **a stupid or foolish person** [名] うすのろ、間抜け

Sean felt like a *dolt* after he answered his professor's question incorrectly.

関連語 dolt : stupid [st(j)úːpid]
doltには stupid（愚かな）な特徴がある。

TRANSLATION | 例 文 の 訳

demur	投票に反対するのは私の権利だ。
	デイビッドが彼女にプロポーズすると、彼女は迷わず承諾した。
deplete	軍隊は食料の供給を急激に減らした。
deplore	大統領はソマリアの子供たちの死を悼む声明を出した。
divulge	フレッドは親友に自分の秘密を何でも打ち明ける。
dolt	ショーンは教授の質問に間違って答えてしまい、自分が間抜けのように感じた。

euphemism
[júːfəmìzm]

n. the use of a mild or inoffensive expression instead of one that is offensive or aggressive　　　　　[名] 婉曲語法、遠回しな言い方

A tactful person uses *euphemisms* in their daily language.

関連語 euphemism : offense [əféns]
　euphemism には offense（気持ちを害すること、無礼）がない。

euphonious
[juːfóuniəs]

adj. pleasing to the ear　　　　　[形] 耳に心地よい

The *euphonious* music lulled the baby to sleep.

反意語 euphonious : cacophonous [kəkáfənəs]
　euphonious の反意語は cacophonous（耳障りな、不協和音の）

expedite
[ékspədàit]

v. to accelerate or rush a process　　　　　[動] 〜を迅速に進める、はかどらせる

Nat had his VISA application *expedited* so that he could leave the country on time.

関連語 expedite : foot-dragging [fútdræ̀giŋ]
　expedite する人は foot-dragging（遅延、引き延ばし）をすることはない。

expenditure
[ikspénditʃəʳ]

n. the act of spending; that which is spent or used　　　　　[名] 支出、経費；消費

The family maintained careful records of all its *expenditures*.

関連語 expenditure : parsimonious [pɑ̀ːʳsəmóuniəs]
　parsimonious（極度にけちな）な人の辞書に expenditure という言葉はない。

exponent
[ikspóunənt]

n. one that exemplifies or advocates something; a mathematical symbol expressing the raising of a power　　　　　[名] 主導者、支持者；指数

Tracy is an *exponent* of recycling.

関連語 exponent : advocate [ǽdvəkèit]
　exponent は自分の信念を advocate（〜を主張する、擁護する）する人。

TRANSLATION | 例 文 の 訳

euphemism 如才ない人は日常会話で遠回しな表現を使う。
euphonious 心地よい音楽を聞きながら、その赤ん坊は眠った。
expedite ナットは予定通りに出国できるように、ビザの申請手続きを迅速に進めてもらった。
expenditure その家族は、すべての支出を丁寧に記録していた。
exponent トレイシーはリサイクルの支持者だ。

381

figurative
[fígjurətiv]

adj. representing by a figure; metaphorical

[形] 具象的な、象徴的な；比喩的な

The preacher often uses *figurative* language in his sermons.

反意語 figurative : literal [lítʰrəl]
figurative の反意語は literal（文字通りの）

flaunt
[flɔːnt]

v. to display ostentatiously

[動] ～を見せびらかす

Sheila *flaunted* her new dress at the school dance.

反意語 flaunt : ensconce [inskáns]
flaunt の反意語は ensconce（身を隠す）

flounder
[fláundəʳ]

v. to move about or proceed clumsily and ineffectually

[動] まごつく、のたうつ、苦労する、息詰まる、もがく

He *floundered* about the room in his drunken stupor.

反意語 flounder : slide [slaid]
flounder の反意語は slide（滑る、素早く動く）

flourish
[fláːriʃ]

v. to thrive or prosper; to make a sweeping and showy gesture

[動] 繁栄する、活躍する；～を見せびらかす

America *flourished* in wealth during the 1980s.

反意語 flourish : waste away [weist əwéi]
flourish の反意語は waste away（衰弱する、衰えていく）

haphazard
[hæphǽzəʳd]

adj. by chance or random; without planning

[形] 偶然の；無計画の

Nietzsche's essays are written in a *haphazard* manner that confuses the readers.

反意語 haphazard : methodical [məθádikʰl]
haphazard の反意語は methodical（順序だった、整然とした）

TRANSLATION | 例 文 の 訳

figurative	その牧師は説教でよく比喩的な表現を使う。
flaunt	シーラは学校のダンスパーティーで新しいドレスを見せびらかした。
flounder	彼は泥酔して部屋中をのたうち回った。
flourish	アメリカは1980年代に経済的に繁栄した。
haphazard	ニーチェのエッセーは無計画に書かれているので、読者が混乱する。

hyperbole
[haipə́:'bəli]

n. a dramatic exaggeration　　　　　　　　　　　　[名] 誇張法、誇張

The use of *hyperbole* in writing is often intended for comical relief.

関連語 hyperbole : exaggerated [igzǽdʒərèitid]
　　　hyperbole は exaggerated (誇張された) な語法だ。

impecunious
[ìmpikjú:niəs]

adj. habitually poor or without money　　　　[形] 常に金がない、無一文の

My billionaire friend Jeff started off as an *impecunious* inventor living off table scraps.

反意語 impecunious : affluent [ǽflu(:)ənt]
　　　impecunious の反意語は affluent (富裕な、裕福な)

impede
[impí:d]

v. to get in the way of or to slow the progress of
　　　　　　　　　　　　　　　　　　　　　[動] ～を遅らせる、邪魔する

The construction on the bridge *impeded* the morning traffic.

反意語 impede : facilitate [fəsílətèit]
　　　impede の反意語は facilitate (～を促進する)

imperious
[impí°riəs]

adj. having an arrogant attitude; intensely compelling
　　　　　　　　　　　　　　　　　　　　[形] 傲慢な、横柄な；緊急の

Laura silenced her subordinates with an *imperious* glare.

関連語 imperious : humility [hju:míləti]
　　　imperious には humility (謙遜、謙虚) が欠けている。

impermeable
[impə́:'miəbl]

adj. not allowing passage through its surface or substance
　　　　　　　　　　　　　　　　　　　　　　　　　[形] ～を通さない

This new fabric is *impermeable* to wind.

関連語 impermeable : penetrate [pénətrèit]
　　　impermeable なものは penetrate (～を貫く) することができない。

TRANSLATION | 例 文 の 訳

hyperbole 文章中で誇張法を使う場合、喜劇的な効果を狙っていることが多い。

impecunious 億万長者である友人ジェフは、かつては残飯をあさって暮らす無一文の発明家だった。

impede 橋の上の工事が朝の交通を妨げた。

imperious ローラは威圧的な目つきで部下たちを黙らせた。

impermeable この新しい生地は風を通さない。

imperturbable
[ìmpərtə́ːʳbəbl]

adj. serene or extremely calm [形] 動揺しない、冷静な

Gloria remained *imperturbable* before her piano concert relaxedly imagining a grand performance.

反意語 imperturbable : restive [réstiv]
imperturbable の反意語は restive (落ち着きのない、いらいらした)

impervious
[impə́ːʳviəs]

adj. impenetrable; not capable of being disturbed or damaged
[形] ～を通さない；～を受けつけない、損傷しない

The robbers could not open the *impervious* safe even with explosives.

関連語 impervious : damaged [dǽmidʒd]
impervious なものは damaged (損傷を受けた) な状態にならない。

impetuous
[impétʃuəs]

adj. impulsive; marked by violent force of action or manner
[形] 性急な、軽率な；激しい、猛烈な

Gabby's one vice was her habit of *impetuous* shopping.

関連語 impetuous : hesitation [hèzətéiʃən]
impetuous な人の行動には hesitation (ためらい、躊躇) がない。

implacable
[implǽkəbl]

adj. incapable of being appeased or changed
[形] なだめにくい、執念深い、執拗な

There is no use in arguing with Connor because he is *implacable*.

関連語 implacable : compromise [kámprəmàiz]
implacable な人とは compromise (妥協する、歩み寄る) することが難しい。

implode
[implóud]

v. to violently collapse inward [動] 内側に破裂させる、破壊する

The politician's career *imploded* after the drug scandal was uncovered.

関連語 implode : collapse [kəlǽps]
implode の方が collapse (崩壊する) に比べて破壊の強度が高い。

TRANSLATION | 例 文 の 訳

imperturbable	グロリアは落ち着きを失わないために、堂々たる演奏をのんびり思い描きながら、ピアノの演奏会に臨んだ。
impervious	強盗たちは、爆薬を使ってもその頑丈な金庫を開けることができなかった。
impetuous	ギャビーの1つの悪習が衝動買いだった。
implacable	コナーは頑固なので、議論しても無駄だ。
implode	この政治家のキャリアは、薬物スキャンダルが発覚した後、崩壊した。

induce
[ind(j)úːs]

v. **to persuade or influence; to cause to make happen**

[動] 説得して〜する気にさせる、〜を引き起こす

Ivy was *induced* to work harder by the enticement of stock options.

反意語 inducement : deterrent [ditə́ːrənt]

inducement（報酬、わいろ、誘い込むもの）の反意語は deterrent（妨害物、引き止めるもの）

instrumentalist
[ìnstrəméntlist]

n. **one who plays a musical instrument**

[名] 楽器演奏者

The band was composed of one lead singer and three *instrumentalists*.

関連語 instrumentalist : symphony [símfəni]

instrumentalist は symphony（交響曲）を演奏する。

nepotism
[népətìzm]

n. **favoritism based on family relations**

[名] 身内びいき、親族の登用

Uncle Jim exhibited *nepotism* by hiring his irresponsible nephew to work at the store.

関連語 nepotism : relative [rélətiv]

nepotism は relative（親戚）を重用すること。

nocturnal
[nɑktə́ːʳnl]

adj. **related to or active during the night**

[形] 夜行性の、夜の

Owls are *nocturnal* creatures.

反意語 nocturnal : diurnal [daiə́ːʳnl]

nocturnal の反意語は diurnal（昼行性の、昼間の）

opportune
[àpəʳt(j)úːn]

adj. **suitable or appropriate for a certain moment or purpose**

[形] 適切な、好都合な

David waited for the *opportune* moment to make his escape from the prison.

関連語 opportune : convenience [kənvíːnjəns]

opportune と似た意味の名詞に convenience（便利さ、利便性）がある。

TRANSLATION | 例 文 の 訳

induce	アイビーはストックオプションに引かれて、より一生懸命に働く気になった。
instrumentalist	そのバンドは1人のリードシンガーと3人の楽器演奏者で構成されていた。
nepotism	おじのジムは、無責任なおいを雇って店で働かせることで、身びいきを露呈させた。
nocturnal	フクロウは夜行性の動物だ。
opportune	デイビッドは脱獄に好都合なタイミングを待った。

peck [pek]	n. **a short light kiss** [名] 軽いキス In Europe, people give each other a *peck* on the cheek when they greet each other. 関連語 peck : kiss [kis] peckは額や頬にする軽いkiss (キス)。
repel [ripél]	v. **to reject or drive away; to cause distaste** [動] 〜を撃退する、追い払う；不快な気持ちにする The taxi driver's rudeness *repelled* the customer from leaving a tip. 関連語 repel : repugnant [ripʌ́gnənt] repugnant (とても嫌な、嫌悪感を引き起こす) なものはrepelする特徴がある。
repertoire [répəˈtwàːˈ]	n. **the list of artistic pieces (dramas, plays, dances, etc.) that an artist or group can perform** [名] レパートリー Paul has a varied *repertoire* of guitar music that he performs for friends. 関連語 repertoire : play [plei] repertoireとはplay (演奏する、上演する) する曲目、演目のリスト。
replete [riplíːt]	adj. **full of or complete** [形] 〜でいっぱいの、十分な A traditional Greek meal is *replete* with olives and feta. 反意語 repletion : want [wɔ(ː)nt] repletion (充満、充実) の反意語はwant (欠乏、不足)。
repose [ripóuz]	v. **to lie down or take a rest** [動] 横になる、休む n. **rest** [名] 休息、睡眠 Tom's favorite spot to *repose* is in his hammock. Daniel had such a peaceful face in *repose*. 関連語 repose : fatigue [fətíːg] fatigue (疲労) から回復するためにreposeを取る。

TRANSLATION | 例 文 の 訳

peck　　　　ヨーロッパでは挨拶を交わすときに互いの頬に軽くキスをする。
repel　　　　そのタクシー運転手は無礼だったので、乗客はチップを渡さなかった。
repertoire　ポールはギターでさまざまな音楽を演奏し、友人に聞かせている。
replete　　　伝統的なギリシャ料理にはオリーブとフェタチーズがたくさん入っている。
repose　　　トムのお気に入りの休憩場所はハンモックの中だ。
　　　　　　　　ダニエルは、とても穏やかな顔つきで眠っていた。

repudiate
[ripjú:dièit]

v. **to renounce or reject as true; to disown or formally separate from; to refuse to pay a debt**

[動] ～を公式に否定する、拒否する；～と縁を切る；借金の支払いを拒否する

Nicole Kidman *repudiated* the charge that she cheated on Tom Cruise.

反意語 repudiate : concede [kənsí:d]
repudiate の反意語は concede（～を認める、許す）

scatter
[skǽtəʳ]

v. **to disperse in all directions; to strew or divide into random portions**

[動] まき散らす；ばらまく

The wind *scattered* leaves across the yard.

関連語 scattering : overlap [òuvəʳlǽp]
scattering（散乱している）なものは overlap（重なり合う、重複する）することがない。

sophisticate
[səfístəkèit]

v. **to make worldly-wise or complex; to refine**

[動] ～を世慣れさせる、複雑化する；洗練する

n. **one who knows about socially important matters**

[名] 教養人

Heather's parents hoped that the trip to Europe would *sophisticate* her by exposing her to art and culture.

Jane prefers to attend social events that draw *sophisticates*.

反意語 sophisticated : barbaric [bɑ:ʳbǽrik]
sophisticated（洗練された、教養のある）の反意語は barbaric（野蛮な、未開の）

soporific
[sàpərífik]

n. **a drug or agent used to induce sleep**

[名] 催眠剤、睡眠薬

adj. **tending to induce sleep**

[形] 眠くなるような、催眠性の

Norma took a *soporific* for her insomnia.

John was lulled to sleep by that *soporific* movie.

関連語 soporific : sleep [sli:p]
soporific には sleep（睡眠）を引き起こす機能がある。

TRANSLATION | 例 文 の 訳

repudiate ニコール・キッドマンは、トム・クルーズを裏切って浮気をしたという疑惑を公式に否定した。

scatter 風で葉が庭中に散らばった。

sophisticate ヘザーの両親は、ヨーロッパ旅行が彼女を芸術や文化に触れさせ、洗練されたものにすることを望んでいた。

ジェーンは教養人が集まる社交行事に参加するのが好きだ。

soporific ノーマは不眠症なので睡眠薬を飲んだ。

ジョンは、その眠気を催すような映画を見て居眠りしてしまった。

splint
[splint]

n. a device used to support and keep a joint or fractured bone from moving　　　　　　　[名] 添え木、副木

The *splint* was uncomfortable and inconvenient because all her movements were restricted by it.

関連語 splint : mobility [moubílǝti]
splint は mobility (動きやすさ、機動力) を損ねる機能がある。

stealth
[stelθ]

n. the quality of being secretive and covert　　　[名] 秘密の行為、隠密の行為

A leopard uses *stealth* to catch its prey.

関連語 stealth : furtive [fǝ́ːʳtiv]
stealth と似た意味の形容詞に furtive (ひそかな、こっそりなされた) がある。

supercilious
[sùːpǝʳsíliǝs]

adj. showing an arrogant manner　　　　　　[形] ばかにした、横柄な

Matthew's *supercilious* smirk angered his ex-girlfriend.

反意語 supercilious : obsequious [ǝbsíːkwiǝs]
supercilious の反意語は obsequious (こびる、卑屈な)

superficial
[sùːpǝʳfíʃǝl]

adj. relating to the surface; lacking depth; shallow　　　　　　　　　　　　　　[形] 表面的な；うわべだけの；浅い

America is thought to have a *superficial* and materialistic culture.

関連語 superficial : dilettante [dílitàːnt]
dilettante (芸術を道楽でする人、好事家) は専門的な技術がなく、趣味で superficial に芸術を扱うという特徴がある。

superior
[sǝpíǝʳriǝʳ]

adj. upper or better; of higher rank or stature　　　　　　　　　　　　　　[形] 〜より優れている；〜より上位の

Just because something costs more doesn't mean it has *superior* quality.

関連語 superiority : authority [ǝθɔ́ːrǝti]
authority (権力者) は superiority (上位、優越、優位性) を持つという特徴がある。

TRANSLATION | 例文の訳

splint　　添え木は不快で不便だった。そのせいで彼女は、あらゆる動きを制限されてしまったのだ。

stealth　　ヒョウは、ひそかな動きで獲物を捕まえる。

supercilious　　マシューの人を見下したような薄笑いが、彼の昔の恋人を怒らせた。

superficial　　アメリカの文化は表層的で実利本意なものだと考えられている。

superior　　単に値段がより高いからといって、品質がより優れていることにはならない。

supine
[suːpáin]

adj. lying on one's back with face upward; suggesting lethargy or passivity
[形] 仰向けの；怠惰な、無気力な、受け身の

Travis' *supine* answer to everything was always either I don't know or I don't care.

反意語 supine : vigilant [vídʒələnt]
supine の反意語は vigilant（たえず警戒している、油断のない）

taper
[téipəʳ]

v. to progressively narrow or diminish in width
[動] 次第に細くなる；弱まる

I have never liked wearing pants with *tapered* legs.

関連語 taper : width [widθ]
taper は width（幅）が狭くなっていく、狭くすること。

tepid
[tépid]

adj. lukewarm; lacking in enthusiasm or passion
[形] なまぬるい；熱意のない

Heathcliffe's *tepid* style of speaking did little to attract people to him.

反意語 tepid : fervid [fɔ́ːʳvid]
tepid の反意語は fervid（熱烈な、熱情的な）

tortuous
[tɔ́ːʳtʃuəs]

adj. winding or crooked
[形] ねじれた、曲がりくねった

The *tortuous* mountain roads are difficult to drive on.

関連語 tortuous : labyrinth [lǽbərìnθ]
labyrinth（迷路）は tortuous な特徴がある。

typo
[táipou]

n. an error in typing (short for 'typographical error')
[名] タイプミス

One *typo* ruined the entire letter, which I then had to re-type.

関連語 typo : text [tekst]
typo は text（本文）の中にある誤字。

TRANSLATION | 例 文 の 訳

supine トラヴィスは何事にも無気力な答えしか返さず、いつも「わからない」か「かまわない」かしか言わなかった。

taper 私は裾が細いパンツを履きたいと思ったことがない。

tepid ヒースクリフの話し方には熱意が感じられないので、彼が人を引きつけることはほとんどなかった。

tortuous 曲がりくねった山道で車を運転するのは難しい。

typo 1つのタイプミスで手紙全体が台無しになり、私は打ち直さなければならなかった。

vapid
[vǽpid]

adj. lacking taste or flavor; lacking spirit, liveliness, or interest

[形] 味のない；退屈な、つまらない

Sue left the concert because of the *vapid* music.

反意語 vapid : riveting [rívitiŋ]

vapid の反意語は riveting（興味を引き付けられる、とても面白い）

vapor
[véipəʳ]

n. a barely visible gas; something unsubstantial

[名] 蒸気、はかないもの

There was a lot of *vapor* in the air from Michael's cooking.

関連語 vaporization : heat [hi:t]

heat（熱）によって vaporization（蒸発）が発生する。

TRANSLATION | 例 文 の 訳

| vapid | 退屈な音楽を聞かされたので、スーは演奏会を後にした。 |
| vapor | マイケルの料理から、たくさんの湯気が立ち上っていた。 |

390

■ Fill in the blanks with the correct letter that matches the word with its definition.

1. impermeable _____
2. supercilious _____
3. euphonious _____
4. tortuous _____
5. aspirant _____
6. taper _____
7. induce _____
8. flounder _____
9. impecunious _____
10. opportune _____

a. suitable or appropriate for a certain moment or purpose
b. habitually poor or without money
c. winding or crooked
d. to move about or proceed clumsily and ineffectually
e. showing an arrogant manner
f. not allowing passage through its surface or substance
g. to progressively narrow or diminish in width
h. one who seeks or desires to succeed or advance
i. pleasing to the ear
j. to persuade or influence; to cause to make happen

■ Put the correct word in each blank from the list of words below.

11. restive（落ち着きのない、いらいらした）の反意語は_____である。

12. _____には offense がない。

13. _____の反意語は riveting（興味を引き付けられる、とても面白い）である。

14. _____は object（反対）の類義語である。

15. diurnal（昼行性の、昼間の）の反意語は_____である。

16. _____は exaggerated された修辞語法である。

17. _____は resistance（抵抗）の反意語である。

18. _____には sleep を引き起こす機能がある。

19. methodical（順序だった、整然とした）の反意語は_____である。

20. _____な人は humility がない。

a. nocturnal	b. capitulation	c. imperturbable	d. imperious	e. hyperbole
f. demur	g. euphemism	h. vapid	i. soporific	j. implode
k. haphazard	l. expenditure			

Answer key

11. c 12. g 13. h 14. f 15. a 16. e 17. b 18. i 19. k 20. d
1. f 2. e 3. i 4. c 5. h 6. g 7. j 8. d 9. b 10. a

昔の人は覚えた辞書の
ページを食べていたという
伝説があるのを知っていますか？

28th DAY

---

abrade
[əbréid]

v. **to wear away by friction; to irritate**

[動]〜をすり減らす；〔精神的に〜を〕摩耗させる

During the Ice Age, the advance of icebergs *abraded* the continent.

関連語 abraded : friction [fríkʃən]
friction（摩擦）の結果、ものが abraded（摩耗された）な状態になる。

---

acquiesce
[æ̀kwiés]

v. **to yield to or comply with unwillingly or passively**

[動]（不本意ながら）同意する、黙って従う

Sandra *acquiesced* to her parents and gave up her dream to be a dancer.

関連語 acquiesce : intransigent [intrǽnsədʒənt]
intransigent（妥協しない、頑固な）な人は acquiesce することがない。

---

aerate
[ɛ́ə reit]

v. **to supply with oxygen or air**　　　[動]空気にさらす、酸素を供給する

It is important to *aerate* the water in a fish tank.

関連語 aerate : oxygen [ɑ́ksidʒən]
aerate は oxygen（酸素）を通すことをいう。

---

ambiguity
[æ̀mbigjúːəti]

n. **the state of having more than one meaning; uncertainty in meaning**

[名]多義性；意味のあいまいさ

The purpose of contracts is to remove any *ambiguity r*egarding each party's responsibility.

関連語 ambiguous : clarity [klǽrəti]
ambiguous（あいまいな）な表現には clarity（明快さ）が欠けている。

TRANSLATION | 例 文 の 訳

abrade	氷河期に氷山の移動によって大陸が削られた。
acquiesce	サンドラはしぶしぶ両親に同意し、ダンサーになる夢をあきらめた。
aerate	魚の水槽の水に酸素を通すことは重要だ。
ambiguity	契約書の目的は、双方の義務に関するあいまいさをすべて取り除くことにある。

appreciate
[əprí:ʃièit]

v. **to be grateful for; to understand the value or quality of**

[動] 感謝する；価値を認める

More than the flowers and cards, I *appreciated* the visits by my friends when I was ill.

関連語 appreciation : testimonial [tèstəmóuniəl]

testimonial (証明書、推薦文) は appreciation (感謝) を表す。

approbation
[æprəbéiʃən]

n. **formal or official approval; praise**

[名] 認可、是認；賞賛

The soldier's valor in combat earned him the military's highest *approbation*, the Medal of Honor.

類義語 approbation : praise [preiz]

approbation の類義語は praise (賞賛)

appropriate
adj.[əpróupri:t]
v.[əpróuprièit]

adj. **suitable or fitting**

[形] 適切な、妥当な

v. **to set apart for a specific use**

[動] 〜を着服する、横領する

A handshake is *appropriate* when greeting someone.

The baker *appropriated* half of the bakery's monthly flour supply to make bread for his daughter's wedding.

関連語 appropriate : embezzler [imbézlər]

embezzler (横領者) は appropriate する人。

approve
[əprú:v]

v. **to consent or accept as favorable or satisfactory**

[動] 承認する、認める

The committee *approved* the building of a new school.

関連語 approval : applause [əplɔ́:z]

applause (拍手喝采) を送って approval (賛成、支持、賞賛) を表す。

TRANSLATION | 例 文 の 訳

appreciate	病気のとき、花やカードより友達の訪問がありがたかった。
approbation	戦場で勇敢に戦ったその兵士に、軍からの最高の栄誉である名誉勲章が授与された。
appropriate	人に挨拶するときには、握手するといい。
	そのパン職人は、娘の結婚式のパンを作るために、パン店が月々仕入れる小麦粉の半分を着服した。
approve	委員会は新しい学校の建設を承認した。

approximate
[əpráksəmit]

adj. almost exact; quite similar　　　　　　　　[形] およそ〜の；ほぼ〜の

The contractor's *approximate* cost of the renovation was more than the purchase price of the house.

関連語 approximate : precise [prisáis]
　　precise（正確な、まさに）と approximate（およそ）には明確な違いがある。

barbarize
[báːʳbəràiz]

v. to make savage or crude　　　[動] 〜が[を] 野蛮になる[する]、粗野になる[する]

Hedonists are usually accused of *barbarizing* human society.

反意語 barbarize : civilize [sívəlàiz]
　　barbarize の反意語は civilize（文明化する、洗練する）

brazen
[bréizn]

adj. made of brass; marked by unrestrained boldness
　　　　　　　　　　　　　　　　　　[形] 真鍮の；厚顔な、ずうずうしい

Sue showed no remorse in telling her professor a *brazen* lie.

反意語 brazen : modest [mádist]
　　brazen の反意語は modest（控えめな、謙遜した）

cabal
[kəbǽl]

n. a secretive scheme or plot; a group of conspiring plotters
　　　　　　　　　　　　　　　　　　　　　[名] 陰謀；陰謀団、秘密結社

A *cabal* of rebels plotted to overthrow the government.

関連語 cabal : association [əsòusiéiʃən]
　　cabal は密かに結成された association（組織、団体）の一種。

capricious
[kəpríʃəs]

adj. unpredictable or unexpected; changing frequently
　　　　　　　　　　　　　　　　　　　　　[形] 予測できない；気まぐれな

The *capricious* character of forest fires makes it dangerous for the infantry to battle.

関連語 capricious : deliberation [dilìbəréiʃən]
　　capricious な人には deliberation（熟考、熟慮、慎重さ）が欠けている。

TRANSLATION ｜ 例 文 の 訳

approximate	業者が見積もったリフォーム料金の額は、その家の購入価格よりもずっと高かった。
barbarize	快楽主義者はたいてい、人間社会を非文明化するといって非難される。
brazen	スーは教授に厚かましいうそをついたことに何の後悔も見せなかった。
cabal	反乱者たちの秘密結社が、政府転覆の陰謀を図った。
capricious	山火事には予測できない性質があるので、歩兵隊が消火するのは危険だ。

circuitous
[səːˈkjúːətəs]

adj. having a circular or roundabout course; speaking or acting in an indirect manner　　[形] 回り道の、遠回りの；回りくどい、遠回しの

The defendant's plea was *circuitous* and did no good for his case.

関連語 circuitous : directness [diréktnis]
circuitousな言葉には directness（率直、単刀直入）がない。

consolidate
[kənsálədèit]

v. to join together to reduce in number　　[動] 統合する、合併する

The family *consolidated* all their debts into one payment plan.

反意語 consolidate : dissolve [dizálv]
consolidateの反意語は dissolve（解消する、溶かす）

conspire
[kənspáiər]

v. to join in a plot or scheme to do a wrongful or unlawful act　　[動] 共謀する、陰謀をたくらむ

The three tenants *conspired* against their landlord.

関連語 conspiratorial : conniver [kənáivər]
conniver（共謀者）とは conspiratorial（共謀の、陰謀の）である。

dapper
[dǽpər]

adj. stylish and neat in appearance　　[形] こざっぱりした、しゃれた

The *dapper* young man caught Jessica's eye.

反意語 dapper : unkempt [ʌnkémpt]
dapperの反意語は unkempt（だらしない）

debunk
[diːbʌ́ŋk]

v. to expose the falseness or sham of　　[動] ～の誤りを暴露する

The defendant's plea was *debunked* by the witness' testimony.

反意語 debunk : shroud [ʃráud]
debunkの反意語は shroud（真相などを隠す）

TRANSLATION | 例 文 の 訳

circuitous	被告人の申し立ては回りくどく、事件の審理に役立たなかった。
consolidate	その家族は、すべての負債を1回でまとめて返済する計画を立てた。
conspire	3人の小作人は地主を相手に陰謀を図った。
dapper	そのこざっぱりした若者はジェシカの目を引いた。
debunk	被告人の申し立ては、目撃者の証言によって否定された。

decant
[dikǽnt]

v. **to transfer or pour from one vessel into another**

[動] 液体を別の容器に移す

Mrs. Hawes was in the kitchen, *decanting* buttermilk into a bottle.

関連語 decanter : pour [pɔːʳ]

decanter（栓付きのガラスびん）は pour（注ぐ）するための容器。

deceive
[disíːv]

v. **to trick or cheat; to make something untrue seem true**

[動] だます；思い違いをさせる

It is more shameful to mistrust one's friends than to be *deceived* by them.

関連語 deceive : charlatan [ʃáːʳlətn]

charlatan（ペテン師）は deceive するのが特徴。

decelerate
[diːsélərèit]

v. **to slow down or reduce speed**

[動] 〜の速度を落とす、減速する

When the police car appeared around the corner, Miss Bart *decelerated* quickly.

関連語 decelerate : brake [breik]

brake（ブレーキ）には decelerate する機能がある。

demagogue
[déməgàg]

n. **a speaker who appeals to the audience's passions or prejudices**

[名] 扇動者

Demagogues will always exist because people will always look to charismatic people who say what they want to hear.

類義語 demagogue : rabble-rouser [rǽbl-ràuzər]

demagogue の類義語は rabble-rouser（扇動者）

demolish
[dimáliʃ]

v. **to tear down or destroy**

[動] 〜を取り壊す、破壊する

The old residential district was *demolished* to make room for a stadium.

類義語 demolish : dismantle [dismǽntl]

demolish の類義語は dismantle（〜を分解する；解体する）

TRANSLATION | 例 文 の 訳

decant　　ハウズ夫人は台所でバターミルクを瓶に移していた。

deceive　　友人にだまされるよりも、その友人を疑うことのほうが恥ずべきことだ。

decelerate　警察車両が近くに現れると、バートさんはすぐに車を減速した。

demagogue　人は自分が聞きたいことを話してくれるカリスマ性のある人物を常に求めるので、扇動者はいなくならないだろう。

demolish　　その古い居住区はスタジアムの用地を確保するために取り壊された。

deprecate
[déprikèit]

v. **to belittle or express disapproval of**

[動] 軽視する、〜に不賛成を表明する

It is more useful to offer solutions than to just *deprecate* others' ideas.

関連語 self-deprecating : swagger [swǽgəʳ]

self-deprecating(自己を卑下した、控えめな)な人は swagger(いばって歩く、いばる)することがない。

depreciate
[deprí:ʃièit]

v. **to lower the value of; to belittle; to decrease in value or estimation**

[動] 〜の価値を下げる；〜を軽視する；減価償却する

Japan has *depreciated* the yen in hopes of spurring exports.

関連語 depreciation : value [vǽljuː]

depreciation(価値の下落)とは value(価値)の下落をいう。

deprivation
[dèprivéiʃən]

n. **the state of being in want or need; the state of being deprived; loss**

[名] 欠乏、窮乏；はく奪；損失

Food *deprivation* is a problem in many areas in Africa.

反意語 deprivation : surfeit [sɔ́ːʳfit]

deprivation の反意語は surfeit(過剰)

deracinate
[diːrǽsənèit]

v. **to uproot**

[動] 根こそぎにする

The new police chief worked tirelessly to *deracinate* the last vestiges of corruption in his department.

反意語 deracinate : plant [plǽnt]

deracinate の反意語は plant(植物を植える)

edible
[édəbl]

adj. **suitable to be eaten**

[形] 食べられる、食用に適する

Bob's cooking smells bad, but it is *edible*.

関連語 edible : meat [miːt]

meat(肉)は edible だ。

TRANSLATION | 例文の訳

deprecate 他人の考えにただ反対するよりも、解決策を提示するほうが役に立つ。
depreciate 日本は輸出を促進しようと円の価値を下げてきた。
deprivation 食糧の欠乏はアフリカの多くの地域が抱える問題だ。
deracinate 新しい警察署長は、組織内の腐敗を根絶しようと休みなく働いた。
edible ボブの料理の匂いはひどいが、食べられる。

397

elude
[ilú:d]

v. **to avoid or escape**   [動] 〜から逃れる、〜を避ける

The fugitive *eluded* the police by hiding in the swamp.

類義語 elude : evade [ivéid]
elude の類義語は evade (〜を避ける)

enclose
[inklóuz]

v. **to surround on all sides; to put inside**   [動] 〜を囲む；〜を同封する

The family dog was left *enclosed* in his cage while everyone was away.

関連語 enclose : envelope [énvəlòup]
envelope (封筒) には手紙を enclose する機能がある。

encomium
[enkóumiəm]

n. **enthusiastic praise; a formal expression of praise**   [名] 絶賛；賛辞

Pericles' funeral oration was an *encomium* that extolled the virtues of Athenian citizens.

類義語 encomium : eulogy [jú:lədʒi]
encomium の類義語は eulogy (賞賛の言葉、賛辞)

ephemeral
[ifémˀrəl]

adj. **lasting a very brief time**   [形] つかの間の、短命の

The cherry blossoms' *ephemeral* beauty lasts only a few days.

関連語 ephemeral : endure [ind(j)úəˀ]
ephemeral なことは endure (持続する) することがない。

expurgate
[ékspəˀgèit]

v. **to remove or cleanse of something unwanted or offensive**
[動] 不適切な箇所や場面を削除する

The youth group *expurgated* the vulgar graffiti from the walls.

関連語 expurgate : censor [sénsəˀ]
censor (検閲係) は expurgate する。

TRANSLATION | 例 文 の 訳

elude	その逃亡者は沼地に隠れて警察から逃れた。
enclose	その飼い犬は、家族全員が留守の間ケージに入れられたままだった。
encomium	ペリクレスの葬儀での演説は、アテネ市民の美徳をたたえる賛辞だった。
ephemeral	桜の花のはかない美しさは、ほんの数日しか続かない。
expurgate	若者のグループが壁の下品な落書きを消した。

impress
[imprés]

v. **to create a vivid image of; to affect strongly, often favorably**

[動] 印象を与える、感銘を与える；痛感させる

The teacher was *impressed* with the student's study habits.

関連語 impression : stickler [stíklər]
stickler (うるさい人) は人に impression (印象、感銘) を与えられない。

impromptu
[imprámpt(j)uː]

adj. **done on the spot without preparation**　　[形] 即興の

Impromptu skits are usually the most fun for both the audience and actors.

類義語 impromptu : improvisatorial [impràvəzətɔ́ːriəl]
impromptu の類義語は improvisatorial (即興的な)

imprudent
[imprúːdnt]

adj. **thoughtless or unwise; lacking discretion**　　[形] 軽率な、無分別な

Imprudent loans to develop countries resulted in defaults in the 1980's.

関連語 imprudent : discretion [diskréʃən]
imprudent な人には discretion (思慮分別、慎重さ) が欠けている。

impugn
[ìmpjúːn]

v. **to discredit through criticism**　　[動] 非難する

Becky *impugned* Stan's motives for enrolling in a woman's studies course.

反意語 impugn : vindicate [víndəkèit]
impugn の反意語は vindicate (~の正当さを立証する、容疑を晴らす)

insular
[ínsələr]

adj. **relating to an island; having a narrow viewpoint because of isolation**　　[形] 島の、狭量な

Joan's *insular* viewpoints come from being raised in a rural and homogenous area.

反意語 insular : cosmopolitan [kàzməpálətn]
insular の反意語は cosmopolitan (国際的な、国際的な視野を持った)

TRANSLATION | 例 文 の 訳

impress	教師はその生徒の学習の習慣に感銘を受けた。
impromptu	即興の寸劇は、たいていの観客と役者の両方が最も楽しめるものだ。
imprudent	国の開発のための無分別な融資が、1980年代の債務不履行をもたらした。
impugn	ベッキーは、女性学の授業を履修したスタンの動機を非難した。
insular	ジョアンの視野が狭いのは、田舎の多様性に欠ける地域で育ったせいだ。

intuition
[ìnt(j)uːíʃən]

n. **quick and ready insight; immediate apprehension or cognition**

[名] 直感；直感的知覚

Without enough information, Samuel chose to make a decision based on *intuition*.

関連語 intuition : reasonable [ríːzᵊnəbl]

intuition だけで決定を下す人は reasonable（道理をわきまえた、筋の通った）な人ではない。

lapse
[læps]

n. **a minor failure**

[名] ささいなミス

v. **to gradually fall from a previous standard**

[動] 徐々に弱まる

The judge ruled that the defendant merely had a *lapse* in judgement and did not require any disciplinary action.

The patient's heart condition *lapsed* until he finally passed away.

関連語 lapse : error [érəʳ]

lapse はささいな error（誤り）。

loquacious
[loukwéiʃəs]

adj. **wordy or prone to excessive talk**

[形] 多弁な、おしゃべりの

Fredrick was *loquacious* in large groups but seemed to always speak out of nervousness.

反意語 loquacious : taciturn [tǽsətəːʳn]

loquacious の反意語は taciturn（無口な、不愛想な）

moth
[mɔ(ː)θ]

n. **a lepidopterous insect that eats and destroys clothes and grains**

[名] ガ、虫食い

Mary's winter clothes had not been properly packed and were consequently full of *moth* holes.

反意語 moth-eaten : new and fresh [n(j)uː ən freʃ]

moth-eaten（虫に食われた、ぼろぼろの）の反意語は new and fresh（新しく新鮮な）

TRANSLATION ｜ 例 文 の 訳

intuition 十分な情報がないので、サミュエルは直感を基に決定することにした。

lapse 判事の裁定によると、被告人は単にささいな判断ミスを犯しただけであり、いかなる懲戒処分も必要ないという。

その患者の心臓の機能は徐々に弱まり、ついに彼は亡くなった。

loquacious フレデリックは大勢の中にいるとおしゃべりだったが、いつも緊張しながら話しているように見えた。

moth メアリーの冬服は適切に保管されていなかったので、結果的に虫食いの穴だらけになった。

| **mural**
[mjúᵊrəl] | n. a painting done on a wall | [名] 壁画 |

The three-story high *mural* in Manhattan was designed to advocate peace.

関連語 mural : wall [wɔ:l]
mural は wall (壁) に描く絵。

| **paradigmatic**
[pæ̀rədigmǽtik] | adj. relating to an example or pattern | [形] 模範的な、典型的な |

The police officer gave a *paradigmatic* talk about safety precautions.

関連語 paradigmatic : anomaly [ənáməli]
paradigmatic なものは anomaly (例外、変則) には縁がない。

| **paradox**
[pǽrədɑ̀ks] | n. an apparently self-contradictory statement opposed to common sense | [名] 矛盾、逆説、パラドックス |

The term bittersweet is a famous poetic *paradox*.

関連語 paradox : oxymoron [ɑ̀ksimɔ́:rɑn]
oxymoron (矛盾語法) は paradox な語法で構成された修辞学。

| **paragon**
[pǽrəgɑ̀n] | n. an example or model of excellence | [名] 模範、典型 |

Cynthia was a *paragon* of health having balanced diet, exercise, work, and rest.

関連語 paragon : imitate [ímətèit]
paragon を imitate (〜を見習う、手本にする) する。

| **paramount**
[pǽrəmàunt] | adj. supreme in rank or power; of chief concern | [形] 最高位の；最重要な |

Stopping terrorism is the *paramount* goal of world leaders this year.

反意語 paramount : ancillary [ǽnsəlèri]
paramount の反意語は ancillary (補助の、副次的な)

TRANSLATION | 例文の訳

mural マンハッタンにある建物3階分の壁画は、平和を訴えるためにデザインされた。
paradigmatic その警察官は安全上対策についての模範的な話をした。
paradox 「bittersweet (悲喜こもごも)」という言葉は有名な詩的パラドックスだ。
paragon 食事、運動、仕事、休息のバランスがとれているシンシアは、模範的な健康体の持ち主だった。
paramount テロを止めることが、今年の世界の指導者たちの最重要課題だ。

401

piquant
[píːkənt]

adj. **stimulating and pleasant to taste; spicy; provocative or intriguing**

[形] 味などがぴりっとする、食欲をそそる；辛い；興味をそそる、刺激的な

The chili served at the dinner was perfectly *piquant*.

反意語 piquant : insipid [insípid]

piquantの反意語はinsipid（味のない、気の抜けた）

rapt
[ræpt]

adj. **focused or wholly absorbed; carried away or enraptured**

[形] 夢中になっている；没頭している

The audience watched Evel Knievel with *rapt* attention as he attempted to jump the Grand Canyon.

反意語 rapt : distracted [distrǽktid]

raptの反意語はdistracted（注意が散漫な、取り乱した）

reprehensible
[règprihénsəbl]

adj. **worthy of blame or criticism**　　　　　　　　　[形] 非難すべき

Some do not consider stealing food for survival as *reprehensible*.

関連語 reprehensible : censure [sénʃər]

reprehensibleはcensure（非難）を受けて当然だという意味。

reprobate
[réprəbèit]

n. **a morally unprincipled person**　　　　　[名] ろくでなし、道楽者、放蕩者

adj. **condemned or damned as morally corrupt**

[形] 堕落した、節操のない

v. **to disapprove**　　　　　　　　　　　　　　　　　[動] 非難する

The *reprobate* couldn't find a sympathetic ear anywhere.

The criminal's *reprobate* actions caused him to be sentenced to 20 years in prison.

The priest *reprobated* the young children as they were caught spraying graffiti on the church walls.

関連語 reprobate : misbehave [mìsbihéiv]

reprobateはmisbehave（無作法にふるまう、行儀悪くする）する。

TRANSLATION | 例 文 の 訳

piquant　　　夕食で出されたチリは、文句なく食欲をそそるものだった。

rapt　　　　観衆は、イーベル・クニーベルがグランドキャニオンを飛び越えようとする様に釘付けになった。

reprehensible 生きるために食べ物を盗んでも非難すべきではない、と考える人もいる。

reprobate　　その堕落者は、自分の話に共感してくれる人などどこにも見つけられなかった。

犯人は自堕落な行為によって禁固20年の刑を言い渡された。

その牧師が叱ったのは、教会の壁にスプレーで落書きするところを見つかった小さな子供たちだった。

reprove
[riprú:v]

v. to scold or express disapproval of　　　　　　　　[動] 叱る、たしなめる

Little John's crying was *reproved* by his grandmother.

関連語 reprove : reprimand [réprəmænd]
reprimand（～を叱責する、懲戒する）は reprove よりも叱る程度が強い。

repugnance
[ripʌ́gnəns]

n. a strong dislike; something offensive or contradictory

[名] 嫌悪；矛盾

Bats are unjustly regarded with *repugnance* by people.

関連語 repugnant : repel [ripél]
repugnant（とても嫌な、嫌悪感を引き起こす）なものは repel（人を不快な気持ちにする）する特徴がある。

saint
[séint]

n. a person of great virtue and piety that becomes canonized

[名] 聖人のような人、聖人、聖者

Mother Teresa was considered a *saint* because of her tireless work with the poor.

反意語 saint : miscreant [mískriənt]
saint の反意語は miscreant（悪漢、悪者）

straightforward
[strèitfɔ́:ʳwəʳd]

adj. clear and direct; free from obscurity or vagueness

[形] わかりやすい、率直な；明快な

The homework assignment was pretty *straightforward*.

反意語 straightforward : circumlocutory [sə̀:ʳkəmlákjutɔ̀:i]
straightforward の反意語は circumlocutory（回りくどい）

supple
[sʌ́pl]

adj. easily bent; yielding or compliant　　　　　　[形] 柔軟な；素直な

The gymnast's legs were muscular but *supple*.

関連語 supple : rigidity [ridʒídəti]
supple なものには rigidity（堅いこと、剛性、硬直）が欠けている。

TRANSLATION | 例文の訳

reprove	幼いジョンは、泣いているところを祖母にたしなめられた。
repugnance	コウモリは人々に不当に嫌われている。
saint	マザー・テレサは、貧しい人々への飽くなき奉仕によって聖人と見なされた。
straightforward	その宿題はとてもわかりやすいものだった。
supple	その体操選手の脚は、筋肉質だが柔軟だった。

supplicant
[sʌ́plikənt]

n. one who asks humbly and earnestly   [名] 嘆願者

The *supplicant* knelt before the altar and asked God for help.

関連語 supplicant : beseeching [bisíːtʃiŋ]
supplicant とは beseeching (懇願するような) な人のことだ。

suppress
[səprés]

v. to use force to subdue or put down; to conceal or keep secret
[動] 〜を鎮圧する、抑圧する ; 〜を隠す

The authorities *suppressed* the rioters with tear gas and water hoses.

類義語 suppress : quell [kwel]
suppress の類義語は quell (〜を鎮圧する)

tirade
[táireid]

n. a long speech filled with criticism and usually vulgarity
[名] 激しい非難、下品な言葉を含む長演説

The terminated worker went on a *tirade* before marching out of the office.

関連語 tirade : critical [krítikəl]
tirade には critical (批判的な) な特徴がある。

veracious
[vəréiʃəs]

adj. truthful or accurate   [形] 本当の、正確な

The investigative committee's report, criticized as a cover up, was *veracious* and unbiased.

反意語 veracious : fallacious [fəléiʃəs]
veracious の反意語は fallacious (誤った、虚偽の)

TRANSLATION | 例 文 の 訳

supplicant	その嘆願者は祭壇の前にひざまずき、神に助けを求めた。
suppress	当局は催眠ガスと放水ホースで暴徒たちを鎮圧した。
tirade	その解雇された従業員は、長々と一席ぶってから、足早に職場を出て行った。
veracious	調査委員会の報告は、隠蔽だと批判されたものの、正確で公正なものだった。

■ Fill in the blanks with the correct letter that matches the word with its definition.

1. impromptu _____
2. rapt _____
3. depreciate _____
4. aerate _____
5. paradigmatic _____
6. circuitous _____
7. supplicant _____
8. encomium _____
9. acquiesce _____
10. dapper _____

a. energetic and lively praise
b. done on the spot without preparation
c. stylish and neat in appearance
d. one who asks humbly and earnestly
e. having a circular or roundabout course; speaking or acting in an indirect manner
f. to yield to or comply with unwillingly or passively
g. to supply with oxygen or air
h. focused or wholly absorbed; carried away or enraptured
i. to decrease in value or estimation; to belittle
j. relating to an exemplary or illustrating pattern

■ Put the correct word in each blank from the list of words below.

11. censor は_____する。
12. _____は cosmopolitan（国際的な、国際的な視野を持った）の反意語である。
13. envelope は手紙を_____する機能を持つ。
14. repugnant したものには_____する特徴がある。
15. _____は密かに結成された association の一種である。
16. _____な人は discretion を持っていない。
17. fallacious（誤った、虚偽の）の反意語は_____である。
18. embezzler（横領者）は_____する人である。
19. charlatan（ペテン師）は相手を_____する。
20. _____な人は deliberation（熟考、慎重さ）がない。

a. repel	b. expurgate	c. ephemeral	d. veracious	e. appropriate
f. depreciate	g. insular	h. deceive	i. imprudent	j. enclose
k. capricious	l. cabal			

Answer key

20. k	19. h	18. e	17. d	16. i	15. l	14. a	13. j	12. g	11. b
10. c	9. f	8. a	7. d	6. e	5. j	4. g	3. i	2. h	1. b

覚えた単語は酸素のように
取り込んで絶対に放しません。

29th DAY

---

adept
[ədépt]

adj. **highly skilled or experienced**　　　　[形] 熟達した、精通した

The new student is very *adept* at math.

反意語 adept : clumsy [klʌ́mzi]
adept の反意語は clumsy（ぎこちない、不器用な）

---

adore
[ədɔ́ːʳ]

v. **to worship as a deity; to regard with extreme fondness and loving admiration**　　[動] 〜を崇拝する；〜を熱愛する

Hindus *adore* the cow as a symbolic representative of the life-preserving aspect of their religion.

類義語 adore : revere [rivíər]
adore の類義語は revere（〜を崇敬する）

---

anodyne
[ǽnədàin]

n. **a drug that relieves or allays pain**　　　[名] 鎮痛剤

The doctor prescribed a powerful *anodyne* for her backpains.

関連語 anodyne : relieve [rilíːv]
anodyne には relieve（痛みなどを和らげる）する機能がある。

---

apposite
[ǽpəzit]

adj. **highly appropriate or relevant**　　　[形] 適切な

That evidence is very *apposite* to this case.

反意語 apposite : extraneous [ikstréiniəs]
apposite の反意語は extraneous（無関係な、外部からの）

TRANSLATION | 例 文 の 訳

adept	その新入生は数学に長けている。
adore	ヒンドゥー教の信者たちは、命を守るという宗教観を象徴として、牛を崇拝する。
anodyne	医師は彼女の腰痛のために強い鎮痛剤を処方した。
apposite	その証拠は、この事件に非常によく当てはまる。

21st
22nd
23rd
24th
25th
26th
27th
28th
29th
30th

approach
[əpróutʃ]

v. to come closer or nearer to; to approximate

[動] ～に近づく；～に達しようとする

As the hour of departure *approached*, the two lovers held each other closer.

関連語 approach : accost [əkɔ́(:)st]
accost（～に近寄って声をかける）は近づくだけでなく、積極的に approach して声をかけることをいう。

aware
[əwéəʳ]

adj. having knowledge or understanding of; alert to

[形] 知っている、わかっている、気づいている

A soldier must always be *aware* of his surroundings.

類義語 aware : cognizant [kágnəzᵊnt]
aware の類義語は cognizant（認識して、知って）

boor
[buəʳ]

n. a crude or insensitive person; a peasant

[名] 無礼者

My ex-husband is an unpleasant *boor*!

関連語 boor : sensitivity [sènsətívəti]
boor には sensitivity（感じやすさ、感受性）がない。

chaotic
[keiátik]

adj. lacking any order

[形] 混沌とした、無秩序の

The crowds at the World Cup games were *chaotic* and wild.

類義語 chaotic : disordered [disɔ́:ʳdəʳd]
chaotic の類義語は disordered（乱れた）

churlish
[tʃə́(:)ʳliʃ]

adj. rude or vulgar; lacking civil grace

[形] 無作法な、失礼な

It was *churlish* of Cheryl to refuse our dinner invitation.

反意語 churlish : genteel [dʒentí:l]
churlish の反意語は genteel（上品な）

TRANSLATION | 例 文 の 訳

approach 出発時刻が近づくと、2人の恋人たちは強く抱き合った。
aware 兵士は常に自分の周囲の状況をわかっていなければならない。
boor 私の前夫は不愉快な無礼者だった！
chaotic ワールドカップの観客は無秩序で荒れていた。
churlish シェリルは無礼にも、私たちの夕食への招待を断った。

coarse [kɔːrs]	adj. **rough or crude; of poor quality; lacking refinement or taste**
	[形] きめの粗い；粗悪な；粗野な、下品な
	Toby was a tough boy whose *coarse* mannerisms reflected his difficult life.
	反意語 coarse : refined [rifáind]
	coarse の反意語は refined（洗練された）

coerce [kouə́ːrs]	v. **to bring to act by force or threat** [動] 強要する
	The rebels *coerced* the villagers into hiding them from the army.
	類義語 coerce : extort [ikstɔ́ːrt]
	coerce の類義語は extort（取り立てる、せびる）

colander [kʌ́ləndər]	n. **a bowl with perforations used to drain liquids and rinse foods**
	[名] 調理用のざる
	Washing vegetables is much easier if you have a *colander*.
	関連語 colander : drain [drein]
	colander には drain（〜の水を抜く、〜の水気を切る）する機能がある。

compatible [kəmpǽtəbl]	adj. **capable of existing together harmoniously**
	[形] 共存できる、うまが合う；互換できる、両用の
	If you could only see them in their daily life, you would see how truly *compatible* they are.
	反意語 make compatible : polarize [póuləràiz]
	make compatible（互換性を持たせる）の反意語は polarize（〜を分裂させる、二極化させる）

complaisance [kəmpléisns]	n. **the disposition to comply** [名] 愛想のよさ、人のよさ
	Our new housekeeper came highly recommended and was lauded by her previous employers for her *complaisance* and efficiency.
	関連語 complaisance : intractable [intrǽctəbl]
	intractable（手に負えない、扱いにくい）な人には complaisance がない。

TRANSLATION | 例 文 の 訳

coarse	トビーは乱暴な少年で、粗野なふるまいが彼の問題の多い生活を反映していた。
coerce	反乱者たちが村人に、自分たちを軍からかくまうように強要した。
colander	ざるがあれば、野菜を洗うのがずっと楽になる。
compatible	日常生活を見るだけで、どんなに彼らのうまが合っているかがわかるだろう。
complaisance	うちの新しい家政婦は、前の雇用主たちから強く推薦され、人のよさと仕事の能率を賞賛されていた。

corporeal
[kɔːˈrpɔ́ːriəl]

adj. bodily; tangible or material　　　　　　　　　[形] 肉体の；有形の

The ghost was said to be a *corporeal* being, able to take on a physical form and interact with the living.

反意語 corporeal : intangible [intǽndʒəbl]
corporealの反意語はintangible（触れることができない、無形の）

correspond
[kɔ̀ːrəspánd]

v. to communicate by letters; to be in agreement or to match
[動] 〜と文通する；〜に一致する、調和する

I *correspond* with friends in London, Seoul, and Athens nearly everyday.

関連語 correspond : letters [létərz]
correspondはletters（手紙）をやり取りするという意味。

detract
[ditrǽkt]

v. to lower the importance, quality, or value of; to divert or take away from　　　　　[動]（価値・質・名声など）を落とす；〜を減ずる

The unfurnished basement *detracted* from the otherwise charming house.

類義語 detract : devalue [diːvǽljuː]
detractの類義語はdevalue（価値を減らす）

disperse
[dispə́ːrs]

v. to cause to break up or scatter; to scatter or dissipate
[動] 〜を分散させる；分散する

The crowd *dispersed* as the riot police made their way through the demonstration.

反意語 disperse : flock [flɑk]
disperseの反意語はflock（群がる、集まる）

dispirit
[dispírit]

v. to discourage morale or dishearten　[動] 〜の気力をくじく、〜を落胆させる

The team's first game loss *dispirited* their loyal fans.

関連語 dispirit : morale [mərǽl]
dispiritはmorale（士気、やる気）を損ねるという意味。

TRANSLATION | 例 文 の 訳

corporeal　幽霊は肉体を持ち、生者と交流することができる存在と言われていた。

correspond　私はほぼ毎日、ロンドン、ソウル、アテネにいる友人たちと連絡をとり合う。

detract　家具のない地下室が、それさえなければ魅力的なはずのその家の価値を落としていた。

disperse　機動隊がデモに分け入ると、群衆は散っていった。

dispirit　そのチームが初戦で敗退すると、彼らの忠実なファンたちは落胆した。

endow
[indáu]

v. to grant money to for the support of; to furnish with something freely and naturally　[動]～に基金を寄付する；～の才能を与える

The millionaire *endowed* the hospital with enough money to build a new wing.

関連語 endowment : patron [péitrən]
patron（後援者、パトロン）は endowment（寄付）をするスポンサーだ。

engrave
[ingréiv]

v. to impress deeply or form by incision on wood or metal; to carve figures, letters, or designs　[動]～に彫る、刻む

The lovers *engraved* their names into a tree trunk.

関連語 engrave : gouge [gaudʒ]
gouge（～を[丸のみで]掘る、穴を開ける）は engrave に比べて、丸く深く掘るという意味。

enormity
[inɔ́ːʳməti]

n. great wickedness　[名]残虐さ、深刻さ

Picasso captured the *enormity* of the Spanish Civil War in his painting, Guernica.

類義語 enormity : atrocity [ətrásəti]
enormity の類義語は atrocity（残虐行為、暴力行為）

entreat
[intríːt]

v. to ask for or request earnestly　[動]～を請う、懇願する

The peasant *entreated* the King to spare his life.

関連語 entreaty : command [kəmǽnd]
command（命令）は entreaty（懇願）に比べて強圧的な要求だ。

espouse
[ispáuz]

v. to marry; to advocate or support　[動]結婚する；～を支持する

Luis *espouses* Marxism and teaches it to his students.

反意語 espouse : abjure [æbdʒúəʳ]
espouse の反意語は abjure（主義や信条などを捨てる、放棄する）

TRANSLATION | 例 文 の 訳

endow	その億万長者は、新しい病棟を建てられるだけの資金をその病院に寄付した。
engrave	恋人たちは木の幹に自分たちの名前を彫った。
enormity	ピカソは、絵画『ゲルニカ』でスペイン市民戦争の残虐さを表現した。
entreat	農夫は王に命乞いをした。
espouse	ルイスはマルクス主義を支持し、学生に教えている。

estrange
[istréindʒ]

v. to arouse enmity in where there had been friendliness; to remove from an accustomed environment

[動] 〜を仲たがいさせる；離れる、疎遠になる

Constant quarreling over inheritance finally *estranged* the two brothers.

反意語 estrangement : rapprochement [ræprouʃmáːŋ]
estrangement（疎遠）の反意語は rapprochement（和解）

exorbitant
[igzɔ́ːʳbətˀnt]

adj. excessive or exceeding the appropriate limits

[形] 法外な、とんでもない

An *exorbitant* amount of money was paid to the actress for her latest movie.

関連語 exorbitant : moderation [màdəréiʃən]
exorbitant なものには moderation（節度、適度）が欠けている。

extricate
[ékstrəkèit]

v. to free from an entanglement　　　[動] 〜から解放する、救い出す

Kyle *extricated* himself from the situation by leaving the country.

関連語 extricate : snarl [snɑːʳl]
snarl（混乱、紛糾）から extricate する。

havoc
[hǽvək]

n. devastation or widespread destruction; disorder or chaos

[名] 大損害、大混乱

Even brief power outages can cause *havoc* in city life.

反意語 havoc : serenity [sərénəti]
havoc の反意語は serenity（平穏、平静）

hedonist
[híːdənist]

n. one that lives life by the doctrine that pleasure and happiness is the sole good　　　[名] 快楽主義者

It has always been a dream of mine to quit my day job and become a practicing *hedonist*.

反意語 hedonist : ascetic [əsétik]
hedonist の反意語は ascetic（禁欲主義者）

TRANSLATION | 例 文 の 訳

estrange	遺産を巡って絶え間なく言い争った末に、その 2 人の兄弟はとうとう疎遠になった。
exorbitant	最新映画のために、その女優に法外な額の金が支払われた。
extricate	カイルは出国することで、その状況から脱した。
havoc	短期間であっても、停電は都市生活に大混乱を引き起こす可能性がある。
hedonist	仕事を辞めて快楽主義者を実践することが、長年の私の夢の 1 つだった。

411

hypothesis
[haipάθəsis]

n. a testable but improvable theory　　　　[名] 仮説、仮定、推測

The scientist proposed his *hypothesis* before beginning experimentation.

関連語 hypothesis : confirm [kənfə́ːⁿm]
　　hypothesis を confirm(～を確認する)する。

ignominious
[ìgnəmíniəs]

adj. disgraceful or shameful　　　　[形] 不名誉な、恥ずべき

Despite the team's *ignominious* loss, the coach still praised their efforts.

反意語 ignominious : lofty [lɔ́ːfti]
　　ignominious の反意語は lofty(非常に高い、高尚な、尊大な)

incriminate
[inkrímənèit]

v. to suggest that someone is guilty; to bring an accusation against　　　　[動] ～に罪を負わせる；～を有罪にする

Mary *incriminated* the factory by claiming they hired undocumented workers.

反意語 incriminate : exonerate [igzάnərèit]
　　incriminate の反意語は exonerate(～の無実を証明する)

innovate
[ínəvèit]

v. to create or introduce as new; to do something in a new way　　　　[動] ～を刷新する、革新する

Consultants *innovate* procedures to help companies run more efficiently.

反意語 innovative : hidebound [háidbàund]
　　innovative(革新的な)の反意語は hidebound(狭量な、偏屈な)

lubricant
[lúːbrikənt]

n. a substance used to reduce friction or heat between two substances or surfaces　　　　[名] 潤滑油、潤滑剤

If the hinges of the door get squeaky, just apply some oil *lubricant*.

関連語 lubricant : abrasion [əbréiʒ°n]
　　lubricant は abrasion(摩耗)を防ぐ潤滑剤。

TRANSLATION | 例 文 の 訳

hypothesis	その科学者は実験を始める前に仮説を提示した。
ignominious	チームは不名誉な敗戦を喫したが、監督は彼らの努力を賞賛した。
incriminate	メアリーは、不法滞在者を雇用したと主張してその工場を告発した。
innovate	コンサルタント業務内容を改革し、企業がより効率的に運営できるようにする。
lubricant	ドアのちょうつがいがキーキーと音を立て始めたら、潤滑油を少し差せばいい。

monotonous
[mənátⁿəs]

adj. unchanging or tediously uniform; unvarying in tone

[形] 退屈な、単調な；一本調子の

The despised teacher spoke in such a *monotonous* tone as to put her students to sleep.

関連語 monotonous : drone [droun]

低く続くmonotonousな音のことをdrone（ブンブンという音、持続低音）と言う。

oracle
[ɔ́(:)rəkl]

n. one who divines the future

[名] 神官、預言者

In ancient civilizations, people would travel for days to consult the *oracle* about their futures.

関連語 oracle : prophecy [práfəsi]

oracleはprophecy（予言）を与えることができる人。

perplex
[pəᵣpléks]

v. to confuse; to make complicated

[動] ～を当惑させる、悩ませる

Her husband's odd behavior *perplexes* Betty at times.

類義語 perplex : nonplus [nɑnplʌ́s]

perplexの類義語はnonplus（～を当惑させる）

presage
[présidʒ]

v. to foretell or predict the future; to portend

[動] ～を予知する；～の前兆となる

People were amazed when they saw that what the man *presaged* actually came to pass.

関連語 presage : harbinger [háːᵣbindʒəᵣ]

harbinger（前触れ、前兆）はpresageする特徴がある。

propagate
[prápəgèit]

v. to publicize, spread, or disperse; to cause to breed or multiply

[動] ～を広める、普及させる；～を増やす、繁殖させる

Many companies *propagate* their products through television ads to maximize their target audience.

反意語 propagate : check [tʃek]

propagateの反意語はcheck（～を阻止する、抑制する）

TRANSLATION | 例 文 の 訳

monotonous　その教師が嫌われていたのは、話があまりにも一本調子で、生徒が眠ってしまうほどだったからだ。

oracle　古代文明の中で、人々は何日間も旅をして預言者に会い、自分たちの未来について助言を求めた。

perplex　ベティは、夫の奇妙な行動にときどき悩ませられる。

presage　人々は、その男が予告したことが実際に起きるのを見て驚いた。

propagate　多くの企業が自社製品を広めるために、テレビ広告を通じて訴求対象を最大化している。

propensity [prəpénsəti]	n. an intense inclination or tendency　　　　　　　[名] 傾向、性癖 Michael has a *propensity* to spend too much money on beer. 反意語 propensity to dislike : predilection [prìːdᵊlékʃən] 　　propensity to dislike（好みではない、嫌い）の反意語は predilection（好み、偏愛）
reap [riːp]	v. to harvest or obtain　　　　　　　[動] ～を収穫する、手に入れる Local farmers expect to *reap* a rich wheat harvest this year due to very favorable conditions. 関連語 reap : scythe [saið] 　　scythe（草刈り鎌、大鎌）は reap するときに使う大きな鎌。
reconcile [rékənsàil]	v. to harmonize or bring back together　　　[動] ～を調和させる、和解させる The couple *reconciled* their differences and got back together. 反意語 reconciliation : rift [rift] 　　reconciliation（和解、調和）の反意語は rift（亀裂、不和）。
regressive [rigrésiv]	adj. tending to move backward; decreasing in rate as the base decreases　　　　　　　[形] 後退する；（税率などが）逆累進の *Regressive* tax policies unjustly favor the rich. 反意語 regressive : forward [fɔ́ːʳwəʳd] 　　regressive の反意語は forward（前方への、前進の、将来の）
rejoice [ridʒɔ́is]	v. to give or feel great joy　　　　　　　[動] 大喜びする The world *rejoiced* at the end of the World War. 反意語 rejoice : deplore [diplɔ́ːʳ] 　　rejoice の反意語は deplore（嘆く）

TRANSLATION | 例 文 の 訳

propensity	マイケルはビールに金を使いすぎるたちだ。
reap	今年はとても天候がよかったので、地元の農家では小麦の豊作が期待されている。
reconcile	その夫婦は意見の違いをすり合わせ、よりを戻した。
regressive	逆累進課税は不当に金持ちに有利に働く。
rejoice	世界大戦が終わると、全世界が喜んだ。

renovate
[rénəvèit]

v. **to restore or revive to a more lively and better state**

[動] ～を修理する、改装する

Tom was contracted to *renovate* six houses in the downtown area.

類義語 renovate : renew [rin(j)úː]
renovateの類義語はrenew（～を更新する）

reproach
[ripróutʃ]

v. **to criticize or rebuke**　　　　　　　　　[動] 非難する、叱る

n. **disapproval or criticism**　　　　　　　[名] 非難、叱責

The superintendent *reproached* the teacher for her harsh comments during class.

He looked at her with *reproach* in his eyes, disappointed in her behavior.

関連語 reproach : upbraid [ʌpbréid]
upbraid（ひどく叱る、非難する）はreproachよりも非難の程度が強い。

resonant
[rézˀnənt]

adj. **having a rich and continuous sound; echoing**

[形] 鳴り響く；共鳴する

The singer has a *resonant* voice that fills the concert hall.

反意語 resonant : muffled [mʌ́fld]
resonantの反意語はmuffled（はっきり聞こえない）

respire
[rispáiəʳ]

v. **to breathe**　　　　　　　　　　　　　　[動] 呼吸する

It is refreshing to *respire* in the clean mountain air.

関連語 respiration : lung [lʌŋ]
lung（肺）にはrespiration（呼吸）の機能がある。

TRANSLATION | 例 文 の 訳

renovate　トムは、町の中心部にある6軒の家を改装する契約を取った。

reproach　教育長は、授業中の厳しい発言について、その教員を叱責した。
　　　　　　　彼は、彼女の行動に失望して、非難する目で彼女を見た。

resonant　その歌手は、ホール全体に響き渡る声の持ち主だ。

respire　きれいな山の空気を吸うと爽快だ。

slur
[sləːʳ]

v. to speak unclearly or obscurely: to cast unkind remarks on

[動] 〜を不明瞭に発音する；〜を中傷する

n. a slurred utterance; an insulting remark　[名] 不明瞭な発音；中傷、侮辱

The men *slurred* insults at each other.

The lecturer was difficult to understand because he spoke with a *slur*.

関連語 slur : speech [spiːtʃ]
　slurは不明瞭なspeech（話すこと、発言、スピーチ）をいう。

stern
[stə́ːʳn]

adj. harsh in manner; unsmiling or having a harsh or gloomy appearance　[形] 厳格な、厳しい；（表情が）いかめしい、怖い

There was a *stern* expression on Jeff's face when he came home from work that day.

類義語 stern : austere [ɔːstíəʳ]
　sternの類義語はaustere（厳しい、厳格な、質素な）

sturdy
[stə́ːʳdi]

adj. having rugged physical strength; firmly built

[形] 屈強な、たくましい；頑丈な、丈夫な

Mountain climbers require *sturdy* shoes to carry them through rough terrain.

反意語 sturdy : decrepit [dikrépit]
　sturdyの反意語はdecrepit（老朽化した、よぼよぼの）

subordinate
[səbɔ́ːʳdənət]

adj. lower in rank or importance　[形] 下位の、副次的な、補助的な

Top-ranking five-star generals are nevertheless *subordinate* to a civilian president.

反意語 subordinate : principal [prínsəpəl]
　subordinateの反意語はprincipal（主要な、最も重要な）

TRANSLATION | 例 文 の 訳

slur　その男たちは互いを中傷した。
　その講師は発音が不明瞭だったので、話がわかりにくかった。

stern　その日、仕事を終えて帰宅したジェフの顔には、厳しい表情が浮かんでいた。

sturdy　登山者に丈夫な靴が必要なのは、険しい土地を歩き抜けるためだ。

subordinate　最高位の5つ星を与えられた軍司令官でも、文民の大統領より下位の立場にいる。

surreptitious
[sə̀:rəptíʃəs]

adj. **doing something secretly or by stealth**　　[形] 内密の、こそこそした

The run-away slave made a *surreptitious* escape through the South.

反意語 surreptitious : barefaced [bɛ́əˈfèist]
surreptitiousの反意語はbarefaced（ずうずうしい、しらじらしい））

tenable
[ténəbl]

adj. **capable of being defended or supported against assault; based on sound reasoning**

[形] 攻撃に耐えられる；批判に耐えられる、弁護できる

The Themistoclean Wall of Athens was not *tenable* for long and the city fell to the invaders.

反意語 tenable : indefensible [ìndifénsəbl]
tenableの反意語はindefensible（防御できない、弁護の余地がない）
反意語 tenable : unjustifiable [ʌndʒʌ́stəfàiəbl]
tenableの反意語はunjustifiable（弁解できない、正当化できない）

tenacious
[tənéiʃəs]

adj. **persistent in adhering to something**

[形] 固執する、不屈の、断固とした

The *tenacious* girl stubbornly clung to her version of the truth.

関連語 tenacious : yield [ji:ld]
tenaciousな人はyield（譲る、明け渡す）することがない。

tend
[tend]

v. **to be disposed or inclined; to care for or watch over**

[動] 〜する傾向がある；〜を世話する、〜の番をする

The shepherd *tended* his sheep which were scattered about the hillside.

関連語 tend : fuss [fʌs]
fuss（やきもきする）はtendに比べて、過度に世話や心配をするという意味がある。

torpid
[tɔ́:ˈpid]

adj. **deprived of the power of motion or feeling**　[形] 不活発な、無気力な

Jess is just getting over a cold and is a bit *torpid*.

反意語 torpid : ebullient [ibʌ́ljənt]
torpidの反意語はebullient（元気や感情があふれる、元気のいい）

TRANSLATION | 例 文 の 訳

surreptitious　その奴隷は、こっそりと南部を抜けて逃げた。

tenable　アテネのテミストクレスの壁は、長く攻撃に耐えられず、町は侵略者たちの手に落ちた。

tenacious　その頑固な少女は、自分が考える真実に強く固執した。

tend　その羊飼いは、丘の中腹に散らばるヒツジたちの番をした。

torpid　ジェスは、まだ風邪が治りかけなので、あまり元気がない。

unanimity
[jùːnəníməti]

n. the state of complete agreement or unity　　　　　[名] 満場一致

The committee, for once, was in *unanimity*.

反意語 unanimity : schism [sízm]
unanimity の反意語は schism（分裂、分離）

upbraid
[ʌpbréid]

v. to scold or criticize severely　　　　　[動] ひどく叱る、非難する

Upbraided and punished, the children walked sullenly to their rooms.

関連語 upbraid : reproach [ripróutʃ]
upbraid は reproach（非難する）よりも非難の度合いが強い。

venal
[víːnl]

adj. capable of being purchased; corrupt　　　　　[形] 買収できる、腐敗した

One *venal* official does not corrupt an entire government.

関連語 venal : probity [próubəti]
venal な人には probity（正直、誠実）が欠けている。

TRANSLATION | 例 文 の 訳

unanimity	その委員会は、今度ばかりは満場一致でまとまった。
upbraid	ひどく叱られ、罰を受けて、子供たちはすねたまま自分の部屋に歩いて行った。
venal	1人の腐った職員が、政府全体を腐敗させるわけではない。

■ Fill in the blanks with the correct letter that matches the word with its definition.

1. espouse _____
2. sturdy _____
3. monotonous _____
4. complaisance _____
5. propagate _____
6. subordinate _____
7. chaotic _____
8. endow _____
9. coerce _____
10. venal _____

a. unchanging or tediously uniform; unvarying in tone
b. to publicize or transmit; to continue or increase through reproduction
c. the disposition to comply
d. lower in rank or importance
e. to bring to act by force or threat
f. to grant money to for the support of; to furnish with something freely and naturally
g. capable of being purchased; corrupt
h. to marry; to advocate or support
i. lacking any order
j. having rugged physical strength; firmly built

■ Put the correct word in each blank from the list of words below.

11. command は_____と比較して強圧的である。

12. _____なものには moderation が欠けている。

13. _____は不明瞭な speech のことである。

14. extraneous（無関係な）の反意語は_____である。

15. barefaced（ずうずうしい、しらじらしい）の反意語は_____である。

16. gouge は_____に比べて深く掘るという意味である。

17. cognizant（認識して、知って）の類義語は_____である。

18. _____は schism（分裂、分離）の反意語である。

19. revere（～を崇拝する）の類義語は_____である。

20. rift（亀裂、不和）は_____の反意語である。

a.reconciliation	b. aware	c. slur	d. exorbitant	e. apposite
f. surreptitious	g. entreaty	h. compatible	i. perplex	j. engrave
k. adore	l. unanimity			

Answer key

11. g　12. d　13. c　14. e　15. f　16. j　17. b　18. l　19. k　20. a
1. h　2. j　3. a　4. c　5. b　6. d　7. i　8. f　9. e　10. g

419

ついに最終日まで
たどり着きましたね。もう一息です。

30th DAY

---

awl
[ɔ:l]

n. **a pointed tool used to make or put holes in leather or wood**

[名] 千枚通し

The craftsman packed his *awl* with the rest of his equipment.

関連語 awl : pierce [piəʳs]
awl には pierce (〜を突き通す、貫通する) する機能がある。

---

baneful
[béinfəl]

adj. **destructive or harmful**

[形] 災いをもたらす、致命的な、有害な

Racism is a *baneful* ill that is perpetuated by the fear of the unfamiliar.

反意語 baneful : salubrious [səlú:briəs]
baneful の反意語は salubrious (健康によい、快適な)

---

benevolence
[bənévələns]

n. **an act of kindness or generosity**

[名] 善行；善意

The charitable organization praised the *benevolence* of the individual who made a large donation.

反意語 benevolent : malicious [məlíʃəs]
benevolent (慈悲深い、善意の) の反意語は malicious (悪意のある、意地の悪い)

---

bonhomie
[bànəmí:]

n. **well-natured friendliness**

[名] 愛想がいいこと

The police officer was loved by the town for his continuous *bonhomie*.

関連語 bonhomie : amicable [ǽmikəbl]
bonhomie と似た意味の形容詞に amicable (友好的な、平和的な) がある。

TRANSLATION | 例 文 の 訳

awl その職人は、残りの道具といっしょに千枚通しをかばんに詰めた。

baneful 人種差別は、見慣れぬものに対する恐怖心によって生まれる永続的な害悪だ。

benevolence その慈善団体は、多額の寄付をした人物の善行を賞賛した。

bonhomie その警察官はいつも愛想がよく、町の人たちに愛された。

cargo
[káːʳgou]

n. goods in large quantities that are transported via airplane, boat, or truck
[名] 貨物、積み荷

The *cargo* ships that depart the port every morning are always on time.

関連語 cargo : manifest [mǽnəfèst]
「明らかな」という意味の形容詞manifestにはcargoの「積み荷リスト」という意味もある。

caricature
[kǽrikətʃəʳ]

n. an exaggerated representation that distorts features in a comical way
[名] 風刺画、漫画

We had our *caricatures* drawn at the county fair.

関連語 caricature : distortion [distɔ́ːʳʃən]
caricatureはdistortion（ゆがみ、ねじれ、歪曲）を入れて描かれる絵。

coax
[kouks]

v. to patiently persuade through flattery or gentle urging
[動] 〜をなだめすかす、説得する

Kelly tried hard to *coax* her boyfriend into attending the play.

関連語 coax : blandishment [blǽndiʃmənt]
人をcoaxするためにblandishment（追従、甘言）を使う。

defy
[difái]

v. to openly refuse or confront with resistance; to dare or challenge
[動] 〜を無視する、〜に背く；〜に挑む、挑戦する

You deliberately *defied* me and now you will pay the consequences!

反意語 defy : obey [oubéi]
defyの反意語はobey（〜に従う）

deride
[diráid]

v. to ridicule
[動] 〜をあざ笑う、嘲笑する

The teacher *derided* the student's essay, calling it poorly researched and poorly written.

関連語 deride : mockery [mákəri]
derideと似た意味の名詞にmockery（あざけり、からかい）がある。

TRANSLATION | 例 文 の 訳

cargo	貨物船は毎朝必ず時間通りに出港する。
caricature	私たちは郡の祭りで自分たちの似顔絵を描いてもらった。
coax	ケリーはボーイフレンドを劇に参加させようと、懸命になだめすかした。
defy	あなたはわざと私に背いたのだから、今度はその対価を支払ってもらうぞ！
deride	先生は、この生徒の作文を「調べ方が悪い」「文章が下手だ」と嘲笑した。

derivative
[dirívətiv]

adj. taken or obtained from another; unoriginal

[形] 独創性のない、模倣した

The carmaker's latest design was criticized for being *derivative* and unoriginal.

反意語 derivative : precursory [priːkə́ːʳsəri]
derivative の反意語は precursory（先駆の、前兆の）

elevate
[éləvèit]

v. to raise or lift up

[動] ～を持ち上げる、上げる

Michael *elevated* my spirits this morning by calling to say hello.

反意語 elevation : debasement [dibéismənt]
elevation（上昇）の反意語は debasement（低下、堕落）

epicure
[épikjùəʳ]

n. one who takes great pleasure in sensual activities, such as eating and drinking

[名] 美食家

Though he writes for the weekend food page, Jamieson does not consider himself an *epicure*.

関連語 epicure : discriminating [diskrímənèitiŋ]
epicure は食べ物の微妙な味の違いについて普通の人よりも discriminating（識別力のある）だ。

evade
[ivéid]

v. to escape or avoid through stratagem, especially responsibilities, obligations, or questions

[動]（責任・義務・質問などを）回避する、はぐらかす

The governor *evaded* answering the question by changing the subject.

関連語 evade : answer [ǽnsəʳ]
evade は answer（答えること）を回避するという意味。

evict
[ivíkt]

v. to legally force someone out of a property

[動] ～を合法的に立ち退かせる、退去させる

Lori was *evicted* for not paying her rent on time.

関連語 evict : tenant [ténənt]
evict は tenant（賃貸人）を法的手続きを経て立ち退かせるということ。

TRANSLATION | 例 文 の 訳

derivative	その自動車メーカーの最新の意匠は、二番煎じで独創性がないと批判された。
elevate	マイケルは今朝、私にご機嫌うかがいの電話をかけてきて、元気づけてくれた。
epicure	ジェイミーソンは週末の食の記事を書いているが、自分を美食家だとは思っていない。
evade	知事は話題をそらし、その質問への回答をはぐらかした。
evict	ローリが立ち退かされたのは、期日どおりに家賃を払わなかったからだ。

flavor
[fléivər]

n. a distinct taste; a characteristic or quality　　　[名] 風味、味；特徴、質

The *flavor* of the pudding was quite similar to vanilla.

関連語 flavor : gustation [gʌstéiʃən]
gustation（味覚）は flavor を識別する感覚。

garish
[gǽriʃ]

adj. offensively or excessively flashy and showy
[形] けばけばしい、どぎつい、派手な

I couldn't believe the *garish* dress that woman was wearing at the dance!

関連語 garish : colorful [kʌ́lərfəl]
garish は不快なほど colorful（色とりどりの）であることを表す。

halcyon
[hǽlsiən]

adj. peaceful; prosperous　　　[形] 穏やかな；繁栄した

Nostalgia distorts people's memories with false recollections of *halcyon* years past.

反意語 halcyon : tempestuous [tempéstʃuəs]
halcyon の反意語は tempestuous（騒々しい、動乱の）

heed
[hi:d]

v. to give attention to or consider　　　[動] 〜に注意を払う

Smokers don't *heed* the health warnings on cigarette packages.

類義語 heed : hearken [háːrkən]
heed の類義語は hearken（〜に耳を傾ける）

heresy
[hérəsi]

n. a belief, opinion, or doctrine that goes against the church's belief or dogma
[名]（宗教上の）異端、異論

In colonial America, people were burned at the stake for *heresy* and witchery.

反意語 heresy : orthodoxy [ɔ́ːrθədàksi]
heresy の反意語は orthodoxy（通説、定説）

TRANSLATION | 例 文 の 訳

flavor	そのプリンの風味はバニラにとてもよく似ていた。
garish	あの女性がダンスパーティーで着ていたけばけばしいドレスが信じられなかった！
halcyon	ノスタルジーは、過ぎ去った古き良き時代の偽りの思い出によって、人々の記憶を歪めてしまう。
heed	喫煙者は、たばこのパッケージに書かれている健康への警告に注意を払わない。
heresy	植民地時代のアメリカでは、宗教異端者や妖術使いが火あぶりの刑に処せられた。

heretic
[hérətik]

n. one who commits heresy; one who dissents from church dogma

[名] 異教徒、異端者

The *heretics* of the 16th century were executed publicly.

関連語 heretic : unconformity [ʌ̀nkənfɔːˈrməti]
heretic の主張は定説とは unconformity（不整合）を有する。

illustrate
[íləstrèit]

v. to demonstrate or clarify with examples; to provide with pictures

[動]（図表や実例で）説明する；～に挿絵を入れる

The author hired an artist to *illustrate* the cover of his book.

関連語 illustrate : picture [píktʃər]
illustrate とは本や文章と picture（絵、写真）をいっしょに提示すること。

ingrain
[íngrèin]

adj. natural; deep seated

[形] 生まれつきの；根付いている

v. to impress or fix deeply into one's mind or nature

[動]～を（人や心に）植え付ける、浸透させる

Elephants use *ingrain* senses to migrate from one feeding ground to the next.

The importance of education was *ingrained* in me since childhood.

反意語 ingrained : extrinsic [ikstrínsik]
ingrained（深くしみ込んだ、根深い）の反意語は extrinsic（外部からの、外来性の）

ingratiate
[ingréiʃièit]

v. to gain respect or acceptance deliberately with good deeds

[動]～に取り入る、機嫌を取る

To show he was not trying to *ingratiate* himself with Vronsky, Sven promptly added some slightly critical remarks.

反意語 ingratiate : discomfit [diskʌ́mfit]
ingratiate の反意語は discomfit（～をまごつかせる、当惑させる）

TRANSLATION | 例 文 の 訳

heretic	16世紀の異教徒は公然と処刑された。
illustrate	その作家は、自分の本の表紙のために挿し絵画家を雇った。
ingrain	ゾウは生来の感覚を使って、1つの餌場から次の餌場へと移動する。
	教育の重要性は、子供の頃から私の中に植え付けられていた。
ingratiate	自分がブロンスキーに取り入るつもりがないことを示そうと、スベンは急いで少し批判的な言葉を付け加えた。

iridescent
[ìrədésnt]

adj. **giving off different colors in varying lights and angles**

[形] 虹色の、玉虫色の

The *iridescent* material of her dress caught everyone's eyes.

反意語 iridescent : monochromatic [màn³kroumǽtik]

iridescent の反意語は monochromatic（単色の、モノクロの）

irrepressible
[ìriprésəbl]

adj. **impossible to control, restrain, or hold down**

[形] 抑えられない、こらえられない

Sometimes Pat gets the *irrepressible* urge to buy new clothes, and nothing will stop him until he does.

関連語 irrepressible : quell [kwel]

irrepressible なものは quell（〜を鎮圧する、抑える）することができない。

irritate
[írətèit]

v. **to annoy or make angry; to inflame**

[動] 〜をいらいらさせる、怒らせる；〜に炎症を起こさせる

Tom *irritated* his injury by constantly scratching the injured area.

関連語 irritation : balm [bɑːm]

balm（鎮痛剤）は irritation（興奮、炎症）を抑える。

juggernaut
[dʒʌ́gəʳnɔːt]

n. **an unstoppable force that crushes everything in its path**

[名] 巨大な破壊力、不可抗力

The tornadoes of North America are *juggernauts* that destroy hundreds of homes each year.

関連語 juggernaut : unstoppable [ʌnstápəbl]

juggernaut は unstoppable（止められない、抑制できない）だ。

landmark
[lǽndmàːʳk]

n. **an important turning point in history; a prominent object that acts as a guide**

[名] 画期的な出来事、事件；目印となるもの

The biggest *landmark* in the small town was the local church.

関連語 landmark : conspicuous [kənspíkjuəs]

landmark は conspicuous（人目を引く、目立つ）だ。

TRANSLATION | 例 文 の 訳

iridescent	彼女のドレスの玉虫色の生地が、全員の目を引いた。
irrepressible	パットはときどき新しい洋服を買いたい衝動を抑えきれなくなり、どうしようもなくなって買ってしまう。
irritate	トムは患部を常に引っかいていたので、傷が炎症を起こしてしまった。
juggernaut	北米の竜巻は、毎年数百戸の住宅を破壊するほどの巨大な力を持っている。
landmark	その小さな町の最大の目印は、地元の教会だった。

logic
[ládʒik]

n. the science of the principles of reasoning; valid explanation or rationalization　　　　　　　　　　　　　　　　　[名] 論理学；論理

The judges' decisions were sound in *logic* and in law.

関連語 logic : fallacy [fǽləsi]
　　　fallacy（誤った考え、誤った推論）には logic が欠けている。

lug
[lʌg]

v. to carry or pull with extreme effort　　　　[動] 〜を力いっぱい運ぶ、引く

Sally *lugged* her baggage all the way from the airport to downtown, 20 miles away.

関連語 lug : carry [kǽri]
　　　lug は荷物を引っ張って carry（運ぶ、運搬する）するということ。

lurk
[ləːʳk]

v. to lie in wait　　　　　　　　　　　　　　[動] 潜む、待ち伏せする

Young children often believe that monsters *lurk* under their beds.

関連語 lurk : wait [weit]
　　　こっそり待つという意味の lurk は wait（〜を待つ）の一種。

meander
[miǽndəʳ]

v. to wander aimlessly and idly　　　　　　　　[動] あてもなくさまよう

Silvia often spent her afternoons *meandering* through the forest lost in deep thought.

反意語 meander : proceed purposefully [prəsíːd pə́ːʳpəsfuli]
　　　meander の反意語は proceed purposefully（目的を持って進む）

moribund
[mɔ́(ː)rəbʌnd]

adj. being in the final stages of death　　[形] 死にかけている、消滅しかかった

The *moribund* patient asked for his family to stay at his bedside.

反意語 moribund : resurgent [riːsə́ːʳdʒənt]
　　　moribund の反意語は resurgent（蘇る、再起する）

TRANSLATION | 例 文 の 訳

logic	その判事の裁定は、論理的にも法的にも適切だった。
lug	サリーは空港から20マイル離れた中心街まで、はるばる自分の荷物を引っ張っていった。
lurk	幼い子供は、たいてい自分のベッドの下に怪物が潜んでいると信じている。
meander	シルビアは午後によく、物思いにふけりながら森の中を歩き回ることがあった。
moribund	その患者は死にぎわに、家族にそばにいてくれと頼んだ。

parity
[pǽrəti]

n. the quality of being on an equal level in status, value, or amount　　　　　[名] (地位・価値・量などの) 同格、同等、等価

The earnings of women and men are not yet on *parity*, even for equal work.

関連語 parity : equivalent [ikwívələnt]
parityと似た意味の形容詞に equivalent (同等の、同価値の) がある。

parlance
[páːˈləns]

n. a particular manner of speaking　　　　　[名] (ある集団が用いる特有の) 語法、用語、言葉遣い

Legal *parlance* intimidates and deters lay people from carefully reading their contracts.

関連語 parlance : speak [spiːk]
speak (話す) ことを言及する時、parlance (語調、話し方) という単語を使う。

perfidious
[pəˈfídiəs]

adj. faithless or disloyal; having treacherous characteristics　　　　　[形] 不誠実な、不実な；裏切りの

The *perfidious* knight was executed by the king for treason.

関連語 perfidious : loyalty [lɔ́iəlti]
perfidiousな人には loyalty (忠誠、忠実) が欠けている。

perfunctory
[pəˈfʌ́ŋktˀri]

adj. done quickly as a matter of routine; mechanical; lacking enthusiasm or interest　　　　　[形] おざなりの、表面的な、熱意のない

Jack viewed his job as just a *perfunctory* part of his day, preferring to focus his attention on evening outings.

関連語 perfunctory : inspiration [ìnspəréiʃən]
inspiration (霊感、インスピレーション) のない人は、いつも perfunctoryな仕事の処理を行う。

peripatetic
[pèrəpətétik]

adj. moving or traveling around; itinerant　　　　　[形] 歩き回る、旅行して回る；移動する

I lead a *peripatetic* life, jumping from country to country.

反意語 peripatetic : sedentary [sédntèri]
peripateticの反意語は sedentary (移住しない、定住性の)

TRANSLATION | 例 文 の 訳

parity	女性と男性の賃金は、たとえ仕事が同じでも、いまだに同等ではない。
parlance	法律用語のせいで、素人はおじけづいて、契約書を丁寧に読もうとしない。
perfidious	その不誠実な騎士は、反逆罪で王に処刑された。
perfunctory	ジャックは、仕事を単に一日のどうでもいい一部分と見なし、晩に外出することにばかり気が向いていた。
peripatetic	私は、国から国へと飛び回る生活をしている。

peripheral [pərífərəl]	adj. constituting an outer boundary; not of central importance [形] 周辺部にある；核心から離れた、あまり重要でない The driver's impaired *peripheral* vision led to his accident. 反意語 periphery : core [kɔːʳ] periphery（周辺、周囲）の反意語は core（中心、中核）
perjure [pə́ːʳdʒəʳ]	v. to lie deliberately under oath　　　　　　　　　　　[動] 偽証する The mother of the accused *perjured* herself in order to save her son's life. 反意語 perjure : depose [dipóuz] perjure の反意語は depose（～を [宣誓供述書などにより] 証言する）
profundity [prəfʌ́ndəti]	n. wisdom that is profound and obscure　　　　　[名] 深遠な思想、知恵 The *profundities* that he heard as a young boy were now beginning to make sense to him as an adult. 関連語 profundity : glib [glib] glib（口の達者な、ぺらぺらしゃべる）な人には profundity がない。
pry [prai]	v. to impertinently inquire into another's life; to move or lift with a lever　　　　　[動]（他人の生活を）詮索する；～をてこで動かす、上げる Jason was always careful not to *pry* into people's personal lives. 関連語 prying : inquisitive [inkwízətiv] prying（詮索好きな）には、inquisitive（好奇心が強い）よりも必要以上に話題に入り込む、という意味がある。

TRANSLATION | 例 文 の 訳

peripheral	その運転手は、視力が欠けていたために事故に遭った。
perjure	被告人の母親は、息子の命を救おうと法廷で偽証した。
profundity	子供の頃に聞いた深い知恵が、今大人になった彼に意味を持ち始めていた。
pry	ジェイソンは、他人の個人的な生活を詮索しないようにいつも気をつけていた。

purlieu
[pə́ːʳl(j)uː]

n. a district lying on the bounds or outskirts; a frequently visited place　[名] 近隣、周辺；行きつけの場所

After work John and his friends usually get a few drinks at a *purlieu* close to work.

反意語 purlieu : infrequent place [infríːkwənt pleis]
purlieu の反意語は infrequent place（めったに行かない場所）

purloin
[pəʳlɔ́in]

v. to steal; to take by theft　[動] ～を盗む；盗んで手に入れる

The accountant *purloined* from the petty cash box at work.

関連語 purloin : appropriate [əpróuprièit]
purloin は appropriate（～を横領する、着服する）の一種。

redundant
[ridʌ́ndənt]

adj. excessive or superfluous; unnecessarily wordy or repetitive　[形] 余分な、過剰な；冗長な、繰り返しの

Lay-offs were imminent as the merger had made many positions *redundant*.

関連語 redundant : reiterate [riːítərèit]
reiterate（～を何度も繰り返していう）すると redundant なものが含まれる。

refute
[rifjúːt]

v. to prove wrong; to deny and question the accuracy of　[動] ～の誤りを証明する；～を論破する

The president of the company *refuted* the allegations of bribery upon him.

反意語 refute : affirm [əfə́ːrm]
refute の反意語は affirm（～だと断言する、確認する）

scribble
[skríbl]

v. to write quickly and carelessly, usually illegibly　[動] ～を殴り書きする

The note left on the table was *scribbled* and she couldn't read it.

関連語 scribble : write [rait]
scribble は write（～を書く）の一種。

TRANSLATION | 例 文 の 訳

purlieu	仕事の後、ジョンは友人たちと、たいてい職場近くの行きつけの店で酒を2、3杯飲む。
purloin	その会計士は、職場の小さな現金入れからお金を盗んだ。
redundant	合併によって多くの職務が余り、人員解雇が急務となっている。
refute	社長は自分に向けられた贈賄疑惑が誤りであることを立証した。
scribble	テーブルの上に残されたメモは殴り書きされていて、彼女には読めなかった。

scrutinize
[skrúːt^ənàiz]

v. to examine or look closely and carefully

[動] 〜を綿密に調べる、吟味する

Eddie *scrutinized* the phone bill that was much more expensive than he expected.

関連語 scrutinize : observe [əbzə́ːʳv]

scrutinizeはより詳細にobserve（〜を観察する）するということ。

sentient
[sénʃənt]

adj. able to perceive through sense; conscious

[形] 知覚できる、感覚を持った

The robot was designed to be a *sentient* being, with the ability to learn and make decisions on its own.

反意語 sentient : unconscious [ʌnkʌ́nʃəs]

sentientの反意語はunconscious（意識を失った、無意識の）

sprightly
[spráitli]

adj. spirited or having a gay lightness

[形] 活発な、陽気な

The *sprightly* old grandmother pranced around the house.

関連語 sprightly : cavort [kəvɔ́ːʳt]

cavort（浮かれ騒ぐ）することはsprightlyだという特徴がある。

striate
[stráieit]

v. to mark with striae or striations

[動] 筋をつける、縞模様をつける

The barber pole is *striated* and universally recognized.

関連語 striated : groove [gruːv]

striated（筋、縞、溝のある）なものにはgroove（溝）がついている。

stridency
[stráidnsi]

n. the quality of being loud, harsh, and grating

[名] 耳障り、かん高いこと

The *stridency* of an emergency alerts nearby individuals to heed the urgent situation.

関連語 stridency : sound [saund]

stridencyは耳障りなsound（音）のこと。

TRANSLATION | 例 文 の 訳

scrutinize	エディは電話料金の請求書を綿密に調べた。予想よりもはるかに高額だったからだ。
sentient	このロボットは、自分で学習し、判断する能力を持った、感覚のある存在として設計されていた。
sprightly	陽気で年老いた祖母は、家の周りを意気揚々と歩き回った。
striate	理髪店の看板柱は縞模様で、世界的に認識されている。
stridency	緊急警報の耳障りな音は、周辺住民に緊急事態に備えるように警告する。

surfeit
[sə́ːˈfit]

n. an excessive amount; overindulgence in food or drink

[名] 過剰；食べ過ぎ、飲み過ぎ

After the feast, the men who consumed a *surfeit* of food couldn't move for hours.

反意語 surfeit : deprivation [dèprivéiʃən]

surfeitの反意語はdeprivation（欠乏、窮乏）

thrive
[θraiv]

v. to flourish or grow vigorously; to prosper in success or wealth

[動] 健康に育つ；繁栄する

It is a common trait of athletes to *thrive* on pressure and competition.

反意語 thriving : flagging [flǽgiŋ]

thriving（繁栄する、繁盛する）の反意語はflagging（落ち目の、衰えつつある）

trivial
[tríviəl]

adj. unimportant or ordinary

[形] ささいな、ありふれた

One must not concern himself too much with *trivial* matters.

反意語 trivial : substantial [səbstǽnʃəl]

trivialの反意語はsubstantial（相当な、十分な）

turgid
[tə́ːˈdʒid]

adj. swollen or bloated; excessively embellished

[形] 腫れた、膨れた；大げさな、仰々しい

The *turgid* whale carcass could not be removed from the beach.

反意語 turgid : deflated [difléit]

turgidの反意語はdeflated（しぼんだ）

unruly
[ʌnrúːli]

adj. not disciplined or obedient; wild or uncontrolled

[形] 言うことを聞かない、規則に従わない；手に負えない

The *unruly* children ignored the teacher's commands.

類義語 unruly : obstreperous [əbstrépʰrəs]

unrulyの類義語はobstreperous（騒がしい、手に負えない）

TRANSLATION | 例 文 の 訳

surfeit	ごちそうを平らげたあと、食べ過ぎた男たちは何時間も動けなかった。
thrive	プレッシャーと競争を生きがいとするのがスポーツ選手に共通する特性だ。
trivial	ささいなことを過度に心配すべきではない。
turgid	膨張したクジラの死骸を海岸から動かすことはできなかった。
unruly	その子供たちは聞き分けがなく、教師の命令を無視した。

upright
[ʌ́pràit]

adj. **standing up or in a vertical position**　　　［形］直立した、まっすぐに立った

The doll sat *upright* on the nightstand.

反意語 upright : prostrate [prάstreit]
upright の反意語は prostrate（横たわった、寝そべった）

variable
[vέ^əriəbl]

adj. **varying or changing; inconstant**　　　［形］変わりやすい；定まらない

The *variable* weather is rather unpredictable this time of year.

反意語 variable : immutable [imjúːtəbl]
variable の反意語は immutable（不変の）

verify
[vérəfài]

v. **to establish the truth or accuracy of**
［動］〜が正しいことを確認する、証明する

The man's testimony was *verified* by independent witnesses who were also at the scene of the accident.

関連語 verify : accuracy [ǽkjurəsi]
verify はあるものの accuracy（正確さ）を立証するということ。

TRANSLATION | 例 文 の 訳

upright	その人形は、ベッドのサイドテーブルの上に背筋を伸ばして座っていた。
variable	一年のこの時期、天気が変わりやすく、なかなか予測がつかない。
verify	その男性の証言が正しいことが、同じく事故現場にいた別の証人たちによって証明された。

432

■ Fill in the blanks with the correct letter that matches the word with its definition.

1. parlance _____

2. sprightly _____

3. ingratiate _____

4. purloin _____

5. coax _____

6. irritate _____

7. evict _____

8. turgid _____

9. peripatetic _____

10. heresy _____

a. moving or traveling around; itinerant

b. to steal; to take by theft

c. to annoy or make angry; to inflame

d. a belief, opinion, or doctrine that goes against the church's belief or dogma

e. a particular manner of speaking

f. to legally force someone out of a property

g. swollen or bloated; excessively embellished

h. spirited or having a gay lightness

i. to patiently persuade through flattery or gentle urging

j. to gain respect or acceptance deliberately with good deeds

■ Put the correct word in each blank from the list of words below.

11. debasement（低下）は_____の反意語である。

12. _____は、引きずりながら carry するという意味だ。

13. _____は食べ物の微妙な味の違いについて普通の人よりも discriminating だ。

14. deprivation（欠乏、窮乏）の反意語は_____である。

15. _____な人は loyalty を持っていない。

16. mockery の意味を持つ動詞は_____である。

17. resurgent（蘇る、再起する）の反意語は_____である。

18. precursory（先駆の）の反意語は_____である。

19. landmark には_____という特性がある。

20. _____は色が不快になるほど過度に colorful であるという意味である。

a. derivative	b. conspicuous	c. elevation	d. moribund	e. pry	f. epicure
g. surfeit	h. lug	i. deride	j. perfidious	k. garish	l. trivial

Answer key

11. c 12. h 13. f 14. g 15. j 16. i 17. d 18. a 19. b 20. k

1. e 2. h 3. j 4. b 5. i 6. c 7. f 8. g 9. a 10. d

433

Answer Page 436

Questions

across

3. cheerful or happy; floatable
7. having a strong desire or yearning
9. bright; radiant in character
10. to give a conciliatory gift or bribe; to take up liquid by absorbing it
12. a legally authorized delay of payment; a suspension of something
13. to patiently persuade through flattery or gentle urging
15. the use of an excessive quantity of words to express something
17. witty or clever retort
18. to weaken or thin by adding a liquid
19. a humorous poem of around five lines
20. flawless; incapable of sinning or doing wrong

down

1. a surrender or compliance
2. not identified or of unknown authorship
4. impulsive; marked by violent force of action or manner
5. with minimal energy or excitement; listless
6. debased; marked by a vulgarity or by disrespecting something sacred
8. to infer without evidence
11. feeling regret or sadness for having done wrong or caused harm 14. to accelerate or rush a process
14. to accelerate or rash a process
16. to contaminate with a disease or sickness; to corrupt

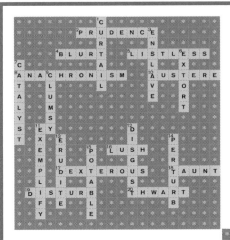

1st Day ～ 10th Day

page 146

11th Day ～ 20th Day

page 290

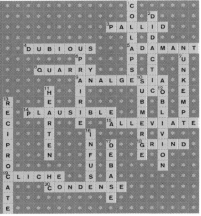

21st Day ～ 30th Day

page 434

Super Vocabulary
Words Pack

abeyance [əbéiəns] ［名］(一時的な) 中止
n. a state in which something is not being operated, momentarily halted

abnegate [ǽbnigèit] ［動］断つ、拒絶する
v. to refuse or reject; to deny

abrogate [ǽbrəgèit] ［動］なくす、廃止する
v. to get rid of or abolish

absolve [æbzálv] ［動］罪を許す
v. to free or pardon of guilt or obligation

acclaim [əkléim] ［動］喝采する
v. to passionately honor someone or something

acclimate [ǽkləmèit] ［動］慣らす、順応させる
v. to adapt to or get used to a new environment or circumstance

accommodate [əkámədèit] ［動］便宜をはかる
v. to have room for; to hold comfortably without crowding

accord [əkɔ́ːrd] ［動］一致する ［名］合意
v. to have no conflict; to be in an agreement
n. an arrangement between two parties where a common understanding is made

address [ədrés] ［動］演説する ［ǽdres］［名］住所
v. to talk to a person or group of people
n. a location for a certain area or a speech given by a person

adumbration [ædʌ́mbreiʃən] ［名］概略を示すこと
n. a partial and guarded disclosure

adversary [ǽdvəˈrsèri] ［名］敵
n. an opponent that one competes with

agenda [ədʒéndə] ［名］議事日程
n. a certain schedule or list of things that someone uses as a guide

aggressive [əgrésiv] ［形］攻撃的な、精力的な
adj. offensive or hostile; bold and energetic

alacritous [əlǽkrətəs] ［形］快活な、熱心な
adj. cheerful and eager

alchemy [ǽlkəmi] ［名］錬金術
n. a false science of chemistry that sought to convert base metals into gold

allege [əlédʒ] ［動］断言する
v. to verbally claim that something has occurred without any proof

alliterate [əlítərèit] ［動］頭韻を踏む
v. to speak or write using the same sound at the beginning of each word

allude [əlúːd] ［動］それとなく言う
v. to speak or imply to something not by direct means

anaerobe [ǽnəròub]［名］無気性生物
n. an organism capable of living without oxygen

anarchist [ǽnəˈkist]［名］無政府主義者
n. a person who believes in, desires, and tries to obtain a society or state without government

anemic [əníːmik]［形］無気力な、元気のない
adj. having little or no vitality or energy

anvil [ǽnvəl]［名］金床、アンビル
n. a heavy iron block used to hammer and shape metals

apophasis [əpάfəsis]［名］陽否陰述（何も言及しないことでそれとなく暗示する語法）
n. the act of referring to something by denying that it will be mentioned

apparel [əpǽrəl]［名］衣服
n. clothing; attire

apprehension [æ̀prihénʃən]［名］懸念、理解、逮捕
n. a sense of panic that something unfortunate will occur; understanding; arrest

assume [əs(j)úːm]［動］仮定する、推定する、責任を負う
v. to conceive that something is truthful; to take on certain responsibilities

astound [əstáund]［動］驚愕させる
v. to surprise or astonish someone

astringent [əstríndʒənt]［名］収斂剤
n. a liquid substance used to close openings, usually to stop blood loss or other bodily fluids

asymmetrical [èisəmétrikəl]［形］非対称の、バランスの取れない
adj. having two sides of a certain object that are not the same; unbalanced

athletics [æθlétiks]［名］運動競技
n. a type of exercise or sport which involves physical activity

attach [ətǽtʃ]［動］付ける
v. to join or associate objects together

avulse [əvʌ́ls]［動］引き裂く
v. to tear apart forcibly

awning [ɔ́ːniŋ]［名］日よけ
n. a type of material used as a cover from rain or sun, erected over a door or window

B

backdrop [bǽkdrὰp]［名］背景
n. the setting; the background

badinage [bæ̀dənάːʒ]［動］からかう　［名］からかい、軽い冗談
v. to verbally taunt someone in a carefree way
n. a playful conversation that involves making fun of one another; banter

ballot [bǽlət] [名]候補者名簿がある投票用紙、候補者名簿
n. a ticket or piece of paper listing the candidates to be voted on during an election

band [bænd] [動]束ねる [名]帯、ベルト、群れ
v. to connect or assemble into a group
n. any type of material that is used to bind an object or hold multiple objects together; a group

banquet [bǽŋkwit] [名]ごちそう
n. an elaborate formal dinner for special occasions

baseboard [béisbɔ̀ːʳd] [名](壁下の) 幅木
n. a border between the wall and the floor found along side the base of the wall

baseness [béisnis] [名]嫌悪感、卑劣さ、下品さ
n. the quality of being vile, disgusting and contemptible

bedeck [bidék] [動]派手に飾る、飾り立てる
v. to adorn or decorate

befuddle [bifʌ́dl] [動]混乱に陥れる
v. to confuse, perplex, or stupefy

benediction [bènədíkʃ°n] [名]祝福、感謝の祈り
n. a blessing; the invocation of a blessing

betray [bitréi] [動]裏切る
v. to break one's trust or promise; to be unfaithful or unloyal

biased [báiəst] [形]偏見を抱いた、偏った
adj. having a preference that impairs impartial judgement

bliss [blis] [名]無上の喜び、至福
n. state of ecstasy or extreme happiness

blizzard [blízəʳd] [名]猛吹雪
n. a heavy snow storm with high winds

blooming [blúːmiŋ] [形]若々しい、栄えている
adj. thriving with youth or health; flourishing

blunder [blʌ́ndəʳ] [名]大失敗、重大なミス
n. a serious error or mistake caused by stupidity or carelessness

boggle [bágl] [動](驚いて) ギョッとする
v. to be overwhelmed with fright or amazement

border [bɔ́ːʳdəʳ] [動]～に接する [名]境界(線)
v. to be along the edges or next to something
n. a boundary or a part that forms the exterior of something

bottleneck [bátlnèk] [動](～の進行を) 妨げる [名]狭い通路、交通渋滞の所
v. to slow down or impede by obstructing
n. a narrow or obstructed passage way

branch [bræntʃ] [名]枝、部門
n. a part or division of a larger whole

bravado [brəváːdou] [名] 虚勢、空威張り
n. a false show of courage

bravura [brəv(j)úʰrə] [名] 華麗な表現 [様式]
n. brilliance in performance style or technique

breezeway [bríːzwèi] [名] (二つの構造物を連結する) 屋根付きの通路
n. a passage way with a roof and no sides that connects two structures

bruit [bruːt] [動] 広める、言いふらす
v. to spread rumors or news

budge [bʌdʒ] [動] ちょっと動く、身動きする
v. to move or push slightly

bungle [bʌ́ŋgl] [動] へまをする、しくじる
v. to botch or manage ineffectively

C

cadge [kædʒ] [動] (人にものを) ねだる、たかる
v. to receive through begging

calcify [kǽlsəfài] [動] 石灰化する
v. to become or transform into a hard stony object through the disposition of calcium salts forming lime

camaraderie [kæ̀mərǽdəri] [名] 友情
n. a sense of trust and closeness that is shared among friends

cameo [kǽmiòu] [名] スターのゲスト出演、カメオ細工
n. a minor role played by a prominent actor in a single scene of a movie; a type of jewelry

capture [kǽptʃəʰ] [動] 捕らえる [名] 捕虜、捕虜にすること
v. to catch or arrest
n. someone that has been caught, or the act of catching someone

cartographer [kɑːʰtágrəfəʰ] [名] 地図製作者
n. someone whose profession is drawing maps

cautious [kɔ́ːʃəs] [形] 用心深い、慎重な
adj. careful, guarded, and wary

centrifuge [séntrəfjùːdʒ] [名] 遠心分離機
n. a machine that uses centrifugal force to separate materials of different densities

charge [tʃɑːʰdʒ] [動] 告発する、(罪を人に) 負わせる
v. to accuse or blame someone of wrongdoing

chisel [tʃízl] [名] 彫刻刀
n. a tool used in sculpting wood or stone

chromatic [kroumǽtik] [形] 色彩の
adj. relating to colors

chronological [krɑ̀nəládʒikəl] ［形］年代順の
adj. portrayed in the same time order as they occurred

circular [sə́ːʳkjələʳ] ［形］円の、円形の、循環の
adj. shaped like a circle

clarion [klǽriən] ［名］クラリオン（昔の吹奏楽器）
n. a medieval brass wind instrument that makes a very high pitched sound

clinch [klintʃ] ［動］しっかり固定させる
v. to hold or grip tightly

cloture [klóutʃəʳ] ［名］討論終結
n. a procedure for closing a discussion and taking a vote in parliament

coeval [kouíːvəl] ［形］同時代［年代］の
adj. existing at the same age or during the same time period

commitment [kəmítmənt] ［名］義務、誓約
n. loyalty to a cause or obligation; a pledge to do something in the future

comply [kəmplái] ［動］応じる、従う
v. to conform to or obey regulations or commands

concatenate [kɑnkǽtᵊnèit] ［動］（～を）鎖状につなぐ
v. to link or connect in a series

conclude [kənklúːd] ［動］結論を出す
v. to reach a decision through facts given as support

concrete [kɑ́nkriːt] ［形］具体的な、明確な ［名］コンクリート
adj. being clear and specific
n. a construction material consisting of a mixture of sand, small stones, cement, and water

condign [kəndáin] ［形］適当な、当然の
adj. appropriate and fitting

condolence [kəndóuləns] ［名］お悔やみ、哀悼の言葉
n. an expression of sympathy for someone's grief, pain, or sorrow

confine [kənfáin] ［動］限定する
v. to restrict something to a limited space

connect [kənékt] ［動］連結する、つなぐ、接続する
v. to join or attach objects together

connoisseur [kɑ̀nəsə́ːʳ] ［名］鑑定家、目きき、くろうと
n. someone who enjoys and is knowledgeable about a particualr subject matter; a person of discriminating taste

constant [kɑ́nstənt] ［名］不変のもの、定数 ［形］不変の、一定な
n. something that never changes; a number or a value in mathematics that is always the same
adj. continuing to occur or happen for a long time

constrain [kənstréin] ［動］拘束する
v. to hold tightly and confine

contain [kəntéin] ［動］含む、包含する
v. to include something inside or as a part

continence [kántənəns] ［名］抑制、自制、節制
n. self restraint and moderation

continuance [kəntínjuəns] ［名］継続、連続
n. condition of permanence or uninterrupted action

contrast [kántræst] ［名］対照、対比
n. the difference between two things when you compare them to one another

converge [kənvə́ːʳdʒ] ［動］集中する、収束する
v. to concentrate on; to meet at a certain place or point

conversant [kənvə́ːʳsᵊnt] ［形］精通した、様々なテーマについて通じている
adj. knowledgeable and able to talk about various subjects

conversion [kənvə́ːʳʒən] ［名］転換
n. the development or procedure of changing something into a different condition or shape

convey [kənvéi] ［動］運ぶ、［意思を］伝達する
v. to deliver to another; to produce data or ideas to be acknowledged or perceived by another

cornucopia [kɔ̀ːʳn(j)ukóupiə] ［名］豊富
n. an abundance, richness, or variety

corrode [kəróud] ［動］腐食する
v. to slowly destroy through some sort of chemical reaction such as rust

coterie [kóutəri] ［名］仲間、同人、グループ
n. a small, select circle of people

countenance [káuntᵊnəns] ［名］表情、支持　［動］容認する、賛同する
n. someone's appearance, usually their facial expressions; encouragement or support
v. to allow or approve of something

counter [káuntəʳ] ［名］（銀行・商店などの）カウンター　［形］反対の、逆の
n. a table or another long flat surface where the undertaking of money, business or food takes place
adj. having to do with reversals or opposing certain acts

courage [kə́ːridʒ] ［名］勇気、度胸
n. a characteristic where one performs dangerous or difficult duties in spite of being afraid

course [kɔːʳs] ［名］進路、方向
n. a route or path that someone or something can follow

courtroom [kɔ́ːʳtrù(ː)m] ［名］法廷
n. a room where a legal preceding takes place

cozen [kʌzn] ［動］だまし取る、だましてさせる
v. to deceive or cheat in a small way

crass [kræs] ［形］卑しい、低俗な
adj. inelegant and vulgar

creek [kri:k] ［名］小川
n. a smaller version of a river or stream

crescendo [kriʃéndou] ［名］(音や声が) だんだん大きくなること
n. a noise that gradually becomes louder

crockery [krάkəri] ［名］瀬戸物、陶磁器類
n. plates and dishes made of clay for eating and serving food

crouch [krautʃ] ［動］かがむ、しゃがむ
v. to stoop with knees bent

crumb [krʌm] ［名］パンくず
n. a very small portion or piece of bread that has fallen off

cunning [kʌ́niŋ] ［形］ずる賢い
adj. having the talent to accomplish things usually through tricks and deception

curate [k(j)uˤrət] ［名］副牧師、助任司祭
n. a clergyman who is an aide to the priest

D

dawdle [dɔ́:dl] ［動］(時間を) 無駄に過ごす
v. to waste time while going somewhere or doing something

decibel [désəbèl] ［名］デシベル (音響測定単位)
n. the unit for measuring sound

declamation [dèkləméiʃən] ［名］雄弁
n. a firm and emphatic statement or speech

deflect [diflékt] ［動］そらす
v. to make something or someone deviate off its original course

demand [dimǽnd] ［動］要求する
v. to strongly ask for something

demotic [dimάtik] ［形］民衆の、庶民の
adj. common or popular; relating to the common people

demystify [di:místəfài] ［動］(〜の) 神秘さを解く
v. to take away the mystery from; to make clear

denial [dináiəl] ［名］否定、拒絶
n. refusal to accept reality or truth

denunciation [dinʌ̀nsiéiʃən] ［名］公然の非難
n. the act of publicly censuring

dependence [dipéndəns] ［名］依存、信頼、従属状態
n. the need for something or on someone in order to sustain oneself

deportation [dìːpɔːˈtéiʃən] ［名］国外追放
n. the expulsion or banishment of a person from a country

descendant [diséndənt] ［名］子孫
n. biological offspring of a given ancestor or ancestors

descent [disént] ［名］降下、下落
n. the act of descending or passing downward

despise [dispáiz] ［動］軽蔑する、嫌う
v. to hate or loathe

detainment [ditéinmənt] ［名］留置
n. a condition where someone or something is forcibly confined in a particular place or area

detrimental [dètrəméntl] ［形］有害な
adj. having a damaging or destructive effect

devote [divóut] ［動］献身する
v. to spend much time and energy on something or someone

diction [díkʃən] ［名］言葉遣い、語法、話し方
n. the manner in which something is expressed in words

diligence [dílədʒəns] ［名］勤勉、精励
n. a steady effort on a given task

diocese [dáiəsis] ［名］司教 [主教] 区
n. the area which a bishop takes controls

dirge [dəːˈdʒ] ［名］葬送歌、哀歌
n. a slow sad song that is usually sung at a funeral

disagreeable [dìsəgríːəbl] ［形］不愉快な、嫌な
adj. being unpleasant

disarm [disáːˈm] ［動］武装を解除する
v. to deprive of weapons or other means of hostility; to render harmless or defenseless

discrepancy [diskrépənsi] ［名］事実や主張の食い違い、不一致
n. difference or divergence in facts or claims

disengage [dìsengéidʒ] ［動］解放する、解く
v. to release something from connection or attachment; to discontinue

disjoint [disdʒɔ́int] ［動］(～の) 関節をはずす、解体する
v. to disconnect; to destroy the logical or chronological coherence of

dismiss [dismís] ［動］解散させる
v. to send away or force someone to leave a job

disquiet [diskwáiət] ［名］心配、不安
n. lack of peace or rest; anxiety or restlessness

dissect [disékt] ［動］解剖する
v. to cut open and examine a body for scientific purposes

doctrine [dáktrin] ［名］信条、教義
n. a series of principles or beliefs

doleful [dóulfəl] ［形］悲しげな、陰うつな
adj. filled with sorrow and grief

dolorous [dálərəs] ［形］悲しそうな、痛ましい
adj. showing sadness, grief, or pain

donor [dóunəʳ] ［名］寄贈者、贈与者
n. one who gives money or goods to fund

downplay [dáunplèi] ［動］軽視する、見くびる
v. to make something seem less significant

doze [douz] ［動］うたた寝をする
v. to sleep lightly, for a short period of time

drill [dril] ［名］ドリル、錐、反復練習
n. a pointed tool for making holes; a way of training through repetition

dutiful [d(j)ú:tifəl] ［形］従順な、本分を守る
adj. willingly obedient to superiors out of a sense of duty

E

eaglet [í:glit] ［名］ワシの子
n. a baby eagle

ebullience [ibʌ́ljəns] ［名］(あふれんばかりの) 熱狂、情熱
n. overflowing exuberance

ecologist [i:kálədʒist] ［名］生態学者、環境保護活動家
n. a person who is studying ecology

eddy [édi] ［名］渦 (巻き) 、反主流
n. a whirlpool of air or water against the main current

effrontery [efrʌ́ntəri] ［名］図々しさ
n. a behavior that is thought of as rude or impolite

egalitarian [igæ̀lətéʳriən] ［形］平等主義の
adj. characterized by the belief that all peple should be equal in political, economic, social, and civil rights

elegiac [èlidʒáiək] ［形］哀歌 (調) の、哀愁を帯びた
adj. expressing sorrow over past events

elicit [ilísit] ［動］引き出す
v. to do or say something to get a response or reaction

elitism [ilíːtizm] ［名］エリート主義、エリート意識
n. a belief that certain people deserve favor on the basis of their perceived superiority

emaciate [iméiʃièit] ［動］ひどく痩せる、やつれさせる
v. to become thin or physically weak

embroider [embrɔ́idəʳ] ［動］刺繍する
v. to stitch a design and put it on clothes or other types of fabrics

energize [énəʳdʒàiz] ［動］活力を吹き込む
v. to fill with energy

ensue [ensúː] ［動］後から続いて起こる
v. to occur immediately after another event

entrancing [entrǽnsiŋ] ［形］うっとりさせる、魅惑的な
adj. charming and delightful enough to cause wonderment

entry [éntri] ［名］入り口、入場
n. a way into a place; admittance

equity [ékwəti] ［名］公平、公正
n. the quality or state of being fair and just

evacuate [ivǽkjuèit] ［動］明け渡す、避難させる
v. to vacate a place or area; to send people out of a dangerous place

exceptional [iksépʃənl] ［形］例外的な、格別の
adj. having qualities that are unusually rare and special

excessive [iksésiv] ［形］過度の
adj. greater than is reasonable or necessary

excitable [iksáitəbl] ［形］興奮しやすい
adj. becoming easily anxious or nervous

exclaim [ikskléim] ［動］大声で急に叫ぶ
v. to express loudly and suddenly

excrete [ikskríːt] ［動］排せつする
v. to discharge from the body

execrable [éksikrəbl] ［形］嫌悪すべき、忌まわしい
adj. deserving of curses and damnation

exhilarate [igzílərèit] ［動］愉快にする
v. to make happy or joyful; to enliven or animate

explicate [ékspləkèit] ［動］詳細に説明する
v. to explain clearly

exquisite [ekskwízit] ［形］立派な、非常に美しい、精巧な
adj. characterized by excellence, beauty, and intricacy

exude [igzúːd] ［動］発散させる
v. to discharge or emit

factorable [fǽktərəbl] ［形］因数分解できる
adj. capable of determining the factors of

factual [fǽktʃuəl] ［形］事実の
adj. being true or authentic

fascinating [fǽsənèitiŋ] ［形］魅力的な、とても面白い
adj. alluring and very interesting

faultfinder [fɔ́:ltfàindəʳ] ［名］あら捜しをする人、やかまし屋
n. one who scolds and criticizes

feign [fein] ［動］（〜を）装う
v. to pretend or deceive

felicitous [filísətəs] ［形］巧みな、適切な
adj. clever or very skillful

fictional [fíkʃənl] ［形］作り事の、虚構の
adj. having to do with things created through the imagination

finicky [fíniki] ［形］好みがうるさい、気難しい
adj. being hard to please

firm [fəːʳm] ［形］堅い、堅固な　［名］会社、商会
adj. having a solid shape
n. an organization that markets or produces products or supplies assistance for which people pay

flare [flɛəʳ] ［動］（火が）明るく燃え上がる
v. to burn or blaze brightly

flatten [flǽtn] ［動］平らにする
v. to make something level or flat; to knock down completely

flint [flint] ［名］火打ち石
n. a piece of quartz which sparks when struck with steel

flip [flip] ［動］さっと裏返す
v. to turn over quickly

florid [flɔ́(:)rid] ［形］赤みのある、血色の良い
adj. having a ruddy complexion

foil [fɔil] ［名］金属の薄片、箔
n. a thin sheet of metal

folly [fáli] ［名］愚行
n. a way of thinking, acting, or behavior that is considered foolish

formality [fɔːʳmǽləti] ［名］形式的な行為
n. a formal action that must be done as part of an official process or a social situation

formidable [fɔ́:rmidəbl] ［形］恐るべき、手ごわい
adj. fearsome or intimidating; inspiring awe or wonder

forsake [fə˞séik] [動] 見捨てる、見放す
v. to abandon or desert

fracture [frǽktʃə˞] [動] 折れる
v. to cause a slight crack or break

fret [fret] [動] いらだつ、悩む
v. to be irritated, vexed, or agitated

friction [fríkʃən] [名] 摩擦、あつれき
n. a force that makes it difficult for things to slide or move against something else

frieze [friːz] [名] フリーズ、帯状の装飾
n. decoration high upon the walls of a room; consisting of a long strip of paper or panel of carving

G

gangly [gǽŋgli] [形] ひょろっとした
adj. tall and lanky with long limbs

garment [gáː˞mənt] [名] 衣服
n. clothing

gasification [gæ̀səfikéiʃən] [名] ガス化、気化
n. the process or act of converting into a gaseous form

gaudy [gɔ́ːdi] [形] 派手で俗っぽい
adj. showy and tacky

gauge [geidʒ] [名] 計量器、計量基準、尺度
n. an instrument that measures and shows the amount of something; a standard dimension, quantity, or capacity

glisten [glísn] [動] 輝く
v. to be shiny

glitch [glitʃ] [名] (機械・計画などの) 欠陥、故障
n. a small error or malfunction

glutton [glʌ́tn] [名] 大食家
n. one who consumes large amounts of food and drink

goad [goud] [動] 追い立てる [名] 突き棒
v. to urge or provoke someone
n. something that makes someone do something

grain [grein] [名] 穀物、粒子、一粒
n. the seeds from cereal crops; the arrangement or a small piece of a substance

grandstand [grǽndstæ̀nd] [動] スタンドプレーをする
v. to show off or act ostentatiously in order to impress

grate [greit] ［動］すりつぶす、きしらせる、イライラさせる
v. to shred into smaller pieces or rub against something and make an annoying sound; to irritate

gravel [grǽvəl] ［名］砂利
n. a collect of very small stones

hack [hæk] ［動］(乱雑に)たたき切る
v. to cut or chop roughly and irregularly

halt [hɔ:lt] ［動］停止する
v. to stop

hapless [hǽplis] ［形］同情に値する、不運な
adj. deserving pity; miserable and unfortunate

heroic [hiróuik] ［形］とても勇敢な、堂々とした
adj. extremely brave and courageous

herpetologist [hə̀:ˈpətálədʒist] ［名］爬虫類学者
n. someone who studies reptiles and amphibians

hieroglyph [hái^ərəglìf] ［名］象形文字
n. ancient writings that consist of pictorial symbols in the form of pictures

hoax [houks] ［名］(人を)だますこと
n. a type of trick

homogeneous [hòumədʒí:niəs] ［形］同種の
adj. having parts of a group that are the same

horn [hɔ:ˈn] ［名］角、ホルン(楽器)、クラクション
n. a type of bone that sticks out from the head of an animal; a musical instrument consisting of a tube; the object in a vehicle that makes a loud warning sound

hypnotic [hipnátik] ［形］催眠(術)の、催眠状態の
adj. tending to cause sleep; having the effect of causing a state of unconsciousness

idolatrize [aidálətràiz] ［動］偶像崇拝する
v. to worship idols

immobilize [imóubəlàiz] ［動］(〜を) 動かなくさせる
v. to stop someone or something from moving

immure [imjúəˈ] ［動］閉じ込める
v. to confine or imprison

450

impalpable [impǽlpəbl] ［形］手でさわっても感じられない、無形の
adj. unable to perceive through the sense of touch

imposter [impástər] ［名］詐欺師
n. someone who is pretending to be someone else in order to trick people

imprecise [ìmprisáis] ［形］不正確な、曖昧な
adj. unclear or inexact

improper [imprápər] ［形］不適切な
adj. being dishonest or doing things that are illegal

impure [impjúər] ［形］汚い、混ざりもののある
adj. having bad qualities, or being contaminated

inadequate [inǽdikwət] ［形］不適切な、不十分な
adj. being incapable of doing something; insufficient

inanimate [inǽnəmət] ［形］活気のない、生命のない
adj. having no vitality; not alive

inclination [ìnklənéiʃən] ［名］傾向、気質、性向
n. an impression or sensation that makes someone want to do a particular thing

indistinct [ìndistíŋkt] ［形］不明瞭な、ぼんやりとした
adj. being unclear or difficult to see or recognize

infer [infə́ːr] ［動］推論する
v. to conclude or guess from facts

infirm [infə́ːrm] ［形］弱い、虚弱な
adj. weak or ill

inflexible [infléksəbl] ［形］曲がらない、確固たる
adj. being unable to change

ingenuity [ìndʒən(j)úːəti] ［名］創造力
n. a talent for making new things; acuteness in devising

ingest [indʒést] ［動］摂取する
v. to eat; to take in through the mouth

inkling [íŋkliŋ] ［名］うすうす感づくこと、ほのめかし
n. a slight hint or a vague notion

insatiable [inséiʃəbl] ［形］飽くことを知らない、強欲な
adj. having a desire or greed that is unable to be satisfied

insubstantial [ìnsəbstǽnʃəl] ［形］実態のない、かすかな.
adj. not seeming real; not very large in size or amount

intelligence [intélədʒns] ［名］知能、理解力
n. the ability to attain and use things that have been learned

invidious [invídiəs] ［形］人のねたみを買うような、気に障る
adj. causing envy or resentment

ire [áiəʳ] ［名］憤怒、深い憤り
n. a strong feeling of anger or rage

irreducible [ìridjú:səbl] ［形］減らせない、削減できない
adj. unable to reduce to a smaller or simpler form

irrelevant [iréləvənt] ［形］不適切な、無関係な
adj. unimportant or unrelated to the topic or situation

J

jamb [dʒæm] ［名］(戸口・窓などの) わき柱
n. a post that forms the upright sides of a window or door

jeer [dʒiəʳ] ［動］あざける、やじる
v. to speak in a way that makes fun of people

jeopardize [dʒépəʳdàiz] ［動］危険にさらす
v. to do something that may cause something to fail or be damaged

K

knack [næk] ［名］技巧、こつ
n. ability and ease in performing a certain task

knave [neiv] ［名］信用のできない人
n. a dishonest or deceitful person

knead [ni:d] ［動］練り上げる
v. to mix or work by using one's hands to press, fold, and stretch something

L

labile [léibil] ［形］変化しやすい、柔軟な
adj. adaptable and welcoming of change

lachrymose [lǽkrəmòus] ［形］涙もろい、涙を催させる
adj. prone to weeping

lackluster [lǽklʌstəʳ] ［形］活気のない、精彩を欠いた
adj. lacking of vitality or brilliance

lambaste [læmbéist] ［動］殴る、厳しく叱る
v. to beat or reprimand harshly

lampoon [læmpú:n] ［名］風刺文
n. a humorous way to criticize something

lank [læŋk] ［形］ひょろ長い
adj. tall and lean

largesse [lɑːˈdʒés] ［名］寛大さ、気前の良さ
n. generous and liberal nature in giving to others

leverage [lévəridʒ] ［名］てこの力、効力、影響力
n. the mechanical advantage of a lever; the power to control a situation or person

lighthearted [laithɑːˈtid] ［形］陽気な、気楽な
adj. untroubled; free of worry or care

linen [línin] ［名］亜麻布、リネン
n. a type of fabric made from flax

linoleum [linóuliəm] ［名］リノリウム（床仕上げ材の一種）
n. a floor covering made of a hardened linseed oil mixture

liquefy [líkwifài] ［動］液化させる
v. to change from either solid or gas form to liquid form

lissome [lísəm] ［形］柔軟な，しなやかな、なおやか
adj. easy to bend or move; slim and limber

literary [lítərèri] ［形］文学の、文学的な
adj. pertaining to literature

locate [loukéit] ［動］（～の場所）を決める
v. to determine or discover the position of

lode [loud] ［名］鉱脈
n. an abundant bed of minerals found in rock formations

longevity [lɑndʒévəti] ［名］寿命、長生き
n. long continuance or duration; the fact of having a long life

loutish [láutiʃ] ［形］ぶこつな、粗野な
adj. boorish and contemptible in attitude or appearance

M

magnanimity [mægnəníməti] ［名］度量の大きいこと、寛大さ
n. the quality of being very liberal and generous

malaise [mæléiz] ［名］何となく気分がすぐれないこと、不快（感）、不調
n. the state of physical unease experienced before an illness; general sense of being ill at ease

manuscript [mǽnjuskrìpt] ［名］原稿、手稿
n. a piece of writing that was written by hand

mar [mɑːˈ] ［動］そこなう、台無しにする
v. to ruin or damage something

margin [mɑːˈdʒin] ［名］余白、限度、縁
n. an area of empty space on paper; the border or edge

mark [mɑːˈk] ［名］マーク、記号
n. a sign that usually has a special meaning

marvel [mάːʳvəl] ［名］驚くべきこと、驚異
n. an extraordinary event that has people in awe

medley [médli] ［名］メドレー（いくつかの原曲を集めて作った混合曲）
n. a musical composition that is made up of songs from various sources

meld [meld] ［動］併合する、混合させる
v. to blend or merge

mercurial [məːʳkjúəriəl] ［形］移り気の、気まぐれな
adj. being volatile and erratic

merit [mérit] ［名］長所、功績
n. a quality that is praiseworthy; achievement or excellence

mill [mil] ［名］製造工場、製粉所
n. a factory where a product is made or where grain is crushed and flour is produced

misgiving [misgíviŋ] ［名］不安、疑い
n. a feeling that something is not right and the result will be bad

misrepresent [mìsreprizént] ［動］不正確に伝える、事実を曲げて述べる
v. to intentionally give misleading representations or information

mite [mait] ［名］ダニ、少量
n. a small parasitic insect that lives on plants and animals; a small amount

montage [mɑntάːʒ] ［名］モンタージュ
n. a composite picture

mortar [mɔ́ːʳtəʳ] ［名］モルタル、しっくい
n. a mixture used to hold bricks together

mortification [mɔ̀ːʳtəfikéiʃən] ［名］屈辱
n. a strong emotion of embarrassment or humiliation

mosaic [mouzéiik] ［名］モザイク
n. a work of art that consists of small pieces of glass, stone embedded in plaster

motley [mάtli] ［形］雑多な、まだらの
adj. having many colors or variety

mourn [mɔːʳn] ［動］嘆く、悲しむ
v. to be sad or grieve over

mull [mʌl] ［動］問題についてじっくり考える
v. to ponder over a problem or question

mumble [mʌ́mbl] ［動］（不明瞭に）つぶやく
v. to speak in an unclear and quiet manner which makes it hard to comprehend

mutate [mjuːtéit] ［動］突然変異する
v. to change as a result of a genetic flaw; to change or alter; to transform

nadir [néidəʳ] ［名］どん底、最下点、天底
n. the lowest point in one's career or life

naif (naive) [nɑːíːf][nɑːíːv] ［形］世間知らずの、純真な
adj. artless and unsophisticated; gullible

narcissism [náːʳsəsìzm] ［名］ナルシシズム、自己愛、自己陶酔
n. excessive love of or admiration of oneself; conceit

naysay [néisèi] ［動］反対する、拒否する
v. to oppose or deny

negligible [néglidʒəbl] ［形］無視してよい、取るに足らない
adj. being unimportant thus ignored

negotiation [nigòuʃiéiʃən] ［名］交渉
n. process of bargaining and conferring in order to reach a mutual agreement

neologism [niːálədʒìzm] ［名］新造語
n. the coining of new words or phrases

noisome [nɔ́isəm] ［形］有害な、不快な
adj. disgusting and loathsome

nonconformist [nɑ̀nkənfɔ́ːʳmist] ［名］非協調主義者
n. someone who refuses to be obligated by common beliefs

nonflammable [nɑ̀nflǽməbl] ［形］不燃性の
adj. incombustible, impossible to set on fire

nonsensical [nɑnsénsikəl] ［形］無意味な、ばかげた
adj. lacking good sense; absurd

novelty [návəlti] ［名］新奇さ、目新しさ
n. newness, quality of being fresh or new

nurture [náːʳtʃəʳ] ［動］養育する
v. to nourish and feed

obituary [oubítʃuèri] ［名］死亡記事、死亡者略歴
n. a notice of a deceased person which often includes a short biography

oblique [əblíːk] ［形］曖昧な、遠回しの、傾いた
adj. obscure and evasive; not straightforward

obsolete [àbsəlíːt] ［形］すたれた、時代遅れの
adj. old and no longer in use

occlude [əklúːd] ［動］塞ぐ
v. to close up or block the way

onerous [ánərəs] ［形］厄介な
adj. burdensome; troublesome or oppressive

oppress [əprés] ［動］圧迫する
v. to handle people in an unfair manner often in a cruel way

ore [ɔːʳ] ［名］鉱石
n. metal found in the earth

organism [ɔ́ːʳgənìzm] ［名］有機体
n. a particular form of life which has a body containing organs or other parts that work in agreement to one another to sustain life

ornate [ɔːʳnéit] ［形］飾り立てた、華美な
adj. having decorative patterns and shapes

oscillation [àsəléiʃən] ［名］振動
n. the act of moving from one place to another

overlook [òuvəʳlúk] ［動］見落とす、見過ごす
v. to miss or ignore

overt [óuvəːʳt] ［形］明白な、公然の
adj. obviously apparent; publicly observable

P

paean [píːən] ［名］賛歌
n. a song of praise

pall [pɔːl] ［動］飽きさせる、興味を失わせる
v. to make dull or lifeless

panegyric [pæ̀nədʒírik] ［名］称賛の演説、賛辞
n. an expression of elaborate praise

panorama [pæ̀nərǽmə] ［名］全景、パノラマ
n. a widespread view of an area

pariah [pəráiə] ［名］社会ののけ者、パーリア（南部インドの最下層民）
n. one that is rejected or despised by society; a social outcast

parochial [pəróukiəl] ［形］視野や度量が狭い、偏狭な
adj. restricted or narrow in outlook or attitude

parody [pǽrədi] ［名］滑稽な物まね、パロディー
n. a humorous imitation of a popuplar work of art or person

pathological [pæ̀θəládʒikəl] ［形］病的な、精神病による
adj. abnormal; relating to mental disorders or behavioral problems

pauper [pɔ́ːpəʳ] ［名］貧困者
n. a very poor person

pebble [pébl] ［名］さざれ石
n. a tiny smooth stone

peep [pi:p] [動] のぞき見する ［名］(小鳥・ネズミなどの) ピーピー [チューチュー]鳴く声
v. to look quickly or secretly
n. a short, weak, and shrill sound

peevish [píːviʃ] [形] 気難しい、イライラした、怒りっぽい
adj. easy to annoy or vex; querulous

pejorative [pidʒɔ́ːrətiv] [形] 軽蔑的な、非難の意を含む
adj. demeaning or belittling

penalty [pénˀlti] ［名］(刑) 罰
n. a punishment for breaking a rule or law

personable [páːˤsˀnəbl] [形] (性格や容姿が) 魅力的な
adj. engaging in personality or pleasing in appearance; attractive

personnel [pə̀ːˤsˀnél] ［名］人員、職員
n. employees of a group, business, or organization

pestle [péstl] ［名］乳棒、すりこぎ
n. a device used to pound or grind substances into powder

piddling [pídliŋ] [形] ささいな、取るに足りない
adj. trivial and frivolous; paltry and trifling

piety [páiəti] ［名］敬虔、信心
n. reverence and devotion to God

pillar [píləˤ] ［名］柱状のもの
n. a solid vertical structure used to support buildings

plain [plein] [形] 平易な、明瞭な、はっきり見える
adj. common and not elaborate; being very clear and distinct

plantation [plæntéiʃən] ［名］((亜)熱帯地方の) 大農園
n. a large piece of farm land used to cultivate several different groups of trees and crops

plastic [plǽstik] [形] 人工的な、不自然な、可塑性のある
adj. artificial or unnatural; flexible or adaptable

plateau [plætóu] ［名］高原
n. a vast area of flat land that is higher than the surrounding area; a period of stability or little change

plight [plait] ［名］悪い状態、苦境、窮状
n. a bad or desperate situation; predicament

posit [pázit] [動] 配置する、仮定する
v. to place in position; to assume the actuality of

possess [pəzés] [動] 所有する、持っている
v. to have as an asset; to own

pragmatic [prægmǽtik] [形] 実用的な
adj. practical, concerned with facts rather than abstract ideas

predisposition [prìːdispəzíʃən] ［名］傾向
n. a tendency or previous inclination

preempt [priémpt] ［動］先取する
v. to take ahead of others

preface [préfis] ［名］序文
n. an introduction to a book which gives information on the work or author

preference [préfᵊrəns] ［名］(他よりも) 好きであること
n. a predilection for something over another

prefiguration [priːfigjəréiʃən] ［名］予示、予想
n. something that foreshadows

preside [prizáid] ［動］統轄する、主宰する
v. to exercise control in a position of authority

prissy [prísi] ［形］やかまし屋の、こうるさい
adj. excessively proper and prim

prologue [próulɔːg] ［名］プロローグ、前口上、発端
n. an introduction or preface

pronounce [prənáuns] ［動］発音する、宣言する
v. to use particular sounds to say a word; to formally state an official opinion

proofread [prúːfriːd] ［動］校正する
v. to check for and correct errors

prophecy [práfəsi] ［名］予言
n. a foretelling or prediction

prosecute [prásəkjùːt] ［動］起訴する
v. to begin or initiate legal action against

protagonist [proutǽgənist] ［名］(芝居や物語の) 主人公
n. the leading figure in a drama or story

protocol [próutəkàl] ［名］(外交上の) 儀礼、典礼
n. a set of rules for correct behavior

providential [pràvədénʃəl] ［形］神意による、天の配剤の
adj. occurring as if by divine intervention

puissance [pjúːəsns] ［名］力、勢力、権力
n. strength, might, or power

punch [pʌntʃ] ［動］(穴あけ具、パンチ、こぶしで) 殴ること
v. a tool for making a hole; a type of impact caused by the use of one's fist

puzzle [pʌzl] ［動］当惑させる、まごつかせる ［名］難問、パズル
v. to confuse or mystify; to perplex
n. a problem or mystery that is difficult to solve

quack [kwæk] ［名］偽医者
n. an untrained person who pretends to be a doctor

quaff [kwɑ:f] ［動］がぶ飲みする
v. to drink with great relish

quail [kwéil] ［動］おじける、ひるむ
v. to shrink back in fear or dread; to cower

qualm [kwɑ:m] ［名］不安、吐き気
n. a sudden feeling of doubt or guilt; nausea

quantify [kwɑ́ntəfài] ［動］量を定める
v. to determine or express the amount or number of

quarantine [kwɔ́:rəntì:n] ［動］（伝染病予防のために）隔離する
v. to isolate for a period of time in order to prevent the spread of contagious disease

quest [kwest] ［名］探求　［動］探し求める
n. a search; an attempt to find something
v. to go in search of; to seek or pursue after

queue [kju:] ［名］おさげ髪、弁髪、待ち行列
n. a single braid of hair; a line as of people waiting for something

---

raconteur [ræ̀kɑntə́:ʳ] ［名］話し上手な人、談話家
n. someone who can skillfully tell a story

raffle [rǽfl] ［名］ラッフル（慈善などを目的とした富くじ）
n. a kind of lottery in which people buy chances to win a prize

rambunctious [ræmbʌ́ŋkʃəs] ［形］手［始末］に負えない、乱暴な、騒々しい
adj. noisy and lively; boisterous

rankle [rǽŋkl] ［動］（人の心を）苦しめる、イライラさせる
v. to irritate or make resentful

ration [rǽʃən] ［名］割当量、配給（量）
n. a fixed allotment of food especially for soldiers

ream [ri:m] ［名］多量、連（紙の取引単位：500枚）
n. a large amount of something; 500 pieces of paper

rebuke [ribjú:k] ［動］強く非難する、叱責する
v. to speak harshly against something

recite [risáit] ［動］暗唱する、朗唱する
v. to repeat text of a writing

recognition [rèkəgníʃən] ［名］表彰、認識
n. the praise or identification of something

recur [rikə́ːʳ] ［動］再発する
v. to happen again

reel [riːl] ［名］巻き枠、リール
n. a device used to spin wire or film around a frame

refugee [rèf(j)udʒíː] ［動］避難者、難民
v. one who flees to a foreign country in search of refuge as a result of war, persecution, or oppression

regard [rigáːʳd] ［動］〜と見なす、考える
v. to consider something in a particular way

regret [rigrét] ［動］後悔する、遺憾に思う
v. to feel remorse or sorrow

rehearsal [rihə́ːʳsᵊl] ［名］リハーサル
n. a practice for a performance

reiterate [riːítərèit] ［動］何度も繰り返し言う
v. to say again for emphasis

relate [riléit] ［動］話す、物語る、（〜の）間の関係を説明する
v. to tell; to show a relationship between two things

relegate [rélagèit] ［動］左遷する
v. to lower one's position

reluctance [riláktəns] ［名］気が進まないこと、不承不承
n. the act or state of being unwilling

repeal [ripíːl] ［名］廃止、撤廃
n. the act of revoking an official act

repulse [ripʌ́ls] ［動］撃退する
v. to repel or drive back

restrict [ristríkt] ［動］制限する
v. to have a limit for something

resuscitate [risʌ́sətèit] ［動］蘇生させる
v. to revive from unconsciousness

retract [ritrǽkt] ［動］（前言などを）取り消す
v. to withdraw or take back something said or done

reveal [rivíːl] ［動］明らかにする、さらけ出す
v. to make aware or to show

rigid [rídʒid] ［形］硬直した、厳格な
adj. not easy to change; strict

rooted [rúːtid] ［形］根付いた、定着した
adj. firmly fixed or established

sabbatical [səbǽtikəl] ［名］研究休暇、サバティカル
n. a release from normal teaching duties granted to a professor, as for study or travel

salutation [sæ̀ljətéiʃən] ［名］あいさつの言葉
n. a greeting

salvage [sǽlvidʒ] ［動］救助する ［名］海難救助、サルベージ
v. to save property from destruction
n. saving things from a disaster at sea

sap [sæp] ［動］（活力などを）徐々に奪う
v. to drain or weaken

scholarly [skálərli] ［形］学術的な、学問的な
adj. having an intellectual manner

scrappy [skrǽpi] ［形］けんか好きな、攻戦的な
adj. willing to fight or argue; aggressive

selective [siléktiv] ［形］選択的な
adj. characterized by careful choice; discriminating

self-effacing [sélfiféisiŋ] ［形］控えめな、でしゃばらない
adj. humble and modest; reluctant to draw attention to oneself

shaft [ʃæft] ［名］（エレベーターなどの）シャフト、（鉱山の）立て坑
n. a long narrow vertical passage

shrill [ʃril] ［形］金切り声の、かん高い.
adj. having a high and unpleasant sound

slide [slaid] ［動］滑る
v. to move smoothly and quickly across a surface

slope [sloup] ［名］傾斜
n. an incline or slant

solution [səljúːʃən] ［名］解答、溶液
n. an answer or conclusion to a problem; a liquid with another substance dissolved in it

sonata [sənáːtə] ［名］ソナタ
n. a musical piece that consists of one musical instrument and a piano

sonnet [sánit] ［名］ソネット（14行詩）
n. a rhyming poem that is made up of 14 lines with each line containing 14 syllables

spectrum [spéktrəm] ［名］スペクトル（光がプリズムを通過するとき生じる7色の色帯）
n. a range of colors resulting from a light that is separated when passing through a prism

stagnant [stǽgnənt] ［形］流れない、停滞した
adj. not flowing; motionless

stamina [stǽmənə] ［名］持久力、根気、スタミナ
n. physical or moral endurance and strength

standardize [stǽndərdàiz] ［動］標準化する
v. to make features common, systematic, or standard

stanza [sténzə] ［名］節、連（詩を構成する単位）
n. a division of a poem

stark [stɑːʳk] ［形］完全な、荒涼たる
adj. absolute or complete; desolate

stint [stint] ［動］出し惜しむ ［名］（仕事・活動などに従事していた）期間
v. to be frugal or use sparingly
n. a period of time spent doing something

stock [stɑk] ［名］在庫品、備蓄
n. surplus that is stored up for later use

stockade [stɑkéid] ［名］防御柵、（米軍の）営倉
n. a barrier made of wooden posts for defensive purposes; a military prison

storyteller [stɔ́ːritèləʳ] ［名］語り手
n. a person who tells or writes about an event usually to entertain

strand [strænd] ［動］座礁させる
v. to leave in a difficult or helpless position or an unfavorable place

strict [strikt] ［形］厳格な
adj. rigid or exact; expecting discipline and severity

stylus [stáiləs] ［名］スタイラスペン、（レコードの）針
n. the needle used to read a record on a record player

subject [sʌ́bdʒikt] ［名］主題、（国王・君主の下にいる）国民、臣民.
n. the topic of conversation, writing, etc. ; a person under control

subpoena [səbpíːnə] ［名］召喚状
n. a letter or document that requires a person to attend court

subservience [səbsə́ːʳviəns] ［名］服従
n. willingness to serve another's purposes

subtle [sʌ́tl] ［形］とらえがたい、微妙な
adj. elusive or obscure; hard to pinpoint

superfluous [suːpə́ːʳfluəs] ［形］必要以上の、余分の
adj. more than what is needed; extraneous

supersede [sùːpəʳsíːd] ［動］（～に）取って代わる
v. to take the place of or take over

susceptibility [səsèptəbíləti] ［名］影響を受けやすいこと、感受性
n. feelings or emotions that are easily affected

suspend [səspénd] ［動］延期する、保留する、（一時）中止する
v. to postpone or discontinue

symphony [símfəni] ［名］交響曲、調和
n. four separate movements or musical pieces played by an orchestra; harmony

tamper [tǽmpəʳ] ［動］不正に［みだりに］変更する、改ざんする
v. to foolishly play or tinker with

tantalize [tǽntəlàiz] ［動］(見せびらかして)じらす
v. to tease or torment by presenting something desirable but making it unattainable

tapestry [tǽpistri] ［名］タペストリー、壁掛け
n. a thick piece of cloth that usually contains a picture woven or sewn in it and is often hung on walls

taxing [tǽksiŋ] ［形］骨の折れる、厄介な
adj. being very demanding or stressful

tear [tɛəʳ] ［動］引き裂く
v. to pull apart or divide

temper [témpəʳ] ［名］気質、怒り
n. a habitual state of mind or manner of feeling; a mood of anger

temporize [témpəràiz] ［動］時間を稼ぐ、(即決をしないで)ぐずぐずする
v. to do something less important so as to give extra time to make a decision

terror [térəʳ] ［名］恐怖
n. a strong feeling of fear

therapeutic [θèrəpjúːtik] ［形］治療上の、治療学の
adj. relating to the treatment of disease

tinge [tindʒ] ［動］色味を帯びる
v. to infuse something with color, taste, or shade

torpor [tɔ́ːʳpəʳ] ［名］不活発、無気力
n. inactivity due to lack of vigor and energy

tout [taut] ［動］押し売りする
v. to solicit in an aggresive manner

transcend [trænsénd] ［動］超越する
v. to rise above

travesty [trǽvəsti] ［名］滑稽化、戯画化
n. a representation that is grossly exaggerated to the point of ridicule

tribute [tríbjuːt] ［名］(尊敬や感謝を表す) 言葉、賛辞
n. declaration of esteem, respect, and admiration

turbulent [tɔ́ːʳbjulənt] ［形］荒れ狂う、騒然とした
adj. having a lot of change, disorder, or violence; stormy

turpitude [tɔ́ːʳpit(j)ùːd] ［名］卑劣さ、非道徳性、邪悪
n. wickedness, vileness, or depravity

typical [típikəl] ［形］典型的な、象徴的な
adj. normal and usual; symbolic

unconventional [ʌ̀nkənvénʃənl] ［形］慣習にとらわれない、自由な
adj. not conforming to conventional standards or accepted rules

understate [ʌ̀ndəˈstéit] ［動］控えめに言う、軽視する
v. to indicate that something is less influential than it really is

undeserved [ʌ̀ndizə́ːˈvd] ［形］受けるに値しない、不相応な
adj. unfair or unjustifiable; unmerited

unexceptionable [ʌ̀niksépʃʰnəbl] ［形］申し分のない
adj. beyond any reasonable objection

unfettered [ʌ̀nfétəˈd] ［形］拘束されない、制限されていない
adj. being independent from rules or authority; unrestricted

unimpeachable [ʌ̀nimpíːtʃəbl] ［形］非難できない、非の打ちどころのない
adj. beyond doubt or reproach

uninspired [ʌ̀ninspáiəˈd] ［形］独創性のない
adj. deficient in creativity

unlikely [ʌ̀nláikli] ［形］見込みのない、ありそうもない
adj. not likely to be or happen

unreflective [ʌ̀nrifléktiv] ［形］無分別な
adj. irrational or unthinking

unsophisticated [ʌ̀nsəfístəkèitid] ［形］純朴な、世慣れていない
adj. having very little experience and refinement

unsubstantial [ʌ̀nsəbstǽnʃəl] ［形］非現実的な、内容が貧弱な
adj. scanty in amount or degree; without foundation

unwieldy [ʌ̀nwíːldi] ［形］(形・大きさなどのせいで) 動かしにくい、扱いにくい
adj. difficult to move or handle because of size, shape, or design; awkward

unwitting [ʌ̀nwítiŋ] ［形］偶然の、意図的でない、知らない
adj. not intended; not knowing

utilize [júːtəlàiz] ［動］利用する
v. to apply something to use

valediction [væ̀lədíkʃən] ［名］告別の辞、別れの言葉
n. a speech or phrase bidding farewell

varnish [váːˈniʃ] ［名］(塗料の) ニス、ワニス
n. a translucent glossy coating that protects surfaces from air and moisture

vendee [vendíː] ［名］買い手
n. one who buys or purchases

venerate [vénərèit] [動] 尊敬する
v. to honor or respect with great reverence

venom [vénəm] [名] 毒
n. a poison that is found in animals such as snakes, bees, and scorpions

ventilate [véntəlèit] [動] 換気する
v. to enable new air to circulate

verdict [vɔ́ːʳdikt] [名] 評決、裁定
n. the outcome of a trial

verse [vəːʳs] [名] 詩、詩の1行 [節・連]
n. a poem, stanza, or line

vicissitude [visísət(j)ùːd] [名] 変化、変遷
n. a change, mutation, or alternation

victimize [víktimàiz] [動] 被害者にする、(不当に)苦しめる
v. to make a victim of; to treat someone in a deliberately unfair way

vitiate [víʃièit] [動] 損なう、道徳的地位を低下させる
v. to impair; to debase in moral status

vitriolic [vìtriálik] [形] しんらつな、痛烈な
adj. bitter and harsh in tone

W

waffle [wάfl] [動] 曖昧なことを言う [書く]
v. to speak or write vaguely and evasively

warmonger [名] [wɔ́ːʳmʌ̀ŋgəʳ] 主戦論者
n. one who advocates war

warrant [wɔ́(ː)rənt] [動] 正当化する
v. to justify or show sufficient grounds for

watchful [wάtʃfəl] [形] 用心深い、警戒する
adj. carefully observant or attentive

watt [wɑt] [名] ワット (電力の単位)
n. calibration for electrical power

wax [wæks] [名] 密ろう、ワックス、激怒 [動] 増大する
n. a substance that is used to make candles with; a protective layer of coating for certain surfaces; rage
v. to increase in size, number, or strength

welter [wéltəʳ] [名] ごちゃ混ぜ、寄せ集め、混乱
n. a confusing, jumbled mass; a muddle

whet [ʰwet] [動] (刃物などを) 研ぐ
v. to make sharp

whiff [ʰwif] [名] (風・煙などの) ひと吹き
n. a brief gentle gust of air

winnow [wínou] [動] 選り分ける
v. to examine and then separate useful things from those that are not

withdraw [wiðdrɔ́ː] [動] 引き抜く
v. to take out or extract

woo [wuː] [動] 求愛する
v. to court or seek favor

wordsmith [wɔ́ːʳdsmìθ] [名] 文章家
n. a skilled or professional writer

wordy [wɔ́ːʳdi] [形] 言葉が冗長な
adj. using too many words; verbose

worldly [wɔ́ːʳldli] [形] この世の、世俗的な
adj. being experienced in social activities, relating to the practical rather than the spiritual aspects of life

---

Y

yoke [jouk] [動] 結び付ける [名] 束縛、くびき
v. to join securely together
n. bondage

Z

zealot [zélət] [名] 熱狂者
n. one who is excessively enthusiastic; a fanatic

Super Vocabulary
Words Roots & Prefixes

Words Roots and Prefixes A

a, an — not, without

abandon 162
abase 177
abash 177
abate 177, 235
abeyance 438
abrade 392
abrasion 412
abridge 335
abuse 367
achromatic 108, 192
acquiescec392
albinism 148, 240

albino 148
alibi 192
align 220, 249
allay 262
alleviate 262, 368
aloof 32, 336
amorphous 336
anachronism 3
anaerobe 439
analgesia 163
anarchist 170, 439
anemic 439

anesthetic 119, 300
anodyne 406
anomalous 336
anomaly 401
anonymous 364
apathetic 148, 178, 232
aseptic 149
aside 136, 194
avoid 122

ab — away from

abbreviate 191
abdicate 103, 207
aberrant 118
abet 118, 238
abhor 191
abide 191
abject 248

abjure 248, 410
abnegate 438
abode 300
aboveboard 31, 195
abrogate 93, 232, 438
abscond 2
absolve 438

absorb 31
absorbing 129
abstain 234
abstemious 45, 109, 122
abstract 45, 252
abstruse 89, 191

ac, acr, acu — sharp, bitter

acerbic 118
acme 292

acrid 335
acrimonious 320

acute 234

ad — to, toward

adamant 162
addict 103
addicted 103
address 438
adept 406
adhere 192
adjust 71, 248

admirable 292
admire 101
admonish 306, 311
adoration 267
adroitness 122
adulate 2, 153, 274
adulterate 2

adumbration 438
adventurous 27
adversary 438
advertent 31
advocate 59, 381

aesthet — feeling

aesthete 45

ag, act — to do

aggrandize 234
agitate 198, 248

aggravate 234, 262

aggrieve 235, 293

agog — to lead

demagogue 396

pedagogue 96

agon — to struggle

agonize 335

antagonize 59

protagonist 458

ali, alter — other

alibi 192

alienable 162

inalienable 162

alt — high

exalt 166

ambi — both, around

ambiguity 392
ambivalent 148

ambiguous 309, 392

unambiguous 199

ang, anx — to strangle, to hang

anger 167, 241
anxiety 308

disentangle 166, 188
estrange 411

estrangement 241, 411

anim — breath, mind, life

animate 220
animation 220

inanimate 451

unanimity 216, 418

Words Roots and Prefixes **B**

bat — to beat

abate 177, 235 debate 151 exacerbate 153, 234

be — thoroughly, to make

bedeck 440
befuddle 440
behavior 262
belabor 249
beleaguer 263, 282
belie 263

belief 200
belligerent 277
beloved 277
bequest 75
berate 22, 320
beseeching 404

besmirch 32
betray 440
browbeat 3, 278
misbehave 9, 402
obedient 112, 323

belli, bell — beauty, war

belligerent 277

bene — good, well

beneficial 292 benevolence 420 benevolent 268

bi — two

abide 191
arbitrator 138
biased 440
dubious 152

exorbitant 411
flexibility 162, 269
indubitable 109
obituary 455

probity 28, 329, 418
rubicund 170, 304

bio — life, living organisms

antibiotic 370 symbiosis 302 symbiotic 302

bol, bl — to throw

blizzard 440
blurt 32, 86
bluster 33
bolster 278

crumble 4, 209
dabble 151
dabbler 151
embolden 177, 196, 349

hyperbole 153, 383
parable 355
pebble 456
scribble 429

caco	bad, wrong

cacophonous 325, 381   cacophony 221

capit	head

capitulation 379   capitulate 41, 379

car	wheel; to roll

cargo 315, 421   carry 426   cart 278
carouse 17

carn	flesh

carnal 259

cata	down

catastrophe 24

cede, ceed, cess	to go, to yield

concede 180, 387   accessible 89, 191   unnecessary 54
precede 125   cessation 33
precedent 125, 260   excessive 447
proceed 426   intercessor 79, 110

ceive, cept	to take

deceive 120, 396   inception 376   susceptibility 462
deception 196   perceive 65, 329   unexceptionable 464
exceptional 447

cel — sky

celebrity 365

cens — to assess; tax

censor 398   censure 402

chrom — color

achromatic 108, 192   chromatic 441   monochromatic 425

chron — time

anachronism 3   chronological 442   chronology 3

cide, cis — to kill, to cut

accident 143   imprecise 451   precise 394
accidental 66   incision 70   precision 199
cistern 47   narcissism 455   vicissitude 313, 465
concise 113, 251, 347   precis 113

circum — around

circumference 236   circumlocutory 403   circumspect 215, 321
circumlocution 8, 321   circumscribe 274, 321   circumvent 322

clud, clus, claus — to close

recluse 107, 215

co, con, col, cor — with, together

accolade 52, 206   coda 124, 221   collude 279, 339
accommodate 438   coerce 408   colonnade 351
beacon 150   coeval 442   combust 338
coagulant 231, 322   cogent 236, 324   combustible 338
coagulate 150   colander 152   comfort 293
coalesce 164   collapse 279   comfortable 119

comity 379
command 307, 410
commencement 33
commend 307
commitment 148, 442
commodious 165, 307, 339
commonplace 307
commonsensical 125, 307
commotion 99, 308
comparable 308
compatible 97, 408
compendious 308
complacence 308
complain 90, 308
complaisance 408
complexity 309, 324
complimentary 183
compliment 309
comply 371, 442
compose 309
comprehend 24, 309
compress 310
compression 310
compromise 310, 384
compunction 310
compunctious 322
concatenate 442
concavity 357
conceal 251, 380
concede 180, 387
concentrate 165, 251, 296
conciliate 95, 100, 251
conciliatory 251, 277, 361
concise 113, 251, 347
conclude 442
concord 135, 251, 311
concrete 442
concur 38, 252
condemn 252
condense 45, 252, 345
condescend 252
condign 442
condolence 442
condone 253
confession 293
confine 442

confirm 263, 293, 412
conform 294
conformation 336
conformity 294
confront 322
confuse 294
confusion 208, 294
congeal 294
congenial 294
congruent 294
conjecture 114, 310
connect 442
connive 76
conniver 76, 395
connoisseur 442
consent 180
consequence 257
conservative 226
conserve 13
consolidate 395
conspicuous 269, 425
conspiratorial 76, 395
conspire 395
constancy 68, 172, 259
constant 442
constellation 207
constitute 207
constrain 271, 443
constrict 307, 339
consummate 237
contagion 339
contain 443
contemptible 78
contentment 5
continence 443
continuance 443
contract 265
contraction 351
contradictory 82, 322
contrast 195, 443
contravene 366
contrite 322, 336
control 95
contumacious 112, 323
convalesce 216, 295
convenience 385

converge 443
conversant 443
conversion 443
convert 323
convey 28, 443, 323
conviction 152
convince 236, 324
convivial 90, 216
convoluted 309, 324
convulsion 351, 366
cooperate 279, 339
copious 287, 379
cornucopia 443
coronation 242, 366
corporeal 202, 409
correspond 409
corrode 326, 443
corruptionist 229
coterie 443
decorum 142
discomfit 6, 424
discommode 6, 31, 282
discompose 6, 212
discontent 6
encomiast 280
encomium 398
excoriate 78, 223
inconsequential 4
inconsonant 251
inconspicuous 273, 343
incorrigible 104, 226
incorruptible 195
nonconformist 455
protocol 458
raconteur 459
rancon 179, 286
reconcile 414
reconciliation 414
recondite 215
reconnoiter 215
succor 203
unconformity 424
unconscious 430
unconventional 464

contra, counter — against, opposite

contradictory 82, 322
contrast 195, 443
contravene 366

counter 443
counterfeit 366
countermand 367

cor(d) — heart

accord 438
concord 135, 251, 311

core 428
discord 181

incorrigible 104, 226
rancor 179, 286

corp(or) — body

corporeal 19, 202, 409

cosm — world

cosmopolitan 33, 358, 399

cre, cret — to discern

accrete 220

crescendo 444

excrete 447

cred — to believe

credence 105

credulous 128, 367

discredit 17

crit, cris — to discern

critical 404

criticize 95

cruc — cross

crucial 4

cult — to take care

cultivate 295

cultivated 229

cur, course — to run

con**cur** 38, 252
curate 444
curb 340
curmudgeon 379
cursory 180

curt 4
curtail 5, 325, 357
dis**cur**sive 18
ex**cur**sive 48
mer**cur**ial 454

pre**cur**sor 373
pre**cur**sory 373, 422
re**cur** 460
course 279, 443

cycl — circle, wheel

en**cycl**opedia 308

Words Roots and Prefixes **D**

de — from, down, away

debacle 352
debase 151
debilitate 152
debunk 395
decant 396
decanter 396
deceitful 174
deceive 120, 396
decelerate 396
deception 196
deceptive 196
decode 295
decorate 46
decorous 221, 315
decorum 142
decrepit 222, 416
defend 72, 134
defer 134
deferential 24
deferrable 134
defile 134
definitive 135
deflated 431
deflect 444
defuse 135, 296
defy 421
dehydrate 196

deject 253
dejection 183, 253
delay 266
deliberate 156, 179, 265
deliberation 394
delirium 208
delusion 43, 295
demand 444
demean 368
demolish 396
demolition 90
demur 380
demystify 444
denial 444
denounce 253, 306, 311
denunciation 444
deny 5
depart 2
dependence 445
deplete 380
deplore 299, 380, 414
deploy 165, 251
deportation 444
depose 165, 428
deprave 153
deprecate 397
depreciate 397

deprivation 397, 431
deracinate 397
deride 421
derision 114, 155
derivative 422
descend 26
descendant 445
descent 445
desecrate 17
desire 155
destruction 90, 396
detach 62
detainment 445
detection 367
deter 76
determination 76
deterrent 120
detour 77, 359
detract 409
devalue 409
devastate 120
devote 138, 445
inter**de**pendent 302
self-**de**nial 194
self-**de**precating 397

demo · people

demotic 444

dia · through, across, between

diaphanous 180, 185
encyclopedia 308

incendiary 198, 248
mediate 79, 110

mediation 310
quotidian 358

dict · to speak

contradictory 82, 322
diction 445
dictionary 299

indict 65
interdict 75, 79, 374
predict 113, 245

prediction 113, 194
valediction 107, 464
verdict 465

dign · worth

condign 442

dignify 368

dis, dys, dif · away, not, negative

diffidence 135
disabuse 352
disaffected 5
disaggregate 164
disagreeable 445
disarm 445
disavow 5, 180
discern 6
discerner 234
discerning 6, 22
discharge 181
disclosure 181
discomfit 6, 424
discommode 6, 31, 282
discompose 6, 212
discontent 6
discord 181
discredit 17
discrepancy 445
discrete 18
discretion 399
discretionary 270
discriminate 18, 371

discriminating 422
discursive 18
disdain 18
disembodied 19
disembody 19
disengage 445
disentangle 166, 188
disgorge 279
disgruntle 19
disguise 19
disgust 19, 239
disinclination 119
disinfection 149
disingenuous 20
disintegrate 35, 162
disinter 368
disinterest 35
disjoint 445
dislike 184, 191
dismantle 35
dismiss 445
disordered 407
disparage 35

disparate 35, 308
dispassionate 10, 36
disperse 409
dispirit 409
dispose 139
disprove 36, 288
dispute 36, 99, 226
disquiet 445
disregard 36
disrespect 37, 297
disrupt 37, 201
dissect 446
dissemble 37
disseminate 37
dissent 38, 180, 252
dissimulate 76
dissipate 136
dissociate 132
dissolute 47, 168
dissolve 47, 395
dissonance 135
dissuade 41, 48
distillate 136

Words Roots and Prefixes

evasive 284
evict 422
exacerbate 153, 234
exacting 84, 217
exaggerate 153, 383
exalt 166
examine 79
exceptional 447
excerpt 197
excessive 447
excitable 447
exclaim 447
excoriate 78, 223
excrete 447
exculpate 192, 224
excursive 48
excuse 87
execrable 447
execrate 106, 166
exemplary 7
exemplify 107, 206

exempt 49, 184
exhaust 139, 208
exhilarate 447
exhort 208
exhortation 81
exhortative 208, 245
exile 96
exonerate 227, 341, 412
exorbitant 411
exotic 109, 353
expansive 27
expedite 353, 381
expenditure 381
expense 98
experience 53, 156
explanation 266
explicate 447
exponent 59, 381
express 149, 203
expurgate 398
exquisite 447

extant 64
extenuate 369
extinct 64
extinguish 78, 370
extol 78, 223
extort 78, 408
extortionist 78
extract 91
extraneous 91, 406
extraordinary 91, 269
extravagant 92
extricate 411
extrinsic 92, 211, 298, 424
extrovert 182, 185
exude 447
exultant 20, 120
inescapable 110
inevitable 122
overexpose 123
overexposure 123, 227
unexceptionable 464

equi	equal	
equipoise 8, 217	equivalent 427	equivocation 20, 41
equity 447	equivocate 20	

erg, urg	to work	
energize 447	energy 314	urge 245

err	to wander	
aberrant 118	erratic 306, 326	error 400
errant 279		

esce	to begin	
acquiesce 392	coalesce 164	convalesce 216, 295

eu	well, good	
eulogize 268, 280	euphemism 141, 381	euphonious 381
eulogy 398		

ev	time, age
coeval 442	longevity 453

exter, extra	outside of	
dexterous 62, 249	extraneous 91, 406	extravagant 92
extract 91	extraordinary 91, 269	

Words Roots and Prefixes **F**

fa, fess	to speak
affability 132	confession 293

fac, fic, fec, fect	to make, to do	
affect 22	factorable 447	official 156
artifact 149	factual 448	officious 141
disaffected 5	fecundity 224	ossification 25
disinfection 149	fictional 448	ratification 82
effectiveness 225	gasification 449	satisfaction 84
facile 208, 378	infect 370	significant 243, 301
facilitate 208, 312, 383	infection 370	soporific 244, 387
faction 224, 250	munificent 316	unaffected 98

fan	to show
fantastic 354	

fed, fid	to trust	
diffidence 135	fidelity 369	perfidious 68, 427

fer	to carry	
circumference 236	effervesce 137	preference 458
defer 134	infer 217, 451	proffer 70, 331
deferrable 134		

480

fin — to end

confine 442   definitive 135   infinite 139, 208

flect, flex — to bend

deflect 444   flexibility 162, 269   inflexible 451
unreflective 301, 464   flexible 25

fort — strong

effort 345   fortify 8

fract, frag — to break

fracture 75, 449   refractory 10, 143   fragile 154

fug — to flee

centrifuge 441   subterfuge 202

fus — to pour

confuse 294   effusive 237   profuse 170, 331
confusion 208, 294   infuse 41, 238   refuse 241, 268
defuse 135   obfuscate 141, 212, 298   suffuse 143

Words Roots and Prefixes G

gen — race, birth, kind

disingenuous 20   generous 168   indigent 25
engender 238   genuine 56, 171, 327   ingenious 239
general 7   homogeneous 108, 450   ingenuity 344, 451
generosity 178   indigenous 109, 353   oxygen 392

ger, gest	to carry

exaggerate 153, 383
forgery 366

ingest 451
swagger 160, 397

gno	to know

ignore 35, 178

graph, gram	to write

cartographer 441
choreograph 338

choreography 338
epigram 223

lexicographer 299
petrography 96

greg	group, gather

disaggregate 164

gregarious 107, 336

gregariousness 107, 215

gress, grad	to step

aggressive 438
digress 48, 237

digressive 18
progress 54

regressive 414
transgress 173

Words Roots and Prefixes

hap	to fall

haphazard 57, 382

hapless 450

mishap 24

hod, od	way

methodical 382

homo	same

homogeneous 108, 450

hum, hom	earth

hum**ble** 298

hyper	over, above

hyper**bole** 153, 383

hypo	beneath, under

hypo**thesis** 412

Words Roots and Prefixes ▌

ign	fire

ign**ite** 113, 313

il, in, im	into, not

il**literate** 281
il**lluminate** 298
il**lustrate** 424
im**bibe** 259
im**itate** 401
im**maculate** 99
im**manent** 92, 298
im**material** 11, 298
im**minent** 299
im**mobilize** 450
im**mune** 313
im**munity** 203, 313
im**mure** 450
im**mutable** 313, 432
im**pact** 354
im**palpable** 451
im**partial** 138
im**passion** 138
im**passive** 8, 151, 354
im**peccable** 104, 354

im**pecunious** 133, 345, 383
im**pede** 208, 343, 383
im**penetrable** 223
im**perative** 139
im**perious** 12, 298, 383
im**permeable** 383
im**perturbable** 217, 384
im**pervious** 174, 384
im**petuous** 40, 265, 384
im**placable** 384
im**plant** 51
im**plode** 279, 384
im**poster** 451
im**precise** 451
im**press** 399
im**pression** 399
im**promptu** 399
im**proper** 451
im**prove** 103
im**providence** 114, 357

im**provisatorial** 399
im**prudence** 285
im**prudent** 399
im**pugn** 376, 399
im**puissance** 351
im**pure** 451
in**ability** 27
in**adequate** 451
in**alienable** 162
in**ane** 167
in**animate** 451
in**attentive** 31
in**augurate** 156
in**auguration** 156
in**auspicious** 344
in**cendiary** 198, 248
in**cense** 198, 343
in**cipient** 210
in**cision** 70
in**cite** 210, 228

inter, intro	between	

Words Roots and Prefixes J

jac, ject	to throw	
abject 248	dejection 183	reject 257, 345
conjecture 114, 310	object 16	subject 237, 462
deject 253	objection 380	

jud	law
judicious 110, 133, 243	prejudiced 35

jur	to swear	
abjure 248, 410	perjure 165, 428	perjury 57

Words Roots and Prefixes L

lav, luv, lut, lot	to wash	
dilute 296	irresolution 76	solution 461
dissolute 47, 168	lavish 67, 328	
irresoluteness 204	resolute 41, 94, 173	

leg, lect, lig	to gather, read, choose, or send; law	
allege 438	diligence 445	negligible 455
allegiance 10	intelligence 451	relegate 460
delegate 367	intelligible 154	selective 461
delegation 367	negligent 239	

lev	light, not heavy	
alleviate 262, 368	elevation 422	leverage 453
elevate 422	irrelevant 452	relevant 272

liber, liver — free

liberal 168   liberality 168   libertine 47, 168

libr — balance

calibrate 263

lic — to permit

elicit 446   licentious 199

liter — letter

alliterate 438   literal 80, 140, 382   obliterate 283
illiterate 281   literary 453

log — speech, word

apologist 134   epilogue 223   neologism 193, 455
apologize 336   eulogize 268, 280   prologue 458
chronological 442   logic 426   syllogism 36, 288
ecologist 167, 446

logy — science, study

anthology 74   chronology 3   eulogy 398

loqu, locut — to speak

grandiloquent 167   circumlocution 8, 321   circumlocutory 403
loquacious 203, 400

luc, lumin — light

elucidate 7   lucid 212   translucent 157, 174
illuminate 298   luminary 222, 299
ineluctable 110   pellucid 284

mir | wonder

admirable 292

admire 101

mirth 9, 263

mis | bad, wrong

misanthrope 9, 297
misbehave 9, 402
mischievous 10, 150, 306
miscreant 23, 403

misdemeanor 23
misgiving 454
mishap 24

mislead 41
misrepresent 454

mit, miss | to send

commitment 148, 442
dismiss 445
manumit 39, 173, 327
mitigate 81

permit 372
remiss 285, 301
submission 375
submissive 65

summit 317
unlimited 274, 321
vomit 279

mob, mot, mov | to move

commotion 99, 308
emotion 121
immotilize 450

mobility 388
motility 189
motivate 81

move 105, 254, 276, 281
promote 343
remove 77, 283

mono | one, alone

monochromatic 425

monotonous 413

mony | state, condition

parsimony 243

testimony 57

morph | shape

amorphous 336

mort | death

mortification 454

488

mut	to change	
im**mut**able 313, 432	**mut**ate 454	

Words Roots and Prefixes N

nai, nat	born	
naif (naive) 455 **nai**ve 225, 257	**nat**ion 314	**nat**ty 95, 360

neg	to deny	
ab**neg**ate 438	**neg**ligent 239	**neg**ligible 455

nomin, nomen	name	
ig**nomin**ious 412		

non	not	
a**non**ymous 364 **non**flammable 338, 455	**non**conformist 455 **non**descript 269	**non**entity 257 **non**sensical 253, 455

not(e)	known	
notable 355 **note** 338	**not**ice 32	**not**iceable 97

nov	new	
in**nov**ate 412 in**nov**ative 412	**nov**elty 346, 455	re**nov**ate 415

Words Roots and Prefixes

ob	in the way	
obdurate 112	obscurity 365	obtuse 95
obfuscate 141, 212, 298	obsequious 24, 388	obtuseness 95
object 16	obsess 24	obviate 54
objection 380	obsolete 455	
obliterate 283	obstinate 10, 53	
oblivion 283	obstreperous 95, 431	
obscure 24	obstruct 54	

oc, of, op	against	
offend 141	officious 141	oppress 455
offense 141, 381		

ont, ent	being
nonentity 257	

onym	name
anonymous 364	

op	eye
myopia 186, 342	synopsis 217

oper	to work
cooperate 279, 339	

or	mouth	
adoration 267	oracle 413	oratory 185
adore 406	orate 185	

ord — to arrange

disordered 407
extraordinary 91, 269

insubordinate 65, 375
order 139, 367

orderly 3, 228, 350
subordinate 416

Words Roots and Prefixes P

pan — all

deadpan 151, 354
expansive 27

panegyric 456
panorama 456

pantechnicon 54

para — beside

paradigmatic 401
paradox 401

paragon 401
paramount 149, 401

paranoia 355

pass — to step

trespass 94, 130

path — feeling, disease, suffering

antipathy 74, 132
apathetic 148, 178, 232

pathological 456

sympathetic 318

ped, pod, pus — foot

expedite 353, 381
impede 208, 343, 383

impediment 77

pedestrian 124

pel, puls — to push

repel 386, 403

repulse 460

pend — to weigh, to hang

compendious 308
dependence 445

dependency 103
expenditure 381

interdependent 302
suspend 462

per — through, intensive

asperity 378
imperative 139
impermeable 383
imperturbable 217, 384
impervious 384
intemperate 91
perceive 65, 329
peremptory 342
perfidious 68, 427

perforate 142
performance 326
permanency 166
permanent 326
permit 372
pernicious 372
perplex 413
persevere 240
perspicacious 372

persuade 10
pertinacity 10
pertinent 11, 272, 298
perturb 11, 332
pervade 11
pervasive 11
prosper 345
prosperity 186
prosperous 345

peri — around

peripatetic 427

peripheral 65, 428

periphery 428

pet — to seek; small

impetuous 40, 265, 384

petty 97

phon — sound

cacophonous 325, 381
cacophony 221

euphonious 381

symphony 385, 462

po, pos — to put, to place

apostasy 349, 369
apostate 349
overexpose 123
overexposure 123, 227
ponder 285
ponderous 40, 183

pontificate 257
posit 457
possess 457
posture 98
predisposition 458
preponderance 125

preponderant 216
preposterous 125, 307
repose 79, 386
unprepossessing 89

port — to carry

deportation 444
support 96

rapport 181

supportive 202

Words Roots and Prefixes

Words Roots and Prefixes R

rap, rav	to seize	
entrap 91, 245	rapport 181	rapprochement 241
rapacious 358		

re	back, again	
disregard 36	relapse 214, 271	repudiate 387
disrespect 37, 297	relate 460	repugnance 403
irreducible 452	relative 385	repugnant 386, 403
irrepressible 55, 425	release 92, 271	repulse 460
irresoluteness 204	relegate 460	rescind 12, 182
irresolution 76	relevant 272	reserved 27
react 122	relief 203	resilience 27
reassure 187	relieve 272, 406	resist 41
rebuke 459	religion 344	resonant 415
recalcitrant 140, 200	relinquish 272, 330	respect 55
recant 200	reluctance 187, 460	respiration 415
recidivism 214, 271	reluctant 187	respire 415
reciprocate 215	remember 112	respite 41, 198
recite 459	remiss 285, 301	resplendence 137, 181
recognition 459	remonstrance 316, 316	resplendent 42
reconcile 414	remonstrator 48	responsible 209
reconciliation 414	remorse 127, 142, 316	restive 55, 384
recondite 215	remove 77, 283	restored 121
reconnoiter 215	remunerate 317	restrain 55
recur 460	remunerative 317	restraint 199
redolent 127	renew 415	restrict 460
redoubtable 127	renounce 372	resurgence 69
redundant 429	renovate 415	resurgent 69, 426
refined 143, 408	repartee 83, 359	resuscitate 460
refractory 10, 143	repatriate 222, 359	retain 70, 162, 331
refuse 241, 268	repeal 82, 460	retaliate 70
refute 429	repel 386, 403	retard 50, 70
regard 127, 460	repertoire 386	retort 83, 359
regressive 414	replete 386	retract 460
regret 460	repletion 386	reveal 460
rehabilitate 216	repose 79, 386	revive 84
rehabilitation 216, 295	reprehensible 402	reward 272
rehearsal 460	represented 367	rewarding 7, 272
reiterate 429, 460	reprimand 403	unremarkable 346
reject 257, 345	reproach 415, 418	unrepentant 310, 347
rejoice 380, 414	reprobate 9, 242, 402	
rejuvenate 101	reprove 403	

494

reg, rect — rule; right, direct

rid, ris — to laugh

rog, rogat — to ask

Words Roots and Prefixes S

sacr, secr — holy

sci(o) — to know

sed, sid, sess — to follow

sist, sta — to stand

soci — to join; company

associate 32
association 394

dissociate 132
sociable 90, 141, 216

society 324

solv, solut — to release

absolve 438
dissolve 47, 395
solvent 47, 302

dissolute 47, 168
irresoluteness 204
irresolution 76

resolute 41, 94, 173
solution 461

somn — sleep

somnolence 118, 317

soph — wisdom

sophisticate 387

sophistication 239

unsophisticated 464

spect — to look

circumspect 215, 321
disrespect 37, 297

prospect 271
respect 55

spectrum 461

sper, spir — to breathe

asperity 378
aspirant 378
conspiratorial 76, 395
conspire 395
dispirit 409

inspiration 427
inspire 41, 238
prosper 345
prosperity 186
prosperous 345

respiration 415
respire 415
spiritual 259
uninspired 464

stru, struct — to build

destruction 90, 396

instruct 51

obstruct 54

Words Roots and Prefixes T

tail — to cut

curtail 5, 325, 357

tend, tens, tent — extend, stretch

advertent 31
attendant 83
attentive 41
contented 19
discontent 6
inattentive 31
intensify 66, 111, 201, 304

intent 66
latent 67
ostentation 240
patent 69, 228
penitent 142
penitential 347
portentous 11

potentate 69
stentorian 128, 224
tend 39, 417
tender 376
tendinous 171
tension 158

term — end, limit

determination 76

terminate 376

termination 376

terr — to frighten

deterrent 120, 385

terror 463

tor, tort — to twist

desultory 62
distort 48
distortion 48, 421
extort 78, 408

extortionist 78
retort 83, 359
torpid 417
torpor 463

torrid 129, 276
tortuous 198, 389

tract — to drag, draw

abstract 45, 252
attracted 24
attractive 89
contract 265
contraction 351, 366

detract 409
distract 48, 402
extract 91
intractable 93, 408
protract 5, 357

retract 460
tractable 160

Words Roots and Prefixes U

urb	city	
urban 207	urbane 175	urbanity 74

us, ut	to use	
abuse 367 usual 100	usurp 72	utilize 464

Words Roots and Prefixes V

vac, vag, void	empty	
avoid 11, 122 evacuate 447 vaccinate 203	vaccination 203, 313 vagrant 144	vague 116, 232 void 376

val, vail	strong, worth	
devalue 409 equivalent 427 prevail 126 prevalent 126	valediction 107, 464 valiance 274 valiant 274	valid 128 valuables 43 value 151, 397

ver	true	
veracious 280, 404 verdant 347	verdict 432, 465	

verb	word	
verbose 251, 347	verbosity 304	

via, vey, voy	way	
convey 28, 443 obviate 54	purvey 12	trivial 53, 431

Words Roots and Prefixes **W**

Index

concede 180, 387
concentrate 165, 251, 296
conciliate 95, 100, 251
conciliatory 251, 277, 361
concise 113, 251, 347
conciseness 217
conclude 442
concord 135, 251, 311
concrete 442
concur 38, 252
condemn 252
condense 252, 345
condensed 45, 252
condescend 252
condescending 252
condign 442
condolence 442
condone 253
confession 293
confine 442
confirm 263, 293, 412
conform 294
conformation 336
conformity 294
confront 322
confuse 294
confusion 208, 294
congeal 294
congenial 294
congruent 294
conjecture 114, 310
connect 442
connive 76
conniver 76, 395
connoisseur 442
consent 180
consequence 257
conservative 226
conserve 13
consolidate 395
conspicuous 269, 425
conspiratorial 76, 395
conspire 395
constancy 68, 172, 259
constant 442
constellation 207
constitute 207
constrain 271, 443

constrict 339
constricted 307, 339
consummate 237
contagion 339
contain 443
contemptible 78
contentment 5
contented 19
continence 443
continuance 443
contract 265
contraction 351, 366
contradictory 82, 322
contrast 195, 443
contravene 366
contrite 322, 336
control 95
contumacious 112, 323
convalesce 216, 295
convenience 385
convention 323
conventional 323
converge 443
conversant 443
conversion 443
convert 323
convey 28, 443
conviction 152, 323
convince 236, 324
convivial 90, 216
convoluted 309, 324
convulsion 351, 366
cool 225
cooperate 279, 339
copious 287, 379
copy 227
coquette 182, 351
core 428
cornucopia 443
coronation 242, 366
corporeal 19, 202, 409
correspond 409
corrode 326, 443
corruptionist 229
cosmopolitan 33, 358, 399
cosset 34, 244
coterie 443
countenance 252, 443

counter 443
counterfeit 366
countermand 367
country 17
courage 443
course 144, 279, 443
court 34
courtroom 443
coven 34
covenant 350
cover 4
covetous 358
coward 133
cowardice 25, 61
cower 207
cozen 444
cramp 165
cramped 165
crass 443
craven 151
credence 105
credulous 128, 367
creek 444
creep 105, 244
crescendo 444
crest 120
crestfallen 20, 120
crime 23
cringe 352
critical 404
criticize 95
crockery 444
cronyism 339
croon 340
crouch 444
crucial 4
crumb 444
crumble 4, 209
crutch 47
crux 47
cryptic 61, 264
cuisine 50
culpable 279
cultivate 295
cultivated 229
cunning 444
curate 444
curb 340

curmudgeon 379
cursory 180
curt 4
curtail 5, 325, 357
cut 197

dignify 368
digress 48, 237
digressive 18
dilapidate 121
dilapidated 121
dilate 265
dilettante 265, 388
diligence 445
dilute 296
dimension 294
diminish 136, 296
diminution 296
din 311
dingy 352
diocesan 5
diocese 445
dire 325
directness 395
dirge 445
disabuse 352
disaffected 5
disaggregate 164
disagreeable 445
disarm 445
disavow 5, 180
discern 6
discerner 234
discerning 6, 22
discharge 181
disclosure 181
discomfit 6, 424
discommode 6, 31, 282
discompose 6, 212
discontent 6
discord 181
discredit 17
discrepancy 445
discrete 18
discretion 399
discretionary 270
discriminate 18, 371
discriminating 422
discursive 18
disdain 18
disembodied 19
disembody 19
disengage 445
disentangle 166, 188

disgorge 279
disgruntle 19
disgruntled 19
disguise 19
disgust 19, 239
disinclination 119
disinfection 149
disingenuous 20
disintegrate 35, 162
disinter 368
disinterest 35
disinterested 35
disjoint 445
dislike 184, 191, 313
dismantle 35, 396
dismiss 445
disordered 407
disparage 35
disparate 35, 308
dispassionate 10, 36
disperse 409
dispirit 409
dispose favorably 139
disprove 36, 288
dispute 36, 99, 226
disquiet 445
disregard 36
disrespect 37, 297
disrupt 37, 201
dissect 446
dissemble 37
disseminate 37
dissent 38, 180, 252
dissimulate 76
dissipate 136
dissociate 132
dissolute 47, 168
dissolve 47, 395
dissonance 135
dissuade 41, 48, 316
distillate 136
distinction 168
distort 48
distortion 48, 421
distract 48
distracted 402
distraught 309, 340
distress 199, 368

distressed 335
disturb 90
ditch 62
ditty 296
diurnal 385
divergent 136, 194
divestiture 364
divide 287
divulge 251, 380
dizziness 361
doctrine 445
dodder 222
dogged 237
doggerel 237
doleful 446
dolorous 446
dolt 380
donor 446
doubt 105
doubtful 109
dour 48
douse 368
downplay 446
downpour 63
doyen 63
doze 446
drab 181
draconian 152
draconic 294
drain 152, 408
drainage 322
drama 258
drawl 63
dread 352
drench 368
drift 304
drill 446
drivel 253
drizzle 295
droll 302, 340
drone 413
droop 137
drudgery 7, 272
dry 165
dubious 152, 323
dulcet 325
dull 332
dune 325

incite 210, 228
inclement 211
inclination 451
incogitant 211
inconsequential 4
inconsonant 251
inconspicuous 273, 343
incontrovertible 36, 226
incorrigible 104, 226
incorruptible 195
incriminate 412
inculpate 227, 341
incumbent 185
indefensible 227, 417
indetection 367
indict 65
indifferent 108, 194
indigenous 109, 353
indigent 25
indistinct 451
indoctrinate 96
indolent 109, 128, 301
indomitable 109, 172
indubitable 109
induce 385
inducement 120, 385
induct 181
indulge 45, 109
ineluctable 110
inept 122
inert 122
inescapable 110
inevitable 122
infect 370
infection 370
infer 217, 451
infinite 139, 208
infirm 451
inflame 139
inflexible 451
information 37, 215, 264
infrequent place 429
infuse 41, 238
ingenious 239
ingenue 239
ingenuity 344, 451
ingest 451
ingrain 424

ingrained 424
ingratiate 424
inherent 211
inhibit 211
inimical 193, 227
inimitable 227
iniquitous 255
iniquity 255
injure 67
inkling 451
innovate 412
innovative 412
inquisitive 428
insatiable 451
insensible 22
insight 22
insipid 40, 402
insolent 40
insoluble 47
insouciance 273
insouciant 40
inspiration 427
inspire 41, 238
instigate 51
instill 51
institute 93
instruct 51
instrumentalist 385
insubordinate 65, 375
insubstantial 451
insular 33, 399
intangible 65, 329, 409
integral 65
intelligence 451
intelligible 154
intemperate 91
intensify 66, 111, 201, 304
intent 66
intentional 66
intercessor 79, 110
interdependent 302
interdict 75, 79, 374
interest 256, 370
interpreter 174
interrogate 79
intimate 80, 339
intimidate 80
intimidation 78

intractable 93, 408
intransigent 392
intrepid 76, 93
intricacy 93
introductory 357
intrude 94
intrusive 60
intuition 400
inure 51
inured 51, 273
invective 17, 52, 206, 309
inveigle 370
investigate 52, 329
inveterate 52
invidious 451
invigorate 66, 71
inviolable 66
inviolate 330
invulnerable 67
irascible 57, 158, 184
ire 452
iridescent 425
irk 256
irreducible 452
irrelevant 452
irrepressible 55, 425
irresoluteness 204
irresolution 76
irritate 425
irritation 277, 425
issue 151

J

jaded 123, 227
jamb 452
jargon 235
jaundice 139
jaunty 160
jeer 452
jejune 256
jeopardize 452
jest 52, 273
jingoism 314
jittery 94
jocund 228, 256
jolt 281
jovial 52, 256

513

meander 426
meaningful 167
measly 184
meat 397
mediate 79, 110
mediation 310
mediocre 111
mediocrity 111
medley 454
meek 112, 123
meet 71, 144
meld 360, 454
mellifluous 282
melody 221
membrane 300, 342
menace 355
mend 269
mendacious 269
mentor 210, 371
merchandise 327
mercurial 454
merit 454
metaphor 140
meteoric 68, 107
methodical 382
meticulous 81
metrical 170
miff 94, 349
mildness 378
milk 91
mill 454
mince 185
mineral 271
minuscule 328
minute 328
mirth 9, 263
misanthrope 9, 297
misbehave 9, 402
mischievous 10, 150, 306
miscreant 23, 403
misdemeanor 23
miser 24, 375
misgiving 454
mishap 24
mislead 41
misleading 41
misrepresent 454
misunderstood 179

mite 454
mitigate 81
mnemonic 112
mob 169
mobility 388
mockery 212, 338, 421
moderate 111
moderation 411
modest 111, 394
modesty 185
modicum 111
moisture 17, 98, 311
mollify 249, 263, 282
momentous 300
money 331
monochromatic 425
monotonous 413
montage 454
moral restraint 199
morale 409
moratorium 328
morbid 140, 347
mordant 312, 328
moribund 69, 426
morose 52, 228, 256
mortar 454
mortification 454
mosaic 454
moth 400
moth-eaten 400
motility 189
motivate 81
motley 454
mottle 94, 163
mottled 94
mourn 454
mouth 214
move 254, 281
move ahead willingly 276
move swiftly 105, 244
move unidirectionally 215
muffle 140
muffled 140, 168, 415
mulish 269
mull 454
mumble 454
mundane 91, 269
munificent 316

mural 401
murmur 371
museum 149
music 282
mutate 454
myopia 186, 342
myopic 6

N

nadir 292, 455
naif (naive) 455
naive 225, 257
narcissism 455
narrow 75
narrowness 134
nation 314
natty 95, 360
naysay 455
nebulous 199
nefarious 140, 218
negligent 239
negligible 455
negotiation 171, 455
neologism 193, 455
nepotism 385
nervousness 153
nettle 95
new and fresh 400
nibble 168, 183
nicety 199
nitpick 95
nitpicker 95
noble 200, 346
nocturnal 385
noisome 292, 455
nomad 300
nonconformist 455
nondescript 269
nonentity 257
nonflammable 338, 455
nonplus 413
nonsensical 253, 455
nose 115
notable 238, 355
notable success 238, 355
note 338
notice 32
noticeable 97

novelty 346, 455
noxious 82, 158
nuance 168
nucleate 157
nudge 112, 330
numb 273, 300
nurture 455

O

obdurate 112
obedient 112, 323
obey 140, 200, 421
obfuscate 141, 212, 298
obituary 455
object 16
objection 380
obligate 270
obligatory 270
oblige 282
oblique 455
obliterate 283
oblivion 283
obscure 24
obscurity 365
obsequious 24, 388
observe 430
obsess 24
obsessed 24
obsolete 455
obstinate 10, 53
obstreperous 95, 431
obstruct 54
obtuse 95
obtuseness 95
obviate 54
occlude 455
occult 69, 228, 320
ode 123
odious 19, 239
offbeat 46, 141, 196
offend 141, 231
offense 141, 381
offhand 301
official 156
officious 141
offish 141
ominous 239
onerous 455

opacity 157
opaque 180, 185
opine 240, 285
opportune 385
oppress 456
opulent 25
oracle 413
orate 185
oratory 185
order 139, 367
orderly 3, 228
orderly arrangement 350
ore 456
organism 456
original work 54
originality 55, 307
ornate 456
orthodox 82
orthodoxy 82, 423
oscillation 456
ossification 25
ossify 25
ostentation 240
ostracize 96
oust 185
outgoing 182, 185
outmaneuver 212
overbearing 123
overexpose 123
overexposure 123, 227
overindulge 50, 123
overlap 18, 387
overlook 456
overt 8, 456
overture 124
oxygen 392
oxymoron 82, 322, 401

P

pacific 6, 212
pacify 6
paean 456
pain 119, 122
painstaking 372
palatable 84, 212
palatial 108
pall 456
palliate 283

pallid 283
palmy 186
palpable 266, 283
palter 250, 284
paltry 243, 301
pan 183
panache 270
panegyric 456
panorama 456
pantechnicon 54
parable 355
paradigmatic 401
paradox 401
paragon 401
paramount 149, 401
paranoia 355
pariah 456
parity 427
parlance 427
parochial 456
parody 456
paroxysm 54
parrot 55
parry 142
parse 142
parsimonious 21, 92, 96, 316, 381
parsimony 243
partial 10, 36
partisan 10
pastiche 54
patent 69, 228
pathological 456
patron 96, 410
patronize 96, 252
pattern 286
paucity 213
paunchy 25, 115
pauper 456
pebble 456
peccadillo 200
peck 386
pedagogue 96
pedantic 228
pedestrian 124
peep 457
peeve 124
peevish 457
pejorative 457

react 122
realized 210
ream 459
reap 414
reasonable 400
reassure 187
rebel 170
rebuke 459
recalcitrant 140, 200
recant 200
recidivism 214, 271
reciprocate 215
recite 459
reckless 215
recluse 107, 215
recognition 459
reconcile 414
reconciliation 414
recondite 215
reconnoiter 215
rectify 229
rectitude 173, 229, 255
recur 460
redolent 127
redoubtable 127
redundant 429
reel 460
refined 143, 408
refractory 10, 143
refugee 460
refuse 241, 268
refute 429
regard 127, 460
regimen 242
regressive 414
regret 460
regular 346
rehabilitate 216
rehabilitation 216, 295
rehearsal 460
reign 242, 366
reiterate 429, 460
reject 257, 345
rejoice 380, 414
rejuvenate 101
relapse 214, 271
relate 460
relative 385

release 92, 271
relegate 460
relevant 272
relief 203
relieve 272, 406
religion 344
relinquish 272, 330
reluctance 187, 460
reluctant 187
remember 112
remiss 285, 301
remonstrance 316
remonstrator 48, 316
remorse 127, 142, 316
remove 283
remove impediment 77
remunerate 317
remunerative 317
rend 269, 286
renew 415
renounce 372
renovate 415
repartee 83, 359
repatriate 222, 359
repeal 82, 460
repel 386, 403
repertoire 386
replete 386
repletion 386
repose 79, 386
reprehensible 402
represented 367
reprimand 403
reproach 415, 418
reprobate 9, 242, 402
reprove 403
repudiate 387
repugnance 403
repugnant 386, 403
repulse 460
rescind 12, 182
reserved 27
resilience 27
resist 41
resistance 379
resolute 41, 94, 173
resonant 415
respect 55

respiration 415
respire 415
respite 41, 198
resplendence 137, 181
resplendent 42
responsible 209
restive 55, 384
restored 121
restrain 55
restraint 199
restrict 460
resurgence 69
resurgent 69, 426
resuscitate 460
retain 70, 162, 331
retaliate 70
retard 50, 70
reticence 83
reticent 83, 237, 303
retinue 83
retort 83, 359
retract 460
retrench 98, 254
reveal 460
revere 55, 406
reverent 255
revive 84
reward 272
rewarding work 7, 272
ribald 12, 114
rickety 216
rift 414
righteous 242
rigid 460
rigidity 403
rile 272, 338
riot 359
rioter 359
river 166
riveting 332, 390
rock 96
roil 230, 242
roisterer 17
roof 285
rooted 460
roster 56, 159
route 77, 359
routine 87, 98

rubicund 170, 304
rude 373
rudiment 127
rue 127, 316
ruffian 245
ruin 221
ruminate 301
ruminative 301
ruse 196
rustic 56, 175, 270

S

sabbatical 461
sabotage 202
saboteur 37, 201
saccharine 118
safeguard 143
sagacious 242
sagacity 242
sage 243
saint 23, 403
salient 273
salmon 210
salubrious 14, 301, 420
salutary 264
salutation 461
salvage 461
salve 232, 302
sanctify 17
sanctimonious 62, 286
sanction 344, 374
sanguine 12, 34
sap 461
satiate 84
satiated 84
satisfaction 84
satisfy 84, 362
saturate 98
saturated 98
savor 84
savory 84, 212, 335
savvy 85
scan 170
scant 170, 364
scanty 303
scarce 187
scatter 157, 387
scattering 387

scene 246
scent 127, 282
scheme 374
schism 216, 418
scholarly 228, 461
scintillate 243
scintillating 92, 243
scorn 257, 345
scrappy 461
scribble 429
scrupulous 28
scrutinize 430
sculpt 28
sculpture 27
scurrilous 56
scythe 414
seal 90
secondary 216
secrete 31
secure 230
sedate 230, 242
sedentary 427
sedulous 109, 128
see 267
seemly 12, 114
selective 461
self-denial 194
self-deprecating 397
self-effacing 461
sensation 273
sensitivity 407
sentence 142
sentient 430
sentimental 23
sentinel 56
separate 360
sere 23, 374
serendipity 345
serene 218, 345
serenity 90, 235, 318, 411
seriousness 369
sermon 356, 374
servile 12
severity 81, 152, 283
shackle 70, 166
shaft 461
sham 171
shape 282

shard 188
shift 206, 243
shiftiness 329
shirk 258, 268
shorten 340
shrill 461
shroud 395
shun 375
sidereal 128
signal 346
significant 243, 301
silver 288
similarity 371
simpleton 242
sin 200
sincere 286
sincerity 20, 26, 286
sinew 171
sinewy 171
sing 340
sip 244, 360
skeptic 72, 128, 367
skimp 243
skimpy 331
skirt 258
skit 258
slacken 100, 158
slake 159
slate 365
sleep 387
slew 213
slide 382, 461
slight 34, 244
slippery 192
slipshod 258, 372
slope 461
slothful 16
slouch 360
slovenly 95, 258, 360
slow 63
sluggard 28
slur 416
sly 85
smart 100
smell 254
smirk 28, 258
smother 360
smug 28, 138

smuggle 28
smugness 28, 258
snarl 166, 188, 411
sneer 114
snobbish 143
snub 18, 29, 34
soak 159, 310
sober 129, 214
sobriety 201, 317
sociable 90, 141, 216
society 324
solemn 273
solemn utterance 52, 273
solicitous 273
solidify 287
solution 461
solvent 47, 302
somber 302, 340
somnolence 118, 317
sonata 461
song 296
sonnet 461
soothe 361
sop 251, 361
sophisticate 387
sophisticated 387
sophistication 239
soporific 244, 387
sordid 346
sorrow 45, 209
sound 430
soundness 316
sparse 287, 379
Spartan 46, 68, 188
spat 186
spate 188
speak 32, 33, 172, 257, 371, 427
specialist 151
specious 128
spectrum 461
speculate 114, 310
speech 197, 416
spelunker 33, 171
spendthrift 114, 357
spindly 154
sprited 248
spiritual 259
spleen 287

splendor 99
splint 388
spoilage 126
spontaneous 346
sporadic 346
spot 94, 253
sprightly 61, 430
spry 120
spurious 56, 327
spurn 57, 196
spurned 277
squabble 99
squalid 99
squall 99, 308
squalor 99
squander 13
stability 124, 159, 277
stabilize 274
staff 159
stagnant 461
staid 160
stalemate 171
stalk 317
stalwart 172
stamina 461
stammer 172
stand erect 360
standard 118
standardize 461
stanza 462
star 128, 207
stark 462
startle 189
stasis 189
stay aloft 276
steadfast 13
stealth 181, 388
steep 115
steepness 115
stench 115
stentorian 128, 224
sterile 129, 347
stern 416
stickler 217, 399
stiff 230
stifle 50, 172
stimulant 244
stimulate 297

stingy 375
stint 462
stir 113, 259
stirring 29
stock 462
stockade 462
stodgy 332
stoic 11, 332
story 355
storyteller 462
stouthearted 27
straightforward 403
strand 462
strength 137, 152, 234
stress 262
striate 430
striated 341, 430
strict 462
strict limitation 80
stridency 430
striking 358
strut 13, 160
student 157
stultify 29
stultifying 29
stunt 295
stupid 372, 380
sturdy 416
stylus 462
subdue 172
subdued 109
subject 237, 462
subjugate 173
sublime 201
submerge 201, 350
submission 375
submissive 65
subordinate 416
subpoena 462
subservience 462
subside 201
subsidiary 202
subsidy 202
substantial 202, 431
subterfuge 202
subtle 462
subvert 202
success 238, 355

English Conversational Ability Test
国際英語会話能力検定

● E-CATとは…
英語が話せるようになるための
テストです。インターネット
ベースで、30分であなたの発
話力をチェックします。

www.ecatexam.com

● iTEP®とは…
世界各国の企業、政府機関、アメリカの大学
300校以上が、英語能力判定テストとして採用。
オンラインによる90分のテストで文法、リー
ディング、リスニング、ライティング、スピー
キングの5技能をスコア化。iTEP®は、留学、就
職、海外赴任などに必要な、世界に通用する英
語力を総合的に評価する画期的なテストです。

www.itepexamjapan.com

Hackers Super Vocabulary
ハッカーズ・スーパーボキャブラリー

2023年2月1日　第1刷発行
2023年8月1日　第3刷発行

著　者　David Cho

発行者　浦　　晋亮

発行所　IBCパブリッシング株式会社
　　　　〒162-0804 東京都新宿区中里町29番3号 菱秀神楽坂ビル
　　　　Tel. 03-3513-4511　Fax. 03-3513-4512
　　　　www.ibcpub.co.jp

印刷所　株式会社シナノパブリッシングプレス

© 2002 Hackers Language Research Institute Co., Ltd.
© IBC Publishing, Inc. 2023

Printed in Japan

落丁本・乱丁本は、小社宛にお送りください。送料小社負担にてお取り替えいたします。
本書の無断複写（コピー）は著作権法上での例外を除き禁じられています。

ISBN978-4-7946-0748-5